AA

Motorist' BRITAIN

Scale 1:250,000
or 3.95 miles to 1 inch

43rd edition June 2021 © AA Media Limited 2021
Revised version of the atlas formerly known as *Complete Atlas of Britain*. Original edition printed 1979.

All cartography in this atlas edited, designed and produced by the Mapping Services Department of AA Media Limited (A05788).

This atlas contains Ordnance Survey data © Crown copyright and database right 2021 and Royal Mail data © Royal Mail copyright and database right 2021. Contains public sector information licensed under the Open Government Licence v3.0. Ireland mapping contains data available from openstreetmap.org © under the Open Database License found at opendatacommons.org

Published by AA Media Limited, whose registered office is Grove House, Lutyens Close, Basingstoke, Hampshire RG24 8AG, UK. Registered number 06112600.

ISBN: 978 0 7495 8269 2

A CIP catalogue record for this book is available from The British Library.

Disclaimer: The contents of this atlas are believed to be correct at the time of the latest revision, it will not contain any subsequent amended, new or temporary information including diversions and traffic control or enforcement systems. The publishers cannot be held responsible or liable for any loss or damage occasioned to any person acting or refraining from action as a result of any use or reliance on material in this atlas, nor for any errors, omissions or changes in such material. This does not affect your statutory rights.

The publishers would welcome information to correct any errors or omissions and to keep this atlas up to date. Please write to the Atlas Editor, AA Media Limited, Grove House, Lutyens Close, Basingstoke, Hampshire RG24 8AG, UK.
E-mail: *roadatlasfeedback@aamediagroup.co.uk*

Acknowledgements: AA Media Limited would like to thank the following for information used in the creation of this atlas: Cadw, English Heritage, Forestry Commission, Historic Scotland, National Trust and National Trust for Scotland, RSPB, The Wildlife Trust, Scottish Natural Heritage, Natural England, The Countryside Council for Wales. Award winning beaches from 'Blue Flag' and 'Keep Scotland Beautiful' (summer 2019 data): for latest information visit *www.blueflag.org* and *www.keepscotlandbeautiful.org*. Transport for London (Central London Map), Nexus (Newcastle district map). Ireland mapping: Republic of Ireland census 2016 © Central Statistics Office and Northern Ireland census 2016 © NISRA (population data); Irish Public Sector Data (CC BY 4.0) (Gaeltacht); Logainm.ie (placenames); Roads Service and Transport Infrastructure Ireland.
Printed by Walstead Peterborough, UK

Contents

Map pages	inside front cover
Route planner	II–VII
Motorways	VIII–XIV
Restricted junctions	VIII–XI
M25 London Orbital motorway	XII
M6 Toll motorway	XIII
Smart motorways	XIV
Road map symbols	1
Road maps	2–115
Britain 1:250,000 scale	2–111
Some islands are shown at slightly smaller scales	
Ireland 1:1,000,000 scale	112–115
District maps	116–127
Birmingham	116–117
Glasgow	118–119
London	120–123
Manchester	124–125
Tyne & Wear	126–127
Street map symbols	128
Town plans	129–141
Central London street map and index	142–157
Index to place names	158–194
County, administrative area map	158
Place name index	159–194

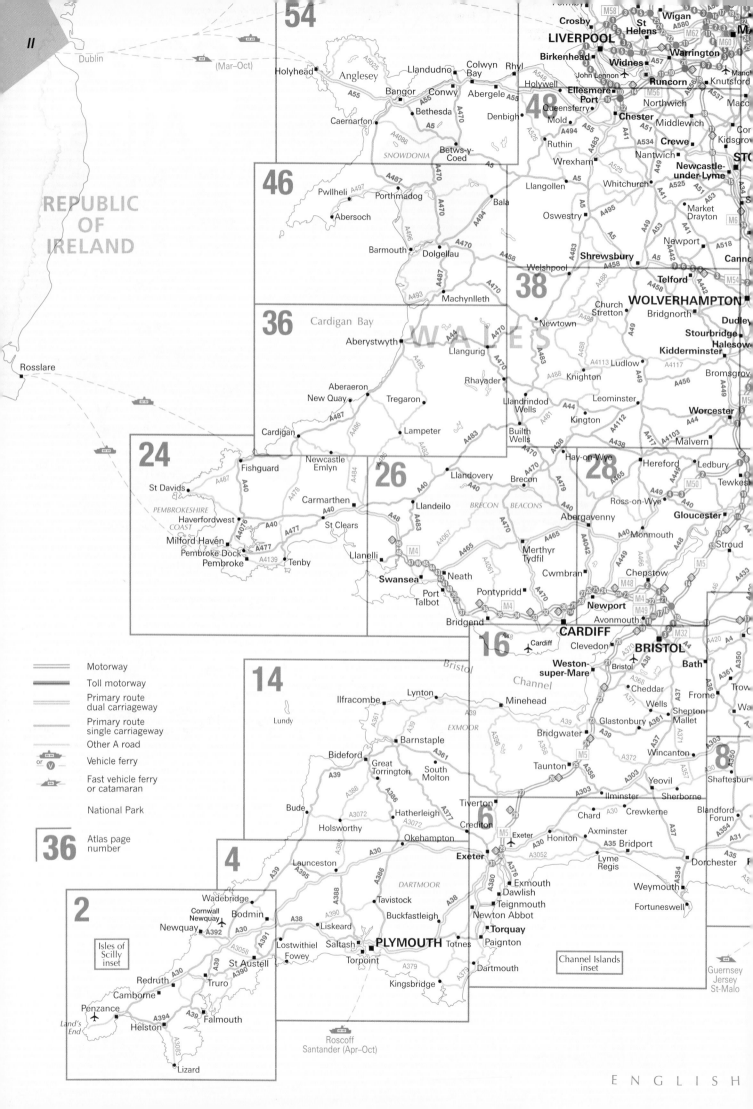

Motorway

Toll motorway

Primary route dual carriageway

Primary route single carriageway

Other A road

Vehicle ferry

Fast vehicle ferry or catamaran

National Park

36 Atlas page number

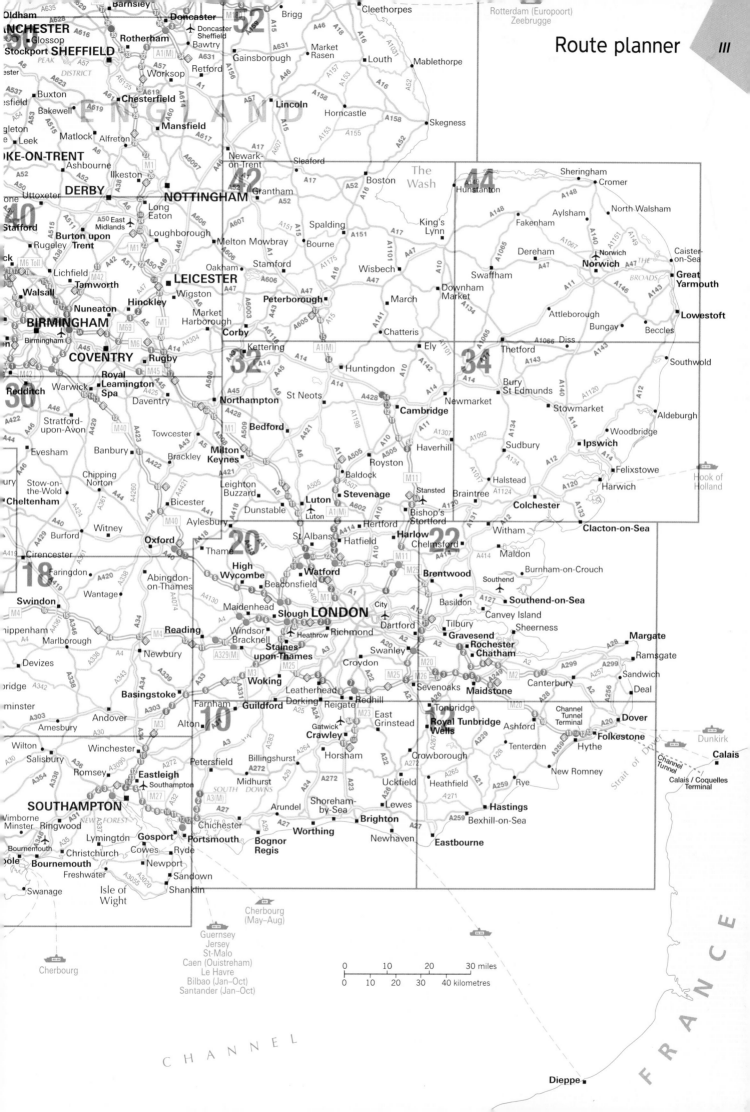

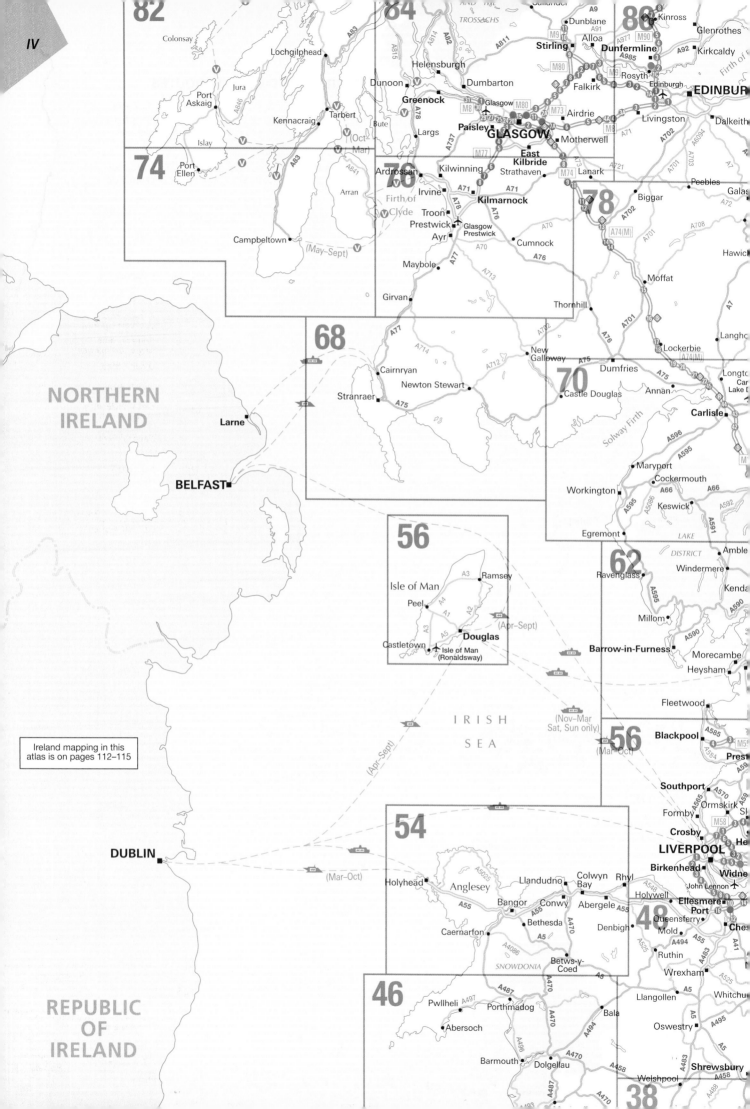

IV

82

84

80

Colonsay

Lochgilphead

AND THE
TROSSACHS

Dunblane
A9

Callander

Kinross

Glenrothes

Stirling

Dunfermline

Kirkcaldy

Helensburgh

Alloa

Falkirk

Rosyth

Edinburgh

EDINBURGH

Jura

Dunoon

Dumbarton

Airdrie

Livingston

Dalkeith

Port
Askaig

Kennacraig

Tarbert

Greenock

Largs

Glasgow

GLASGOW

Paisley

Motherwell

Islay

Bute

Port
Ellen

74

Arran

Campbeltown

(May–Sept)

76

Ardrossan

Irvine

Kilwinning

East
Kilbride

Strathaven

Lanark

Peebles

Galas

Troon

Kilmarnock

Prestwick

Ayr

Glasgow
Prestwick

Cumnock

78

Biggar

Hawick

Maybole

Girvan

Thornhill

Moffat

Langho

68

Cairnryan

New
Galloway

Lockerbie

Stranraer

Newton Stewart

70

Dumfries

Longto

Car
Lake D

Castle Douglas

Annan

NORTHERN
IRELAND

Larne

Carlisle

BELFAST

Solway Firth

Maryport

Cockermouth

Workington

Keswick

56

Egremont

LAKE

Ireland mapping in this
atlas is on pages 112–115

Isle of Man

Ramsey

DISTRICT

Amble

62

Ravenglass

Windermere

Peel

Kenda

Millom

Castletown

Douglas

(Apr–Sept)

Isle of Man
(Ronaldsway)

Morecambe

Barrow-in-Furness

Heysham

IRISH

(Nov–Mar
Sat, Sun only)

Fleetwood

56

Blackpool

SEA

Pres

(Mar–Oct)

Southport

Ormskirk

Sl

(Apr–Sept)

Formby

54

Crosby

He

LIVERPOOL

DUBLIN

(Mar–Oct)

Birkenhead

Widne

Holyhead

Anglesey

Llandudno

Colwyn
Bay

Rhyl

John Lennon

Holywell

Ellesmere
Port

**REPUBLIC
OF
IRELAND**

Bangor

Conwy

Abergele

Denbigh

Mold

Che

Bethesda

Queensferry

Caernarfon

Betws-y-Coed

Ruthin

Wrexham

SNOWDONIA

Llangollen

Whitchu

46

Pwllheli

Porthmadog

Bala

Oswestry

Abersoch

Welshpool

Barmouth

Dolgellau

Shrewsbury

38

EMERGENCY DIVERSION ROUTES

In an emergency it may be necessary to close a section of motorway or other main road to traffic, so a temporary sign may advise drivers to follow a diversion route. To help drivers navigate the route, black symbols on yellow patches may be permanently displayed on existing direction signs, including motorway signs. Symbols may also be used on separate signs with yellow backgrounds.

Legend:

- Motorway
- Toll motorway
- Primary route dual carriageway
- Primary route single carriageway
- Other A road
- or V Vehicle ferry
- Fast vehicle ferry or catamaran
- National Park

80 Atlas page number

Scale: 0 — 10 — 20 — 30 miles
0 — 10 — 20 — 30 — 40 kilometres

Map labels:

Dunbar, Eyemouth, Berwick-upon-Tweed, Coldstream, Kelso, Wooler, Jedburgh, Alnwick, Amble, NORTHUMBERLAND, Otterburn, Ashington, Morpeth, Newcastle, North Shields, Tynemouth, South Shields, NEWCASTLE UPON TYNE, Corbridge, Hexham, Gateshead, SUNDERLAND, Brampton, Consett, Chester-le-Street, Durham, Alston, Hartlepool, Penrith, Bishop Auckland, Middlesbrough, Barnard Castle, Stockton-on-Tees, Brough, Darlington, Guisborough, Whitby, Richmond, Durham Tees Valley, NORTH YORK MOORS, Sedbergh, Northallerton, Scarborough, YORKSHIRE DALES, Leyburn, Thirsk, Pickering, Filey, Kirkby Lonsdale, Ripon, Helmsley, Easingwold, Malton, Bridlington, Settle, Driffield, Skipton, Harrogate, York, Market Weighton, Lancaster, Otley, Leeds Bradford, Wetherby, Beverley, Clitheroe, Keighley, BRADFORD, LEEDS, Selby, Withernsea, Burnley, Halifax, Blackburn, KINGSTON UPON HULL, Rochdale, Huddersfield, Wakefield, Goole, Bolton, Bury, Pontefract, Thorne, Scunthorpe, Immingham, Wigan, Oldham, Barnsley, Humberside, Grimsby, MANCHESTER, Doncaster, Brigg, Cleethorpes, Warrington, Glossop, Stockport, SHEFFIELD, Rotherham, Doncaster Sheffield, Market Rasen, Louth, Mablethorpe, Runcorn, Manchester, Knutsford, Bawtry, Gainsborough, PEAK DISTRICT, Worksop, Retford, Lincoln, Northwich, Macclesfield, Buxton, Chesterfield, Horncastle, Skegness, Middlewich, Bakewell, Crewe, Kidsgrove, Leek, Matlock, Alfreton, Mansfield, Newark-on-Trent, Sleaford, STOKE-ON-TRENT, Newcastle-under-Lyme, Ashbourne, Ilkeston, Boston, Sheringham, Cromer, Market Drayton, Stone, Uttoxeter, DERBY, NOTTINGHAM, Grantham, The Wash, Hunstanton, Aylsham, Newport, Stafford, East Midlands, Long Eaton, Loughborough, Spalding, King's Lynn, Fakenham, Dereham, Norwich, Cannock, Burton upon Trent, Rugeley, Melton Mowbray, Bourne, Telford, Lichfield, Tamworth, Oakham, Stamford, Wisbech, Swaffham, Downham Market, Walsall, Wigston, LEICESTER, Peterborough, March

Ferry routes: Amsterdam (IJmuiden), Rotterdam (Europoort) Zeebrugge

Page number boxes: 80, 72, 64, 66, 58, 60, 52, 42, 44, 40

Road numbers (selected): A1, A697, A698, A68, A696, A69, A19, A1068, A171, A170, A166, A165, A1079, A164, A15, A46, A17, A52, A148, A47, M6, M62, M1, M18, M60

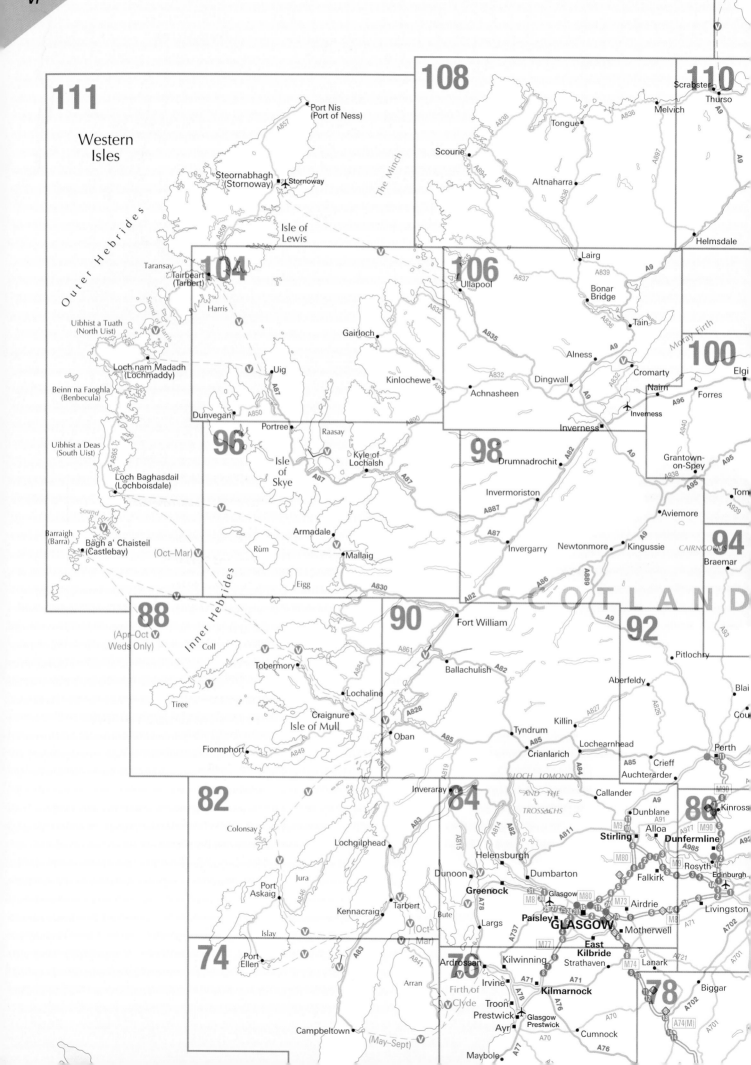

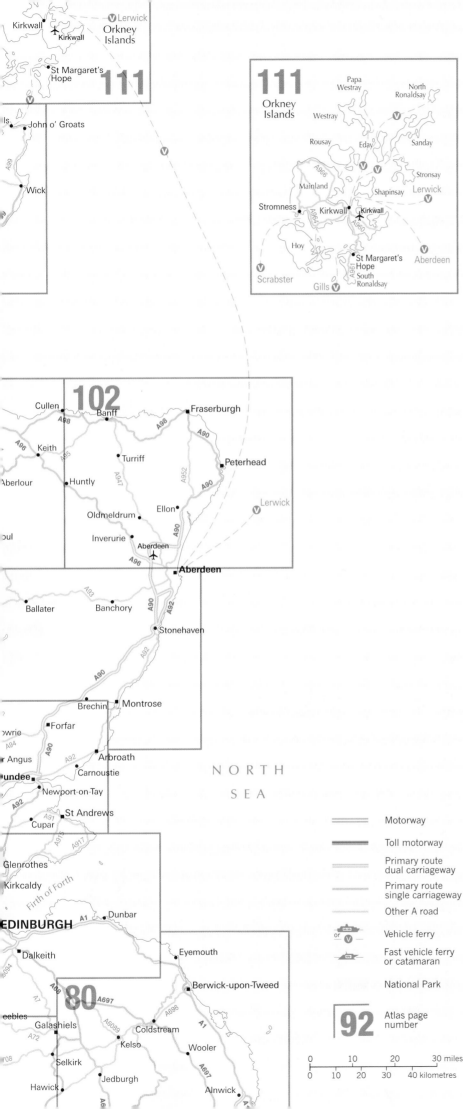

111 Orkney Islands

Kirkwall
Kirkwall
St Margaret's Hope

John o' Groats
Wick

111
Orkney Islands

Papa Westray
North Ronaldsay
Westray
Rousay
Eday
Sanday
Mainland
Stronsay
Shapinsay
Lerwick
Stromness
Kirkwall
Kirkwall
Hoy
St Margaret's Hope
Scrabster
Gills
South Ronaldsay
Aberdeen

111
Shetland Islands

Unst
Yell
Fetlar
Scatsta
Vidlin
Out Skerries
Papa Stour
Whalsay
Mainland
Scalloway
Lerwick
Bressay
Foula
Sumburgh
Fair Isle
Kirkwall
Aberdeen

102

Cullen
Banff
Fraserburgh
Keith
Turriff
Peterhead
Aberlour
Huntly
Oldmeldrum
Ellon
Lerwick
Inverurie
Aberdeen
Aberdeen

Ballater
Banchory
Stonehaven

Brechin
Montrose
Forfar
Angus
Arbroath
Carnoustie
Dundee
Newport-on-Tay
St Andrews
Cupar

NORTH SEA

Glenrothes
Kirkcaldy
Firth of Forth

EDINBURGH
Dunbar
Dalkeith
Eyemouth
Berwick-upon-Tweed

80
Peebles
Galashiels
Coldstream
Selkirk
Kelso
Wooler
Hawick
Jedburgh
Alnwick

FERRY OPERATORS

Hebrides and west coast Scotland
calmac.co.uk
skyeferry.co.uk
western-ferries.co.uk

Orkney and Shetland
northlinkferries.co.uk
pentlandferries.co.uk
orkneyferries.co.uk
shetland.gov.uk/ferries

Isle of Man
steam-packet.com

Ireland
irishferries.com
poferries.com
stenaline.co.uk

North Sea (Scandinavia and Benelux)
dfdsseaways.co.uk
poferries.com

Isle of Wight
wightlink.co.uk
redfunnel.co.uk

Channel Islands
condorferries.co.uk

France and Belgium
brittany-ferries.co.uk
condorferries.co.uk
eurotunnel.com
dfdsseaways.co.uk
poferries.com

Northern Spain
brittany-ferries.co.uk

Motorway

Toll motorway

Primary route dual carriageway

Primary route single carriageway

Other A road

or V Vehicle ferry

Fast vehicle ferry or catamaran

National Park

92 Atlas page number

0   10   20   30 miles
0 10 20 30 40 kilometres

Restricted junctions

Motorway and primary route junctions which have access or exit restrictions are shown on the map pages thus:

M1 London - Leeds

2
Northbound
Access only from A1 (northbound)
Southbound
Exit only to A1 (southbound)

4
Northbound
Access only from A41 (northbound)
Southbound
Exit only to A41 (southbound)

6A
Northbound
Access only from M25 (no link from A405)
Southbound
Exit only to M25 (no link from A405)

7
Northbound
Access only from A414
Southbound
Exit only to A414

17
Northbound
Exit only to M45
Southbound
Access only from M45

19
Northbound
Exit only to M6 (northbound)
Southbound
Exit only to A14 (southbound)

21A
Northbound
Exit only, no access
Southbound
Access only, no exit

24A
Northbound
No exit, access only
Southbound
Access only from A50 (eastbound)

35A
Northbound
Exit only, no access
Southbound
Access only, no exit

43
Northbound
Exit only to M621
Southbound
Access only from M621

48
Northbound
Exit only to A1(M) (northbound)
Southbound
Access only from A1(M) (southbound)

M2 Rochester - Faversham

1
Westbound
No exit to A2 (eastbound)
Eastbound
No access from A2 (westbound)

M3 Sunbury - Southampton

8
Northeastbound
Access only from A303, no exit
Southwestbound
Exit only to A303, no access

10
Northbound
Exit only, no access
Southbound
Access only, no exit

14
Northeastbound
Access from M27 only, no exit
Southwestbound
No access to M27 (westbound)

M4 London - South Wales

For junctions 1 & 2 see London district map on pages 120–123

21
Westbound
Exit only to M48
Eastbound
Access only from M48

23
Westbound
Access only from M48
Eastbound
Exit only to M48

25
Westbound
Exit only, no access
Eastbound
Access only, no exit

25A
Westbound
Exit only, no access
Eastbound
Access only, no exit

29
Westbound
Exit only to A48(M)
Eastbound
Access only from A48(M)

38
Westbound
Exit only, no access
Eastbound
No restriction

39
Westbound
Access only, no exit
Eastbound
No access or exit

42
Westbound
Exit only to A483
Eastbound
Access only from A483

M5 Birmingham - Exeter

10
Northeastbound
Access only, no exit
Southwestbound
Exit only, no access

11A
Northeastbound
Access only from A417 (westbound)
Southwestbound
Exit only to A417 (eastbound)

18A
Northeastbound
Exit only to M49
Southwestbound
Access only from M49

18
Northeastbound
No access, exit only
Southwestbound
No exit, access only

M6 Toll Motorway

See M6 Toll motorway map on page *XIII*

M6 Rugby - Carlisle

3A
Northbound
Exit only to M6 Toll
Southbound
Access only from M6 Toll

4
Northbound
Exit only to M42 (southbound) and A446
Southbound
Exit only to A446

4A
Northbound
Access only from M42 (southbound)
Southbound
Exit only to M42

5
Northbound
Exit only, no access
Southbound
Access only, no exit

10A
Northbound
Exit only to M54
Southbound
Access only from M54

11A
Northbound
Access only from M6 Toll
Southbound
Exit only to M6 Toll

20A
Northbound
No restriction
Southbound
Access only from M56 (eastbound)

20
Northbound
Exit only to M56 (westbound)
Southbound
Access only from M56 (eastbound)

24
Northbound
Access only, no exit
Southbound
Exit only, no access

25
Northbound
Exit only, no access
Southbound
Access only, no exit

30
Northbound
Access only from M61
Southbound
Exit only to M61

31A
Northbound
Exit only, no access
Southbound
Access only, no exit

45
Northbound
Exit only, no access
Southbound
Access only, no exit

M8 Edinburgh - Bishopton

For junctions 7A to 29A see Glasgow district map on pages 118–119

6
Westbound
Exit only, no access
Eastbound
Access only, no exit

6A
Westbound
Access only, no exit
Eastbound
Exit only, no access

7
Westbound
Access only, no exit
Eastbound
Exit only, no access

M9 Edinburgh - Dunblane

2
Northwestbound
Access only, no exit
Southeastbound
Exit only, no access

Northwestbound
Exit only, no access

Southeastbound
Access only, no exit

Northwestbound
Access only, no exit

Southeastbound
Exit only to A905

Northwestbound
Exit only to M876
(southwestbound)

Southeastbound
Access only from M876
(northeastbound)

M11 London - Cambridge

Northbound
Access only from A406
(eastbound)

Southbound
Exit only to A406

Northbound
Exit only, no access

Southbound
Access only, no exit

Northbound
Exit only, no access

Southbound
No direct access,
use jct 8

Northbound
Exit only to A11

Southbound
Access only from A11

Northbound
Exit only, no access

Southbound
Access only, no exit

Northbound
Exit only, no access

Southbound
Access only, no exit

M20 Swanley - Folkestone

Northwestbound
Staggered junction; follow
signs - access only

Southeastbound
Staggered junction; follow
signs - exit only

Northwestbound
Exit only to M26
(westbound)

Southeastbound
Access only from M26
(eastbound)

Northwestbound
Access only from A20

Southeastbound
For access follow signs -
exit only to A20

Northwestbound
No restriction

Southeastbound
For exit follow signs

Northwestbound
Access only, no exit

Southeastbound
Exit only, no access

M23 Hooley - Crawley

Northbound
Exit only to A23
(northbound)

Southbound
Access only from A23
(southbound)

Northbound
Access only, no exit

Southbound
Exit only, no access

M25 London Orbital Motorway

See M25 London Orbital motorway map on
page *XII*

M26 Sevenoaks - Wrotham

Westbound
Exit only to clockwise
M25 (westbound)

Eastbound
Access only from
anticlockwise M25
(eastbound)

Westbound
Access only from M20
(northwestbound)

Eastbound
Exit only to M20
(southeastbound)

M27 Cadnam - Portsmouth

Westbound
Staggered junction; follow
signs - access only from
M3 (southbound). Exit
only to M3 (northbound)

Eastbound
Staggered junction; follow
signs - access only from
M3 (southbound). Exit
only to M3 (northbound)

Westbound
Exit only, no access

Eastbound
Access only, no exit

Westbound
Staggered junction; follow
signs - exit only to M275
(southbound)

Eastbound
Staggered junction; follow
signs - access only from
M275 (northbound)

M40 London - Birmingham

Northwestbound
Exit only, no access

Southeastbound
Access only, no exit

Northwestbound
Exit only, no access

Southeastbound
Access only, no exit

Northwestbound
Exit only to M40/A40

Southeastbound
Access only from
M40/A40

Northwestbound
Exit only, no access

Southeastbound
Access only, no exit

Northwestbound
Access only, no exit

Southeastbound
Exit only, no access

Northwestbound
Access only, no exit

Southeastbound
Exit only, no access

M42 Bromsgrove - Measham

See Birmingham district map on pages
116–117

M45 Coventry - M1

Westbound
Access only from A45
(northbound)

Eastbound
Exit only, no access

Westbound
Access only from M1
(northbound)

Eastbound
Exit only to M1
(southbound)

M48 Chepstow

Westbound
Access only from M4
(westbound)

Eastbound
Exit only to M4
(eastbound)

Westbound
No exit to M4 (eastbound)

Eastbound
No access from M4
(westbound)

M53 Mersey Tunnel - Chester

Northbound
Access only from M56
(westbound). Exit only to
M56 (eastbound)

Southbound
Access only from M56
(westbound). Exit only to
M56 (eastbound)

M54 Telford - Birmingham

Westbound
Access only from M6
(northbound)

Eastbound
Exit only to M6
(southbound)

M56 Chester - Manchester

For junctions 1,2,3,4 & 7 see Manchester
district map on pages 124–125

Westbound
Access only, no exit

Eastbound
No access or exit

Westbound
No exit to M6
(southbound)

Eastbound
No access from M6
(northbound)

Westbound
Exit only to M53

Eastbound
Access only from M53

Westbound
No access or exit

Eastbound
No restriction

M57 Liverpool Outer Ring Road

Northwestbound
Access only, no exit

Southeastbound
Exit only, no access

Northwestbound
Access only from A580
(westbound)

Southeastbound
Exit only, no access

M60 Manchester Orbital

See Manchester district map on pages
124–125

M61 Manchester - Preston

Northwestbound
No access or exit

Southeastbound
Exit only, no access

Northwestbound
Exit only to M6
(northbound)

Southeastbound
Access only from M6
(southbound)

M62 Liverpool - Kingston upon Hull

Westbound
Access only, no exit

Eastbound
Exit only, no access

Westbound
No access to A1(M) (southbound)

Eastbound
No restriction

M65 Preston - Colne

Northeastbound
Exit only, no access

Southwestbound
Access only, no exit

Northeastbound
Access only, no exit

Southwestbound
Exit only, no access

M66 Bury

Northbound
Exit only to A56 (northbound)

Southbound
Access only from A56 (southbound)

Northbound
Exit only, no access

Southbound
Access only, no exit

M67 Hyde Bypass

Westbound
Access only, no exit

Eastbound
Exit only, no access

Westbound
Exit only, no access

Eastbound
Access only, no exit

M69 Coventry - Leicester

Northbound
Access only, no exit

Southbound
Exit only, no access

M73 East of Glasgow

Northbound
No exit to A74 and A721

Southbound
No exit to A74 and A721

Northbound
No access from or exit to A89. No access from M8 (eastbound)

Southbound
No access from or exit to A89. No exit to M8 (westbound)

M74 and A74(M) Glasgow - Gretna

Northbound
Exit only, no access

Southbound
Access only, no exit

Northbound
Access only, no exit

Southbound
Exit only, no access

Northbound
No access from A74 and A721

Southbound
Access only, no exit to A74 and A721

Northbound
Access only, no exit

Southbound
Exit only, no access

Northbound
No access or exit

Southbound
Exit only, no access

Northbound
No restriction

Southbound
Access only, no exit

Northbound
Access only, no exit

Southbound
Exit only, no access

Northbound
Exit only, no access

Southbound
Access only, no exit

Northbound
Exit only, no access

Southbound
Access only, no exit

M77 Glasgow - Kilmarnock

Northbound
No exit to M8 (westbound)

Southbound
No access from M8 (eastbound)

Northbound
Access only, no exit

Southbound
Exit only, no access

Northbound
Access only, no exit

Southbound
Exit only, no access

Northbound
Access only, no exit

Southbound
No restriction

Northbound
Exit only, no access

Southbound
Exit only, no access

M80 Glasgow - Stirling

For junctions 1 & 4 see Glasgow district map on pages 118–119

Northbound
Exit only, no access

Southbound
Access only, no exit

Northbound
Access only, no exit

Southbound
Exit only, no access

Northbound
Exit only to M876 (northeastbound)

Southbound
Access only from M876 (southwestbound)

M90 Edinburgh - Perth

Northbound
No exit, access only

Southbound
Exit only to A90 (eastbound)

Northbound
Exit only to A92 (eastbound)

Southbound
Access only from A92 (westbound)

Northbound
Access only, no exit

Southbound
Exit only, no access

Northbound
Exit only, no access

Southbound
Access only, no exit

Northbound
No access from A912
No exit to A912 (southbound)

Southbound
No access from A912 (northbound).
No exit to A912

M180 Doncaster - Grimsby

Westbound
Access only, no exit

Eastbound
Exit only, no access

M606 Bradford Spur

Northbound
Exit only, no access

Southbound
No restriction

M621 Leeds - M1

Clockwise
Access only, no exit

Anticlockwise
Exit only, no access

Clockwise
No exit or access

Anticlockwise
No restriction

Clockwise
Access only, no exit

Anticlockwise
Exit only, no access

Clockwise
Exit only, no access

Anticlockwise
Access only, no exit

Clockwise
Exit only to M1 (southbound)

Anticlockwise
Access only from M1 (northbound)

M876 Bonnybridge - Kincardine Bridge

Northeastbound
Access only from M80 (northbound)

Southwestbound
Exit only to M80 (southbound)

Northeastbound
Exit only to M9 (eastbound)

Southwestbound
Access only from M9 (westbound)

A1(M) South Mimms - Baldock

Northbound
Exit only, no access

Southbound
Access only, no exit

Northbound
No restriction

Southbound
Exit only, no access

Northbound
Access only, no exit

Southbound
No access or exit

A1(M) Pontefract - Bedale

Northbound
No access to M62
(eastbound)

Southbound
No restriction

Northbound
Access only from M1
(northbound)

Southbound
Exit only to M1
(southbound)

A1(M) Scotch Corner - Newcastle upon Tyne

Northbound
Exit only to A66(M)
(eastbound)

Southbound
Access only from A66(M)
(westbound)

Northbound
No access. Exit only to
A194(M) & A1
(northbound)

Southbound
No exit. Access only from
A194(M) & A1
(southbound)

A3(M) Horndean - Havant

Northbound
Access only from A3

Southbound
Exit only to A3

Northbound
Exit only, no access

Southbound
Access only, no exit

A38(M) Birmingham
Victoria Road (Park Circus)

Northbound
No exit

Southbound
No access

A48(M) Cardiff Spur

Westbound
Access only from M4
(westbound)

Eastbound
Exit only to M4
(eastbound)

Westbound
Exit only to A48
(westbound)

Eastbound
Access only from A48
(eastbound)

A57(M) Manchester
Brook Street (A34)

Westbound
No exit

Eastbound
No access

A58(M) Leeds
Park Lane and Westgate

Northbound
No restriction

Southbound
No access

A64(M) Leeds
Clay Pit Lane (A58)

Westbound
No exit (to Clay Pit Lane)

Eastbound
No access (from Clay Pit
Lane)

A66(M) Darlington Spur

Westbound
Exit only to A1(M)
(southbound)

Eastbound
Access only from A1(M)
(northbound)

A74(M) Gretna - Abington

Northbound
Exit only, no access

Southbound
Access only, no exit

A194(M)
Newcastle upon Tyne

Northbound
Access only from A1(M)
(northbound)

Southbound
Exit only to A1(M)
(southbound)

A12 M25 - Ipswich

Northeastbound
Access only, no exit

Southwestbound
No restriction

Northeastbound
Exit only, no access

Southwestbound
Access only, no exit

Northeastbound
Exit only, no access

Southwestbound
Access only, no exit

Northeastbound
Access only, no exit

Southwestbound
Exit only, no access

Northeastbound
No restriction

Southwestbound
Access only, no exit

Northeastbound
Exit only, no access

Southwestbound
Access only, no exit

Northeastbound
Access only, no exit

Southwestbound
Exit only, no access

Northeastbound
Exit only, no access

Southwestbound
Access only, no exit

Northeastbound
Exit only (for Stratford
St Mary and Dedham)

Southwestbound
Access only

A14 M1 - Felixstowe

Westbound
Exit only to M6 & M1
(northbound)

Eastbound
Access only from M6 &
M1 (southbound)

Westbound
Exit only, no access

Eastbound
Access only, no exit

Westbound
Access only, no exit

Eastbound
Exit only, no access

Westbound
Exit only, no access

Eastbound
Access only from A1
(southbound)

Westbound
Access only, no exit

Eastbound
Exit only, no access

Westbound
No restriction

Eastbound
Access only, no exit

Northeastbound
Access only, no exit

Southwestbound
Exit only, no access

Northeastbound
No restriction

Southwestbound
Access only, no exit

Westbound
Exit only to A11
Access only from A1303

Eastbound
Access only from A11

Westbound
Access only from A11

Eastbound
Exit only to A11

Westbound
Exit only, no access

Eastbound
Access only, no exit

Westbound
Access only, no exit

Eastbound
Exit only, no access

A55 Holyhead - Chester

Westbound
Exit only, no access

Eastbound
Access only, no exit

Westbound
Access only, no exit

Eastbound
Exit only, no access

Westbound
Exit only, no access

Eastbound
No access or exit.

Westbound
No restriction

Eastbound
No access or exit

Westbound
Exit only, no access

Eastbound
No access or exit

Westbound
Exit only to A5104

Eastbound
Access only from A5104

Refer also to atlas pages 20–21. In October 2021 the Ultra Low Emission Zone is due to be extended. For further information visit **tfl.gov.uk/ULEZ**

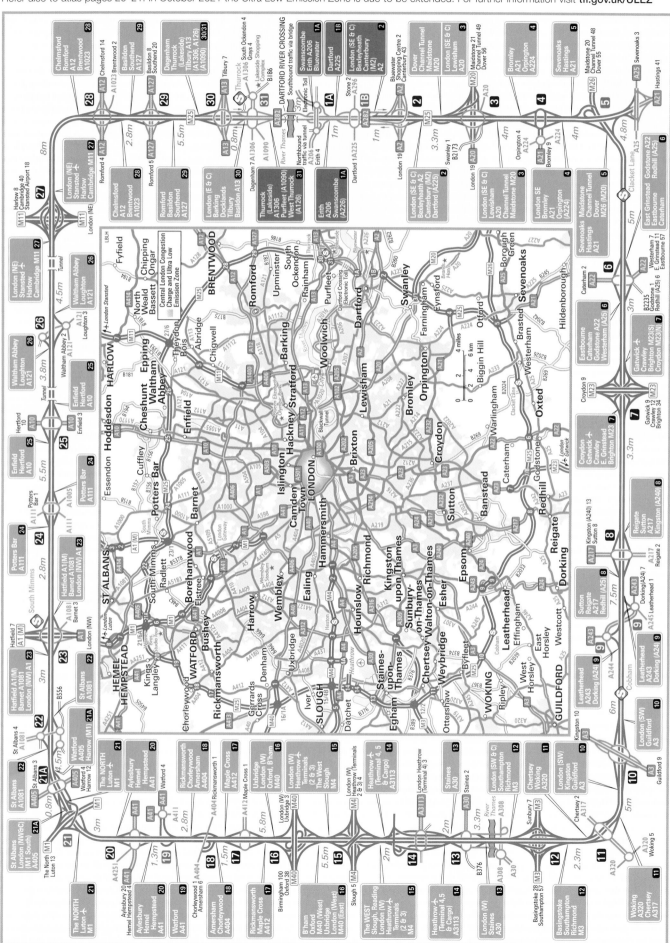

Refer also to atlas page 40

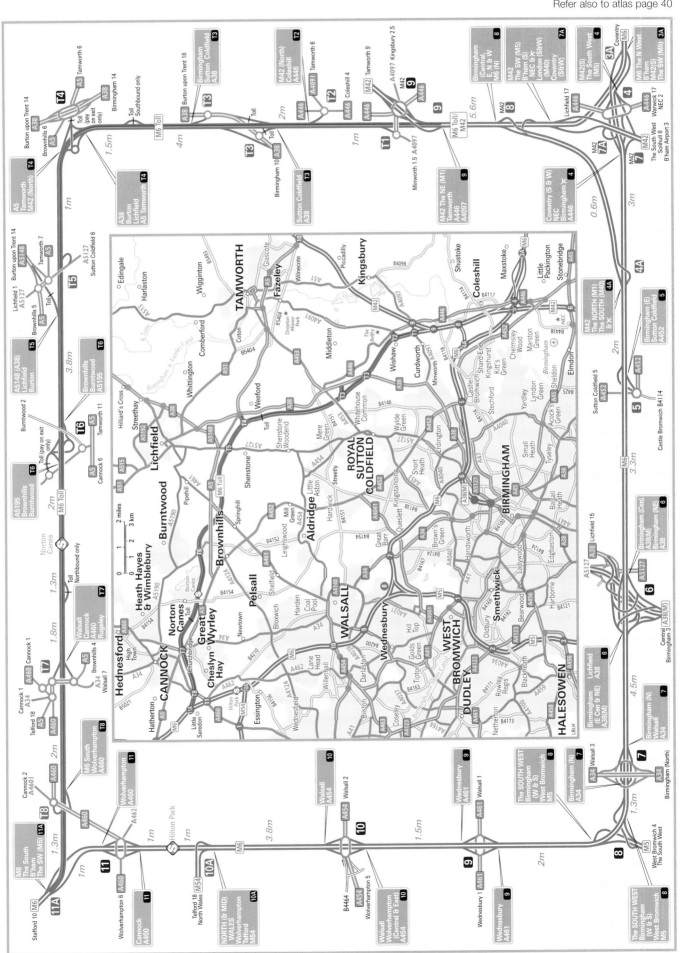

Smart motorways

Since Britain's first motorway (the Preston Bypass) opened in 1958, motorways have changed significantly. A vast increase in car journeys over the last 62 years has meant that motorways quickly filled to capacity. To combat this, the recent development of **smart motorways** uses technology to monitor and actively manage traffic flow and congestion.

How they work

Smart motorways utilise various active traffic management methods, monitored through a regional traffic control centre:

- Traffic flow is monitored using CCTV
- Speed limits are changed to smooth traffic flow and reduce stop-start driving
- Capacity of the motorway can be increased by either temporarily or permanently opening the hard shoulder to traffic
- Warning signs and messages alert drivers to hazards and traffic jams ahead
- Lanes can be closed in the case of an accident or emergency by displaying a red X sign

- Emergency refuge areas are located regularly along the motorway where there is no hard shoulder available

The map shows the main motorway network with the three different types of smart motorway in operation or planned to open over the next five years:

Controlled motorway
Variable speed limits without hard shoulder (the hard shoulder is used in emergencies only)

Hard shoulder running
Variable speed limits with part-time hard shoulder (the hard shoulder is open to traffic at busy times when signs permit)

All lane running
Variable speed limits with hard shoulder as permanent running lane (there is no hard shoulder); this is standard for all new smart motorway schemes since 2013

Standard motorway

Quick tips

- Never drive in a lane closed by a red X

- Keep to the speed limit shown on the gantries
- A solid white line indicates the hard shoulder – do not drive in it unless directed or in the case of an emergency
- A broken white line indicates a normal running lane
- Exit the smart motorway where possible if your vehicle is in difficulty. In an emergency, move onto the hard shoulder where there is one, or the nearest emergency refuge area
- Put on your hazard lights if you break down

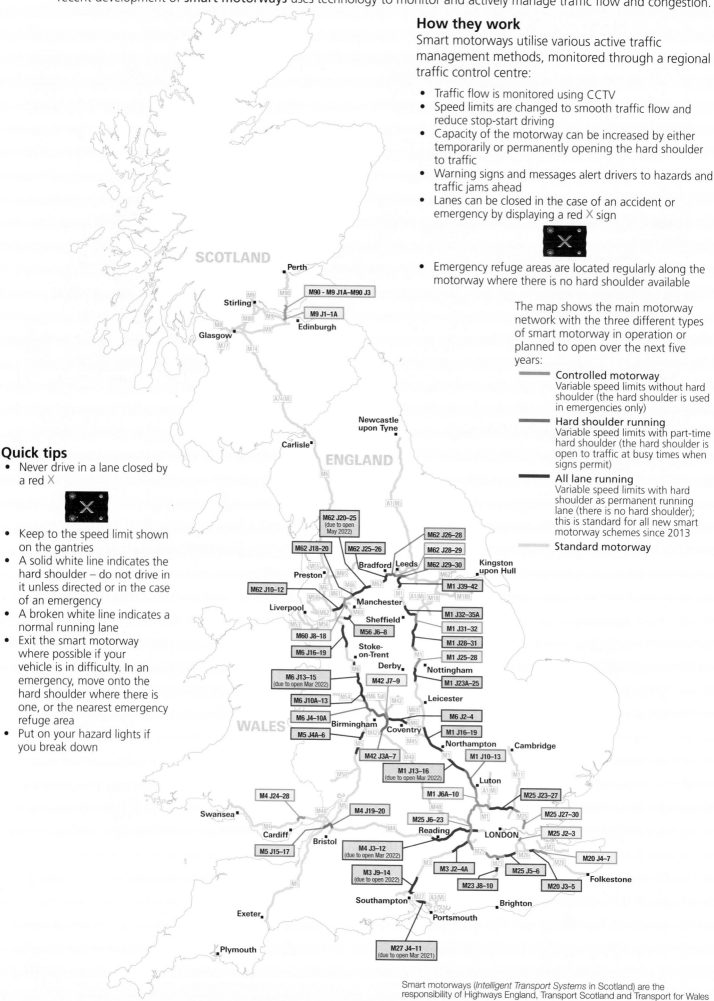

Smart motorways (*Intelligent Transport Systems* in Scotland) are the responsibility of Highways England, Transport Scotland and Transport for Wales

Motoring information

Motorway with number	Primary route service area	Road tunnel	Airport (major/minor), heliport
Toll motorway with toll station	Primary route destination BATH	Road toll, steep gradient (arrows point downhill)	International freight terminal
Motorway junction with and without number	Other A road single/dual carriageway A1123	Distance in miles between symbols	24-hour Accident & Emergency hospital
Restricted motorway junctions	B road single/dual carriageway B2070	Vehicle ferry (all year, seasonal)	Crematorium
Motorway service area, rest area	Minor road more than 4 metres wide, less than 4 metres wide	Fast vehicle ferry or catamaran	Park and Ride (at least 6 days per week)
Motorway and junction under construction	Roundabout	Passenger ferry (all year, seasonal)	City, town, village or other built-up area
Primary route single/dual carriageway	Interchange/junction	Railway line, in tunnel	Height in metres, mountain pass
Primary route junction with and without number	Narrow primary/other A/B road with passing places (Scotland)	Railway station, tram stop, level crossing	Snow gates (on main routes)
Restricted primary route junctions	Road under construction	Preserved or tourist railway	National boundary, county or administrative boundary

Touring information To avoid disappointment, check opening times before visiting

Scenic route	Garden	Waterfall	Motor-racing circuit
Tourist Information Centre	Arboretum	Hill-fort	Air show venue
Tourist Information Centre (seasonal)	Country park	Roman antiquity	Ski slope (natural, artificial)
Visitor or heritage centre	Showground	Prehistoric monument	National Trust site
Picnic site	Theme park	Battle site with year 1066	National Trust for Scotland site
Caravan site (AA inspected)	Farm or animal centre	Preserved or tourist railway	English Heritage site
Camping site (AA inspected)	Zoological or wildlife collection	Cave or cavern	Historic Scotland site
Caravan & camping site (AA inspected)	Bird collection	Windmill, monument or memorial	Cadw (Welsh heritage) site
Abbey, cathedral or priory	Aquarium	Beach (award winning)	Other place of interest
Ruined abbey, cathedral or priory	RSPB site	Lighthouse	Boxed symbols indicate attractions within urban area
Castle	National Nature Reserve (England, Scotland, Wales)	Golf course	World Heritage Site (UNESCO)
Historic house or building	Local nature reserve	Football stadium	National Park and National Scenic Area (Scotland)
Museum or art gallery	Wildlife Trust reserve	County cricket ground	Forest Park
Industrial interest	Forest drive	Rugby Union national stadium	Sandy beach
Aqueduct or viaduct	National trail	International athletics stadium	Heritage coast
Vineyard, brewery or distillery	Viewpoint	Horse racing, show jumping	Major shopping centre

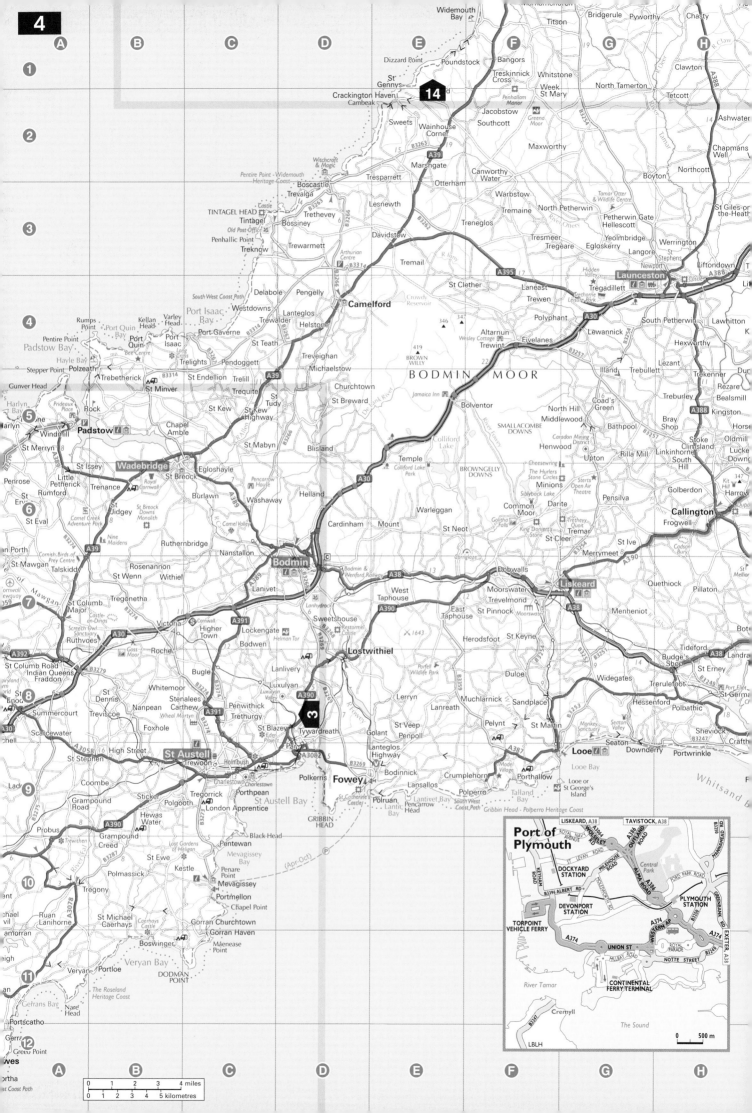

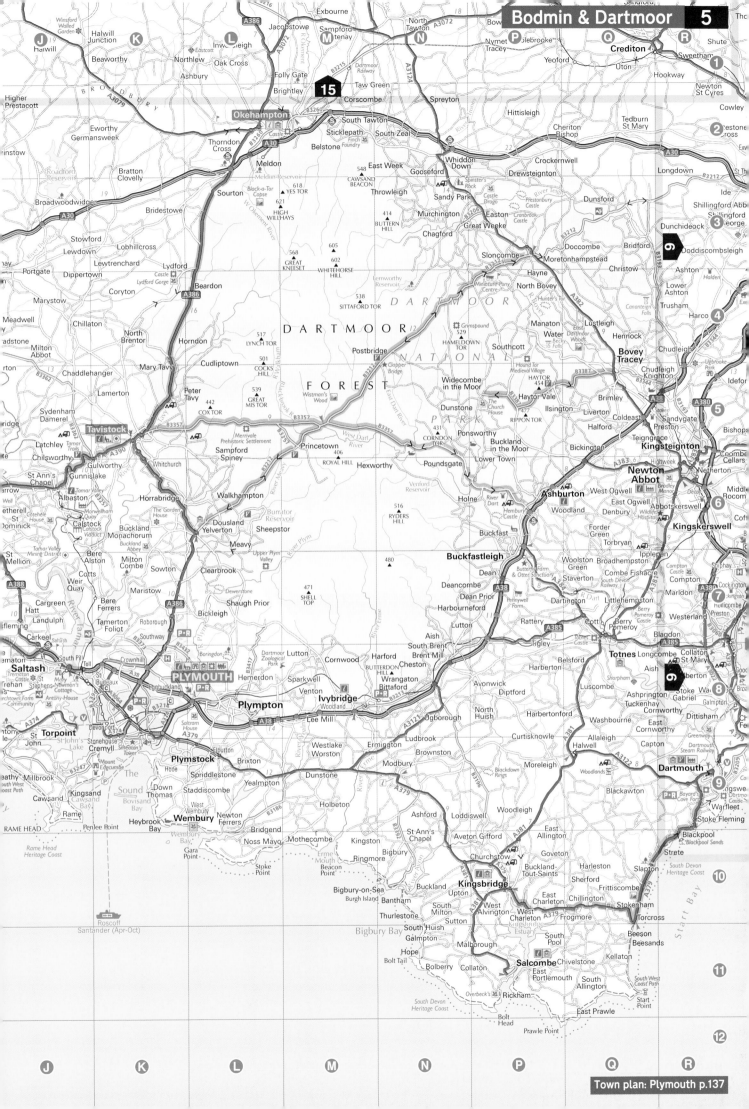

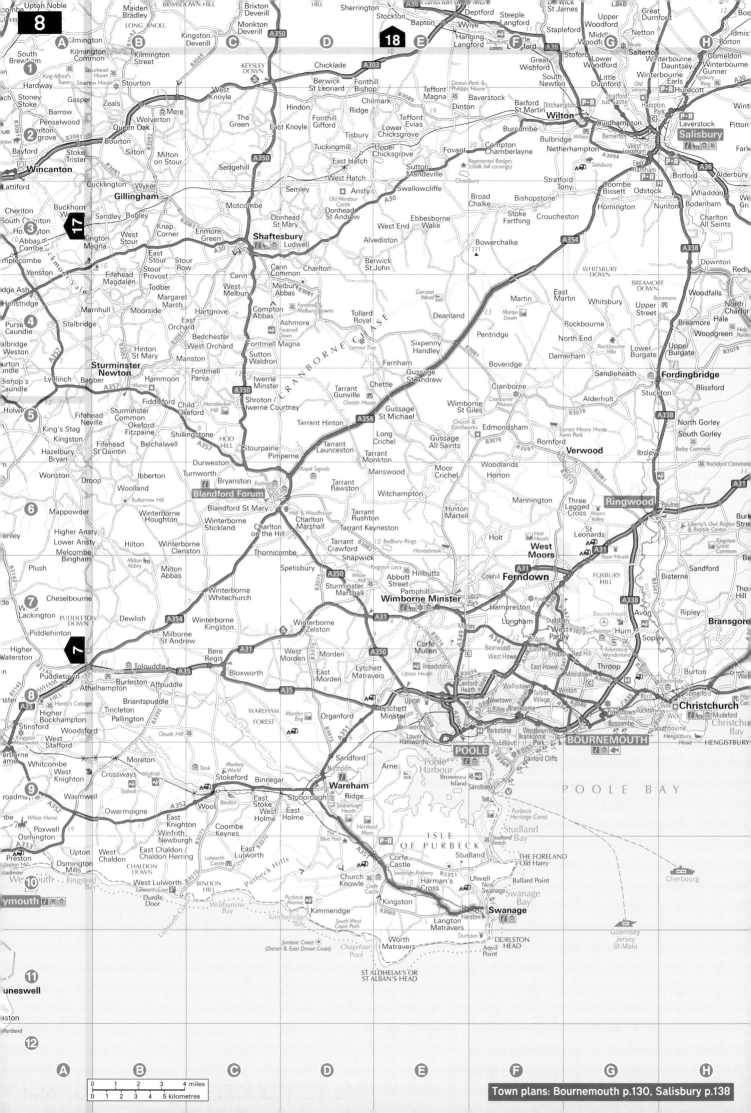

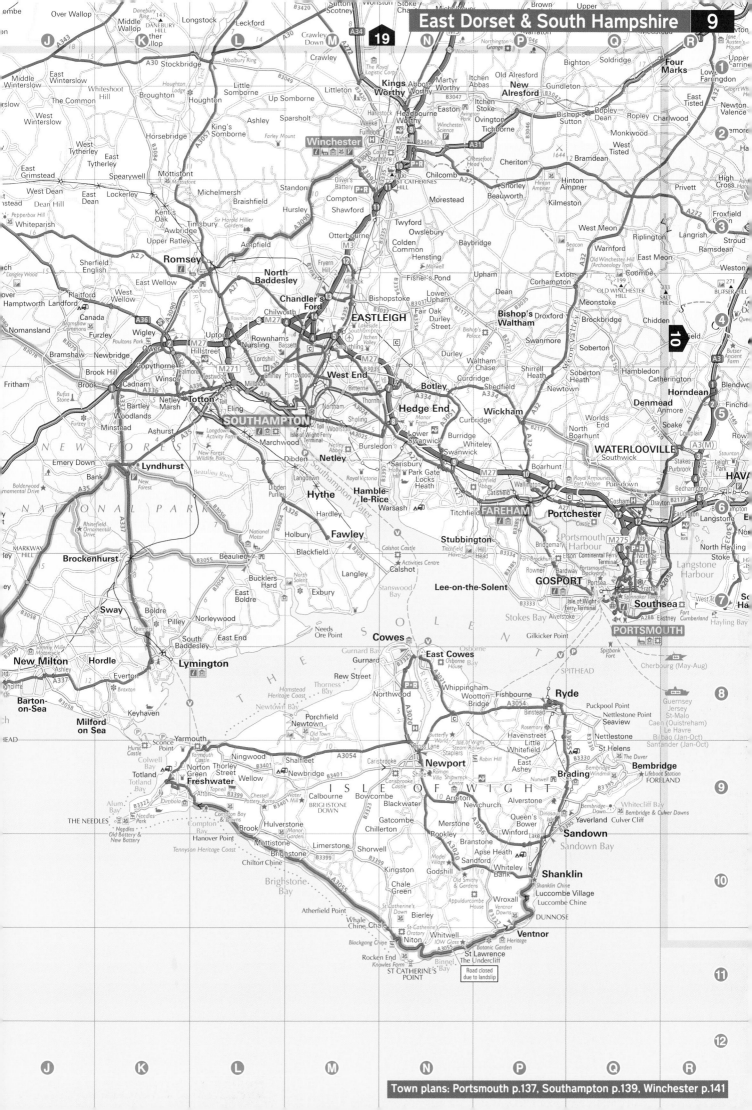

Town plan: Royal Tunbridge Wells p.138

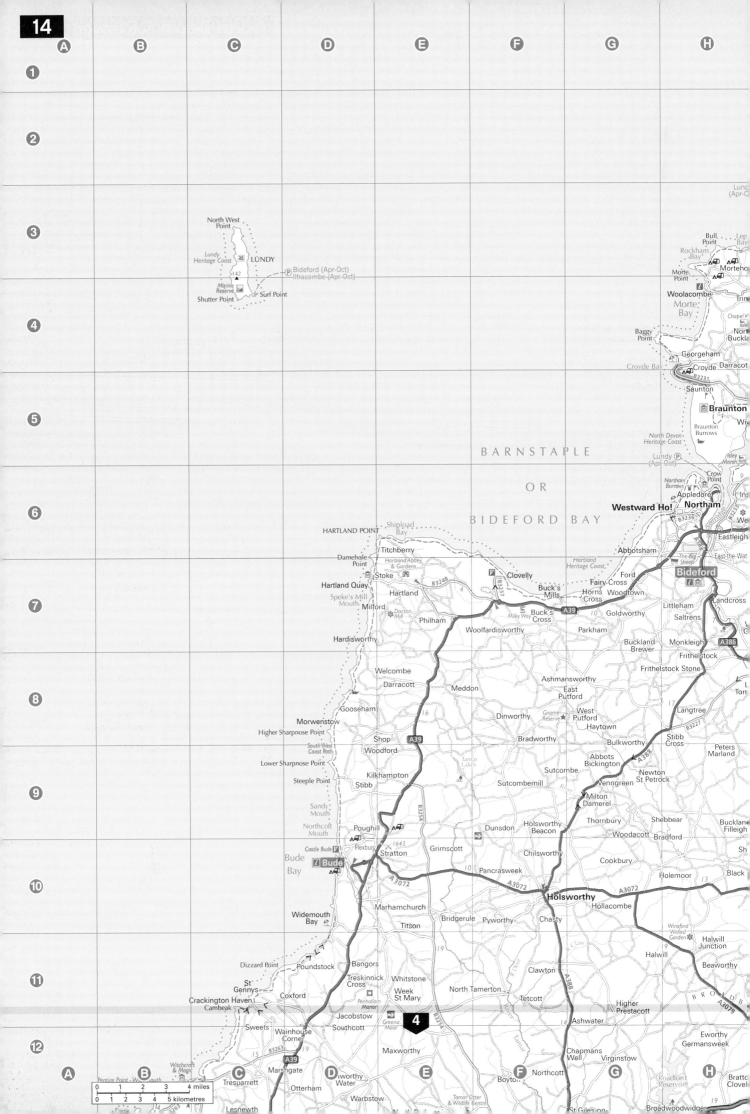

A B C D E F G H

1
2
3
4
5
6
7
8
9
10
11
12

North West
Point

*Lundy
Heritage Coast*   LUNDY

▲142   ℗ Bideford (Apr-Oct)
*Marine   Ilfracombe (Apr-Oct)
Reserve*
Shutter Point   ⚓ Surf Point

Bull
Point   Lep
Bay
Rockham
Bay   Morteho
Morte.
Point   Morteho
Woolacombe   Trin
Morte:
Bay   *Chapel V*
Baggy
Point   Nort
Buckla
Georgeham
Croyde   Darracot
Croyde Bay   Saunton
Braunton
Braunton
Burrows   Wr

B A R N S T A P L E

O R   North Devon
Heritage Coast   Lundy ℗
(Apr-Oct)   Isley
Marsh
Crow
Point   Ins
B I D E F O R D   B A Y   *Northam
Burrows*   Appledore
Westward Ho!   **Northam**   We
B3236
Eastleigh

HARTLAND POINT   Shipload
Bay   Abbotsham   East-the-Wat
The Big
Sheep
Damehole
Point   Titchberry   *Hartland Abbey
& Gardens*   *Hartland
Heritage Coast*   Ford   **Bideford**
Stoke   Clovelly   Fairy
Cross   Woodtown   Landcross
Hartland Quay   Hartland   B3248   Buck's   Horns
Mills   Cross
*Speke's Mill
Mouth*   Milford   Milky Way   Buck's   A39   10   Goldworthy   Littleham   Saltrens
*Docton
Mill*   Philham   Cross   Parkham   Monkleigh   A386
Hardisworthy   Woolfardisworthy   Buckland
Brewer   Frithelstock
Frithelstock
Stone   Torr

Welcombe   Meddon   Ashmansworthy   Langtree
Darracott   East
Putford   B3227
Dinworthy   *Gnome   West
Reserve* ★   Putford   Stibb
Cross   Peters
Gooseham   Haytown   Marland
Morwenstow   Bradworthy   Bulkworthy
Higher Sharpnose Point   Shop   A39   Abbots   A388   Newton
*South West   Woodford   Bickington   St Petrock
Coast Path*   *Tamar
Lakes*   Sutcombe   Venngreen
Lower Sharpnose Point   Kilkhampton   Sutcombemill   Milton   Thornbury   Shebbear   Buckland
Filleigh
Steeple Point   Stibb   *River*   Damerel   Woodacott   Bradford
Sandy   Dunsdon   Holsworthy   Chilsworthy   Cookbury   Sh
Mouth   Beacon
Northcott   Poughill   ▲V   Holemoor
Mouth   Grimscott   Chilsworthy   13   Black
Castle Bude   Flexbury   ▲1643   Pancrasweek   A3072   Winsford
Stratton   Walled
Bude   Marhamchurch   10   **Holsworthy**   A3072   Garden
Bude   A3072   Hollacombe   Halwill
Bay   Junction
Widemouth   Titson   Bridgerule   Pyworthy   Chasty   Halwill   Beaworthy
Bay   North Tamerton   Tetcott
Dizzard Point   Poundstock   Bangors   Whitstone   Clawton   Higher   BROAD
St   Treskinnick   Week   Prestacott   A3079
Gennys   Cross   St Mary   *Penhallam   Ashwater   Roadford
Crackington Haven   Coxford   Manor*   Chapmans   Eworthy   Clovel
Cambeak   Jacobstow   *Greena   B3254   Well   Germansweek
Sweets   Southcott   Moor*   4   14   Virginstow   Bratto
Wainhouse   Maxworthy   *Tamar Otter   St Giles-on-   Broadwoodwidger
A39   Corner   & Wildlife Centre*

*Witchcraft
& Magic*

4

A   B   C   D   E   F   G   H
Pentire Point - Wadebridge
Tresparrett   Marshgate   Diworthy   Boyton   Northcott
Otterham   Water
0 1 2 3   4 miles   Warbstow
0 1 2 3 4 5 kilometres   Lesnewth

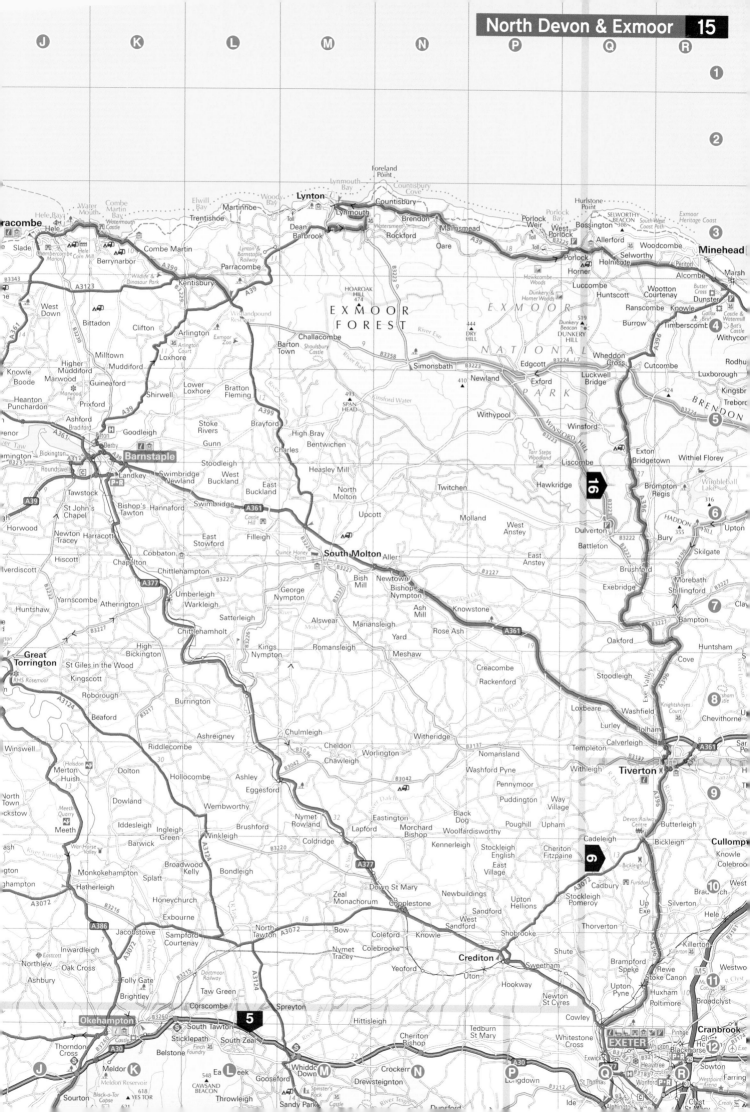

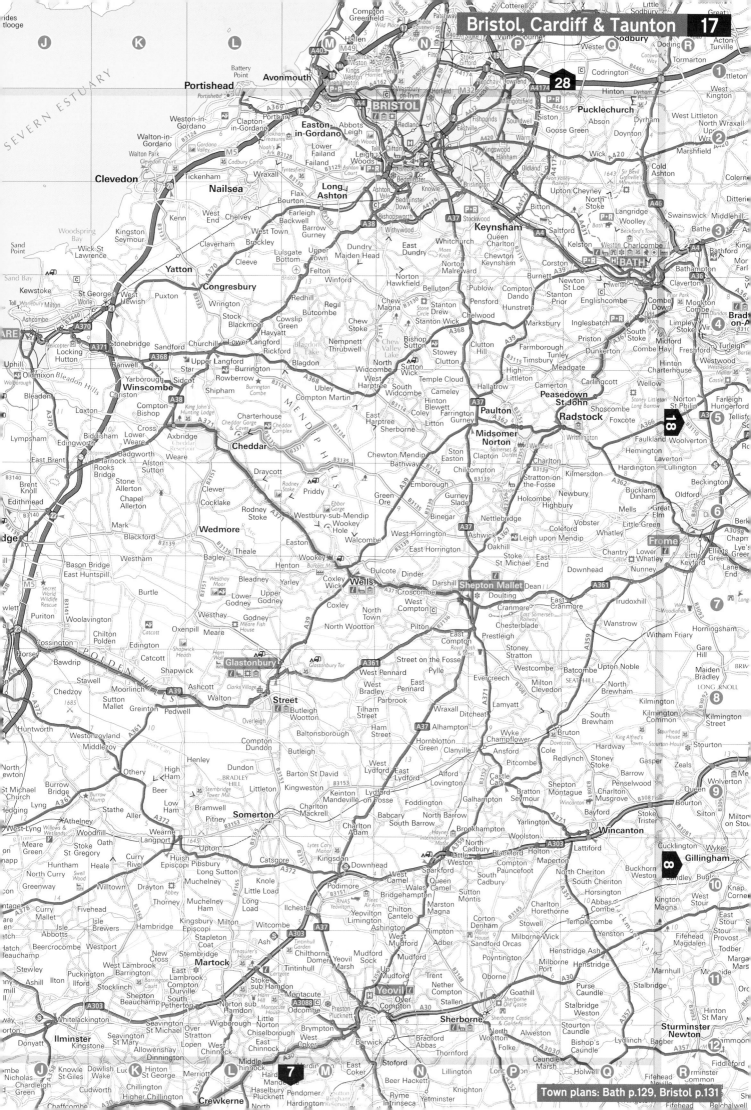

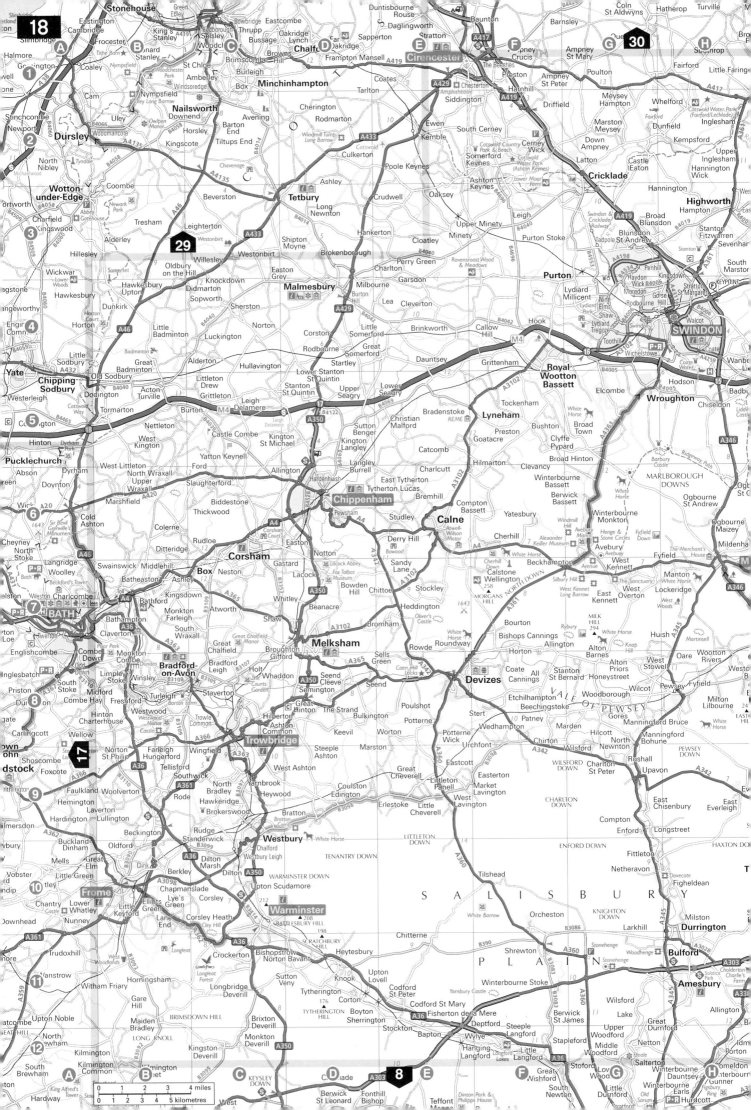

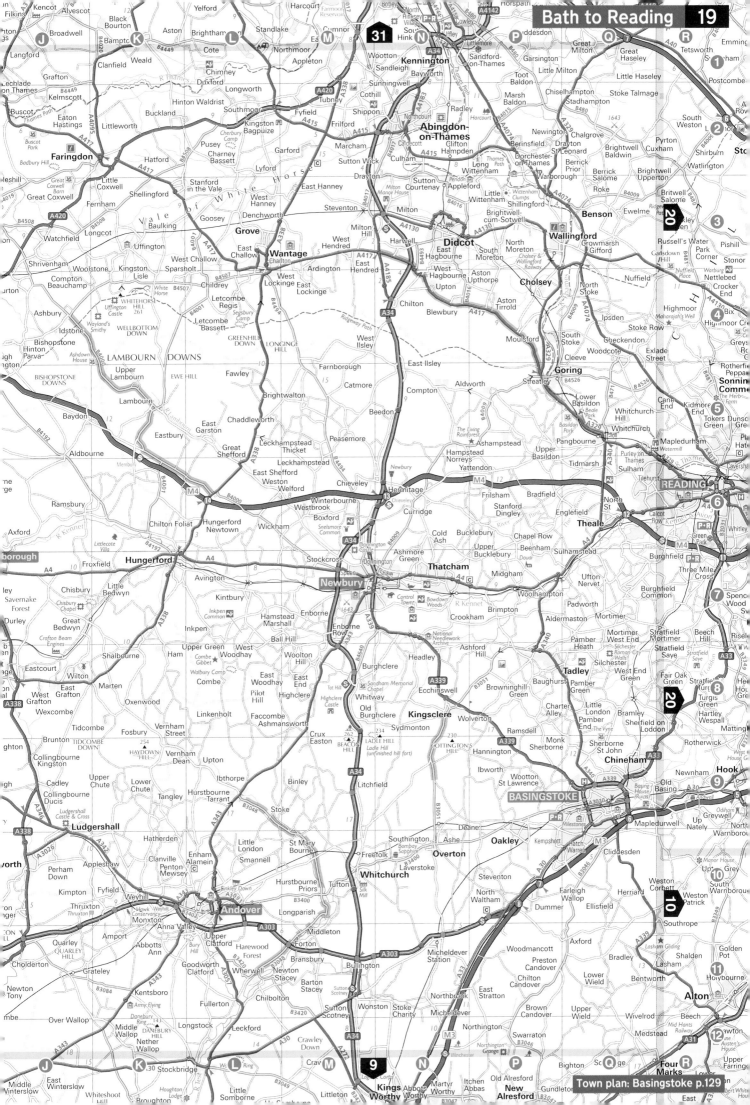

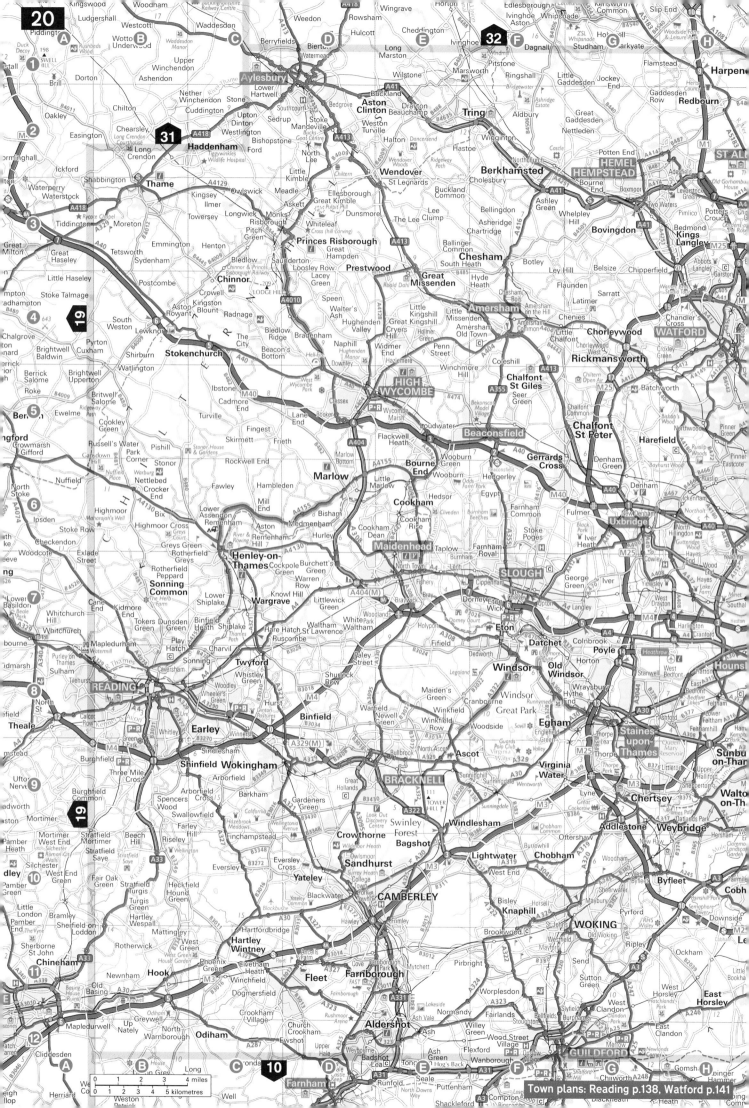

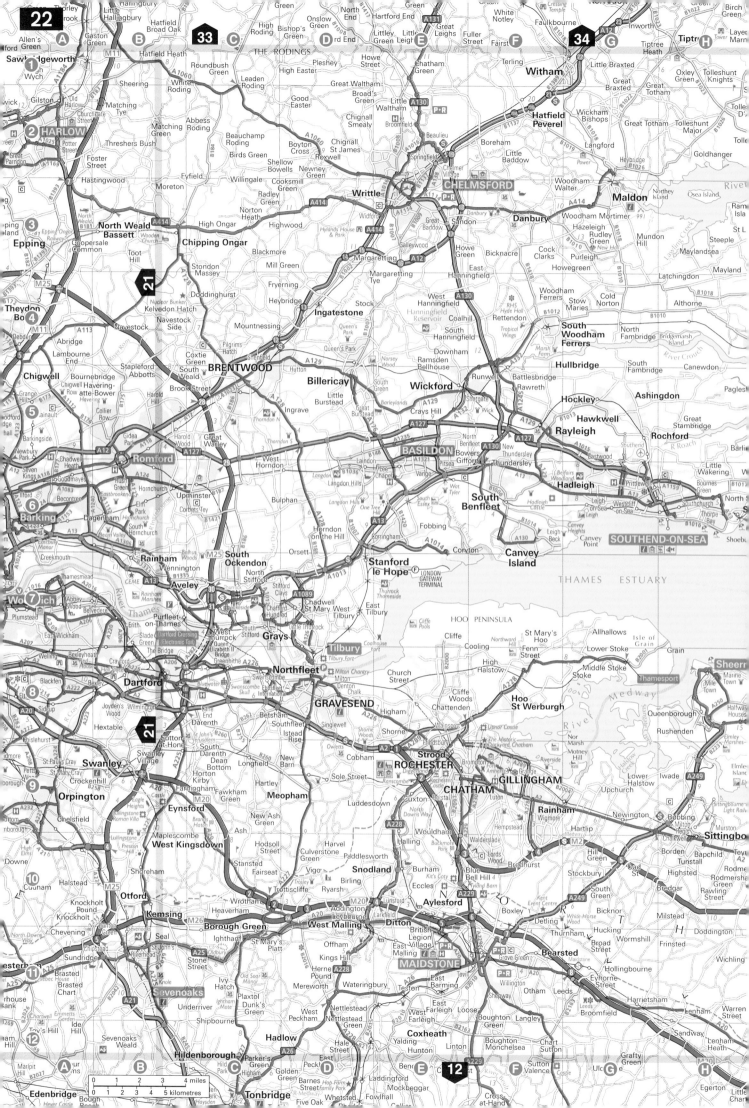

Town plan: Canterbury p.131

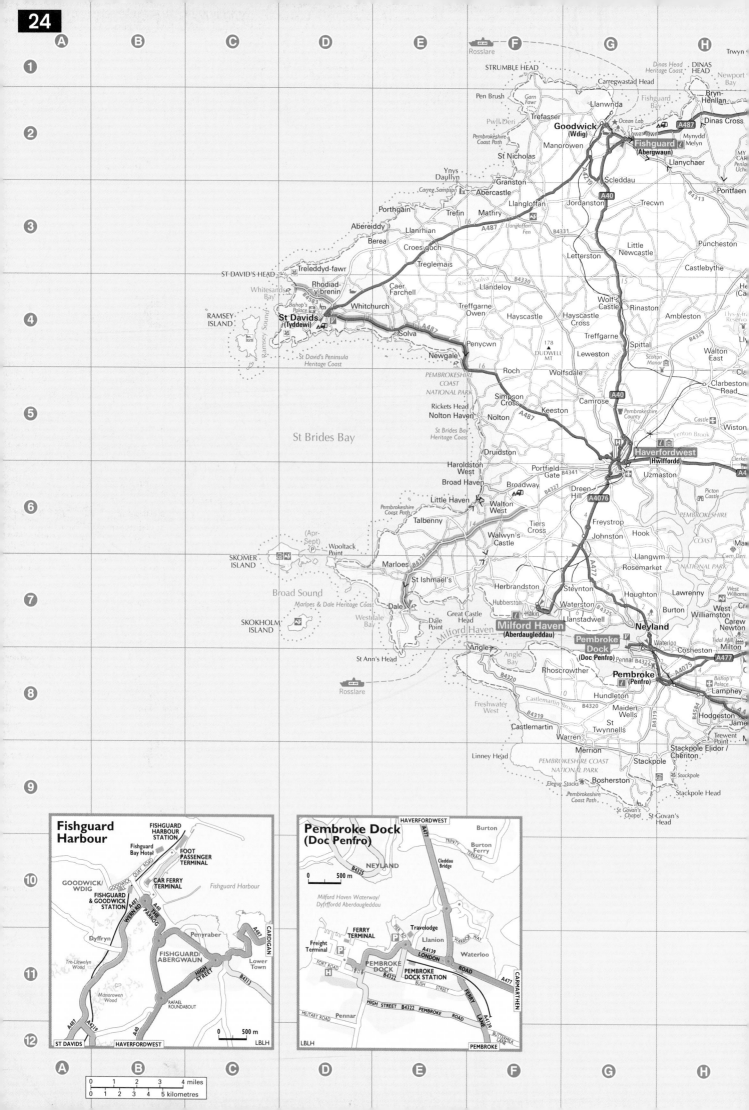

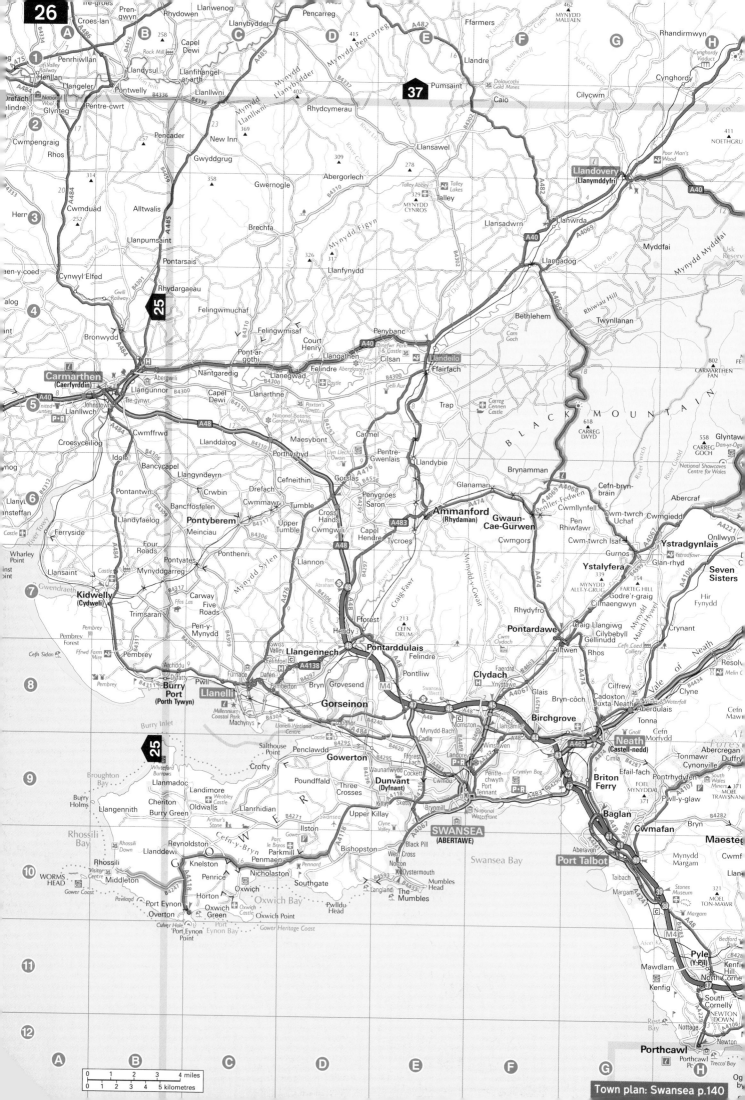

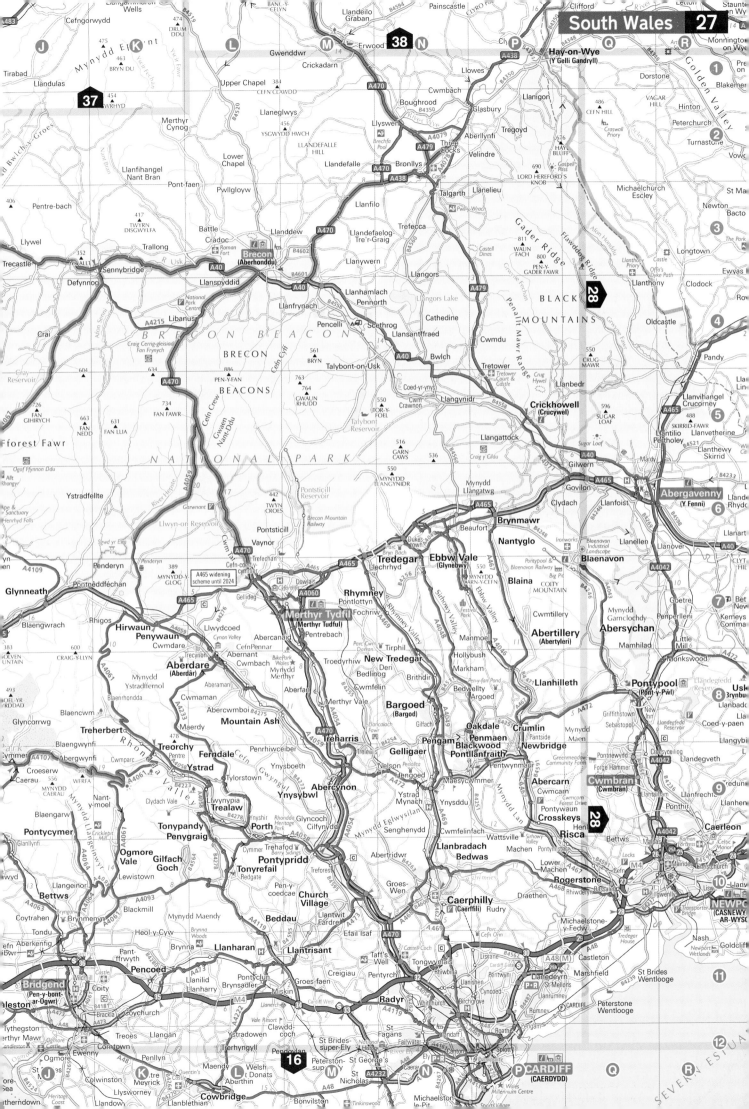

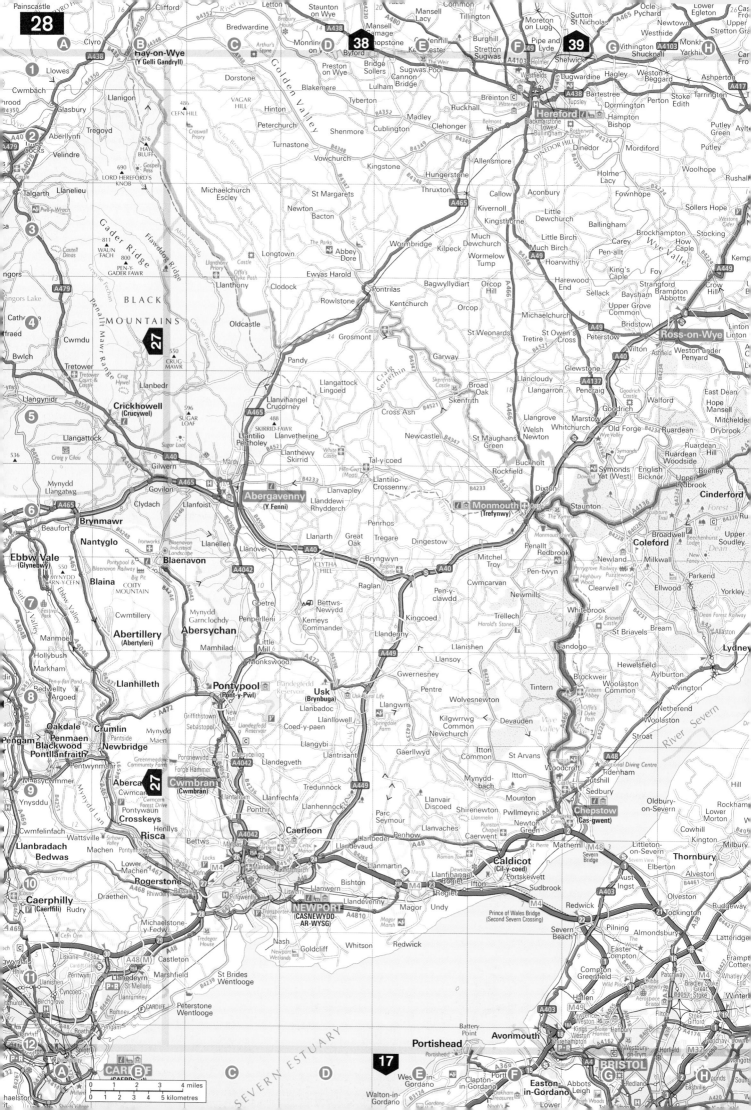

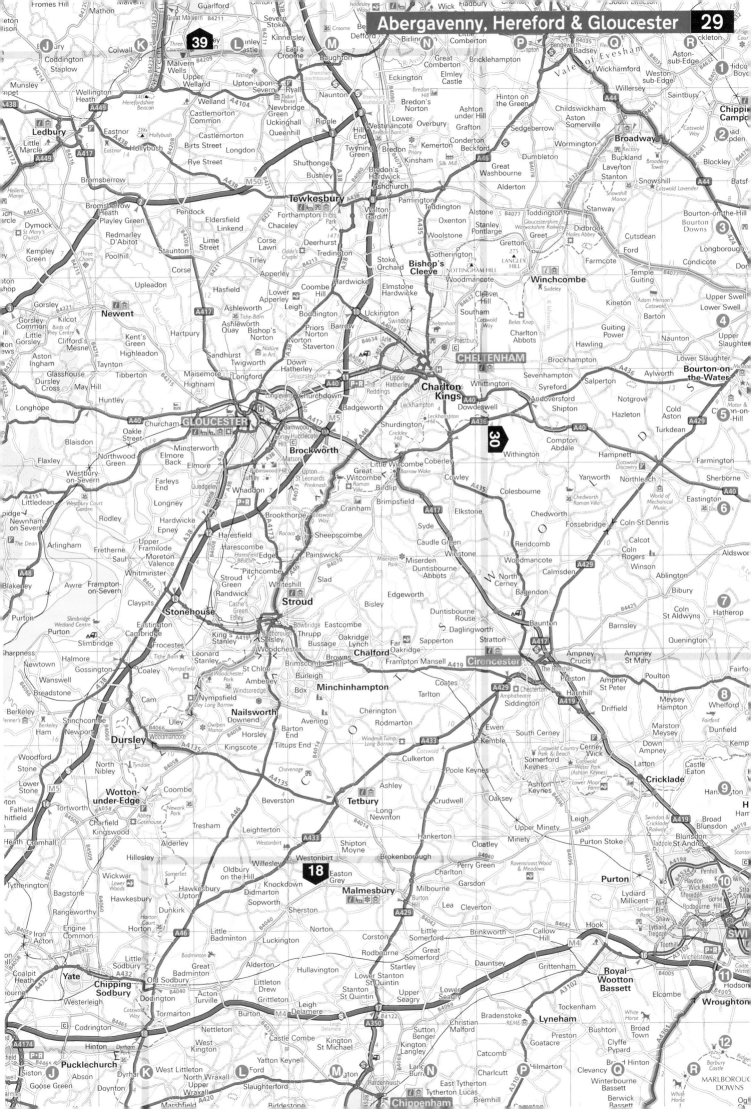

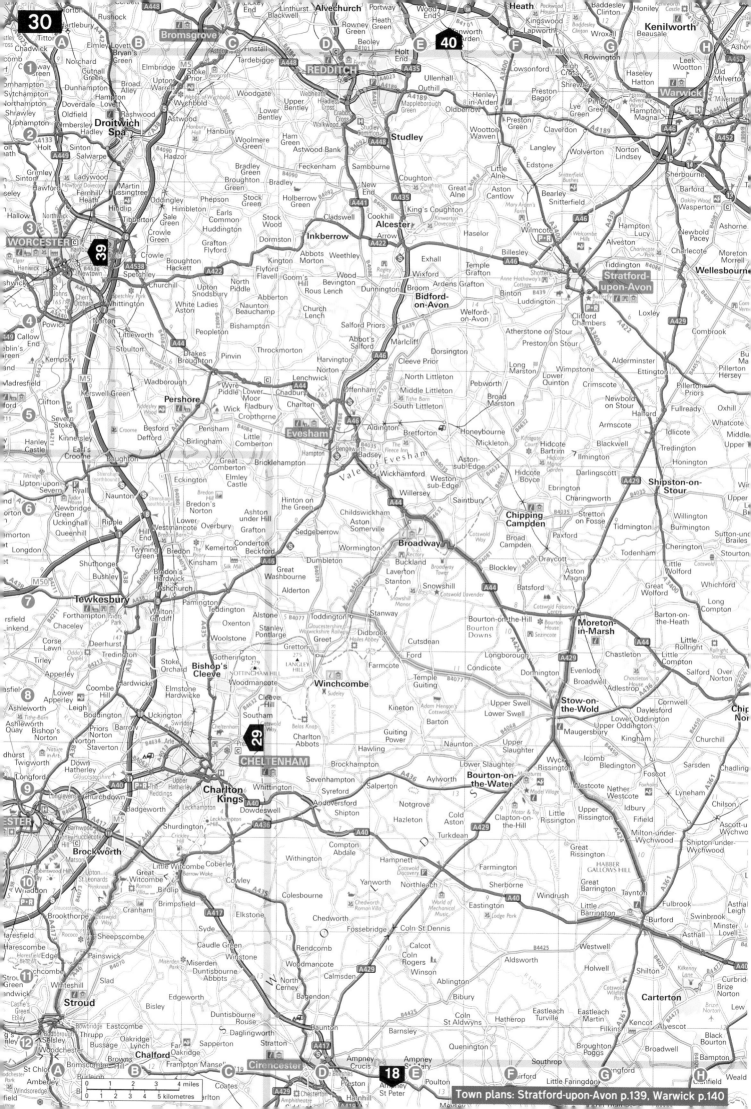

Town plans: Stratford-upon-Avon p.139, Warwick p.140

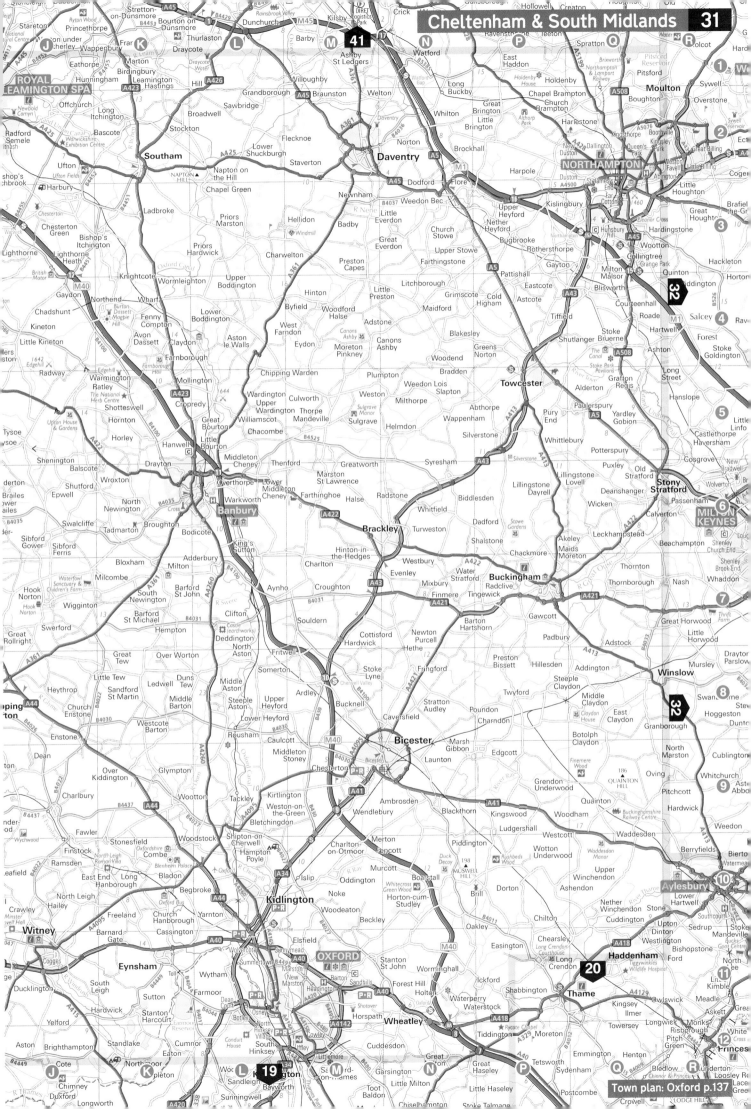

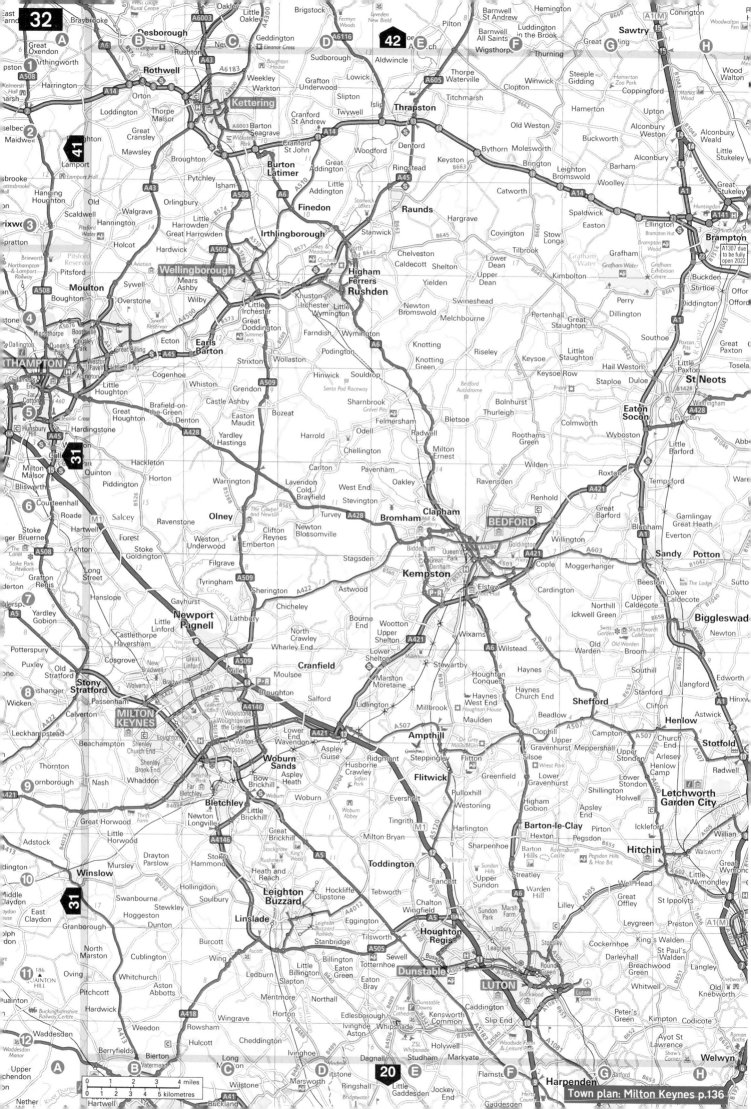

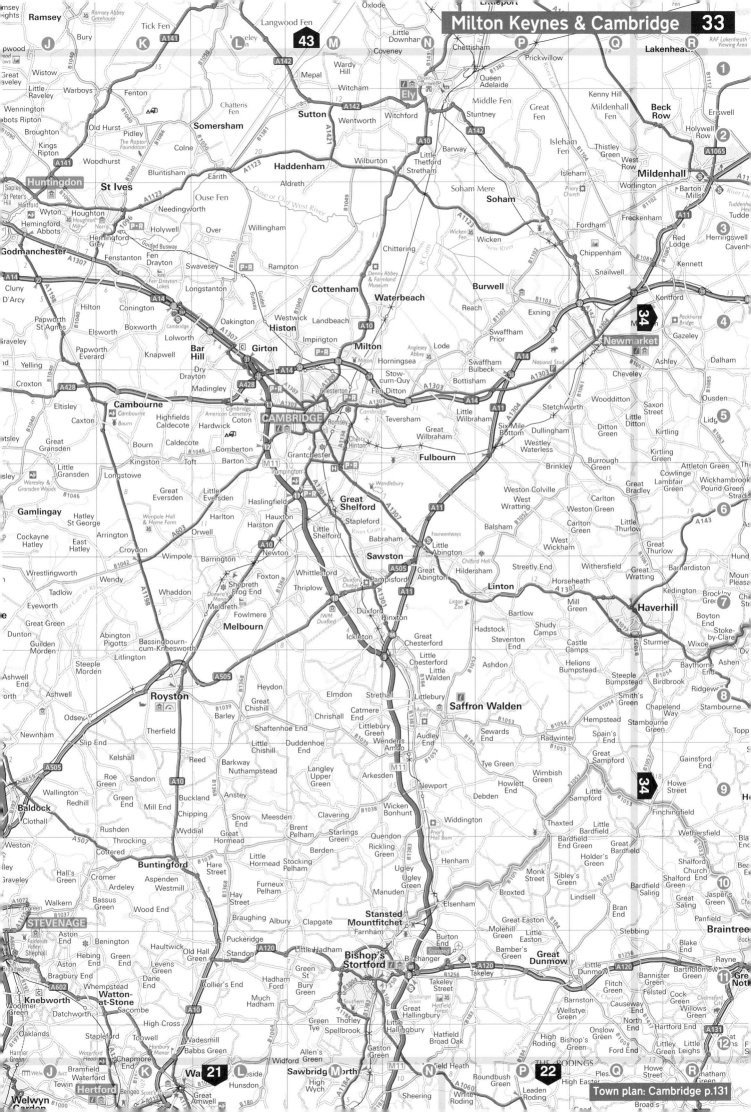

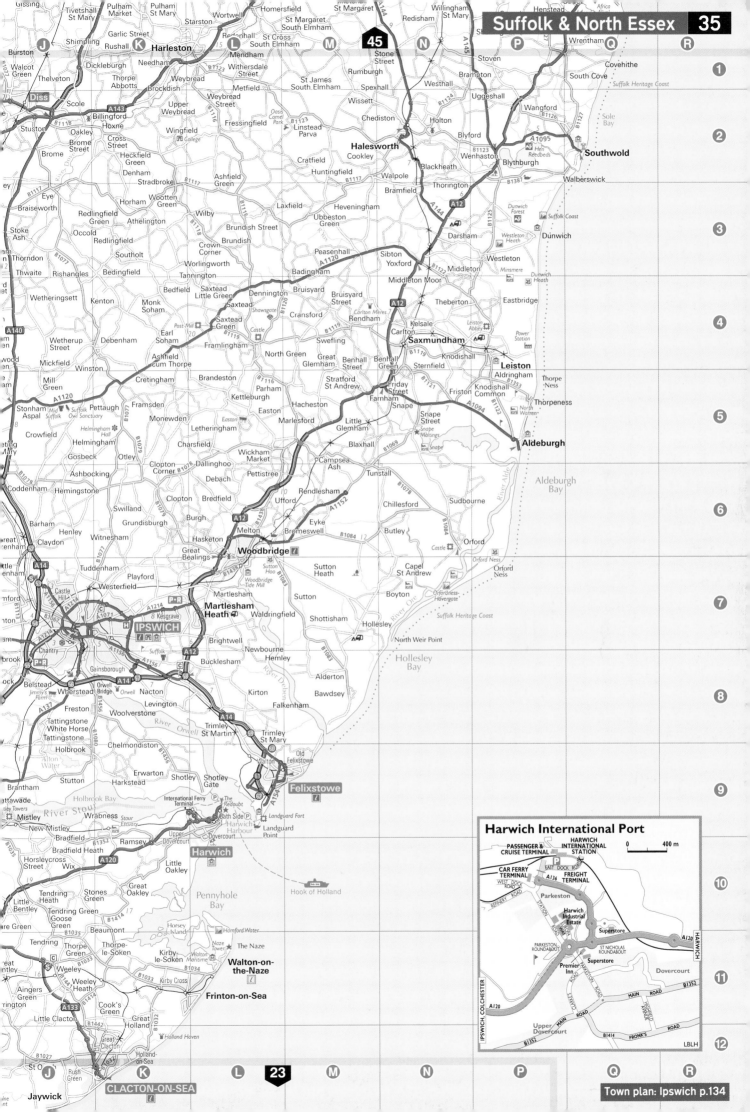

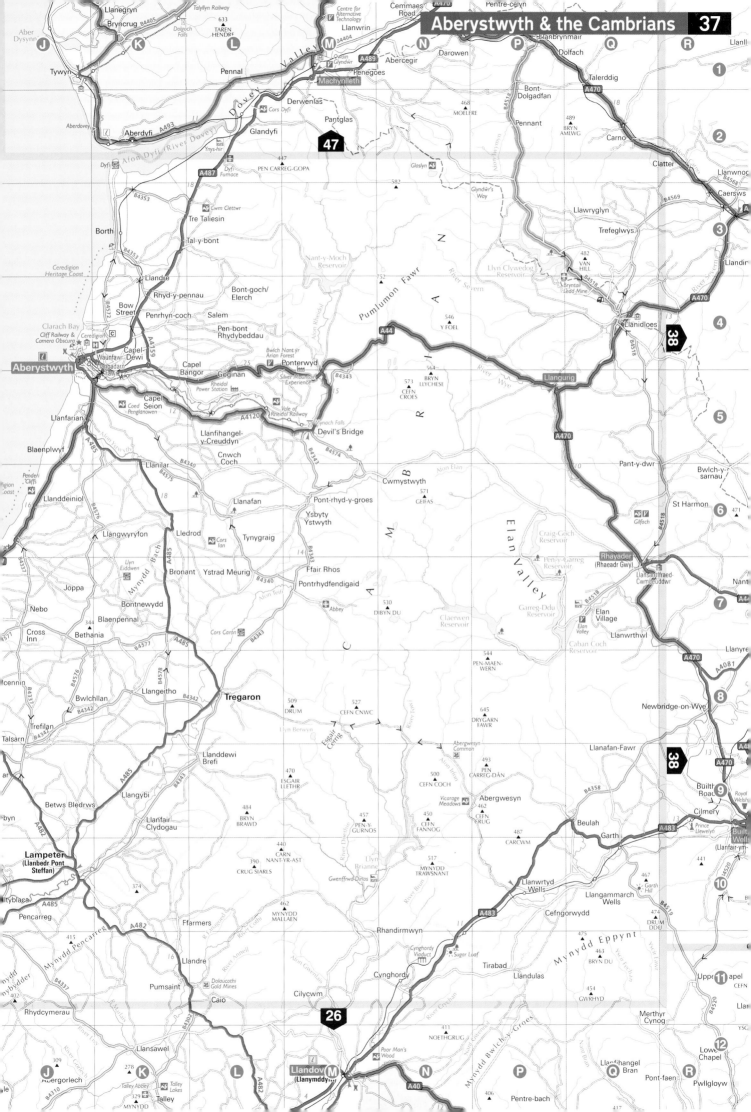

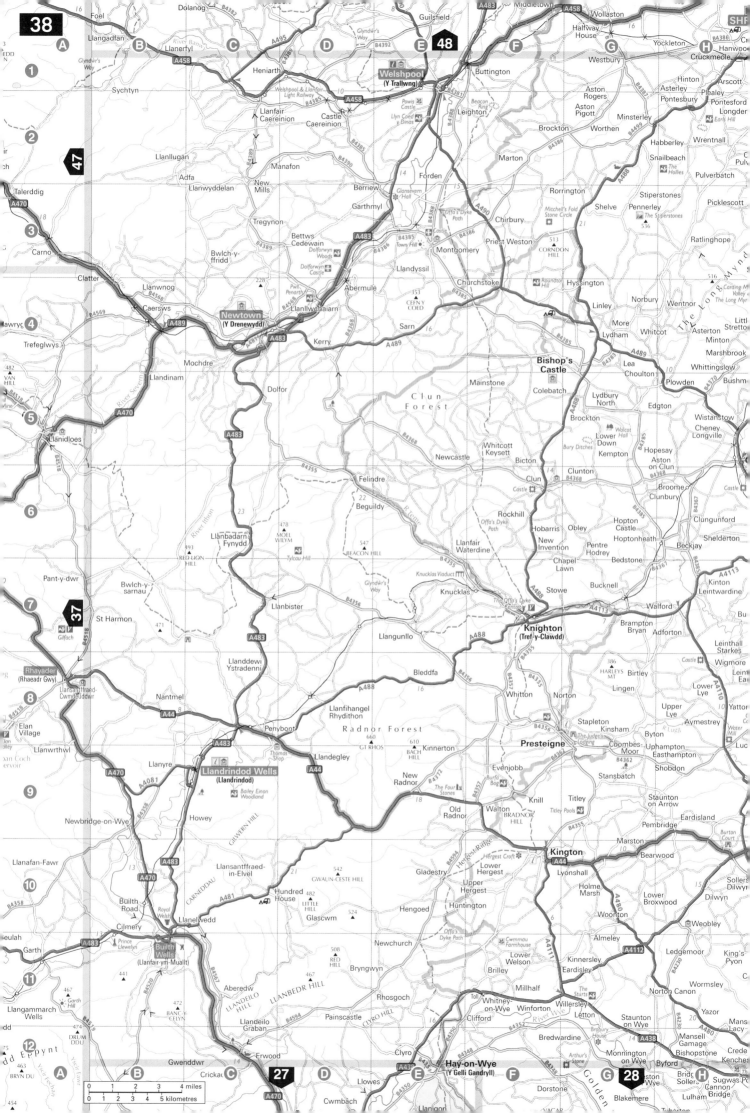

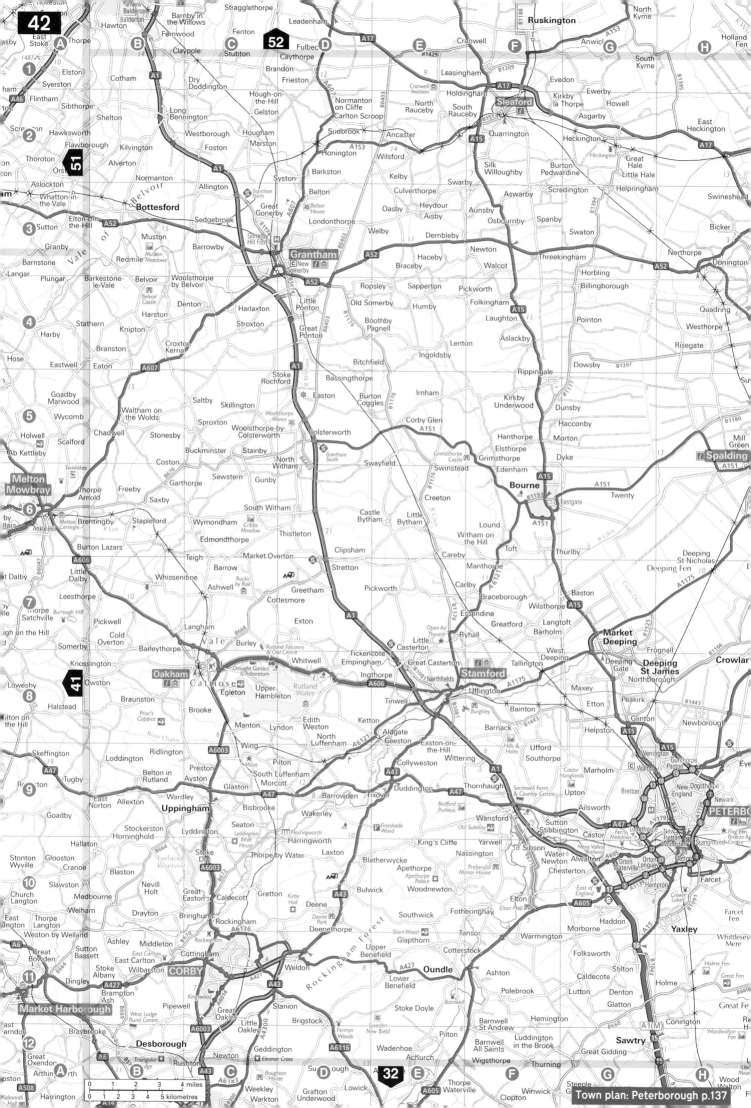

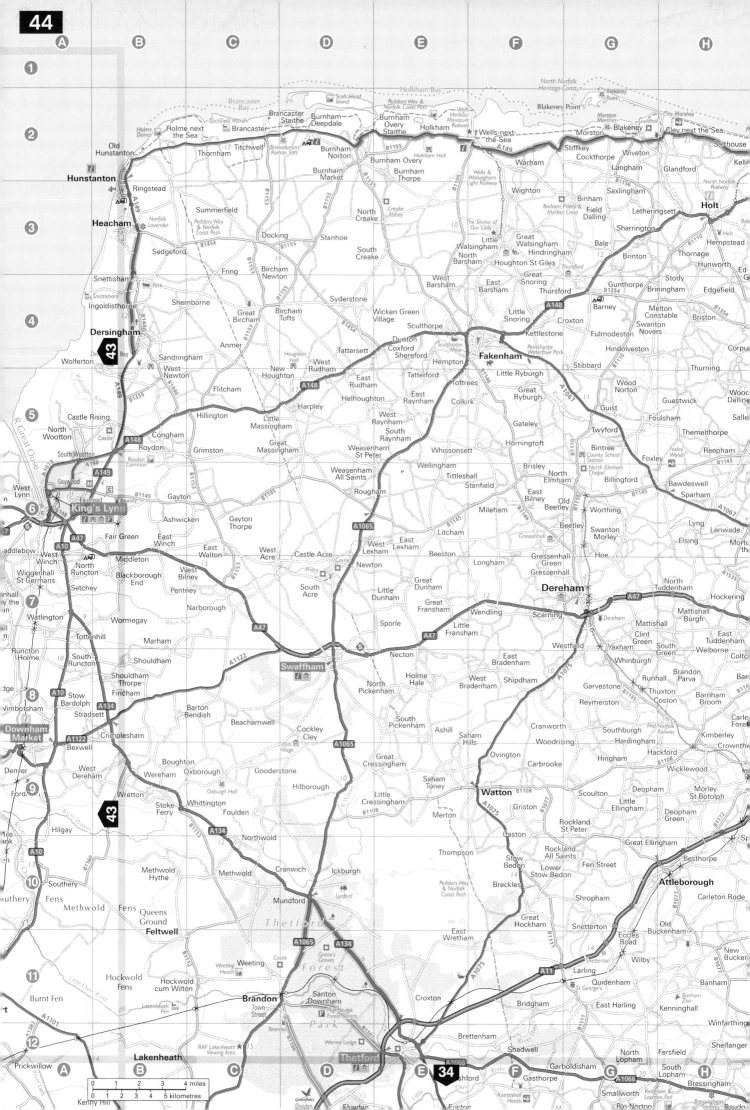

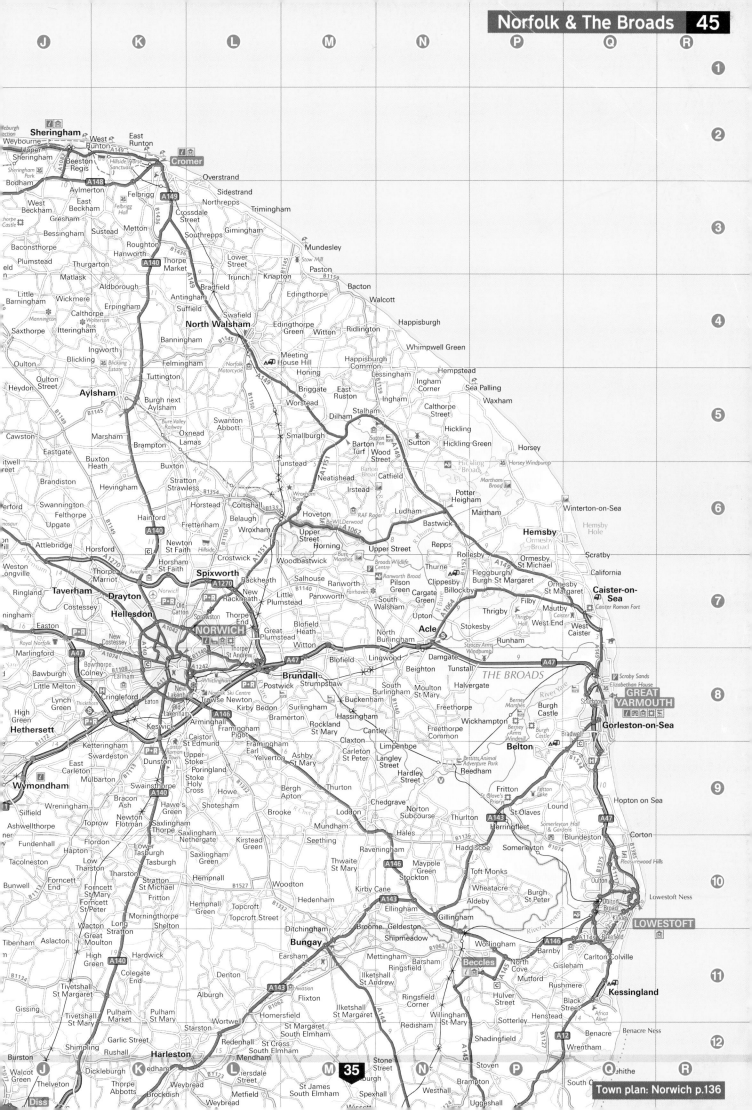

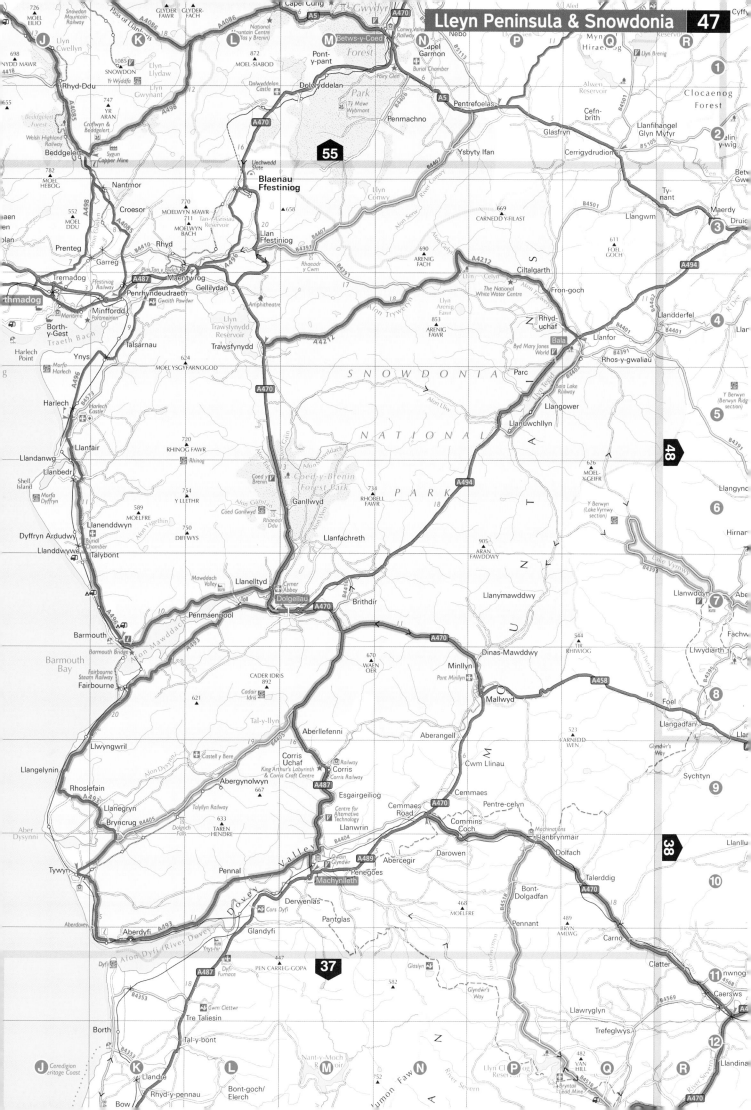

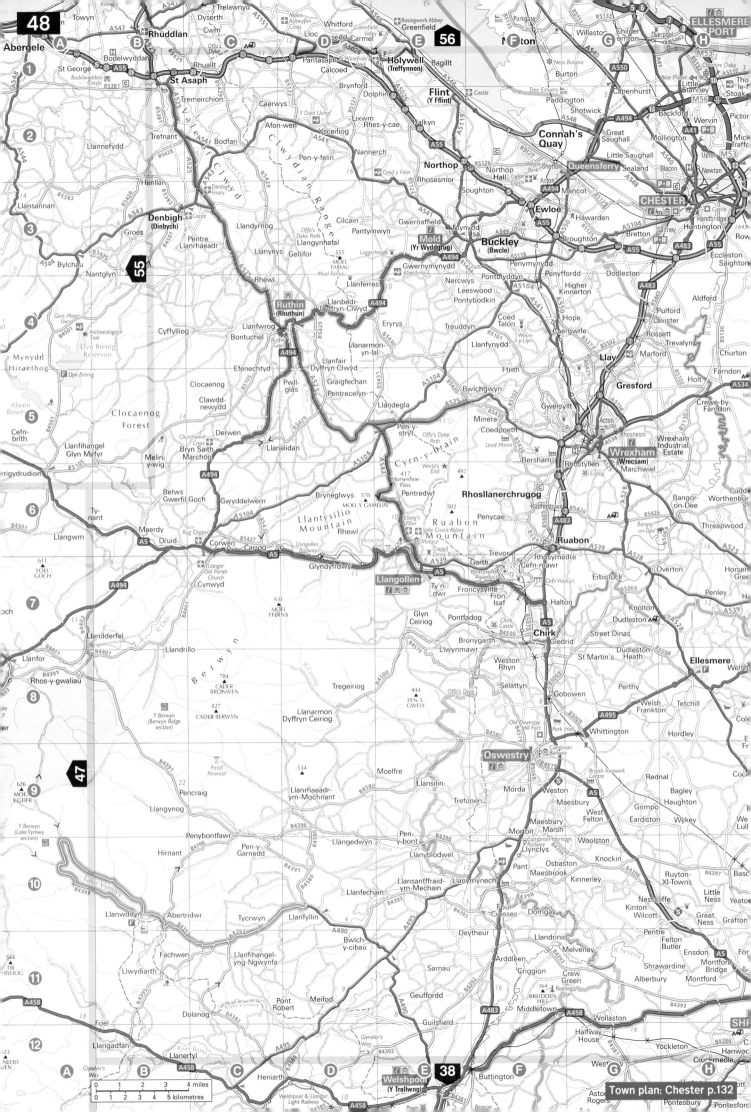

Skeffling
HUMBER
Kilnsea
Spurn Heritage Coast
Spurn Point
SPURN HEAD
Spurn Heritage Coast
61

GRIMSBY
West Marsh
Little Coates
Nunsthorpe
Scartho
Bradley
Scartho
Cleethorpes
Old Clee
Thrunscoe
The Jungle Zoo
Cleethorpes Coast Light Railway
Humberston
altham
New Waltham
Holton le Clay
oldby Beck
Waltham
Brigsley
Ashby cum Fenby
Grainsby
East endale
Waithe
Tetney
North Thoresby
B1201
North Cotes
Marshchapel
Donna Nook
Tetney Marshes
Wold Newton
Ludborough
Fulstow
Grainthorpe
Lincolnshire Wolds Railway
North Somercotes
A1031
North Ormsby
Covenham St Bartholomew
Covenham Reservoir
Conisholme
Saltfleet
Utterby
Covenham St Mary
Yarburgh
Saltfleetby - Theddlethorpe Dunes
Fotherby
Alvingham
North Cockerington
Saltfleetby St Clement
Kelstern
A631
South Elkington
Welton le Wold
Rushmoor
South Cockerington
Saltfleetby St Peter
Saltfleetby All Saints
Theddlethorpe St Helen
A1157
Louth
Grimoldby
B1200
Theddlethorpe All Saints
Seal Sanctuary & Wildlife Centre
Hallington
Raithby
Little Carlton
Manby
Great Carlton
Mablethorpe
athorpe
Withcall
A153
Tathwell
A16
Legbourne
North Reston
Gayton le Marsh
Trusthorpe
Donington on Bain
Haugham
Little Cawthorpe
South Reston
Withern
A1104
Sutton on Sea
Sandilands
ceby
Asterby
Cadwell Park
Burwell
Muckton
Authorpe
Maltby le Marsh
A1111
A52
Scamblesby
Oxcombe
White Pit
Belleau
Aby
Watermill & Wildfowl
Beesby
Saleby
Markby
Belchford
South Ormsby
Swaby
South Thoresby
Huttoft
West Ashby
Tetford
Brinkhill
Rigsby
Alford
Bilsby
Thurlby
B1449
Anderby
On Your Marques
Salmonby
Harrington
Sutterby
Well
A1104
B1196
Farlesthorpe
Mumby
Fulletby
Somersby
Bag Enderby
Langton
Ulceby
Cumberworth
Chapel Point
Horncastle
Greetham
Ashby Puerorum
Aswardby
A1028
Willoughby
Hogsthorpe
Chapel St Leonards
High Toynton
A158
Hagworthingham
Sausthorpe
Skendleby
Sloothby
Habertoft
Addlethorpe
Fantasy Island
Ingoldmells
Mareham on the Hill
Snipe Dales
Lymn
Partney
Welton le Marsh
Ingoldmells Point
Hameringham
Mavis Enderby
Raithby
A16
Scremby
Candlesby
Lincolnshire Coast Light Railway
Roughton
Moorby
Old Bolingbroke
Hundleby
Spilsby
Ashby by Partney
Orby
Gunby Hall
Wood Enderby
Miningsby
Bolingbroke Castle
Toynton All Saints
Halton Holegate
Monksthorpe
Bratoft
Burgh le Marsh
A158
Natureland Seal Sanctuary
East Kirkby
Revesby
Lincolnshire Aviation
East Keal
B1195
Great Steeping
Northcote
Irby in the Marsh
Village Church Farm
Skegness
gsby
Mareham le Fen
Stickford
Keal Cotes
Little Steeping
Firsby
Croft
umby
New Bolingbroke
Stickney
New Leake
Thorpe St Peter
Wainfleet All Saints
A52
Tumby Woodside
ARK
Eastville
Friskney
Wainfleet St Mary
Wainfleet Haven
Britain in Flight
New York
East Fen
Lincolnshire
Gibraltar Point
West Fen Northlands
B1183
Leake Common Side
Gipsey Bridge
Frithville
Sibsey Trader Windmill
Sibsey
Wrangle
Fishtoft Drove
B1184
Old Leake
angrick
Hilldyke
Leverton
Anton's Gowt
Benington

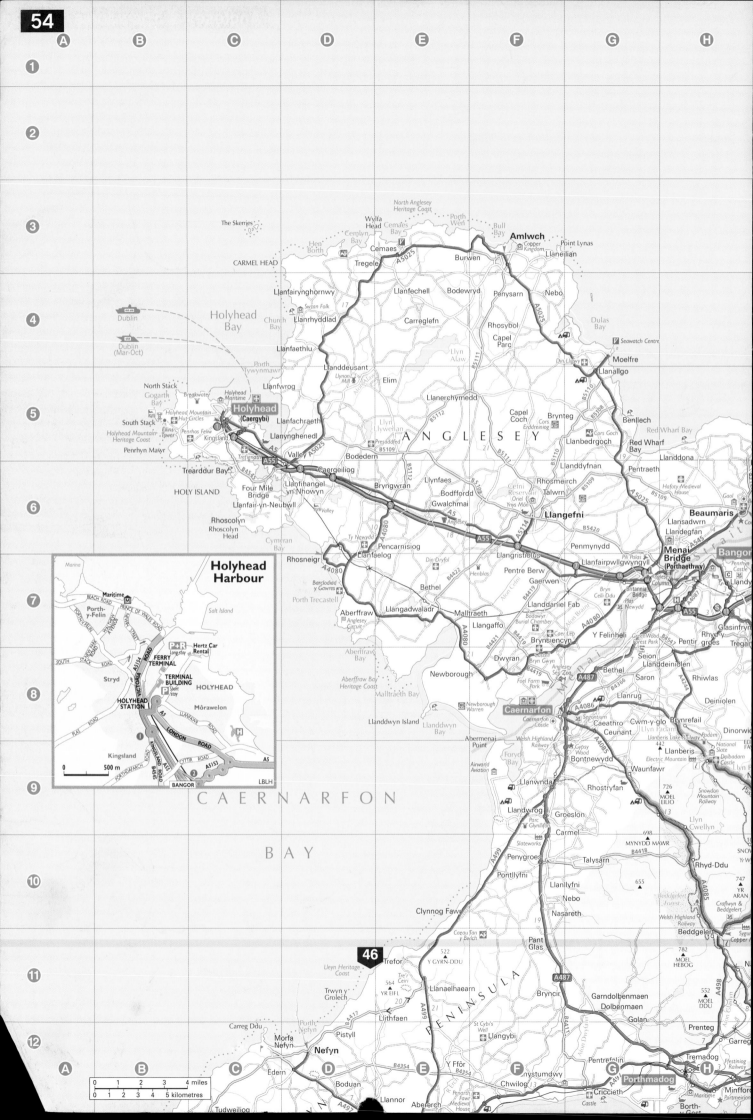

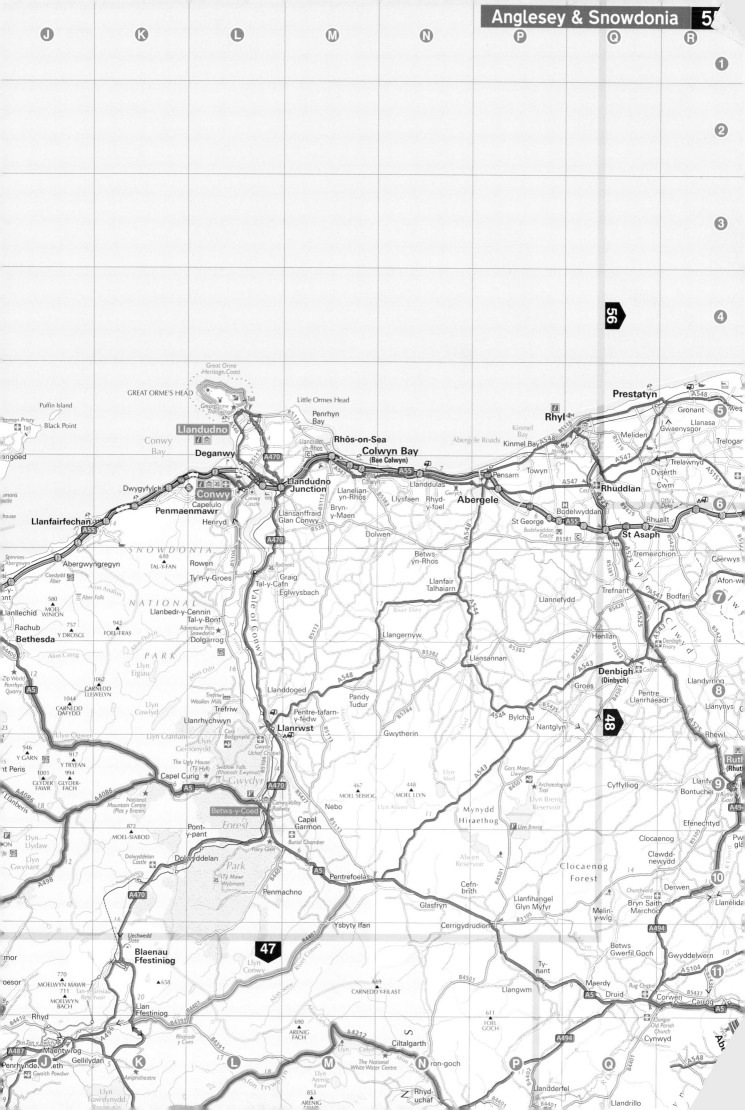

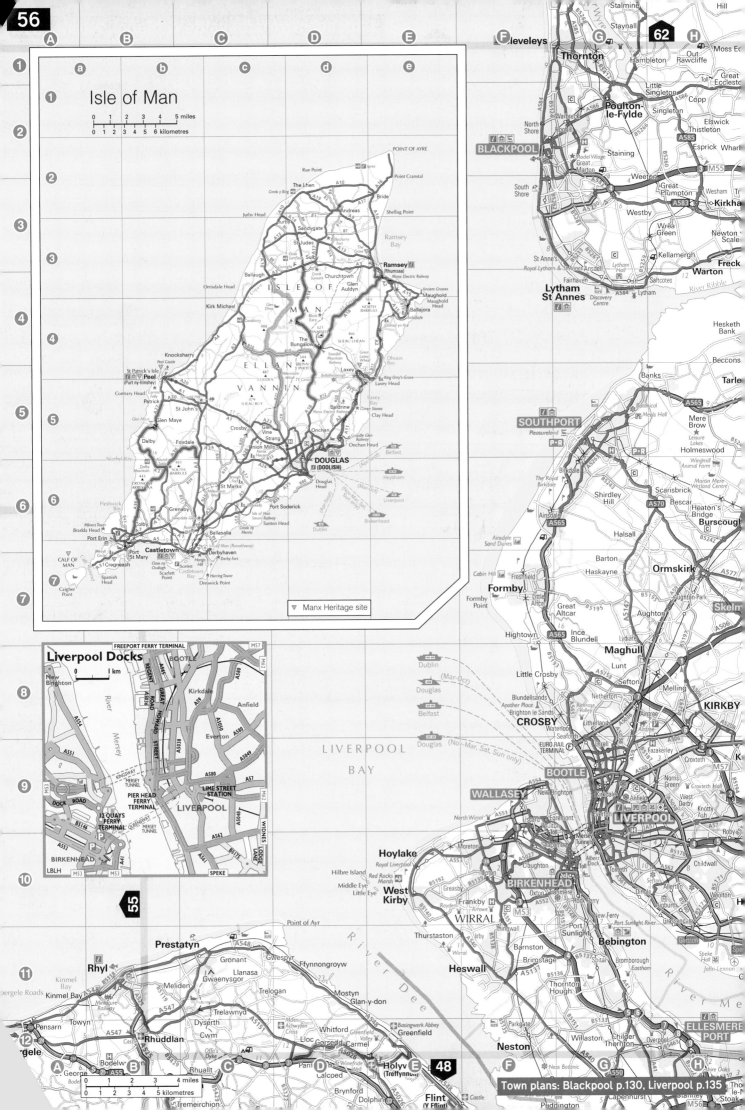

Isle of Man

0 1 2 3 4 5 miles
0 1 2 3 4 5 6 kilometres

▽ Manx Heritage site

Liverpool Docks

0   1 km

FREEPORT FERRY TERMINAL

BOOTLE

New Brighton

River Mersey

KIRKDALE

REGENT ROAD

GREAT HOWARD STREET

A565

A59

Anfield

Everton

A5038

A580

A5049

A5080

KINGSWAY
MERSEY TUNNEL

PIER HEAD FERRY TERMINAL

12 QUAYS FERRY TERMINAL

DOCK ROAD

Toll

QUEENSWAY
MERSEY TUNNEL

LIME STREET STATION

LIVERPOOL

A57

A5047

BIRKENHEAD

LBLH

B5146

M53

A41

Toll

A553

WIDNES LODGE LANE

B5178

SPEKE

55

LIVERPOOL BAY

Dublin

(Mar-Oct)

Douglas

Belfast

Douglas (Nov-Mar, Sat, Sun only)

Town plans: Blackpool p.130, Liverpool p.135

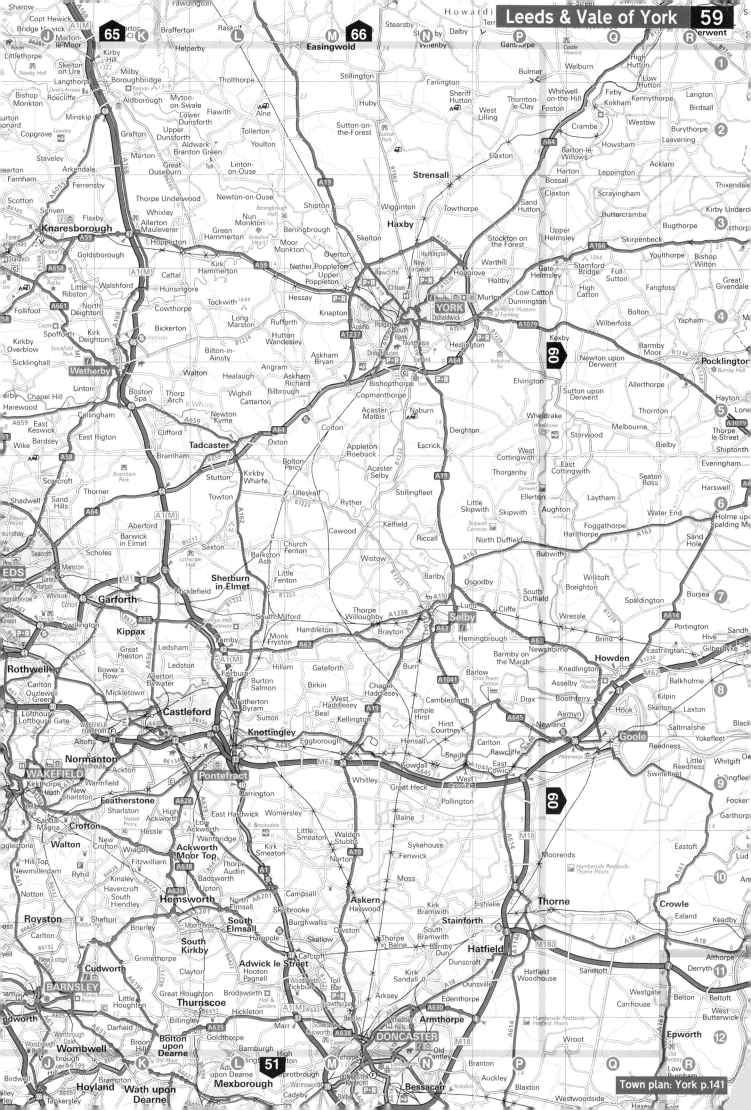

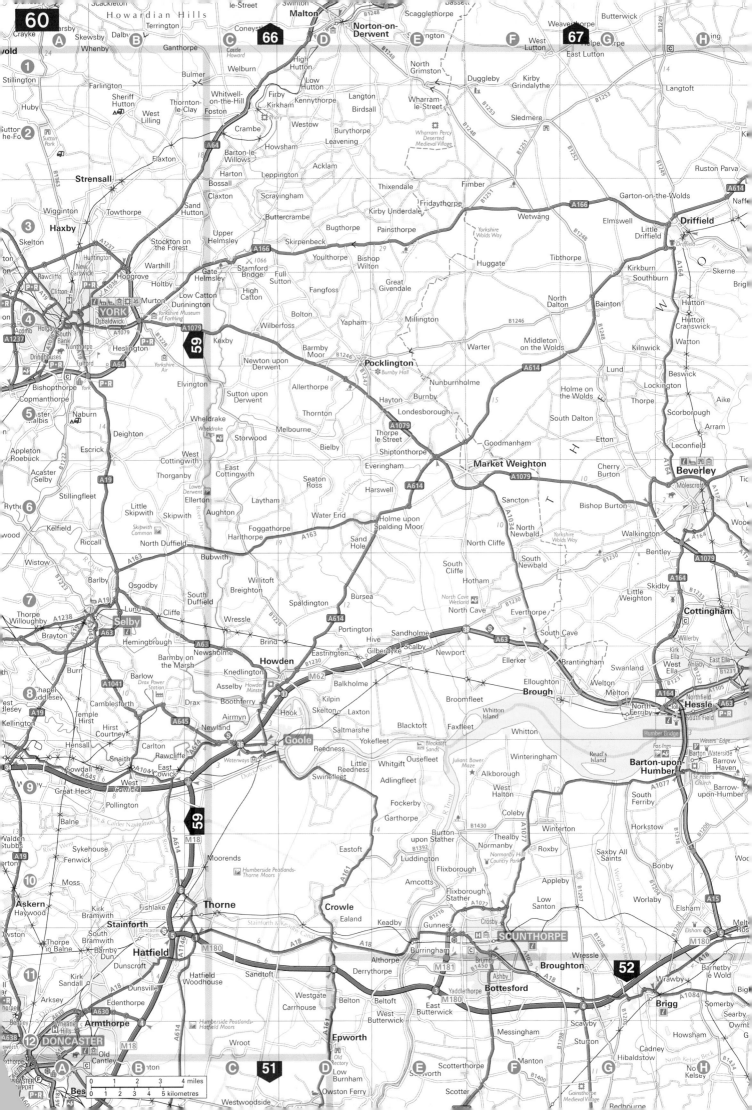

Port of Hull

BRIDLINGTON

A165 · PRESTON ROAD · SOUTHCOATES LANE · MARFLEET AVENUE · ORANGE ROAD

KINGSTON UPON HULL

A1033 · SOUTHCOATES ROUNDABOUT · NORTHERN GATEWAY RBT · A1033 · MARFLEET ROUNDABOUT · HEDON ROAD · SOMERDEN ROUNDABOUT · HEDON · A62 · A63 · Alexandra Dock · King George Dock · QE Dock · Gate · Gate

Marfleet

TERMINAL 2 · TERMINAL 1

KINGSTON TERMINAL

River Humber

0   1 km

LBLH

J   K   67   L   M   N   P   Q   R

Burton Fleming · Grindale · Buckton · Bempton · North Landing · Flamborough Cliffs · Selwicks Bay · FLAMBOROUGH HEAD

A165 · B1255 · B1259 · Flamborough

Sewerby · Hall & Gardens · Bondville Miniature Village

Bridlington

BRIDLINGTON BAY

Rudston · Monolith · Boynton · Bessingby · Hilderthorpe · Carnaby

Haisthorpe · Thornholme · A1038 · Bridlington

Burton Agnes · Norman Manor House · Harpham · Fraisthorpe

Gransmoor · Barmston

Great Kelk · Lissett · B1242

Gembling · Ulrome

Foston on the Wolds · Skipsea Castle · Skipsea

Beeford

North Frodingham · A165 · Dunnington · Atwick

Bewholme

Honeysuckle Farm · B1242

Hornsea · Hornsea Mere

Brandesburton · Seaton · A1035 · Sigglesthorne · Goxhill · Rolston

Foss Hill · Catwick · Mappleton · Mappleton Sands

Leven · High Farm · Long Riston · Rise · Great Hatfield · B1242

Routh · A1035 · Arnold · Great Cowden

Skirlaugh · New Ellerby · Marton · Withernwick

Veel · Old Ellerby · West Newton · Aldbrough

Wawne · A165 · Swine · Coniston · Burton Constable Hall · Flinton · B1238 · B1242

Dunswell · Ganstead · Wyton · Sproatley · Humbleton · Hilston

Bransholme · Bilton · Lelley · Owstwick · Tunstall

A1033 · B1237 · Sutton-on-Hull · A165 · B1238 · Preston · Elstronwick · Roos · B1242

Newland · Stoneferry · Marfleet · A1033 · Burton Pidsea · Rimswell · Owthorne

International Ferry Terminal · **Hedon** · Burstwick · B1362 · Halsham · Lighthouse · **Withernsea**

KINGSTON UPON HULL · Paull · Thorngumbald · Keyingham · Hollym

Fort Paull · A1033 · Ottringham · Winestead · Holmpton

New Holland · Patrington · A1033

Goxhill · Patrington Haven · Welwick

East Halton · Weeton · B1445 · Easington · Skeffling

B1206 · Thornton Abbey & Gatehouse · North Killingholme · Spurn Heritage Coast

Thornton Curtis · South Killingholme · Kilnsea · Spurn Point

A1077 · Ulceby Skitter · A1077 · Immingham Dock

Ulceby · A160 · A1173 · **Immingham** · Spurn Heritage Coast

Habrough · A180 · SPURN HEAD

Croxton · Kirmington · B1211 · B1210 · Stallingborough · A180 · **GRIMSBY** · Rotterdam (Europoort) Zeebrugge

52 · Keelby · Healing · West Marsh · **Cleethorpes** · **53**

Great Limber · Riby · Great Coates · Little Coates · Nunsthorpe · Old Clee · Thrunscoe · The Jungle Zoo · Cleethorpes Coast Light Railway

Aylesby · B1210 · A16 · A1098

A1173 · Clixby · Irby upon Humber · Bradley · Scartho · B1219 · **Humberston**

Humberside · A18 · Swallow · **Waltham** · Laceby · **New Waltham** · Tetney Marshes

Cabor · Cabourne · Arnoldby le Beck · Brigsley · Holton le Clay · A1031 · Tetney

Swaby · Cuxwold · Beelsby · A18 · Ashby cum Fenby · Waithe · North Cotes

B1205 · Hatcliffe · Donna

J   K   L   M   N   P   Q   R

Town plan: Kingston upon Hull p.134

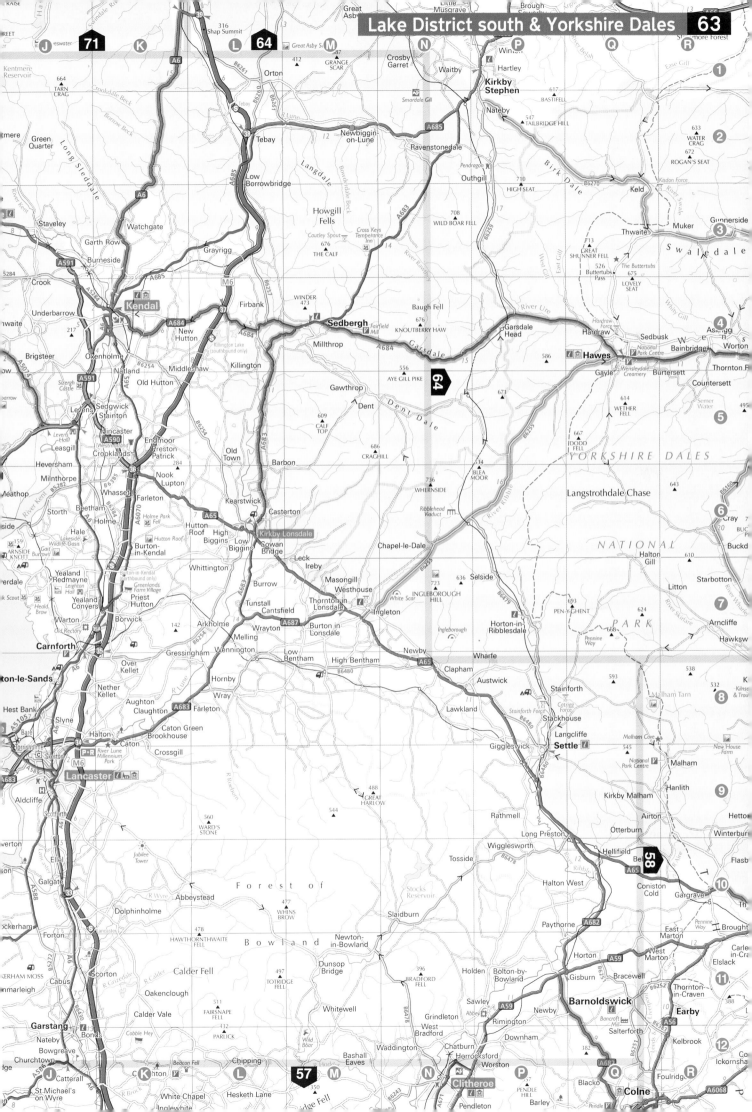

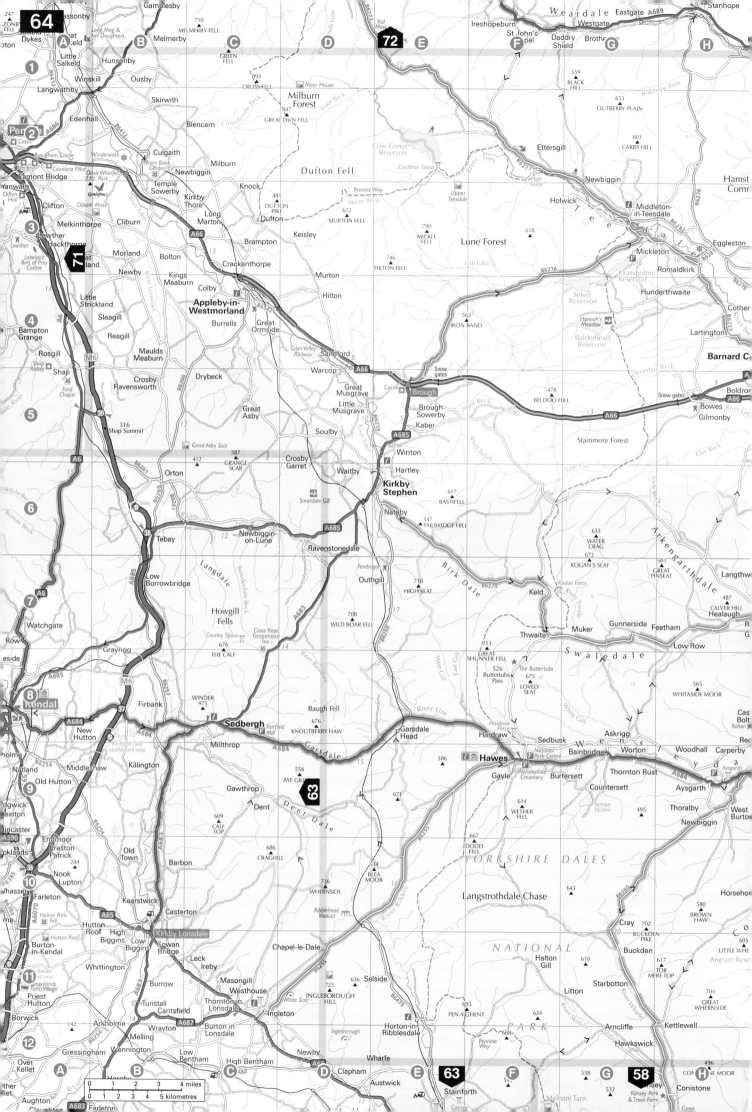

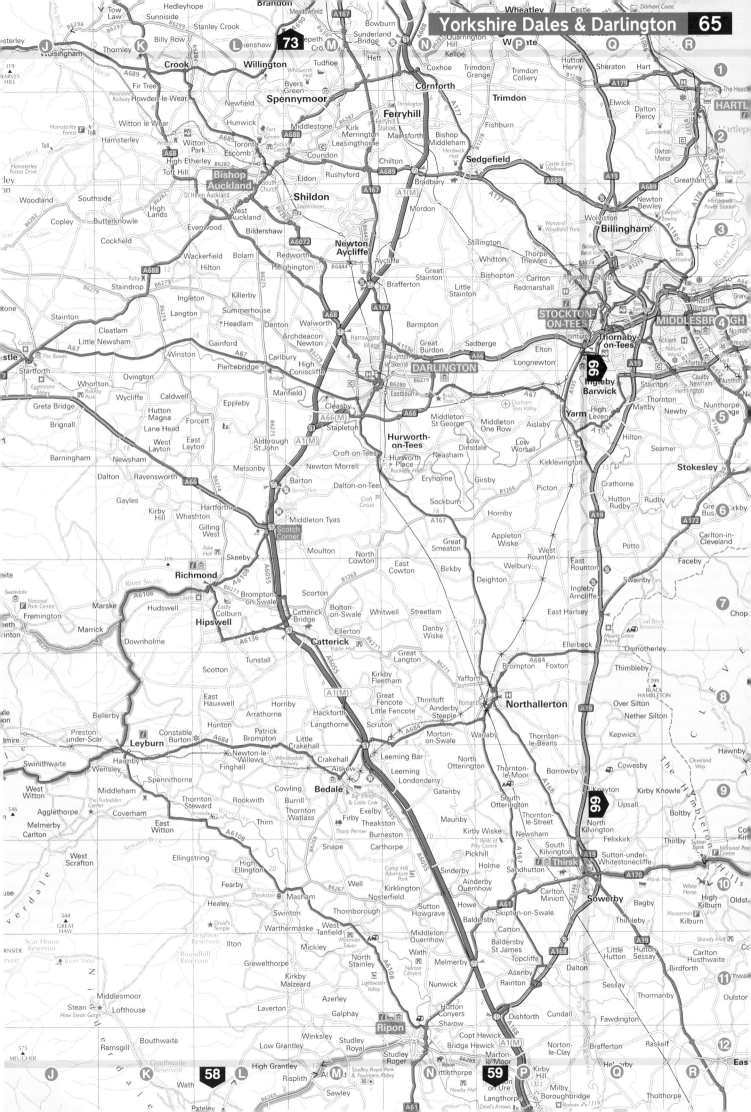

Scarborough (inset)

WHITBY

Peasholm Park
Alexandra Gardens
Bowls Centre
North Sands
North Bay
Cricket Ground
Royal Albert Park
Castle Hill
Scarborough Castle (Ruins)
Coastguard Station
Fire Sta
St Mary's
YMCA
Friarage School
Longwestgate
Luna Park
Old Harbour
Balmoral Centre
Lifeboat Station
West Pier
East Pier
Town Hall
Vincent's Pier
Brunswick
Olympia Leisure
Grand Hotel
South Bay
South Sands
Cliff Bridge
Rotunda Art Gallery
Stephen Joseph
SCARBOROUGH STATION
Courts
Police Sta
Woodend Creative Workspace
Superstore

PICKERING, MALTON
WESTBOROUGH
FILEY

Scarborough

0   200 m

LBLH

Main map

North Yorkshire and Cleveland Heritage Coast
Goldsborough
Overdale Wyke
Lythe
Sandsend
Sandsend Wyke
East Barnby
Dunsley
Newholm
Whitby
Saltwick Bay
Ruswarp
Stainsacre
Aislaby
Briggswath
Sneaton
High Hawsker
Sleights
Iburndale
Ugglebarnby
Ness Point or North Cheek
Grosmont
Robin Hood's Bay
Blue Bank
Fylingthorpe
Robin Hood's Bay
Falling Foss
Old Peak or South Cheek
Ravenscar
Yorkshire's Railway
Eller Beck
292
Staintondale
Shire Horse Centre
Hayburn Wyke
Harwood Dale
Cloughton Wyke
M O O R S
Cloughton
Hole of Horcum
Blakey Topping
Cromer Point
Cleveland Way
Burniston
Bickley
Broxa
Silpho
visham
Bridestones
Dalby Forest Drive
Langdale End
Hackness
Suffield
Scalby
Newby
North Bay Railway
239
North Riding Forest Park
River Derwent
Castle
Dalby Forest
Sea Cut
Falsgrave
Scarborough
Standale Rigg
Forge Valley Wood
Oliver's Mount
Toll
West Ayton
East Ayton
Betton
A170
P+R
A165
Osgodby
Cayton Bay
Sawdon
Eastfield
P+R
The Wyke
Wilton
Ebberston
Ruston
Hutton Buscel
Irton
Crossgates
Ebberston
Snainton
Wykeham
Seamer
Cayton
Allerston
Brompton-by-Sawdon
Lebberston
Filey Brigg
Yedingham
The Carrs
Willerby
Gristhorpe
Filey
Folkton
Muston
Sherburn
Staxton
Flixton
Filey Bay
Scampston
Hall & Gardens
Knapton
East Heslerton
Potter Brompton
Ganton
Yorkshire Wolds Way
Hunmanby
Ilington
West Knapton
West Heslerton
Fordon
Reighton
Flamborough Head Heritage Coast
Wintringham
Wold Newton
Speeton
Bempton Cliffs
Thornwick Bay
Thorpe Bassett
Foxholes
Burton Fleming
Buckton
North Landing
Scagglethorpe
Weaverthorpe
Butterwick
Bempton
Settrington
West Lutton
Helperthorpe
Thwing
Grindale
Flamborough
Flamborough Cliffs
Selwicks Bay
North Grimston
Helperthorpe
East Lutton
60
61
FLAMBOROUGH HEAD
Duggleby
Kirby Grindalythe
Langtoft
Rudston
Monolith
Boynton
Bondville Miniature Village
Bridlington

A64 **A169** **A171** **A165** **A170** **A1039** **B1415** **B1410** **B1416** **B1417** **B1258** **B1261** **B1249** **B1253** **B1255** **B1229** **B1259**

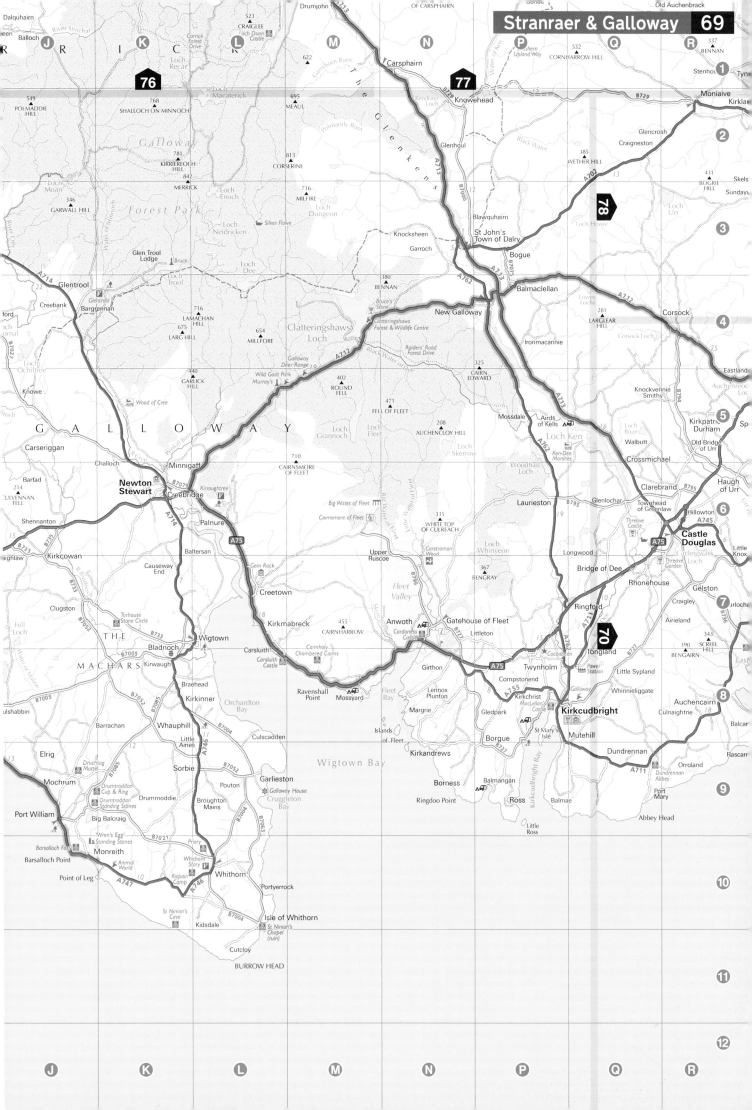

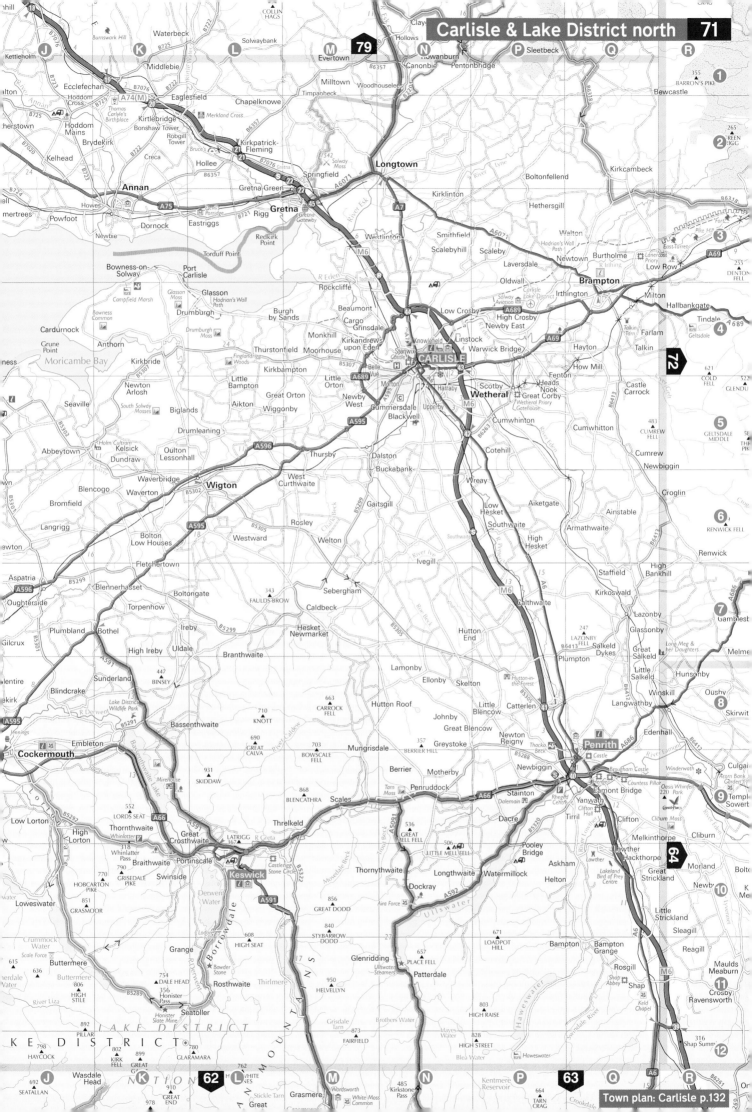

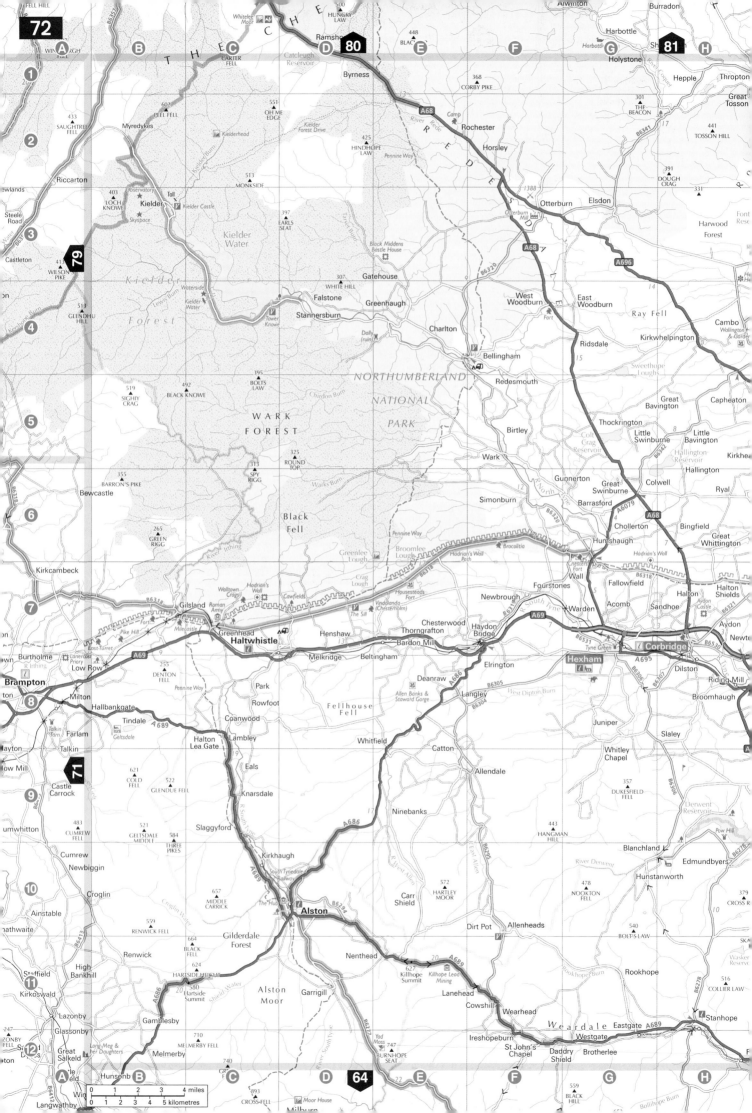

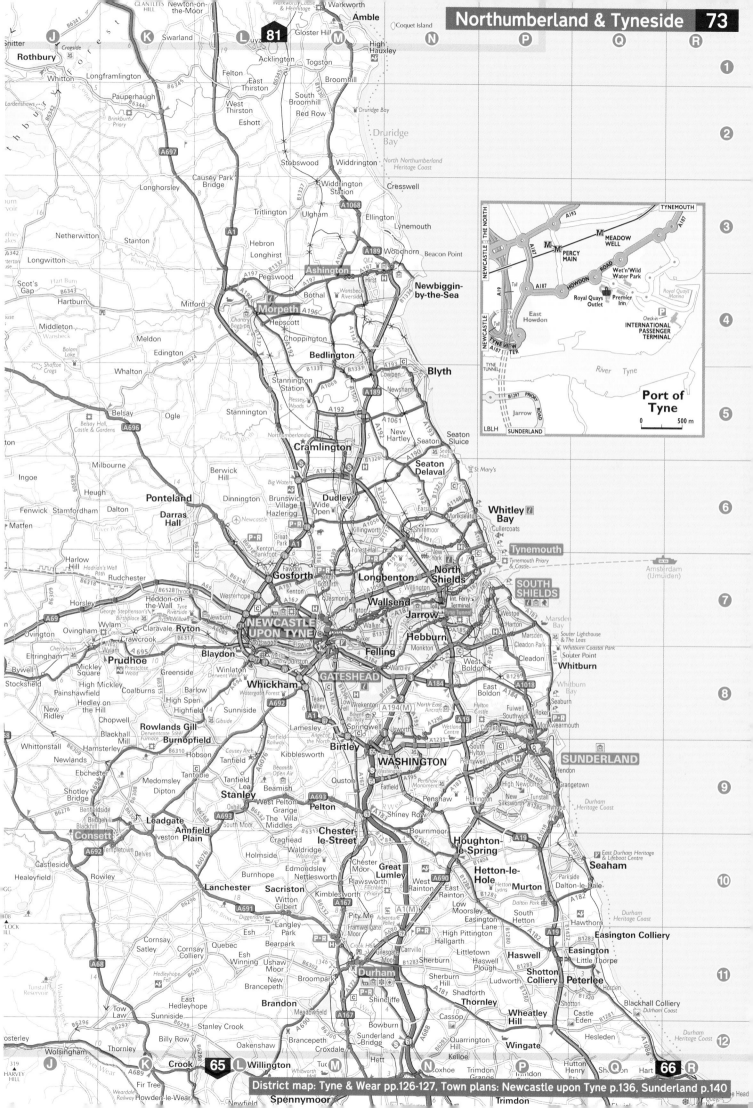

Port of Tyne

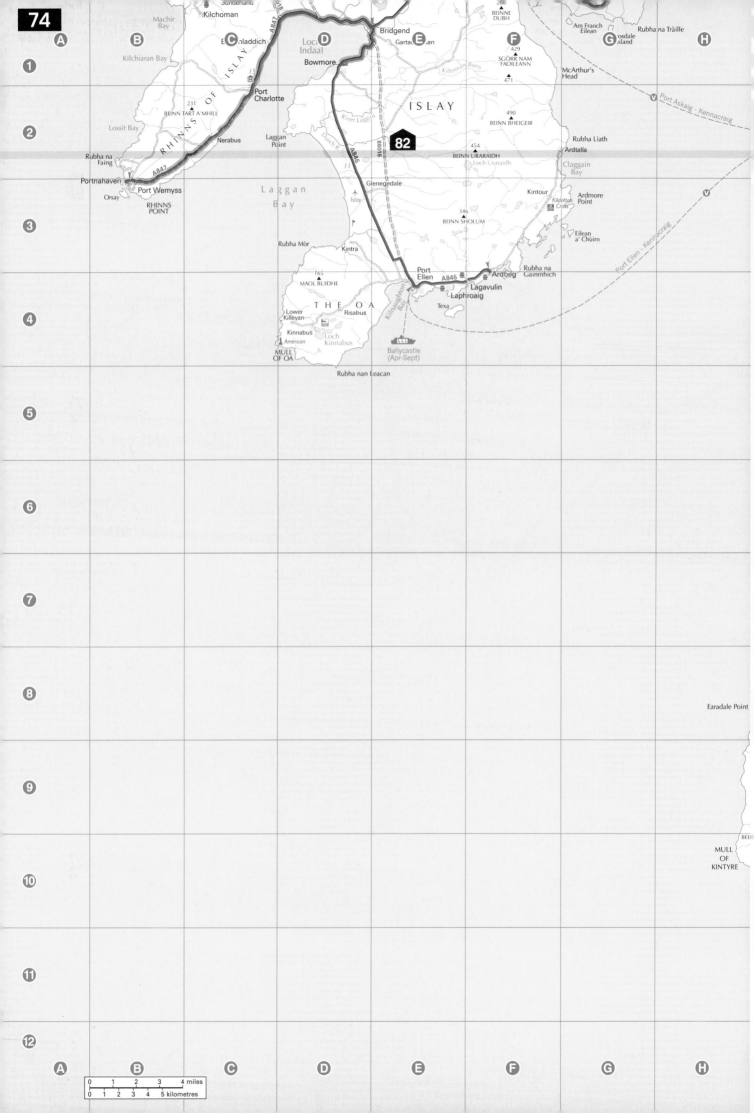

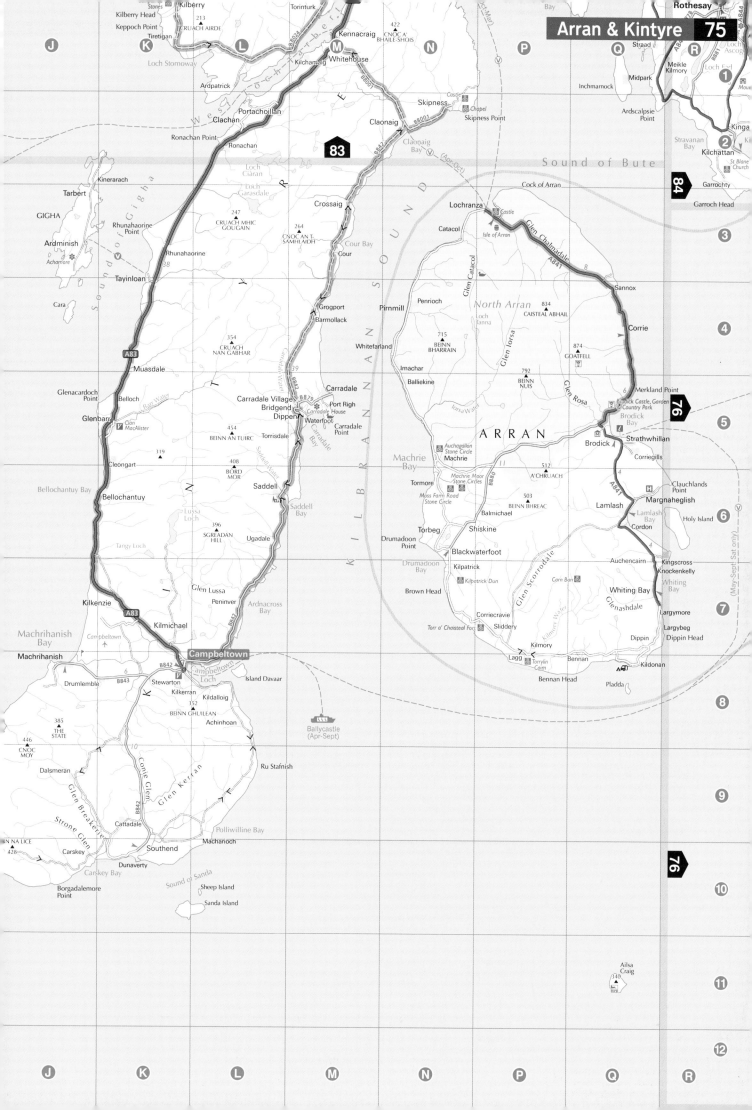

Rothesay

J K L M N P Q R

83

84

76

76

Kilberry Head
Keppoch Point
Tiretigan
Stones
Kilberry
CRUACH AIRDE
213
Torinturk
Kennacraig
422
CNOC A'
BHAILE-SHOIS
Whitehouse
Kilchamaig
Loch Stornoway
Ardpatrick
Portachoillan
Clachan
Ronachan Point
Ronachan
Skipness
Castle
Chapel
Skipness Point
Claonaig
Claonaig
Bay
Sound of Bute
Straad
Midpark
Inchmarnock
Meikle
Kilmory
Ardscalpsie
Point
Kinga
Stravanan
Bay
Kilchattan
St Blane
Church
Garrochty
Garroch Head

Kinerarach
Tarbert
GIGHA
Ardminish
Achamore
Cara
Rhunahaorine
Point
Rhunahaorine
Tayinloan
Crossaig
Cour Bay
Cour
Grogport
Barmollack
247
CRUACH MHIC
GOUGAIN
264
CNOC AN T-
SAMHLAIDH
Lochranza
Castle
Isle of Arran
Catacol
Glen Chalmadale
Cock of Arran
Sannox
Corrie
Merkland Point
8

Muasdale
354
CRUACH
NAN GABHAR
Carradale
Port Righ
Carradale House
Carradale
Point
North Arran
Pirnmill
Penrioch
834
CAISTEAL ABHAIL
Loch
Tanna
Whitefarland
715
BEINN
BHARRAIN
874
GOATFELL
792
BEINN
NUIS
Glen Iorsa
Glen Rosa
Brodick Castle, Garden
& Country Park
Brodick
Bay

Glenacardoch
Point
Belloch
Glenbarr
Clan MacAlister
Cleongart
Bellochantuy Bay
Bellochantuy
454
BEINN AN TUIRC
Torrisdale
Carradale Village
Bridgend
Dippen
Waterfoot
Saddell
319
408
BORD
MOR
Ugadale
Imachar
Balliekine
A'CHRUACH
512
ARRAN
Machrie
Bay
Auchagallon
Stone Circle
Machrie
Tormore
Machrie Moor
Stone Circles
Moss Farm Road
Stone Circle
BEINN BHREAC
503
Strathwhillan
Brodick
Corriegills
Clauchlands
Point
Margnaheglish
Lamlash
Lamlash
Bay
Cordon
Holy Island

Lussa
Loch
396
SGREADAN
HILL
Tangy Loch
Saddell
Bay
Glen Lussa
Peninver
Ardnacross
Bay
Torbeg
Shiskine
Balmichael
Drumadoon
Point
Blackwaterfoot
Drumadoon
Bay
Kilpatrick
Kilpatrick Dun
Brown Head
Corriecravie
Sliddery
Torr a' Chaisteal Fort
Lagg
Kilmory
Torrylin
Cairn
Bennan
Auchencairn
Knockenkelly
Whiting Bay
Glenashdale
Largymore
Largybeg
Dippin
Dippin Head
Kildonan
Pladda
Glen Scorrodale
Bennan Head

Kilkenzie
Machrihanish Bay
Machrihanish
Drumlemble
B843
Stewarton
Kilkerran
Kildalloig
Kilmichael
Campbeltown
Campbeltown
Loch
Island Davaar
352
BEINN GHUILEAN
Achinhoan
Ballycastle
(Apr-Sept)
Ru Stafnish

385
THE STATE
446
CNOC MOY
Dalsmeran
Glen Breakerie
Strone Glen
N NA LICE
428
Carskey
Carskey Bay
Borgadalemore
Point
Conie Glen
Glen Kerran
Cattadale
Southend
Dunaverty
Macharioch
Polliwilline Bay
Sound of Sanda
Sheep Island
Sanda Island

Ailsa
Craig
340

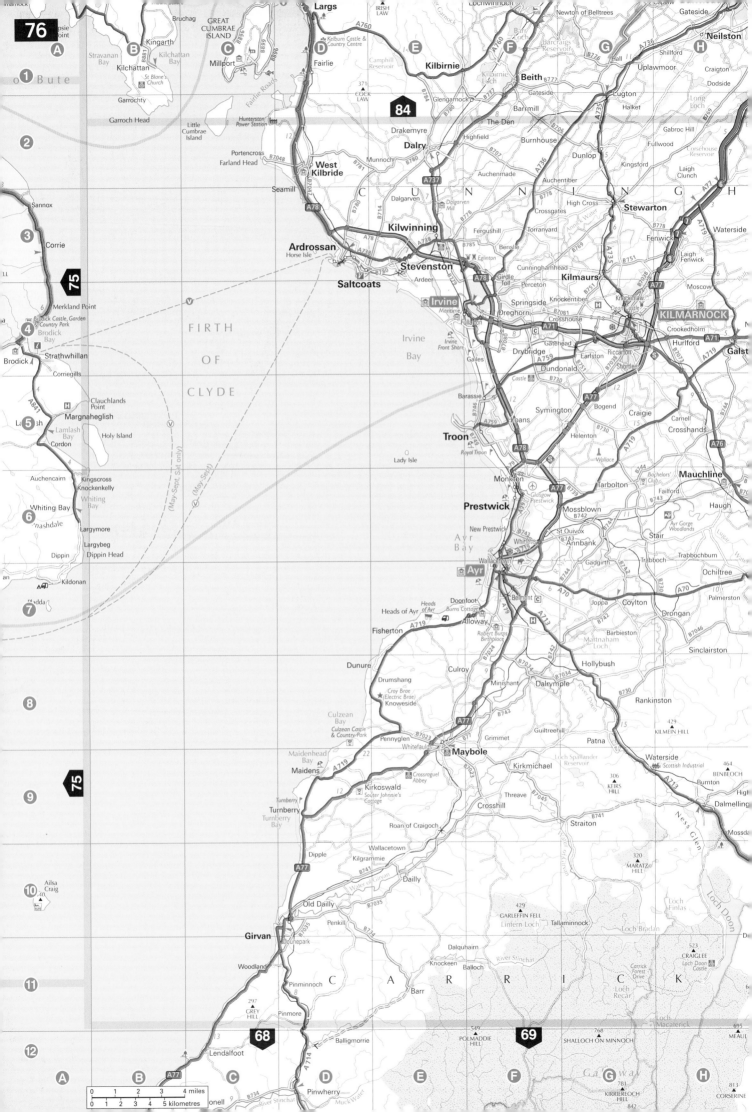

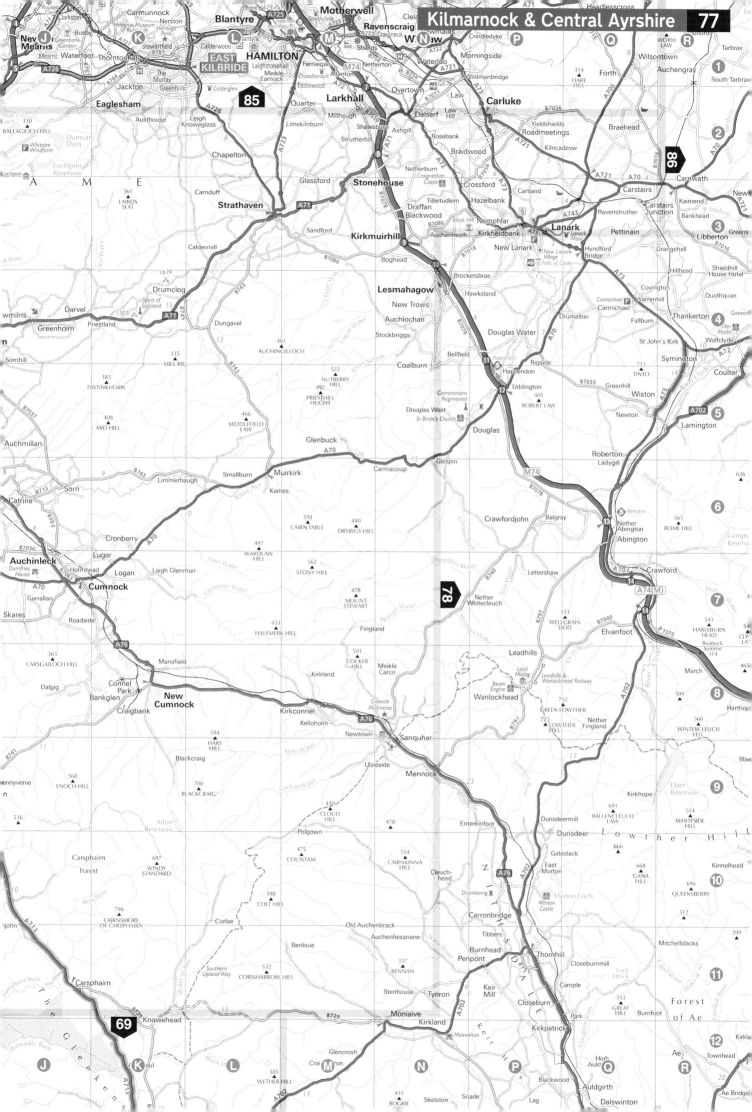

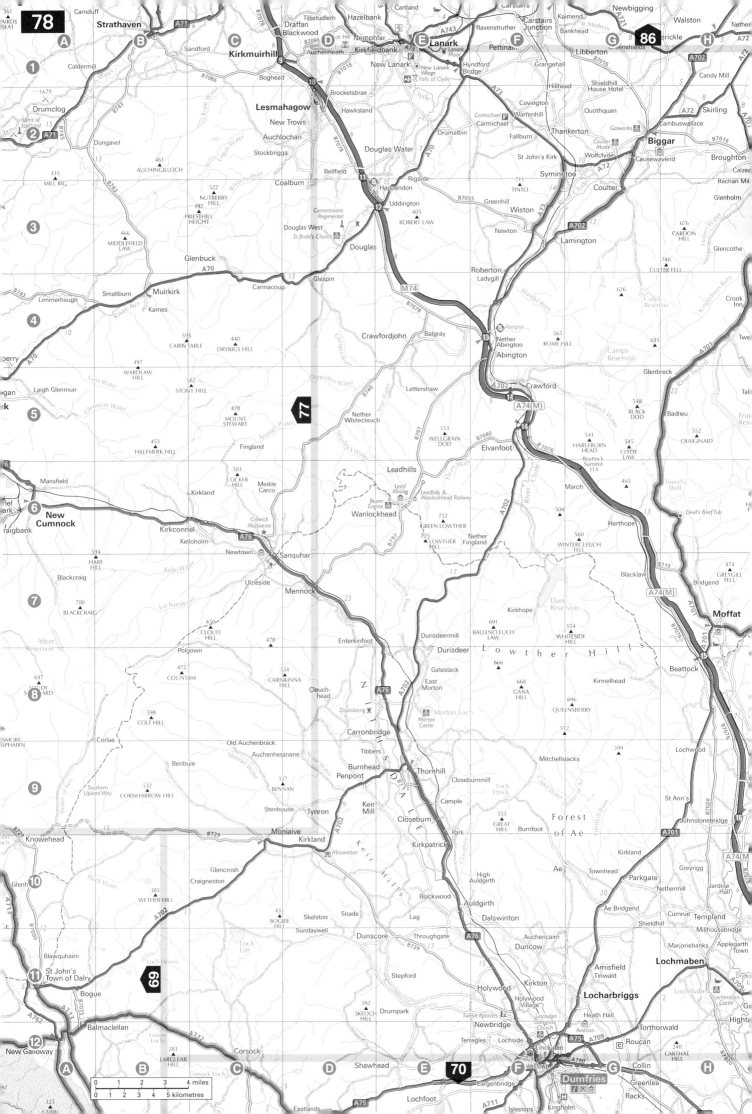

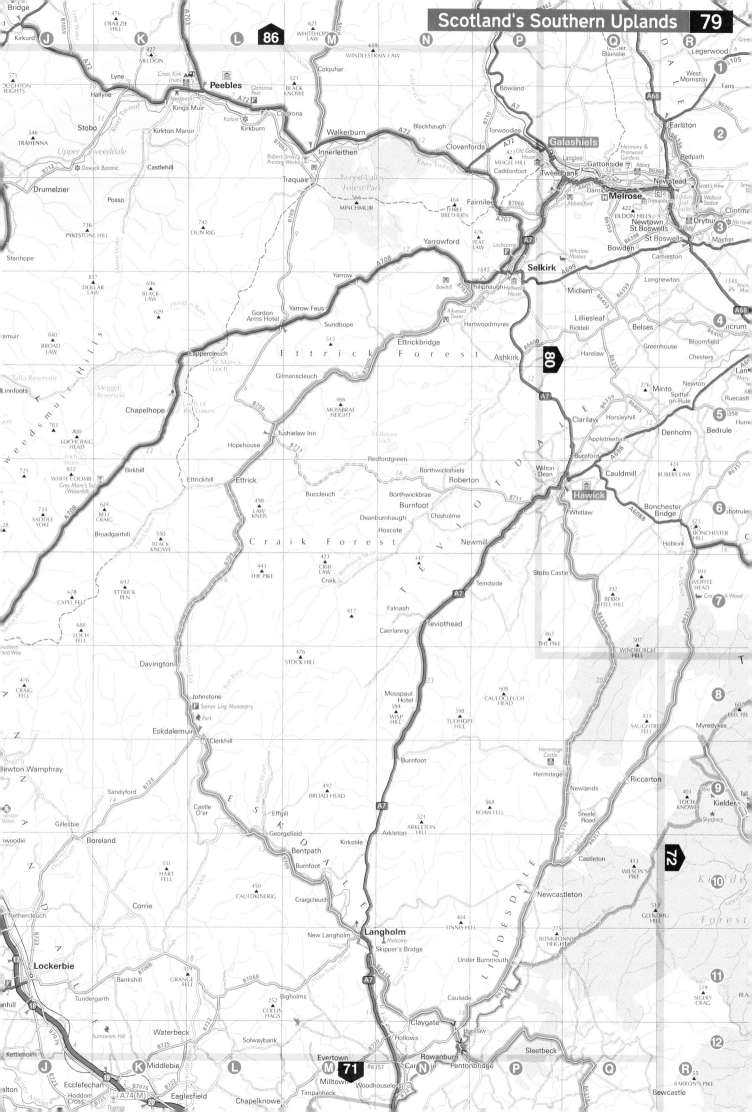

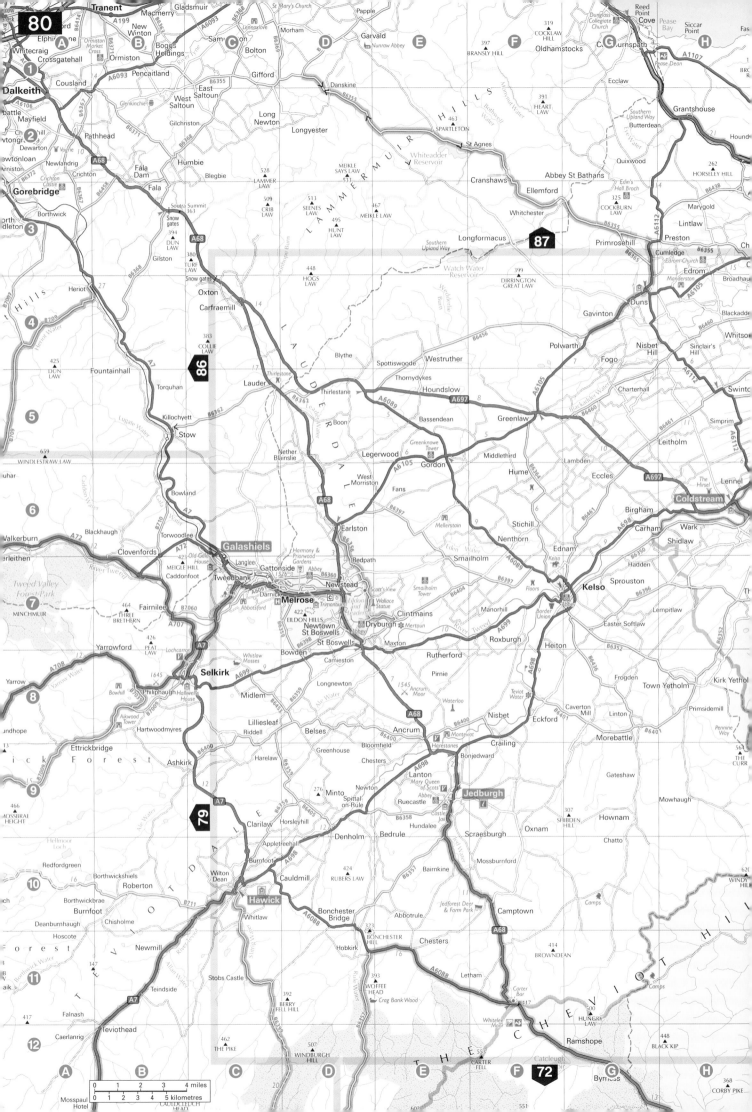

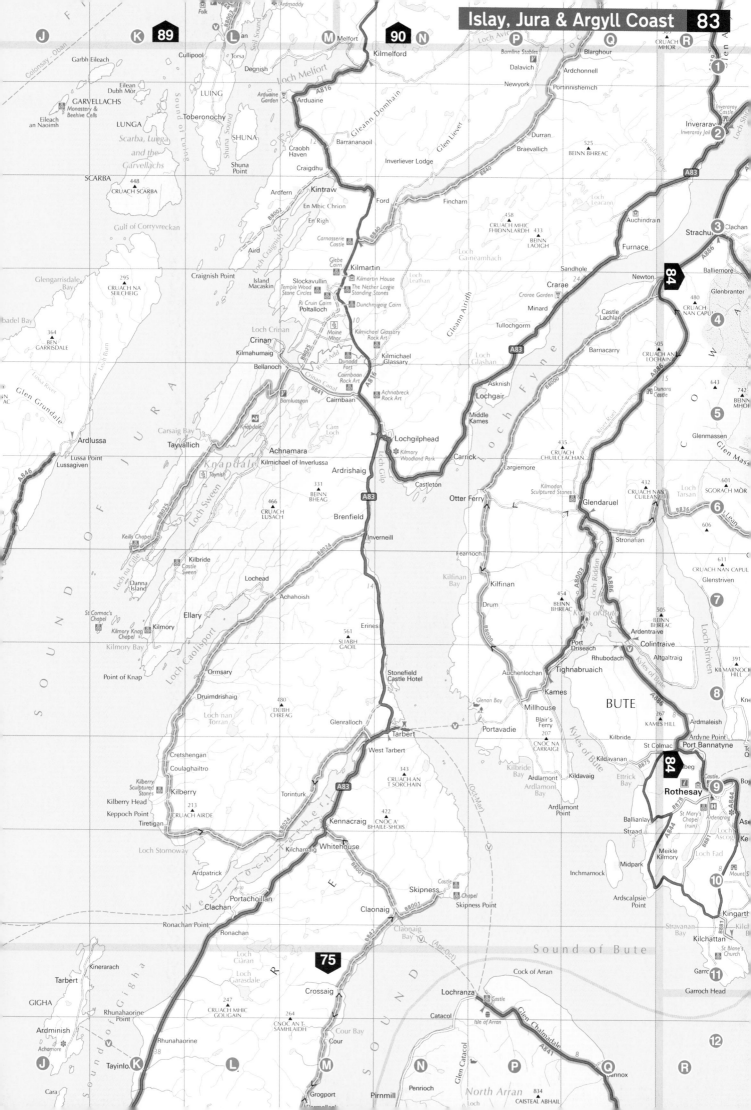

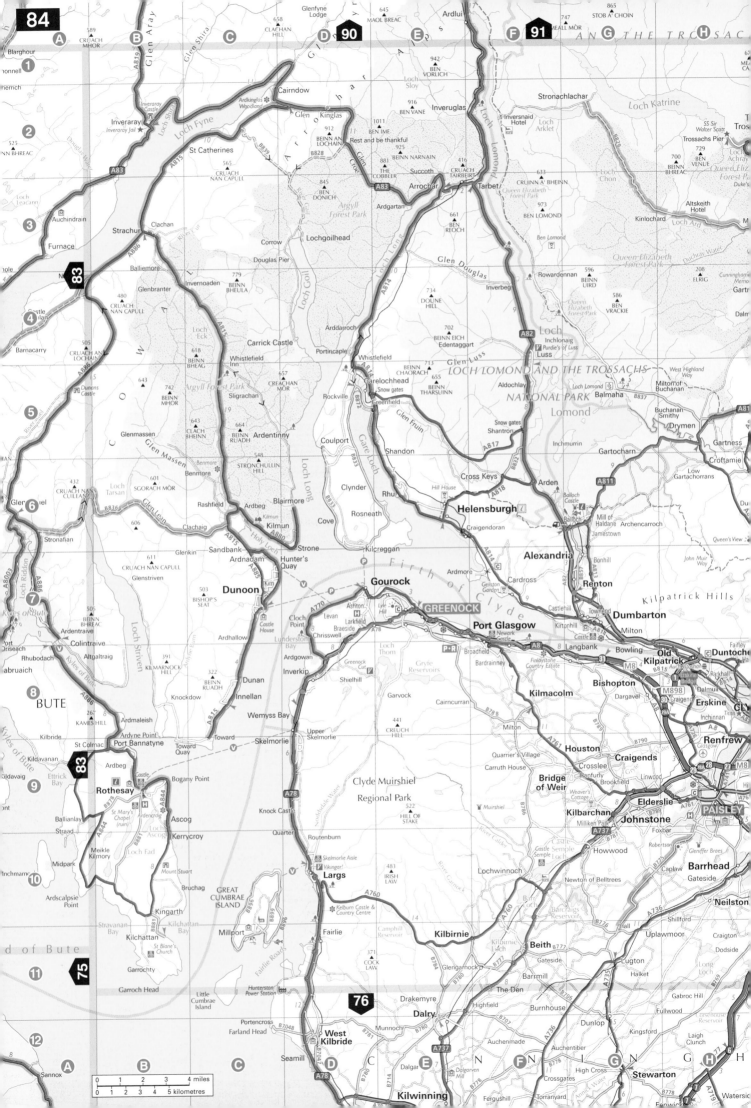

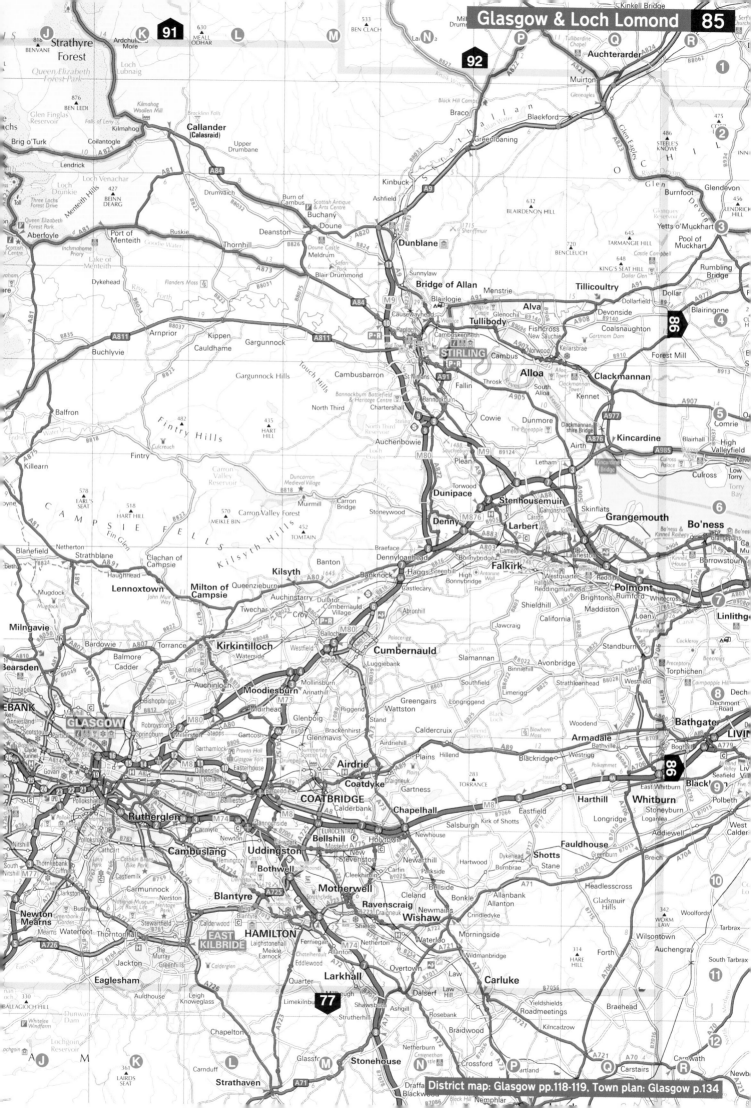

A   B   C   D   E   F   G   H

1

2

3

Eilean Mòr

Rubha
Mòr

Rubha
Sgor-innis

4

Cliad
Bay

Bousd   Sorisdale

B8072

Arnabost

Grishipoll

Clabhach

Loch
Clad

B8071

Coll - Oban

Hogh Bay   Ballyhaugh   Arinagour

COLL

Totronald

Feall
Bay   Coll

Acha

5

Bàgh a' Chaisteil
(Castlebay)

(Apr-Oct, Weds only)

Arileod   Uig

B8010

Eilean
Ornsay

Caliach Point

Calga
Art a
Natur

Calgary Point

Crossapol
Bay   Loch Breachacha

Rubha
Fàsachd

Calgary Bay

Gunna

6

Rubha Port
Bhiosd   Clachan
Mòr

Caoles

Rubha Dubh

Treshnish Point   Ens

Balephetrish
Bay

B8069

Ruaig

Rubh' a' Chaoil

Loch
Bhasapoll

Hough
Bay

Ballevullin   Cornoigmore

B8068

Kenovay

Gott
Bay

Fladda

7

Kilkenneth

Tiree

Lunga

Moss   Heylipoll

B8065

Scarinish

TRESHNISH
ISLES

Gometra

Middleton

B8068

Crossapol

TIREE

Barrapoll

Hynish Bay

Loch a'
Phuill   B8067   Balemartine

Mannal

Bac Mòr or Dutchman's Cap

8

Rinn
Thorbhais

Balephuil
Bay   Hynish

Bac Beag

Staffa

Fingal's

Little Colons

Loch

Isle o

9

10

Rubha nan Cearc

IONA

Iona Abbey
& Nunnery

Kintra

Baile Mòr

MacLean's Cross

Fionnphort

Ardnglas

St Columba
Exhibition
Centre

Bur

ROSS O

11

Soa Island

Erraid

Arc

Ru

Ar

12

Torran Rocks

A   B   C   D   E   F   G   H

0   1   2   3   4 miles
0   1   2   3   4   5 kilometres

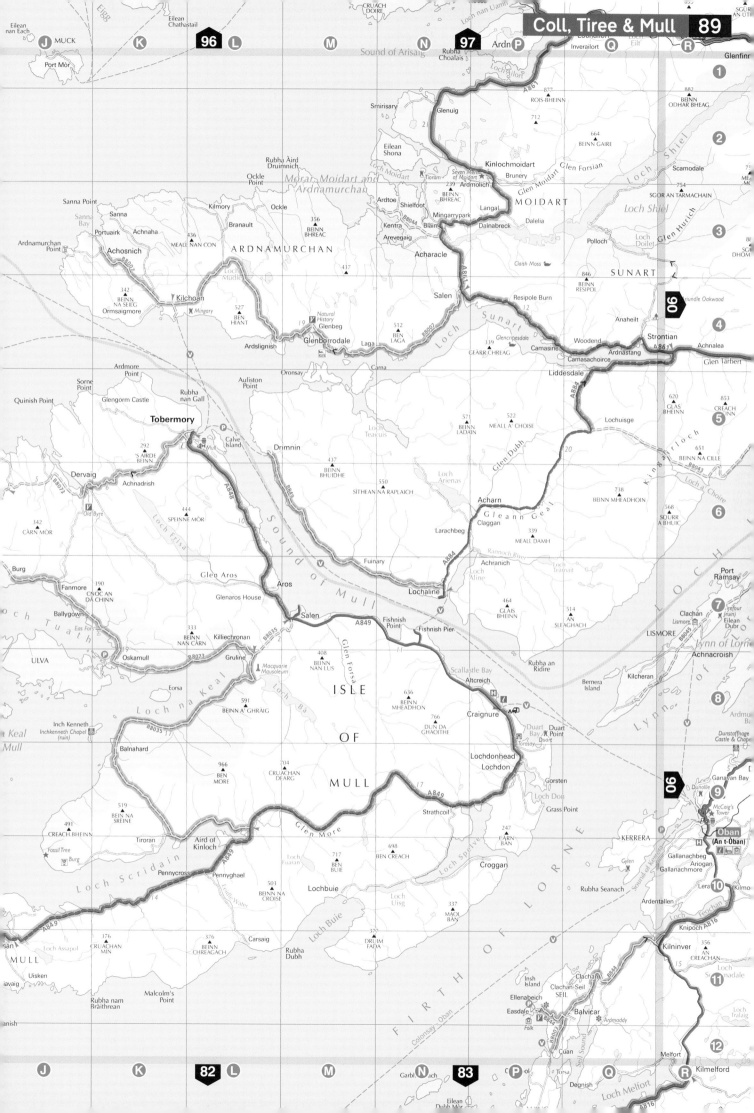

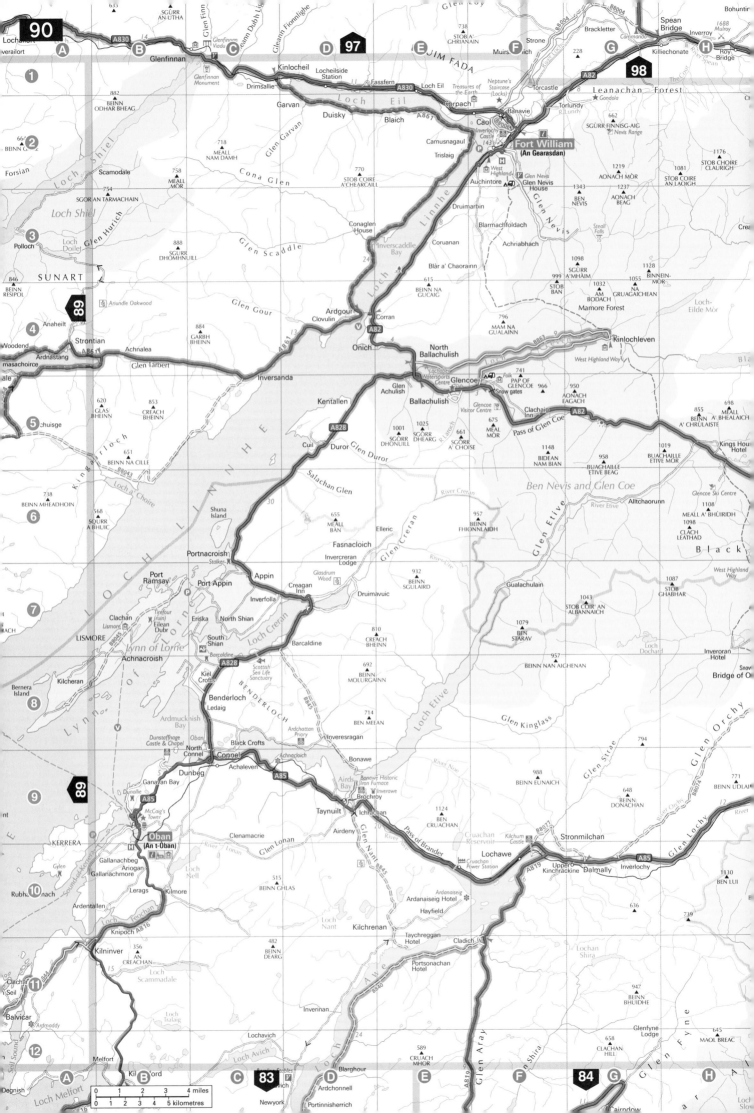

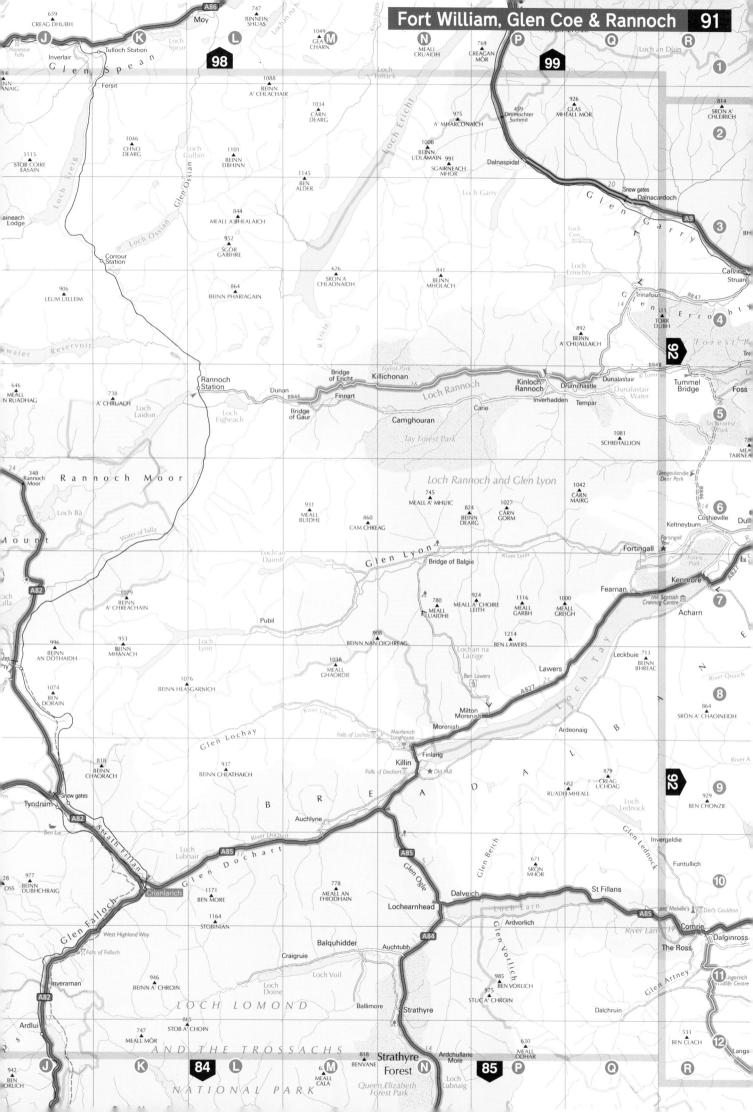

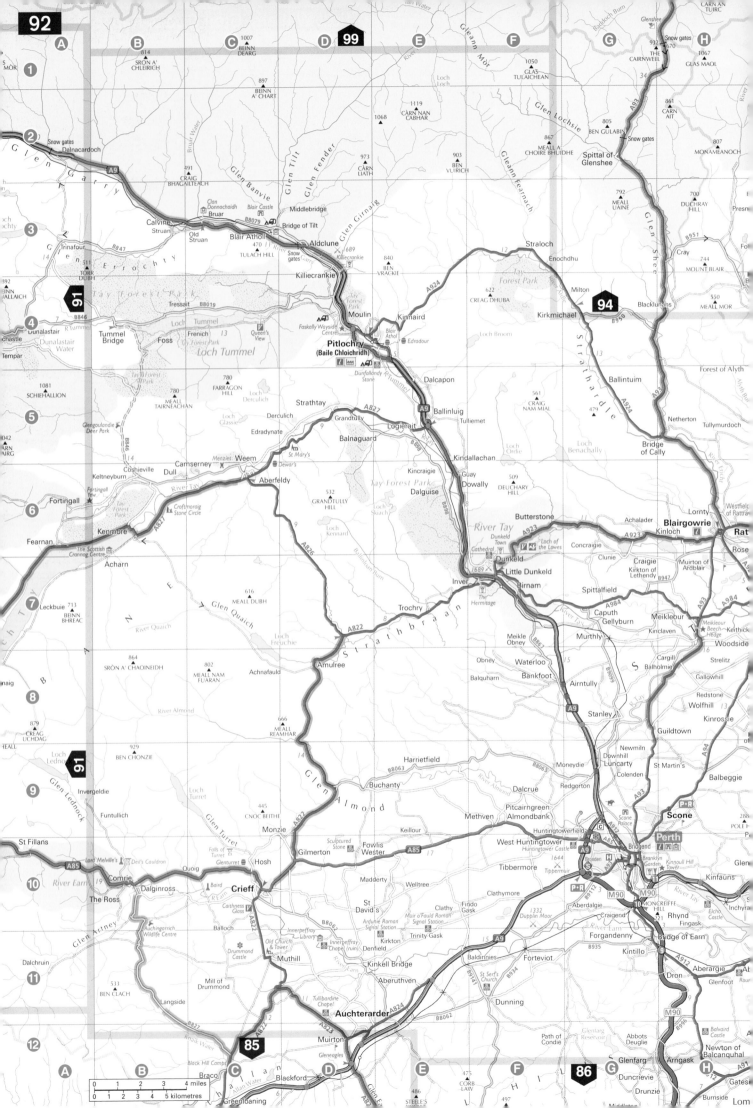

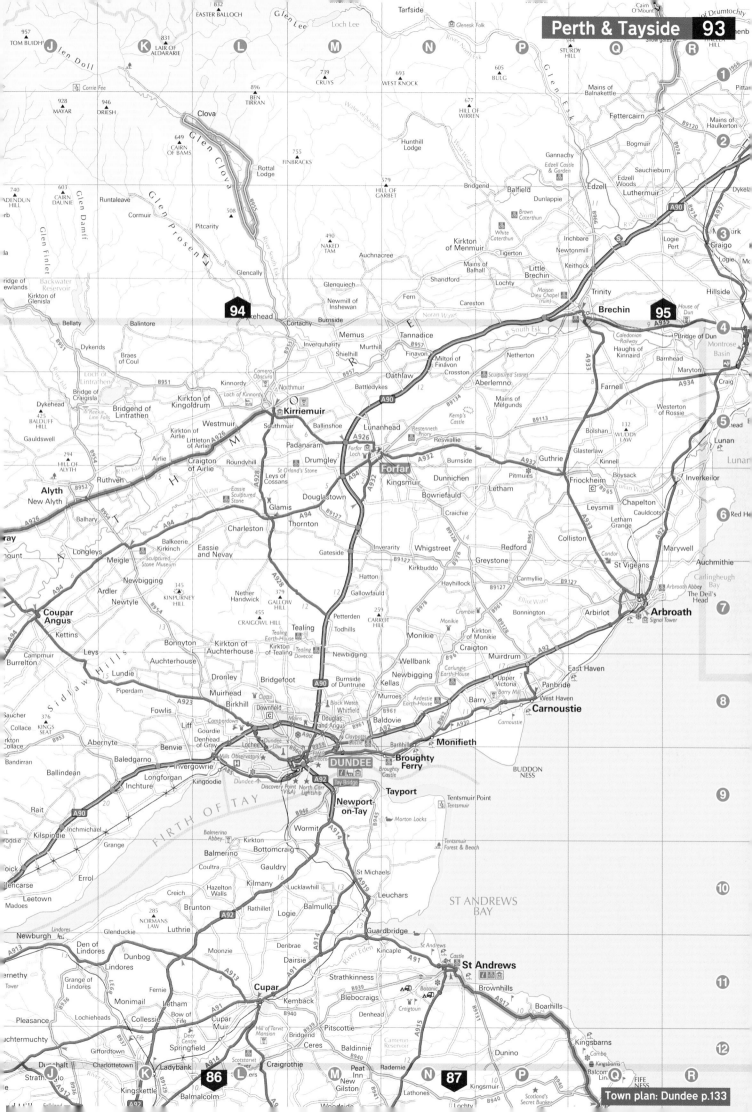

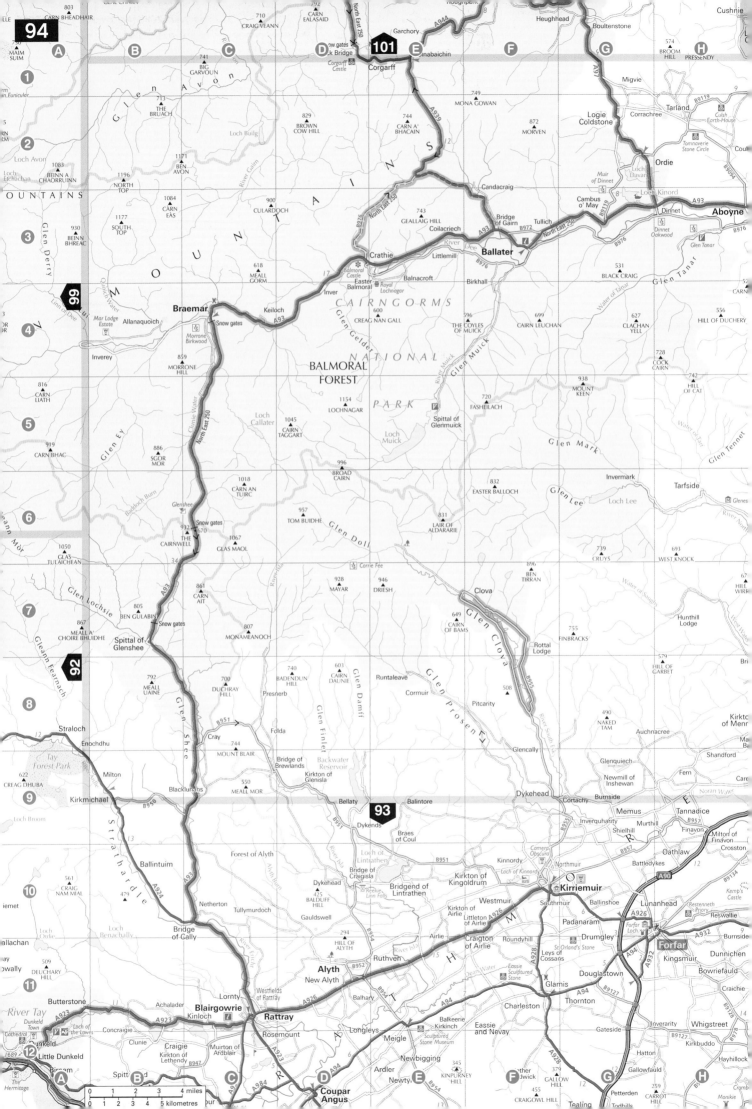

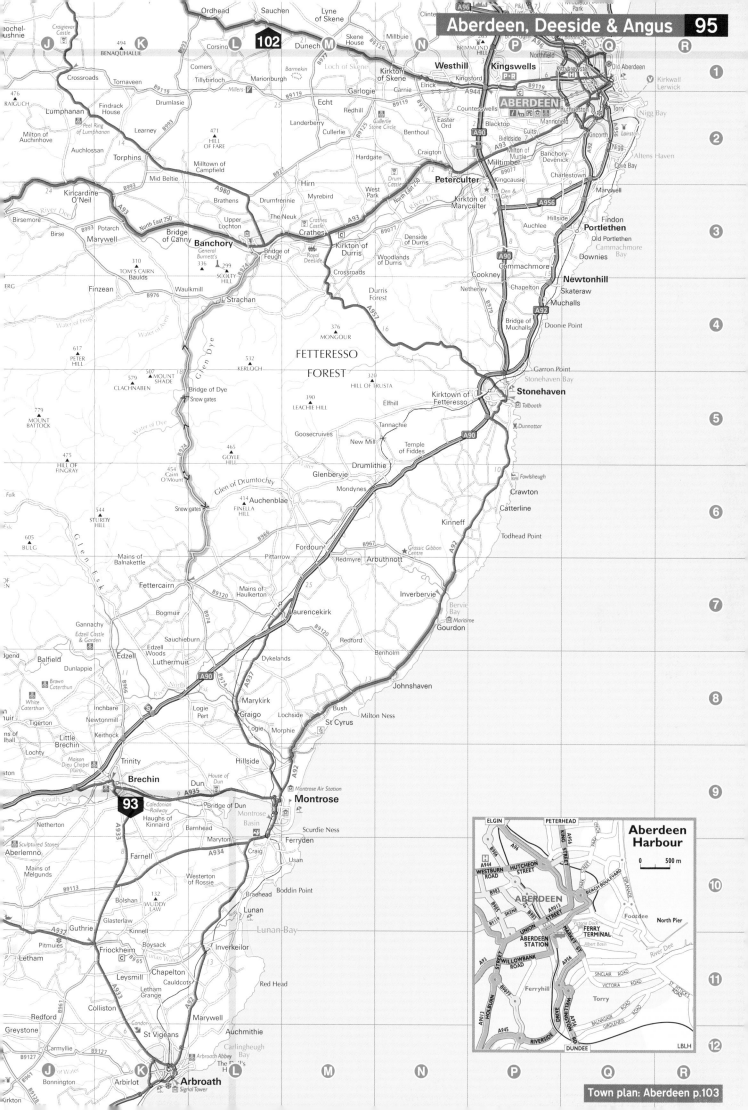

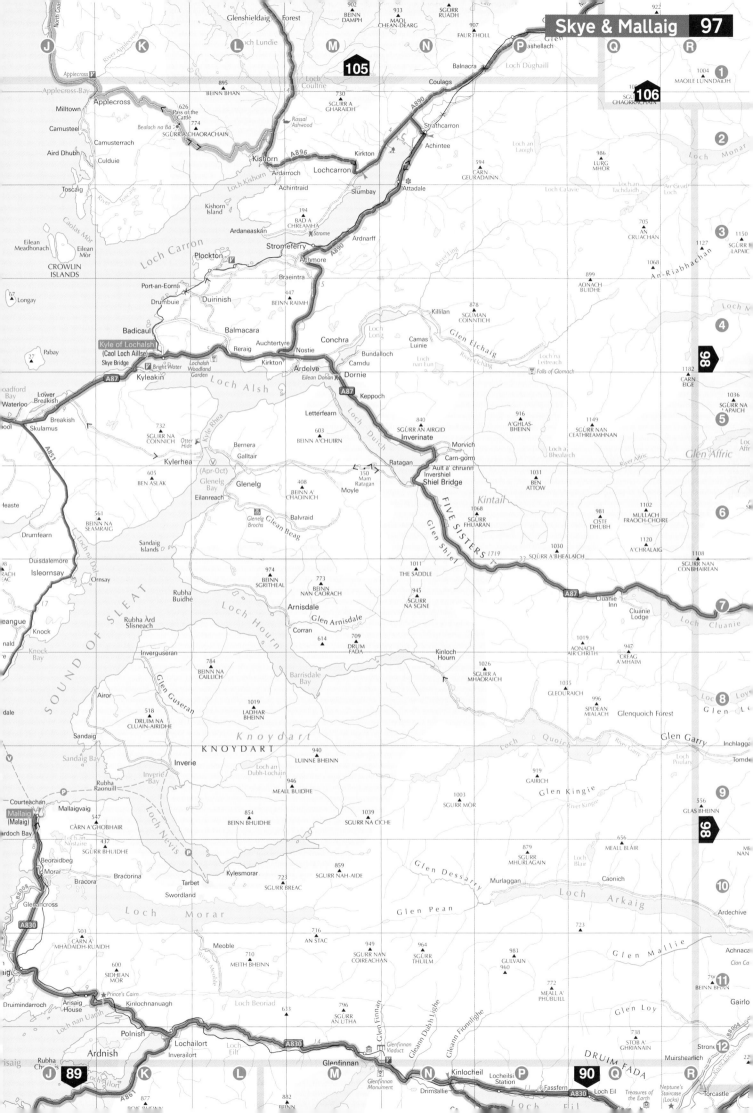

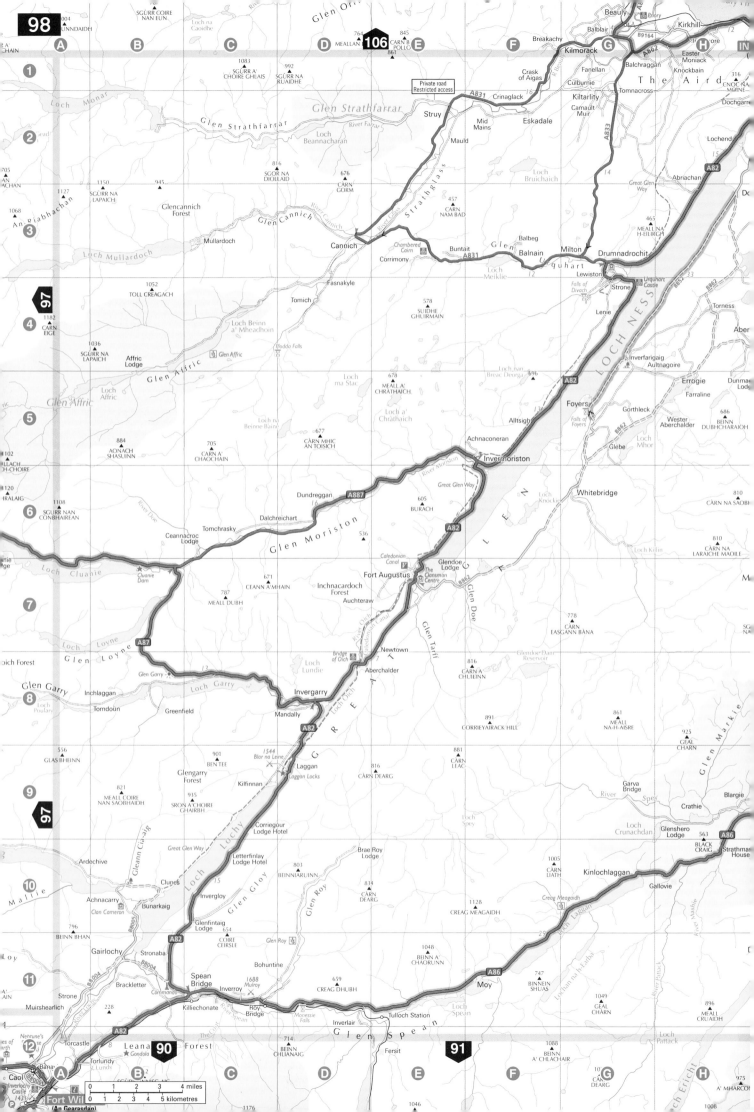

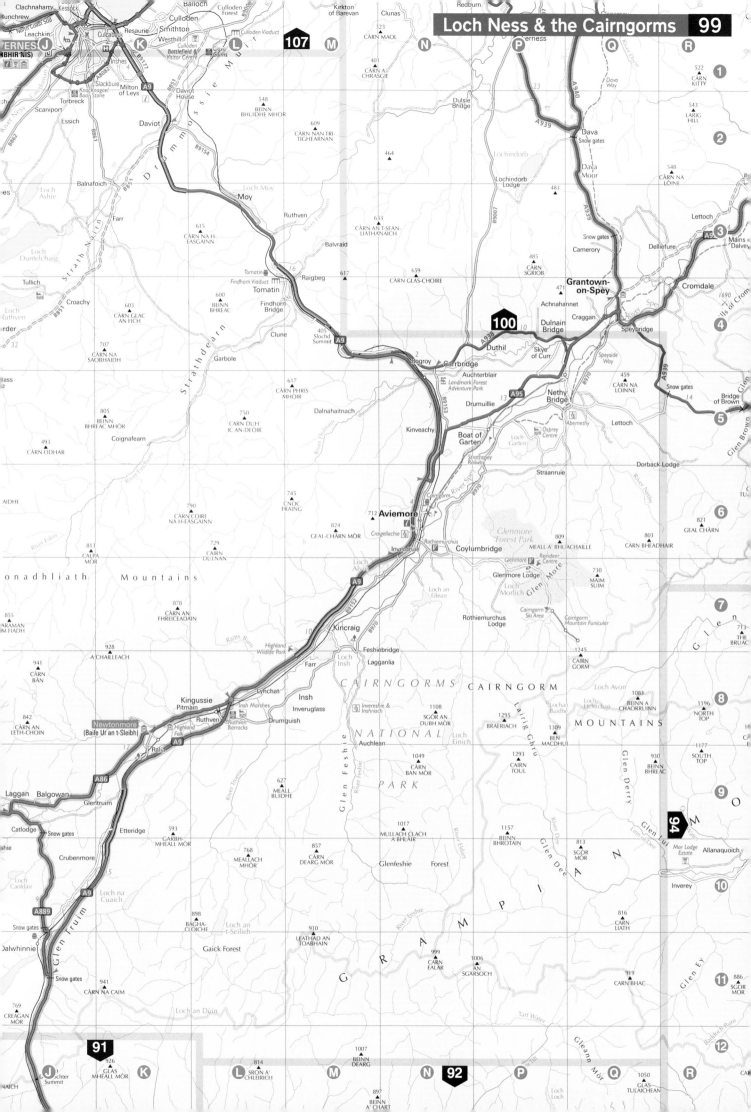

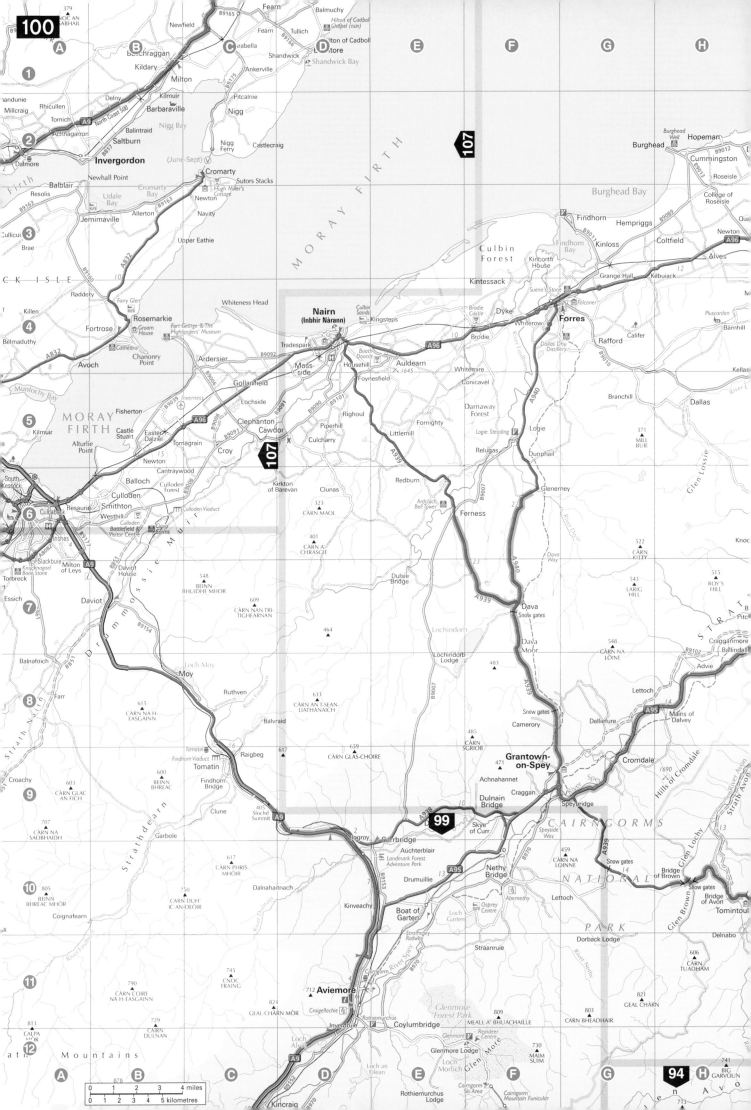

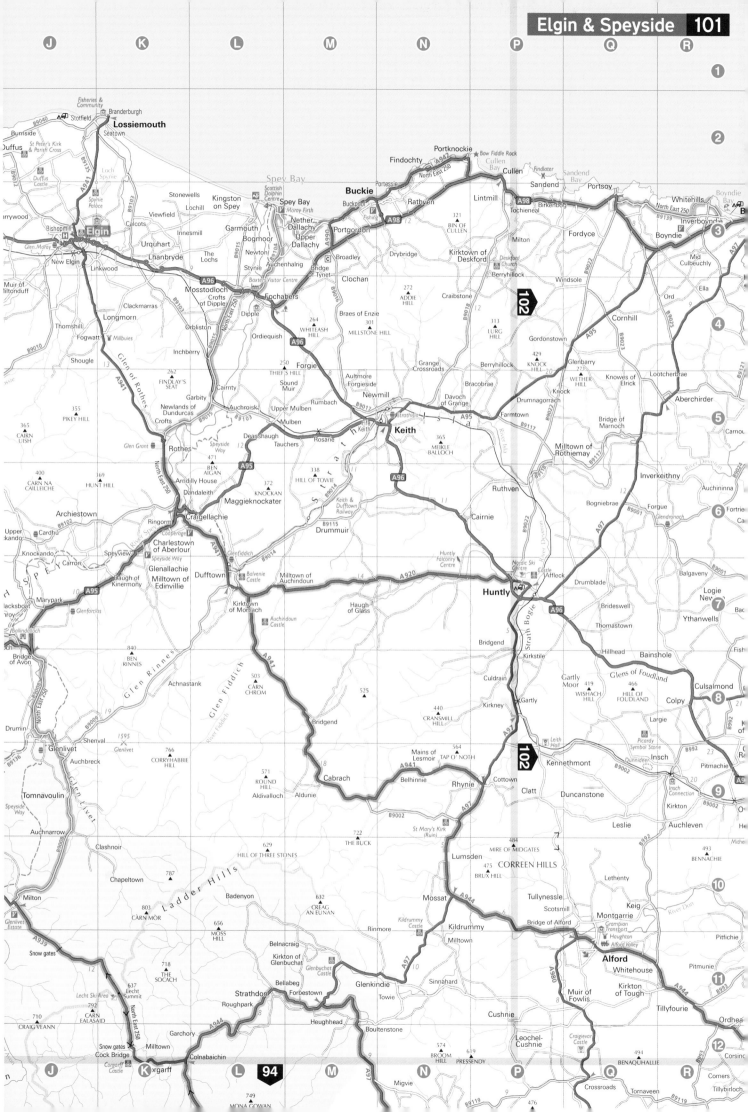

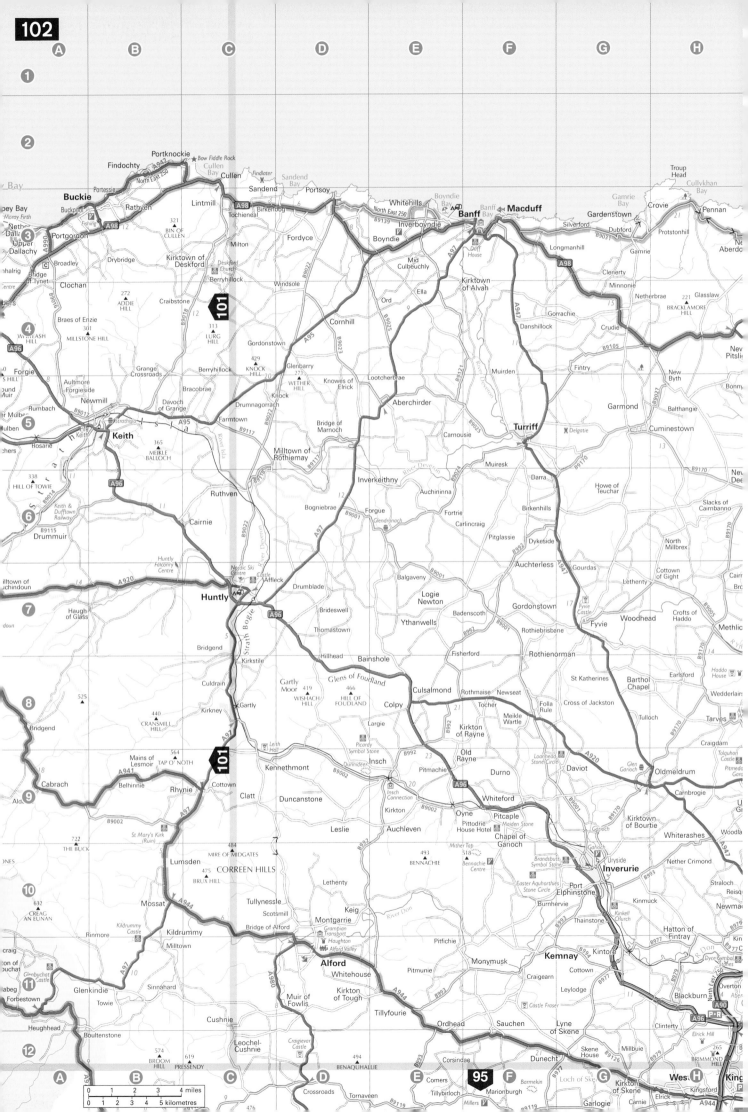

Port plan: Aberdeen p.95

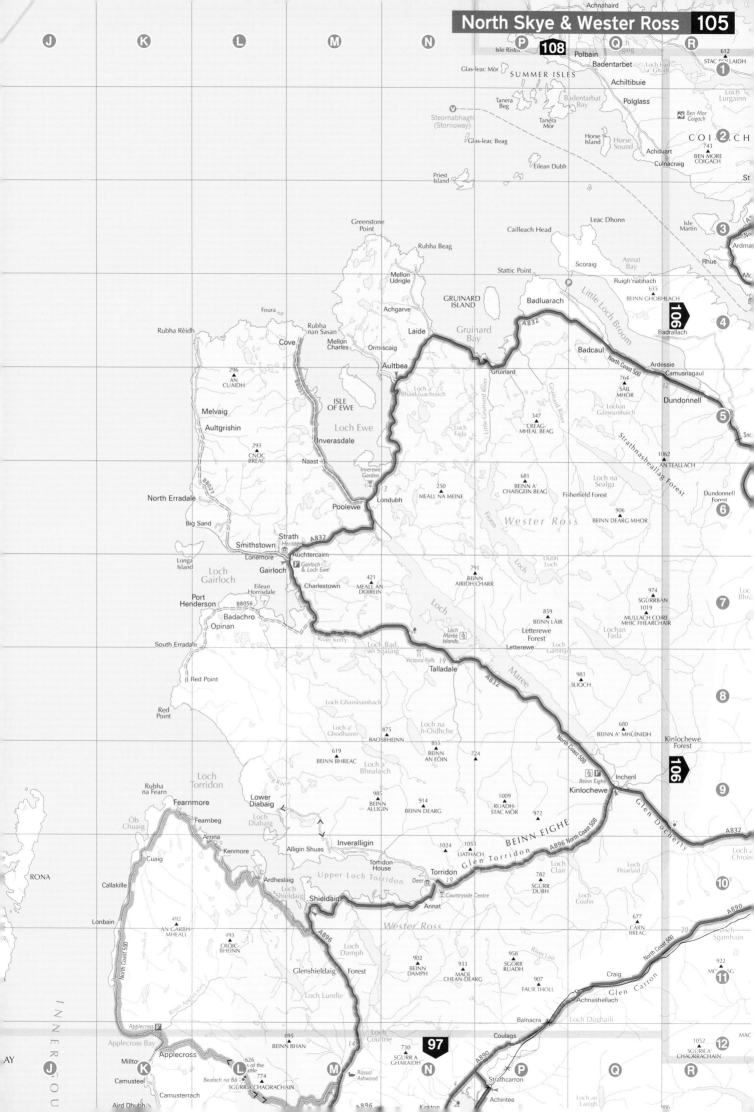

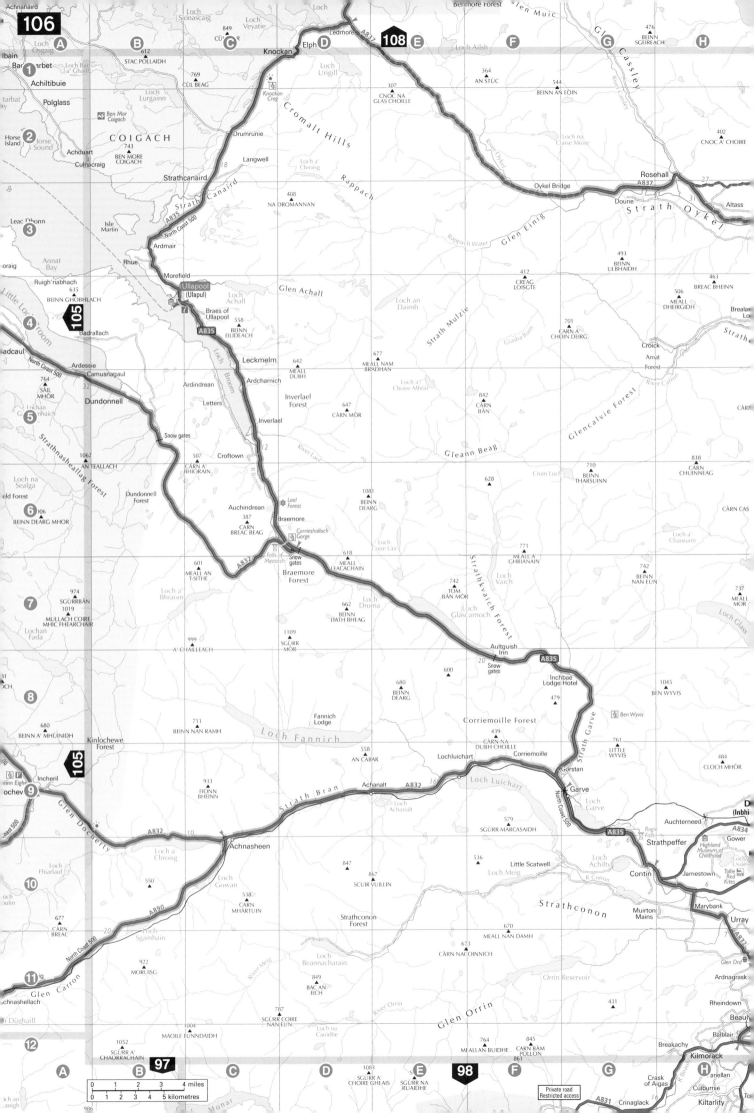

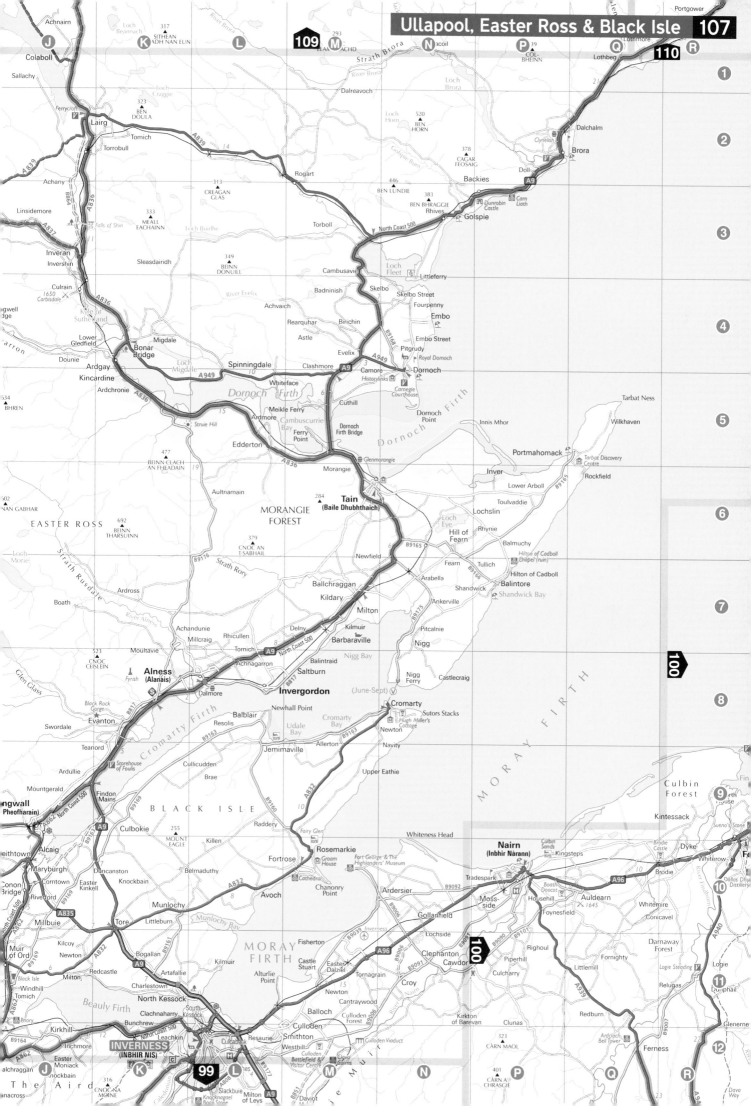

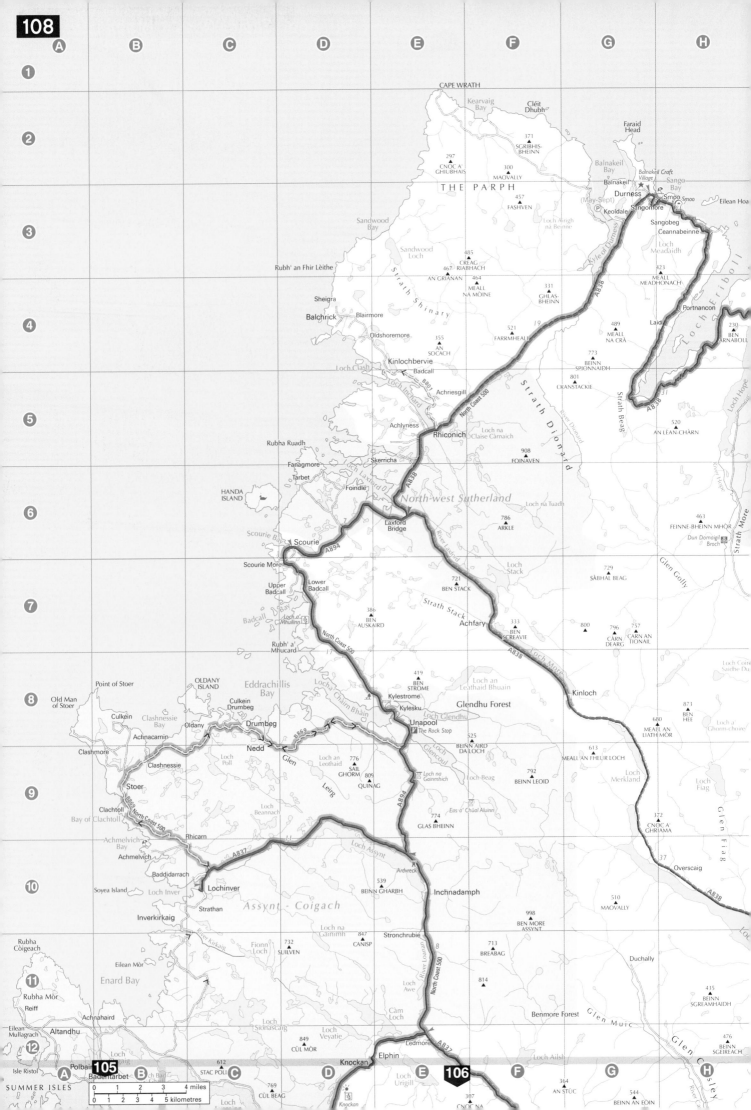

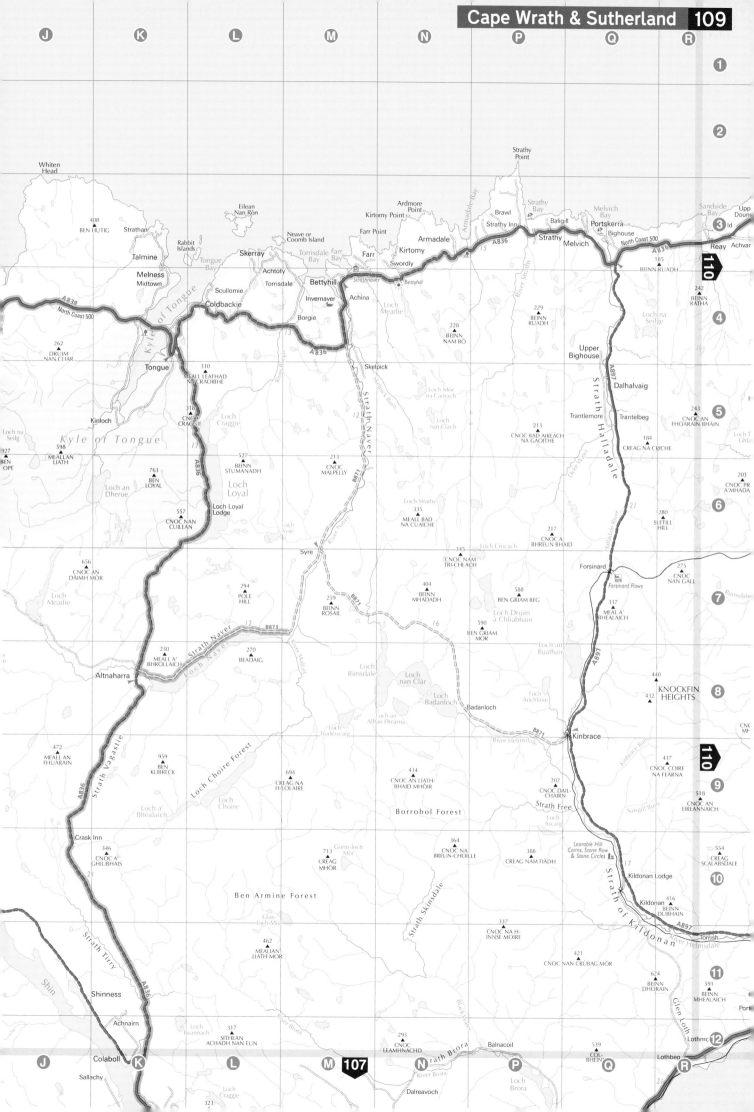

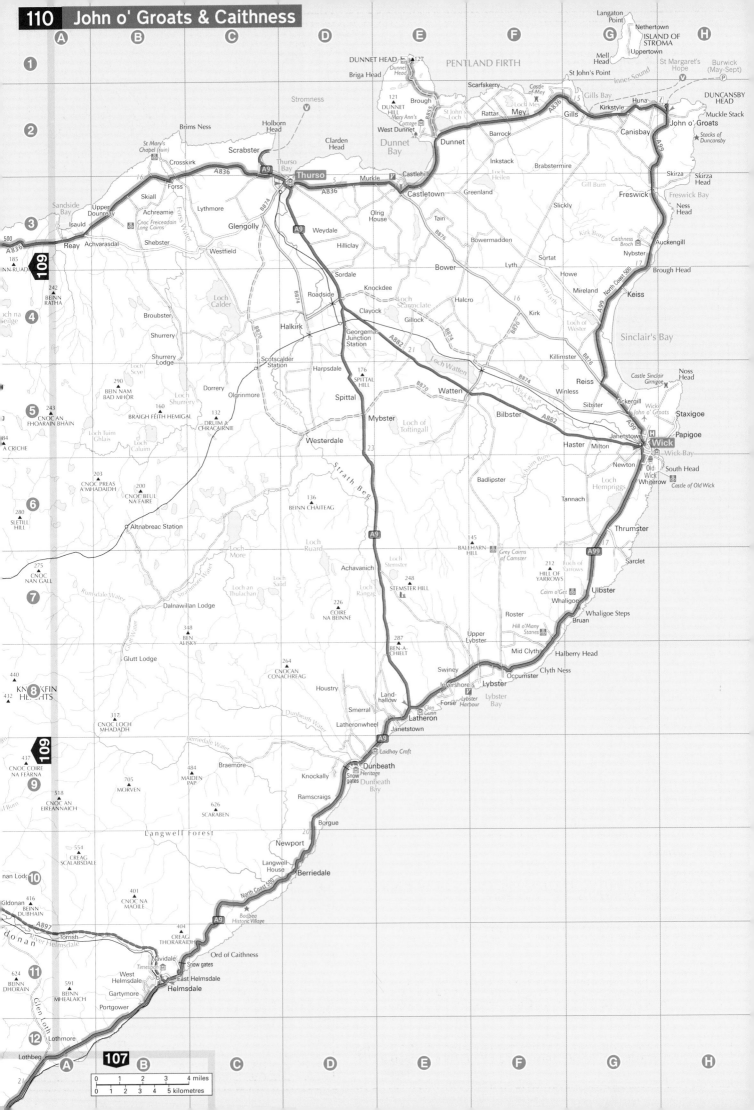

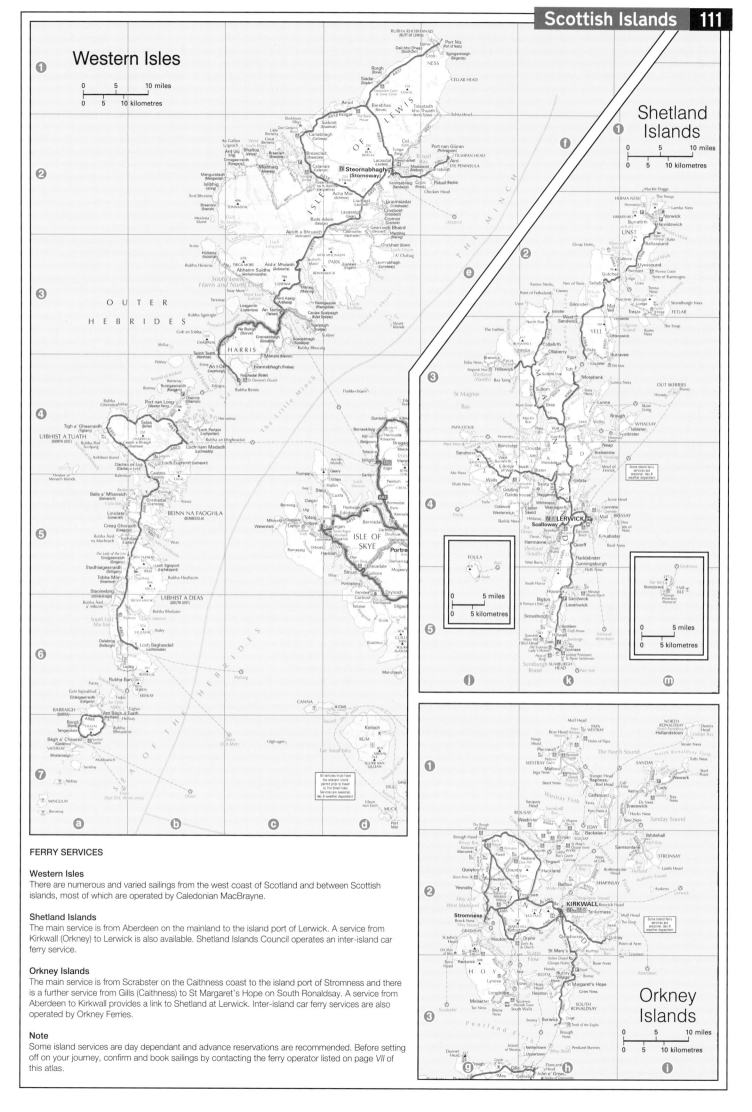

Western Isles

0   5   10 miles
0   5   10 kilometres

Shetland Islands

0   5   10 miles
0   5   10 kilometres

Orkney Islands

0   5   10 miles
0   5   10 kilometres

FERRY SERVICES

Western Isles

There are numerous and varied sailings from the west coast of Scotland and between Scottish islands, most of which are operated by Caledonian MacBrayne.

Shetland Islands

The main service is from Aberdeen on the mainland to the island port of Lerwick. A service from Kirkwall (Orkney) to Lerwick is also available. Shetland Islands Council operates an inter-island car ferry service.

Orkney Islands

The main service is from Scrabster on the Caithness coast to the island port of Stromness and there is a further service from Gills (Caithness) to St Margaret's Hope on South Ronaldsay. A service from Aberdeen to Kirkwall provides a link to Shetland at Lerwick. Inter-island car ferry services are also operated by Orkney Ferries.

Note

Some island services are day dependant and advance reservations are recommended. Before setting off on your journey, confirm and book sailings by contacting the ferry operator listed on page VII of this atlas.

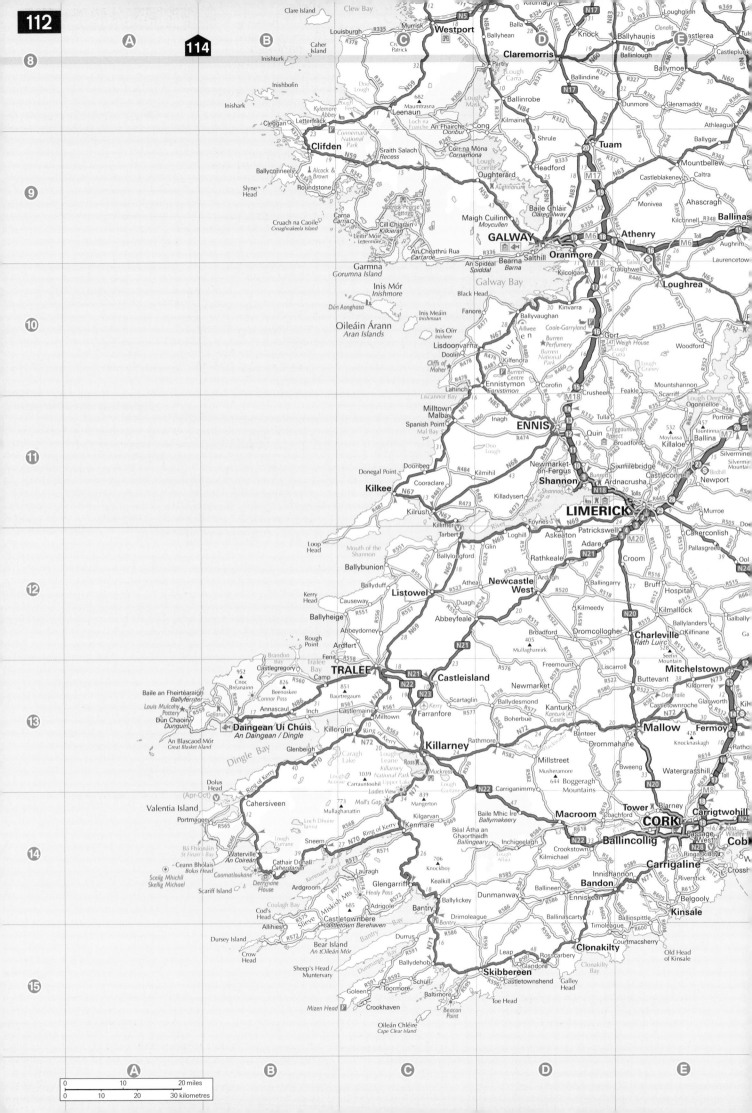

115

IRISH
SEA

CELTIC
SEA

	Toll-free motorway			B road (Northern Ireland)
	Toll motorway and plaza			Distance in miles between symbols (Northern Ireland)
	Motorway junctions with and without number			Minor road
	Restricted motorway junctions			Road tunnel, with toll
	Motorway service area			Road under construction
	National primary route (Republic of Ireland)			Airport (major/minor)
	National secondary route (Republic of Ireland)			International boundary
	Regional route (Republic of Ireland)			Vehicle ferry
	Distance in kilometres between symbols (Republic of Ireland)			Fast vehicle ferry or catamaran
	Primary route (Northern Ireland)			Gaeltacht (Irish language area)
	A road (Northern Ireland)			For key to touring information see page 1

To reflect the distances shown on road signs, distances are shown in miles in Northern Ireland and kilometres in the Republic of Ireland.

16 kilometres = 10 miles

Ireland index

Abbeydorney......C12
Abbeyfeale......D12
Abbeyleix......G11
Adamstown......H12
Adare......D12
Adrigole......C14
Aghalee......J5
Ahascragh......E9
Ahoghill......J4
Allenwood......H9
Allihies......B15
An Bun Beag......E4
An Charraig......E5
An Cheathrú Rua......C9
An Clochán Liath......E4
An Coireán......B14
An Daingean......B13
An Fál Carrach......F3
An Fhairche......C9
Annahilt......J6
Annalong......J7
Annascaul......B13
Annestown......G13
An Rinn......G13
An Spidéal......D9
Antrim......J5
Ardagh......D12
Ardara......E5
Ardee......H8
Ardfert......C12
Ardfinnan......F12
Ardglass......K6
Ardgroom......B14
Ardmore......F14
Ardnacrusha......E11
Arklow......J11
Armagh......H6
Armoy......J3
Arvagh......G7
Ashbourne......J9
Ashford......J10
Askeaton......D12
Athea......D12
Athboy......H8
Athenry......E9
Athleague......E8
Athlone......F9
Athy......H10
Augher......G6
Aughnacloy......H6
Aughrim......E9
Aughrim......J11
Avoca......J11

Bagenalstown......H11
Baile an Fheirtéaraigh......B13
Baile Chláir......D9
Baile Mhic Íre......D14
Baile na Finne......F4
Bailieborough......H7
Balbriggan......J8
Balla......D8
Ballacolla......G11
Ballaghaderreen......E7
Ballina......D7
Ballina......E11
Ballinafad......E7
Ballinagar......G9
Ballinagh......G7
Ballinamallard......G6
Ballinamore......F7
Ballinascarty......D14
Ballinasloe......E9
Ballindaggan......H12
Ballindine......D8
Ballineen......D14
Ballingarry......D12
Ballingarry......G12
Ballingeary......D14
Ballinlough......E8
Ballinrobe......D8
Ballinspittle......E14
Ballintra......F5
Ballivor......H9
Ballon......H11
Ballybay......H7
Ballybofey......F5
Ballybunion......C12
Ballycanew......J11
Ballycarry......K5

Ballycastle......J3
Ballycastle......C6
Ballyclare......J5
Ballyclerahan......F12
Ballyconneely......B9
Ballyconnell......G7
Ballycotton......F14
Ballycumber......F9
Ballydehob......C15
Ballydesmond......D13
Ballyduff......C12
Ballyduff......F13
Ballyfarnon......E7
Ballyferriter......B13
Ballygally......J4
Ballygar......E9
Ballygawley......H6
Ballygawley......E6
Ballygowan......K5
Ballyhack......H13
Ballyhaise......G7
Ballyhalbert......K5
Ballyhaunis......E8
Ballyhean......D8
Ballyheige......C12
Ballyjamesduff......G8
Ballylanders......E12
Ballylickey......C14
Ballyliffin......G3
Ballylongford......C12
Ballylynan......H10
Ballymacarbry......F13
Ballymahon......F8
Ballymakeery......D14
Ballymena......J4
Ballymoe......E8
Ballymoney......H4
Ballymore......F9
Ballymore Eustace......H10
Ballymote......E7
Ballynacarrigy......G8
Ballynahinch......J6
Ballynure......J5
Ballyporeen......F13
Ballyragget......G11
Ballyroan......G10
Ballysadare......E6
Ballyshannon......F5
Ballyvaughan......D10
Ballywalter......K5
Balrothery......J8
Baltimore......C15
Baltinglass......H10
Banagher......F10
Banbridge......J6
Bandon......E14
Bangor......K5
Bangor Erris......C7
Bansha......F12
Banteer......D13
Bantry......C14
Barna......D9
Béal an Mhuirthead......B6
Béal Átha an Ghaorthaidh......D14
Bearna......D9
Belcoo......F6
Belfast......J5
Belgooly......E14
Bellaghy......H4
Belleek......F6
Belmullet......B6
Belturbet......G7
Benburb......H6
Bennettsbridge......G12
Beragh......G5
Bessbrook......J6
Bettystown......J8
Birr......F10
Blacklion......F6
Blackwater......J12
Blarney......E14
Blessington......H10
Boherbue......D13
Borris......H12
Borris-in-Ossory......F10
Borrisokane......F10
Borrisoleigh......F11
Boyle......E7
Bray......J10
Bridgetown......H13

Brittas......J9
Broadford......E11
Broadford......D12
Broughshane......J4
Bruff......E12
Bunbeg......E4
Bunclody......H11
Buncrana......G3
Bundoran......E6
Bunmahon......G13
Bunnyconnellan......D7
Bushmills......H3
Buttevant......E13
Bweeng......E13

Cadamstown......F10
Caherconlish......E12
Caherdaniel......B14
Cahersiveen......B14
Cahir......F12
Caledon......H6
Callan......G12
Caltra......E9
Camp......B13
Carndonagh......G3
Cappawhite......F12
Cappoquin......F13
Carlanstown......H8
Carlingford......J7
Carlow......H11
Carna......C9
Carnew......J11
Carnlough......J4
Carragh......H9
Carraig Airt......F3
Carraroe......C9
Carrick......E5
Carrickfergus......K5
Carrickmacross......H7
Carrickmore......G5
Carrick-on-Shannon......F7
Carrick-on-Suir......G12
Carrigaline......E14
Carrigallen......F7
Carriganimmy......D13
Carrigart......F3
Carrigtwohill......E14
Carryduff......J5
Cashel......F12
Castlebar......D8
Castlebellingham......J7
Castleblakeney......E9
Castlebridge......J12
Castleblayney......H7
Castlecomer......G11
Castleconnell......E11
Castlederg......G5
Castledermot......H11
Castlegregory......B13
Castleisland......C13
Castlemaine......C13
Castlemartyr......F14
Castleplunket......E8
Castlepollard......G8
Castlerea......E8
Castlerock......H3
Castletownbere......B15
Castletownroche......E13
Castletownshend......D15
Castlewellan......J6
Cathair Dónall......B14
Causeway......C12
Cavan......G7
Celbridge......H9
Charlestown......D7
Charleville......E12
Cill Charthaigh......E5
Cill Chiaráin......C9
Clady......G5
Clane......H9
Clara......G9
Claregalway......D9
Claremorris......D8
Clashmore......F13
Claudy......G4
Cleggan......B8
Clifden......B9
Cliffoney......E6
Cloghan......F10
Clogheen......F13
Clogher......G6

Clogherhead......J8
Clogh Mills......J4
Clonakilty......D15
Clonaslee......G10
Clonbur......C9
Clondalkin......J9
Clonea......G13
Clones......G7
Clonmany......G3
Clonmel......F12
Clonmellon......H8
Clonroche......H12
Clough......K6
Cloughjordan......F11
Cloyne......F14
Coachford......D14
Coalisland......H5
Cobh......E14
Coleraine......H3
Collinstown......G8
Collon......H8
Collooney......E7
Comber......K5
Cong......D9
Convoy......F4
Cookstown......H5
Coole......G8
Cooraclare......C11
Cootehill......G7
Cork......E14
Cornamona......C9
Corr na Móna......C9
Corrofin......D10
Courtmacsherry......E15
Courtown......J11
Craughwell......E10
Creeslough......F4
Croithlí......E4
Crolly......E4
Crookhaven......C15
Crookstown......D14
Croom......E12
Crossakeel......H8
Crosshaven......E14
Crossmaglen......H7
Crossmolina......D7
Crumlin......J5
Crusheen......D10
Culdaff......G3
Cullybackey......J4
Culmore......G4
Curracloe......J12
Curry......E7
Cushendall......J4
Cushendun......J3

Daingean......G9
Daingean Uí Chúis......B13
Delvin......G8
Derrinturn......H9
Derry......G4
Derrygonnelly......F6
Derrylin......G6
Dervock......H3
Dingle......B13
Doagh......J5
Donabate......J9
Donaghadee......K5
Donaghmore......H5
Donaghmore......H5
Donegal......F5
Donemana......G4
Doneraile......D13
Doolin......C10
Doon......C11
Doonbeg......C11
Downings......F3
Downpatrick......K6
Dowra......F6
Draperstown......H5
Drimoleague......D14
Drogheda......J8
Droichead Nua......H9
Dromahair......E6
Dromara......J6
Dromcollogher......D12
Dromiskin......J7
Drommahane......E13
Dromod......F8
Dromore......J6

Dromore......G5
Dromore West......D6
Drumaness......K6
Drumfries......G3
Drumkeeran......F7
Drumlish......F8
Drumquin......G5
Drumshanbo......F7
Drumsna......F7
Duagh......C12
Dublin......J9
Duleek......J8
Dunboyne......J9
Dún Chaoin......A13
Dundalk......J7
Dundonald......K5
Dundrum......F12
Dunfanaghy......F3
Dungannon......H5
Dungarvan......G13
Dungiven......H4
Dunglow......E4
Dungourney......F14
Dunkineely......E5
Dún Laoghaire......J9
Dunlavin......H10
Dunleer......J8
Dunloy......J4
Dunmanway......D14
Dunmore......E8
Dunmore East......H13
Dunquin......A13
Dunshaughlin......H9
Durrow......G11
Durrow......G9
Durrus......C15
Dysart......E9

Easky......D6
Edenderry......H9
Edgeworthstown......G8
Eglinton......G4
Elphin......F8
Emyvale......H6
Enfield......H9
Ennis......D11
Enniscorthy......H12
Enniscrone......D6
Enniskean......D14
Enniskillen......F6
Ennistymon......D10
Eyrecourt......F10

Falcarragh......F3
Fanore......D10
Farranfore......C13
Feakle......E11
Fenagh......F7
Fenit......B13
Ferbane......F10
Fermoy......E13
Ferns......J12
Fethard......F12
Fethard......H13
Fintona......G6
Fintown......F4
Fivemiletown......G6
Foxford......D7
Foynes......D12
Freemount......D13
Frenchpark......E8
Freshford......G11

Galbally......E12
Galway......D9
Garrison......F6
Garvagh......H4
Gilford......J6
Glandore......D15
Glanmire......E14
Glanworth......E13
Glaslough......H6
Glassan......F9
Gleann Cholm Cille......E5
Glenamaddy......E8
Glenarm......J4
Glenavy......J5
Glenbeigh......B13
Glencolumbkille......E5
Glenealy......J10
Glengarriff......C14
Glenties......E5

Glin......D12
Golden......F12
Goleen......C15
Goresbridge......H11
Gorey......J11
Gort......D10
Gorteen......E7
Gortin......G4
Gowran......G11
Graiguenamanagh......H12
Granard......G8
Grange......E6
Greencastle......H3
Greencastle......J7
Greenore......J7
Greyabbey......K5
Greystones......J10
Gulladuff......H4

Hacketstown......H11
Headford......D9
Hillsborough......J6
Hilltown......J6
Holycross......F11
Holywood......K5
Hospital......E12
Howth......J9

Inagh......D11
Inch......B13
Inchigeelagh......D14
Inishcrone......D6
Innishannon......E14
Irvinestown......F6

Johnstown......G11

Kanturk......D13
Keadue......F7
Keady......H6
Kealkill......C14
Keel......B7
Kells......J4
Kells......H8
Kenmare......C14
Kesh......F5
Kilbeggan......G9
Kilcar......E5
Kilcock......H9
Kilcolgan......D10
Kilconnell......E9
Kilcoole......J10
Kilcormac......F10
Kilcullen......H10
Kildare......H10
Kildorrery......E13
Kilfenora......D10
Kilfinane......E12
Kilgarvan......C14
Kilkee......C11
Kilkeel......J7
Kilkenny......G11
Kilkieran......C9
Kill......H9
Kill......G13
Killadysert......D11
Killala......D6
Killaloe......E11
Killarney......C13
Killashandra......G7
Killeagh......F14
Killenaule......F12
Killimer......C11
Killiney......J9
Killinick......J13
Killorglin......C13
Killough......K6
Killucan......G9
Killurin......G10
Killybegs......E5
Killyleagh......K6
Kilmacanogue......J10
Kilmacrenan......F3
Kilmacthomas......G13
Kilmaganny......G12
Kilmaine......D8
Kilmallock......E12
Kilmanagh......G11
Kilmeedy......D12
Kilmichael......D14
Kilmihil......C11
Kilmore Quay......H13

Kilmuckridge......J12
Kilpedder......J10
Kilrea......H4
Kilrush......C11
Kilsheelan......G12
Kiltegan......H11
Kiltimagh......D8
Kilworth......E13
Kingscourt......H7
Kinlough......F5
Kinnegad......G9
Kinnitty......F10
Kinsale......E14
Kinvarra......D10
Kircubbin......K5
Knock......D8
Knockcroghery......F8

Lahinch......C10
Lanesborough......F8
Laragh......J10
Larne......K4
Lauragh......C14
Laurencetown......F10
Leap......D15
Leenaun......C8
Leighlinbridge......H11
Leitrim......B9
Leitrim......F7
Leixlip......H9
Letterfrack......B8

Letterkenny......F4
Lifford......G4
Limavady......H4
Limerick......E11
Lisbellaw......G6
Lisburn......J5
Liscarroll......D13
Lisdoonvarna......D10
Lismore......F13
Lisnaskea......G6
Listowel......C12
Loghill......D12
Londonderry......G4
Longford......F8
Longwood......H9
Loughbrickland......J6
Loughglinn......E8
Loughrea......E10
Louisburgh......C8
Lucan......J9
Lurgan......J6
Lusk......J9

Macroom......D14
Maghera......H4
Magherafelt......H5
Maguiresbridge......G6
Maigh Cuilinn......D9
Malahide......J9
Málainn Mhóir......E5
Malin......G3

112

0   10   20 miles
0 10 20 30 kilometres

Malin More E5
Mallow E13
Manorhamilton F6
Markethill H6
Martinstown J4
Maynooth H9
Mayobridge J6
Midleton F14
Milford F4
Millstreet D13
Milltown C13
Milltown Malbay C11
Mitchelstown E13
Moate F9
Mohill F7
Monaghan H6
Monasterevin G10
Moneymore H5
Monivea E9
Mooncoin G13
Mountbellew E9
Mountcharles F5
Mountmellick G10
Mountrath G10
Mountshannon E10
Moville G3
Moy H6
Moycullen D9
Moynalty H8
Mucklagh G9
Muff G4

Muine Bheag H11
Mullagh H8
Mullaghmore E6
Mullinahone G12
Mullinavat G12
Mullingar G9
Mulranny C7
Murrisk C8
Murroe E11

Naas H10
Na Dúnaibh F3
Naul J8
Navan H8
Nenagh E11
Newbawn H12
Newbliss G7
Newbridge H10
Newcastle J6
Newcastle J10
Newcastle West ...D12
New Inn F12
Newmarket D13
Newmarket-on-
 Fergus D11
Newport C7
Newport E11
New Ross H12
Newry J6
Newtownabbey J5
Newtownards K5

Newtownbutler G7
Newtown-
 cunningham G4
Newtownforbes F8
Newtownhamilton .H6
Newtownmount-
 kennedy J10
Newtownstewart ...G5
Nobber H8

Ogonnelloe E11
Oilgate H12
Oldcastle G8
Omagh G5
Omeath J7
Oola E12
Oranmore D9
Oughterard D9

Pallasgreen E12
Partry D8
Passage East H13
Passage West E14
Patrickswell E12
Pettigo F5
Piltown G12
Plumbridge G5
Pomeroy G5
Portadown H6
Portaferry K6
Portarlington G10

Portavogie K6
Portballintrae H3
Portglenone H4
Port Laoise G10
Portlaw G13
Portmagee B14
Portmarnock J9
Portnablagh F3
Portnoo E4
Portroe E11
Portrush H3
Portstewart H3
Portumna E10
Poyntzpass J6
Prosperous H9

Quin D11

Raharney G9
Ramelton F4
Randalstown J5
Raphoe G4
Rasharkin H4
Rathangan H10
Rathcoole J9
Rathcormac E13
Rathdowney G11
Rathdrum J10
Rathfriland J6
Rathkeale D12
Ráth Luirc E12

Rathmore D13
Rathmullan G4
Rathnew J10
Rathvilly H11
Ratoath J9
Recess C9
Rhode G9
Ring G13
Ringaskiddy E14
Riverchapel J11
Riverstick E14
Rochfortbridge ...G9
Rockcorry H7
Roosky F8
Rosbercon H12
Roscommon F8
Roscrea F10
Rosscarbery D15
Rosses Point E6
Rosslare J13
Rosslare Harbour .J13
Rosslea G6
Rossnowlagh E5
Rostrevor J7
Roundstone B9
Roundwood J10
Rush J9

Saintfield K6
St Johnston G4
Sallins H9

Rathmore D13
Salthill D9
Scarriff E11
Scartaglin C13
Schull C15
Seskinore G5
Shanagarry F14
Shannon D11
Shannonbridge ...F9
Shercock H7
Shillelagh H11
Shinrone F10
Shrule D9
Silvermines E11
Sion Mills G5
Sixmilebridge D11
Skerries J8
Skibbereen D15
Slane H8
Sligo E6
Smithborough G6
Sneem B14
Spanish Point C11
Spiddal D9
Sraith Salach C9
Stewartstown H5
Stoneyford G12
Strabane G4
Stradbally G10
Stradone G7
Strandhill E6
Strangford K6

Stranorlar F5
Strokestown F8
Summerhill H9
Swan G11
Swanlinbar F6
Swinford D7
Swords J9

Taghmon H12
Tagoat J13
Tallaght J9
Tallow F13
Tandragee J6
Tarbert C12
Templemore F11
Termonfeckin J8
Thomastown G12
Thurles F11
Timahoe G10
Timoleague D15
Tinahely J11
Tipperary F12
Tobercurry E7
Tobermore H4
Toomevara F11
Toormore C15
Tower E14
Tralee C13
Tramore G13
Trim H8
Tuam D9

Tubbercurry E7
Tulla D11
Tullamore G9
Tullow H11
Tulsk E8
Turlough D7

Urlingford G11
Virginia G8

Warrenpoint J7
Waterford G13
Watergrasshill E13
Waterville B14
Wellingtonbridge .H13
Westport C8
Wexford J12
Whitegate E14
Whitehead K5
Wicklow J10
Woodenbridge J11
Woodford E10

Youghal F14

For Central London see pages 142–151

The Ultra Low Emission Zone (ULEZ) is due to be extended in October 2021.
For further information visit tfl.gov.uk/ULEZ

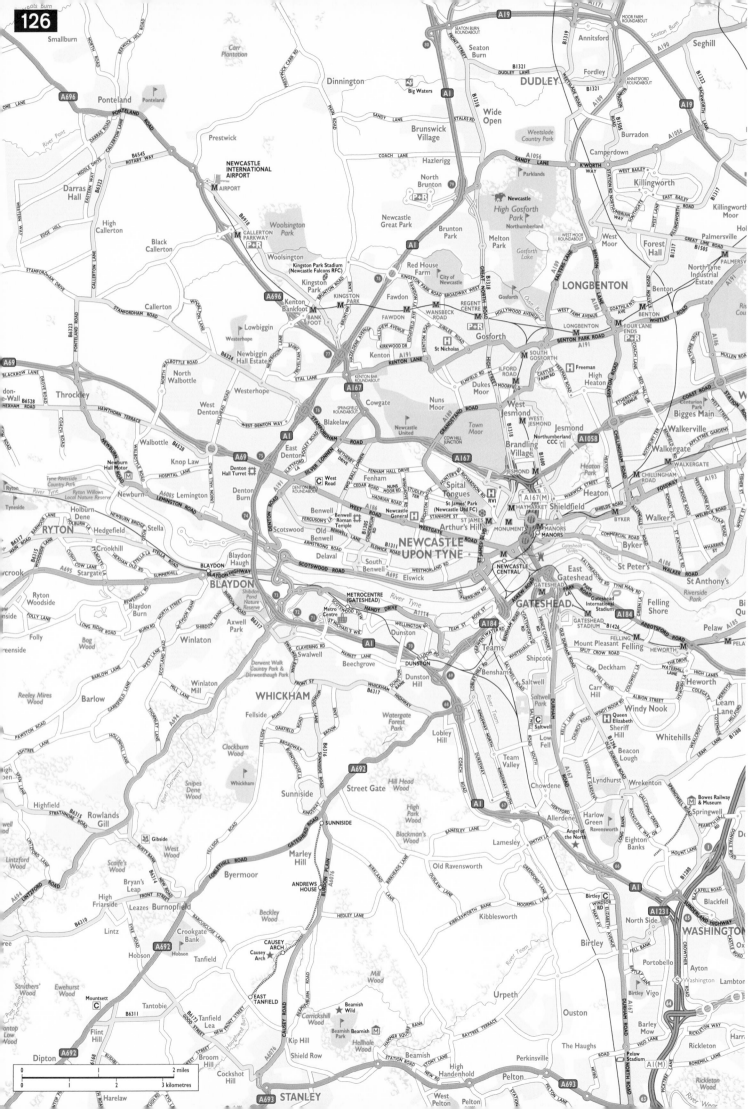

NORTH

SEA

Amsterdam (IJmuiden)

WHITLEY BAY
Whitley Bay
Links Art Gallery
Whitley Bay

East Holywell
Bates Cottages
Holywell
Earsdon
Monkseaton
West Monkseaton
WEST MONKSEATON
Shiremoor
SHIREMOOR
Murton
Backworth
Blackworth Hall
Benton Square
NORTHUMBERLAND PARK
West Allotment
New York
New York Road
Silver Fox Way
Billy Mill
West Chirton
Stephenson Railway
NORTH SHIELDS
Preston
Tynemouth
TYNEMOUTH
Tynemouth Priory & Castle
King Edwards Bay
Longsands South
Blue Reef
Cullercoats
CULLERCOATS
Marden
Marden Park Nature Reserve
North Tyneside General

Willington Square
Holy Cross
Willington
Howdon
Silverlink Roundabout
North Tyneside Steam Railway
Howdon Interchange
Waterville Road
Meadow Well
Percy Main
NORTH SHIELDS
South Shields
SOUTH SHIELDS
Arbeia Roman Fort & Museum
The Lawe
Sandhaven
Mill Dam
CHICHESTER
Westoe
Cauldwell
Harton
Harton Nook
Marsden
Marsden Rock
Marsden Bay
Souter Lighthouse & The Leas
Whitburn Coastal Park

WALLSEND
Segedunum Roman Fort & Baths
Point Pleasant
Willington Quay
East Howdon
HADRIAN ROAD
HOWDON
Royal Quays
International Passenger Terminal
Tyne Tunnel
River Tyne

JARROW
Jarrow Hall
St Paul's Monastery
East Jarrow
Tyne Dock
Temple Town
Dean Rd
TYNE DOCK
South Tyneside General
West Harton
Whiteleas
Biddick Hall
South Shields
BROCKLEY WHINS
Brockley Whins
Shields Road
Cleadon Park
South Shields
Cleadon
Whitburn
South Bents

Hebburn Colliery
HEBBURN
Hebburn New Town
Monkton
Primrose
Fellgate
Hedworth
FELLGATE
Boldon Colliery
West Boldon
East Boldon
Cleadon
Whitburn
Seaburn
Whitburn Bay

Riverside Park
Wardley
Folingsby
Heworth
George Washington
Usworth
North East Aircraft
Downhill
Witherwack
Marley Pots
High Southwick
Southwick
Monkwearmouth
STADIUM OF LIGHT
Roker
Seaburn
Carley Hill

Testos Roundabout
Boldon
Greyhound Stadium
Fulwell

Concord
Sulgrave
Albany
Hertburn
Washington Old Hall
Washington Village
Barmston
Teal Farm
Hylton Castle
Castletown
Hylton Plantation
South Hylton
SOUTH HYLTON
Pennywell
Ford
Sunderland Royal
University
SUNDERLAND
Bishopwearmouth
Millfield
Pallion
Ayre's Quay
Northern Spire Bridge
Queen Alexandra Bridge
Low Southwick
Deptford
Stadium of Light (Sunderland AFC)
National Glass Centre
Sunderland Harbour
St Peter's
Park Lane

Columbia
Biddick
Fatfield
Mount Pleasant
Penshaw Monument
Herrington Country Park
Washington Wetland Centre
New Herrington
Shiney Row
Biddick Gill Wood
Hastings Hill
Grindon
Thorney Close
Silksworth Sports Complex & Ski Centre
Middle Herrington
East Herrington
New Silksworth
Silksworth
High Barnes
Barnes Park
Ashbrooke
Humbledon
Springwell
Plains Farm
Farringdon
Hendon
Sunderland Eye Infirmary
Hillview
Grangetown
Ryhope Colliery
Ryhope

River Wear

Town, port and airport plans

Motorway and junction	One-way, gated/ closed road	Railway station	Toilet, with facilities for the less able
Primary road single/ dual carriageway and numbered junction	Restricted access road	Preserved or tourist railway	Car park, with electric charging point
A road single/ dual carriageway and numbered junction	Pedestrian area	Light rapid transit system station	Park and Ride (at least 6 days per week)
B road single/ dual carriageway	Footpath	Level crossing	Bus/coach station
Local road single/ dual carriageway	Road under construction	Tramway	Hospital, 24-hour Accident & Emergency hospital
Other road single/ dual carriageway, minor road	Road tunnel	Airport, heliport	Beach (award winning)
Building of interest	Lighthouse	Railair terminal	City wall
Ruined building	Castle	Theatre or performing arts centre	Escarpment
Tourist Information Centre	Castle mound	Cinema	Cliff lift
Visitor or heritage centre	Monument, memorial, statue	Abbey, chapel, church	River/canal, lake
World Heritage Site (UNESCO)	Post Office	Synagogue	Lock, weir
Museum	Public library	Mosque	Viewpoint
English Heritage site	Shopping centre	Golf course	Park/sports ground
Historic Scotland site	Shopmobility	Racecourse	Cemetery
Cadw (Welsh heritage) site	Football stadium	Nature reserve	Woodland
National Trust site	Rugby stadium	Aquarium	Built-up area
National Trust Scotland site	County cricket ground	Showground	Beach

Central London street map (see pages 142–151)

London Underground station	London Overground station
Docklands Light Railway (DLR) station	Central London Congestion Charge and Ultra Low Emission boundary*

Royal Parks

Green Park	Park open 5am–midnight. Constitution Hill and The Mall closed to traffic Sundays and public holidays 8am–dusk.
Hyde Park	Park open 5am–midnight. Park roads closed to traffic midnight–5am.
Kensington Gardens	Park open 6am–dusk.
Regent's Park	Park open 5am–dusk. Park roads closed to traffic midnight–7am, except for residents.
St James's Park	Park open 5am–midnight. The Mall closed to traffic Sundays and public holidays 8am–dusk.
Victoria Tower Gardens	Park open dawn–dusk.

Traffic regulations in the City of London include security checkpoints and restrict the number of entry and exit points.

Note: Oxford Street is closed to through-traffic (except buses & taxis) 7am–7pm Monday–Saturday.

Central London Congestion Charge Zone (CCZ)

You need to pay a daily charge for driving or parking a vehicle on public roads in this central London area. Payment permits entry, travel within and exit from the CCZ by the vehicle as often as required on that day.

In June 2020, due to the coronavirus pandemic, temporary changes were made to the charges and times of operation and these continue to be under review. At the time of printing you must pay a £15 daily charge if you drive within the zone 07:00-22:00, every day, except Christmas Day (25 December).

For up to date information on the CCZ, exemptions, discounts or ways to pay, visit **tfl.gov.uk/modes/driving/congestion-charge**

Ultra Low Emission Zone (ULEZ)

Most vehicles in Central London, including cars and vans, need to meet minimum exhaust emission standards or drivers must pay a daily charge to drive within the zone. It applies to the same area covered by the Congestion Charge and operates 24 hours a day, every day of the year, except Christmas Day (25 December). The charge is £12.50 for motorcycles, cars and vans and is in addition to the Congestion Charge.

*From 25th October 2021 the ULEZ boundary will be extended from central London to include the area up to, but not including, the North Circular Road (A406) and South Circular Road (A205).

Please note the maps in this atlas show the zone in operation at the time of going to print.

For further information visit **tfl.gov.uk/ULEZ**

In addition the Low Emission Zone (LEZ) operates across Greater London, 24 hours every day of the year and is aimed at the most heavy-polluting vehicles. It does not apply to cars or motorcycles. For details visit **tfl.gov.uk/LEZ**

Town Plans

Aberdeen 103
Aberystwyth....................36
Basingstoke...................129
Bath...........................129
Birmingham....................130
Blackpool 130
Bournemouth...................130
Bradford......................130
Brighton 131
Bristol 131
Cambridge 131
Canterbury 131
Cardiff........................132
Carlisle.......................132
Chester 132
Coventry 132
Derby 133
Dundee 133
Edinburgh 133
Exeter 133
Glasgow 134
Ipswich 134
Kingston upon Hull 134
Leeds 134
Leicester 135
Liverpool 135
LONDON..................142–151
Manchester 135

Middlesbrough..................135
Milton Keynes 136
Newcastle upon Tyne 136
Newquay 3
Norwich 136
Nottingham....................136
Oxford 137
Peterborough 137
Plymouth 137
Portsmouth 137
Ramsgate 23
Reading 138
Royal Tunbridge Wells 138
Salisbury 138
Scarborough 67
Sheffield......................138
Shrewsbury 139
Southampton 139
Stoke-on-Trent (Hanley) 139
Stratford-upon-Avon 139
Sunderland....................140
Swansea 140
Taunton 140
Warwick 140
Watford 141
Winchester 141
Worcester 141
York...........................141

Ferry Ports

Aberdeen Harbour 95
Dover, Port of..................12
Fishguard Harbour...............24
Harwich International Port.......35
Heysham Harbour.................62
Holyhead Harbour................54
Hull, Port of...................61
Liverpool Docks.................56
Newhaven Harbour................11
Pembroke Dock...................24
Plymouth, Port of................4
Port of Tyne....................73
Portsmouth Harbour..............10

Channel Tunnel

Folkestone Terminal 13
Calais / Coquelles Terminal 13

Central London

Basingstoke | Bath

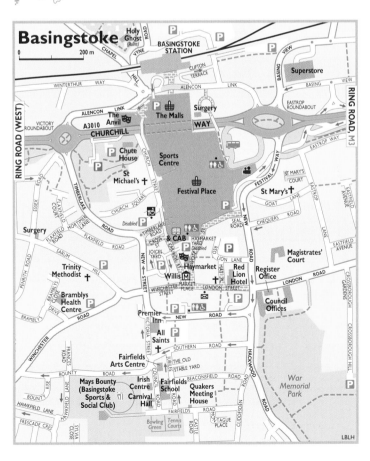

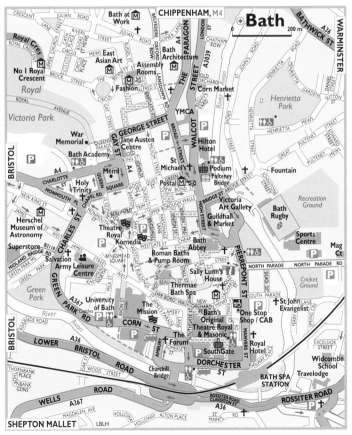

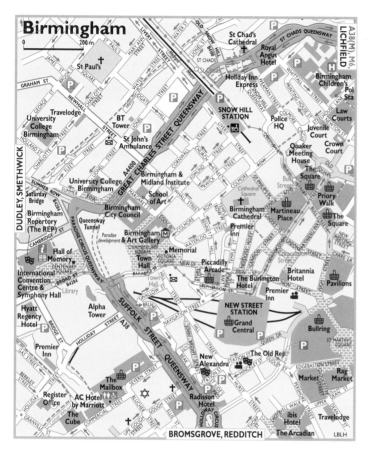

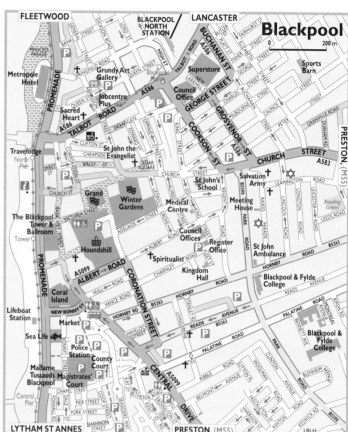

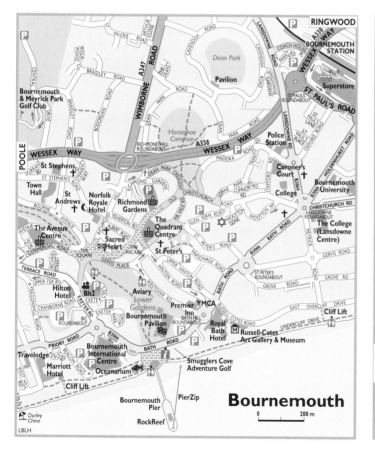

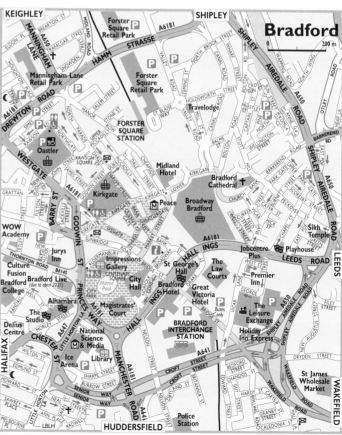

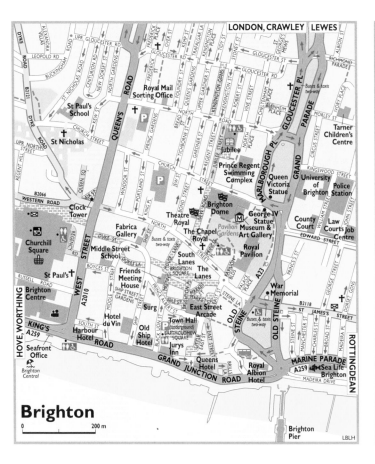

Brighton

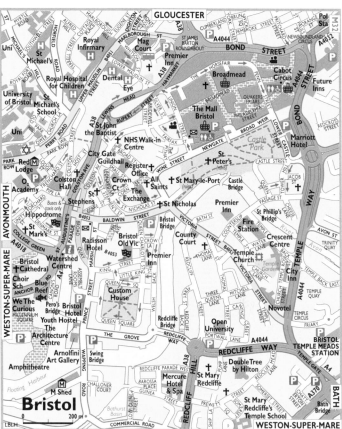

Bristol

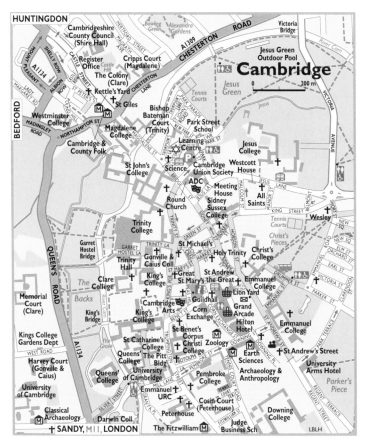

Cambridge

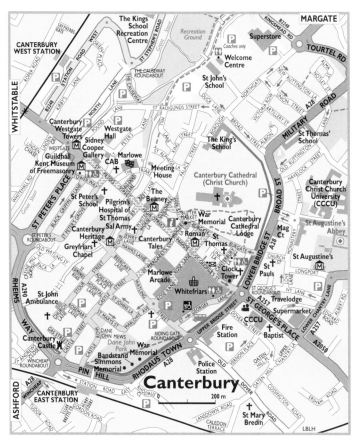

Canterbury

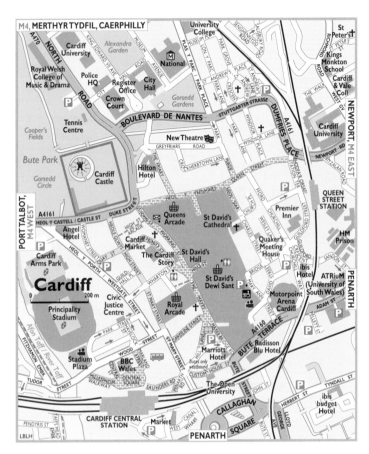

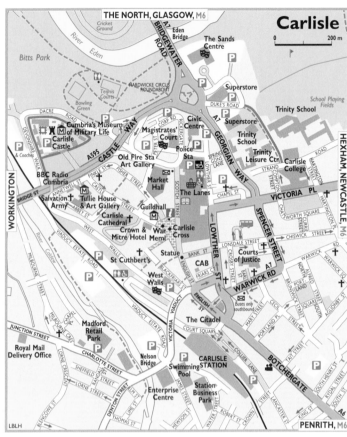

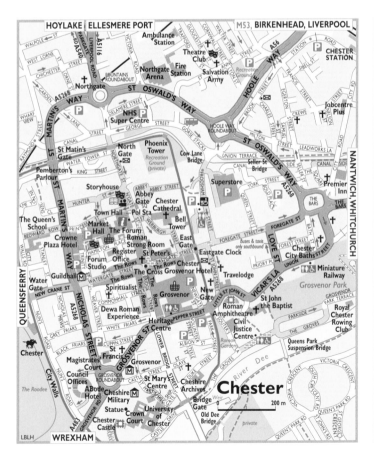

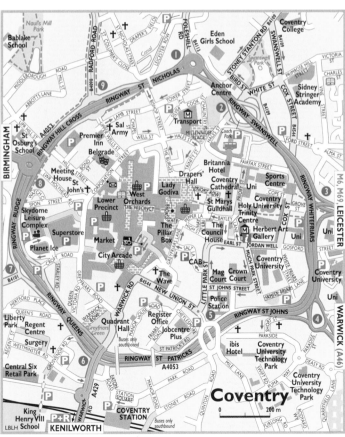

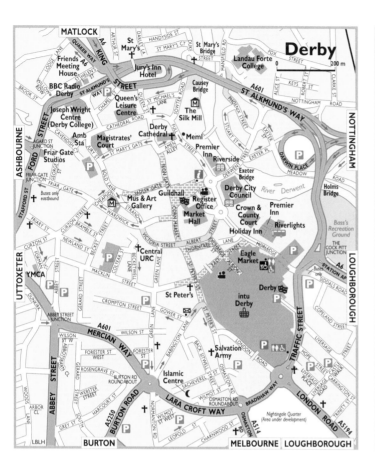

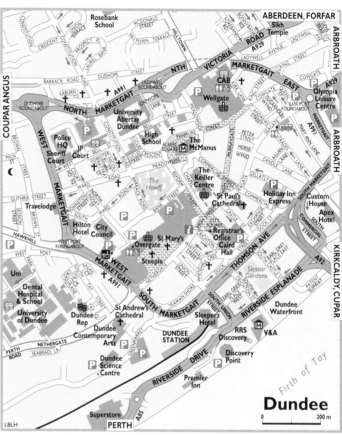

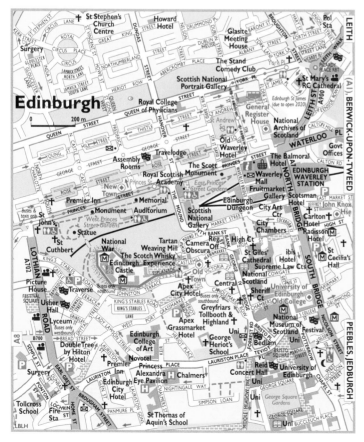

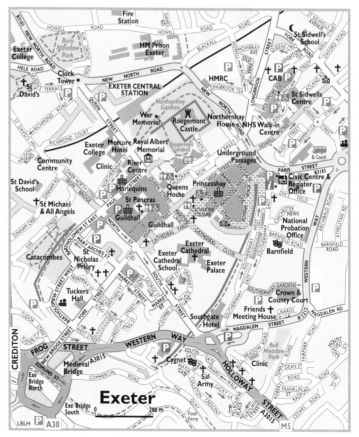

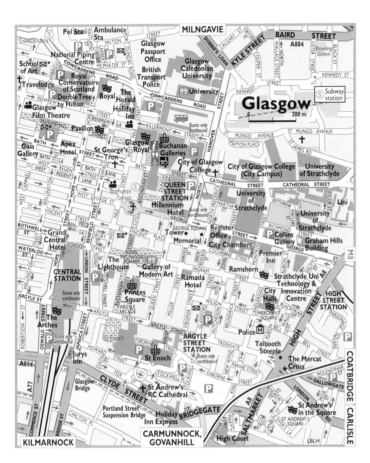

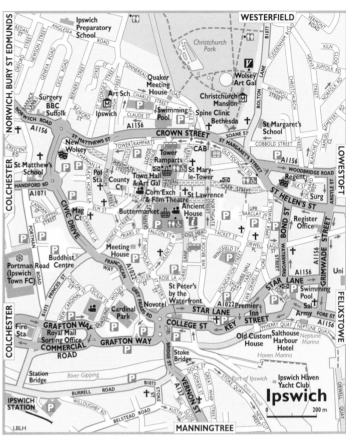

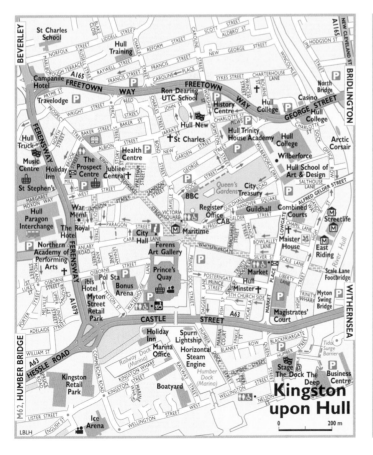

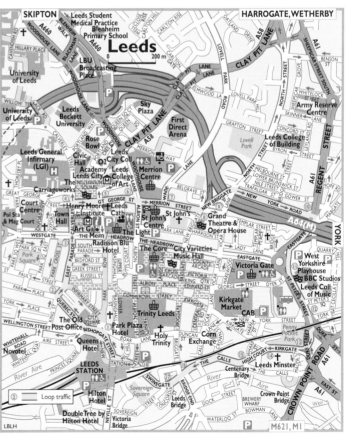

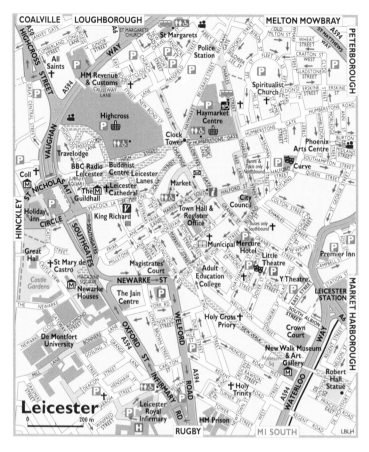

Leicester

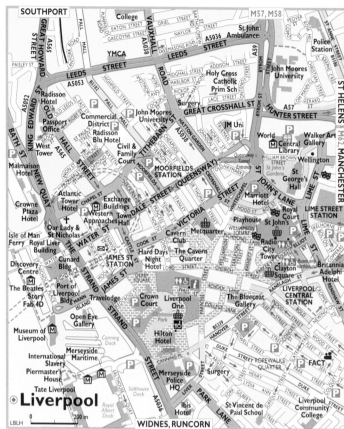

Liverpool

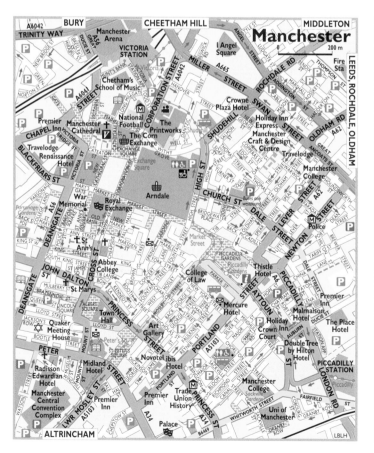

Manchester

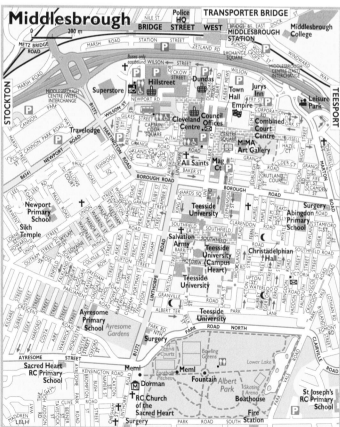

Middlesbrough

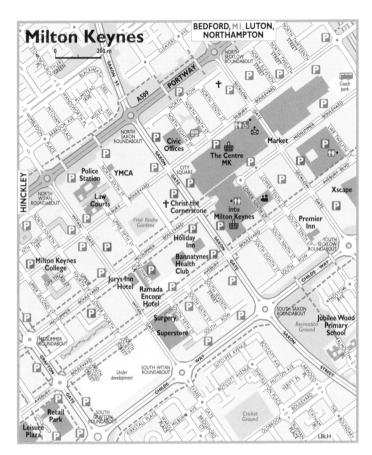

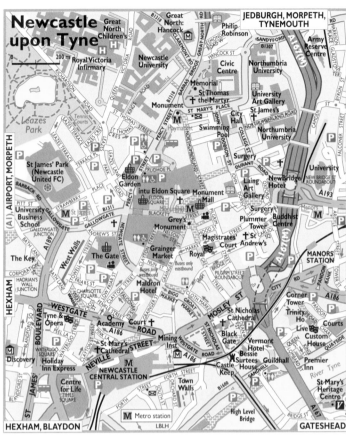

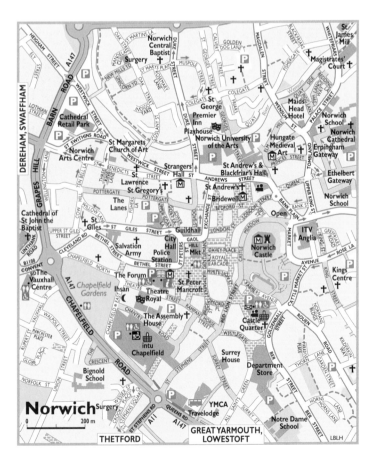

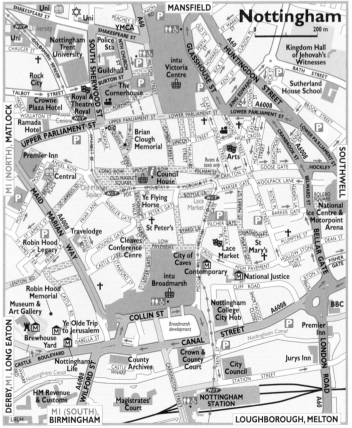

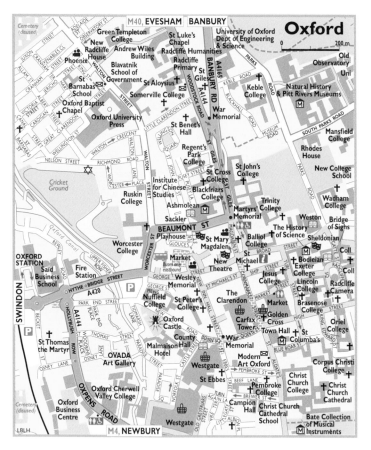

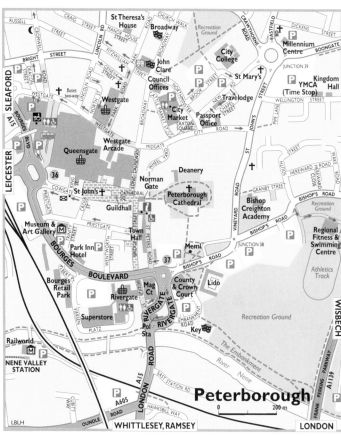

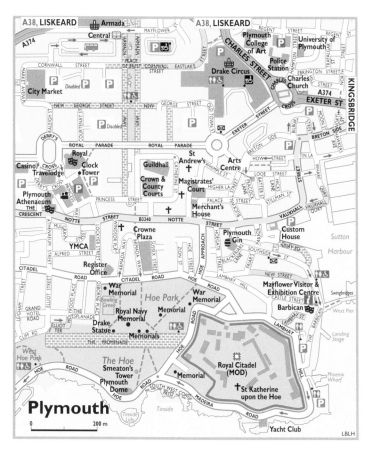

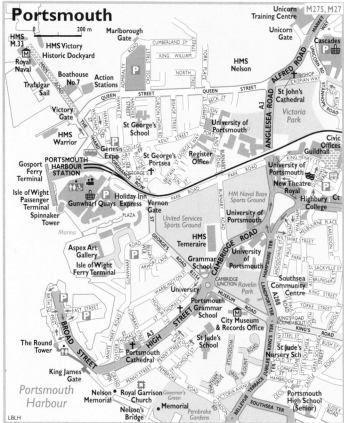

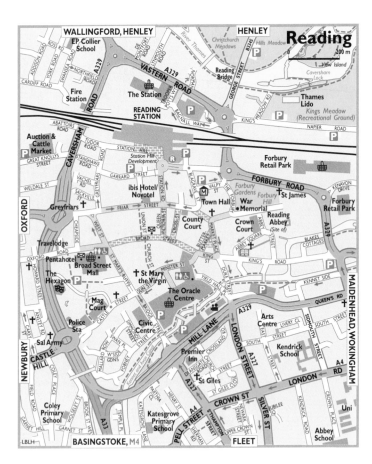

Reading

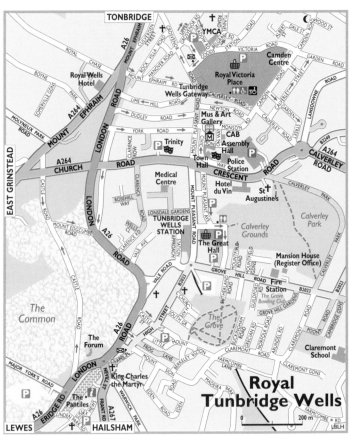

Royal Tunbridge Wells

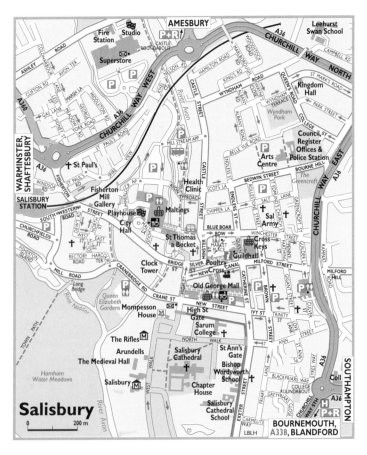

Salisbury

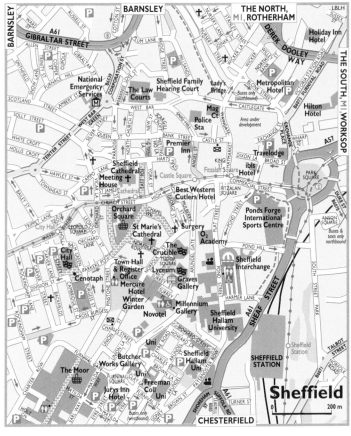

Sheffield

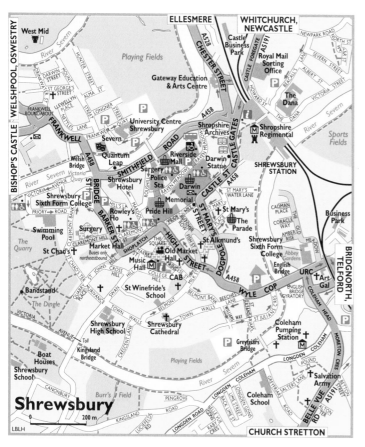

Shrewsbury

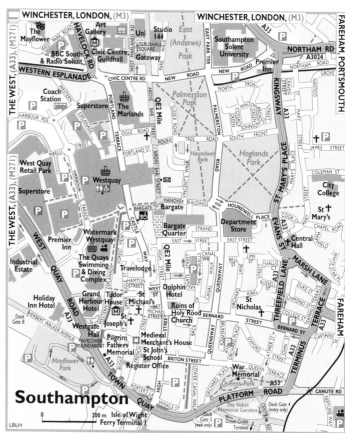

Southampton

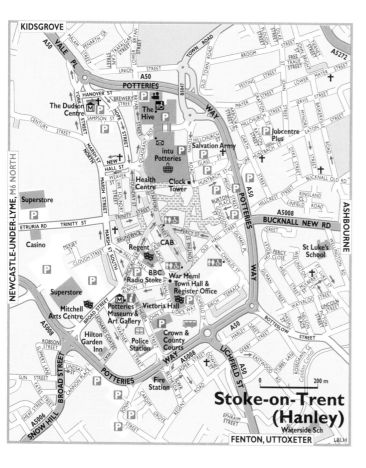

Stoke-on-Trent (Hanley)

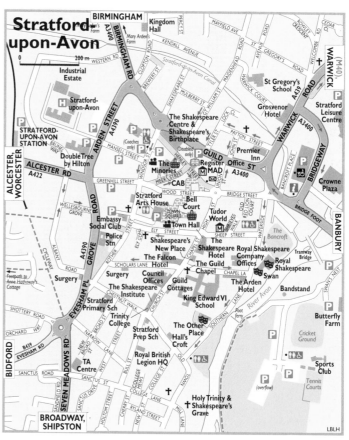

Stratford-upon-Avon

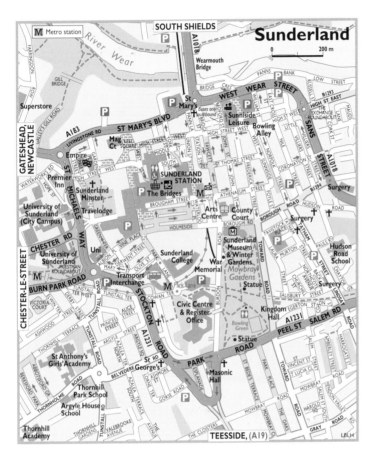

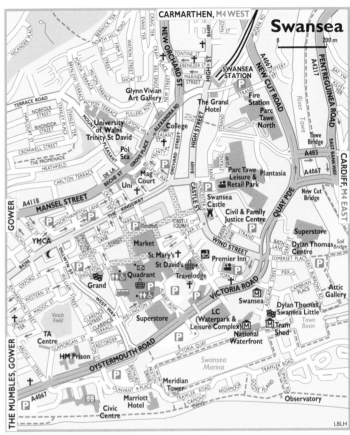

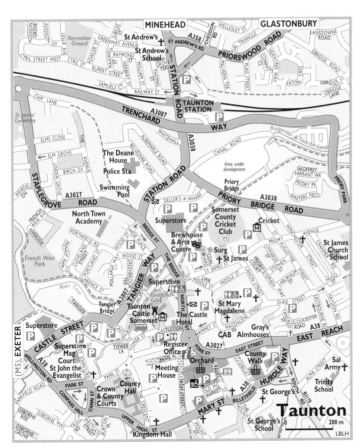

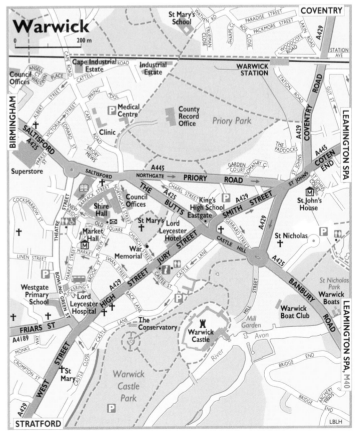

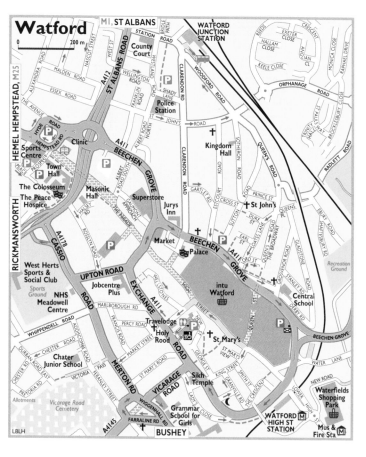

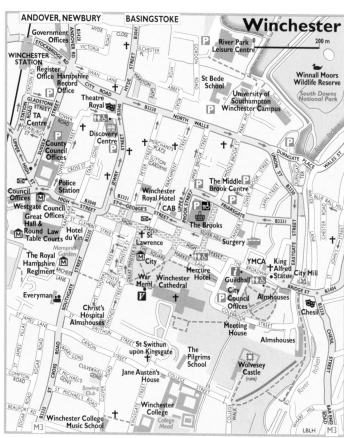

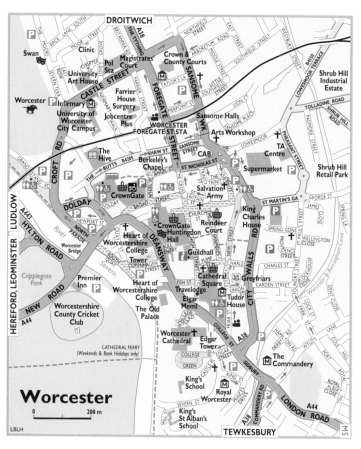

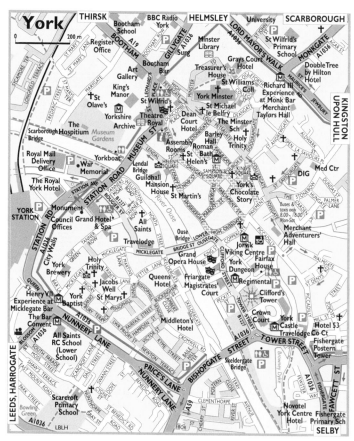

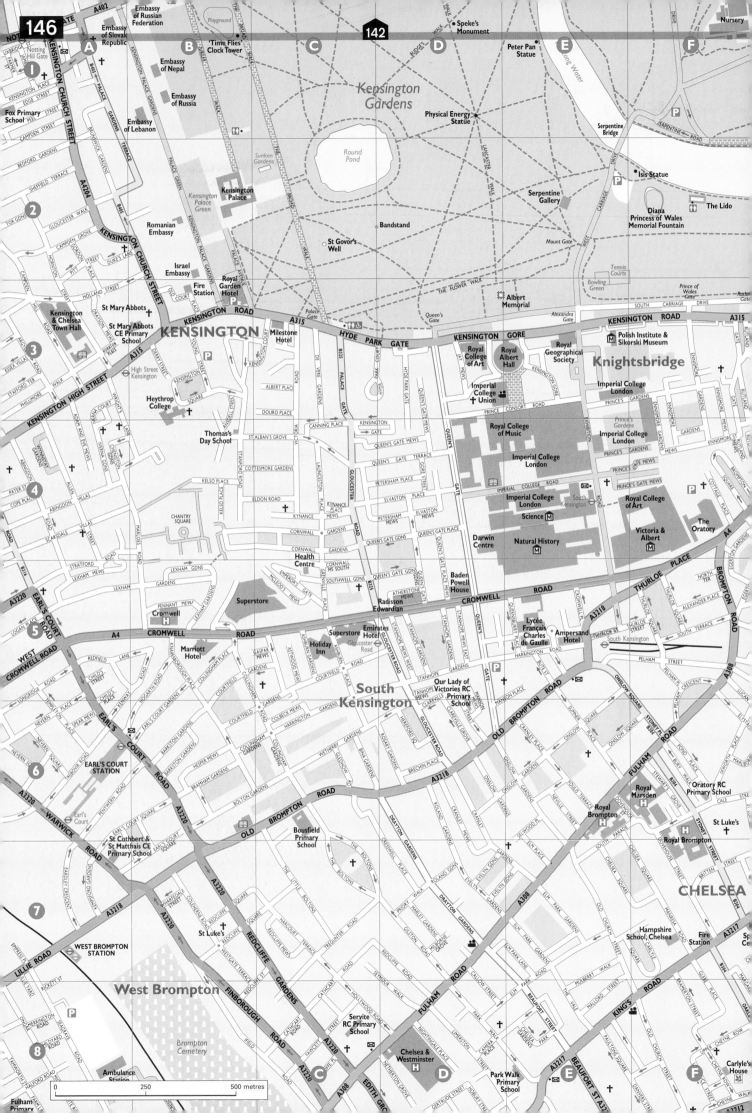

This index lists street and station names, and top places of tourist interest shown in red. Names are listed in alphabetical order and written in full, but may be abbreviated on the map. Each entry is followed by its Postcode District and then the page number and grid reference to the square in which the name is found. Names are asterisked (*) in the index where there is insufficient space to show them on the map.

A

Abbey Gardens NW8 — 142 C1
Abbey Orchard Street SW1P — 148 B4
Abbey Road NW8 — 142 D1
Abbey Street SE1 — 150 B7
Abchurch Lane EC4N — 145 L7
Abercorn Close NW8 — 142 C1
Abercorn Place NW8 — 142 C1
Aberdeen Place NW8 — 142 E3
Aberdour Street SE1 — 149 M5
Abingdon Road W8 — 146 A4
Abingdon Street SW1P — 148 C3
Abingdon Villas W8 — 146 A4
Ackroyd Drive E3 — 151 L1
Acorn Walk SE16 — 151 K5
Acton Street WC1X — 144 E2
Adam and Eve Mews W8 — 146 A3
Adam's Row W1K — 143 K8
Adam Street WC2N — 144 D8
Addington Street SE1 — 148 E3
Addle Hill EC4V — 145 H7
Adelina Grove E1 — 150 F1
Adeline Place WC1B — 144 B5
Adler Street E1 — 150 D2
Admiral Place SE16 — 151 K5
Admiral Walk W9 — 142 A4
Adpar Street W2 — 142 E4
Agar Street WC2N — 144 D8
Agdon Street EC1V — 145 H3
Agnes Street E14 — 151 L2
Ainsty Street SE16 — 151 G6
Air Street W1B — 144 A8
Alaska Street SE1 — 148 F2
Albany Road SE5 — 149 L8
Albany Street NW1 — 143 L1
Albemarle Street W1S — 143 L8
Albermarle Way EC1V — 145 H4
Alberta Street SE17 — 149 H6
Albert Bridge SW3 — 147 G8
Albert Embankment SE1 — 148 D7
Albert Gardens E1 — 151 H3
Albert Gate SW1X — 147 H2
Albert Place W8 — 146 C3
Albion Gate W2 — 143 G7
Albion Place EC1M — 145 H4
Albion Street SE16 — 151 G7
Albion Street W2 — 143 G7
Aldenham Street NW1 — 144 A1
Aldermanbury EC2V — 145 K6
Alderney Mews SE1 — 149 K4
Alderney Street SW1V — 147 L6
Aldford Street W1K — 143 J8
Aldgate EC3M — 150 B3
Aldgate ⊖ EC3M — 150 B3
Aldgate East ⊖ E1 — 150 C2
Aldgate High Street E1 — 150 B3
Aldgate Square EC3N — 150 B3
Aldsworth Close W9 — 142 B4
Aldwych WC2E — 144 E7
Alexander Place SW7 — 146 F5
Alexander Street W2 — 142 A6
Alexandra Gate SW7 — 146 E3
Alfred Mews WC1E — 144 B4
Alfred Place WC1E — 144 B4
Alfred Road W2 — 142 A5
Alice Street SE1 — 149 M4
Alie Street E1 — 150 C3
Allen Street W8 — 146 A4
Allhallows Lane EC4R — 145 L8
Allington Street SW1E — 147 M4
Allitsen Road NW8 — 142 F1
Allsop Place NW1 — 143 H4
Alma Square NW8 — 142 D1
Alpha Place SW3 — 147 G8
Alsace Road SE17 — 149 M7
Alscot Road * SE1 — 150 C8
Alvey Street SE17 — 149 M6
Ambergate Street SE17 — 149 H7
Amberley Road W9 — 142 A4
Ambrosden Avenue SW1P — 148 A4
Amelia Street SE17 — 149 J6
America Square EC3N — 150 B3
America Street SE1 — 149 J2
Ampton Street WC1X — 144 E2
Amwell Street EC1R — 144 F2
Anchorage Point E14 — 151 M6
Andover Place NW6 — 142 B1
Angel ⊖ N1 — 145 G1
Angela Hooper Place * SW1E — 148 A4
Angel Junction N1 — 145 G1
Angel Lane EC4R — 145 L8
Angel Street EC1A — 145 J6
Ann Moss Way SE16 — 150 F8
Ann's Close SW1X — 147 J3
Ansdell Street W8 — 146 B4
Antill Terrace E1 — 151 H2
Antizan Street E1 — 150 B2
Apple Tree Yard SW1Y — 144 A8
Appold Street EC2A — 145 M4
Apsley Gate W1J — 147 J2
Apsley House & Wellington Museum W1J — 147 K2
Aquinas Street SE1 — 149 G1
Arbour Square E1 — 151 H2
Archangel Street SE16 — 151 J7
Archer Street W1B — 144 B7
Arch Street SE1 — 149 J4
Arden Estate N1 — 145 M1
Argyle Square WC1H — 144 D2
Argyle Street WC1H — 144 D2
Argyll Road W8 — 146 A3
Argyll Street W1F — 143 M6
Arlington Street SW1A — 147 M1
Arlington Way EC1R — 145 G2
Arne Street WC2H — 144 D6
Arneway Street SW1P — 148 B5
Arnhem Place E14 — 151 M8
Arnold Estate SE1 — 150 C7
Arnside Street SE17 — 149 K8
Artesian Road W11 — 142 A6
Arthur Street EC4V — 145 L7
Artichoke Hill E1 — 150 E4
Artillery Lane E1 — 150 A1
Artillery Row SW1P — 148 B4
Arundel Street WC2R — 144 F7

Ashbridge Street NW8 — 142 F4
Ashburn Gardens SW7 — 146 C5
Ashburn Place SW7 — 146 C5
Ashby Street EC1V — 145 H2
Asher Way E1W — 150 D4
Ashfield Street E1 — 150 E2
Ashley Place SW1P — 147 M4
Ashmill Street NW1 — 142 F4
Ashmole Street SW8 — 148 F8
Ashworth Road W9 — 142 B2
Assam Street E1 — 150 C2
Assembly Passage * E1 — 151 G1
Astell Street SW3 — 147 G6
Aston Street E14 — 151 K1
Astwood Mews SW7 — 146 C5
Atherstone Mews SW7 — 146 D5
Attneave Street WC1X — 144 F3
Augustus Street NW1 — 143 L1
Aulton Place SE11 — 149 G7
Austin Friars EC2N — 145 L6
Australia Gate SW1A — 147 M3
Austral Street SE11 — 149 H5
Ave Maria Lane EC1A — 145 H6
Avery Farm Row SW1W — 147 K6
Avery Row W1K — 143 L7
Avrybook Street W1U — 143 J5
Aylesbury Road SE17 — 149 L7
Aylesbury Street EC1R — 145 H4
Aylesford Street SW1V — 148 B7
Aylward Street E1 — 151 G2
Ayres Street SE1 — 149 K2

B

Babmaes Street SW1Y — 144 B8
Bache's Street N1 — 145 L2
Back Church Lane E1 — 150 D3
Back Hill EC1R — 145 G4
Bacon Grove SE1 — 150 B8
Bainbridge Street WC1A — 144 C6
Bakers Mews W1U — 143 J6
Baker's Row EC1R — 145 G4
Baker Street NW1 — 143 H4
Baker Street W1U — 143 J5
Balcombe Street NW1 — 143 G3
Balderton Street W1K — 143 J7
Baldwin's Gardens EC1N — 144 F5
Baldwin Street EC1V — 145 L2
Bale Road E1 — 151 J1
Balfe Street N1 — 144 D1
Balfour Mews W1K — 143 K8
Balfour Place W1K — 143 K8
Balfour Street SE17 — 149 K5
Baltic Street East EC1Y — 145 J3
Baltic Street West EC1Y — 145 J4
Balvaird Place SW1V — 148 C7
Bank ⊖ EC2R — 145 L6
Bank End SE1 — 149 K1
Bankside SE1 — 145 J8
Banner Street EC1Y — 145 K3
Banqueting House SW1A — 148 C2
Banyard Road SE16 — 150 E8
Barbican EC1A — 145 J4
Barbican ⊖ EC1A — 145 J5
Barbican Estate EC2Y — 145 J5
Barge House Street SE1 — 149 G1
Bark Place W2 — 142 B7
Barkston Gardens SW5 — 146 B6
Barley Corn Way E14 — 151 L4
Barlow/Congreve Estate SE17 — 149 M5
Barlow Place W1J — 143 L7
Barlow Street SE17 — 149 L5
Barnardo Street E1 — 151 H3
Barnby Street NW1 — 144 A1
Barnes Street E14 — 151 J2
Barnham Street SE1 — 150 A6
Baron's Place SE1 — 149 G3
Baron Street N1 — 145 G1
Barrett Street W1U — 143 K6
Barrow Hill Estate NW8 — 142 F1
Barrow Hill Road NW8 — 142 F1
Barter Street WC1A — 144 D5
Bartholomew Close EC1A — 145 J5
Bartholomew Lane EC2R — 145 L6
Bartholomew Street SE1 — 149 L5
Bartlett Court EC4A — 145 G6
Barton Street SW1P — 148 C4
Basil Street SW3 — 147 H4
Basin Approach E14 — 151 K3
Basinghall Avenue EC2V — 145 K5
Basinghall Street EC2V — 145 K5
Bastwick Street EC1V — 145 J3
Bateman's Buildings W1D — 144 B6
Bateman Street W1D — 144 B6
Bath Street EC1V — 145 K2
Bath Terrace SE1 — 149 J4
Bathurst Mews W2 — 142 E7
Bathurst Street W2 — 142 E7
Battle Bridge Lane SE1 — 149 M1
Batty Street E1 — 150 D2
Bayley Street WC1B — 144 B5
Baylis Road SE1 — 148 F3
Bayswater W2 — 142 B7
Bayswater Road W2 — 142 E7
Baythorne Street E3 — 151 L1
Beaconsfield Road SE17 — 149 M7
Beak Street W1F — 144 A7
Bear Gardens SE1 — 149 K1
Bear Lane SE1 — 149 H1
Beauchamp Place SW3 — 147 G4
Beaufort Gardens SW3 — 147 G4
Beaufort Street SW3 — 146 D6
Beaumont Place W1T — 144 A3
Beaumont Street W1G — 143 K4
Beccles Street E14 — 151 M3
Beckett Street SE1 — 149 L3
Beckway Street SE17 — 149 M6
Bedale Street SE1 — 149 L1
Bedford Avenue WC1B — 144 C5
Bedford Gardens W8 — 146 A2
Bedford Place WC1N — 144 D4

Bedford Row WC1R — 144 E4
Bedford Square WC1B — 144 B5
Bedford Street WC2E — 144 D7
Bedford Way WC1H — 144 C3
Bedlow Close NW8 — 142 F3
Beech Street EC2Y — 145 J4
Beeston Place SW1W — 147 L4
Belgrave Mews North * SW1X — 147 J3
Belgrave Mews South * SW1X — 147 K4
Belgrave Place SW1X — 147 K4
Belgrave Road SW1V — 147 L5
Belgrave Road SW1V — 148 A6
Belgrave Square SW1X — 147 J3
Belgrove Street WC1H — 144 D2
Bell Lane E1 — 150 B1
Bell Street NW1 — 142 F4
Bell Yard WC2A — 144 F6
Belvedere Road SE1 — 148 E2
Benjamin Street EC1M — 145 H4
Bennett Street SW1A — 147 M1
Ben Jonson Road E1 — 151 J1
Ben Smith Way SE16 — 150 D7
Benson Quay E1W — 150 F4
Bentinck Mews W1U — 143 K6
Bentinck Street W1U — 143 K6
Bere Street E1W — 151 H3
Bergen Square SE16 — 151 K8
Berkeley Mews W1H — 143 H6
Berkeley Square W1J — 143 L8
Berkeley Street W1J — 143 L8
Bermondsey ⊖ ⊜ SE16 — 150 E7
Bermondsey Spa SE16 — 150 C8
Bermondsey Square SE1 — 150 A8
Bermondsey Street SE1 — 150 A6
Bermondsey Wall East SE16 — 150 E7
Bermondsey Wall Estate SE16 — 150 D7
Bermondsey Wall West SE16 — 150 C6
Bernard Street WC1N — 144 D4
Berners Mews W1T — 144 A5
Berners Place W1F — 144 A6
Berners Street W1T — 144 A5
Bernhardt Crescent NW8 — 142 F3
Berryfield Road SE17 — 149 J6
Berry Street EC1V — 145 H3
Berwick Street W1F — 144 A6
Bessborough Gardens SW1V — 148 C6
Bessborough Street SW1V — 148 B6
Betterton Street WC2H — 144 D6
Bevenden Street N1 — 145 L2
Bevington Street SE16 — 150 D7
Bevin Way WC1X — 144 F1
Bevis Marks EC3A — 150 A2
Bewley Street E1 — 150 F3
Bickenhall Street W1U — 143 H4
Bidborough Street WC1H — 144 C2
Biddulph Road W9 — 142 B2
Big Ben (Elizabeth Tower) SW1A — 148 D3
Bigland Street E1 — 150 E3
Billiter Square EC3M — 150 A3
Billiter Street EC3M — 150 A3
Bina Gardens SW5 — 146 C6
Bingham Place W1U — 143 J4
Binney Street W1K — 143 K7
Birchin Lane EC3V — 145 L7
Birchfield Street E14 — 151 M3
Birde Lane EC4Y — 145 H6
Birkenhead Street N1 — 144 D1
Bishop's Bridge Road W2 — 142 C6
Bishopsgate EC2M — 150 A2
Bishops Square E1 — 150 B1
Bishop's Terrace SE11 — 149 G5
Bittern Street SE1 — 149 J3
Blackall Street EC2A — 145 M3
Blackburne's Mews W1K — 143 J7
Blackfriars ⊜ ⊖ EC4V — 145 H7
Blackfriars Bridge EC4V — 145 H8
Blacklands Terrace SW3 — 147 H6
Black Friars Lane EC4V — 145 H7
Blackfriars Road SE1 — 149 H3
Blackhorse Court SE1 — 149 L4
Black Lion Gate W2 — 142 B8
Black Prince Road SE11 — 148 E6
Blackwood Street SE17 — 149 K6
Blandford Street W1U — 143 H5
Blenheim Street W1S — 143 L7
Bletchley Street N1 — 145 K1
Blomfield Mews W2 — 142 C5
Blomfield Road W2 — 142 C5
Blomfield Street EC2M — 145 M5
Blomfield Villas W2 — 142 C5
Bloomfield Terrace SW1W — 147 K6
Bloomsbury Square WC1A — 144 D5
Bloomsbury Street WC1B — 144 C5
Bloomsbury Way WC1A — 144 C5
Blount Street E14 — 151 K2
Blue Ball Yard SW1A — 147 M1
Bolden Street SE8 — 151 L8
Bolsover Street W1W — 143 L4
Bolton Gardens SW5 — 146 B6
Bolton Street W1J — 147 L1
Bond Street ⊖ W1C — 143 K6
Bondway SW8 — 148 D8
Bonhill Street EC2A — 145 L4
Bonnington Square SW8 — 148 E8
Boot Street N1 — 145 M2
Borough ⊖ SE1 — 149 K3
Borough High Street SE1 — 149 K3
Borough Road SE1 — 149 H3
Boscobel Place SW1W — 147 K5
Boscobel Street NW8 — 142 E3
Boss Street SE1 — 150 B6
Boston Place NW1 — 143 G3
Botolph Lane EC3R — 145 M7
Boundary Lane SE17 — 149 K8
Boundary Row SE1 — 149 G2
Bourdon Street W1K — 143 L7
Bourlet Close W1W — 143 M5
Bourne Estate EC1N — 144 F4
Bourne Street SW1W — 147 J6
Bourne Terrace W2 — 142 B5
Bouverie Place W2 — 142 F6
Bouverie Street EC4Y — 145 G6
Bowland Yard * SW1X — 147 J3
Bow Lane EC4M — 145 K6

Bowling Green Lane EC1R — 145 G3
Bowling Green Place SE1 — 149 L2
Bowling Green Street SE11 — 148 F8
Bowling Green Walk N1 — 145 M2
Bowsell Street WC1N — 144 D4
Bow Street WC2E — 144 D7
Boyd Street E1 — 150 D3
Boyfield Street SE1 — 149 H3
Boyle Street W1S — 143 M7
Boyson Road SE17 — 149 K8
Brackley Street EC1Y — 145 J4
Bradenham Close SE17 — 149 K8
Brad Street SE1 — 149 G2
Braganza Street SE17 — 149 H7
Braham Street E1 — 150 C3
Bramerton Street SW3 — 146 F7
Bramham Gardens SW5 — 146 B6
Branch Road E14 — 151 J3
Brandon Estate SE17 — 149 H8
Brandon Street SE17 — 149 K6
Brangton Road SE11 — 148 F7
Bray Crescent SE16 — 151 H6
Bray Place SW3 — 147 H6
Bread Street EC4M — 145 K6
Bream's Buildings EC4A — 144 F6
Brechin Place SW7 — 146 D6
Breezer's Hill E1W — 150 D4
Brendon Street W1H — 143 G5
Bressenden Place SW1W — 147 L4
Brettell Street SE17 — 149 L7
Brewers Green SW1H — 148 A3
Brewer Street W1F — 144 A7
Brewhouse Lane E1W — 150 F6
Brewhouse Walk SE16 — 151 J5
Brick Court WC2R — 144 F7
Brick Lane E1 — 150 C1
Brick Street W1J — 147 K2
Bridewell Place EC4V — 145 H7
Bridgeman Street NW8 — 142 F1
Bridge Place SW1V — 147 L5
Bridgeport Place E1W — 150 D4
Bridge Street SW1A — 148 D3
Bridgewater Street EC2Y — 145 J4
Bridgeway Street NW1 — 144 A1
Bridle Lane W1F — 144 A7
Bridstow Place W2 — 142 A6
Brightlingsea Place E14 — 151 L4
Brill Place NW1 — 144 C1
Briset Street EC1M — 145 H4
Bristol Gardens W9 — 142 B4
Britannia Street WC1X — 144 E2
Britannia Walk N1 — 145 L2
Britannia Way N1 — 145 K1
Britten Street SW3 — 146 F7
Britton Street EC1M — 145 H4
Broadbent Street W1K — 143 L7
Broadgate Circle EC2M — 145 M5
Broadley Street NW1 — 142 F4
Broadley Terrace NW1 — 142 F4
Broadstone Place W1U — 143 J5
Broad Walk NW1 — 143 K1
Broad Walk W2 — 143 H7
Broadwall SE1 — 149 G1
Broadway SW1H — 148 B3
Broadwick Street W1F — 144 A7
Brockham Street SE1 — 149 K4
Brodlove Lane E1W — 151 H3
Bromley Street E1 — 151 J2
Brompton Place SW3 — 147 G4
Brompton Road SW3 — 147 G4
Brompton Road SW7 — 146 F5
Brompton Road SW3 — 146 F4
Bronti Close SE17 — 149 K7
Brook Drive SE11 — 149 G5
Brooke Street EC1N — 144 F5
Brook Gate W2 — 143 H8
Brook Mews North W2 — 142 D7
Brook's Mews W1K — 143 K7
Brook Street W1K — 143 K7
Brook Street W2 — 142 E7
Brown Heart Gardens W1K — 143 K7
Browning Mews W1G — 143 K5
Browning Street SE17 — 149 K6
Brownlow Mews WC1N — 144 E3
Brownlow Street WC1V — 144 E5
Brown Street W1H — 143 G6
Brunel Road SE16 — 151 G6
Brune Street E1 — 150 B1
Brunswick Close SE1 — 150 A6
Brunswick Gardens W8 — 146 A1
Brunswick Place N1 — 145 L2
Brunswick Quay SE16 — 151 J8
Brunswick Square WC1N — 144 D3
Brunswick Street WC1N — 144 D3
Brunton Place E14 — 151 K3
Brushfield Street E1 — 150 B1
Bruton Lane W1J — 143 L8
Bruton Place W1J — 143 L8
Bruton Street W1J — 143 L8
Bryan Road SE16 — 151 K6
Bryanstone Mews West W1H — 143 G5
Bryanston Mews East W1H — 143 H5
Bryanston Place W1H — 143 G5
Bryanston Square W1H — 143 H5
Bryanston Street W1C — 143 H7
Buck Hill Walk W2 — 142 E8
Buckingham Gate SW1E — 147 L3
Buckingham Mews SW1E — 147 M3
Buckingham Palace SW1A — 147 L3
Buckingham Palace Road SW1W — 147 L5
Buckingham Place SW1E — 147 M3
Buckland Street N1 — 145 L1
Buckle Street E1 — 150 C2
Bucknall Street WC2H — 144 C6
Buckters Rents SE16 — 151 J5
Budge's Walk W2 — 146 D1
Bulleid Way SW1V — 147 L5
Bulstrode Street W1U — 143 K5
Bunhill Row EC1Y — 145 L3
Burdett Estate E14 — 151 M1
Burdett Road E14 — 151 L2
Burgess Street E14 — 151 M1
Burge Street SE1 — 149 L4
Burlington Arcade W1J — 143 M8
Burlington Gardens W1S — 143 M8
Burnhouse Place SW3 — 147 J6
Burnsall Street SW3 — 147 G6

Burnside Close SE16 — 151 J5
Burrell Street SE1 — 149 H1
Burslem Street E1 — 150 D3
Burton Grove SE17 — 149 L7
Burton Street WC1H — 144 C3
Burwood Place W2 — 143 G6
Bury Close SE16 — 151 H5
Bury Court EC3A — 150 A2
Bury Place WC1A — 144 D5
Bury Street EC3A — 150 A2
Bury Street SW1Y — 148 A1
Bury Walk SW3 — 146 F6
Bushell Street E1W — 150 D5
Bush Lane EC4V — 145 L7
Butcher Row E14 — 151 J3
Bute Street SW7 — 146 E5
Butler Place SW1H — 148 B4
Butler's Wharf SE1 — 150 C6
Buttesland Street N1 — 145 L2
Byefield Close SE16 — 151 K6
Bylands Close SE16 — 151 J5
Byng Place WC1E — 144 B4
Byng Street E14 — 151 M6
Byward Street EC3R — 150 A4
Bywater Place SE16 — 151 K5
Bywater Street SW3 — 147 G6

C

Cabbell Street NW1 — 142 F5
Cable Street E1 — 150 F3
Cadiz Street SE17 — 149 K7
Cadogan Gardens SW3 — 147 H5
Cadogan Gate SW1X — 147 H5
Cadogan Lane SW1X — 147 J4
Cadogan Place SW1X — 147 J4
Cadogan Square SW1X — 147 H5
Cadogan Street SW3 — 147 G6
Caledonian Road N1 — 144 D1
Caledonia Street N1 — 144 D1
Cale Street SW3 — 146 F6
Callow Street SW3 — 146 D7
Calshot Street N1 — 144 E1
Calthorpe Street WC1X — 144 E3
Cambridge Circus WC2H — 144 C7
Cambridge Gardens NW6 — 142 A1
Cambridge Gate NW1 — 143 L3
Cambridge Road NW6 — 142 A1
Cambridge Road NW6 — 142 A2
Cambridge Square W2 — 142 F6
Cambridge Street SW1V — 147 L6
Cambridge Terrace NW1 — 143 L2
Cambridge Terrace Mews NW1 — 143 L3
Camdenhurst Street E14 — 151 K2
Camera Place SW10 — 146 D8
Camomile Street EC3A — 150 A2
Campden Grove W8 — 146 A2
Campden Hill Road W8 — 146 A2
Campden Street W8 — 146 A1
Camperdown Street E1 — 150 C3
Canada Estate SE16 — 151 G7
Canada Gate SW1A — 147 M3
Canada Street SE16 — 151 H7
Canada Water ⊖ ⊜ SE16 — 151 G7
Canada Wharf SE16 — 151 L5
Canal Street SE5 — 149 L8
Canary Riverside E14 — 151 L4
Candle Street E1 — 151 K1
Canning Place W8 — 146 C4
Cannon Drive E14 — 151 M4
Cannon Street EC4N — 145 K7
Cannon Street ⊖ ⊜ EC4R — 145 K7
Cannon Street Road E1 — 150 E3
Canon Beck Road SE16 — 151 G6
Canon Row W1A — 148 D3
Canton Street E14 — 151 M3
Capeners Close * SW1X — 147 J3
Capland Street NW8 — 142 E3
Capper Street WC1E — 144 A4
Capstan Way SE16 — 151 K5
Carbis Road E14 — 151 L2
Carburton Street W1W — 143 L4
Cardigan Street SE11 — 148 F6
Cardington Street NW1 — 144 A2
Carey Street WC2A — 144 F6
Carlisle Avenue EC3N — 150 B3
Carlisle Lane SE1 — 148 F4
Carlisle Place SW1P — 147 M5
Carlisle Street W1D — 144 B6
Carlos Place W1K — 143 K7
Carlton Gardens SW1Y — 148 B2
Carlton Hill NW6 — 142 B1
Carlton House Terrace SW1Y — 148 B1
Carlton Street SW1J — 147 L1
Carlton Vale NW6 — 142 A1
Carlton Vale NW6 — 142 B1
Carlyle Square SW3 — 146 F7
Carmelite Street EC4Y — 145 G7
Carnaby Street W1F — 143 M7
Caroline Place W2 — 142 B7
Caroline Street E1 — 151 H3
Caroline Terrace SW1W — 147 J5
Carpenter Street W1K — 143 K7
Carrington Street W1J — 147 L1
Carr Street E14 — 151 K1
Carteret Street SW1H — 148 B3
Carter Lane EC4V — 145 H7
Carter Place SE17 — 149 K7
Carter Street SE17 — 149 J7
Carthusian Street EC1M — 145 J4
Carting Lane WC2R — 144 D8
Cartwright Gardens WC1H — 144 C2
Cartwright Street E1 — 150 C4
Casey Close NW8 — 142 F3
Casson Street E1 — 150 C1
Castellain Road W9 — 142 B3
Castlebrook Close SE11 — 149 G5
Castle Lane SW1E — 147 M4
Catesby Street SE17 — 149 L6
Cathay Street SE16 — 150 F7
Cathcart Road SW10 — 146 C8
Cathedral Walk SW1E — 147 M4
Catherine Place SW1E — 147 M4
Catherine Street WC2E — 144 D7
Cato Street W1H — 143 G5
Causton Street SW1P — 148 B6

Cavell Street E1 150 F1
Cavendish Avenue NW8 142 E1
Cavendish Place W1G 143 L6
Cavendish Square W1G 143 L6
Cavendish Street N1 145 L1
Caversham Street SW3 147 G8
Caxton Street SW1H 148 B4
Cayton Street EC1V 145 K2
Centaur Street SE1 148 F4
Central Street EC1V 145 J2
Chadwell Street EC1R 145 G1
Chadwick Street SW1P 148 B4
Chagford Street NW1 143 H4
Chalton Street NW1 144 B1
Chambers Street SE16 150 D7
Chamber Street E1 150 C3
Chambers Wharf SE16 150 D6
Chancel Street SE1 149 H1
Chancery Lane WC2A 144 F5
Chancery Lane ⊖ WC1V 144 F5
Chandos Place WC2N 144 C8
Chandos Street W1G 143 L5
Chantry Square W8 146 B4
Chapel Market * N1 144 F1
Chapel Street NW1 142 F5
Chapel Street SW1X 147 K3
Chaplin Close SE1 149 G3
Chapman Street E1 150 E3
Chapter Road SE17 149 H7
Chapter Street SW1P 148 B6
Chargrove Close SE16 151 H6
Charing Cross ⇌ ⊖ WC2N 148 D1
Charing Cross Road WC2H 144 B6
Charing Cross Road WC2N 144 C7
Charlbert Street NW8 142 F1
Charles II Street SW1Y 144 B8
Charles Square N1 145 M2
Charles Street W1J 147 K1
Charleston Street SE17 149 K6
Charlotte Road EC2A 145 M3
Charlotte Street W1T 144 A4
Charlwood Place SW1V 148 A6
Charlwood Street SW1V 147 M7
Charlwood Street SW1V 148 A6
Charrington Street NW1 144 B1
Charterhouse Square EC1M 145 H4
Charterhouse Street EC1M 145 G5
Chart Street N1 145 L2
Chaseley Street E14 151 J2
Chatham Street SE17 149 L5
Cheapside EC2V 145 K6
Chelsea Bridge SW1W 147 K8
Chelsea Bridge Road SW1W 147 J7
Chelsea Embankment SW3 147 G8
Chelsea Manor Gardens SW3 146 F7
Chelsea Manor Street SW3 147 G7
Chelsea Park Gardens SW3 146 E8
Chelsea Physic Garden SW3 147 H8
Chelsea Square SW3 146 E7
Cheltenham Terrace SW3 147 H6
Chenies Mews WC1E 144 B4
Chenies Street WC1E 144 B4
Cheniston Gardens W8 146 A4
Chepstow Place W2 142 A7
Chepstow Road W2 142 A6
Chequer Street EC1Y 145 K3
Cherbury Street N1 145 L1
Cherry Garden Street SE16 150 E7
Chesham Close SW1X 147 J4
Chesham Place SW1X 147 J4
Chesham Street SW1X 147 J4
Chester Close SW1X 147 K3
Chester Close North NW1 143 L2
Chester Close South NW1 143 L2
Chesterfield Gardens W1J 147 K1
Chesterfield Hill W1J 143 K8
Chesterfield Street W1J 147 K1
Chester Gate NW1 143 L2
Chester Mews SW1X 147 K3
Chester Place NW1 143 L1
Chester Road NW1 143 K2
Chester Row SW1W 147 K5
Chester Square SW1W 147 K4
Chester Square Mews SW1W 147 K4
Chester Street SW1X 147 K4
Chester Terrace NW1 143 L2
Chester Way SE11 149 G6
Cheval Place SW7 147 G4
Cheval Street E14 151 M7
Cheyne Gardens SW3 147 G8
Cheyne Row SW3 146 F8
Cheyne Walk SW3 146 F8
Chicheley Street SE1 148 E2
Chichester Road NW6 142 A1
Chichester Road W2 142 C5
Chichester Street SW1V 148 A7
Chicksand Street E1 150 C1
Chigwell Hill E1W 150 E4
Child's Place SW5 146 A5
Child's Street SW5 146 A5
Chiltern Street W1U 143 J4
Chilworth Mews W2 142 D6
Chilworth Street W2 142 D6
China Hall Mews SE16 151 G8
Chinatown W1D 144 B7
Chippenham Mews W9 142 A4
Chiswell Street EC1Y 145 K4
Chitty Street W1T 144 A4
Christchurch Street SW3 147 G8
Christian Street E1 150 D3
Christina Street EC2A 145 M3
Christopher Close SE16 151 H6
Christopher Street EC2A 145 L4
Chudleigh Street E1 151 H2
Chumleigh Street SE5 149 M8
Churchill Gardens Road SW1V 147 L7
Churchill War Rooms SW1A 148 C3
Church Street NW8 142 F4
Church Way NW1 144 B2
Churchyard Row SE11 149 H5
Churton Place SW1V 148 A6
Churton Street SW1V 148 A6
Circus Road NW8 142 E1
Cirencester Square W2 142 A5
City Garden Row N1 145 J1
City Road EC1V 145 J1
City Road EC1Y 145 L3
City Thameslink ⇌ EC4M 145 H6
Clabon Mews SW1X 147 H5
Clack Street SE16 151 G8
Clanricarde Gardens W2 142 A8
Clarkson Row NW1 143 M1
Claremont Square N1 144 F1
Clarence Gardens NW1 143 L2
Clarence Mews SE16 151 G6
Clarendon Gardens W9 142 D4

Clarendon Gate W2 142 F7
Clarendon Place W2 142 F7
Clarendon Street SW1V 147 L6
Clareville Grove SW7 146 D6
Clareville Street SW7 146 D6
Clarges Mews W1J 147 L1
Clarges Street W1J 147 L1
Clark Street E1 150 F2
Clarkson Row NW1 143 M1
Claverton Street SW1V 148 A7
Clave Street E1W 150 F5
Clay Street W1U 143 H5
Clayton Street SE11 148 F8
Cleaver Square SE11 149 G7
Cleaver Street SE11 149 G7
Clegg Street E1W 150 F5
Clemence Street E14 151 L2
Clements Lane EC4N 145 L7
Clement's Road SE16 150 E8
Clenston Mews W1H 143 H6
Clere Street EC2A 145 L3
Clerkenwell Close EC1R 145 G3
Clerkenwell Green EC1R 145 G4
Clerkenwell Road EC1M 145 G4
Cleveland Gardens W2 142 C6
Cleveland Mews W1T 143 M4
Cleveland Place SW1Y 148 A1
Cleveland Row SW1A 148 A2
Cleveland Square W2 142 C6
Cleveland Street W1T 143 M4
Cleveland Terrace W2 142 D6
Clifford Street W1S 143 M7
Clifton Gardens W9 142 C4
Clifton Place SE16 151 G6
Clifton Place W2 142 E7
Clifton Road W9 142 D3
Clifton Street EC2A 145 M3
Clifton Villas W9 142 C4
Clink Street SE1 149 K1
Clipper Close SE16 151 H6
Clipstone Mews W1W 143 M4
Clipstone Street W1W 143 L4
Cliveden Place SW1W 147 J5
Cloak Lane EC4R 145 K7
Cloth Fair EC1A 145 J5
Cloth Street EC1A 145 J5
Cluny Place SE1 150 A8
Cobb Street E1 150 B2
Cobourg Street NW1 144 A2
Coburg Close SW1P 148 A5
Cochrane Mews NW8 142 E1
Cochrane Street NW8 142 E1
Cock Lane EC1A 145 H5
Cockspur Street SW1Y 148 C1
Codling Close * E1W 150 D5
Coin Street SE1 149 G1
Coke Street E1 150 D2
Colbeck Mews SW7 146 C6
Colebrook Row N1 145 H1
Coleherne Road SW10 146 B7
Coleman Street EC2R 145 L6
Cole Street SE1 149 K3
Coley Street WC1X 144 F3
College Hill EC4R 145 K7
College Street EC4R 145 K7
Collett Road SE16 150 D8
Collier Street N1 144 E1
Collingham Gardens SW5 146 B6
Collingham Place SW5 146 B5
Collingham Road SW5 146 B5
Colnbrook Street SE1 149 H4
Colombo Street SE1 149 H1
Colonnade WC1N 144 D4
Coltman Street E14 151 K2
Commercial Road E1 150 D2
Commercial Road E14 151 K3
Commercial Street E1 150 B1
Compton Street EC1V 145 H3
Concert Hall Approach SE1 148 E2
Conder Street E14 151 K2
Conduit Mews W2 142 E6
Conduit Place W2 142 E6
Conduit Street W1S 143 L7
Congreve Street SE17 149 M5
Connaught Close W2 142 F7
Connaught Square W2 143 G6
Connaught Street W2 143 G6
Cons Street SE1 149 G2
Constitution Hill SW1A 147 L3
Content Street SE17 149 K5
Conway Street W1T 143 M4
Cookham Crescent SE16 151 H6
Cook's Road SE17 149 H8
Coombs Street N1 145 J1
Cooper's Lane Estate NW1 144 B1
Cooper's Row EC3N 150 B3
Copenhagen Place E14 151 L2
Cope Place W8 146 A4
Copley Court SE17 149 J8
Copley Street E1 151 H2
Copperfield Road E3 151 K1
Copperfield Street SE1 149 J2
Copthall Avenue EC2R 145 L6
Coptic Street WC1A 144 C5
Coral Street SE1 149 G3
Coram Street WC1H 144 C3
Cork Square E1W 150 E5
Cork Street W1S 143 M8
Corlett Street NW1 142 F5
Cornhill EC3V 145 L6
Cornwall Gardens SW7 146 C4
Cornwall Mews South SW7 146 C5
Cornwall Road SE1 148 F1
Cornwall Road SE1 149 G2
Cornwall Street E1 150 E3
Cornwall Terrace Mews NW1 143 H4
Cornwood Drive E1 151 G2
Coronet Street N1 145 M2
Corporation Row EC1R 145 G3
Corsham Street N1 145 L2
Cosser Street SE1 148 F4
Cosway Street NW1 143 G4
Cottage Place SW3 146 F4
Cottesmore Gardens W8 146 B4
Cottons Lane SE1 149 M1
Coulson Street SW3 147 H6
Counter Street SE1 149 M1
County Street SE1 149 K5
Courtenay Square SE11 148 F7
Courtenay Street SE11 148 F6
Courtfield Gardens SW5 146 B5
Courtfield Mews * SW5 146 C5
Courtfield Road SW7 146 C5
Court Street E1 150 E1
Cousin Lane SE1 145 K8

Covent Garden ⊖ WC2E 144 D7
Covent Garden WC2E 144 D7
Coventry Street W1D 144 B8
Cowcross Street EC1M 145 H4
Cowper Street EC2A 145 L3
Crail Row SE17 149 L5
Cramer Street W1U 143 J5
Crampton Street SE17 149 J6
Cranbourn Street WC2H 144 C7
Cranleigh Street NW1 144 A1
Cranley Gardens SW7 146 D6
Cranley Mews SW7 146 D6
Cranley Place SW7 146 E6
Cranston Estate N1 145 L1
Cranwood Street EC1V 145 L2
Craven Hill W2 142 D7
Craven Hill Gardens W2 142 D7
Craven Road W2 142 D7
Craven Street WC2N 148 D1
Craven Terrace W2 142 D7
Crawford Passage EC1R 145 G3
Crawford Place W1H 143 G5
Crawford Street W1H 143 G5
Creechurch Lane EC3A 150 A3
Creed Lane EC4V 145 H7
Cresswell Place SW10 146 D6
Cressy Place E1 151 G1
Crestfield Street WC1H 144 D2
Crimscott Street SE1 150 A8
Crispin Street E1 150 B1
Cromer Street WC1H 144 D2
Crompton Street W2 142 D4
Cromwell Mews * SW7 146 E5
Cromwell Place SW7 146 E5
Cromwell Road SW5 146 B5
Cromwell Road SW7 146 E5
Crondall Court N1 145 M1
Crondall Street N1 145 L1
Cropley Street N1 145 K1
Crosby Row SE1 149 L3
Cross Lane EC3R 150 A4
Crosswall EC3N 150 B3
Crowder Street E1 150 E3
Crucifix Lane SE1 150 A6
Cruikshank Street WC1X 144 F1
Crutched Friars EC3N 150 A3
Cuba Street E14 151 M6
Cubitt Street WC1X 144 E2
Culford Gardens SW3 147 H6
Culling Road SE16 150 F7
Cullum Street EC3M 145 M7
Culross Street W1K 143 J8
Culworth Street NW8 142 F1
Cumberland Gardens WC1X 144 F2
Cumberland Gate W2 143 H7
Cumberland Market NW1 143 L2
Cumberland Street SW1V 147 L6
Cumberland Terrace NW1 143 K1
Cumberland Terrace Mews NW1 143 L1
Cumberland Wharf SE16 151 G6
Cumming Street N1 144 E1
Cundy Street SW1W 147 K6
Cunningham Place NW8 142 E3
Cureton Street SW1P 148 C6
Curlew Street SE1 150 B6
Cursitor Street EC4A 144 F6
Curtain Road EC2A 145 M3
Curtain Road EC2A 145 M4
Curzon Gate W2 147 K2
Curzon Street W1J 147 K1
Cuthbert Street W2 142 E4
Cutler Street EC3A 150 A2
Cynthia Street N1 144 F1
Cypress Place W1T 144 A4
Cyrus Street EC1V 145 H3

D

Dacre Street SW1H 148 B3
Dakin Place E1 151 J1
Dallington Street EC1V 145 H3
Damien Street E1 150 F2
Dane Street WC1R 144 E5
Dansey Place W1D 144 B7
Dante Road SE11 149 H5
Danvers Street SW3 146 F8
D'Arblay Street W1F 144 A6
Dartford Street SE17 149 K8
Dartmouth Street SW1H 148 B3
Darwin Street SE17 149 L5
Date Street SE17 149 K7
Davenant Street E1 150 D1
Daventry Street NW1 142 F4
Davidge Street SE1 149 H3
Davies Mews W1K 143 K7
Davies Street W1K 143 K7
Dawes Street SE17 149 L6
Dawson Place W2 142 A7
Deal Porters Way SE16 151 G8
Deal Street E1 150 D1
Dean Bradley Street SW1P 148 C5
Dean Close SE16 151 H6
Deancross Street E1 150 F3
Deanery Street W1K 147 K1
Dean Farrar Street SW1H 148 B3
Dean Ryle Street SW1P 148 C5
Dean's Buildings SE17 149 L6
Dean Stanley Street SW1P 148 C4
Dean Street W1D 144 B6
Dean's Yard SW1P 148 C4
Decima Street SE1 149 M4
Deck Close SE16 151 J6
Defoe Close SE16 151 K7
Delamere Street W2 142 C5
Delamere Terrace W2 142 B4
De Laune Street SE17 149 H7
Delaware Road W9 142 B3
Dellow Street E1 150 F3
Delverton Road SE17 149 H7
Denbigh Place SW1V 147 M6
Denbigh Street SW1V 147 M6
Denbigh Street SW1V 148 A6
Denman Street W1D 144 B7
Denmark Street WC2H 144 C6
Denny Close SE11 149 G6
Denny Street SE11 149 G6
Denyer Street SW3 147 G5
Derby Gate SW1A 148 D3
Derby Street W1J 147 K1
Dering Street W1S 143 L6
Derry Street W8 146 B3
De Vere Gardens W8 146 C3
Deverell Street SE1 149 L4
Devonport Street E1 151 G3

Devonshire Close W1G 143 K4
Devonshire Mews South W1G 143 K4
Devonshire Mews West W1G 143 K4
Devonshire Place W1G 143 K4
Devonshire Place Mews W1G 143 K4
Devonshire Row EC2M 150 A2
Devonshire Square EC2M 150 A2
Devonshire Street W1G 143 K4
Devonshire Terrace W2 142 D7
De Walden Street W1G 143 K5
Dickens Estate SE16 150 D7
Dickens Square SE1 149 K4
Dilke Street SW3 147 H8
Dingley Place EC1V 145 K2
Dingley Road EC1V 145 J2
Disney Place SE1 149 K2
Distaff Lane EC4V 145 J7
Distin Street SE11 148 F6
Dockhead SE1 150 C7
Dockley Road SE16 150 D8
Dock Street E1 150 D4
Doddington Grove SE17 149 H7
Doddington Place SE17 149 H8
Dodson Street SE1 149 G3
Dod Street E14 151 M2
Dolben Street SE1 149 H2
Dolland Street SE11 148 E7
Dolphin Square SW1V 148 A7
Dolphin Square SW1V 148 B7
Dombey Street WC1N 144 E4
Dominion Drive SE16 151 H7
Dominion Street EC2A 145 L5
Donegal Street N1 144 F1
Dongola Road E1 151 J1
Donne Place SW3 147 G5
Doon Street SE1 148 F1
Dora Street E14 151 L2
Doric Way NW1 144 B2
Dorset Rise EC4Y 145 G7
Dorset Square NW1 143 H4
Dorset Street W1U 143 H5
Doughty Mews WC1N 144 E3
Doughty Street WC1N 144 E3
Douglas Street SW1P 148 B6
Douro Place W8 146 C3
Douthwaite Square * E1W 150 D5
Dovehouse Street SW3 146 E6
Dover Street W1J 147 L1
Dover Street W1S 143 L8
Dowgate Hill EC4R 145 K7
Downfield Close W9 142 B4
Downing Street SW1A 148 C2
Down Street W1J 147 K2
Downtown Road SE16 151 K6
D'Oyley Street SW1X 147 J5
Draco Street SE17 149 J8
Drake Close SE16 151 H6
Draycott Avenue SW3 147 G5
Draycott Place SW3 147 H6
Draycott Terrace SW3 147 H5
Drayson Mews W8 146 A3
Drayton Gardens SW10 146 D6
Druid Street SE1 150 A6
Druid Street SE1 150 B6
Drummond Crescent NW1 144 B2
Drummond Gate * SW1V 148 B6
Drummond Road SE16 150 E8
Drummond Street NW1 144 A3
Drury Lane WC2B 144 D6
Dryden Court SE11 149 G5
Dryden Street WC2B 144 D6
Duchess Mews W1G 143 L5
Duchess Street W1B 143 L5
Duchy Street SE1 149 G1
Duckett Street E1 151 J1
Duck Lane W1F 144 B6
Dufferin Street EC1Y 145 K4
Duke of Wellington Place SW1W 147 K3
Duke of York Square SW3 147 H6
Duke of York Street SW1Y 148 A1
Duke Shore Wharf E14 151 K4
Duke's Lane W8 146 A2
Duke's Place EC3A 150 B2
Duke's Road WC1H 144 C2
Duke Street W1K 143 K7
Duke Street W1U 143 J6
Duke Street Hill SE1 149 L1
Duke Street St James's SW1Y 148 A1
Dunbar Wharf E14 151 L4
Duncannon Street WC2N 144 C8
Duncan Terrace N1 145 H1
Dundee Street E1W 150 E5
Dundee Wharf E14 151 L4
Dunelm Street E1 151 H2
Dunlop Place SE16 150 C8
Dunraven Street W1K 143 H7
Dunster Court EC3R 150 A3
Duplex Ride SW1X 147 H3
Durand's Wharf SE16 151 L6
Durham Row E1 151 J1
Durham Street SE11 148 E7
Durham Terrace W2 142 A6
Dyott Street WC1A 144 C6
Dysart Street EC2A 145 M4

E

Eagle Court EC1M 145 H4
Eagle Street WC1R 144 E5
Eamont Street * NW8 143 G1
Eardley Crescent SW5 146 A7
Earlham Street WC2H 144 C7
Earl's Court ⇌ ⊖ SW5 146 A6
Earl's Court Gardens SW5 146 B6
Earl's Court Road SW5 146 A6
Earl's Court Square SW5 146 A6
Earlstoke Street EC1V 145 H2
Earl Street EC2A 145 M4
Earnshaw Street WC2H 144 C6
East Arbour Street E1 151 H2
Eastbourne Mews W2 142 D6
Eastbourne Terrace W2 142 D6
Eastcastle Street W1W 144 A6
Eastcheap EC3M 145 M7
Eastfield Street E14 151 K1
East India Dock Road E14 151 M3
East Lane SE16 150 D6
Easton Street WC1X 144 F3
East Poultry Avenue EC1A 145 H5
East Road N1 145 L2
East Smithfield E1W 150 C4
East Street SE17 149 K6
East Tenter Street E1 150 C3
Eaton Close SW1W 147 J5

Eaton Gate SW1W 147 J5
Eaton Lane SW1W 147 L4
Eaton Mews North SW1W 147 J5
Eaton Mews South SW1W 147 K5
Eaton Mews West SW1W 147 K5
Eaton Place SW1X 147 J4
Eaton Row SW1W 147 K4
Eaton Square SW1W 147 K5
Eaton Terrace SW1W 147 J5
Ebbisham Drive SW8 148 E8
Ebury Bridge SW1W 147 K6
Ebury Bridge Road SW1W 147 K7
Ebury Mews SW1W 147 K5
Ebury Square SW1W 147 K6
Ebury Street SW1W 147 K5
Eccleston Bridge SW1W 147 L5
Eccleston Mews SW1X 147 K4
Eccleston Place SW1W 147 L5
Eccleston Square SW1V 147 L6
Eccleston Street SW1X 147 K4
Edbrooke Road W9 142 A3
Edge Street W8 146 A1
Edgware Road W2 142 F5
Edgware Road ⊖ NW1 142 F5
Edinburgh Gate SW1X 147 H3
Edith Grove SW10 146 C8
Edwards Mews W1H 143 J6
Egerton Crescent SW3 146 F5
Egerton Gardens SW3 146 F5
Egerton Terrace SW3 147 G4
Eglington Court SE17 149 J7
Elba Place SE17 149 K5
Eldon Road W8 146 B4
Eldon Street EC2M 145 L5
Eleanor Close SE16 151 H6
Elephant & Castle SE1 149 J4
Elephant & Castle ⊖ SE1 149 J5
Elephant Lane SE16 150 F6
Elephant Road SE17 149 J5
Elf Row E1W 151 G3
Elgar Street SE16 151 K7
Elgin Avenue W9 142 B2
Elgin Mews North W9 142 C2
Elgin Mews South W9 142 C2
Elia Mews N1 145 H1
Elia Street N1 145 H1
Elim Estate SE1 149 M3
Elim Street SE1 149 M3
Elizabeth Bridge SW1V 147 L6
Elizabeth Street SW1W 147 K5
Ellen Street E1 150 D3
Elliott's Row SE11 149 H5
Ellis Street SW1X 147 J5
Elmfield Way W9 142 A4
Elm Park Gardens SW10 146 E7
Elm Park Lane SW3 146 E7
Elm Park Road SW3 146 E8
Elm Place SW7 146 E7
Elms Mews W2 142 D7
Elm Street WC1X 144 F4
Elm Tree Road NW8 142 E2
Elnathan Mews W9 142 B4
Elsa Street E1 151 J1
Elsted Street SE17 149 L6
Elvaston Mews SW7 146 D4
Elvaston Place SW7 146 D4
Elverton Street SW1P 148 B5
Ely Place EC1N 145 G5
Elystan Place SW3 147 G6
Elystan Street SW3 146 F6
Embankment ⊖ WC2N 148 D1
Embankment Gardens SW3 147 H8
Embankment Place WC2N 148 D1
Emba Street SE16 150 D7
Emerald Street WC1N 144 E4
Emerson Street SE1 149 J1
Emery Hill Street SW1P 148 A5
Emery Street SE1 149 G3
Emperor's Gate SW7 146 C5
Empire Square SE1 149 L3
Empress Place SW6 146 A7
Endell Street WC2H 144 C6
Endsleigh Gardens WC1H 144 B3
Endsleigh Place WC1H 144 B3
Endsleigh Street WC1H 144 B3
Enford Street W1H 143 G5
English Grounds SE1 149 M1
Enid Street SE16 150 C8
Ennismore Gardens SW7 146 F3
Ennismore Gardens Mews SW7 146 F3
Ennismore Mews SW7 146 F3
Ennismore Street SW7 146 F4
Ensign Street E1 150 D4
Epworth Street EC2A 145 L3
Erasmus Street SW1P 148 C6
Errol Street EC1Y 145 K4
Essendine Road W9 142 A3
Essex Street WC2R 144 F7
Essex Villas W8 146 A3
Europa Place EC1V 145 J2
Euston ⇌ ⊖ NW1 144 B2
Euston Road NW1 144 B3
Euston Square NW1 144 B2
Euston Square ⊖ NW1 144 A3
Euston Street NW1 144 A3
Evelyn Gardens SW7 146 D7
Evelyn Walk N1 145 L1
Eversholt Street NW1 144 A1
Everton Mews NW1 143 M2
Ewer Street SE1 149 J2
Ewhurst Close E1 151 G1
Exchange Square EC2A 145 M4
Exeter Street WC2E 144 D7
Exhibition Road SW7 146 E3
Exmouth Market EC1R 145 G3
Exon Street SE17 149 M6
Exton Street SE1 148 F2
Eyre Street Hill EC1R 144 F4

F

Fairclough Street E1 150 D3
Fair Street SE1 150 B6
Falmouth Road SE1 149 K4
Fann Street EC1M 145 J4
Fanshaw Street N1 145 M1
Farmer Street W8 146 A1
Farm Lane SW6 146 A8
Farm Street W1K 143 K8
Farnham Place SE1 149 J1
Farrance Street E14 151 M3
Farringdon ⇌ ⊖ EC1M 145 G4
Farringdon Lane EC1R 145 G4
Farringdon Road EC1R 144 F3

Farringdon Street EC1M......145 H5
Farrins Rents SE16......151 J5
Farrow Place SE16......151 K7
Farthing Fields * E1W......150 F5
Fashion Street E1......150 B1
Faunce Street SE17......149 H7
Fawcett Street SW10......146 C6
Featherstone Street EC1Y......145 L3
Fenchurch Avenue EC3M......150 A3
Fenchurch Buildings EC3M......150 A3
Fenchurch Place EC3M......150 A3
Fenchurch Street EC3M......150 A3
Fenchurch Street ⇌ EC3M......150 A3
Fendall Street SE1......150 B8
Fenning Street SE1......149 M2
Fentiman Road SW8......148 D8
Fernsbury Street WC1X......144 F2
Fetter Lane EC4A......145 G6
Fieldgate Street E1......150 D2
Fielding Street SE17......149 J7
Field Street WC1X......144 E1
Finborough Road SW10......146 B8
Finch Lane EC3V......145 L6
Finland Street SE16......151 K8
Finsbury Circus EC2M......145 L5
Finsbury Estate EC1R......145 G3
Finsbury Market EC2A......145 M4
Finsbury Square EC2A......145 L4
Finsbury Street EC2Y......145 L4
First Street SW3......147 G5
Fishermans Drive SE16......151 J4
Fisher Street WC1R......144 D5
Fisherton Street NW8......142 E3
Fish Street Hill EC3R......145 L7
Fitzalan Street SE11......148 F5
Fitzhardinge Street W1H......143 J6
Fitzroy Square W1T......143 M4
Fitzroy Street W1T......143 M4
Flamborough Street E14......151 J3
Flank Street E1......150 C4
Flaxman Terrace WC1H......144 C3
Fleet Street EC4A......145 G6
Fleming Road SE17......149 H8
Fletcher Street E1......150 D3
Flint Street SE17......149 L6
Flitcroft Street WC2H......144 C6
Flockton Street SE16......150 D7
Flood Street SW3......147 G7
Flood Walk SW3......147 G7
Floral Street WC2E......144 D7
Foley Street W1W......143 M5
Forbes Street E1......150 D3
Fordham Street E1......150 D2
Ford Square E1......150 F2
Fore Street EC2Y......145 K6
Formosa Street W9......142 C4
Forset Street W1H......143 G6
Forsyth Gardens SE17......149 H8
Fort Street E1......150 B1
Fortune Street EC1Y......145 K4
Forum Magnum Square SE1......148 E3
Foster Lane EC2V......145 J6
Foulis Terrace SW7......146 E6
Foundry Close SE16......151 J5
Fournier Street E1......150 B1
Fowey Close E1W......150 E5
Frampton Street NW8......142 E4
Francis Street SW1P......148 A5
Franklin's Row SW3......147 H6
Frazier Street SE1......149 G3
Frean Street SE16......150 C8
Frederick Close W2......143 G7
Frederick Street WC1X......144 E2
Frederic Mews * SW1X......147 J3
Freemantle Street SE17......149 M6
Friday Street EC4V......145 J7
Friend Street EC1V......145 H2
Frith Street W1D......144 B6
Fulbourne Street E1......150 E1
Fulford Street SE16......150 F7
Fulham Road SW10......146 D8
Fulham Road SW3......146 F6
Furnival Street EC4A......144 F5
Fynes Street SW1P......148 B5

G

Gabriel's Wharf SE1......149 G1
Gainsford Street SE1......150 B6
Galleon Close SE16......151 G6
Galsworthy Avenue E14......151 K2
Galway Street EC1V......145 K2
Gambia Street SE1......149 H2
Garden Road NW8......142 D1
Garden Row SE1......149 H4
Garden Street E1......151 H1
Garden Terrace * SW1V......148 B6
Garden Walk EC2A......145 M3
Gard Street EC1V......145 J2
Garford Street E14......151 M4
Garnault Place EC1R......145 G3
Garnet Street E1W......150 F4
Garrett Street EC1Y......145 K3
Garrick Street WC2E......144 C7
Garterway SE16......151 H7
Garway Road W2......142 B6
Gaspar Mews SW7......146 C5
Gataker Street * SE16......150 E8
Gate Mews SW7......146 F3
Gateforth Street NW8......142 F3
Gate Mews NW1......143 L3
Gatesborough Street * EC2A......145 M3
Gate Street WC2A......144 E5
Gatliff Road SW1W......147 K7
Gaunt Street SE1......149 J4
Gayfere Street SW1P......148 C4
Gaywood Street SE1......149 H4
Gaza Street SE17......149 H7
Gedling Place SE1......150 C7
Gee Street EC1V......145 J3
George Mathers Road SE11......149 H5
George Row SE16......150 C7
George Street W1H......143 H6
George Yard W1K......143 K7
Geraldine Street SE1......149 H4
Gerald Road SW1W......147 K5
Gerrard Street W1D......144 B7
Gerridge Street SE1......149 G3
Gertrude Street SW10......146 D8
Gibson Road SE11......148 E5
Gilbert Place WC1A......144 C5
Gilbert Road SE11......149 G5
Gilbert Street W1K......143 K7
Gildea Street W1W......143 L5

Gillingham Street SW1V......147 M5
Gill Street E14......151 L3
Gilston Road SW10......146 D7
Giltspur Street EC1A......145 H5
Gladstone Street SE1......149 H4
Glamis Place E1W......151 G4
Glamis Road E1W......151 G4
Glasgow Terrace SW1V......147 M7
Glasshill Street SE1......149 J3
Glasshouse Street W1B......144 A7
Glasshouse Walk SE11......148 D7
Glasshouse Yard EC1......145 J4
Glebe Place SW3......146 F7
Gledhow Road SW5......146 C6
Glentworth Street NW1......143 H4
Globe Pond Road SE16......151 J5
Globe Street SE1......149 K3
Gloucester Court * EC3R......150 A4
Gloucester Gardens W2......142 C6
Gloucester Mews W2......142 D6
Gloucester Mews West W2......142 C6
Gloucester Place NW1......143 H3
Gloucester Place W1U......143 H5
Gloucester Place Mews W1U......143 H5
Gloucester Road SW7......146 C4
Gloucester Road ⊖ SW7......146 C5
Gloucester Square W2......142 E6
Gloucester Street SW1V......147 M7
Gloucester Terrace W2......142 B5
Gloucester Terrace W2......142 D6
Gloucester Walk W8......146 A4
Gloucester Way EC1R......145 G2
Glyn Street SE11......148 E7
Godfrey Street SW3......147 G6
Goding Street SE11......148 D7
Godliman Street EC4V......145 J7
Godwin Close * N1......145 K1
Golden Hinde II SE1......149 L1
Golden Jubilee Bridge WC2N......148 D1
Golden Lane EC1Y......145 J4
Golden Square W1F......144 A7
Golding Street E1......150 E3
Goldney Road W9......142 A4
Goldsmith Street EC2V......145 K6
Gomm Road SE16......151 G8
Goodge Place W1T......144 A5
Goodge Street W1T......144 A5
Goodge Street ⊖ W1T......144 B5
Goodwin Close SE16......150 C8
Gordon Place W8......146 A2
Gordon Square WC1H......144 B3
Gordon Street WC1H......144 B3
Gore Street SW7......146 D4
Goring Street * EC3A......150 A2
Gosfield Street W1W......143 L5
Goslett Yard WC2H......144 B6
Goswell Road EC1V......145 H1
Gough Street WC1X......144 F3
Goulston Street E1......150 B2
Gower Mews WC1E......144 B5
Gower Place NW1......144 A3
Gower Street WC1E......144 B3
Gower's Walk E1......150 D2
Gracechurch Street EC3V......145 M7
Grafton Mews W1T......143 M4
Grafton Place NW1......144 B2
Grafton Street W1S......143 L8
Grafton Way W1T......144 A4
Graham Street N1......145 J1
Graham Terrace SW1W......147 J6
Granby Terrace NW1......143 M1
Grand Avenue EC1A......145 H5
Grange Road SE1......150 B8
Grange Walk SE1......150 A8
Grange Yard SE1......150 B8
Grantully Road W9......142 B2
Granville Place W1H......143 J6
Granville Road NW6......142 A1
Granville Square WC1X......144 F2
Grape Street WC2H......144 C6
Gravel Lane E1......150 B2
Gray's Inn Road WC1X......144 D2
Gray's Inn Square WC1R......144 F5
Gray Street SE1......149 G3
Great Castle Street W1G......143 L6
Great Central Street NW1......143 G4
Great Chapel Street W1D......144 B6
Great College Street SW1P......148 C4
Great Cumberland Place W1H......143 H6
Great Dover Street SE1......149 K3
Great Eastern Street EC2A......145 M3
Great George Street SW1P......148 C3
Great Guildford Street SE1......149 J1
Great James Street WC1N......144 E4
Great Marlborough Street W1F......143 M7
Great Maze Pond SE1......149 L2
Great Newport Street WC2H......144 C7
Greatorex Street E1......150 D1
Great Ormond Street WC1N......144 D4
Great Percy Street WC1X......144 F2
Great Peter Street SW1P......148 B4
Great Portland Street W1W......143 L4
Great Portland Street ⊖ W1W......143 L4
Great Pulteney Street W1F......144 A7
Great Queen Street WC2B......144 D6
Great Russell Street WC1B......144 C5
Great Scotland Yard SW1A......148 C1
Great Smith Street SW1P......148 C4
Great Suffolk Street SE1......149 H2
Great Sutton Street EC1V......145 H4
Great Swan Alley EC2R......145 L6
Great Titchfield Street W1W......143 M4
Great Tower Street EC3M......145 M7
Great Tower Street EC3R......150 A4
Great Winchester Street EC2N......145 L6
Great Windmill Street W1D......144 B7
Greek Street W1D......144 B6
Greenacre Square SE16......151 J6
Green Bank E1W......150 E5
Greenberry Street NW8......142 F1
Greencoat Place SW1P......148 A5
Green Coat Row SW1P......148 A4
Greenfield Road E1......150 D2
Greenham Close SE1......148 F3
Green Park ⊖ W1J......147 M1
Greenwell Street W1W......143 L4
Greet Street SE1......149 G2
Grenade Street E14......151 L4
Grendon Street NW8......142 F3
Grenville Place SW7......146 C5
Gresham Street EC2V......145 J6
Gresse Street W1T......144 B5
Greville Street EC1N......145 G5

Greycoat Place SW1P......148 B4
Greycoat Street SW1P......148 B4
Grigg's Place SE1......150 A8
Grosvenor Bridge SW8......147 L8
Grosvenor Crescent SW1X......147 J3
Grosvenor Crescent Mews SW1X......147 J3
Grosvenor Gardens SW1W......147 L4
Grosvenor Gardens Mews East SW1W......147 L4
Grosvenor Gardens Mews North SW1W......147 L4
Grosvenor Gardens Mews South * SW1W......147 L4
Grosvenor Gate W1K......143 H8
Grosvenor Hill W1K......143 L7
Grosvenor Place SW1X......147 K3
Grosvenor Road SW1V......147 L8
Grosvenor Square W1K......143 J7
Grosvenor Street W1K......143 K7
Grosvenor Terrace SE5......149 J8
Grove End Road NW8......142 D2
Guildhouse Street SW1V......147 M5
Guilford Street WC1N......144 D4
Guinness Square SE1......149 M5
Gulliver Street SE16......151 K8
Gunpowder Square EC4A......145 G6
Gun Street E1......150 B1
Gunthorpe Street E1......150 C2
Gutter Lane EC2V......145 J6
Guy Street SE1......149 L3

H

Haberdasher Street N1......145 L2
Haddonhall Estate SE1......149 M4
Hainton Close E1......150 F3
Halcrow Street * E1......150 F2
Half Moon Street W1J......147 L1
Halford Road SW6......146 A8
Halkin Place SW1X......147 J4
Halkin Street SW1X......147 K3
Halley Street E14......151 K1
Hallfield Estate W2......142 C6
Hall Place W2......142 E4
Hall Road NW8......142 D2
Hall Street EC1V......145 H2
Halpin Place SE17......149 M6
Halsey Street SW3......147 G5
Hamilton Close NW8......142 D2
Hamilton Close SE16......151 K7
Hamilton Gardens NW8......142 D2
Hamilton Place W1J......147 K2
Hamilton Terrace NW8......142 C1
Hammett Street EC3N......150 B4
Hampden Close NW1......144 B1
Hampden Gurney Street W2......143 H6
Hampstead Road NW1......143 M2
Hampton Street SE17......149 J6
Hanbury Street E1......150 C1
Hand Court WC1V......144 E5
Handel Street WC1N......144 D3
Hankey Place SE1......149 L3
Hannibal Road E1......151 G1
Hanover Square W1S......143 L6
Hanover Street W1S......143 L7
Hans Crescent SW3......147 H3
Hanson Street W1W......143 M4
Hans Place SW1X......147 H4
Hans Road SW3......147 G4
Hans Street SW1X......147 H4
Hanway Place W1T......144 B6
Hanway Street W1T......144 B6
Harbet Road W2......142 F5
Harcourt Street W1H......143 G5
Harcourt Terrace SW10......146 C7
Hardinge Street E1W......151 G3
Hardwick Street EC1R......145 G2
Hardwidge Street SE1......149 M2
Hardy Close SE16......151 H6
Harewood Place W1G......143 L6
Harewood Row NW1......143 G4
Harewood Avenue NW1......143 G4
Harrington Gardens SW7......146 C6
Harrington Road SW7......146 E5
Harrington Square NW1......143 M1
Harrington Street NW1......143 L2
Harrison Street WC1H......144 D2
Harrods SW1X......147 G4
Harrowby Street W1H......143 G6
Harrow Lane E14......151 M7
Harrow Place E1......150 B2
Harrow Road W2......142 A4
Hart Street EC3R......150 A3
Hasker Street SW3......147 G5
Hastings Street WC1N......144 C2
Hatfields SE1......149 G1
Hatherley Grove W2......142 B6
Hatteraick Road SE16......151 G6
Hatton Garden EC1N......145 G4
Hatton Street W2......142 E4
Hatton Wall EC1N......145 G4
Havering Street E1......151 H3
Haverstock Street N1......145 J1
Hawke Place * SE16......151 H6
Haydon Street EC3N......150 B3
Hayes Place NW1......143 G4
Hay Hill W1J......143 L8
Hayles Street SE11......149 H5
Haymarket SW1Y......144 B8
Hayne Street EC1A......145 J4
Hay's Lane SE1......149 M1
Hay's Mews W1J......143 L8
Haywood Place EC1R......145 J3
Headfort Place SW1X......147 K3
Head Street E1......151 H2
Hearnshaw Street E14......151 K2
Hearn Street EC2A......145 M4
Heathcote Street WC1N......144 E3
Heddon Street W1B......143 M7
Heddon Street W1S......144 A7
Hedger Street SE11......149 H5
Heiron Street SE17......149 J8

Hellings Street E1W......150 D5
Helmet Row EC1V......145 K3
Helsinki Square SE16......151 L8
Henderson Drive NW8......142 E3
Heneage Lane EC3A......150 A3
Heneage Street E1......150 C1
Henrietta Place W1G......143 L6
Henrietta Street WC2E......144 D7
Henriques Street E1......150 D2
Henshaw Street SE17......149 L5
Herbal Hill EC1R......145 G4
Herbert Crescent SW1X......147 H4
Herbrand Street WC1H......144 C3
Hercules Road SE1......148 F4
Hereford Road W2......142 A6
Hereford Square SW7......146 D6
Hermitage Street W2......142 E5
Hermitage Wall E1W......150 D5
Hermit Street EC1V......145 H2
Heron Place SE16......151 K5
Heron Quay E14......151 M5
Herrick Street SW1P......148 C6
Hertford Street W1J......147 K2
Hertsmere Road E14......151 M4
Hesper Mews SW5......146 B6
Hessel Street E1......150 E3
Hewett Street EC2A......145 M3
Heygate Street SE17......149 J5
Hide Place SW1P......148 B6
High Holborn WC1V......144 E5
High Street Kensington ⊖ W8......146 A3
Hildyard Road SW6......146 A8
Hilliards Court E1W......150 F5
Hillingdon Street SE17......149 J8
Hill Road NW8......142 D1
Hills Place W1F......143 M6
Hill Street W1J......143 K8
Hinde Street W1U......143 K6
Hind Grove E14......151 M3
Hindgrove Area E14......151 M3
Hithe Grove SE16......151 G8
HMS Belfast SE1......150 A5
Hobart Place SW1W......147 K4
Hobury Street SW10......146 D8
Hogarth Road SW5......146 B6
Holbein Mews SW1W......147 J6
Holbein Place SW1W......147 J6
Holborn EC1N......145 G5
Holborn ⊖ WC2B......144 E5
Holborn Circus EC1N......145 G5
Holborn Viaduct EC1A......145 G5
Holford Street WC1X......144 F2
Holland Street SE1......149 H1
Holland Street W8......146 A3
Hollen Street W1F......144 A6
Holles Street W1C......143 L6
Hollywood Road SW10......146 C8
Holyoak Road SE11......149 H5
Holyrood Street SE1......149 M2
Holyrood Street SE1......150 A6
Holywell Row EC2A......145 M4
Homefield Street * N1......145 M1
Homer Row W1H......143 G5
Homer Street W1H......143 G5
Hooper Street E1......150 D3
Hopetown Street E1......150 C1
Hopkins Street W1F......144 A7
Hopton Street SE1......149 H1
Hopwood Road SE17......149 L8
Hornton Place W8......146 A3
Hornton Street W8......146 A2
Horse & Dolphin Yard W1D......144 B7
Horseferry Road E14......151 J3
Horseferry Road SW1P......148 B4
Horse Guards Avenue SW1A......148 C2
Horse Guards Parade SW1A......148 C2
Horse Guards Road SW1A......148 C2
Horselydown Lane SE1......150 B6
Horsley Street SE17......149 K8
Hosier Lane EC1A......145 H5
Hothfield Place SE16......151 G8
Hotspur Street SE11......148 F6
Houghton Street WC2A......144 E6
Houndsditch EC3A......150 A2
Houses of Parliament SW1A......148 D3
Howick Place SW1E......148 A4
Howland Street W1T......144 A4
Howland Way SE16......151 K7
Howley Place W2......142 D4
Hoxton Square N1......145 M2
Hoxton Street N1......145 M1
Hudson's Place SW1V......147 M5
Hugh Mews SW1V......147 L6
Hugh Street SW1V......147 L6
Hugh Street SW1V......147 L6
Hull Close SE16......151 J6
Hull Street EC1V......145 J2
Hungerford Bridge SE1......148 E1
Hunter Close SE1......149 M4
Hunter Street WC1N......144 D3
Huntley Street WC1E......144 A4
Huntsman Street SE17......149 M6
Huntsworth Mews NW1......143 H3
Hurley Crescent SE16......151 H6
Hutching's Street E14......151 M7
Hutton Street EC4Y......145 G7
Hyde Park W2......147 G1
Hyde Park Corner W1J......147 K2
Hyde Park Corner ⊖ W1J......147 K2
Hyde Park Court SW7......146 D3
Hyde Park Crescent W2......142 F6
Hyde Park Gardens W2......142 F7
Hyde Park Gardens Mews W2......142 F7
Hyde Park Gate SW7......146 C3
Hyde Park Gate SW7......146 D3
Hyde Park Square W2......142 F7
Hyde Park Street W2......142 F7

I

Idol Lane EC3R......145 M7
Ifield Road SW10......146 B8
Iliffe Street SE17......149 J6
Iliffe Yard SE17......149 J6
Imperial College Road SW7......146 D4
Imperial War Museum SE1......149 G4
India Street EC3N......150 B3
Ingestre Place W1F......144 A7
Inglebert Street EC1R......145 G2
Ingram Close SE11......148 E5
Inner Circle NW1......143 J2
Inverness Terrace W2......142 B6
Inverness Terrace Gate W2......142 C8
Invicta Plaza SE1......149 H1

Inville Road SE17......149 L7
Ironmonger Lane EC2V......145 K6
Ironmonger Row EC1V......145 K2
Irving Street WC2N......144 C8
Isambard Place SE16......151 G6
Island Row E14......151 K3
Iverna Court W8......146 A4
Iverna Gardens W8......146 A4
Ives Street SW3......147 G5
Ivor Place NW1......143 G4
Ixworth Place SW3......146 F6

J

Jacob Street SE1......150 C6
Jamaica Gate SE16......150 F8
Jamaica Road SE1......150 C7
Jamaica Road SE16......150 E7
Jamaica Street E1......151 G2
Jamaica Wharf SE1......150 C6
James Street W1U......143 K6
James Street WC2E......144 D7
Jameson Street W8......146 A1
Jamuna Close E14......151 K1
Janeway Street SE16......150 D7
Jardine Road E1W......151 J4
Java Wharf SE1......150 C6
Jay Mews SW7......146 D3
Jermyn Street SW1Y......144 A8
Jerome Crescent NW8......142 F3
Jewery Street EC3N......150 B3
Joan Street SE1......149 G2
Jockey's Fields WC1R......144 E4
Johanna Street SE1......148 F3
John Adam Street WC2N......144 D8
John Carpenter Street EC4Y......145 G7
John Fisher Street E1......150 C4
John Islip Street SW1P......148 C5
John Prince's Street W1G......143 L6
John Roll Way SE16......150 D7
John Ruskin Street SE5......149 J8
John's Mews WC1N......144 E4
Johnson's Place SW1V......148 A7
Johnson Street E1......151 G3
John Street WC1N......144 E4
Joiner Street SE1......149 L1
Jonathan Street SE11......148 E6
Jubilee Place SW3......147 G6
Jubilee Street E1......151 G2
Jubilee Walk W8......146 B1
Judd Street WC1H......144 C2
Junction Mews W2......142 F5
Juxon Street SE11......148 E5

K

Katherine Close SE16......151 H5
Kean Street WC2B......144 E6
Keel Close SE16......151 J6
Keeley Street WC2B......144 E6
Keeton's Road SE16......150 E7
Kell Street SE1......149 H3
Kelso Place W8......146 B4
Kemble Street WC2B......144 E6
Kempsford Gardens SW5......146 A7
Kempsford Road SE11......149 G6
Kendall Place W1U......143 J5
Kendal Street W2......143 G6
Kennet Street E1W......150 D5
Kenning Street SE16......151 G6
Kennings Way SE11......149 G7
Kennington ⊖ SE11......149 H7
Kennington Lane SE11......148 E7
Kennington Oval SE11......148 E8
Kennington Park Gardens SE11......149 G8
Kennington Park Place SE11......149 G7
Kennington Park Road SE11......149 G7
Kennington Road SE1......148 F4
Kennington Road SE11......149 G5
Kennnington Oval SE11......148 F8
Kenrick Place W1U......143 J5
Kensington Church Street W8......146 A1
Kensington Court W8......146 B3
Kensington Gardens W2......146 C1
Kensington Gardens Square W2......142 B6
Kensington Gate W8......146 C4
Kensington Gore SW7......146 E3
Kensington High Street W8......146 A4
Kensington Palace W8......146 B2
Kensington Palace Gardens W8......146 B1
Kensington Palace Gardens W8......146 B2
Kensington Place W8......146 A1
Kensington Road SW7......147 G3
Kensington Road W8......146 B3
Kensington Square W8......146 B3
Kenton Street WC1H......144 C3
Kenway Road SW5......146 A6
Keystone Close N1......144 D1
Keyworth Street SE1......149 H4
Kia Oval (Surrey County Cricket Ground) SE11......148 F8
Kilburn Park Road NW6......142 A2
Kildare Terrace W2......142 A6
Killick Street N1......144 E1
Kinburn Street SE16......151 H6
Kinder Street E1......150 E2
King & Queen Wharf SE16......151 H5
King and Queen Street SE17......149 K6
King Charles Street SW1A......148 C2
King David Lane E1......151 G3
Kingdom Street W2......142 C5
King Edward Street EC1A......145 J6
King Edward Walk SE1......149 G4
King James Street SE1......149 H3
Kingly Street W1F......143 M7
King's Arms Yard EC2R......145 L6
King's Bench Street SE1......149 H2
Kingscote Street EC4V......145 H7
King's Cross ⇌ N1C......144 D1
King's Cross Road WC1X......144 E2
King's Cross Square N1C......144 D1
King's Cross St Pancras ⊖ N1C......144 D1
Kingsgate Walk * SW1E......148 A4
King's Head Yard SE1......149 L1
King's Mews WC1N......144 F4
Kingsmill Terrace NW8......142 E1
King Square EC1V......145 J2
King's Road SW3......146 E8
King's Scholars Passage SW1P......148 A5
King's Stairs Close SE16......150 F6
King Street WC2E......144 D7
King Street SW1Y......148 L8

King Street EC2V 145 K6
Kingsway WC2B 144 E6
King William Street EC4N 145 L7
Kinnerton Place North * SW1X 147 J3
Kinnerton Place South * SW1X 147 J3
Kinnerton Street SW1X 147 J3
Kinnerton Yard * SW1X 147 J3
Kipling Estate SE1 ....149 L3
Kipling Street SE1 ....149 L3
Kirby Estate SE16 ....150 D7
Kirby Grove SE1 ....149 M3
Kirby Street EC1N 145 G4
Knaresborough Place SW5 ....146 B5
Knightrider Street EC4V 145 H7
Knightsbridge SW1X 147 H3
Knightsbridge ⊖ SW3 ....147 H3
Knox Street W1H 143 H4
Kynance Mews SW7 ....146 C4
Kynance Place SW7 ....146 C4

L

Lackington Street EC2A 145 L4
Lafone Street SE1 ....150 B6
Lagado Mews SE16 ....151 H5
Lambeth Bridge SW1P 148 D5
Lambeth High Street SE1 ....148 E5
Lambeth Hill EC4V 145 J7
Lambeth North ⊖ SE1 ....148 F3
Lambeth Palace Road SE1 ....148 E4
Lambeth Road SE1 ....148 F4
Lambeth Walk SE11 ....148 F5
Lamb's Conduit Street WC1N 144 E4
Lamb's Passage EC1Y 145 K4
Lamb Street E1 ....150 B1
Lamb Way SE1 ....150 A7
Lamlash Street SE11 ....149 H5
Lanark Place W9 ....142 D3
Lanark Road W9 ....142 B1
Lancaster Gate W2 ....142 D7
Lancaster Gate W2 ....142 D7
Lancaster Gate ⊖ W2 ....142 E7
Lancaster Mews W2 ....142 D7
Lancaster Place WC2E 144 E7
Lancaster Street SE1 ....149 H3
Lancaster Terrace W2 ....142 E7
Lancaster Walk W2 ....142 D8
Lancelot Place SW7 ....147 G3
Lancing Street NW1 ....144 B2
Lanesborough Place * SW1X 147 J3
Langdale Street E1 ....150 E3
Langford Place NW8 ....142 D1
Langham Place W1B 143 L5
Langham Street W1W 143 L5
Langham Street W1W 143 M5
Langley Lane SW8 ....148 D8
Langley Street WC2H 144 C7
Langton Close WC1X 144 E3
Lanhill Road W9 ....142 A3
Lansdowne Place SE1 ....149 L4
Lant Street SE1 ....149 J3
Larcom Street SE17 ....149 K6
Lauderdale Road W9 ....142 B3
Laud Street SE11 ....148 E7
Launcelot Street SE1 ....148 F3
Launceston Place W8 ....146 C4
Laurence Pountney Lane EC4V 145 L7
Lavender Road SE16 ....151 K5
Lavender Wharf SE16 ....151 K4
Lavington Street SE1 ....149 J1
Lawn Lane SW8 ....148 D8
Lawrence Street SW3 ....146 F8
Lawrence Wharf SE16 ....151 L6
Law Street SE1 ....149 L4
Laxton Place NW1 ....143 L3
Laystall Street EC1R 144 F4
Leadenhall Street EC3A 150 A3
Leadenhall Street EC3V 145 M6
Leake Street SE1 ....148 E2
Leather Lane EC1N 145 G4
Leathermarket Street SE1 ....149 M3
Leeke Street WC1X 144 E2
Lees Place W1K 143 J7
Leicester Square ⊖ WC2H 144 C7
Leicester Square WC2H 144 C7
Leicester Street WC2H 144 B7
Leigh Street WC1H 144 C3
Leinster Gardens W2 ....142 C6
Leinster Mews W2 ....142 C7
Leinster Place W2 ....142 C7
Leinster Square W2 ....142 A7
Leinster Terrace W2 ....142 C7
Leman Street E1 ....150 C3
Lennox Gardens SW1X 147 G4
Lennox Gardens Mews SW1X 147 G5
Leonard Street EC2A 145 L3
Leopold Estate E3 ....151 M1
Leopold Estate E3 ....151 L1
Leroy Street SE1 ....149 M5
Lever Street EC1V 145 J2
Lewisham Street SW1H 148 B3
Lexham Gardens W8 ....146 A5
Lexham Mews W8 ....146 A5
Lexington Street W1F 144 A7
Leyden Street E1 ....150 B2
Leydon Close SE16 ....151 H5
Library Street SE1 ....149 H3
Lidlington Place NW1 ....144 A1
Lilestone Street NW8 ....142 F4
Lilley Close E1W 150 D5
Lillie Road SW6 ....146 A7
Lillie Yard SW6 ....146 A7
Limeburner Lane EC4M 145 H6
Lime Close E1W 150 D5
Limehouse Causeway E14 ....151 L4
Limehouse Link E14 ....151 L3
Limehouse ≷ E14 ....151 J3
Limerston Street SW10 ....146 D7
Lime Street EC3M 145 M7
Lincoln's Inn Fields WC2A 144 E6
Linden Gardens W2 ....142 A8
Lindley Street E1 ....150 F1
Lindsay Square SW1V 148 B7
Lindsey Street EC1A 145 H4
Linhope Street NW1 ....143 H3
Linsey Street SE16 ....150 D8
Lisle Street WC2H 144 B7
Lisson Green Estate NW8 ....142 F3
Lisson Grove NW1 ....143 G4
Lisson Grove NW8 ....142 F3
Lisson Street NW1 ....142 F4
Litchfield Street WC2H 144 C7
Little Argyll Street W1F 143 M6
Little Britain EC1A 145 J5

Little Chester Street SW1X 147 K4
Little George Street SW1P 148 C3
Little Marlborough Street W1F 143 M6
Little New Street EC4A 145 G6
Little Portland Street W1G 143 L6
Little Russell Street WC1A 144 C5
Little St James's Street SW1A 147 M2
Little Sanctuary SW1A 148 C3
Little Somerset Street E1 ....150 B3
Little Titchfield Street W1W 143 M5
Liverpool Grove SE17 ....149 K7
Liverpool Street EC2M 145 M5
Liverpool Street ≷ ⊖ EC2M 145 M5
Lizard Street EC1V 145 K3
Llewellyn Street SE16 ....150 D7
Lloyd Baker Street WC1X 144 F2
Lloyd's Avenue EC3N 150 B3
Lloyd Square WC1X 144 F2
Lloyds Row EC1R 145 G2
Lloyd Street WC1X 144 F2
Locksfield Estate E14 ....151 L2
Locksley Street E14 ....151 L1
Lockyer Street SE1 ....149 L3
Lodge Road NW8 ....142 F3
Loftie Street SE16 ....150 D7
Logan Place W8 ....146 A5
Lolesworth Close E1 ....150 B1
Lollard Street SE11 ....148 F5
Lollard Street SE11 ....148 F6
Loman Street SE1 ....149 J2
Lomas Street E1 ....150 D1
Lombard Lane EC4Y 145 G6
Lombard Street EC3V 145 L7
London Bridge EC4R 145 L8
London Bridge ≷ ⊖ SE1 ....149 L1
London Bridge Street SE1 ....149 L1
London Dungeon SE1 ....148 E2
London Eye SE1 ....148 E2
London Mews W2 ....142 E6
London Road SE1 ....149 H4
London Street EC3R 150 A3
London Street W2 ....142 E6
London Transport
    Museum WC2E 144 D7
London Wall EC2M 145 K5
London Zoo ZSL NW1 ....143 J1
Long Acre WC2E 144 D7
Longford Street NW1 ....143 L3
Long Lane EC1A 145 J5
Long Lane SE1 ....149 L3
Longmoore Street SW1V 147 M5
Longridge Road SW5 ....146 A5
Longville Road SE11 ....149 H5
Long Walk SE1 ....150 A8
Long Yard WC1N 144 E4
Lord North Street SW1P 148 C4
Lord's Cricket Ground NW8 ....142 E2
Lorenzo Street WC1X 144 E1
Lorrimore Road SE17 ....149 J8
Lorrimore Square SE17 ....149 H8
Lothbury EC2R 145 L6
Loughborough Street SE11 ....148 F7
Lovat Lane EC3R 145 M7
Love Lane EC2V 145 K6
Lovell Place SE16 ....151 K7
Lowell Street E14 ....151 K2
Lower Belgrave Street SW1W 147 K4
Lower Grosvenor Place SW1W 147 L4
Lower James Street W1F 144 A7
Lower John Street W1F 144 A7
Lower Marsh SE1 ....148 F3
Lower Road SE16 ....151 G7
Lower Sloane Street SW1W 147 J6
Lower Thames Street EC3R 150 A4
Lower Thames Street EC3R 145 M8
Lowndes Close * SW1X 147 J4
Lowndes Place SW1X 147 J4
Lowndes Square SW1X 147 H3
Lowndes Street SW1X 147 J4
Lucan Place SW3 ....146 F5
Lucey Road SE16 ....150 C8
Ludgate Circus EC4M 145 H6
Ludgate Hill EC4M 145 H6
Luke Street EC2A 145 M3
Lukin Street E1 ....151 G3
Lumley Street W1K 143 K7
Lupus Street SW1V 147 L7
Lupus Street SW1V 148 B7
Luton Street NW8 ....142 E4
Luxborough Street W1U 143 J4
Lyall Mews SW1X 147 J4
Lyall Street SW1X 147 J4
Lyons Place NW8 ....142 E3
Lytham Street SE17 ....149 K7

M

Macclesfield Road EC1V 145 J2
Macclesfield Street * W1D 144 B7
Mace Close E1W 150 E5
Macklin Street WC2B 144 D6
Mackworth Street NW1 ....143 M2
Macleod Street SE17 ....149 K7
Madame Tussauds NW1 ....143 J4
Maddox Street W1S 143 M7
Magdalen Street SE1 ....149 M2
Magee Street SE11 ....148 F8
Maguire Street SE1 ....150 C6
Maida Avenue W9 ....142 D4
Maida Vale W9 ....142 C2
Maida Vale ⊖ W9 ....142 C2
Maiden Lane SE1 ....149 K1
Maiden Lane WC2E 144 D7
Major Road SE16 ....150 D7
Makins Street SW3 ....147 G6
Malet Street WC1E 144 B4
Mallord Street SW3 ....146 E8
Mallory Street NW8 ....142 F3
Mallow Street EC1V 145 L3
Malta Street EC1V 145 H3
Maltby Street SE1 ....150 B7
Manchester Square W1U 143 J6
Manchester Street W1U 143 J5
Manciple Street SE1 ....149 L3
Mandeville Place W1U 143 K6
Manette Street W1D 144 B6
Manilla Street E14 ....151 M6
Manningford Close EC1V 145 H2
Manor Place SE17 ....149 J7
Manresa Road SW3 ....146 F7
Mansell Street E1 ....150 C3
Mansfield Mews W1G 143 L5
Mansfield Street W1G 143 L5
Mansion House ⊖ EC4V 145 K7

Manson Mews SW7 ....146 D5
Manson Place SW7 ....146 D6
Mapleleaf Square SE16 ....151 J6
Maples Place E1 ....150 F1
Maple Street W1T 143 H7
Marble Arch W1C 143 H7
Marchmont Street WC1H 144 C3
Margaret Street W1W 143 L6
Margaretta Terrace SW3 ....146 F7
Margery Street WC1X 144 F3
Marigold Street SE16 ....150 E7
Marine Street SE16 ....150 C7
Market Mews W1J 147 K1
Market Place W1W 143 M6
Markham Square SW3 ....147 G6
Markham Street SW3 ....147 G6
Mark Lane EC3R 150 A4
Marlborough Gate W2 ....142 E7
Marlborough Place NW8 ....142 C1
Marlborough Road SW1A 148 A2
Marlborough Street SW3 ....146 F6
Marloes Road W8 ....146 B4
Marlow Way SE16 ....151 H6
Maroon Street E14 ....151 K2
Marshall Street W1F 144 A7
Marshalsea Road SE1 ....149 K2
Marsham Street SW1P 148 C5
Marsh Wall E14 ....151 M5
Martha's Buildings EC1V 145 K3
Martha Street E1 ....150 F3
Martin Lane EC4V 145 L7
Maryland Road W9 ....142 A4
Marylands Road W9 ....142 A4
Marylebone ≷ ⊖ NW1 ....143 G4
Marylebone Flyover W2 ....142 E5
Marylebone High Street W1U 143 K5
Marylebone Lane W1U 143 K6
Marylebone Road NW1 ....143 G4
Marylebone Street W1G 143 K5
Marylee Way SE11 ....148 F6
Masjid Lane E14 ....151 M2
Mason Street SE17 ....149 M5
Massinger Street SE17 ....149 M6
Masters Street E1 ....151 J1
Matlock Street E14 ....151 J2
Matthew Parker Street SW1H 148 C3
Maunsel Street SW1P 148 B5
Mayfair Place W1J 147 L1
Mayflower Street SE16 ....150 F7
Mayford Estate NW1 ....144 A1
Maynards Quay E1W 150 F4
May's Court WC2N 144 C8
McAuley Close SE1 ....148 F4
McLeod's Mews SW7 ....146 C5
Meadcroft Road SE11 ....149 G8
Meadcroft Road SE11 ....149 H8
Meadow Road SW8 ....148 E8
Meadow Row SE1 ....149 J5
Mead Row SE1 ....148 F4
Meakin Estate SE1 ....149 M4
Mecklenburgh Square WC1N 144 E3
Medway Street SW1P 148 B5
Meeting House Alley E1W 150 E5
Melcombe Place NW1 ....143 G4
Melcombe Street W1U 143 H4
Melina Place NW8 ....142 D2
Melior Street SE1 ....149 M2
Melton Street NW1 ....144 A2
Memorial Gates SW1W 147 K3
Mepham Street SE1 ....148 F2
Mercer Street WC2H 144 C7
Merchant Square W2 ....142 E5
Merlin Street EC1R 144 F2
Mermaid Court SE1 ....149 K2
Merrick Square SE1 ....149 K4
Merrington Road SW6 ....146 A8
Merrow Street SE17 ....149 L7
Methley Street SE11 ....149 G7
Meymott Street SE1 ....149 G2
Micawber Street N1 ....145 K1
Micklethwaite Road SW6 ....146 A8
Middlesex Street E1 ....150 A1
Middlesex Street E1 ....150 B2
Middle Street EC1A 145 J5
Middle Temple WC2R 144 F7
Middle Temple Lane EC4Y 144 F7
Middleton Drive SE16 ....151 H6
Midland Road NW1 ....144 C1
Midship Close SE16 ....151 H6
Milborne Grove SW10 ....146 D7
Milcote Street SE1 ....149 H3
Miles Street SW8 ....148 D8
Milford Lane WC2R 144 F7
Milk Street EC2V 145 K6
Milk Yard E1W 151 G4
Millbank SW1P 148 D4
Millennium Bridge SE1 ....145 J8
Millennium Harbour E14 ....151 M6
Milligan Street E14 ....151 L4
Millman Mews WC1N 144 E4
Millman Street WC1N 144 E4
Mill Place E14 ....151 K3
Millstream Road SE1 ....150 B7
Mill Street SE1 ....150 C6
Mill Street W1S 143 L7
Milner Street SW3 ....147 G5
Milton Street EC2Y 145 K4
Milverton Street SE11 ....149 G7
Mincing Lane EC3M 150 A4
Minera Mews SW1W 147 J5
Minories EC3N 150 B3
Mitchell Street EC1V 145 J3
Mitre Road SE1 ....149 G2
Mitre Street EC3A 150 A3
Molyneux Street W1H 143 G5
Monck Street SW1P 148 C4
Monkton Street SE11 ....149 G5
Monkwell Square EC2Y 145 K5
Monmouth Place W2 ....142 A6
Monmouth Road W2 ....142 A6
Monmouth Street WC2H 144 C6
Montague Close SE1 ....149 L1
Montague Place EC3R 144 C5
Montague Street WC1B 144 C5
Montagu Mansions W1H 143 H5
Montagu Mews North W1H 143 H5
Montagu Mews West W1H 143 H5
Montagu Place W1H 143 H5
Montagu Row W1U 143 H5
Montagu Square W1H 143 H5
Montagu Street W1H 143 H5
Montford Place SE11 ....148 F7
Montpelier Square SW7 ....147 G3
Montpelier Street SW7 ....147 G3
Montpelier Walk SW7 ....146 G3

Montrose Place SW1X 147 K3
Monument ⊖ EC4R 145 L7
Monument Street EC3R 145 L7
Monument Street EC3R 145 M7
Monza Street E1W 151 G4
Moodkee Street SE16 ....151 G7
Moore Street SW3 ....147 H5
Moorfields EC2Y 145 L5
Moorgate EC2R 145 L6
Moorgate ⊖ ≷ EC2Y 145 L5
Moor Lane EC2Y 145 K5
Moor Street W1D 144 C7
Mora Street EC1V 145 K2
Morecambe Street SE17 ....149 K6
Moreland Street EC1V 145 H2
More London SE1 ....150 A5
Moreton Place SW1V 148 A6
Moreton Street SW1V 148 A6
Moreton Terrace SW1V 148 A6
Morgan's Lane SE1 ....149 M2
Morgan's Lane SE1 ....150 A5
Morley Street SE1 ....149 G3
Mornington Crescent NW1 ....143 M1
Mornington Place NW1 ....143 L1
Mornington Terrace NW1 ....143 L1
Morocco Street SE1 ....150 A7
Morpeth Terrace SW1P 147 M5
Morris Street E1 ....150 F3
Morshead Road W9 ....142 A2
Mortimer Market WC1E 144 A4
Mortimer Street W1T 144 A5
Mortimer Street W1W 143 M5
Morton Place SE1 ....148 F4
Morwell Street WC1B 144 B5
Moscow Place W2 ....142 B7
Moscow Road W2 ....142 B7
Mossop Street SW3 ....147 G5
Motcomb Street SW1X 147 J4
Mount Gate W2 ....146 E2
Mount Mills EC1V 145 J3
Mount Pleasant WC1X 144 F4
Mount Row W1K 143 K8
Mount Street W1K 143 K8
Mount Street Mews W1K 143 K8
Mount Terrace E1 ....150 E1
Moxon Street W1U 143 J5
Mulberry Street E1 ....150 D2
Mulberry Walk SW3 ....146 E8
Mulready Street NW8 ....142 F4
Mundy Street N1 ....145 M2
Munster Square NW1 ....143 L3
Munton Road SE17 ....149 K5
Murphy Street SE1 ....148 F3
Murray Grove N1 ....145 K1
Musbury Street E1 ....151 G2
Muscovy Street EC3N 150 A4
Museum of London EC2Y 145 J5
Museum Street WC1A 144 C6
Myddelton Passage EC1R 145 G2
Myddelton Square EC1R 145 G2
Myddelton Street EC1R 145 G3
Myrdle Street E1 ....150 D2

N

Naoroji Street WC1X 144 F2
Napier Grove N1 ....145 K1
Narrow Street E14 ....151 K4
Nash Street NW1 ....143 L2
Nassau Street W1W 143 M5
Nathaniel Close * E1 ....150 C2
National Portrait
    Gallery WC2H 144 C8
Natural History Museum SW7 ....146 E4
Neal Street WC2H 144 C6
Neathouse Place * SW1V 147 M5
Neckinger SE1 ....150 C8
Needleman Street SE16 ....151 H7
Nelson Close NW6 ....142 A1
Nelson Place N1 ....145 H1
Nelson's Column WC2N 144 C8
Nelson Square SE1 ....149 H2
Nelson Street E1 ....150 E2
Nelson Terrace N1 ....145 H1
Neptune Street SE16 ....151 G7
Nesham Street E1W 150 D4
Netherton Grove SW10 ....146 D8
Netley Street NW1 ....143 M2
Nevern Place SW5 ....146 A6
Nevern Square SW5 ....146 A6
Neville Street SW7 ....146 E6
Newark Street E1 ....150 E2
New Atlas Wharf E14 ....151 M8
New Bond Street W1S 143 L7
New Bond Street W1S 143 L8
New Bridge Street EC4V 145 H6
New Broad Street EC2M 145 M5
New Burlington Street W1S 143 M7
Newburn Street SE11 ....148 F7
Newbury Street EC1A 145 J5
Newcastle Place W2 ....142 E5
New Cavendish Street W1G 143 L5
New Change EC4M 145 J6
New Church Road SE5 ....149 L8
Newcomen Street SE1 ....149 L2
New Compton Street WC2H 144 C6
Newcourt Street NW8 ....142 F1
Newell Street E14 ....151 L3
New Fetter Lane EC4A 145 G6
Newgate Street EC1A 145 H6
New Globe Walk SE1 ....145 J8
New Goulston Street E1 ....150 B2
Newham's Row SE1 ....150 A7
Newington Butts SE1 ....149 H5
Newington Causeway SE1 ....149 J4
New Kent Road SE1 ....149 K5
Newlands Quay E1W 150 F4
Newman Street W1T 144 A5
New North Place EC2A 145 M3
New North Road N1 ....145 L1
New North Street WC1N 144 D4
New Oxford Street WC1A 144 C6
Newport Street SE11 ....148 E5
New Quebec Street W1H 143 H6
New Ride SW7 ....146 E3
New Road E1 ....150 E2
New Row WC2N 144 C7
New Spring Gardens Walk SE1 ....148 D7
New Square WC2A 144 F6
New Street EC2M 150 A2
New Street Square EC4A 145 G6
Newton Road W2 ....142 A6
Newton Street WC2B 144 D5
New Union Street EC2Y 145 K5

Nicholas Lane EC3V 145 L7
Nicholson Street SE1 ....149 H1
Nightingale Place SW10 ....146 D8
Nile Street N1 ....145 K2
Nine Elms Lane SW8 ....148 C8
Noble Street EC2V 145 J6
Noel Road * N1 ....145 J1
Noel Street W1F 144 A6
Norbiton Road E14 ....151 L2
Norfolk Crescent W2 ....143 G6
Norfolk Place W2 ....142 E6
Norfolk Square W2 ....142 E6
Norman Street EC1V 145 J3
Norris Street SW1Y 144 B8
Northampton Road EC1R 145 G3
Northampton Square EC1V 145 H2
North Audley Street W1K 143 J7
North Bank NW8 ....142 F2
Northburgh Street EC1V 145 H3
North Carriage Drive W2 ....143 F7
Northdown Street N1 ....144 D1
Northey Street E14 ....151 K4
North Gower Street NW1 ....144 A2
Northington Street WC1N 144 E4
North Mews WC1N 144 E4
North Ride W2 ....143 G7
North Row W1K 143 J7
North Terrace SW3 ....146 F5
Northumberland Alley EC3N 150 B3
Northumberland
    Avenue WC2N 148 C1
Northumberland Place W2 ....142 A6
Northumberland Street WC2N 148 C1
North Wharf Road W2 ....142 E5
Northwick Terrace NW8 ....142 D3
Norway Gate SE16 ....151 K7
Norway Place E14 ....151 L3
Norwich Street EC4A 144 F5
Nottingham Place W1U 143 J4
Nottingham Street W1U 143 J4
Notting Hill Gate W11 ....142 A8
Notting Hill Gate ⊖ W11 ....146 A1
Nugent Terrace NW8 ....142 D1
Nutford Place W1H 143 G6

O

Oakden Street SE11 ....149 G5
Oakington Road W9 ....142 A3
Oak Lane E14 ....151 L3
Oakley Close EC1V 145 H1
Oakley Gardens SW3 ....147 G8
Oakley Square NW1 ....144 A1
Oakley Street SW3 ....146 F8
Oak Tree Road NW8 ....142 F2
Oat Lane EC2V 145 J5
Occupation Road SE17 ....149 J6
Ocean Square E1 ....151 J1
Ocean Street E1 ....151 J1
Odessa Street SE16 ....151 L7
Ogle Street W1W 143 M5
Old Bailey EC4M 145 H6
Old Barrack Yard SW1X 147 J3
Old Bond Street W1S 143 M8
Old Broad Street EC2N 145 M6
Old Brompton Road SW5 ....146 B6
Old Brompton Road SW7 ....146 D6
Old Burlington Street W1S 143 M7
Oldbury Place W1U 143 J4
Old Castle Street E1 ....150 B2
Old Cavendish Street W1G 143 L6
Old Church Road E1 ....151 H2
Old Church Street SW3 ....146 E7
Old Compton Street W1D 144 B7
Old Court Place W8 ....146 B3
Old Gloucester Street WC1N 144 D4
Old Jamaica Road SE16 ....150 C7
Old Jewry EC2R 145 K6
Old Kent Road SE1 ....149 M5
Old Marylebone Road NW1 ....143 G5
Old Montague Street E1 ....150 C1
Old North Street WC1X 144 E4
Old Paradise Street SE11 ....148 E5
Old Park Lane W1J 147 K2
Old Pye Street SW1P 148 B4
Old Queen Street SW1H 148 B3
Old Square WC2A 144 F6
Old Street EC1V 145 K3
Old Street ≷ ⊖ EC1Y 145 L3
Old Street Junction EC1Y 145 L3
Oliver's Yard EC1Y 145 L3
Olney Road SE17 ....149 J8
O'Meara Street SE1 ....149 K2
Omega Place N1 ....144 D1
Onega Gate SE16 ....151 K8
Ongar Road SW6 ....146 A8
Onslow Gardens SW7 ....146 D6
Onslow Square SW7 ....146 E5
Onslow Square SW7 ....146 E6
Ontario Street SE1 ....149 J4
Ontario Way E14 ....151 M4
Opal Street SE11 ....149 H6
Orange Place SE16 ....151 G8
Orange Square SW1W 147 K6
Orange Street E1W 150 D5
Orange Street WC2H 144 B8
Orb Street SE17 ....149 L6
Orchardson Street NW8 ....142 E4
Orchard Street W1H 143 J6
Orde Hall Street WC1N 144 E4
Orient Street SE11 ....149 H5
Orme Court W2 ....142 B8
Orme Lane W2 ....142 B8
Orme Square Gate W2 ....142 B8
Ormond Close WC1N 144 D4
Ormonde Gate SW3 ....147 H7
Ormond Yard SW1Y 144 A8
Orsett Mews W2 ....142 C6
Orsett Street SE11 ....148 E6
Orsett Terrace W2 ....142 C5
Orton Street E1W 150 D5
Osbert Street SW1V 148 B6
Osborn Street E1 ....150 C2
Oslo Square SE16 ....151 K7
Osnaburgh Street NW1 ....143 L3
Osnaburgh Terrace NW1 ....143 L3
Ossington Buildings W1U 143 J5
Ossington Street W2 ....142 A7
Ossulston Street NW1 ....144 B1
Oswin Street SE11 ....149 H5
Othello Close SE11 ....149 H6
Otto Street SE17 ....149 H8
Outer Circle NW1 ....143 H3
Outer Circle NW1 ....143 K1

Oval ⊖ SE11....148 F8
Oval Way SE11....148 E7
Ovington Square SW3....147 G4
Ovington Street SW3....147 G5
Owen Street EC1V....145 G1
Oxendon Street SW1Y....144 B8
Oxford Circus ⊖ W1B....143 M6
Oxford Road NW6....142 A1
Oxford Square W2....142 F6
Oxford Street W1C....143 L6
Oxford Street WC1A....144 A6

P

Pace Place E1....150 E3
Pacific Wharf SE16....151 H5
Paddington ⊖ W2....142 D6
Paddington Green W2....142 E5
Paddington Street W1U....143 J5
Pageant Crescent SE16....151 K5
Page Street SW1P....148 B5
Paget Street EC1V....145 H2
Pakenham Street WC1X....144 E3
Palace Avenue W8....146 B2
Palace Court W2....142 A7
Palace Gardens Terrace W8....146 A1
Palace Gate W8....146 C3
Palace Green W8....146 B2
Palace of Westminster SW1A....148 D3
Palace Place SW1E....147 M4
Palace Street SW1E....147 M4
Pall Mall SW1Y....148 A1
Pall Mall East SW1Y....148 B1
Palmer Street SW1H....148 B3
Pancras Lane EC4N....145 K6
Pancras Road N1C....144 C1
Panton Street SW1Y....144 B8
Paradise Street SE16....150 E7
Paradise Walk SW3....147 H8
Pardoner Street SE1....149 L4
Pardon Street EC1V....145 H3
Parfett Street E1....150 D2
Paris Garden SE1....149 G1
Park Crescent W1B....143 K4
Park Crescent Mews West W1G....143 K4
Parker's Row SE1....150 C7
Parker Street WC2B....144 D6
Park Lane W1K....143 H7
Park Lane W1....147 J1
Park Place SW1A....147 M1
Park Place Villas W2....142 D4
Park Road NW1....143 H3
Park Square East NW1....143 L3
Park Square Mews NW1....143 K3
Park Square West NW1....143 K3
Park Street SE1....149 K1
Park Street W1K....143 J7
Park Village East NW1....143 L1
Park Walk SW10....146 D8
Park West Place W2....143 G6
Parliament Street SW1A....148 C2
Parry Street SW8....148 D8
Passmore Street SW1W....147 J6
Paternoster Square....145 J6
Pater Street W8....146 A4
Pattina Walk SE16....151 K5
Paul Street EC2A....145 M4
Paultons Square SW3....146 E8
Paveley Street NW1....143 G3
Pavilion Road SW1X....147 H3
Pavilion Street SW1X....147 H4
Paxton Terrace SW1V....147 L7
Peabody Avenue SW1V....147 L7
Peabody Estate SE1....149 J1
Peacock Street SE17....149 J6
Pearl Street E1W....150 F5
Pearman Street SE1....149 G3
Pear Tree Court EC1R....145 G3
Peartree Lane E1W....151 G4
Pear Tree Street EC1V....145 J3
Peel Street W8....146 A1
Peerless Street EC1V....145 K2
Pelham Crescent SW7....146 F6
Pelham Place SW7....146 F5
Pelham Street SW7....146 F5
Pelier Street SE17....149 K8
Pemberton Row EC4A....145 G6
Pembridge Gardens W2....142 A8
Pembridge Place W2....142 A7
Pembridge Square W2....142 A7
Pembridge Villas W11....142 A7
Pembroke Close SW1X....147 J3
Penang Street E1W....150 F5
Penfold Place NW8....142 F5
Penfold Street NW8....142 E4
Pennant Mews W8....146 B5
Pennington Street E1W....150 D4
Pennyfields E14....151 M4
Penrose Grove SE17....149 J7
Penrose Street SE17....149 J7
Penton Place SE17....149 H6
Penton Rise WC1X....144 E2
Penton Street N1....144 F1
Pentonville Road N1....144 E1
Penywern Road SW5....146 A6
Pepper Street SE1....149 J2
Pepys Street EC3N....150 A4
Percival Street EC1V....145 H3
Percy Circus WC1X....144 F2
Percy Street W1T....144 B5
Perkin's Rents SW1P....148 B4
Perryn Road SE16....150 E7
Petersham Mews SW7....146 D4
Petersham Place SW7....146 C4
Peter Street W1F....144 B7
Peto Place NW1....143 L4
Petticoat Lane E1....150 B2
Petty France SW1H....148 A3
Petty Wales EC3R....150 A4
Petyward SW3....147 G6
Phelp Street SE17....149 L7
Phene Street SW3....147 G8
Phillimore Walk W8....146 A3
Philpot Lane EC3M....145 M7
Philpot Street E1....150 E2
Phipp's Mews SW1W....147 L5
Phipp Street EC2A....145 M3
Phoenix Place WC1X....144 F3
Phoenix Road NW1....144 B1
Phoenix Street WC2H....144 C6
Piccadilly W1J....143 L8
Piccadilly Arcade SW1Y....147 M1
Piccadilly Circus W1B....144 A8
Piccadilly Circus ⊖ W1J....144 B8

Pickard Street EC1V....145 J2
Picton Place W1U....143 K6
Pier Head E1W....150 E6
Pigott Street E14....151 M3
Pilgrimage Street SE1....149 L3
Pimlico ⊖ SW1V....148 B6
Pimlico Road SW1W....147 J6
Pinchin Street E1....150 D3
Pindar Street EC2A....145 M4
Pindock Mews W9....142 B3
Pine Street EC1R....144 F3
Pitfield Street N1....145 M1
Pitsea Street E1....151 H3
Pitt's Head Mews W1J....147 K2
Pitt Street W8....146 A2
Pixley Street E14....151 L2
Platina Street * EC2A....145 L3
Plover Way SE16....151 K8
Plumbers Row E1....150 D2
Plumtree Court EC4A....145 G5
Plympton Street NW8....142 F4
Pocock Street SE1....149 H2
Poland Street W1F....144 A6
Pollen Street W1S....143 L7
Pollitt Drive NW8....142 E3
Polperro Mews SE11....149 G5
Polygon Road NW1....144 B1
Pond Place SW3....146 F6
Ponler Street E1....150 E3
Ponsonby Place SW1P....148 C6
Ponsonby Terrace SW1P....148 C6
Ponton Road * SW1V....148 B8
Pont Street SW1X....147 H4
Poolmans Street SE16....151 H6
Pope Street SE1....150 B7
Poplar Place W2....142 B7
Poppin's Court EC4A....145 H6
Porchester Gardens W2....142 B7
Porchester Gate W2....142 C8
Porchester Place W2....143 G6
Porchester Road W2....142 B5
Porchester Square W2....142 B6
Porchester Terrace W2....142 C7
Porchester Terrace North W2....142 C6
Porlock Street SE1....149 L3
Porter Street NW1....143 H4
Porteus Road W2....142 D5
Portland Place W1B....143 K4
Portland Place W1B....143 L5
Portland Square E1W....150 E5
Portland Street SE17....149 L7
Portman Close W1H....143 J6
Portman Mews South W1H....143 J6
Portman Square W1H....143 J6
Portman Street W1H....143 J6
Portpool Lane EC1N....144 F4
Portsea Place W2....143 G6
Portsmouth Street WC2A....144 E6
Portsoken Street E1....150 B3
Portugal Street WC2A....144 E6
Potier Street SE1....149 L4
Potters Fields SE1....150 B6
Pottery Street SE16....150 F7
Poultry EC2V....145 K6
Powis Place WC1N....144 D4
Praed Mews W2....142 E6
Praed Street W2....142 E6
Pratt Walk SE1....148 E5
Premier Place E14....151 M4
Prescot Street E1....150 C3
Preston Close SE1....149 M5
Price's Street SE1....149 H1
Prideaux Place WC1X....144 F2
Primrose Street EC2A....150 A1
Prince Albert Road NW8....142 F1
Prince Consort Road SW7....146 D3
Princelet Street E1....150 C1
Prince of Wales Gate SW7....146 F4
Princes Arcade SW1Y....144 A8
Prince's Gardens SW7....146 E3
Prince's Gate Mews SW7....146 E4
Princes Riverside
   Road SE16....151 H5
Prince's Square W2....142 A7
Princess Road NW6....142 A1
Princess Street SE1....149 H4
Princes Street W1B....143 L6
Prince's Street EC2R....145 L6
Princeton Street WC1R....144 E5
Prioress Street SE1....149 L4
Priory Green Estate N1....144 E1
Priory Walk SW10....146 D7
Proctor Street WC1V....144 E5
Prospect Place E1W....151 G5
Prospect Street SE16....150 E7
Provident Court W1K....143 J7
Provost Street N1....145 L1
Prusom Street E1W....150 F5
Pudding Lane EC3R....145 M7
Pumphouse Mews E1....150 D3
Purbrook Street SE1....150 B7
Purcell Street N1....145 M1
Purchese Street NW1....144 B1

Q

Quebec Way SE16....151 J7
Queen Anne's Gate SW1H....148 B3
Queen Anne Street W1G....143 K5
Queen Elizabeth Street SE1....150 B6
Queen Mother Gate W2....147 J2
Queensborough Terrace W2....142 C7
Queensbury Place SW7....146 E5
Queen's Gardens W2....142 C7
Queen's Gate SW7....146 D3
Queen's Gate SW7....146 D4
Queen's Gate Gardens SW7....146 D5
Queen's Gate Mews SW7....146 D4
Queen's Gate Place SW7....146 D4
Queen's Gate
   Place Mews SW7....146 D4
Queen's Gate Terrace SW7....146 C4
Queen's Mews W2....142 B7
Queen Square WC1N....144 D4
Queen's Row SE17....149 K7
Queen Street EC4N....145 K7
Queen Street W1J....147 L1
Queen Street Place EC4R....145 K7
Queen's Walk SE1....150 A5
Queen's Walk SW1A....147 M2
Queensway W2....142 B6
Queensway ⊖ W2....142 B7
Queen Victoria Street EC4V....145 J7
Quick Street N1....145 H1

R

Raby Street E14....151 K2
Radcliffe Road SE1....150 B8
Radcot Street SE11....149 G7
Radnor Mews W2....142 E6
Radnor Place W2....142 F6
Radnor Street EC1V....145 K3
Radnor Walk SW3....147 G7
Railway Approach SE1....149 L1
Railway Avenue SE16....151 G6
Railway Street N1....144 D1
Raine Street E1W....150 F5
Ralston Street SW3....147 H7
Ramillies Place W1F....143 M6
Ramillies Street W1F....143 M6
Rampart Street E1....150 E2
Rampayne Street SW1V....148 B6
Randall Road SE11....148 D6
Randall Row SE11....148 E6
Randolph Avenue W9....142 B1
Randolph Crescent W9....142 C3
Randolph Gardens NW6....142 B1
Randolph Mews W9....142 D4
Randolph Road W9....142 C4
Ranelagh Grove SW1W....147 K6
Ranelagh Road SW1V....148 A7
Rangoon Street * EC3N....150 B3
Ranston Street NW8....142 F4
Raphael Street SW7....147 G3
Ratcliffe Cross Street E1W....151 J3
Ratcliffe Lane E14....151 J3
Rathbone Place W1T....144 B5
Rathbone Street W1T....144 A5
Raven Row E1....150 F1
Ravensdon Street SE11....149 G7
Ravey Street EC2A....145 M3
Rawlings Street SW3....147 G5
Rawstorne Street EC1V....145 H2
Ray Street EC1R....145 G4
Reardon Place E1W....150 F5
Reardon Street E1W....150 E5
Rectory Square E1....151 H1
Redan Place W2....142 B6
Redburn Street SW3....147 G7
Redcastle Close E1W....151 G4
Redcliffe Gardens SW10....146 B7
Redcliffe Mews SW10....146 C7
Redcliffe Place SW10....146 C8
Redcliffe Road SW10....146 C7
Redcliffe Square SW10....146 B7
Redcliffe Street SW10....146 B8
Redcross Way SE1....149 K2
Redesdale Street SW3....147 G7
Redfield Lane SW5....146 A6
Redhill Street NW1....143 L1
Red Lion Row SE5....149 K8
Red Lion Square WC1R....144 E5
Red Lion Street WC2B....144 E5
Redman's Road E1....151 G1
Red Place W1K....143 J7
Redriff Road SE16....151 J8
Redworth Street SE11....149 G6
Reeves Mews W1K....143 J8
Regal Close E1....150 D1
Regan Way N1....145 M1
Regency Street SW1P....148 B5
Regent Place W1B....144 A7
Regent's Park ⊖ W1B....143 L4
Regent's Park NW1....143 J1
Regent's Park Estate NW1....143 L2
Regent Square WC1H....144 D2
Regent Street SW1Y....144 B8
Regent Street W1S....143 M7
Relton Mews SW7....147 G4
Remington Street N1....145 H1
Remnant Street WC2A....144 E6
Renforth Street SE16....151 G7
Renfrew Road SE11....149 H5
Rennie Street SE1....149 H1
Rephidim Street SE1....149 M4
Repton Street E14....151 K2
Reveley Square SE16....151 K7
Rex Place W1K....143 J8
Rhodeswell Road E14....151 L2
Rich Street E14....151 M3
Rickett Street SW6....146 A8
Ridgemount Street WC1E....144 B4
Ridgemount Gardens WC1E....144 B4
Riding House Street W1W....143 M5
Riley Road SE1....150 B7
Ripley's Believe It or Not! W1J....144 B8
Risborough Street SE1....149 J2
Risdon Street SE16....151 G7
Rissinghill Street N1....144 F1
River Street EC1R....144 F2
Rivington Street EC2A....145 M3
Robert Adam Street W1U....143 J6
Roberts Close SE16....151 J7
Robert Street NW1....143 L2
Rochester Row SW1P....148 A5
Rochester Street SW1P....148 B5
Rockingham Street SE1....149 J4
Rocliffe Street N1....145 H1
Roding Mews E1W....150 D5
Rodmarton Street W1U....143 H5
Rodney Place SE17....149 K5
Rodney Road SE17....149 K5
Rodney Street N1....144 E1
Roger Street WC1N....144 E4
Roland Gardens SW7....146 D6
Roland Way SE17....149 L7
Romford Street E1....150 E2
Romilly Street W1D....144 B7
Romney Street SW1P....148 C5
Rood Lane EC3M....145 M7
Ropemaker Road SE16....151 K7
Ropemaker Street EC2Y....145 L4
Roper Lane SE1....150 B7
Rope Street SE16....151 K8
Rope Walk Gardens E1....150 E2
Rosary Gardens SW7....146 D6
Roscoe Street EC1Y....145 K4
Rose Alley SE1....145 K8
Rosemoor Street SW3....147 G6
Rose Street WC2E....144 C7
Rossmore Road NW1....143 G3
Rotary Street SE1....149 H3
Rotherhithe ⊖ SE16....151 G6
Rotherhithe Old Road SE16....151 J6
Rotherhithe Street SE16....151 J4
Rotherhithe Tunnel SE16....151 J5
Rothsay Street SE1....149 M4
Rotten Row W2....146 F2

Rouel Road SE16....150 C8
Roupell Street SE1....149 G2
Royal Albert Hall SW7....146 E3
Royal Avenue SW3....147 H6
Royal Hospital Road SW3....147 H7
Royal Mint Street E1....150 C4
Royal Oak ⊖ W2....142 B5
Royal Oak Yard SE1....150 A7
Royal Opera House WC2E....144 D7
Royal Road SE17....149 H8
Royal Street SE1....148 E3
Rudolph Road NW6....142 A1
Rugby Street WC1N....144 E4
Rum Close E1W....150 F4
Rupack Street SE16....150 F7
Rupert Street W1D....144 B7
Rushworth Street SE1....149 H2
Russell Court SW1A....148 A2
Russell Square WC1B....144 C4
Russell Square ⊖ WC1B....144 D4
Russell Street WC2B....144 D7
Russia Dock Road SE16....151 K6
Rutherford Street SW1P....148 B5
Rutland Gardens SW7....147 G3
Rutland Gate SW7....146 F4
Rutland Mews SW7....146 F4
Rutland Street SW7....146 F4
Ryder Street SW1Y....148 A1

S

Sackville Street W1S....144 A8
Saffron Hill EC1N....145 G4
Saffron Street EC1N....145 G4
Sail Street SE11....148 F5
St Agnes Place SE11....149 G8
St Alban's Grove W8....146 B4
St Alban's Street SW1Y....144 B8
St Alphage Garden EC2Y....145 K5
St Andrews Hill EC4V....145 H7
St Andrew's Place NW1....143 L3
St Andrew Street EC4A....145 G5
St Anne's Court W1F....144 B6
St Ann's Street SW1P....148 C4
St Anselm's Place W1K....143 K7
St Barnabas Street SW1W....147 K6
St Botolph Street EC3N....150 B2
St Bride Street EC4A....145 G6
St Chad's Street WC1H....144 D2
St Clare Street EC3N....150 B3
St Clements Lane WC2A....144 E6
St Cross Street EC1N....145 G4
St Dunstan's Hill EC3R....145 M8
St Dunstan's Lane EC3R....145 M7
St Elmos Road SE16....151 J7
St Ermin's Hill SW1H....148 B3
St George's Circus SE1....149 H3
St George's Drive SW1V....147 M6
St George's Estate E1....150 D3
St George's Lane * EC3R....145 M7
St George's Road SE1....149 G3
St George's Square SW1V....148 B7
St George Street W1S....143 L7
St Giles High Street WC2H....144 C6
St Helen's Place EC3A....145 M6
St James Market * SW1Y....144 B8
St James's Park ⊖ SW1H....148 B3
St James's Park SW1A....148 B3
St James's Place SW1A....147 M2
St James's Road SE16....150 D8
St James's Square SW1Y....148 A1
St James's Street SW1A....147 M1
St James Walk EC1R....145 G3
St John's Lane EC1M....145 H4
St John's Place EC1M....145 H4
St John's Square EC1V....145 H4
St John Street EC1V....145 H2
St John's Wood High Street NW8....142 F1
St John's Wood Road NW8....142 E3
St Katharine's Way E1W....150 C5
St Leonard's Terrace SW3....147 H7
St Loo Avenue SW3....147 G8
St Luke's Close EC1V....145 K3
St Luke's Street SW3....146 F6
St Manningtree E1....150 C2
St Mark Street E1....150 C3
St Martin's Lane WC2N....144 C7
St Martin's le Grand EC1A....145 J6
St Martin's Street WC2N....144 C8
St Mary at Hill EC3R....145 M8
St Mary Axe EC3A....150 A3
St Marychurch Street SE16....150 F7
St Mary's Gardens SE11....149 G5
St Mary's Terrace W2....142 D4
St Mary's Walk SE11....149 G5
St Matthew Street SW1P....148 B4
St Michael's Street W2....142 E6
St Olav's Square SE16....150 F7
St Oswald's Place SE11....148 E7
St Oswulf Street * SW1P....148 C6
St Pancras International ⊖ N1C....144 C1
St Paul's ⊖ EC1A....145 J6
St Paul's Avenue SE16....151 J5
St Paul's Cathedral EC4M....145 J6
St Paul's Churchyard EC4M....145 J6
St Paul's Way E1....151 L1
St Petersburgh Mews W2....142 B7
St Petersburgh Place W2....142 B7
St Saviours Wharf SE1....150 C6
St Stephen's Gardens W2....142 A5
St Swithin's Lane EC4N....145 L7
St Thomas Street SE1....149 L2
St Vincent Street W1U....143 J5
Salamanca Street SE1....148 D6
Salem Road W2....142 B7
Sale Place W2....142 F5
Salisbury Court EC4Y....145 G6
Salisbury Place W1H....143 H4
Salisbury Street NW8....142 F4
Salmon Lane E14....151 J2
Salter Road SE16....151 K5
Salter Street E14....151 M4
Samford Street NW8....142 F4
Sampson Street E1W....150 D5
Sancroft Street SE11....148 F6
Sandland Street WC1R....144 E5
Sandpiper Close SE16....151 L6
Sandwich Street WC1H....144 C2
Sandy's Row E1....150 B1
Sans Walk EC1R....145 G3
Sardinia Street WC2A....144 E6
Savage Gardens EC3N....150 A4
Savile Row W1S....143 M7
Savoy Hill WC2R....144 E8

Savoy Place WC2R....144 D8
Savoy Street WC2E....144 E7
Sawyer Street SE1....149 J2
Scala Street W1T....144 A5
Scandrett Street E1W....150 E5
Scarborough Street E1....150 C3
Scarsdale Villas W8....146 A4
Schooner Close * SE16....151 H6
Science Museum SW7....146 E4
Scoresby Street SE1....149 H2
Scotch House Junction SW1X....147 H3
Scotland Place SW1A....148 C1
Scott Ellis Gardens NW8....142 E2
Scott Lidgett Crescent SE16....150 D7
Scrutton Street EC2A....145 M3
Seaford Street WC1H....144 D2
Seagrave Road SW6....146 A8
Sea Life London Aquarium SE1....148 E3
Searles Road SE1....149 L5
Sebastian Street EC1V....145 H2
Secker Street SE1....148 F2
Sedan Way SE17....149 M6
Sedding Street SW1X....147 J5
Seddon Street WC1X....144 E3
Seething Lane EC3N....150 A4
Sekforde Street EC1R....145 H3
Selfridges W1A....143 J6
Selsey Street E14....151 M1
Selwood Place SW7....146 E6
Semley Place SW1W....147 K6
Senior Street W2....142 B4
Senrab Street E1....151 H2
Serle Street WC2A....144 F6
Serpentine Bridge W2....146 E1
Serpentine Road W2....146 F2
Seth Street SE16....151 G7
Settles Street E1....150 D2
Seven Dials WC2H....144 C6
Seville Street SW1X....147 H3
Sevington Street W9....142 A3
Seward Street EC1V....145 J3
Seymour Mews W1H....143 J6
Seymour Place W1H....143 G5
Seymour Street W1H....143 H6
Seymour Street W2....143 G7
Seymour Walk SW10....146 C7
Shad Thames SE1....150 B6
Shad Thames SE1....150 C6
Shadwell ⊖ E1....150 F3
Shadwell Gardens E1....150 F3
Shaftesbury Avenue W1D....144 B7
Shaftesbury Avenue WC2H....144 C6
Shaftesbury Street N1....145 K1
Shakespeare's Globe SE1....145 J8
Shand Street SE1....150 A6
Sharsted Street SE17....149 H7
Shaw Crescent E14....151 K2
Shawfield Street SW3....147 G7
Sheffield Terrace W8....146 A2
Sheldon Square W2....142 D5
Shelmerdine Close E3....151 M1
Shelton Street WC2H....144 D6
Shepherdess Walk N1....145 K1
Shepherd Street W1J....147 K1
Sheraton Street W1F....144 B6
Sherborne Lane EC4N....145 L7
Sherwood Street W1D....144 A7
Ship and Mermaid Row SE1....149 M2
Shipwright Road SE16....151 K7
Shirland Road W9....142 A3
Shoe Lane EC4A....145 G5
Shorter Street EC3N....150 B4
Shorts Gardens WC2H....144 C6
Short Street SE1....149 G2
Shoulder of Mutton Alley E14....151 K4
Shouldham Street W1H....143 G5
Shroton Street NW1....142 F4
Siddons Lane W1H....143 H4
Sidmouth Street WC1N....144 D3
Sidney Square E1....150 F2
Sidney Street E1....150 F1
Silex Street SE1....149 H3
Silk Street EC2Y....145 K4
Silver Walk SE16....151 K5
Silvester Street SE1....149 K3
Singer Street EC2A....145 L3
Sir John Soane's Museum WC2A....144 E5
Sir Simon Milton Square SW1V....147 L4
Skinner Place * SW1W....147 J6
Skinners Lane EC4V....145 K7
Skinner Street EC1R....145 G3
Slippers Place SE16....150 F8
Sloane Avenue SW3....147 G6
Sloane Court East SW3....147 J6
Sloane Court West SW3....147 J6
Sloane Gardens SW1W....147 J6
Sloane Square ⊖ SW1W....147 J6
Sloane Street SW1X....147 H5
Sloane Terrace SW1X....147 J5
Smeaton Street E1W....150 E5
Smithfield Street EC1A....145 H5
Smith Square SW1P....148 C4
Smith Street SW3....147 G7
Smith Terrace SW3....147 G7
Smithy Street E1....151 G1
Snowden Street EC2A....145 M4
Snow Hill EC1A....145 H5
Snowsfields SE1....149 L2
Soho Square W1D....144 B6
Soho Street W1D....144 B6
Somerford Way SE16....151 K7
Somers Crescent W2....142 F6
Somerset House WC2R....144 E7
Somerstown Estate NW1....144 A1
Sondes Street SE17....149 L7
South & West Africa Gate SW1A....148 A3
Southall Place SE1....149 L3
Southampton Buildings WC2A....144 F5
Southampton Place WC1A....144 D5
Southampton Row WC1B....144 D4
Southampton Street WC2E....144 D7
South Audley Street W1K....143 K8
South Carriage Drive SW1X....147 H3
South Carriage Drive SW7....146 F3
South Eaton Place SW1W....147 J5
Southern Street N1....144 E1
South Kensington ⊖ SW7....146 E4
South Kensington SW7....146 E5
South Lambeth Road SW8....148 D8
South Molton Lane W1K....143 K7
South Molton Street W1K....143 K7
South Parade SW3....146 E7
South Place EC2M....145 L5
South Sea Street SE16....151 L8
South Square WC1R....144 F5

South Street W1K 147 J1
South Tenter Street E1 150 C3
South Terrace SW7 146 F5
Southwark ⊖ SE1 149 H2
Southwark Bridge SE1 145 K8
Southwark Bridge Road SE1 149 J3
Southwark Park Road SE16 150 E8
Southwark Street SE1 149 H1
Southwell Gardens SW7 146 C5
South Wharf Road W2 142 E6
Southwick Mews W2 142 F6
Southwick Place W2 142 F6
Southwick Street W2 142 F6
Sovereign Close E1W 150 F4
Sovereign Crescent SE16 151 J4
Spanish Place W1U 143 J5
Spa Road SE16 150 C8
Spear Mews SW5 146 A6
Spelman Street E1 150 C1
Spence Close SE16 151 K7
Spencer Street EC1V 145 H2
Spenser Street SW1E 148 A4
Spert Street E14 151 J4
Spital Square E1 150 A1
Spring Gardens SW1A 148 C1
Spring Street W2 142 E6
Spurgeon Street SE1 149 L4
Spur Road SE1 148 F3
Stables Way SE11 148 F7
Stable Yard Road SW1A 148 A2
Stacey Street WC2H 144 C6
Stafford Place SW1E 147 M3
Stafford Road NW6 142 A2
Stafford Street W1S 143 M8
Stafford Terrace W8 146 A3
Stainer Street SE1 149 L2
Staining Lane EC2V 145 K6
Stainsby Road E14 151 M2
Stalham Street SE16 150 F8
Stamford Street SE1 149 G1
Stanford Place SE1 149 M6
Stanford Road W8 146 B4
Stanford Street * SW1V 148 B6
Stanhope Close * SE16 151 H6
Stanhope Gardens SW7 146 D5
Stanhope Gate W1K 147 K1
Stanhope Mews W7 146 D5
Stanhope Mews East SW7 146 D5
Stanhope Mews West SW7 146 D5
Stanhope Place W2 143 G7
Stanhope Place Gate W2 143 G7
Stanhope Row W1J 147 K1
Stanhope Street NW1 143 M1
Stanhope Terrace W2 142 E7
Stannary Street SE11 149 G7
Staples Close SE16 151 J5
Staple Street SE1 149 L3
Starcross Street NW1 144 A2
Star Street W2 142 F6
Station Approach SE1 148 F3
Stave Yard Road SE16 151 J4
Stead Street SE17 149 K6
Steedman Street SE17 149 J5
Steel's Lane E1 151 G3
Steeres Way SE16 151 K7
Stephenson Way NW1 144 A3
Stephen Street W1T 144 B5
Stepney Green E1 151 H1
Stepney High Street E1 151 J1
Stepney Way E1 150 E1
Sterling Street SW7 147 G3
Stevedore Street E1W 150 E5
Stevens Street SE1 150 A7
Steward Street * E1 150 B1
Stewart's Grove SW3 146 F6
Stew Lane EC4V 145 J7
Stillington Street SW1P 148 A5
Stockholm Way E1W 150 D5
Stocks Place E14 151 M3
Stone Buildings WC2A 144 F5
Stonecutter Street EC4A 145 G6
Stoney Lane E1 150 B2
Stoney Street SE1 149 K1
Stopford Road SE17 149 J7
Store Street WC1E 144 B5
Storey's Gate SW1H 148 C3
Storks Road SE16 150 D8
Stoughton Close SE11 148 E6
Stourcliffe Street W1H 143 G6
Strafford Street E14 151 M6
Strand WC2R 144 D8
Stratford Place W1C 143 K6
Stratford Road W8 146 A5
Stratheam Place W2 142 F7
Stratton Street W1J 147 L1
Strutton Ground SW1P 148 B4
Strype Street * E1 150 B2
Stuart Road NW6 142 A2
Stukeley Street WC2B 144 D6
Sturgeon Street SE17 149 J7
Sturge Street SE1 149 J3
Sturt Street N1 145 K1
Stutfield Street E1 150 D3
Sudley Street N1 145 H1
Sudrey Street SE1 149 J3
Suffolk Lane EC4V 145 L7
Suffolk Street SW1Y 144 B8
Sugar Lane SE16 150 D7
Sugar Quay Walk EC3R 150 A4
Sullivan Road SE11 149 G5
Summercourt Road E1 151 G2
Summers Street EC1R 144 F4
Sumner Place SW7 146 E6
Sumner Street SE1 149 J1
Sunderland Terrace W2 142 A6
Sun Passage SE16 150 D8
Sun Street EC2M 145 M4
Sun Street Passage EC2M 145 M5
Surrendale Place W9 142 A4
Surrey Quays Road SE16 151 H7
Surrey Row SE1 149 H2
Surrey Square SE17 149 M6
Surrey Street WC2E 144 E7
Surrey Water Road SE16 151 H6
Sussex Gardens W2 142 E6
Sussex Mews East W2 142 E7
Sussex Mews NW1 143 H3
Sussex Place W2 142 E6
Sussex Square W2 142 E7
Sussex Street SW1V 147 L7
Sutherland Avenue W9 142 A4
Sutherland Row SW1V 147 L6
Sutherland Square SE17 149 J7
Sutherland Street SW1V 147 L7
Sutton Row W1D 144 B6
Sutton Street E1 151 G3

Suttons Way EC1Y 145 K4
Swain Street NW8 142 F3
Swallow Place W1B 143 L6
Swallow Street W1B 144 A8
Swan Lane EC4R 145 L8
Swan Mead SE1 149 M4
Swan Street SE1 149 K3
Swan Road SE16 151 G6
Swan Walk SW3 147 H8
Swedenborg Gardens E1 150 E4
Sweeney Crescent SE1 150 C7
Swinton Street WC1X 144 E2
Sydney Place SW7 146 F6
Sydney Street SW3 146 F6
Symons Street SW3 147 H6

T

Tabard Gardens Estate SE1 149 L3
Tabard Street SE1 149 L3
Tabernacle Street EC2A 145 L3
Tachbrook Street SW1V 148 A6
Talbot Road W2 142 A6
Talbot Square W2 142 E6
Talbot Yard SE1 149 L2
Tallis Street EC4Y 145 G7
Tamworth Street SW6 146 A8
Tanner Street SE1 150 A7
Taplow Street N1 145 K1
Tarling Street E1 150 F3
Tarver Road SE17 149 H7
Tatum Street SE17 149 M6
Taunton Place NW1 143 G3
Tavistock Place WC1H 144 C3
Tavistock Square WC1H 144 C3
Tavistock Street WC2E 144 D7
Taviton Street WC1H 144 B3
Teak Close SE16 151 K6
Tedworth Square SW3 147 H7
Telford Terrace SW1V 147 M7
Temeraire Street SE16 151 G6
Temple ⊖ WC2R 144 F7
Temple Avenue EC4Y 145 G7
Temple Lane EC4Y 145 G7
Temple Place WC2R 144 F7
Templeton Place SW5 146 A5
Tench Street E1W 150 E5
Tenniel Close W2 142 C7
Tennis Street SE1 149 L2
Tenterden Street W1S 143 L6
Tenterground E1 150 B1
Teredo Street SE16 151 J8
Terminus Place SW1V 147 L4
Thame Road SE16 151 H6
Thanet Street WC1H 144 C2
Thavies Inn EC4A 145 G6
Thayer Street W1U 143 K5
The Arches WC2N 144 D8
The Boltons SW10 146 C7
The British Library NW1 144 C2
The British Museum WC1B 144 C5
The Broad Walk W2 142 B8
The Broad Walk W8 146 C2
The Cut SE1 149 G2
Theed Street SE1 149 G2
The Flower Walk W2 146 D3
The Grange SE1 150 B8
The Highway E1W 150 E4
The Little Boltons SW10 146 C7
The Mall SW1A 148 C2
The Mitre E14 151 L3
The Monument EC3R 145 L7
The National Gallery WC2N 144 C8
Theobald's Road WC1X 144 E4
Theobald Street SE1 149 L5
The Oval (Surrey County
   Cricket Ground) SE11 148 F8
The Shard SE1 149 L2
The Vale SW3 146 E8
Thirleby Road SW1P 148 A4
Thomas More Street E1W 150 D4
Thomas Road E14 151 M2
Thoresby Street N1 145 K1
Thorney Street SW1P 148 C5
Thornton Place W1H 143 H4
Thrale Street SE1 149 K1
Thrawl Street E1 150 C1
Threadneedle Street EC2R 145 L6
Three Colt Street E14 151 L6
Three Oak Lane SE1 150 B6
Throgmorton Avenue EC2N 145 L6
Throgmorton Street EC2N 145 L6
Thurland Road SE16 150 D8
Thurloe Place SW7 146 F5
Thurloe Square SW7 146 F5
Thurloe Street SW7 146 F5
Tichbourne Row W2 142 F6
Tiller Road E14 151 M8
Tillman Street E1 150 E3
Tilney Street W1J 147 K1
Timber Pond Road SE16 151 J4
Tinsley Road E1 151 G1
Tinworth Street SE11 148 D6
Tisdall Place SE17 149 L6
Tite Street SW3 147 H8
Tiverton Street SE1 149 J4
Token House Yard EC2R 145 L6
Tolmer's Terrace E1 151 K2
Tolmin Street SE1 149 J3
Tonbridge Street WC1H 144 D2
Tooley Street SE1 149 L1
Tooley Street SE1 150 B6
Tor Gardens W8 146 A2
Torquay Street W2 142 A5
Torrens Street EC1V 145 G1
Torrington Place E1W 150 D5
Torrington Place WC1E 144 B4
Torrington Square WC1E 144 B4
Tothill Street SW1H 148 B3
Tottenham Court Road W1T 144 A4
Tottenham Court Road ⊖ W1D 144 B6
Tottenham Street W1T 144 A5
Toulmin Street SE1 149 J3
Tower Bridge EC3N 150 B5
Tower Bridge Approach EC3N 150 B5
Tower Bridge Road SE1 150 A7
Tower Bridge Wharf E1W 150 C5
Tower Gateway ⊖ EC3N 150 B4
Tower Hill EC3N 150 B4
Tower Hill ⊖ EC3N 150 B4
Tower of London EC3N 150 B4

Tower Place EC3R 150 A4
Tower Street WC2H 144 C7
Townsend Street SE17 149 M5
Toynbee Street E1 150 B1
Trafalgar Gardens E1 151 H1
Trafalgar Square WC2N 144 C8
Trafalgar Street SE17 149 L7
Transept Street NW1 142 F5
Trebeck Street W1J 147 L1
Trebovir Road SW5 146 A6
Tregunter Road SW10 146 C7
Trenton Road SE16 150 E8
Tresham Crescent NW8 142 F3
Trevor Place SW7 147 G3
Trevor Square SW7 147 G3
Trevor Street SW7 147 G3
Trinidad Street E14 151 M4
Trinity Church Square SE1 149 K3
Trinity Square EC3N 150 B4
Trinity Street SE1 149 K3
Trump Street EC2V 145 K6
Tudor Street EC4Y 145 G7
Tufton Street SW1P 148 C4
Tunnel Road SE16 151 G6
Turks Row SW3 147 J6
Turner's Road E3 151 L2
Turner Street E1 150 E2
Turnmill Street EC1N 145 G4
Turpentine Lane SW1V 147 L7
Turquand Street SE17 149 K6
Tyers Gate SE1 149 M3
Tyers Street SE11 148 E7
Tyers Terrace SE11 148 E7
Tyron Street SW3 147 H6
Tysoe Street EC1R 145 G3

U

Udall Street SW1P 148 A5
Ufford Street SE1 149 G2
Ulster Place NW1 143 K4
Umberston Street E1 150 E2
Undershaft EC3A 150 A2
Underwood Road N1 145 K2
Underwood Street N1 145 K1
Union Street SE1 149 H2
University Street WC1E 144 A4
Upbrook Mews W2 142 D6
Upper Belgrave Street SW1X 147 K4
Upper Berkeley Street W1H 143 H6
Upper Brook Street W1K 143 J7
Upper Cheyne Row SW3 146 F8
Upper Grosvenor Street W1K 143 J8
Upper Ground SE1 148 F1
Upper Harley Street NW1 143 K3
Upper James Street W1F 144 A7
Upper John Street W1F 144 A7
Upper Marsh SE1 148 E3
Upper Montagu Street W1H 143 H5
Upper St Martin's Lane WC2H 144 C7
Upper Tachbrook Street SW1V 148 A5
Upper Thames Street EC4V 145 J7
Upper Wimpole Street W1G 143 K4
Upper Woburn Place WC1H 144 B2
Urlwin Street SE5 149 J8
Uxbridge Street W8 146 A1

V

Valentine Place SE1 149 G3
Vandon Passage SW1H 148 A3
Vandon Street SW1H 148 A4
Varden Street E1 150 E2
Varndell Street NW1 143 M2
Vauban Street SE16 150 C8
Vaughan Street SE16 151 L7
Vaughan Way E1W 150 D5
Vauxhall ⇄ ⊖ SW8 148 D7
Vauxhall Bridge SW1V 148 C7
Vauxhall Bridgefoot SE1 148 D7
Vauxhall Bridge Road SW1V 147 M5
Vauxhall Cross SE1 148 D7
Vauxhall Grove SW8 148 D8
Vauxhall Street SE11 148 E6
Vauxhall Walk SE11 148 E6
Venables Street W2 142 E4
Vere Street W1G 143 K6
Vernon Place WC1A 144 D5
Vernon Rise WC1X 144 E2
Verulam Street WC1X 144 F4
Vestry Street N1 145 L2
Victoria ⇄ ⊖ SW1V 147 L5
Victoria & Albert Museum SW7 146 F4
Victoria Embankment SW1A 148 D2
Victoria Embankment WC2R 144 F7
Victoria Gate W2 142 F7
Victoria Road W8 146 C4
Victoria Square SW1W 147 L4
Victoria Street SW1E 147 L4
Victory Place SE17 149 K5
Victory Way SE16 151 K7
Vigo Street W1S 143 M8
Villa Street SE17 149 L7
Villiers Street WC2N 144 D8
Vincent Close SE16 151 K7
Vincent Square SW1P 148 B5
Vincent Street SW1P 148 B5
Vincent Terrace N1 145 H1
Vince Street EC1V 145 L2
Vine Court E1 150 D1
Vinegar Street E1W 150 E5
Vine Hill EC1R 144 F4
Vine Lane SE1 150 A6
Violet Hill NW8 142 C1
Virgil Street SE1 148 E4
Virginia Street E1W 150 D4
Viscount Street EC2Y 145 J4

W

Wadding Street SE17 149 K6
Wakefield Street WC1H 144 D3
Wakeling Street E14 151 J3
Wakley Street EC1V 145 H2
Walbrook EC4N 145 L7
Walcorde Avenue SE17 149 K6
Walcot Square SE11 149 G5
Walden Street E1 150 E2
Waley Street E1 151 J1

Wallwood Street E14 151 M1
Walnut Tree Walk SE11 148 F5
Walpole Street SW3 147 H6
Walter Terrace E1 151 H2
Walton Place SW3 147 H4
Walton Street SW3 147 G4
Walworth Place SE17 149 K7
Walworth Road SE17 149 J5
Wandsworth Road SW8 148 C8
Wansey Street SE17 149 J6
Wapping ⊖ E1W 150 F5
Wapping High Street E1W 150 E6
Wapping Lane E1W 150 F4
Wapping Wall E1W 151 G5
Warden's Grove SE1 149 J2
Wardour Street W1F 144 B6
Warner Street EC1R 144 F4
Warren Street W1T 143 M4
Warren Street ⊖ NW1 143 M3
Warrington Crescent W9 142 C3
Warrington Gardens W9 142 C4
Warwick Avenue W9 142 B3
Warwick Avenue ⊖ W9 142 C4
Warwick Crescent W2 142 C5
Warwick House Street SW1Y 148 B1
Warwick Lane EC4M 145 H6
Warwick Place W9 142 C4
Warwick Road SW5 146 A6
Warwick Row SW1E 147 L4
Warwick Square SW1V 147 M6
Warwick Street W1B 144 A7
Warwick Way SW1V 147 L6
Waterhouse Square EC1N 145 G5
Waterloo ⇄ ⊖ SE1 148 F2
Waterloo Bridge SE1 148 E1
Waterloo Bridge WC2R 144 E8
Waterloo East ⇄ SE1 149 G2
Waterloo Place SW1Y 148 B1
Waterloo Road SE1 148 F1
Waterloo Street SE1 149 G2
Waterman Way E1W 150 E5
Waterside Close SE16 150 D7
Watling Street EC4N 145 K7
Watney Street E1 150 F3
Watts Street E1W 150 E5
Waveney Close E1W 150 D5
Waverton Street W1J 143 K8
Weavers Lane SE1 150 A6
Webber Row SE1 149 G3
Webber Street SE1 149 H3
Webb Street SE1 150 A8
Webster Road SE16 150 D8
Weighhouse Street W1K 143 K7
Welbeck Street W1G 143 K5
Welbeck Way W1G 143 K6
Welland Mews E1W 150 E5
Wellclose Square E1 150 D4
Wellesley Street E1 151 H2
Wellesley Terrace N1 145 K2
Wellington Arch W1J 147 K2
Wellington Place NW8 142 E2
Wellington Road NW8 142 E1
Wellington Street WC2E 144 D7
Wells Mews W1T 144 A5
Wells Street W1T 144 A5
Wells Way SE5 149 M8
Wenlock Road N1 145 K1
Wenlock Street N1 145 K1
Wentworth Street E1 150 B2
Werrington Street NW1 144 A1
Wesley Street W1G 143 K5
West Arbour Street E1 151 G2
Westbourne Crescent W2 142 D7
Westbourne Gardens W2 142 B6
Westbourne Gate W2 142 E7
Westbourne Grove W2 142 A6
Westbourne Grove Terrace W2 142 B6
Westbourne Park Road W2 142 A5
Westbourne Park Villas W2 142 A5
Westbourne Street W2 142 E7
Westbourne Terrace W2 142 D6
Westbourne Terrace Mews W2 142 C6
Westbourne Terrace Road W2 142 C5
West Brompton ⇄ ⊖ SW5 146 A7
West Carriage Drive W2 146 E2
Westcott Road SE17 149 H8
West Cromwell Road SW5 146 A5
Western Place SE16 151 G6
Westferry ⊖ E14 151 M4
Westferry Circus E14 151 M5
Westferry Road E14 151 M5
West Gardens E1W 150 F4
Westgate Terrace SW10 146 B7
West Halkin Street SW1X 147 J4
West Harding Street EC4A 145 G6
West India Avenue E14 151 M5
West India Dock Road E14 151 M3
Westland Place N1 145 K2
West Lane SE16 150 E7
Westminster ⊖ SW1A 148 D3
Westminster Abbey SW1P 148 C3
Westminster Bridge SE1 148 D3
Westminster Bridge Road SE1 148 F3
Westmoreland Place SW1V 147 L7
Westmoreland Road SE17 149 K8
Westmoreland Street W1G 143 K5
Westmoreland Terrace SW1V 147 L7
Weston Rise WC1X 144 E1
Weston Street SE1 149 M2
Weston Street SE1 149 M3
Westport Street E1 151 H2
West Poultry Avenue EC1A 145 H5
West Road SW3 147 H7
West Smithfield EC1A 145 H5
West Square SE11 149 H4
West Street WC2H 144 C7
West Tenter Street E1 150 C3
West Warwick Place SW1V 147 M6
Westway W2 142 B5
Wetherby Gardens SW5 146 C6
Weyhill Road E1 150 D2
Weymouth Mews W1G 143 L5
Weymouth Street W1G 143 K5
Wharfdale Road * N1 144 D1
Wharfdale Street SW10 146 B7
Wharf Road N1 145 J1
Wharton Street WC1X 144 F2
Wheatley Street W1G 143 K5
Whetstone Park WC2A 144 E5
Whidborne Street WC1H 144 D2
Whiskin Street EC1R 145 G2
Whitcomb Street WC2H 144 B8
Whitechapel ⇄ ⊖ E1 150 E1
Whitechapel Estate E1 150 C4
Whitechapel High Street E1 150 C2

Whitechapel Road E1 150 D1
Whitecross Street EC1Y 145 K3
Whitefriars Street EC4Y 145 G6
Whitehall SW1A 148 C2
Whitehall Court SW1A 148 D2
Whitehall Place SW1A 148 D1
White Hart Street SE11 149 G6
White Hart Yard SE1 149 L2
Whitehaven Street NW8 142 F4
Whitehead's Grove SW3 147 G6
White Horse Lane E1 151 H1
Whitehorse Road E1 151 J1
Whitehorse Road E1 151 J3
White Horse Street W1J 147 L1
White Kennett Street E1 150 B2
White Lion Hill EC4V 145 H7
White Lion Street N1 144 F1
White's Grounds SE1 150 A7
White's Row E1 150 B1
White Tower Way E1 151 J1
Whitfield Place W1T 144 A4
Whitfield Street W1T 144 A4
Whitgift Street SE11 148 E5
Whittaker Street SW1W 147 J6
Whittlesey Street SE1 149 G2
Wicker Street E1 150 E3
Wickham Close E1 151 G1
Wickham Street SE11 148 E7
Wicklow Street WC1X 144 E2
Widegate Street E1 150 A1
Widley Road W9 142 A3
Wigmore Place W1G 143 K5
Wigmore Street W1U 143 K6
Wigton Place SE11 149 G7
Wilbraham Place SW1X 147 J5
Wilcox Place * SW1E 148 A4
Wild Court WC2B 144 E6
Wild's Rents SE1 149 M4
Wild Street WC2B 144 D6
Wilfred Street SW1E 147 M4
Wilkes Street E1 150 B1
William IV Street WC2N 144 C8
William Mews SW1X 147 H3
William Road NW1 143 M3
Willow Place SW1P 148 A5
Willow Street EC2A 145 M3
Wilmington Square WC1X 144 F3
Wilmington Street WC1X 144 F2
Wilson Grove SE16 150 E7
Wilson Street EC2A 145 L4
Wilton Crescent SW1X 147 J3
Wilton Mews SW1X 147 K4
Wilton Place SW1X 147 J3
Wilton Road SW1V 147 M5
Wilton Row SW1X 147 J3
Wilton Street SW1X 147 K4
Wimpole Mews W1G 143 K5
Wimpole Street W1G 143 K5
Winchester Street SW1V 147 L6
Winchester Walk SE1 149 K1
Wincott Street SE11 149 G5
Windmill Road SE11 148 F7
Windmill Street W1T 144 B5
Windrose Close SE16 151 H6
Windsor Terrace N1 145 K1
Wine Close E1W 150 F5
Winnett Street W1D 144 B7
Winsland Mews W2 142 E6
Winsland Street W2 142 E6
Winsley Street W1W 144 A6
Winthrop Street E1 150 E1
Woburn Place WC1H 144 C3
Woburn Square WC1H 144 C4
Wodeham Gardens E1 150 E1
Wolfe Crescent SE16 151 H7
Wolseley Street SE1 150 C6
Woodbridge Street EC1R 145 G3
Woodchester Square W9 142 A4
Woodfall Street SW3 147 H7
Woodland Crescent SE16 151 H7
Woodseer Street E1 150 C1
Woods Mews W1K 143 J7
Woods Place SE1 150 A8
Woodstock Street W1C 143 K6
Wood Street EC2V 145 K6
Woolaston Close SE1 149 J5
Wooler Street SE17 149 L7
Wootton Street SE1 149 G2
Worgan Street SE11 148 E6
Worgan Street * SE16 151 H8
Wormwood Street EC2M 145 M5
Worship Street EC2A 145 M4
Wren Street WC1X 144 F3
Wright's Lane W8 146 A3
Wyatt Close SE16 151 L7
Wyclif Street EC1V 145 H2
Wymering Road W9 142 A2
Wynard Terrace SE11 148 F7
Wyndham Place W1H 143 H5
Wyndham Street W1H 143 G4
Wynnstay Gardens W8 146 A4
Wynyatt Street EC1V 145 H2
Wythburn Place W1H 143 H6

Y

Yalding Road * SE16 150 C8
Yardley Street WC1X 144 F2
Yeoman's Row SW3 147 G4
York Boulevard WC2N 144 D8
York Bridge NW1 143 J3
York Gate NW1 143 J4
York Road SE1 148 E2
Yorkshire Road E14 151 K3
York Square E14 151 J2
York Street W1H 143 G5
York Street W1U 143 H5
York Terrace East NW1 143 J4
York Terrace West NW1 143 J4
York Way N1 144 D1
Young Street W8 146 B3

Z

Zoar Street SE1 149 J1
ZSL London Zoo NW1 143 J1

This index lists places appearing in the main map section of the atlas in alphabetical order. The reference following each name gives the atlas page number and grid reference of the square in which the place appears. The map shows counties, unitary authorities and administrative areas, together with a list of the abbreviated name forms used in the index. The top 100 places of tourist interest are indexed in **red**, World Heritage sites in **green**, motorway service areas in **blue**, airports in **blue** *italic* and National Parks in green *italic*.

Scotland

Abers	Aberdeenshire
Ag & B	Argyll and Bute
Angus	Angus
Border	Scottish Borders
C Aber	City of Aberdeen
C Dund	City of Dundee
C Edin	City of Edinburgh
C Glas	City of Glasgow
Clacks	Clackmannanshire (1)
D & G	Dumfries & Galloway
E Ayrs	East Ayrshire
E Duns	East Dunbartonshire (2)
E Loth	East Lothian
E Rens	East Renfrewshire (3)
Falk	Falkirk
Fife	Fife
Highld	Highland
Inver	Inverclyde (4)
Mdloth	Midlothian (5)
Moray	Moray
N Ayrs	North Ayrshire
N Lans	North Lanarkshire (6)
Ork	Orkney Islands
P & K	Perth & Kinross
Rens	Renfrewshire (7)
S Ayrs	South Ayrshire
S Lans	South Lanarkshire
Shet	Shetland Islands
Stirlg	Stirling
W Duns	West Dunbartonshire (8)
W Isls	Western Isles (Na h-Eileanan an Iar)
W Loth	West Lothian

Wales

Blae G	Blaenau Gwent (9)
Brdgnd	Bridgend (10)
Caerph	Caerphilly (11)
Cardif	Cardiff
Carmth	Carmarthenshire
Cerdgn	Ceredigion
Conwy	Conwy
Denbgs	Denbighshire
Flints	Flintshire
Gwynd	Gwynedd
IoA	Isle of Anglesey
Mons	Monmouthshire
Myr Td	Merthyr Tydfil (12)
Neath	Neath Port Talbot (13)
Newpt	Newport (14)
Pembks	Pembrokeshire
Powys	Powys
Rhondd	Rhondda Cynon Taf (15)
Swans	Swansea
Torfn	Torfaen (16)
V Glam	Vale of Glamorgan (17)
Wrexhm	Wrexham

Channel Islands & Isle of Man

Guern	Guernsey
Jersey	Jersey
IoM	Isle of Man

England

BaNES	Bath & N E Somerset (18)
Barns	Barnsley (19)
BCP	Bournemouth, Christchurch and Poole (20)
Bed	Bedford
Birm	Birmingham
Bl w D	Blackburn with Darwen (21)
Bolton	Bolton (22)
Bpool	Blackpool
Br & H	Brighton & Hove (23)
Br For	Bracknell Forest (24)
Bristl	City of Bristol
Bucks	Buckinghamshire
Bury	Bury (25)
C Beds	Central Bedfordshire
C Brad	City of Bradford
C Derb	City of Derby
C KuH	City of Kingston upon Hull
C Leic	City of Leicester
C Nott	City of Nottingham

C Pete	City of Peterborough
C Plym	City of Plymouth
C Port	City of Portsmouth
C Sotn	City of Southampton
C Stke	City of Stoke-on-Trent
C York	City of York
Calder	Calderdale (26)
Cambs	Cambridgeshire
Ches E	Cheshire East
Ches W	Cheshire West and Chester
Cnwll	Cornwall
Covtry	Coventry
Cumb	Cumbria
Darltn	Darlington (27)
Derbys	Derbyshire
Devon	Devon
Donc	Doncaster (28)
Dorset	Dorset
Dudley	Dudley (29)
Dur	Durham
E R Yk	East Riding of Yorkshire
E Susx	East Sussex
Essex	Essex
Gatesd	Gateshead (30)
Gloucs	Gloucestershire
Gt Lon	Greater London
Halton	Halton (31)
Hants	Hampshire
Hartpl	Hartlepool (32)
Herefs	Herefordshire
Herts	Hertfordshire
IoS	Isles of Scilly
IoW	Isle of Wight
Kent	Kent
Kirk	Kirklees (33)
Knows	Knowsley (34)
Lancs	Lancashire
Leeds	Leeds
Leics	Leicestershire
Lincs	Lincolnshire
Lpool	Liverpool
Luton	Luton

M Keyn	Milton Keynes
Manch	Manchester
Medway	Medway
Middsb	Middlesbrough
N Linc	North Lincolnshire
N Som	North Somerset
N Tyne	North Tyneside (35)
N u Ty	Newcastle upon Tyne
N York	North Yorkshire
NE Lin	North East Lincolnshire
Nhants	Northamptonshire
Norfk	Norfolk
Notts	Nottinghamshire
Nthumb	Northumberland
Oldham	Oldham (36)
Oxon	Oxfordshire
R & Cl	Redcar & Cleveland
Readg	Reading
Rochdl	Rochdale (37)
Rothm	Rotherham (38)
Rutlnd	Rutland
S Glos	South Gloucestershire (39)
S on T	Stockton-on-Tees (40)
S Tyne	South Tyneside (41)
Salfd	Salford (42)
Sandw	Sandwell (43)
Sefton	Sefton (44)
Sheff	Sheffield
Shrops	Shropshire
Slough	Slough (45)
Solhll	Solihull (46)
Somset	Somerset
St Hel	St Helens (47)
Staffs	Staffordshire
Sthend	Southend-on-Sea
Stockp	Stockport (48)
Suffk	Suffolk
Sundld	Sunderland
Surrey	Surrey
Swindn	Swindon
Tamesd	Tameside (49)
Thurr	Thurrock (50)
Torbay	Torbay
Traffd	Trafford (51)
W & M	Windsor & Maidenhead (52)
W Berk	West Berkshire
W Susx	West Sussex
Wakefd	Wakefield (53)
Warrtn	Warrington (54)
Warwks	Warwickshire
Wigan	Wigan (55)
Wilts	Wiltshire
Wirral	Wirral (56)
Wokham	Wokingham (57)
Wolves	Wolverhampton (58)
Worcs	Worcestershire
Wrekin	Telford & Wrekin (59)
Wsall	Walsall (60)

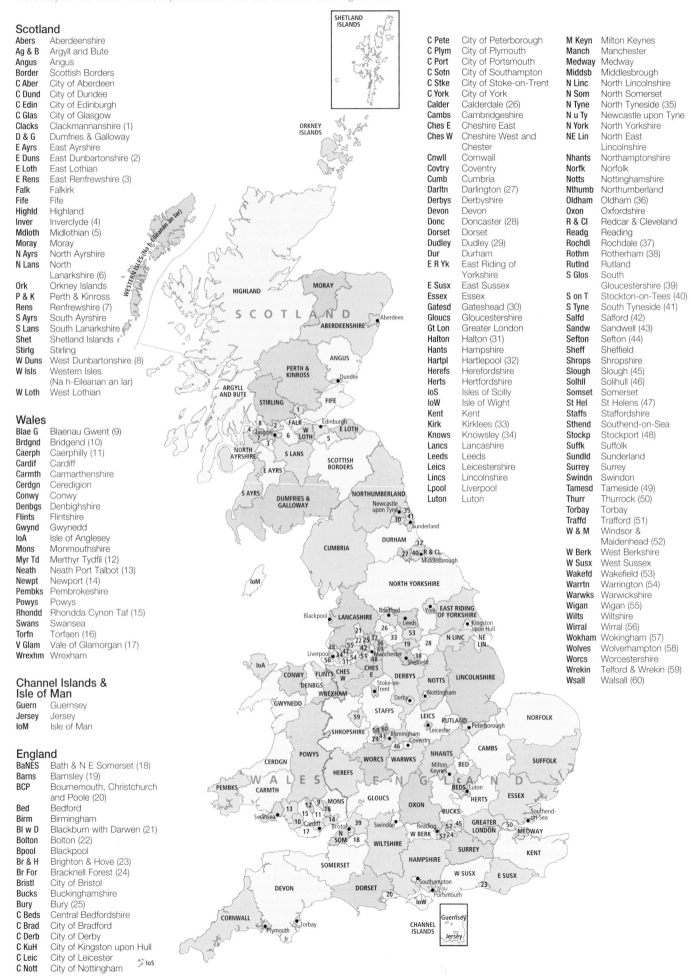

A

Abbas Combe *Somset* 17 Q10
Abberley *Worcs* 39 N8
Abberley Common *Worcs* 39 N8
Abberton *Essex* 34 G11
Abberton *Worcs* 30 C4
Abbess Roding *Essex* 22 C2
Abbeydale *Sheff* 50 H4
Abbey Dore *Herefs* 28 D3
Abbey Green *Staffs* 50 C8
Abbey St Bathans *Border* 87 P9
Abbeystead *Lancs* 63 K10
Abbeytown *Cumb* 71 J5
Abbey Village *Lancs* 57 M4
Abbey Wood *Gt Lon* 21 P7
Abbotrule *Border* 80 E10
Abbots Bickington *Devon* 14 G9
Abbots Bromley *Staffs* 40 E3
Abbotsbury *Dorset* 7 N6
Abbots Deuglie *P & K* 92 G12
Abbotsham *Devon* 14 H6
Abbotskerswell *Devon* 6 B8
Abbots Langley *Herts* 20 H3
Abbots Leigh *N Som* 17 M2
Abbotsley *Cambs* 32 H5
Abbots Morton *Worcs* 30 D3
Abbots Ripton *Cambs* 32 H2
Abbot's Salford *Warwks* 30 E4
Abbots Worthy *Hants* 9 N2
Abbotts Ann *Hants* 19 K11
Abbott Street *Dorset* 8 E7
Abdon *Shrops* 39 L5
Aberaeron *Cerdgn* 36 G7
Aberaman *Rhondd* 27 L8
Aberangell *Gwynd* 47 N8
Aberarder *Highld* 99 J4
Aberargie *P & K* 92 H11
Aberarth *Cerdgn* 36 H7
Aberavon *Neath* 26 G10
Abercanaid *Myr Td* 27 M7
Abercarn *Caerph* 27 P9
Abercastle *Pembks* 24 F3
Abercegir *Powys* 47 N10
Aberchalder *Highld* 98 D8
Aberchirder *Abers* 102 E5
Abercorn *W Loth* 86 C6
Abercraf *Powys* 26 H6
Abercregan *Neath* 26 H9
Abercwmboi *Rhondd* 27 L8
Abercych *Pembks* 36 D11
Abercynon *Rhondd* 27 M9
Aberdalgie *P & K* 92 G10
Aberdare *Rhondd* 27 L8
Aberdaron *Gwynd* 46 C6
Aberdeen *C Aber* 95 Q1
Aberdeen Airport *C Aber* 103 J11
Aberdour *Fife* 86 E5
Aberdulais *Neath* 26 G8
Aberdyfi *Gwynd* 47 K11
Aberedw *Powys* 38 C11
Abereiddy *Pembks* 24 E3
Abererch *Gwynd* 46 G4
Aberfan *Myr Td* 27 M8
Aberfeldy *P & K* 92 C6
Aberffraw *IoA* 54 E7
Aberford *Leeds* 59 K6
Aberfoyle *Stirlg* 85 J3
Abergavenny *Mons* 28 C6
Abergele *Conwy* 55 P6
Abergorlech *Carmth* 26 D3
Abergwesyn *Powys* 37 P9
Abergwili *Carmth* 25 Q5
Abergwynfi *Neath* 27 J9
Abergwyngregyn *Gwynd* 55 J7
Abergynolwyn *Gwynd* 47 L9
Aberkenfig *Brdgnd* 27 J11
Aberlady *E Loth* 87 J6
Aberlemno *Angus* 93 N5
Aberllefenni *Gwynd* 47 M8
Aberllynfi *Powys* 27 N2
Aberlour, Charlestown of *Moray* 101 K6
Abermule *Powys* 38 D4
Abernant *Carmth* 25 N4
Abernant *Rhondd* 27 L7
Abernethy *P & K* 92 H11
Abernyte *P & K* 93 J8
Aberporth *Cerdgn* 36 D9
Abersoch *Gwynd* 46 E6
Abersychan *Torfn* 28 B7
Aberthin *V Glam* 16 D2
Abertillery *Blae G* 27 P7
Abertridwr *Caerph* 27 N10
Abertridwr *Powys* 48 B10
Aberuthven *P & K* 92 E11
Aberystwyth *Cerdgn* 37 J4
Abingdon-on-Thames *Oxon* 19 N2
Abinger Common *Surrey* 10 H2
Abinger Hammer *Surrey* 10 H1
Abington *Nhants* 32 A5
Abington *S Lans* 78 F4
Abington Pigotts *Cambs* 33 K7
Abington Services *S Lans* 78 F4
Abingworth *W Susx* 10 H6
Ab Kettleby *Leics* 41 Q3
Ablington *Gloucs* 30 E11
Abney *Derbys* 50 G5
Aboyne *Abers* 95 J3
Abhainn Suidhe *W Isls* 111 c3
Abram *Wigan* 57 L8
Abriachan *Highld* 98 H2
Abridge *Essex* 21 P4
Abronhill *N Lans* 85 N7
Abson *S Glos* 17 Q2
Abthorpe *Nhants* 31 N5
Aby *Lincs* 53 L7
Acaster Malbis *C York* 59 N5
Acaster Selby *N York* 59 M6
Accrington *Lancs* 57 N3
Acha *Ag & B* 88 F5
Achahoish *Ag & B* 83 L4
Achalader *P & K* 92 G6
Achaleven *Ag & B* 90 C9
Acha Mor *W Isls* 111 d2
Achanalt *Highld* 106 D9
Achandunie *Highld* 107 J3
Achany *Highld* 107 J3
Acharacle *Highld* 89 N3
Acharn *Highld* 89 P6
Acharn *P & K* 92 B6
Achavanich *Highld* 110 E7
Achduart *Highld* 105 Q2
Achfary *Highld* 108 F7
Achgarve *Highld* 105 N4
A'Chill *Highld* 96 C8
Achiltibuie *Highld* 105 Q1
Achina *Highld* 109 M4
Achinhoan *Ag & B* 75 L8
Achintee *Highld* 97 N2
Achintraid *Highld* 97 L2
Achlyness *Highld* 108 E5
Achmelvich *Highld* 108 B10
Achmore *Highld* 97 M3
Achmore *W Isls* 111 d2
Achnacarnin *Highld* 108 B8
Achnacloich *Highld* 96 H7
Achnaconeran *Highld* 98 F5
Achnacroish *Ag & B* 90 B7
Achnadrish *Ag & B* 89 K6
Achnafauld *P & K* 92 D8
Achnagarron *Highld* 107 L8
Achnaha *Highld* 89 K3
Achnahaird *Highld* 108 A11
Achnahannet *Highld* 100 F9
Achnairn *Highld* 109 K12
Achnalea *Highld* 90 B4
Achnamara *Ag & B* 83 L5
Achnasheen *Highld* 106 C10
Achnashellach *Highld* 105 Q11
Achnastank *Moray* 101 K8
Achosnich *Highld* 89 K3
Achranich *Highld* 89 P6
Achreamie *Highld* 110 B3
Achriabhach *Highld* 90 F3
Achriesgill *Highld* 108 E5
Achtoty *Highld* 109 M3
Achurch *Nhants* 42 E12
Achvaich *Highld* 107 L4
Achvarasdal *Highld* 110 B3
Ackergill *Highld* 110 G5
Acklam *Middsb* 66 C4
Acklam *N York* 60 D2
Ackleton *Shrops* 39 P3
Acklington *Nthumb* 73 M1
Ackton *Wakefd* 59 K9
Ackworth Moor Top *Wakefd* 59 K10
Acle *Norfk* 45 N7
Acock's Green *Birm* 40 E10
Acol *Kent* 23 P9
Acomb *C York* 59 M4
Acomb *Nthumb* 72 G7
Aconbury *Herefs* 28 F3
Acton *Ches E* 49 L5
Acton *Gt Lon* 21 K7
Acton *Staffs* 49 P7
Acton *Suffk* 34 E7
Acton *Wrexhm* 48 G5
Acton Beauchamp *Herefs* 39 M11
Acton Bridge *Ches W* 49 L1
Acton Burnell *Shrops* 39 K2
Acton Green *Herefs* 39 M11
Acton Round *Shrops* 39 L3
Acton Scott *Shrops* 39 J4
Acton Trussell *Staffs* 40 C4
Acton Turville *S Glos* 18 B5
Adbaston *Staffs* 49 N9
Adber *Dorset* 17 N11
Adbolton *Notts* 51 N12
Adderbury *Oxon* 31 L7
Adderley *Shrops* 49 M7
Addiewell *W Loth* 86 B9
Addingham *C Brad* 58 E4
Addington *Bucks* 31 Q8
Addington *Gt Lon* 21 M9
Addington *Kent* 22 D10
Addiscombe *Gt Lon* 21 M9
Addlestone *Surrey* 20 G9
Addlethorpe *Lincs* 53 N9
Adeyfield *Herts* 20 H2
Adfa *Powys* 38 C2
Adforton *Herefs* 38 H7
Adisham *Kent* 23 N11
Adlestrop *Gloucs* 30 G8
Adlingfleet *E R Yk* 60 E9
Adlington *Lancs* 57 L6
Admaston *Staffs* 40 D3
Admaston *Wrekin* 49 L11
Adpar *Cerdgn* 36 E12
Adsborough *Somset* 16 H9
Adscombe *Somset* 16 G8
Adstock *Bucks* 31 Q7
Adstone *Nhants* 31 N4
Adversane *W Susx* 10 H5
Advie *Highld* 100 H8
Adwick le Street *Donc* 59 M11
Adwick upon Dearne *Donc* 51 L1
Ae *D & G* 78 G10
Ae Bridgend *D & G* 78 G10
Afan Forest Park *Neath* 26 H8
Affleck *Abers* 102 D7
Affpuddle *Dorset* 8 B8
Affric Lodge *Highld* 98 B5
Afon-wen *Flints* 48 D2
Afton *IoW* 9 L9
Agglethorpe *N York* 65 J9
Aigburth *Lpool* 56 H10
Aike *E R Yk* 60 H5
Aiketgate *Cumb* 71 P6
Aikton *Cumb* 71 L5
Ailsworth *C Pete* 42 G9
Ainderby Quernhow *N York* 65 N10
Ainderby Steeple *N York* 65 N8
Aingers Green *Essex* 35 J11
Ainsdale *Sefton* 56 F6
Ainstable *Cumb* 71 Q6
Ainsworth *Bury* 57 N6
Ainthorpe *N York* 66 G6
Aintree *Sefton* 56 H8
Ainville *W Loth* 86 D9
Aird *Ag & B* 83 L3
Aird *D & G* 68 E7
Aird *Highld* 96 H9
Aird *W Isls* 111 e2
Àird a' Mhulaidh *W Isls* 111 c3
Àird Asaig *W Isls* 111 c3
Aird Dhubh *Highld* 97 J2
Airdeny *Ag & B* 90 D9
Airdrie *N Lans* 85 N9
Airdriehill *N Lans* 85 N9
Airds of Kells *D & G* 69 P5
Àird Uig *W Isls* 111 c2
Airidh a bhruaich *W Isls* 111 c3
Airieland *D & G* 70 C4
Airlie *Angus* 93 K5
Airmyn *E R Yk* 60 C8
Airntully *P & K* 92 G8
Airor *Highld* 97 J8
Airth *Falk* 85 Q5
Airton *N York* 58 B3
Aisby *Lincs* 42 E3
Aisby *Lincs* 52 C5
Aish *Devon* 5 N7
Aish *Devon* 6 A10
Aisholt *Somset* 16 G8
Aiskew *N York* 65 M9
Aislaby *N York* 66 H9
Aislaby *N York* 67 J4
Aislaby *S on T* 65 P5
Aisthorpe *Lincs* 52 D7
Aith *Shet* 111 k4
Akeld *Nthumb* 81 K8
Akeley *Bucks* 31 P6
Akenham *Suffk* 35 J6
Alberbury *Shrops* 48 G11
Albourne *W Susx* 11 K6
Albrighton *Shrops* 39 P2
Albrighton *Shrops* 49 J10
Alburgh *Norfk* 45 L11
Albury *Herts* 33 M10
Albury *Surrey* 10 G1
Albury Heath *Surrey* 10 G2
Alcaig *Highld* 107 J10
Alcaston *Shrops* 39 J5
Alcester *Warwks* 30 E3
Alciston *E Susx* 11 P8
Alcombe *Somset* 16 C7
Alconbury *Cambs* 32 H2
Alconbury Weald *Cambs* 32 H2
Alconbury Weston *Cambs* 32 H2
Aldborough *N York* 59 K2
Aldborough *Norfk* 45 K4
Aldbourne *Wilts* 19 J5
Aldbrough *E R Yk* 61 L6
Aldbrough St John *N York* 65 L5
Aldbury *Herts* 20 F2
Aldcliffe *Lancs* 63 J9
Aldclune *P & K* 92 D3
Aldeburgh *Suffk* 35 P5
Aldeby *Norfk* 45 P10
Aldenham *Herts* 21 J4
Alderbury *Wilts* 8 H2
Alderford *Norfk* 45 J6
Alderholt *Dorset* 8 G5
Alderley *Gloucs* 29 K10
Alderley Edge *Ches E* 57 Q12
Aldermans Green *Covtry* 41 J10
Aldermaston *W Berk* 19 P7
Alderminster *Warwks* 30 G4
Aldershot *Hants* 20 D12
Alderton *Gloucs* 30 D7
Alderton *Nhants* 31 Q5
Alderton *Suffk* 35 M8
Alderton *Wilts* 18 C4
Aldfield *N York* 58 H1
Aldford *Ches W* 48 H4
Aldgate *Rutlnd* 42 E8
Aldham *Essex* 34 F10
Aldham *Suffk* 34 H7
Aldingbourne *W Susx* 10 E8
Aldingham *Cumb* 62 F7
Aldington *Kent* 13 K3
Aldington *Worcs* 30 E5
Aldington Corner *Kent* 13 K3
Aldivalloch *Moray* 101 M9
Aldochlay *Ag & B* 84 F5
Aldreth *Cambs* 33 M3
Aldridge *Wsall* 40 D7
Aldringham *Suffk* 35 P5
Aldsworth *Gloucs* 30 F11
Aldunie *Moray* 101 M9
Aldwark *Derbys* 50 G8
Aldwark *N York* 59 L2
Aldwick *W Susx* 10 E9
Aldwincle *Nhants* 32 E1
Aldworth *W Berk* 19 P5
Alexandria *W Duns* 84 G7
Aley *Somset* 16 G8
Alfington *Devon* 6 F4
Alfold *Surrey* 10 G3
Alfold Crossways *Surrey* 10 G3
Alford *Abers* 102 D11
Alford *Lincs* 53 M8
Alford *Somset* 17 N9
Alfreton *Derbys* 51 K9
Alfrick *Worcs* 39 N10
Alfrick Pound *Worcs* 39 N10
Alfriston *E Susx* 11 P9
Algarkirk *Lincs* 43 J3
Alhampton *Somset* 17 P8
Alkborough *N Linc* 60 F9
Alkham *Kent* 13 N2
Alkmonton *Derbys* 50 F12
Allaleigh *Devon* 5 Q9
Allanaquoich *Abers* 94 B4
Allanbank *N Lans* 85 P10
Allanton *Border* 81 J4
Allanton *N Lans* 85 P10
Allanton *S Lans* 85 M11
Allaston *Gloucs* 28 H7
Allbrook *Hants* 9 M4
All Cannings *Wilts* 18 F8
Allendale *Nthumb* 72 F9
Allen End *Warwks* 40 F7
Allenheads *Nthumb* 72 F10
Allen's Green *Herts* 33 M10
Allensmore *Herefs* 28 F2
Allenton *C Derb* 41 J2
Aller *Devon* 15 N7
Aller *Somset* 17 K9
Allerby *Cumb* 70 H7
Allercombe *Devon* 6 E4
Allerford *Somset* 16 B6
Allerston *N York* 67 J10
Allerthorpe *E R Yk* 60 D5
Allerton *C Brad* 58 E7
Allerton *Highld* 107 M8
Allerton *Lpool* 56 H10
Allerton Bywater *Leeds* 59 K8
Allerton Mauleverer *N York* 59 K3
Allesley *Covtry* 40 H10
Allestree *C Derb* 51 J11
Allexton *Leics* 42 B9
Allgreave *Ches E* 50 C7
Allhallows *Medway* 22 G7
Alligin Shuas *Highld* 105 M10
Allington *Dorset* 7 L4
Allington *Lincs* 42 C3
Allington *Wilts* 18 D5
Allington *Wilts* 18 F8
Allington *Wilts* 18 H11
Allithwaite *Cumb* 62 H6
Alloa *Clacks* 85 P4
Allonby *Cumb* 70 H7
Alloway *S Ayrs* 76 F7
Allowenshay *Somset* 17 K12
All Stretton *Shrops* 39 J3
Alltchaorunn *Highld* 90 G6
Alltsigh *Highld* 98 F5
Alltwalis *Carmth* 25 Q3
Alltwen *Neath* 26 G7
Alltyblaca *Cerdgn* 36 H10
Almeley *Herefs* 38 G11
Almington *Staffs* 49 N8
Almodington *W Susx* 10 D9
Almondbank *P & K* 92 F9
Almondbury *Kirk* 58 F10
Almondsbury *S Glos* 28 H11
Alne *N York* 59 L2
Alness *Highld* 107 L8
Alnham *Nthumb* 81 L11
Alnmouth *Nthumb* 81 P11
Alnwick *Nthumb* 81 P10
Alperton *Gt Lon* 21 J6
Alphamstone *Essex* 34 E9
Alpheton *Suffk* 34 E6
Alphington *Devon* 6 C5
Alport *Derbys* 50 G7
Alpraham *Ches E* 49 L4
Alresford *Essex* 34 H11
Alrewas *Staffs* 40 F5
Alsager *Ches E* 49 P4
Alsop en le Dale *Derbys* 50 F9
Alston *Cumb* 72 D10
Alston *Devon* 7 J3
Alstone *Gloucs* 29 N3
Alstonefield *Staffs* 50 F9
Alston Sutton *Somset* 17 K6
Alswear *Devon* 15 M7
Altandhu *Highld* 108 A12
Altarnun *Cnwll* 4 F4
Altass *Highld* 106 H3
Altcreich *Ag & B* 89 N8
Altgaltraig *Ag & B* 83 Q8
Althorne *Essex* 22 H4
Althorpe *N Linc* 60 E11
Altnabreac Station *Highld* 110 B6
Altnaharra *Highld* 109 K8
Altofts *Wakefd* 59 J9
Alton *Derbys* 51 J7
Alton *Hants* 10 B3
Alton *Staffs* 50 E11
Alton Barnes *Wilts* 18 G8
Alton Pancras *Dorset* 7 Q3
Alton Priors *Wilts* 18 G8
Alton Towers *Staffs* 50 E11
Altrincham *Traffd* 57 P10
Altskeith Hotel *Stirlg* 84 H3
Alva *Clacks* 85 P4
Alvanley *Ches W* 49 J1
Alvaston *C Derb* 41 K2
Alvechurch *Worcs* 40 D11
Alvecote *Warwks* 40 G6
Alvediston *Wilts* 8 E3
Alveley *Shrops* 39 N5
Alverdiscott *Devon* 15 J7
Alverstoke *Hants* 9 P7
Alverstone *IoW* 9 P9
Alverthorpe *Wakefd* 58 H9
Alverton *Notts* 42 B2
Alves *Moray* 100 H3
Alvescot *Oxon* 30 H12
Alveston *S Glos* 28 H10
Alveston *Warwks* 30 G3
Alvingham *Lincs* 53 K5
Alvington *Gloucs* 28 H8
Alwalton *C Pete* 42 G10
Alweston *Dorset* 17 P12
Alwinton *Nthumb* 81 J11
Alwoodley *Leeds* 58 H6
Alyth *P & K* 93 J6
Am Bàgh a Tuath *W Isls* 111 a7
Ambergate *Derbys* 51 J9
Amberley *Gloucs* 29 L8
Amberley *W Susx* 10 G7
Amble *Nthumb* 81 Q12
Amblecote *Dudley* 40 B9
Ambler Thorn *C Brad* 58 E8
Ambleside *Cumb* 62 G2
Ambleston *Pembks* 24 H4
Ambrosden *Oxon* 31 N9
Amcotts *N Linc* 60 E10
Amersham *Bucks* 20 F4
Amersham Common *Bucks* 20 F4
Amersham Old Town *Bucks* 20 F4
Amersham on the Hill *Bucks* 20 F4
Amesbury *Wilts* 18 H11
Amhuinnsuidhe *W Isls* 111 c3
Amington *Staffs* 40 G6
Amisfield *D & G* 78 G11
Amlwch *IoA* 54 F3
Ammanford *Carmth* 26 E6
Amotherby *N York* 66 G11
Ampfield *Hants* 9 L3
Ampleforth *N York* 66 E10
Ampney Crucis *Gloucs* 30 E12
Ampney St Mary *Gloucs* 18 G1
Ampney St Peter *Gloucs* 18 F1
Amport *Hants* 19 K11
Ampthill *C Beds* 32 E8
Ampton *Suffk* 34 E3
Amroth *Pembks* 25 K7
Amulree *P & K* 92 D8
Amwell *Herts* 21 J2
Anaheilt *Highld* 89 Q4
Ancaster *Lincs* 42 D3
Ancells Farm *Hants* 20 D11
Ancroft *Nthumb* 81 L5
Ancrum *Border* 80 E8
Ancton *W Susx* 10 F9
Anderby *Lincs* 53 N8
Andover *Hants* 19 L10
Andoversford *Gloucs* 30 D9
Andreas *IoM* 56 d2
Anerley *Gt Lon* 21 M9
Anfield *Lpool* 56 H9
Angarrack *Cnwll* 2 F7
Angelbank *Shrops* 39 L7
Angle *Pembks* 24 F8
Anglesey *IoA* 54 F5
Anglesey Abbey *Cambs* 33 N4
Angmering *W Susx* 10 H8
Angram *N York* 59 M5
Ankerville *Highld* 107 N7
Ankle Hill *Leics* 41 Q4
Anlaby *E R Yk* 60 H8
Anmer *Norfk* 44 C4
Anmore *Hants* 9 Q5
Annan *D & G* 71 K3
Annandale Water Services *D & G* 78 H9
Annat *Highld* 105 N10
Annathill *N Lans* 85 M8
Anna Valley *Hants* 19 L11
Annbank *S Ayrs* 76 G6
Anne Hathaway's Cottage *Warwks* 30 F3
Annfield Plain *Dur* 73 L9
Anniesland *C Glas* 85 J8
Ansdell *Lancs* 56 G3
Ansford *Somset* 17 P9
Ansley *Warwks* 40 H8
Anslow *Staffs* 40 G3
Anslow Gate *Staffs* 40 G3
Anstey *Herts* 33 L9
Anstey *Leics* 41 M6
Anstruther *Fife* 87 L2
Ansty *W Susx* 11 L5
Ansty *Warwks* 41 K10
Ansty *Wilts* 8 E3
An Tairbeart *W Isls* 111 c3
Anthorn *Cumb* 71 K4
Antingham *Norfk* 45 L4
An t-Ob *W Isls* 111 c4
Antonine Wall 85 P7
Anton's Gowt *Lincs* 43 J1
Antony *Cnwll* 5 J8
Antrobus *Ches W* 57 M11
Anwick *Lincs* 52 G12
Anwoth *D & G* 69 N7
Aperfield *Gt Lon* 21 N10
Apethorpe *Nhants* 42 E10
Apley *Lincs* 52 G8
Apperknowle *Derbys* 51 J5
Apperley *Gloucs* 29 M3
Appin *Ag & B* 90 C7
Appleby *N Linc* 60 G10
Appleby-in-Westmorland *Cumb* 64 C4
Appleby Magna *Leics* 40 H5
Appleby Parva *Leics* 40 H6
Applecross *Highld* 97 J2
Appledore *Devon* 14 H6
Appledore *Devon* 16 E12
Appledore *Kent* 13 J4
Appleford *Oxon* 19 N3
Applegarth Town *D & G* 78 H11
Appleshaw *Hants* 19 K10
Appleton *Halton* 57 K10
Appleton *Oxon* 19 M1
Appleton *Warrtn* 57 L11
Appleton-le-Moors *N York* 66 G9
Appleton-le-Street *N York* 66 G11
Appleton Roebuck *N York* 59 M6
Appleton Thorn *Warrtn* 57 M11
Appleton Wiske *N York* 65 P6
Appletreehall *Border* 80 C10
Appletreewick *N York* 58 D3
Appley *Somset* 16 E10
Apse Heath *IoW* 9 P10
Apsley End *C Beds* 32 G9
Apuldram *W Susx* 10 D9
Arabella *Highld* 107 N7
Arbirlot *Angus* 93 Q7
Arborfield *Wokham* 20 C9
Arborfield Cross *Wokham* 20 C9
Arbourthorne *Sheff* 51 J4
Arbroath *Angus* 93 Q7
Arbuthnott *Abers* 95 N6
Archddu *Carmth* 25 Q8
Archdeacon Newton *Darltn* 65 M4
Archencarroch *W Duns* 84 G6
Archiestown *Moray* 101 J6
Arclid *Ches E* 49 P3
Ardallie *Abers* 103 L7
Ardanaiseig Hotel *Ag & B* 90 E10
Ardaneaskan *Highld* 97 L3
Ardarroch *Highld* 97 L2
Ardbeg *Ag & B* 74 F4
Ardbeg *Ag & B* 84 C6
Ardcharnich *Highld* 106 C5
Ardchiavaig *Ag & B* 89 J11
Ardchonnel *Ag & B* 83 P1
Ardchronie *Highld* 107 K5
Ardchullarie More *Stirlg* 91 N12
Arddarroch *Ag & B* 84 D4
Arddleen *Powys* 48 F11
Ard Dorch *Highld* 96 G4
Ardechive *Highld* 98 A10
Ardeer *N Ayrs* 76 E4
Ardeley *Herts* 33 K10
Ardelve *Highld* 97 M4
Arden *Ag & B* 84 F6
Ardens Grafton *Warwks* 30 E4
Ardentallen *Ag & B* 90 B10
Ardentinny *Ag & B* 84 D5
Ardentraive *Ag & B* 83 Q7
Ardeonaig *Stirlg* 91 P8
Ardersier *Highld* 107 N10
Ardessie *Highld* 105 Q5
Ardfern *Ag & B* 83 M3
Ardfernal *Ag & B* 82 H8
Ardgartan *Ag & B* 84 E3
Ardgay *Highld* 107 K4
Ardgour *Highld* 90 D4
Ardgowan *Inver* 84 D8
Ardhasig *W Isls* 111 c3
Ardheslaig *Highld* 105 L10
Ardindrean *Highld* 106 C5
Ardingly *W Susx* 11 M4
Ardington *Oxon* 19 M3
Ardlamont *Ag & B* 83 P9
Ardleigh *Essex* 34 H10
Ardleigh Heath *Essex* 34 H10
Ardler *P & K* 93 J7
Ardley *Oxon* 31 M8
Ardlui *Ag & B* 91 J12
Ardlussa *Ag & B* 83 J5
Ardmair *Highld* 106 B3
Ardmaleish *Ag & B* 84 B8
Ardminish *Ag & B* 75 J3
Ardmolich *Highld* 89 P2

Ardmore Ag & B 84 F7
Ardmore Highld 107 L5
Ardnadam Ag & B 84 C7
Ardnagrask Highld 106 H11
Ardnamurchan Highld 89 L3
Ardnarff Highld 97 M3
Ardnastang Highld 89 Q4
Ardpatrick Ag & B 83 L10
Ardrishaig Ag & B 83 M6
Ardross Highld 107 K7
Ardrossan N Ayrs 76 D3
Ardslignish Highld 89 L4
Ardtalla Ag & B 82 G11
Ardtoe Highld 89 M3
Arduaine Ag & B 83 M2
Ardullie Highld 107 J9
Ardvasar Highld 96 H8
Ardvorlich P & K 91 P10
Ardvourlie W Isls 111 c3
Ardwell D & G 68 F9
Ardwick Manch 57 Q9
Areley Kings Worcs 39 P7
Arevegaig Highld 89 N3
Arford Hants 10 D3
Argoed Caerph 27 N8
Argyll Forest Park Ag & B 84 D3
Aribruach W Isls 111 c3
Aridhglas Ag & B 88 H10
Arileod Ag & B 88 E5
Arinagour Ag & B 88 F5
Ariogan Ag & B 90 B10
Arisaig Highld 97 J11
Arisaig House Highld 97 J11
Arkendale N York 59 K2
Arkesden Essex 33 M9
Arkholme Lancs 63 L7
Arkleton D & G 79 N10
Arkley Gt Lon 21 K4
Arksey Donc 59 M11
Arkwright Town Derbys 51 K6
Arle Gloucs 29 N4
Arlecdon Cumb 70 G10
Arlesey C Beds 32 H9
Arleston Wrekin 49 M12
Arley Ches E 57 M11
Arlingham Gloucs 29 J6
Arlington Devon 15 K4
Arlington E Susx 12 B8
Armadale Highld 96 H8
Armadale Highld 109 N3
Armadale W Loth 85 Q8
Armathwaite Cumb 71 Q6
Arminghall Norfk 45 L8
Armitage Staffs 40 E4
Armley Leeds 58 H7
Armscote Warwks 30 G5
Armthorpe Donc 59 N12
Arnabost Ag & B 88 F4
Arncliffe N York 64 G12
Arncroach Fife 87 K2
Arndilly House Moray 101 M5
Arne Dorset 8 E9
Arnesby Leics 41 N8
Arngask P & K 92 H12
Arnisdale Highld 97 L11
Arnish Highld 104 H11
Arniston Mdloth 86 G9
Arnol W Isls 111 d1
Arnold E R Yk 61 J6
Arnold Notts 51 N10
Arnprior Stirlg 85 K4
Arnside Cumb 63 J6
Aros Ag & B 89 L7
Arrad Foot Cumb 62 F6
Arram E R Yk 60 H5
Arran N Ayrs 75 P5
Arrathorne N York 65 L8
Arreton IoW 9 N9
Arrina Highld 105 L10
Arrington Cambs 33 K6
Arrochar Ag & B 84 E3
Arrow Warwks 30 E3
Arscott Shrops 38 H1
Artafallie Highld 107 K11
Arthington Leeds 58 H5
Arthingworth Nhants 41 Q10
Arthrath Abers 103 K7
Artrochie Abers 103 L8
Arundel W Susx 10 G8
Asby Cumb 70 H10
Ascog Ag & B 84 B9
Ascot W & M 20 E9
Ascott-under-Wychwood
Oxon 30 H9
Asenby N York 65 P11
Asfordby Leics 41 P4
Asfordby Hill Leics 41 Q4
Asgarby Lincs 42 G2
Ash Kent 22 C9
Ash Kent 23 P10
Ash Somset 17 L11
Ash Surrey 20 E12
Ashampstead W Berk 19 P5
Ashbocking Suffk 35 K6
Ashbourne Derbys 50 F10
Ashbrittle Somset 16 E11
Ashburton Devon 5 P6
Ashbury Devon 15 J11
Ashbury Oxon 19 J4
Ashby N Linc 52 C2
Ashby by Partney Lincs 53 L9
Ashby cum Fenby NE Lin 53 J4
Ashby de la Launde Lincs 52 F11
Ashby-de-la-Zouch Leics 41 J4
Ashby Folville Leics 41 P5
Ashby Magna Leics 41 M9
Ashby Parva Leics 41 M9
Ashby Puerorum Lincs 53 K8
Ashby St Ledgers Nhants 31 M1
Ashby St Mary Norfk 45 M9
Aschurch Gloucs 29 N3
Ashcombe Devon 6 C6
Ashcombe N Som 17 J4
Ashcott Somset 17 L8
Ashdon Essex 33 P8
Ashdown Forest E Susx 11 P4
Ashe Hants 19 N10
Asheldham Essex 23 J3
Ashen Essex 34 C8
Ashendon Bucks 31 P10
Asheridge Bucks 20 F3
Ashfield Herefs 28 H4
Ashfield Stirlg 85 N3

Ashfield cum Thorpe Suffk 35 K4
Ashfield Green Suffk 35 L3
Ashford Devon 5 N9
Ashford Devon 15 J5
Ashford Kent 13 J2
Ashford Surrey 20 H8
Ashford Bowdler Shrops 39 K7
Ashford Carbonell Shrops 39 K7
Ashford Hill Hants 19 P8
Ashford in the Water Derbys 50 G6
Ashgill S Lans 77 N2
Ash Green Surrey 20 E12
Ash Green Warwks 41 J9
Ashill Devon 6 E1
Ashill Norfk 44 E8
Ashill Somset 17 J11
Ashingdon Essex 22 G5
Ashington Nthumb 73 M4
Ashington Somset 17 N11
Ashington W Susx 11 J7
Ashkirk Border 79 P4
Ashleworth Gloucs 29 L4
Ashleworth Quay Gloucs 29 L4
Ashley Cambs 34 B5
Ashley Ches E 57 P11
Ashley Devon 15 L9
Ashley Gloucs 29 N9
Ashley Hants 9 J8
Ashley Hants 9 L2
Ashley Kent 13 P1
Ashley Nhants 42 B11
Ashley Staffs 49 N7
Ashley Wilts 18 B7
Ashley Green Bucks 20 F3
Ash Magna Shrops 49 K7
Ashmansworth Hants 19 M8
Ashmansworthy Devon 14 F8
Ashmore Dorset 8 D4
Ashmore Green W Berk 19 N6
Ashorne Warwks 30 H3
Ashover Derbys 51 J8
Ashow Warwks 40 H12
Ashperton Herefs 28 H1
Ashprington Devon 5 Q8
Ashreigney Devon 15 L9
Ash Street Suffk 34 G7
Ashtead Surrey 21 J10
Ash Thomas Devon 6 D1
Ashton Cnwll 2 F9
Ashton Devon 6 B6
Ashton Herefs 39 K8
Ashton Inver 84 D7
Ashton Nhants 31 Q4
Ashton Nhants 42 F11
Ashton Common Wilts 18 D8
Ashton Hayes Ches W 49 J2
Ashton-in-Makerfield Wigan 57 L8
Ashton Keynes Wilts 18 F2
Ashton under Hill Worcs 30 C6
Ashton-under-Lyne Tamesd 50 C2
Ashton Vale Bristl 17 N3
Ashurst Hants 9 K5
Ashurst Kent 11 P3
Ashurst Lancs 57 J7
Ashurst W Susx 11 J6
Ashurst Wood W Susx 11 N3
Ash Vale Surrey 20 E11
Ashwater Devon 5 J2
Ashwell Herts 33 J8
Ashwell Rutlnd 42 C7
Ashwell End Herts 33 J8
Ashwellthorpe Norfk 45 J9
Ashwick Somset 17 P6
Ashwicken Norfk 44 B6
Askam in Furness Cumb 62 E6
Askern Donc 59 M10
Askerswell Dorset 7 M4
Askett Bucks 20 D3
Askham Cumb 71 Q10
Askham Notts 51 Q6
Askham Bryan C York 59 M5
Askham Richard C York 59 M5
Asknish Ag & B 83 P5
Askrigg N York 64 G8
Askwith N York 58 F5
Aslackby Lincs 42 F4
Aslacton Norfk 45 J11
Aslockton Notts 51 Q11
Aspatria Cumb 71 J7
Aspenden Herts 33 K10
Aspley Guise C Beds 32 D9
Aspley Heath C Beds 32 D9
Aspull Wigan 57 L7
Asselby E R Yk 60 C8
Assington Suffk 34 F8
Assington Green Suffk 34 C6
Astbury Ches E 49 Q3
Astcote Nhants 31 P4
Asterby Lincs 53 J7
Asterley Shrops 38 G1
Asterton Shrops 38 H4
Asthall Oxon 30 H10
Asthall Leigh Oxon 30 H10
Astle Highld 107 M4
Astley Shrops 49 K10
Astley Warwks 40 H9
Astley Wigan 57 M8
Astley Worcs 39 P8
Astley Abbots Shrops 39 N3
Astley Bridge Bolton 57 N6
Astley Cross Worcs 39 P8
Aston Birm 40 E9
Aston Ches E 49 L6
Aston Ches W 57 K12
Aston Derbys 50 F4
Aston Flints 48 F3
Aston Herts 33 J11
Aston Oxon 31 J12
Aston Rothm 51 L4
Aston Shrops 39 P4
Aston Shrops 49 K9
Aston Staffs 40 B3
Aston Staffs 49 N6
Aston Wokham 20 C6
Aston Wrekin 49 L12
Aston Abbotts Bucks 32 C11
Aston Botterell Shrops 39 L5
Aston-by-Stone Staffs 40 B2
Aston Cantlow Warwks 30 E3
Aston Clinton Bucks 20 E2
Aston Crews Herefs 29 J4

Aston End Herts 33 J11
Aston Fields Worcs 40 C12
Aston Flamville Leics 41 L8
Aston Ingham Herefs 29 J4
Aston le Walls Nhants 31 L4
Aston Magna Gloucs 30 G7
Aston Munslow Shrops 39 K5
Aston on Clun Shrops 38 H6
Aston Pigott Shrops 38 G2
Aston Rogers Shrops 38 G2
Aston Rowant Oxon 20 B4
Aston Somerville Worcs 30 D6
Aston-sub-Edge Gloucs 30 F6
Aston Tirrold Oxon 19 N4
Aston-upon-Trent Derbys 41 K2
Aston Upthorpe Oxon 19 N4
Astwick C Beds 32 H8
Astwood M Keyn 32 D7
Astwood Worcs 30 C2
Astwood Bank Worcs 30 D2
Aswarby Lincs 42 F3
Aswardby Lincs 53 L9
Atcham Shrops 39 K1
Athelhampton Dorset 8 B8
Athelington Suffk 35 K3
Athelney Somset 17 J9
Athelstaneford E Loth 87 K6
Atherington Devon 15 K7
Atherstone Warwks 40 H7
Atherstone on Stour Warwks 30 G4
Atherton Wigan 57 M8
Atlow Derbys 50 G10
Attadale Highld 97 N3
Attercliffe Sheff 51 J3
Atterley Shrops 39 L2
Atterton Leics 41 J7
Attingham Park Shrops 49 K12
Attleborough Norfk 44 H10
Attleborough Warwks 41 J8
Attlebridge Norfk 45 J6
Attleton Green Suffk 34 C6
Atwick E R Yk 61 K4
Atworth Wilts 18 C7
Aubourn Lincs 52 D10
Auchbreck Moray 101 J9
Auchedly Abers 103 J8
Auchenblae Abers 95 M6
Auchenbowie Stirlg 85 N5
Auchencairn D & G 70 D5
Auchencairn D & G 78 F11
Auchencairn N Ayrs 75 Q6
Auchencrow Border 87 Q9
Auchendinny Mdloth 86 F9
Auchengray S Lans 86 B10
Auchenhalrig Moray 101 M3
Auchenheath S Lans 77 N3
Auchenhessnane D & G 77 N11
Auchenlochan Ag & B 83 P8
Auchenmade N Ayrs 76 F2
Auchenmalg D & G 68 G8
Auchentiber N Ayrs 76 F2
Auchindrain Ag & B 83 Q3
Auchindrean Highld 106 C6
Auchininna Abers 102 E6
Auchinleck E Ayrs 77 J7
Auchinloch N Lans 85 L8
Auchinstarry N Lans 85 M7
Auchintore Highld 90 F7
Auchiries Abers 103 M7
Auchlean Highld 99 M9
Auchlee Abers 95 P3
Auchleven Abers 102 E9
Auchlochan S Lans 77 N4
Auchlossan Abers 95 J2
Auchlyne Stirlg 91 M9
Auchmillan E Ayrs 77 J5
Auchmithie Angus 93 R6
Auchmuirbridge Fife 86 E3
Auchnacree Angus 94 H8
Auchnagatt Abers 103 J7
Auchnarrow Moray 101 J9
Auchnotteroch D & G 68 D7
Auchroisk Moray 101 L5
Auchterarder P & K 92 E12
Auchteraw Highld 98 E7
Auchterblair Highld 99 N5
Auchtercairn Highld 105 M7
Auchterderran Fife 86 E3
Auchterhouse Angus 93 L8
Auchterless Abers 102 F7
Auchtermuchty Fife 93 J12
Auchterneed Highld 106 H9
Auchtertool Fife 86 E4
Auchtertyre Highld 97 L4
Auchtubh Stirlg 91 N11
Auckengill Highld 110 G3
Auckley Donc 51 P1
Audenshaw Tamesd 50 B2
Audlem Ches E 49 M6
Audley Staffs 49 P5
Audley End Essex 33 N8
Audley End House &
Gardens Essex 33 N8
Audnam Dudley 40 B9
Aughton E R Yk 60 C6
Aughton Lancs 56 H7
Aughton Lancs 63 K8
Aughton Rothm 51 L4
Aughton Wilts 19 J9
Aughton Park Lancs 56 H7
Auldearn Highld 100 E4
Aulden Herefs 39 J10
Auldgirth D & G 78 E10
Auldhouse S Lans 77 K2
Ault a' chruinn Highld 97 N5
Aultbea Highld 105 N5
Aultgrishin Highld 105 L5
Aultguish Inn Highld 106 F8
Ault Hucknall Derbys 51 L7
Aultmore Moray 101 M5
Aultnagoire Highld 98 H4
Aultnamain Highld 107 L6
Aunsby Lincs 42 F3
Aust S Glos 28 G10
Austerfield Donc 51 P2
Austrey Warwks 40 H5
Austwick N York 63 N8
Authorpe Lincs 53 L7
Avebury Wilts 18 G6
Avebury Trusloe Wilts 18 G6
Aveley Thurr 22 C7
Avening Gloucs 29 M8
Averham Notts 51 Q9

Aveton Gifford Devon 5 N10
Aviemore Highld 99 N6
Avington W Berk 19 L7
Avoch Highld 107 L10
Avon Hants 8 G7
Avonbridge Falk 85 Q8
Avon Dassett Warwks 31 K4
Avonmouth Bristl 28 F12
Avonwick Devon 5 P8
Awbridge Hants 9 K3
Awliscombe Devon 6 F3
Awre Gloucs 29 J7
Awsworth Notts 51 L11
Axbridge Somset 17 L5
Axford Hants 19 Q11
Axford Wilts 19 J6
Axminster Devon 6 H3
Axmouth Devon 6 H5
Aycliffe Dur 65 M3
Aydon Nthumb 72 H7
Aylburton Gloucs 28 H8
Aylesbeare Devon 6 D4
Aylesbury Bucks 20 D1
Aylesby NE Lin 52 H3
Aylesford Kent 22 E10
Aylesham Kent 23 N11
Aylestone C Leic 41 M7
Aylestone Park C Leic 41 N7
Aylmerton Norfk 45 K3
Aylsham Norfk 45 K5
Aylton Herefs 28 H2
Aylworth Gloucs 30 E9
Aymestrey Herefs 38 H8
Aynho Nhants 31 L7
Ayot St Lawrence Herts 32 H12
Ayr S Ayrs 76 F7
Aysgarth N York 64 H9
Ayshford Devon 16 E11
Ayside Cumb 62 H5
Ayston Rutlnd 42 C9
Ayton Border 81 J3
Azerley N York 65 M11

B

Babbacombe Torbay 6 C9
Babbs Green Herts 33 L12
Babcary Somset 17 N9
Babraham Cambs 33 N6
Babworth Notts 51 P5
Backaland Ork 111 h1
Backfolds Abers 103 L5
Backford Ches W 48 H2
Backies Highld 107 N3
Back of Keppoch Highld 97 J11
Backwell N Som 17 L3
Baconsthorpe Norfk 45 J3
Bacton Herefs 28 D3
Bacton Norfk 45 M4
Bacton Suffk 34 H4
Bacup Lancs 57 Q4
Badachro Highld 105 L7
Badanloch Highld 109 N8
Badbury Swindn 18 H5
Badby Nhants 31 M3
Badcall Highld 108 E5
Badcaul Highld 105 Q4
Baddeley Edge C Stke 50 B9
Baddeley Green C Stke 50 B9
Baddesley Clinton Warwks 40 G11
Baddesley Ensor Warwks 40 H7
Baddidarrach Highld 108 C10
Baddinsgill Border 86 D10
Badenscoth Abers 102 F7
Badentarbet Highld 105 J2
Badenyon Abers 101 L10
Badger Shrops 39 N3
Badgeworth Gloucs 29 M5
Badgworth Somset 17 K5
Badicaul Highld 97 K4
Badingham Suffk 35 M3
Badlesmere Kent 23 J11
Badlieu Border 78 H5
Badlipster Highld 110 F6
Badluarach Highld 105 P4
Badninish Highld 107 M4
Badrallach Highld 105 Q4
Badsey Worcs 30 D5
Badshot Lea Surrey 10 D1
Badsworth Wakefd 59 L10
Badwell Ash Suffk 34 G3
Bagber Dorset 17 Q12
Bagby N York 66 C10
Bag Enderby Lincs 53 K8
Bagendon Gloucs 30 D11
Bàgh a' Chaisteil W Isls 111 a7
Bagillt Flints 48 E1
Baginton Warwks 41 J11
Baglan Neath 26 G9
Bagley Shrops 48 H9
Bagley Somset 17 L7
Bagnall Staffs 50 B10
Bagshot Surrey 20 E10
Bagstone S Glos 29 J3
Bagworth Leics 41 K6
Bagwyllydiart Herefs 28 E4
Baildon C Brad 58 F6
Baildon Green C Brad 58 F6
Baile Ailein W Isls 111 d2
Baile a' Mhanaich W Isls 111 b5
Baile Mòr Ag & B 88 G10
Baillieston C Glas 85 L9
Bainbridge N York 64 G9
Bainshole Abers 102 D8
Bainton C Pete 42 F8
Bainton E R Yk 60 G4
Baintown Fife 86 G2
Bairnkine Border 80 E10
Bakewell Derbys 50 G7
Bala Gwynd 47 Q4
Balallan W Isls 111 d2
Balbeg Highld 98 G3
Balbeggie P & K 92 H9
Balblair Highld 106 H12
Balblair Highld 107 L8
Balby Donc 51 M1
Balcary D & G 70 D5
Balchraggan Highld 98 G3
Balchrick Highld 108 D4
Balcombe W Susx 11 L4
Balcomie Links Fife 87 M1

Baldersby N York 65 N10
Baldersby St James N York 65 P11
Balderstone Lancs 57 L3
Balderton Notts 52 B12
Baldinnie Fife 93 M12
Baldinnies P & K 92 F11
Baldock Herts 33 J9
Baldock Services Herts 32 H9
Baldovie C Dund 93 M8
Baldrine IoM 56 d5
Baldslow E Susx 12 F7
Bale Norfk 44 G3
Baledgarno P & K 93 K9
Balemartine Ag & B 88 C7
Balerno C Edin 86 D8
Balfarg Fife 86 F2
Balfield Angus 95 J8
Balfour Ork 111 h2
Balfron Stirlg 85 J5
Balgaveny Abers 102 E7
Balgonar Fife 86 B4
Balgowan D & G 68 F9
Balgowan Highld 99 J9
Balgown Highld 104 E8
Balgracie D & G 68 D7
Balgray S Lans 78 E4
Balham Gt Lon 21 L8
Balhary P & K 93 J6
Balholmie P & K 92 H8
Baligill Highld 109 P3
Balintore Angus 93 K4
Balintore Highld 107 P7
Balintraid Highld 107 M8
Balivanich W Isls 111 b5
Balkeerie Angus 93 K6
Balkholme E R Yk 60 D8
Ballachulish Highld 90 E5
Ballajora IoM 56 e4
Ballantrae S Ayrs 68 E3
Ballasalla IoM 56 b6
Ballater Abers 94 F3
Ballaugh IoM 56 c3
Ballchraggan Highld 107 M7
Ballencrieff E Loth 87 J6
Ballevullin Ag & B 88 B7
Ball Green C Stke 50 B9
Ball Haye Green Staffs 50 C9
Ball Hill Hants 19 M8
Ballianlay Ag & B 83 Q9
Ballidon Derbys 50 G9
Balliekine N Ayrs 75 N5
Balliemore Ag & B 84 B3
Balligmorrie S Ayrs 68 G2
Ballimore Stirlg 91 M11
Ballindalloch Moray 101 J7
Ballindean P & K 93 J9
Ballinger Common Bucks 20 E3
Ballingham Herefs 28 G3
Ballingry Fife 86 E3
Ballinluig P & K 92 E5
Ballinshoe Angus 93 M5
Ballintuim P & K 92 G5
Balloch Highld 107 M11
Balloch N Lans 85 M7
Balloch P & K 92 C10
Balloch S Ayrs 76 F11
Balloch W Duns 84 G6
Balls Cross W Susx 10 F5
Balls Green E Susx 11 P3
Ballygown Ag & B 89 J7
Ballygrant Ag & B 82 E9
Ballyhaugh Ag & B 88 E5
Balmacara Highld 97 L4
Balmaclellan D & G 69 P4
Balmae D & G 69 P9
Balmaha Stirlg 84 G5
Balmalcolm Fife 86 G1
Balmangan D & G 69 P9
Balmedie Abers 103 K10
Balmerino Fife 93 L10
Balmichael N Ayrs 75 P6
Balmore E Duns 85 K8
Balmuchy Highld 107 P6
Balmule Fife 86 E5
Balmullo Fife 93 M10
Balnacoil Highld 109 P12
Balnacra Highld 97 P2
Balnacroft Abers 94 E3
Balnafoich Highld 99 K2
Balnaguard P & K 92 E5
Balnahard Ag & B 89 K9
Balnain Highld 98 G3
Balnakeil Highld 108 G3
Balne N York 59 N9
Balquharn P & K 92 F8
Balquhidder Stirlg 91 M11
Balsall Common Solhll 40 G10
Balsall Heath Birm 40 E9
Balscote Oxon 31 K6
Balsham Cambs 33 P6
Baltasound Shet 111 m2
Baltersan D & G 69 K6
Balthangie Abers 102 H5
Baltonsborough Somset 17 M8
Balvicar Ag & B 89 Q11
Balvraid Highld 97 M6
Balvraid Highld 99 M3
Bamber Bridge Lancs 57 K4
Bamber's Green Essex 33 P11
Bamburgh Nthumb 81 N7
Bamburgh Castle Nthumb 81 N7
Bamford Derbys 50 G4
Bampton Cumb 71 Q11
Bampton Devon 16 C10
Bampton Oxon 30 H12
Bampton Grange Cumb 71 Q11
Banavie Highld 90 F2
Banbury Oxon 31 L6
Bancffosfelen Carmth 26 C6
Banchory Abers 95 L3
Banchory-Devenick Abers 95 P2
Bancycapel Carmth 25 P6
Bancyfelin Carmth 25 N5
Bandirran P & K 93 J9
Banff Abers 102 F3
Bangor Gwynd 54 H7
Bangor-on-Dee Wrexhm 48 H6
Bangors Cnwll 14 D11
Banham Norfk 44 H11
Bank Hants 9 K6
Bankend D & G 70 G2
Bankfoot P & K 92 F8
Bankglen E Ayrs 77 L7

Bankhead C Aber 103 J12
Bankhead S Lans 86 B12
Banknock Falk 85 N7
Banks Lancs 56 H5
Bankshill D & G 79 K11
Banningham Norfk 45 K4
Bannister Green Essex 34 B11
Bannockburn Stirlg 85 N5
Banstead Surrey 21 K10
Bantham Devon 5 N10
Banton N Lans 85 M7
Banwell N Som 17 K4
Bapchild Kent 22 H10
Bapton Wilts 18 E12
Barabhas W Isls 111 d1
Barassie S Ayrs 76 F5
Barbaraville Highld 107 M7
Barbieston S Ayrs 76 G7
Barbon Cumb 63 L6
Barbrook Devon 15 M3
Barby Nhants 41 M12
Barcaldine Ag & B 90 D7
Barcombe E Susx 11 N7
Barcombe Cross E Susx 11 N6
Barden Park Kent 12 C2
Bardfield End Green Essex 33 Q9
Bardfield Saling Essex 34 B10
Bardney Lincs 52 G9
Bardon Leics 41 K5
Bardon Mill Nthumb 72 E7
Bardowie E Duns 85 K8
Bardrainney Inver 84 F8
Bardsea Cumb 62 F7
Bardsey Leeds 59 J5
Bardsey Island Gwynd 46 B7
Bardwell Suffk 34 F3
Bare Lancs 63 J8
Barfad D & G 69 J6
Barford Norfk 45 J8
Barford Warwks 30 H2
Barford St John Oxon 31 K7
Barford St Martin Wilts 8 F2
Barford St Michael Oxon 31 K7
Barfrestone Kent 23 N12
Bargeddie N Lans 85 L9
Bargoed Caerph 27 N8
Bargrennan D & G 69 J4
Barham Cambs 32 G2
Barham Kent 23 N12
Barham Suffk 35 J6
Bar Hill Cambs 33 L4
Barholm Lincs 42 F7
Barkby Leics 41 N5
Barkby Thorpe Leics 41 N5
Barkestone-le-Vale Leics 41 R1
Barkham Wokham 20 C9
Barking Gt Lon 21 N6
Barking Suffk 34 H6
Barkingside Gt Lon 21 N5
Barking Tye Suffk 34 H6
Barkisland Calder 58 D9
Barkla Shop Cnwll 2 H5
Barkston Lincs 42 D2
Barkston Ash N York 59 L7
Barkway Herts 33 L9
Barlanark C Glas 85 L9
Barlaston Staffs 50 F12
Barlavington W Susx 10 F6
Barlborough Derbys 51 L5
Barlby N York 59 N7
Barlestone Leics 41 K6
Barley Herts 33 L8
Barley Lancs 57 P1
Barleythorpe Rutlnd 42 C8
Barling Essex 22 H5
Barlings Lincs 52 F8
Barlochan D & G 70 D4
Barlow Derbys 51 J6
Barlow Gatesd 73 K8
Barlow N York 59 N8
Barmby Moor E R Yk 60 D4
Barmby on the Marsh E R Yk 59 P8
Barmollack Ag & B 75 M4
Barmouth Gwynd 47 K7
Barmpton Darltn 65 N4
Barmston E R Yk 61 K3
Barnacarry Ag & B 83 Q4
Barnack C Pete 42 F8
Barnard Castle Dur 65 J4
Barnard Gate Oxon 31 K11
Barnardiston Suffk 34 B7
Barnbarroch D & G 70 D4
Barnburgh Donc 59 L12
Barnby Suffk 45 P11
Barnby Dun Donc 59 N11
Barnby in the Willows Notts 52 C11
Barnby Moor Notts 51 P6
Barncorkrie D & G 68 E11
Barnes Gt Lon 21 K7
Barnes Street Kent 12 D1
Barnet Gt Lon 21 K4
Barnetby le Wold N Linc 52 F2
Barney Norfk 44 G4
Barnham Suffk 34 E2
Barnham W Susx 10 F8
Barnham Broom Norfk 44 H8
Barnhead Angus 93 R4
Barnhill C Dund 93 N8
Barnhill Moray 100 H4
Barnhills D & G 68 D5
Barningham Dur 65 J4
Barningham Suffk 34 F2
Barnoldby le Beck NE Lin 52 H3
Barnoldswick Lancs 63 Q11
Barns Green W Susx 10 H5
Barnsley Barns 59 J11
Barnsley Gloucs 30 E12
Barnstaple Devon 15 K5
Barnston Essex 33 Q11
Barnston Wirral 56 F11
Barnstone Notts 41 Q1
Barnt Green Worcs 40 D11
Barnton C Edin 86 E7
Barnton Ches W 49 M1
Barnwell All Saints Nhants 42 F12
Barnwell St Andrew Nhants 42 F11
Barnwood Gloucs 29 M5
Barr S Ayrs 76 E11
Barra W Isls 111 a7
Barra Airport W Isls 111 a6
Barrachan D & G 69 J8
Barraigh W Isls 111 a7
Barrananaoil Ag & B 83 M2

Barrapoll Ag & B 88 B7
Barrasford Nthumb 72 G6
Barrhead E Rens 84 H10
Barrhill S Ayrs 68 H3
Barrington Cambs 33 L6
Barrington Somset 17 K11
Barripper Cnwll 2 F7
Barrmill N Ayrs 84 F11
Barrock Highld 110 F2
Barrow Gloucs 29 M4
Barrow Lancs 57 N2
Barrow Rutlnd 42 C7
Barrow Somset 17 Q9
Barrow Suffk 34 C4
Barrowby Lincs 42 C3
Barrowden Rutlnd 42 D9
Barrowford Lancs 57 Q2
Barrow Gurney N Som 17 M3
Barrow Haven N Linc 60 H9
Barrow-in-Furness Cumb 62 E8
Barrow Island Cumb 62 E8
Barrow-upon-Humber N Linc 60 H9
Barrow upon Soar Leics 41 M4
Barrow upon Trent Derbys 41 J2
Barry Angus 93 P8
Barry V Glam 16 F3
Barry Island V Glam 16 F3
Barsby Leics 41 P5
Barsham Suffk 45 N11
Barston Solhll 40 G10
Bartestree Herefs 28 G1
Barthol Chapel Abers 102 H8
Bartholomew Green Essex 34 C11
Barthomley Ches E 49 N5
Bartley Hants 9 K5
Bartley Green Birm 40 D10
Bartlow Cambs 33 P7
Barton Cambs 33 L5
Barton Ches W 49 J5
Barton Gloucs 30 E8
Barton Lancs 56 G7
Barton Lancs 57 K2
Barton N York 65 M6
Barton Oxon 31 M11
Barton Torbay 6 C8
Barton Bendish Norfk 44 B8
Barton End Gloucs 29 L8
Barton Hartshorn Bucks 31 N7
Barton in Fabis Notts 41 M2
Barton in the Beans Leics 41 K6
Barton-le-Clay C Beds 32 F9
Barton-le-Street N York 66 G11
Barton-le-Willows N York 60 C2
Barton Mills Suffk 34 C3
Barton-on-Sea Hants 9 J8
Barton-on-the-Heath Warwks 30 G7
Barton Park Services N York 65 L6
Barton St David Somset 17 M9
Barton Seagrave Nhants 32 C2
Barton Stacey Hants 19 M11
Barton Town Devon 15 L4
Barton Turf Norfk 45 M5
Barton-under-Needwood Staffs 40 G4
Barton-upon-Humber N Linc 60 H9
Barton Waterside N Linc 60 H9
Barvas W Isls 111 d1
Barway Cambs 33 N2
Barwell Leics 41 K8
Barwick Devon 15 K10
Barwick Somset 17 M12
Barwick in Elmet Leeds 59 K6
Baschurch Shrops 48 H10
Bascote Warwks 31 K2
Bashall Eaves Lancs 63 N12
Basildon Essex 22 E5
Basingstoke Hants 19 Q9
Baslow Derbys 50 H6
Bason Bridge Somset 17 J7
Bassaleg Newpt 28 C10
Bassendean Border 80 E5
Bassenthwaite Cumb 71 K8
Bassett C Sotn 9 M4
Bassingbourn-cum-Kneesworth Cambs 33 K7
Bassingham Lincs 52 C10
Bassingthorpe Lincs 42 D5
Bassus Green Herts 33 K10
Baston Lincs 42 G7
Bastwick Norfk 45 N6
Batchworth Herts 20 G5
Batcombe Dorset 7 N3
Batcombe Somset 17 Q8
Batford Herts 21 J1
Bath BaNES 17 Q3
Bathampton BaNES 18 B7
Bathealton Somset 16 E10
Batheaston BaNES 18 B7
Bathford BaNES 18 B7
Bathgate W Loth 86 B8
Bathley Notts 51 Q8
Bathpool Cnwll 4 G5
Bathpool Somset 16 H10
Bath Side Essex 35 L9
Bathville W Loth 85 Q9
Bathway Somset 17 N5
Batley Kirk 58 G9
Batsford Gloucs 30 F7
Battersby N York 66 E6
Battersea Gt Lon 21 L7
Battisford Suffk 34 G6
Battisford Tye Suffk 34 G6
Battle E Susx 12 E6
Battle Powys 27 L3
Battledykes Angus 93 M5
Battlefield Shrops 49 K11
Battlesbridge Essex 22 F5
Battleton Somset 16 C10
Baughton Worcs 29 M1
Baughurst Hants 19 P8
Baulds Abers 95 K4
Baulking Oxon 19 K3
Baumber Lincs 52 H8
Baunton Gloucs 30 D12
Baverstock Wilts 8 E2
Bawburgh Norfk 45 J8
Bawdeswell Norfk 44 H6
Bawdrip Somset 17 J8
Bawdsey Suffk 35 M8
Bawtry Donc 51 P3
Baxenden Lancs 57 P4
Baxterley Warwks 40 H7

Bay Highld 104 C10
Bayble W Isls 111 e2
Baybridge Hants 9 N3
Baycliff Cumb 62 F7
Baydon Wilts 19 K5
Bayford Herts 21 L2
Bayford Somset 17 Q9
Bayhead W Isls 111 a4
Baylham Suffk 34 H6
Baysham Herefs 28 G4
Bayston Hill Shrops 39 J1
Baythorne End Essex 34 C8
Bayton Worcs 39 M7
Bayworth Oxon 19 N1
Beachampton Bucks 31 Q6
Beachamwell Norfk 44 C8
Beachy Head E Susx 12 C10
Beacon Devon 6 G2
Beacon End Essex 34 F10
Beacon Hill Notts 52 B11
Beacon Hill Surrey 10 E3
Beacon's Bottom Bucks 20 C4
Beaconsfield Bucks 20 F5
Beaconsfield Services Bucks 20 F6
Beadlam N York 66 F9
Beadlow C Beds 32 F8
Beadnell Nthumb 81 P8
Beaford Devon 15 K8
Beal N York 59 M8
Beal Nthumb 81 M6
Bealsmill Cnwll 4 H5
Beaminster Dorset 7 L3
Beamish Dur 73 M9
Beamish Open Air Museum Dur 73 L9
Beamsley N York 58 E4
Beanacre Wilts 18 D7
Beanley Nthumb 81 M9
Beardon Devon 5 L4
Beare Green Surrey 11 J2
Bearley Warwks 30 F3
Bearpark Dur 73 M11
Bearsden E Duns 85 J8
Bearsted Kent 22 F11
Bearstone Shrops 49 N7
Bearwood BCP 8 F7
Bearwood Birm 40 D9
Bearwood Herefs 38 H10
Beattock D & G 78 H8
Beauchamp Roding Essex 22 C2
Beauchief Sheff 51 J5
Beaufort Blae G 27 N6
Beaulieu Essex 22 E2
Beaulieu Hants 9 L7
Beauly Highld 107 J11
Beaumaris IoA 54 H6
Beaumaris Castle IoA 54 H6
Beaumont Cumb 71 M4
Beaumont Essex 35 J10
Beaumont Jersey 7 b2
Beaumont Leys C Leic 41 M6
Beausale Warwks 40 G12
Beauworth Hants 9 P3
Beaworthy Devon 14 H11
Beazley End Essex 34 C10
Bebington Wirral 56 G11
Beccles Suffk 45 N11
Becconsall Lancs 57 J4
Beckbury Shrops 39 N2
Beckenham Gt Lon 21 M9
Beckermet Cumb 62 B2
Beckfoot Cumb 70 H5
Beckford Worcs 29 N2
Beckhampton Wilts 18 G7
Beckingham Lincs 52 C11
Beckingham Notts 51 R3
Beckington Somset 18 B9
Beckjay Shrops 38 H6
Beckley Oxon 31 M10
Beck Row Suffk 34 B2
Beck Side Cumb 62 E6
Beckton Gt Lon 21 N7
Beckwithshaw N York 58 H4
Becontree Gt Lon 21 P6
Bedale N York 65 M9
Bedchester Dorset 8 C4
Beddau Rhondd 27 M10
Beddgelert Gwynd 54 H11
Beddingham E Susx 11 N8
Beddington Gt Lon 21 L9
Beddington Corner Gt Lon 21 L9
Bedfield Suffk 35 K4
Bedford Bed 32 F6
Bedgrove Bucks 20 D2
Bedhampton Hants 10 B8
Bedingfield Suffk 35 K3
Bedlam N York 58 H2
Bedlington Nthumb 73 M5
Bedlinog Myr Td 27 M8
Bedminster Bristl 17 N2
Bedminster Down Bristl 17 N3
Bedmond Herts 20 H3
Bednall Staffs 40 C4
Bedrule Border 80 E10
Bedstone Shrops 38 G7
Bedwas Caerph 27 N10
Bedwellty Caerph 27 N8
Bedworth Warwks 41 J9
Beeby Leics 41 P6
Beech Hants 10 B3
Beech Staffs 49 Q7
Beech Hill W Berk 20 B9
Beechingstoke Wilts 18 G8
Beedon W Berk 19 N5
Beeford E R Yk 61 J4
Beeley Derbys 50 H7
Beelsby NE Lin 52 H3
Beenham W Berk 19 P7
Beer Devon 6 G5
Beer Somset 17 M9
Beercrocombe Somset 17 J11
Beer Hackett Dorset 7 N2
Beesands Devon 5 Q11
Beesby Lincs 53 M7
Beeson Devon 5 Q11
Beeston C Beds 32 G7
Beeston Ches W 49 K4
Beeston Leeds 58 H7
Beeston Norfk 44 F7
Beeston Notts 51 M12
Beeston Regis Norfk 45 J2
Beeswing D & G 70 E2

Beetham Cumb 63 J6
Beetham Somset 6 H1
Beetley Norfk 44 F6
Begbroke Oxon 31 L10
Begelly Pembks 25 K7
Beguildy Powys 38 E6
Beighton Norfk 45 N8
Beighton Sheff 51 K4
Beinn Na Faoghla W Isls 111 b5
Beith N Ayrs 84 F11
Bekesbourne Kent 23 M11
Belaugh Norfk 45 L6
Belbroughton Worcs 40 B11
Belchalwell Dorset 8 B4
Belchamp Otten Essex 34 D8
Belchamp St Paul Essex 34 D8
Belchamp Walter Essex 34 D8
Belchford Lincs 53 J8
Belford Nthumb 81 M7
Belgrave C Leic 41 N6
Belhaven E Loth 87 M6
Belhelvie Abers 103 K10
Belhinnie Abers 101 N9
Bellabeg Abers 101 L11
Bellanoch Ag & B 83 M5
Bellaty Angus 93 J4
Bell Busk N York 58 B3
Belleau Lincs 53 L7
Bell End Worcs 40 C11
Bellerby N York 65 K8
Belle Vue Cumb 71 M4
Belle Vue Wakefd 59 J9
Bellfield S Lans 78 D2
Bellfields Surrey 20 F11
Bellingdon Bucks 20 F3
Bellingham Nthumb 72 F4
Belloch Ag & B 75 K5
Bellochantuy Ag & B 75 K6
Bell o' th' Hill Ches W 49 K6
Bellshill N Lans 85 M10
Bellshill Nthumb 81 N7
Bellside N Lans 85 N10
Bellsquarry W Loth 86 C8
Bells Yew Green E Susx 12 C3
Belluton BaNES 17 N4
Belmaduthy Highld 107 K10
Belmont Bl w D 57 M6
Belmont Gt Lon 21 K10
Belmont S Ayrs 76 F7
Belmont Shet 111 m2
Belnacraig Abers 101 M11
Belper Derbys 51 J10
Belsay Nthumb 73 K5
Belses Border 80 D8
Belsford Devon 5 P8
Belsize Herts 20 G4
Belstead Suffk 35 J8
Belstone Devon 5 M2
Belthorn Bl w D 57 N4
Beltinge Kent 23 M9
Beltingham Nthumb 72 E7
Beltoft N Linc 52 B3
Belton Leics 41 K4
Belton Lincs 42 D3
Belton N Linc 52 B3
Belton Norfk 45 P9
Belton House Lincs 42 D3
Belton in Rutland Rutlnd 42 B9
Belvedere Gt Lon 21 P7
Belvoir Leics 42 B4
Bembridge IoW 9 Q9
Bemerton Wilts 8 G2
Bempton E R Yk 67 P12
Benacre Suffk 45 Q12
Benbecula W Isls 111 b5
Benbecula Airport W Isls 111 b5
Benbuie D & G 77 M11
Benderloch Ag & B 90 C8
Benenden Kent 12 F4
Benfieldside Dur 73 J9
Bengeo Herts 21 L1
Bengeworth Worcs 30 D5
Benhall Green Suffk 35 N5
Benhall Street Suffk 35 N5
Benholm Abers 95 N7
Beningbrough N York 59 M3
Benington Herts 33 J11
Benington Lincs 43 L2
Benllech IoA 54 G5
Benmore Ag & B 84 C6
Bennan N Ayrs 75 Q7
Ben Nevis Highld 90 G3
Benniworth Lincs 52 H7
Benover Kent 12 E1
Ben Rhydding C Brad 58 F5
Benslie N Ayrs 76 F3
Benson Oxon 19 Q3
Benthoul C Aber 95 N2
Bentley Donc 59 M11
Bentley E R Yk 60 H7
Bentley Hants 10 C2
Bentley Suffk 35 J8
Bentley Warwks 40 H8
Bentpath D & G 79 M10
Bentwichen Devon 15 M5
Bentworth Hants 19 Q11
Benvie Angus 93 K8
Benville Dorset 7 M3
Benwick Cambs 43 K11
Beoley Worcs 40 E12
Beoraidbeg Highld 97 J10
Bepton W Susx 10 D6
Berden Essex 33 M10
Berea Pembks 24 E3
Bere Alston Devon 5 J6
Bere Ferrers Devon 5 K7
Bere Regis Dorset 8 C8
Bergh Apton Norfk 45 M9
Berinsfield Oxon 19 P2
Berkeley Gloucs 29 J8
Berkhamsted Herts 20 F2
Berkley Somset 18 B10
Berkswell Solhll 40 G10
Bermondsey Gt Lon 21 M7
Bernera Highld 97 M5
Bernisdale Highld 104 E11
Berrick Prior Oxon 19 Q2
Berrick Salome Oxon 19 Q3
Berriedale Highld 110 D10
Berrier Cumb 71 N9
Berriew Powys 38 D2
Berrington Shrops 39 K2
Berrington Worcs 39 L8
Berrington Green Worcs 39 L8

Berrow Somset 16 H6
Berrow Green Worcs 39 N9
Berryfields Bucks 20 C1
Berryhillock Moray 101 P3
Berryhillock Moray 101 P5
Berrynarbor Devon 15 K3
Berry Pomeroy Devon 5 Q7
Bersham Wrexhm 48 F5
Bersted W Susx 10 E9
Berwick E Susx 11 P8
Berwick Bassett Wilts 18 G6
Berwick Hill Nthumb 73 L6
Berwick St James Wilts 18 F11
Berwick St John Wilts 8 D3
Berwick St Leonard Wilts 8 D2
Berwick-upon-Tweed Nthumb 81 L4
Bescar Lancs 56 H6
Besford Worcs 30 B5
Bessacarr Donc 51 N1
Bessingby E R Yk 61 K2
Bessingham Norfk 45 J3
Besthorpe Norfk 44 H10
Besthorpe Notts 52 B9
Bestwood Village Notts 51 M10
Beswick E R Yk 60 H5
Betchworth Surrey 21 K12
Bethania Cerdgn 37 J7
Bethel Gwynd 54 G8
Bethel IoA 54 E7
Bethersden Kent 12 H3
Bethesda Gwynd 55 J8
Bethesda Pembks 25 J5
Bethlehem Carmth 26 F4
Bethnal Green Gt Lon 21 M6
Betley Staffs 49 N6
Betsham Kent 22 C8
Betteshanger Kent 23 P11
Bettiscombe Dorset 7 K3
Bettisfield Wrexhm 49 J8
Bettws Brdgnd 27 J10
Bettws Newpt 28 C10
Bettws Cedewain Powys 38 D3
Bettws Ifan Cerdgn 36 E10
Bettws-Newydd Mons 28 D7
Bettyhill Highld 109 M4
Betws Bledrws Cerdgn 37 K9
Betws Gwerfil Goch Denbgs 48 B6
Betws-y-Coed Conwy 55 L9
Betws-yn-Rhos Conwy 55 N6
Beulah Cerdgn 36 E10
Beulah Powys 37 Q9
Bevercotes Notts 51 P6
Beverley E R Yk 60 H6
Beverston Gloucs 29 M9
Bewcastle Cumb 71 Q1
Bewdley Worcs 39 P7
Bewerley N York 58 F2
Bewholme E R Yk 61 K4
Bexhill-on-Sea E Susx 12 E8
Bexley Gt Lon 21 P8
Bexleyheath Gt Lon 21 P8
Bexwell Norfk 43 Q9
Beyton Suffk 34 F4
Beyton Green Suffk 34 F4
Bhaltos W Isls 111 c2
Bhatarsaigh W Isls 111 a7
Bibury Gloucs 30 E11
Bicester Oxon 31 N9
Bickenhill Solhll 40 F10
Bicker Lincs 42 H3
Bickerstaffe Lancs 57 J7
Bickerton N York 59 K4
Bickford Staffs 40 B5
Bickington Devon 5 Q6
Bickington Devon 15 J6
Bickleigh Devon 5 L7
Bickleigh Devon 6 C2
Bickley Ches W 49 K6
Bickley Gt Lon 21 N9
Bickley N York 67 K8
Bicknacre Essex 22 F3
Bicknoller Somset 16 F8
Bicknor Kent 22 G10
Bicton Shrops 38 F5
Bicton Shrops 49 J11
Bidborough Kent 11 C2
Biddenden Kent 12 G3
Biddenham Bed 32 E6
Biddestone Wilts 18 C6
Biddisham Somset 17 K5
Biddlesden Bucks 31 N6
Biddulph Staffs 50 B8
Biddulph Moor Staffs 50 B8
Bideford Devon 14 H6
Bidford-on-Avon Warwks 30 E4
Bielby E R Yk 60 D5
Bieldside C Aber 95 P2
Bierley IoW 9 N10
Bierton Bucks 32 B12
Big Balcraig D & G 69 K9
Bigbury Devon 5 N10
Bigbury-on-Sea Devon 5 N10
Bigby Lincs 52 F3
Biggar S Lans 78 G2
Biggin Derbys 50 F8
Biggin Hill Gt Lon 21 N10
Biggleswade C Beds 32 H7
Bigholms D & G 79 M11
Bighouse Highld 109 Q3
Bighton Hants 9 Q1
Biglands Cumb 71 L5
Bignor W Susx 10 F6
Bigrigg Cumb 70 G11
Big Sand Highld 105 L6
Bigton Shet 111 k5
Bilborough C Nott 51 M11
Bilbrook Somset 16 D7
Bilbrough N York 59 M5
Bilbster Highld 110 F5
Bildershaw Dur 65 L3
Bildeston Suffk 34 G6
Billericay Essex 22 D5
Billesdon Leics 41 Q7
Billesley Warwks 30 F3
Billingborough Lincs 42 G4
Billinge St Hel 57 K8
Billingford Norfk 44 H5
Billingford Norfk 44 G6
Billingham S on T 66 C3
Billinghay Lincs 52 G11
Billingley Barns 59 K12
Billingshurst W Susx 10 H5

Billingsley Shrops 39 N5
Billington C Beds 32 D11
Billington Lancs 57 N2
Billockby Norfk 45 N7
Billy Row Dur 73 L12
Bilsborrow Lancs 57 K2
Bilsby Lincs 53 M8
Bilsham W Susx 10 F9
Bilsington Kent 13 K3
Bilsthorpe Notts 51 N8
Bilston Mdloth 86 F8
Bilston Wolves 40 C8
Bilstone Leics 41 J6
Bilton E R Yk 61 K7
Bilton N York 58 H3
Bilton Warwks 41 L11
Bilton-in-Ainsty N York 59 L4
Binbrook Lincs 52 H5
Bincombe Dorset 7 P6
Binegar Somset 17 N6
Binfield Br For 20 D8
Binfield Heath Oxon 20 C7
Bingfield Nthumb 72 H6
Bingham Notts 51 P11
Bingley C Brad 58 E6
Binham Norfk 44 G3
Binley Covtry 41 J10
Binley Hants 19 M9
Binley Woods Warwks 41 K11
Binnegar Dorset 8 C9
Binniehill Falk 85 P8
Binscombe Surrey 10 F2
Binstead IoW 9 P8
Binsted Hants 10 C2
Binsted W Susx 10 F8
Binton Warwks 30 H4
Bintree Norfk 44 G5
Birch Essex 34 F11
Birchall Staffs 50 C9
Bircham Newton Norfk 44 C4
Bircham Tofts Norfk 44 C4
Birchanger Essex 33 N11
Birchanger Green Services Essex 33 N11
Birch Cross Staffs 40 E2
Bircher Herefs 39 J8
Birchfield Birm 40 E8
Birch Green Essex 34 F11
Birchgrove Cardif 27 N11
Birchgrove Swans 26 F8
Birchgrove W Susx 11 N4
Birchington Kent 23 P9
Birchley Heath Warwks 40 H8
Birchover Derbys 50 G8
Birch Services Rochdl 57 Q7
Birch Vale Derbys 50 D4
Birchwood Lincs 52 D9
Birch Wood Somset 16 H12
Birchwood Warrtn 57 M9
Bircotes Notts 51 N3
Birdbrook Essex 34 B8
Birdforth N York 66 C11
Birdham W Susx 10 D9
Birdingbury Warwks 31 K1
Birdlip Gloucs 29 N6
Birdsall N York 60 E2
Birds Edge Kirk 58 G11
Birds Green Essex 22 C2
Birdsgreen Shrops 39 P5
Birdsmoorgate Dorset 7 K3
Birdwell Barns 51 J1
Birgham Border 80 G6
Birichin Highld 107 M4
Birkby N York 65 N7
Birkdale Sefton 56 G6
Birkenbog Abers 102 C3
Birkenhead Wirral 56 G10
Birkenhead (Queensway) Tunnel Lpool 56 G10
Birkenhills Abers 102 F6
Birkenshaw Kirk 58 G8
Birkhall Abers 94 F4
Birkhill Angus 93 L8
Birkhill D & G 79 K6
Birkin N York 59 M8
Birley Herefs 39 J10
Birley Carr Sheff 51 J3
Birling Kent 22 D10
Birlingham Worcs 30 C5
Birmingham Birm 40 E9
Birmingham Airport Solhll 40 F10
Birnam P & K 92 F7
Birness Abers 103 K8
Birse Abers 95 J3
Birsemore Abers 95 J3
Birstall Kirk 58 G8
Birstall Leics 41 N5
Birstwith N York 58 G3
Birtley Gatesd 73 M9
Birtley Herefs 38 G8
Birtley Nthumb 72 F5
Birts Street Worcs 29 K2
Bisbrooke Rutlnd 42 C9
Biscathorpe Lincs 52 H6
Bisham W & M 20 D6
Bishampton Worcs 30 C4
Bish Mill Devon 15 M7
Bishop Auckland Dur 65 L2
Bishopbridge Lincs 52 E5
Bishopbriggs E Duns 85 K8
Bishop Burton E R Yk 60 G6
Bishop Middleham Dur 65 N2
Bishopmill Moray 101 J3
Bishop Monkton N York 59 J2
Bishop Norton Lincs 52 E5
Bishopsbourne Kent 23 M11
Bishops Cannings Wilts 18 F7
Bishop's Castle Shrops 38 G4
Bishop's Caundle Dorset 17 Q12
Bishop's Cleeve Gloucs 29 N4
Bishop's Frome Herefs 39 M11
Bishops Green Essex 33 Q12
Bishop's Hull Somset 16 G10
Bishop's Itchington Warwks 31 K3
Bishops Lydeard Somset 16 G9
Bishop's Norton Gloucs 29 L4
Bishop's Nympton Devon 15 N7
Bishop's Offley Staffs 49 P9
Bishop's Stortford Herts 33 M11
Bishop's Sutton Hants 9 Q2
Bishop's Tachbrook Warwks 30 H2
Bishop's Tawton Devon 15 K6
Bishopsteignton Devon 6 B7

Bishopstoke Hants 9 M4
Bishopston Swans 26 D10
Bishopstone Bucks 20 C2
Bishopstone E Susx 11 P9
Bishopstone Herefs 38 H12
Bishopstone Kent 23 N9
Bishopstone Swindn 19 J4
Bishopstone Wilts 8 F3
Bishopstrow Wilts 18 D11
Bishop Sutton BaNES 17 N4
Bishop's Waltham Hants 9 P4
Bishopswood Somset 6 H1
Bishop's Wood Staffs 49 Q12
Bishopsworth Bristl 17 N3
Bishop Thornton N York 58 H2
Bishopthorpe C York 59 N5
Bishopton Darltn 65 P4
Bishopton Rens 84 G8
Bishop Wilton E R Yk 60 D3
Bishton Newpt 28 D10
Bishton Staffs 40 D4
Bisley Gloucs 29 M7
Bisley Surrey 20 F10
Bissoe Cnwll 2 H7
Bisterne Hants 8 H6
Bitchfield Lincs 42 E4
Bittadon Devon 15 J4
Bittaford Devon 5 N8
Bitterley Shrops 39 K6
Bitterne C Sotn 9 M5
Bitteswell Leics 41 M9
Bitton S Glos 17 P3
Bix Oxon 20 B6
Bixter Shet 111 k4
Blaby Leics 41 M7
Blackadder Border 80 H4
Blackawton Devon 5 Q9
Blackborough Devon 6 E3
Blackborough End Norfk 43 Q7
Black Bourton Oxon 30 H12
Blackboys E Susx 11 Q6
Blackbrook Derbys 51 J10
Blackbrook St Hel 57 K9
Blackbrook Staffs 49 N7
Blackburn Abers 102 H11
Blackburn Bl w D 57 M4
Blackburn W Loth 86 B8
Blackburn with Darwen Services Bl w D 57 M4
Blackcraig E Ayrs 77 K9
Black Crofts Ag & B 90 C8
Blackdog Abers 103 K11
Black Dog Devon 15 N9
Blackdown Dorset 7 K3
Blackfen Gt Lon 21 P8
Blackfield Hants 9 M7
Blackford P & K 85 P2
Blackford Somset 17 K6
Blackford Somset 17 P10
Blackfordby Leics 41 J4
Blackhall C Edin 86 E7
Blackhall Colliery Dur 73 Q11
Blackhall Mill Gatesd 73 K9
Blackhaugh Border 79 N2
Blackheath Gt Lon 21 M7
Blackheath Sandw 40 C9
Blackheath Suffk 35 N2
Blackheath Surrey 10 G2
Blackhill Abers 103 M4
Blackhill Abers 103 M6
Blackhill Dur 73 J9
Blackhill of Clackriach Abers 103 J6
Blackhorse Devon 6 C4
Blacklaw D & G 78 G7
Blackley Manch 57 Q8
Blacklunans P & K 94 C9
Blackmarstone Herefs 28 F2
Blackmill Brdgnd 27 K10
Blackmoor Hants 10 C4
Blackmoor N Som 17 L4
Blackmoorfoot Kirk 58 E10
Blackmore Essex 22 C3
Blackmore End Essex 34 C9
Black Mountains 27 Q4
Blackness Falk 86 C6
Blacknest Hants 10 C2
Black Notley Essex 34 C11
Blacko Lancs 57 Q1
Black Pill Swans 26 E10
Blackpool Bpool 56 F2
Blackpool Zoo Bpool 56 G2
Blackridge W Loth 85 P9
Blackrod Bolton 57 L6
Blacksboat Moray 101 J7
Blackshaw D & G 70 G3
Blackshaw Head Calder 58 C8
Blackstone W Susx 11 K6
Black Street Suffk 45 Q11
Blackthorn Oxon 31 N9
Blackthorpe Suffk 34 E4
Blacktoft E R Yk 60 E8
Blacktop C Aber 95 P2
Black Torrington Devon 14 H10
Blackwall Derbys 50 G10
Blackwall Tunnel Gt Lon 21 M7
Blackwater Cnwll 2 H6
Blackwater Hants 20 D10
Blackwater IoW 9 N9
Blackwater Somset 16 H11
Blackwaterfoot N Ayrs 75 N6
Blackwell Cumb 71 N5
Blackwell Derbys 50 E6
Blackwell Derbys 51 K8
Blackwell Warwks 30 G5
Blackwell Worcs 40 C11
Blackwood Caerph 27 N8
Blackwood D & G 78 E10
Blackwood S Lans 77 N3
Blacon Ches W 48 H2
Bladnoch D & G 69 K8
Bladon Oxon 31 K10
Blaenannerch Cerdgn 36 D10
Blaenau Ffestiniog Gwynd 47 L3
Blaenavon Torfn 27 Q7
Blaenavon Industrial Landscape Torfn 27 P7
Blaencwm Rhondd 27 K8
Blaenffos Pembks 25 L2
Blaengarw Brdgnd 27 J9
Blaengwrach Neath 27 J7
Blaengwynfi Neath 27 J9

Blaenpennal Cerdgn 37 K7
Blaenplwyf Cerdgn 37 J5
Blaenporth Cerdgn 36 D10
Blaenrhondda Rhondd 27 K8
Blaenwaun Carmth 25 L4
Blaen-y-coed Carmth 25 N4
Blagdon N Som 17 M4
Blagdon Somset 16 G11
Blagdon Torbay 6 B9
Blagdon Hill Somset 16 G11
Blaich Highld 90 E2
Blain Highld 89 N3
Blaina Blae G 27 P7
Blair Atholl P & K 92 C3
Blair Drummond Stirlg 85 M3
Blairgowrie P & K 92 H6
Blairhall Fife 86 B5
Blairingone P & K 86 B3
Blairlogie Stirlg 85 N4
Blairmore Ag & B 84 D6
Blairmore Highld 108 D4
Blair's Ferry Ag & B 83 P8
Blaisdon Gloucs 29 J5
Blakebrook Worcs 39 P6
Blakedown Worcs 39 Q6
Blake End Essex 34 B11
Blakemere Ches W 49 K2
Blakemere Herefs 28 D1
Blakenall Heath Wsall 40 D7
Blakeney Gloucs 29 J7
Blakeney Norfk 44 G2
Blakenhall Ches E 49 N6
Blakenhall Wolves 40 B7
Blakesley Nhants 31 N4
Blanchland Nthumb 72 H10
Blandford Forum Dorset 8 C6
Blandford St Mary Dorset 8 C6
Blanefield Stirlg 85 J7
Blankney Lincs 52 F10
Blantyre S Lans 85 L10
Blàr a' Chaorainn Highld 90 F3
Blarghour Ag & B 83 Q1
Blargie Highld 98 H6
Blarmachfoldach Highld 90 F3
Blaston Leics 42 B10
Blatherwycke Nhants 42 D10
Blawith Cumb 62 F5
Blawquhairn D & G 69 N3
Blaxhall Suffk 35 M5
Blaxton Donc 51 P2
Blaydon Gatesd 73 L8
Bleadney Somset 17 L7
Bleadon N Som 17 J5
Blean Kent 23 L10
Bleasby Notts 51 Q10
Blebocraigs Fife 93 M11
Bleddfa Powys 38 E8
Bledington Gloucs 30 G9
Bledlow Bucks 20 C3
Bledlow Ridge Bucks 20 C4
Blegbie E Loth 87 J9
Blencarn Cumb 64 B2
Blencogo Cumb 71 K6
Blendworth Hants 10 B7
Blenheim Palace Oxon 31 K10
Blennerhasset Cumb 71 J7
Bletchingdon Oxon 31 L9
Bletchingley Surrey 21 M12
Bletchley M Keyn 32 C9
Bletchley Shrops 49 L8
Bletchley Park Museum M Keyn 32 C9
Bletherston Pembks 25 J5
Bletsoe Bed 32 E5
Blewbury Oxon 19 N4
Blickling Norfk 45 K4
Blidworth Notts 51 N9
Blidworth Bottoms Notts 51 N9
Blindcrake Cumb 71 J8
Blindley Heath Surrey 11 M2
Blisland Cnwll 4 D5
Blissford Hants 8 H5
Bliss Gate Worcs 39 N7
Blisworth Nhants 31 Q4
Blithbury Staffs 40 E4
Blockley Gloucs 30 F7
Blofield Norfk 45 M8
Blofield Heath Norfk 45 M7
Blo Norton Norfk 34 G2
Bloomfield Border 80 D8
Blore Staffs 50 F10
Bloxham Oxon 31 K7
Bloxholm Lincs 52 F11
Bloxwich Wsall 40 C7
Bloxworth Dorset 8 C8
Blubberhouses N York 58 F3
Blue Anchor Somset 16 D7
Blue Bell Hill Kent 22 E10
Blue John Cavern Derbys 50 F4
Blundellsands Sefton 56 F8
Blundeston Suffk 45 Q10
Blunham C Beds 32 G6
Blunsdon St Andrew Swindn 18 G3
Bluntington Worcs 40 B11
Bluntisham Cambs 33 K2
Blurton C Stke 50 B11
Blyborough Lincs 52 D5
Blyford Suffk 35 N2
Blymhill Staffs 49 P11
Blyth Notts 51 N4
Blyth Nthumb 73 N5
Blyth Bridge Border 86 D12
Blythburgh Suffk 35 P2
Blythe Border 80 D6
Blythe Bridge Staffs 50 C11
Blyth Services Notts 51 N3
Blyton Lincs 52 C5
Boarhills Fife 93 P11
Boarhunt Hants 9 P6
Boarstall Bucks 31 N10
Boath Highld 107 J7
Boat of Garten Highld 99 P5
Bobbing Kent 22 H9
Bobbington Staffs 39 P4
Bocking Essex 34 C11
Bocking Churchstreet Essex 34 C10
Boddam Abers 103 M6
Boddam Shet 111 k5
Boddington Gloucs 29 M4
Bodedern IoA 54 D5
Bodelwyddan Denbgs 55 Q6
Bodenham Herefs 39 K11
Bodenham Wilts 8 H3

Bodenham Moor Herefs 39 K11
Bodewryd IoA 54 E4
Bodfari Denbgs 48 C2
Bodffordd IoA 54 F6
Bodham Norfk 45 J3
Bodiam E Susx 12 F5
Bodicote Oxon 31 L6
Bodinnick Cnwll 4 E9
Bodle Street Green E Susx 12 D7
Bodmin Cnwll 3 N3
Bodmin Moor Cnwll 4 F5
Bodsham Kent 13 L2
Boduan Gwynd 46 E4
Bodwen Cnwll 4 E9
Bogallan Highld 107 K11
Bogbrae Abers 103 L8
Bogend S Ayrs 76 G5
Boggs Holdings E Loth 87 J7
Boghall Mdloth 86 F8
Boghall W Loth 86 B8
Boghead S Lans 77 N3
Bogmoor Moray 101 L3
Bogmuir Abers 95 K7
Bogniebrae Abers 102 D6
Bognor Regis W Susx 10 E9
Bogroy Highld 99 N4
Bogue D & G 69 P3
Bohortha Cnwll 3 J8
Bohuntine Highld 98 D11
Bolam Dur 65 L3
Bolberry Devon 5 N11
Boldmere Birm 40 E8
Boldre Hants 9 K7
Boldron Dur 65 J5
Bole Notts 52 B6
Bolehill Derbys 50 H9
Bolham Devon 16 C12
Bolham Water Devon 6 F1
Bolingey Cnwll 2 H5
Bollington Ches E 50 C5
Bolney W Susx 11 L5
Bolnhurst Bed 32 F5
Bolnore W Susx 11 M5
Bolshan Angus 93 Q5
Bolsover Derbys 51 L6
Bolsterstone Sheff 50 H2
Boltby N York 66 C9
Bolton Bolton 57 N7
Bolton Cumb 64 B3
Bolton E Loth 87 K8
Bolton E R Yk 60 D4
Bolton Nthumb 81 M10
Bolton Abbey N York 58 E4
Bolton-by-Bowland Lancs 63 P11
Boltonfellend Cumb 71 P2
Boltongate Cumb 71 L7
Bolton-le-Sands Lancs 63 J8
Bolton Low Houses Cumb 71 K6
Bolton-on-Swale N York 65 M7
Bolton Percy N York 59 M6
Bolton upon Dearne Barns 51 L1
Bolventor Cnwll 4 E5
Bomere Heath Shrops 49 J10
Bonar Bridge Highld 107 K4
Bonawe Ag & B 90 D9
Bonby N Linc 60 G10
Boncath Pembks 25 L2
Bonchester Bridge Border 80 D10
Bondleigh Devon 15 L10
Bonds Lancs 63 J12
Bo'ness Falk 86 B6
Boney Hay Staffs 40 D5
Bonhill W Duns 84 G7
Boningale Shrops 39 P2
Bonjedward Border 80 E9
Bonkle N Lans 85 P10
Bonnington Angus 93 P7
Bonnington Kent 13 K3
Bonnybank Fife 86 G2
Bonnybridge Falk 85 N7
Bonnykelly Abers 103 J5
Bonnyrigg Mdloth 86 G8
Bonnyton Angus 93 L7
Bonsall Derbys 50 H8
Bonshaw Tower D & G 71 K2
Bont-Dolgadfan Powys 47 P10
Bont-goch Cerdgn 37 L4
Bontnewydd Cerdgn 37 K7
Bontnewydd Gwynd 54 G9
Bontuchel Denbgs 48 C4
Bonvilston V Glam 16 E2
Boode Devon 15 J5
Booker Bucks 20 D5
Boon Border 80 D5
Boosbeck R & Cl 66 F4
Boose's Green Essex 34 E9
Boot Cumb 62 E3
Boothby Graffoe Lincs 52 E10
Boothby Pagnell Lincs 42 D4
Boothferry E R Yk 60 C8
Boothstown Salfd 57 N8
Boothtown Calder 58 E8
Boothville Nhants 32 B4
Bootle Cumb 62 C5
Bootle Sefton 56 G9
Boraston Shrops 39 L8
Bordeaux Guern 6 c1
Borden Kent 22 G10
Bordon Hants 10 C3
Boreham Essex 22 F2
Boreham Street E Susx 12 D7
Borehamwood Herts 21 J4
Boreland D & G 79 J10
Boreraig Highld 104 B10
Borgh W Isls 111 a7
Borgh W Isls 111 d1
Borgie Highld 109 M4
Borgue D & G 69 P9
Borgue Highld 110 D9
Borley Essex 34 E7
Borneskitaig Highld 104 E7
Borness D & G 69 N9
Boroughbridge N York 59 K2
Borough Green Kent 22 C11
Borrowash Derbys 41 K1
Borrowby N York 65 Q9
Borrowdale Cumb 71 L11
Borrowstoun Falk 86 B6
Borstal Medway 22 E9
Borth Cerdgn 37 K3
Borthwick Mdloth 86 H9
Borthwickbrae Border 79 N6

Borthwickshiels Border 79 N6
Borth-y-Gest Gwynd 47 J4
Borve Highld 104 F11
Borve W Isls 111 a7
Borve W Isls 111 c3
Borve W Isls 111 d1
Borwick Lancs 63 K7
Bosbury Herefs 39 M12
Boscastle Cnwll 4 D3
Boscombe BCP 8 G8
Boscombe Wilts 18 H11
Bosham W Susx 10 D8
Bosherston Pembks 24 G9
Bosley Ches E 50 B7
Bossall N York 60 C3
Bossiney Cnwll 4 D3
Bossingham Kent 13 M1
Bossington Somset 16 B6
Bostock Green Ches W 49 M2
Boston Lincs 43 K2
Boston Spa Leeds 59 K5
Boswinger Cnwll 3 L7
Botallack Cnwll 2 B8
Botany Bay Gt Lon 21 L4
Botesdale Suffk 34 H2
Bothal Nthumb 73 M4
Bothamsall Notts 51 P6
Bothel Cumb 71 J7
Bothenhampton Dorset 7 L5
Bothwell S Lans 85 L10
Bothwell Services (southbound) S Lans 85 M10
Botley Bucks 20 F3
Botley Hants 9 N5
Botley Oxon 31 L11
Botolph Claydon Bucks 31 Q8
Botolphs W Susx 11 J8
Bottesford Leics 42 B3
Bottesford N Linc 52 C3
Bottisham Cambs 33 N5
Bottomcraig Fife 93 L10
Bottoms Calder 58 B9
Botusfleming Cnwll 5 J7
Botwnnog Gwynd 46 D5
Bough Beech Kent 11 P1
Boughrood Powys 27 N2
Boughton Nhants 31 Q2
Boughton Norfk 44 B9
Boughton Notts 51 P7
Boughton Aluph Kent 13 K1
Boughton Green Kent 22 F12
Boughton Lees Kent 13 K1
Boughton Monchelsea Kent 22 F12
Boughton Street Kent 23 K10
Bouldon Shrops 39 K5
Boulmer Nthumb 81 Q10
Boultenstone Abers 101 M12
Boultham Lincs 52 D9
Bourn Cambs 33 K5
Bournbrook Birm 40 D10
Bourne Lincs 42 F6
Bournebridge Essex 21 P5
Bourne End Bucks 20 E6
Bourne End C Beds 32 D7
Bourne End Herts 20 G3
Bournemouth BCP 8 G8
Bournemouth Airport BCP 8 G7
Bournes Green Sthend 22 H6
Bournheath Worcs 40 C11
Bournmoor Dur 73 N9
Bournville Birm 40 D10
Bourton Dorset 8 B2
Bourton Oxon 31 J4
Bourton Shrops 39 L3
Bourton Wilts 18 F7
Bourton on Dunsmore Warwks 41 K12
Bourton-on-the-Hill Gloucs 30 F7
Bourton-on-the-Water Gloucs 30 F9
Bousd Ag & B 88 G4
Bouth Cumb 62 G5
Bouthwaite N York 65 K12
Boveridge Dorset 8 F4
Bovey Tracey Devon 5 Q5
Bovingdon Herts 20 G3
Bow Devon 15 M10
Bow Gt Lon 21 M6
Bow Ork 111 h3
Bow Brickhill M Keyn 32 C9
Bowbridge Gloucs 29 M7
Bowburn Dur 73 N12
Bowcombe IoW 9 M9
Bowd Devon 6 F5
Bowden Border 80 D7
Bowden Hill Wilts 18 D7
Bowdon Traffd 57 N10
Bower Highld 110 E3
Bowerchalke Wilts 8 F3
Bowermadden Highld 110 F3
Bowers Staffs 49 P8
Bowers Gifford Essex 22 E6
Bowershall Fife 86 C4
Bower's Row Leeds 59 K8
Bowes Dur 64 H5
Bowgreave Lancs 63 J12
Bowhouse D & G 70 G3
Bowland Border 79 P1
Bowley Herefs 39 K10
Bowlhead Green Surrey 10 E3
Bowling C Brad 58 F7
Bowling W Duns 84 G8
Bowmanstead Cumb 62 F3
Bowmore Ag & B 82 D10
Bowness-on-Solway Cumb 71 K3
Bowness-on-Windermere Cumb 62 H3
Bow of Fife Fife 93 K12
Bowriefauld Angus 93 N6
Bow Street Cerdgn 37 K4
Bowthorpe Norfk 45 K8
Box Gloucs 29 M8
Box Wilts 18 C7
Boxford Suffk 34 F7
Boxford W Berk 19 M6
Boxgrove W Susx 10 E8
Boxley Kent 22 F10
Boxmoor Herts 20 G3
Boxted Essex 34 G9
Boxted Suffk 34 D6
Boxted Cross Essex 34 G9

Boxworth Cambs......33 K4
Boyden Gate Kent......23 N9
Boylestone Derbys......40 F1
Boyndie Abers......102 E3
Boyndlie Abers......103 J3
Boynton E R Yk......61 K1
Boysack Angus......93 Q6
Boythorpe Derbys......51 J6
Boyton Cnwll......4 H2
Boyton Suffk......35 N7
Boyton Wilts......18 D11
Boyton Cross Essex......22 D2
Boyton End Suffk......34 C7
Bozeat Nhants......32 C5
Brabourne Kent......13 L2
Brabourne Lees Kent......13 L3
Brabstermire Highld......110 G2
Bracadale Highld......96 D2
Braceborough Lincs......42 F7
Bracebridge Heath Lincs......52 E9
Bracebridge Low Fields Lincs......52 D9
Braceby Lincs......42 E3
Bracewell Lancs......63 Q11
Brackenfield Derbys......51 J8
Brackenhirst N Lans......85 M8
Brackla Brdgnd......27 K11
Bracklesham W Susx......10 D10
Brackletter Highld......98 B11
Brackley Nhants......31 N6
Bracknell Br For......20 E9
Braco P & K......85 N2
Bracobrae Moray......101 P5
Bracon Ash Norfk......45 K9
Bracora Highld......97 K10
Bracorina Highld......97 K10
Bradbourne Derbys......50 G9
Bradbury Dur......65 N2
Bradden Nhants......31 N5
Bradeley C Stke......49 Q5
Bradenham Bucks......20 D4
Bradenham Norfk......44 F8
Bradenstoke Wilts......18 E5
Bradfield Devon......6 E2
Bradfield Essex......35 J9
Bradfield Norfk......45 L4
Bradfield Sheff......50 H3
Bradfield Combust Suffk......34 E5
Bradfield Green Ches E......49 M4
Bradfield Heath Essex......35 J10
Bradfield St Clare Suffk......34 E5
Bradfield St George Suffk......34 E5
Bradford C Brad......58 F7
Bradford Devon......14 G10
Bradford Abbas Dorset......17 N12
Bradford Leigh Wilts......18 C8
Bradford-on-Avon Wilts......18 C8
Bradford-on-Tone Somset......16 G10
Bradford Peverell Dorset......7 P4
Bradiford Devon......15 K5
Brading IoW......9 Q9
Bradley Derbys......50 G10
Bradley Hants......19 Q11
Bradley NE Lin......53 J3
Bradley Staffs......49 Q11
Bradley Wolves......40 C8
Bradley Worcs......30 C2
Bradley Green Worcs......30 C2
Bradley in the Moors Staffs......50 D11
Bradley Stoke S Glos......28 H11
Bradmore Notts......41 N2
Bradninch Devon......6 D3
Bradnop Staffs......50 D9
Bradpole Dorset......7 L4
Bradshaw Calder......58 E8
Bradstone Devon......4 H4
Bradwall Green Ches E......49 N3
Bradwell Derbys......50 F5
Bradwell Essex......34 D11
Bradwell M Keyn......32 B8
Bradwell Norfk......45 Q8
Bradwell-on-Sea Essex......23 J3
Bradwell Waterside Essex......23 J2
Bradworthy Devon......14 F8
Brae Highld......107 L9
Brae Shet......111 k3
Braeface Falk......85 N7
Braehead Angus......95 L10
Braehead D & G......69 K8
Braehead S Lans......77 Q2
Braeintra Highld......97 M3
Braemar Abers......94 C4
Braemore Highld......106 C9
Braemore Highld......110 C9
Brae Roy Lodge Highld......98 D10
Braeside Inver......84 D7
Braes of Coul Angus......93 K4
Braes of Enzie Moray......101 M4
Braes of Ullapool Highld......106 C4
Braeswick Ork......111 i1
Braevallich Ag & B......83 P2
Braewick Shet......111 j3
Brafferton Darltn......65 N4
Brafferton N York......66 B12
Brafield-on-the-Green
Nhants......32 B5
Bragar W Isls......111 d1
Bragbury End Herts......33 J11
Braidwood S Lans......77 P2
Brailsford Derbys......50 G11
Braintree Essex......34 C11
Braiseworth Suffk......35 J3
Braishfield Hants......9 L3
Braithwaite C Brad......58 E6
Braithwaite Cumb......71 K10
Braithwell Donc......51 L3
Bramber W Susx......11 J7
Bramcote Warwks......41 K9
Bramdean Hants......9 Q3
Bramerton Norfk......45 L8
Bramfield Herts......21 L1
Bramfield Suffk......35 N3
Bramford Suffk......35 J7
Bramhall Stockp......50 B4
Bramham Leeds......59 K5
Bramhope Leeds......58 G5
Bramley Hants......19 Q8
Bramley Leeds......58 G6
Bramley Rothm......51 L3
Bramley Surrey......10 G2
Bramling Kent......23 N11
Brampford Speke Devon......6 C3
Brampton Cambs......32 H3
Brampton Cumb......64 C9

Brampton Cumb......71 Q4
Brampton Lincs......52 B7
Brampton Norfk......45 K5
Brampton Rothm......51 K1
Brampton Suffk......35 P1
Brampton Abbotts Herefs......28 H4
Brampton Ash Nhants......42 B11
Brampton Bryan Herefs......38 G7
Brampton-en-le-Morthen
Rothm......51 L4
Bramshall Staffs......40 D2
Bramshaw Hants......9 J4
Bramshott Hants......10 D4
Bramwell Somset......17 L9
Branault Highld......89 L3
Brancaster Norfk......44 C2
Brancaster Staithe Norfk......44 D2
Brancepeth Dur......73 L12
Branchill Moray......100 G5
Brandelsby N York......66 E11
Branderburgh Moray......101 K2
Brandesburton E R Yk......61 J5
Brandeston Suffk......35 L5
Brandiston Norfk......45 J6
Brandon Dur......73 M11
Brandon Lincs......42 C1
Brandon Suffk......44 D11
Brandon Warwks......41 K11
Brandon Parva Norfk......44 H8
Brandsby N York......66 E11
Brandy Wharf Lincs......52 E4
Bran End Essex......33 Q10
Branksome BCP......8 F8
Branksome Park BCP......8 F8
Bransbury Hants......19 M11
Bransby Lincs......52 C7
Branscombe Devon......6 G5
Bransford Worcs......39 P10
Bransgore Hants......8 H7
Bransholme C KuH......61 J7
Bransley Shrops......39 M7
Branston Leics......42 B4
Branston Lincs......52 E9
Branston Staffs......40 G4
Branston Booths Lincs......52 F9
Branstone IoW......9 P10
Brant Broughton Lincs......52 D11
Brantham Suffk......35 J9
Branthwaite Cumb......70 H9
Branthwaite Cumb......71 L7
Brantingham E R Yk......60 G8
Branton Nthumb......81 N1
Branton Green N York......59 K2
Branxton Nthumb......81 J6
Brassington Derbys......50 G9
Brasted Kent......21 P11
Brasted Chart Kent......21 P11
Brathens Abers......95 L3
Bratoft Lincs......53 M9
Brattleby Lincs......52 D7
Bratton Wilts......18 D9
Bratton Wrekin......49 L11
Bratton Clovelly Devon......5 K2
Bratton Fleming Devon......15 L5
Bratton Seymour Somset......17 P9
Braughing Herts......33 L10
Braunston Nhants......31 M2
Braunston Rutlnd......42 B8
Braunton Devon......14 H5
Brawby N York......66 G11
Brawl Highld......109 Q3
Bray W & M......20 E7
Braybrooke Nhants......41 Q9
Brayford Devon......15 M5
Bray Shop Cnwll......4 H5
Brayton N York......59 N7
Braywick W & M......20 E7
Breachwood Green Herts......32 G11
Breacleit W Isls......111 c2
Breaclete W Isls......111 c2
Breadsall Derbys......51 J11
Breadstone Gloucs......29 J8
Breage Cnwll......2 F9
Breakachy Highld......106 H12
Breakish Highld......97 J5
Brealangwell Lodge Highld......106 H4
Bream Gloucs......28 H7
Breamore Hants......8 H4
Brean Somset......16 H5
Breanais W Isls......111 b2
Brearton N York......58 H3
Breascleit W Isls......111 c2
Breasclete W Isls......111 c2
Breaston Derbys......41 L2
Brechfa Carmth......26 C3
Brechin Angus......95 K9
Breckles Norfk......44 F10
Brecon Powys......27 L3

Bredbury Stockp......50 B3
Brede E Susx......12 G6
Bredenbury Herefs......39 L10
Bredfield Suffk......35 L6
Bredgar Kent......22 G10
Bredhurst Kent......22 F10
Bredon Worcs......29 N2
Bredon's Hardwick Worcs......29 M2
Bredon's Norton Worcs......29 N2
Bredwardine Herefs......38 G12
Breedon on the Hill Leics......41 K3
Breich W Loth......85 Q10
Breightmet Bolton......57 N7
Breighton E R Yk......60 C7
Breinton Herefs......28 F2
Bremhill Wilts......18 E6
Brenchley Kent......12 D2
Brendon Devon......15 M3
Brenfield Ag & B......83 M6
Brenish W Isls......111 b2
Brent Cross Gt Lon......21 K6
Brent Eleigh Suffk......34 F7
Brentford Gt Lon......21 J7
Brentingby Leics......42 B6
Brent Knoll Somset......17 J6
Brent Mill Devon......5 N8
Brent Pelham Herts......33 M10
Brentwood Essex......22 C5
Brenzett Kent......13 J5
Brenzett Green Kent......13 J5
Brereton Staffs......40 D4
Brereton Green Ches E......49 P3
Bressay Shet......111 k4

Bressingham Norfk......34 H1
Bretby Derbys......40 H3
Bretford Warwks......41 K11
Bretforton Worcs......30 E5
Bretherton Lancs......57 J3
Brettabister Shet......111 k4
Brettenham Norfk......44 F12
Brettenham Suffk......34 F6
Bretton C Pete......42 G9
Bretton Flints......48 G3
Brewood Staffs......40 B6
Briantspuddle Dorset......8 B8
Brickendon Herts......21 L2
Bricket Wood Herts......20 H3
Brick Houses Sheff......50 H5
Bricklehampton Worcs......29 N1
Bride IoM......56 e2
Bridekirk Cumb......71 J8
Bridestowe Devon......5 L3
Brideswell Abers......102 D7
Bridford Devon......5 Q3
Bridge Kent......23 M11
Bridgefoot Angus......93 L8
Bridgehampton Somset......17 N10
Bridge Hewick N York......65 N12
Bridgehill Dur......73 K9
Bridgemary Hants......9 P6
Bridgend Abers......101 P7
Bridgend Ag & B......75 M5
Bridgend Ag & B......82 E9
Bridgend Angus......95 J8
Bridgend Brdgnd......27 J11
Bridgend Cerdgn......36 C10
Bridgend D & G......78 H7
Bridgend Devon......5 L9
Bridgend Fife......93 L12
Bridgend Moray......101 M8
Bridgend P & K......92 G10
Bridgend W Loth......86 C7
Bridgend of Lintrathen Angus......93 K5
Bridge of Alford Abers......102 D10
Bridge of Allan Stirlg......85 N4
Bridge of Avon Moray......100 H10
Bridge of Avon Moray......101 J7
Bridge of Balgie P & K......91 N7
Bridge of Brewlands Angus......94 C9
Bridge of Brown Highld......100 H10
Bridge of Cally P & K......92 H5
Bridge of Canny Abers......95 K3
Bridge of Craigisla Angus......93 J5
Bridge of Dee C Aber......95 P2
Bridge of Dee D & G......70 C4
Bridge of Don C Aber......103 K12
Bridge of Dun Angus......93 R4
Bridge of Dye Abers......95 K5
Bridge of Earn P & K......92 G11
Bridge of Ericht P & K......91 M5
Bridge of Feugh Abers......95 L3
Bridge of Gairn Abers......94 F3
Bridge of Gaur P & K......91 M5
Bridge of Marnoch Abers......102 D5
Bridge of Muchalls Abers......95 P4
Bridge of Orchy Ag & B......91 J8
Bridge of Tilt P & K......92 D3
Bridge of Tynet Moray......101 M3
Bridge of Walls Shet......111 j4
Bridge of Weir Rens......84 G9
Bridgerule Devon......14 E10
Bridge Sollers Herefs......28 E1
Bridge Street Suffk......34 E6
Bridgetown Somset......16 C9
Bridge Trafford Ches W......49 J2
Bridgham Norfk......44 F11
Bridgnorth Shrops......39 N4
Bridgwater Somset......16 H8
Bridgwater Services Somset......17 J8
Bridlington E R Yk......61 K2
Bridport Dorset......7 L4
Bridstow Herefs......28 G4
Brierfield Lancs......57 Q2
Brierley Barns......59 K1
Brierley Gloucs......28 H6
Brierley Hill Dudley......40 B9
Brigg N Linc......52 E3
Briggate Norfk......45 M5
Briggswath N York......67 J6
Brigham Cumb......70 H9
Brigham E R Yk......61 J4
Brighouse Calder......58 F9
Brighstone IoW......9 M10
Brighthampton Oxon......31 K12
Brightley Devon......15 K11
Brightling E Susx......12 D6
Brightlingsea Essex......34 H12
Brighton Br & H......11 L8
Brighton City Airport W Susx......11 K8
Brighton le Sands Sefton......56 F8
Brightons Falk......85 Q7
Brightwalton W Berk......19 M5
Brightwell Suffk......35 L7
Brightwell Baldwin Oxon......19 Q2
Brightwell-cum-Sotwell
Oxon......19 P3
Brightwell Upperton Oxon......19 Q2
Brignall Dur......65 J5
Brig o'Turk Stirlg......85 J2
Brigsley NE Lin......53 J3
Brigsteer Cumb......63 J4
Brigstock Nhants......42 D11
Brill Bucks......31 P10
Brill Cnwll......2 G9
Brilley Herefs......38 F11
Brimfield Herefs......39 K8
Brimfield Cross Herefs......39 K8
Brimington Derbys......51 K6
Brimley Devon......5 Q5
Brimpsfield Gloucs......29 N6
Brimpton W Berk......19 P7
Brimscombe Gloucs......29 M8
Brimstage Wirral......56 F11
Brincliffe Sheff......51 J4
Brind E R Yk......60 C7
Brindister Shet......111 j4
Brindle Lancs......57 L4
Brineton Staffs......49 P11
Bringhurst Leics......42 B10
Bringsty Common Herefs......39 M10
Brington Cambs......32 F2
Brinian Ork......111 h2
Briningham Norfk......44 G4
Brinkhill Lincs......53 L8
Brinkley Cambs......33 Q6
Brinklow Warwks......41 K10
Brinkworth Wilts......18 E4

Brinscall Lancs......57 L5
Brinsley Notts......51 L10
Brinsworth Rothm......51 K3
Brinton Norfk......44 G3
Brisley Norfk......44 F6
Brislington Brist!......17 N3
Brissenden Green Kent......12 H3
Bristol Brist!......17 N2
Bristol Airport N Som......17 M3
Bristol Zoo Gardens Brist!......17 N2
Briston Norfk......44 H4
Britannia Lancs......58 B9
Britford Wilts......8 H2
Brithdir Caerph......27 N7
Brithdir Gwynd......47 M7
British Legion Village Kent......22 E11
Briton Ferry Neath......26 G9
Britwell Salome Oxon......19 R3
Brixham Torbay......6 C10
Brixton Devon......5 L9
Brixton Gt Lon......21 L8
Brixton Deverill Wilts......18 C11
Brixworth Nhants......41 Q12
Brize Norton Oxon......30 H11
Brize Norton Airport Oxon......30 H11
Broad Alley Worcs......30 B1
Broad Blunsdon Swindn......18 G3
Broadbottom Tamesd......50 C3
Broadbridge W Susx......10 D8
Broadbridge Heath W Susx......11 J4
Broad Campden Gloucs......30 F6
Broad Carr Calder......58 E9
Broad Chalke Wilts......8 F3
Broadclyst Devon......6 D4
Broadfield Inver......84 F8
Broadford Highld......96 H5
Broadford Bridge W Susx......10 H6
Broadgairhill Border......79 K6
Broad Green Worcs......39 P10
Broadhaugh Border......81 J4
Broad Haven Pembks......24 F6
Broadheath Traffd......57 N10
Broadhembury Devon......6 E2
Broadhempston Devon......5 Q7
Broad Hinton Wilts......18 G5
Broadland Row E Susx......12 G6
Broadley Moray......101 M3
Broad Marston Worcs......30 F5
Broadmayne Dorset......7 Q5
Broad Meadow Staffs......49 Q6
Broadmoor Pembks......25 J7
Broadoak Dorset......7 L4
Broad Oak E Susx......12 C5
Broad Oak E Susx......12 G6
Broad Oak Herefs......28 F5
Broad Oak St Hel......57 K9
Broadsands Torbay......6 B10
Broad's Green Essex......22 E2
Broadstairs Kent......23 Q9
Broadstone BCP......8 E8
Broadstone Shrops......39 K4
Broad Street E Susx......12 G6
Broad Street Kent......22 G11
Broad Town Wilts......18 G5
Broadwas Worcs......39 N10
Broadwater Herts......33 J11
Broadwater W Susx......11 J8
Broadwaters Worcs......39 Q6
Broadway Pembks......24 F6
Broadway Somset......17 J11
Broadway Worcs......30 E5
Broadwell Gloucs......28 G6
Broadwell Gloucs......30 G8
Broadwell Oxon......30 G12
Broadwell Warwks......31 L2
Broadwindsor Dorset......7 L3
Broadwood Kelly Devon......15 K10
Broadwoodwidger Devon......5 J3
Brochel Highld......104 H12
Brochroy Ag & B......90 D9
Brockamin Worcs......39 P10
Brockbridge Hants......9 Q4
Brockdish Norfk......35 K1
Brockenhurst Hants......9 K5
Brocketsbrae S Lans......78 D2
Brockford Street Suffk......35 J4
Brockhall Nhants......31 N2
Brockhall Village Lancs......57 N2
Brockham Surrey......21 K12
Brockhampton Gloucs......30 D9
Brockhampton Hants......10 B8
Brockhampton Herefs......28 H3
Brockholes Kirk......58 F11
Brocklesby Lincs......61 K11
Brockley N Som......17 L3
Brockley Suffk......34 D3
Brockley Green Suffk......34 C7
Brockley Green Suffk......34 D6
Brockmoor Dudley......40 B9
Brockton Shrops......38 G5
Brockton Shrops......38 G5
Brockton Shrops......39 L4
Brockweir Gloucs......28 G8
Brockworth Gloucs......29 M5
Brocton Staffs......40 C4
Brodick N Ayrs......75 Q6
Brodie Moray......100 F4
Brodsworth Donc......59 L11
Brogaig Highld......104 F8
Brokenborough Wilts......18 D3
Broken Cross Ches E......50 B6
Brokerswood Wilts......18 C9
Bromborough Wirral......56 G11
Brome Suffk......35 J2
Brome Street Suffk......35 J2
Bromeswell Suffk......35 M6
Bromfield Cumb......71 J6
Bromfield Shrops......39 J6
Bromham Bed......32 E6
Bromham Wilts......18 E7
Bromley Dudley......40 B9
Bromley Gt Lon......21 N9
Bromley Shrops......39 N3
Bromley Cross Bolton......57 N6
Brompton Medway......22 F9
Brompton N York......65 Q9
Brompton-by-Sawdon N York......67 K10
Brompton-on-Swale N York......65 L7
Brompton Ralph Somset......16 E9
Brompton Regis Somset......16 C9
Bromsberrow Gloucs......29 K3
Bromsberrow Heath Gloucs......29 K3

Bromsgrove Worcs......40 C12
Bromyard Herefs......39 M10
Bronant Cerdgn......37 K7
Brongest Cerdgn......36 E10
Bronington Wrexhm......49 J7
Bronllys Powys......27 N2
Bronwydd Carmth......25 P4
Bronygarth Shrops......48 F7
Brook Hants......9 J5
Brook IoW......9 L9
Brook Kent......13 K2
Brook Surrey......10 E3
Brooke Norfk......45 L9
Brooke Rutlnd......42 C8
Brookenby Lincs......52 H4
Brookfield Rens......84 G9
Brookhampton Somset......17 P9
Brook Hill Hants......9 J5
Brookhouse Lancs......63 K8
Brookhouse Rothm......51 L3
Brookhouse Green Ches E......49 P4
Brookhouses Derbys......50 D3
Brookland Kent......13 J4
Brooklands Traffd......57 P10
Brookmans Park Herts......21 K3
Brook Street Essex......22 C5
Brook Street Kent......12 H4
Brookthorpe Gloucs......29 L6
Brookwood Surrey......20 F11
Broom C Beds......32 G8
Broom Rothm......51 K3
Broom Warwks......30 E4
Broome Norfk......45 M10
Broome Shrops......38 H6
Broome Worcs......40 B10
Broomedge Warrtn......57 N10
Broomfield Essex......22 E2
Broomfield Kent......22 G11
Broomfield Kent......23 M9
Broomfield Somset......16 G9
Broomfleet E R Yk......60 F8
Broomhaugh Nthumb......72 H8
Broom Hill Barns......59 K12
Broom Hill Notts......51 M10
Broomhill Nthumb......73 M1
Broompark Dur......73 M11
Brora Highld......107 P2
Broseley Shrops......39 M2
Brotherlee Dur......72 G12
Brotherton N York......59 L8
Brotton R & Cl......66 F4
Broubster Highld......110 B4
Brough Cumb......64 E5
Brough E R Yk......60 F8
Brough Highld......110 E2
Brough Notts......52 B10
Brough Shet......111 m3
Broughall Shrops......49 K7
Brough Lodge Shet......111 m2
Brough Sowerby Cumb......64 E5
Broughton Border......78 H2
Broughton Cambs......33 J2
Broughton Flints......48 G3
Broughton Hants......9 K2
Broughton Lancs......57 K2
Broughton M Keyn......32 C8
Broughton N Linc......52 D2
Broughton N York......58 C4
Broughton N York......66 H11
Broughton Nhants......32 B2
Broughton Oxon......31 K6
Broughton Salfd......57 P8
Broughton V Glam......16 C3
Broughton Astley Leics......41 M8
Broughton Beck Cumb......62 E5
Broughton Gifford Wilts......18 C7
Broughton Green Worcs......30 C2
Broughton Hackett Worcs......30 B3
Broughton-in-Furness Cumb......62 E5
Broughton Mains D & G......69 L9
Broughton Mills Cumb......62 E4
Broughton Moor Cumb......70 H8
Broughton Poggs Oxon......30 G12
Broughty Ferry C Dund......93 N9
Brown Candover Hants......19 P11
Brown Edge Staffs......50 B9
Brownhill Abers......102 H7
Brownhills Fife......93 P11
Brownhills Wsall......40 D6
Browninghill Green Hants......19 P8
Brown Lees Staffs......49 Q4
Brownsea Island Dorset......8 F9
Brown's Green Birm......40 D8
Browns Hill Gloucs......29 M8
Brownston Devon......5 N9
Broxa N York......67 K8
Broxbourne Herts......21 M3
Broxburn E Loth......87 N6
Broxburn W Loth......86 C7
Broxted Essex......33 P10
Bruan Highld......110 G7
Bruar P & K......92 C3
Bruchag Ag & B......84 B10
Bruichladdich Ag & B......82 C10
Bruisyard Suffk......35 M4
Bruisyard Street Suffk......35 M4
Brumby N Linc......52 C2
Brund Staffs......50 E8
Brundall Norfk......45 M8
Brundish Suffk......35 L3
Brundish Street Suffk......35 L3
Brunery Highld......89 P2
Brunswick Village N u Ty......73 M6
Brunthwaite C Brad......58 D5
Bruntingthorpe Leics......41 N9
Brunton Fife......93 K10
Brunton Wilts......19 J9
Brushford Devon......15 L9
Brushford Somset......16 C10
Bruton Somset......17 P8
Bryan's Green Worcs......30 B1
Bryanston Dorset......8 C6
Brydekirk D & G......71 K2
Bryher IoS......2 b2
Brympton Somset......17 M11
Bryn Carmth......26 D8
Bryn Neath......26 H9
Bryn Wigan......57 K8
Brynamman Carmth......26 F6
Brynberian Pembks......25 J2
Bryncir Gwynd......46 H3
Bryn-côch Neath......26 G8
Bryncroes Gwynd......46 D5
Bryncrug Gwynd......47 K9

Bryneglwys Denbgs....48 D6
Brynford Flints....48 D1
Bryn Gates Wigan....57 L8
Bryngwran IoA....54 D6
Bryngwyn Mons....28 D7
Bryngwyn Powys....38 E11
Bryn-Henllan Pembks....24 H2
Brynhoffnant Cerdgn....36 E9
Brynmawr Blae G....27 P6
Bryn-mawr Gwynd....46 D5
Brynmenyn Brdgnd....27 J10
Brynmill Swans....26 E9
Brynna Rhondd....27 L11
Brynrefail Gwynd....54 H8
Brynsadler Rhondd....27 L11
Bryn Saith Marchog Denbgs....48 C5
Brynsiencyn IoA....54 F7
Brynteg IoA....54 G5
Bryn-y-Maen Conwy....55 M6
Bualintur Highld....96 E5
Bubbenhall Warwks....41 J11
Bubwith E R Yk....60 C7
Buccleuch Border....79 M6
Buchanan Smithy Stirlg....84 H5
Buchanhaven Abers....103 M6
Buchanty P & K....92 D9
Buchany Stirlg....85 M3
Buchlyvie Stirlg....85 J4
Buckabank Cumb....71 M6
Buckden Cambs....32 H4
Buckden N York....64 G11
Buckenham Norfk....45 M8
Buckerell Devon....6 F3
Buckfast Devon....5 P6
Buckfastleigh Devon....5 P7
Buckhaven Fife....86 G3
Buckholt Mons....28 F5
Buckhorn Weston Dorset....17 R10
Buckhurst Hill Essex....21 N5
Buckie Moray....101 M3
Buckingham Bucks....31 P7
Buckland Bucks....20 E2
Buckland Devon....5 N10
Buckland Gloucs....30 E7
Buckland Herts....33 K9
Buckland Kent....13 P2
Buckland Oxon....19 K12
Buckland Surrey....21 K12
Buckland Brewer Devon....14 G7
Buckland Common Bucks....20 E3
Buckland Dinham Somset....17 R6
Buckland Filleigh Devon....14 H9
Buckland in the Moor Devon....5 P5
Buckland Monachorum
  Devon....5 K6
Buckland Newton Dorset....7 P2
Buckland Ripers Dorset....7 P6
Buckland St Mary Somset....16 H12
Buckland-Tout-Saints Devon....5 P10
Bucklebury W Berk....19 P6
Bucklers Hard Hants....9 L7
Bucklesham Suffk....35 L8
Buckley Flints....48 F3
Bucklow Hill Ches E....57 N11
Buckminster Leics....42 C5
Bucknall C Stke....50 B10
Bucknall Lincs....52 G9
Bucknell Oxon....31 M8
Bucknell Shrops....38 G7
Buckpool Moray....101 M3
Bucksburn C Aber....103 J12
Buck's Cross Devon....14 F7
Bucks Green W Susx....10 H4
Buckshaw Village Lancs....57 K5
Bucks Horn Oak Hants....10 D2
Buck's Mills Devon....14 F7
Buckton E R Yk....67 P11
Buckton Nthumb....81 M6
Buckworth Cambs....32 G2
Budby Notts....51 N6
Bude Cnwll....14 D10
Budge's Shop Cnwll....4 H8
Budleigh Salterton Devon....6 E6
Budock Water Cnwll....2 H9
Buerton Ches E....49 M6
Bugbrooke Nhants....31 P3
Bugle Cnwll....3 M4
Bugley Dorset....8 B3
Bugthorpe E R Yk....60 D3
Buildwas Shrops....39 L2
Builth Road Powys....38 B10
Builth Wells Powys....38 B11
Bulbridge Wilts....8 G2
Bulford Wilts....18 H11
Bulkeley Ches E....49 K5
Bulkington Warwks....41 K9
Bulkington Wilts....18 D8
Bulkworthy Devon....14 G8
Bullbrook Br For....20 D9
Bullington Hants....19 M11
Bullington Lincs....52 F7
Bulmer Essex....34 D8
Bulmer N York....60 C1
Bulmer Tye Essex....34 D8
Bulphan Thurr....22 D6
Bulwark Abers....103 J6
Bulwell C Nott....51 M11
Bulwick Nhants....42 D10
Bumble's Green Essex....21 N3
Bunacaimbh Highld....97 J11
Bunarkaig Highld....98 B10
Bunbury Ches E....49 K4
Bunchrew Highld....107 K12
Bundalloch Highld....97 M4
Bunessan Ag & B....89 J11
Bungay Suffk....45 M11
Bunnahabhain Ag & B....82 F8
Bunny Notts....41 N2
Buntait Highld....98 E3
Buntingford Herts....33 K10
Bunwell Norfk....45 J10
Burbage Leics....41 K8
Burbage Wilts....19 J8
Burchett's Green W & M....20 D7
Burcombe Wilts....8 F2
Burcott Bucks....32 C11
Bures Essex....34 E9
Burford Oxon....30 G10
Burford Shrops....39 L8
Burg Ag & B....89 J7
Burgess Hill W Susx....11 L6
Burgh Suffk....35 K6
Burgh by Sands Cumb....71 M4

Burgh Castle Norfk....45 P8
Burghclere Hants....19 M8
Burghead Moray....100 H2
Burghfield W Berk....19 Q7
Burghfield Common W Berk....19 Q7
Burgh Heath Surrey....21 K10
Burghill Herefs....39 J12
Burgh Island Devon....5 M10
Burgh le Marsh Lincs....53 N9
Burgh next Aylsham Norfk....45 K5
Burgh on Bain Lincs....52 H6
Burgh St Margaret Norfk....45 P7
Burgh St Peter Norfk....45 P10
Burghwallis Donc....59 M10
Burham Kent....22 E10
Buriton Hants....10 C6
Burland Ches E....49 L5
Burlawn Cnwll....3 M2
Burleigh Gloucs....29 M8
Burlescombe Devon....16 E11
Burleston Dorset....8 B8
Burley Hants....8 H6
Burley Rutlnd....42 C7
Burleydam Ches E....49 L7
Burley Gate Herefs....39 L11
Burley in Wharfedale C Brad....58 F5
Burley Street Hants....8 H6
Burley Wood Head C Brad....58 F5
Burlton Shrops....49 J9
Burmarsh Kent....13 L4
Burmington Warwks....30 H6
Burn N York....59 N8
Burnage Manch....57 Q9
Burnaston Derbys....40 H2
Burnbrae N Lans....85 P10
Burnby E R Yk....60 E5
Burneside Cumb....63 J3
Burneston N York....65 N9
Burnett BaNES....17 P3
Burnfoot Border....79 N6
Burnfoot Border....80 C10
Burnfoot D & G....78 F9
Burnfoot D & G....79 M10
Burnfoot D & G....79 N9
Burnfoot P & K....86 B2
Burnham Bucks....20 E7
Burnham Deepdale Norfk....44 D2
Burnham Market Norfk....44 D2
Burnham Norton Norfk....44 D2
Burnham-on-Crouch Essex....23 J4
Burnham-on-Sea Somset....17 J6
Burnham Overy Norfk....44 D2
Burnham Overy Staithe Norfk....44 D2
Burnham Thorpe Norfk....44 D2
Burnhead D & G....78 E9
Burnhervie Abers....102 F10
Burnhill Green Staffs....39 P3
Burnhope Dur....73 L10
Burnhouse N Ayrs....76 G2
Burniston N York....67 L8
Burnley Lancs....57 Q3
Burnmouth Border....81 K3
Burn of Cambus Stirlg....85 M3
Burnopfield Dur....73 L9
Burnsall N York....58 D2
Burnside Angus....93 M4
Burnside Angus....93 N5
Burnside Fife....86 D1
Burnside Moray....101 J2
Burnside Moray....101 L4
Burnside of Duntrune Angus....93 M8
Burntisland Fife....86 F5
Burnton E Ayrs....76 H9
Burntwood Staffs....40 D5
Burntwood Green Staffs....40 E6
Burnt Yates N York....58 G2
Burnworthy Somset....16 G11
Burpham Surrey....20 G11
Burpham W Susx....10 G8
Burradon Nthumb....81 K11
Burrafirth Shet....111 m2
Burravoe Shet....111 k3
Burray Village Ork....111 h3
Burrells Cumb....64 C4
Burrelton P & K....92 H8
Burridge Devon....7 J2
Burridge Hants....9 N5
Burrill N York....65 M9
Burringham N Linc....52 B2
Burrington Devon....15 L8
Burrington Herefs....38 H7
Burrington N Som....17 L4
Burrough Green Cambs....33 Q6
Burrow Lancs....63 L7
Burrow Somset....16 C7
Burrow Bridge Somset....17 J9
Burrowhill Surrey....20 F10
Burry Green Swans....26 B9
Burry Port Carmth....25 Q8
Burscough Lancs....56 H6
Burscough Bridge Lancs....57 J6
Bursea E R Yk....60 D7
Bursledon Hants....9 N5
Burstall Suffk....34 H7
Burstock Dorset....7 K3
Burston Norfk....45 J12
Burstow Surrey....11 L2
Burstwick E R Yk....61 L8
Burtersett N York....64 F9
Burtholme Cumb....71 Q3
Burthorpe Green Suffk....34 C4
Burtle Somset....17 K7
Burtoft Lincs....43 J3
Burton BCP....8 H8
Burton Ches E....48 G1
Burton Ches W....49 K3
Burton Pembks....24 H7
Burton Somset....16 G7
Burton Wilts....18 B5
Burton Agnes E R Yk....61 J2
Burton Bradstock Dorset....7 L5
Burton-by-Lincoln Lincs....52 D8
Burton Coggles Lincs....42 E5
Burton End Essex....33 N11
Burton Fleming E R Yk....67 K12
Burton Hastings Warwks....41 K9
Burton Hill Wilts....18 D4
Burton-in-Kendal Cumb....63 K7
Burton-in-Kendal Services
  Cumb....63 K7
Burton in Lonsdale N York....63 M7
Burton Joyce Notts....51 N11

Burton Latimer Nhants....32 C2
Burton Lazars Leics....41 Q4
Burton Leonard N York....59 J2
Burton on the Wolds Leics....41 N4
Burton Overy Leics....41 Q7
Burton Pedwardine Lincs....42 G2
Burton Pidsea E R Yk....61 L7
Burton Salmon N York....59 L8
Burton's Green Essex....34 D10
Burton upon Stather N Linc....60 E10
Burton upon Trent Staffs....40 G3
Burton Waters Lincs....52 D8
Burtonwood Warrtn....57 K9
Burtonwood Services Warrtn....57 K9
Burwardsley Ches W....49 K4
Burwarton Shrops....39 L5
Burwash E Susx....12 D5
Burwash Common E Susx....12 D5
Burwash Weald E Susx....12 D5
Burwell Cambs....33 P4
Burwell Lincs....53 K7
Burwen IoA....54 F3
Burwick Ork....111 h3
Bury Bury....57 P6
Bury Cambs....43 J12
Bury Somset....16 C10
Bury W Susx....10 G7
Bury Green Herts....33 M11
Bury St Edmunds Suffk....34 E4
Burythorpe N York....60 D2
Busby E Rens....85 K10
Buscot Oxon....19 J2
Bush Abers....95 M8
Bush Bank Herefs....39 J10
Bushbury Wolves....40 B7
Bushey Herts....21 J4
Bushey Heath Herts....21 J5
Bush Hill Park Gt Lon....21 M4
Bushley Worcs....29 M2
Bushmoor Shrops....38 H5
Bushton Wilts....18 F5
Bussage Gloucs....29 M7
Butcombe N Som....17 M4
Bute Ag & B....83 Q8
Butleigh Somset....17 M9
Butleigh Wootton Somset....17 M8
Butlers Marston Warwks....30 H4
Butley Suffk....35 N6
Buttercrambe N York....60 C3
Butterdean Border....87 P8
Butterknowle Dur....65 K3
Butterleigh Devon....6 C2
Buttermere Cumb....71 J11
Buttershaw C Brad....58 F8
Butterstone P & K....92 F6
Butterton Staffs....49 P7
Butterton Staffs....50 E9
Butterwick Lincs....43 L2
Butterwick N York....66 G11
Butterwick N York....67 L12
Buttington Powys....38 F1
Buttonoak Shrops....39 N6
Buxhall Suffk....34 G5
Buxted E Susx....11 P5
Buxton Derbys....50 D6
Buxton Norfk....45 K5
Buxton Heath Norfk....45 K5
Bwlch Powys....27 N4
Bwlchgwyn Wrexhm....48 F5
Bwlchllan Cerdgn....37 J8
Bwlchtocyn Gwynd....46 E6
Bwlch-y-cibau Powys....48 D11
Bwlch-y-ffridd Powys....38 C3
Bwlch-y-groes Pembks....25 M2
Bwlch-y-sarnau Powys....38 B7
Byers Green Dur....65 L2
Byfield Nhants....31 M4
Byfleet Surrey....20 G10
Byford Herefs....38 H12
Byker N u Ty....73 M7
Bylchau Conwy....55 P8
Byley Ches W....49 N2
Byram N York....59 L8
Byrness Nthumb....72 D1
Bystock Devon....6 D6
Bythorn Cambs....32 F2
Byton Herefs....38 G8
Bywell Nthumb....73 J8
Byworth W Susx....10 F6

C

Cabourne Lincs....52 G3
Cabrach Ag & B....82 G9
Cabrach Moray....101 M9
Cabus Lancs....63 J11
Cadbury Devon....6 C2
Cadbury World Birm....40 D10
Cadder E Duns....85 K8
Caddington C Beds....32 F11
Caddonfoot Border....79 P2
Cadeby Donc....51 L1
Cadeby Leics....41 K7
Cadeleigh Devon....6 C2
Cade Street E Susx....12 C6
Cadgwith Cnwll....2 G11
Cadham Fife....86 F2
Cadishead Salfd....57 N9
Cadle Swans....26 E9
Cadley Lancs....57 K3
Cadley Wilts....18 H7
Cadley Wilts....19 J9
Cadmore End Bucks....20 C5
Cadnam Hants....9 K5
Cadney N Linc....52 E2
Cadoxton V Glam....16 F3
Cadoxton Juxta-Neath Neath....26 G8
Caeathro Gwynd....54 G8
Caenby Lincs....52 E5
Caerau Brdgnd....27 J9
Caerau Cardif....16 F2
Caer Farchell Pembks....24 E4
Caergeiliog IoA....54 D6
Caergwrle Flints....48 F4
Caerlanrig Border....79 N7
Caerleon Newpt....28 D10
Caernarfon Gwynd....54 F8
Caernarfon Castle Gwynd....54 F8
Caerphilly Caerph....27 N10
Caersws Powys....38 B4
Caerwedros Cerdgn....36 F9

Caerwent Mons....28 F10
Caerwys Flints....48 D2
Caio Carmth....37 L11
Cairinis W Isls....111 b5
Cairnbaan Ag & B....83 M5
Cairnbulg Abers....103 L3
Cairncross Border....81 J2
Cairndow Ag & B....84 C2
Cairneyhill Fife....86 C5
Cairngarroch D & G....68 E8
Cairngorms National Park....99 N8
Cairnie Abers....101 N6
Cairnorrie Abers....102 H7
Cairnryan D & G....68 E5
Cairnty Moray....101 L5
Caister-on-Sea Norfk....45 Q7
Caistor Lincs....52 G3
Caistor St Edmund Norfk....45 K8
Calanais W Isls....111 c2
Calbourne IoW....9 M9
Calceby Lincs....53 K7
Calcot Gloucs....30 E11
Calcot Row W Berk....19 R6
Calcots Moray....101 K3
Caldbeck Cumb....71 M7
Caldecote Cambs....33 K5
Caldecote Cambs....42 G11
Caldecott Nhants....32 E3
Caldecott Oxon....19 N2
Caldecott Rutlnd....42 C10
Calderbank N Lans....85 N9
Calder Bridge Cumb....62 B2
Caldercruix N Lans....85 N9
Calder Grove Wakefd....58 H10
Caldermill S Lans....77 L3
Calder Vale Lancs....63 K11
Calderwood S Lans....85 L11
Caldey Island Pembks....25 K9
Caldicot Mons....28 F10
Caldmore Wsall....40 D7
Caldwell N York....65 L5
Calf of Man IoM....56 a7
Calfsound Ork....111 h1
Calgary Ag & B....89 J6
Califer Moray....100 G4
California Falk....85 Q7
California Norfk....45 Q7
Calke Derbys....41 J3
Calke Abbey Derbys....41 J3
Callakille Highld....105 K10
Callander Stirlg....85 K2
Callanish W Isls....111 c2
Callestick Cnwll....2 H5
Calligarry Highld....96 H8
Callington Cnwll....4 H7
Callow Herefs....28 F2
Callow End Worcs....39 Q11
Callow Hill Wilts....18 F4
Calmore Hants....9 K5
Calmsden Gloucs....30 D11
Calne Wilts....18 E6
Calshot Hants....9 N7
Calstock Cnwll....5 J6
Calstone Wellington Wilts....18 F7
Calthorpe Norfk....45 K4
Calthorpe Street Norfk....45 N5
Calthwaite Cumb....71 P7
Calton Staffs....50 E10
Calveley Ches E....49 L4
Calver Derbys....50 G6
Calverhall Shrops....49 L7
Calverleigh Devon....16 C12
Calverley Leeds....58 G6
Calverton M Keyn....32 B8
Calverton Notts....51 N10
Calvine P & K....92 B3
Calzeat Border....78 H2
Cam Gloucs....29 K8
Camasachoirce Highld....89 Q4
Camasine Highld....89 P4
Camas Luinie Highld....97 N4
Camastianavaig Highld....96 F2
Camault Muir Highld....98 G2
Camber E Susx....13 J6
Camberley Surrey....20 E10
Camberwell Gt Lon....21 L7
Camblesforth N York....59 N8
Cambo Nthumb....72 H4
Camborne Cnwll....2 F7
Camborne & Redruth
  Mining District Cnwll....2 G7
Cambourne Cambs....33 K5
Cambridge Cambs....33 M5
Cambridge Gloucs....29 K7
Cambridge Airport Cambs....33 M5
Cambrose Cnwll....2 G6
Cambus Clacks....85 P4
Cambusavie Highld....107 M3
Cambusbarron Stirlg....85 N5
Cambuskenneth Stirlg....85 N4
Cambuslang S Lans....85 L10
Cambus o' May Abers....94 G3
Cambuswallace S Lans....78 G2
Camden Town Gt Lon....21 L6
Cameley BaNES....17 N5
Camelford Cnwll....4 D4
Camelon Falk....85 P6
Camerory Highld....100 F8
Camerton BaNES....17 P5
Camerton Cumb....70 G8
Camghouran P & K....91 N5
Camieston Border....80 D8
Cammachmore Abers....95 P3
Cammeringham Lincs....52 D7
Camore Highld....107 N4
Campbeltown Ag & B....75 N8
Campbeltown Airport Ag & B....75 K7
Cample D & G....78 E9
Campmuir P & K....93 J7
Camps W Loth....86 C8
Campsall Donc....59 M10
Campsea Ash Suffk....35 M5
Campton C Beds....32 G8
Camptown Border....80 F10
Camrose Pembks....24 G5
Camserney P & K....92 C6
Camusnagaul Highld....90 E2
Camusnagaul Highld....105 Q5
Camusteel Highld....97 J2
Camusterrach Highld....97 J2
Canada Hants....9 K4
Candacraig Abers....94 F3

Candlesby Lincs....53 M9
Candy Mill Border....78 H1
Cane End Oxon....20 B7
Canewdon Essex....22 H5
Canford Cliffs BCP....8 F9
Canford Heath BCP....8 F8
Canisbay Highld....110 G2
Canley Covtry....40 H11
Cann Dorset....8 C3
Canna Highld....96 B8
Cann Common Dorset....8 C4
Cannich Highld....98 D3
Cannington Somset....16 H8
Canning Town Gt Lon....21 N7
Cannock Staffs....40 C5
Cannock Chase Staffs....40 C4
Cannon Bridge Herefs....28 E1
Canonbie D & G....71 N1
Canon Frome Herefs....39 M12
Canon Pyon Herefs....39 J11
Canons Ashby Nhants....31 M4
Canonstown Cnwll....2 D8
Canterbury Kent....23 M10
Canterbury Cathedral Kent....23 M10
Cantley Norfk....45 N8
Canton Cardif....16 F2
Cantraywood Highld....107 N11
Cantsfield Lancs....63 L7
Canvey Island Essex....22 F6
Canwick Lincs....52 E9
Canworthy Water Cnwll....4 F2
Caol Highld....90 F2
Caolas Scalpaigh W Isls....111 c3
Caoles Ag & B....88 C6
Caonich Highld....97 Q10
Capel Kent....12 D2
Capel Surrey....11 J2
Capel Bangor Cerdgn....37 K5
Capel Coch IoA....54 F5
Capel Curig Conwy....55 K9
Capel Dewi Carmth....26 C5
Capel Dewi Cerdgn....36 G11
Capel-Dewi Cerdgn....37 K4
Capel Garmon Conwy....55 M9
Capel Hendre Carmth....26 E6
Capel Iwan Carmth....25 M2
Capel-le-Ferne Kent....13 N3
Capel Parc IoA....54 F4
Capel St Andrew Suffk....35 N7
Capel St Mary Suffk....34 H8
Capel Seion Cerdgn....37 K5
Capelulo Conwy....55 L6
Capenhurst Ches W....48 G2
Cape Wrath Highld....108 E1
Capheaton Nthumb....73 J5
Caplaw E Rens....84 G10
Cappercleuch Border....79 K4
Capton Devon....5 Q9
Caputh P & K....92 G7
Caradon Mining District
  Cnwll....4 G5
Carbeth Stirlg....85 J7
Carbis Bay Cnwll....2 D7
Carbost Highld....96 D4
Carbost Highld....104 F11
Carbrook Sheff....51 J3
Carbrooke Norfk....44 F9
Car Colston Notts....51 Q11
Carcroft Donc....59 M11
Cardenden Fife....86 E4
Cardhu Moray....101 J6
Cardiff Cardif....16 G2
Cardiff Airport V Glam....16 E3
Cardiff Gate Services Cardif....27 P11
Cardiff West Services Cardif....27 M11
Cardigan Cerdgn....36 C10
Cardington Bed....32 F7
Cardington Shrops....39 J3
Cardinham Cnwll....4 D6
Cardrain D & G....68 F11
Cardrona Border....79 L2
Cardross Ag & B....84 F7
Cardryne D & G....68 F11
Cardurnock Cumb....71 J4
Careby Lincs....42 F6
Careston Angus....95 J9
Carew Pembks....24 H7
Carew Cheriton Pembks....24 H7
Carew Newton Pembks....24 H7
Carey Herefs....28 G3
Carfin N Lans....85 N10
Carfraemill Border....80 C4
Cargate Green Norfk....45 N7
Cargenbridge D & G....70 F2
Cargill P & K....92 H8
Cargo Cumb....71 M4
Cargreen Cnwll....5 J7
Carham Nthumb....80 H6
Carhampton Somset....16 D7
Carharrack Cnwll....2 G7
Carie P & K....91 P5
Carinish W Isls....111 b5
Carisbrooke IoW....9 N9
Cark Cumb....62 G6
Carkeel Cnwll....5 J7
Càrlabhagh W Isls....111 c2
Carlbury Darltn....65 L4
Carlby Lincs....42 F7
Carleen Cnwll....2 F9
Carleton Forehoe Norfk....44 H8
Carleton-in-Craven N York....58 C4
Carleton Rode Norfk....44 H10
Carleton St Peter Norfk....45 M9
Carlincraig Abers....102 E6
Carlingcott BaNES....17 Q5
Carlisle Cumb....71 N4
Carlisle Lake District Airport
  Cumb....71 P4
Carlops Border....86 D10
Carloway W Isls....111 c2
Carlton Barns....59 J11
Carlton Bed....32 D6
Carlton Cambs....33 Q6
Carlton Leeds....59 J8
Carlton Leics....41 K6
Carlton N York....59 N9
Carlton N York....65 J9
Carlton N York....66 E9
Carlton Notts....51 N11
Carlton S on T....65 P3
Carlton Suffk....35 N4
Carlton Colville Suffk....45 Q11
Carlton Curlieu Leics....41 P7

Carlton Green Cambs 33 Q6
Carlton Husthwaite N York 66 C11
Carlton-in-Cleveland N York 66 C6
Carlton in Lindrick Notts 51 N4
Carlton-le-Moorland Lincs 52 C10
Carlton Miniott N York 65 P10
Carlton-on-Trent Notts 52 B10
Carlton Scroop Lincs 42 D2
Carluke S Lans 77 P2
Carmacoup S Lans 77 N6
Carmarthen Carmth 25 P5
Carmel Carmth 26 D5
Carmel Flints 56 D12
Carmel Gwynd 54 G9
Carmichael S Lans 78 F2
Carmunnock C Glas 85 K10
Carmyle C Glas 85 L9
Carmyllie Angus 93 P7
Carnaby E R Yk 61 K2
Carnbee Fife 87 K2
Carnbo P & K 86 C2
Carn Brea Cnwll 2 G7
Carnbrogie Abers 102 H9
Carndu Highld 97 M4
Carnduff S Lans 77 L3
Carnell E Ayrs 76 H5
Carnforth Lancs 63 J7
Carn-gorm Highld 97 N5
Carnhell Green Cnwll 2 F8
Carnie Abers 95 N2
Carnkie Cnwll 2 G7
Carnkie Cnwll 2 G8
Carno Powys 47 Q11
Carnock Fife 86 C4
Carnon Downs Cnwll 3 J7
Carnousie Abers 102 E5
Carnoustie Angus 93 P8
Carnwath S Lans 86 B11
Carol Green Solhll 40 H11
Carperby N York 64 H9
Carradale Ag & B 75 M5
Carradale Village Ag & B 75 M5
Carrbridge Highld 99 N4
Carrefour Jersey 7 b1
Carreglefn IoA 54 E4
Carr Gate Wakefd 58 H8
Carrhouse N Linc 60 D11
Carrick Ag & B 83 N5
Carrick Castle Ag & B 84 D4
Carriden Falk 86 B6
Carrington Mdloth 86 G9
Carrington Traffd 57 N9
Carrog Denbgs 48 C6
Carron Falk 85 P6
Carron Moray 101 J7
Carronbridge D & G 78 E8
Carron Bridge Stirlg 85 M6
Carronshore Falk 85 P6
Carr Shield Nthumb 72 E10
Carrutherstown D & G 70 H2
Carruth House Inver 84 F9
Carrville Dur 73 N11
Carsaig Ag & B 89 L11
Carseriggan D & G 69 J5
Carsethorn D & G 70 G4
Carshalton Gt Lon 21 L9
Carsington Derbys 50 G9
Carskey Ag & B 75 J10
Carsluith D & G 69 L8
Carsphairn D & G 77 J11
Carstairs S Lans 77 Q3
Carstairs Junction S Lans 77 Q3
Carterton Oxon 30 H11
Carthew Cnwll 3 M5
Carthorpe N York 65 N10
Cartland S Lans 77 P3
Cartmel Cumb 62 H6
Carway Carmth 26 C7
Cashe's Green Gloucs 29 L7
Cassington Oxon 31 L11
Cassop Dur 73 N12
Castel Guern 6 b2
Casterton Cumb 63 L6
Castle Acre Norfk 44 D7
Castle Ashby Nhants 32 C5
Castlebay W Isls 111 a7
Castle Bolton N York 65 J8
Castle Bromwich Solhll 40 F9
Castle Bytham Lincs 42 E6
Castlebythe Pembks 24 H3
Castle Caereinion Powys 38 D2
Castle Camps Cambs 33 P8
Castle Carrock Cumb 71 Q5
Castlecary Falk 85 N7
Castle Cary Somset 17 P9
Castle Combe Wilts 18 C5
Castlecraig Highld 107 N8
Castle Donington Leics 41 K3
Castle Douglas D & G 70 C3
Castle Eaton Swindn 18 G2
Castle Eden Dur 73 Q12
Castleford Wakefd 59 K8
Castle Frome Herefs 39 M11
Castle Gresley Derbys 40 H4
Castle Hedingham Essex 34 D9
Castlehill Border 79 K2
Castlehill Highld 110 E3
Castle Hill Suffk 35 J7
Castlehill W Duns 84 G7
Castle Howard N York 66 G12
Castle Kennedy D & G 68 F7
Castle Lachlan Ag & B 83 Q4
Castlemartin Pembks 24 F8
Castlemilk C Glas 85 K10
Castlemorton Worcs 29 L2
Castlemorton Common
  Worcs 29 K2
Castle O'er D & G 79 L9
Castle Rising Norfk 43 Q6
Castleside Dur 73 J10
Castle Stuart Highld 107 M11
Castlethorpe M Keyn 32 B7
Castleton Ag & B 83 N6
Castleton Derbys 50 F4
Castleton N York 66 F6
Castleton Newpt 27 Q11
Castleton Rochdl 58 B11
Castletown Highld 110 E3
Castletown IoM 56 b7
Castletown Sundld 73 P8
Castley N York 58 H6
Caston Norfk 44 F9

Castor C Pete 42 G9
Catacol N Ayrs 75 N3
Catcliffe Rothm 51 K3
Catcomb Wilts 18 E5
Catcott Somset 17 K8
Caterham Surrey 21 M11
Catfield Norfk 45 N6
Catford Gt Lon 21 M8
Catforth Lancs 57 J2
Cathcart C Glas 85 K10
Cathedine Powys 27 N4
Catherington Hants 10 B8
Catherston Leweston Dorset 7 K4
Catisfield Hants 9 P6
Catlodge Highld 99 J9
Catmere End Essex 33 M8
Catmore W Berk 19 M5
Caton Lancs 63 K8
Caton Green Lancs 63 K8
Catrine E Ayrs 77 J6
Catsfield E Susx 12 E7
Catsgore Somset 17 M10
Catshill Worcs 40 C11
Cattadale Ag & B 75 K9
Cattal N York 59 K4
Cattawade Suffk 34 H9
Catterall Lancs 57 J1
Catterick N York 65 M7
Catterick Bridge N York 65 M7
Catterlen Cumb 71 P8
Catterline Abers 95 P6
Catterton N York 59 L5
Catteshall Surrey 10 F2
Catthorpe Leics 41 M10
Cattistock Dorset 7 N3
Catton N York 65 P11
Catton Nthumb 72 E8
Catwick E R Yk 61 J5
Catworth Cambs 32 F3
Caudle Green Gloucs 29 N6
Caulcott Oxon 31 L8
Cauldcots Angus 93 Q6
Cauldhame Stirlg 85 L4
Cauldmill Border 80 C10
Cauldon Staffs 50 E10
Cauldwell Derbys 40 G4
Caulkerbush D & G 70 F4
Caulside D & G 79 P11
Caundle Marsh Dorset 17 P12
Caunton Notts 51 Q8
Causeway End D & G 69 K7
Causeway End Essex 34 B11
Causewayend S Lans 78 G2
Causewayhead Stirlg 85 N4
Causeyend Abers 103 K10
Causey Park Bridge Nthumb 73 L2
Cavendish Suffk 34 D7
Cavenham Suffk 34 C3
Caversfield Oxon 31 M8
Caversham Readg 20 B8
Caverswall Staffs 50 C11
Caverton Mill Border 80 G8
Cawdor Highld 100 D5
Cawood N York 59 M6
Cawsand Cnwll 5 J9
Cawston Norfk 45 J5
Cawthorne Barns 58 H11
Caxton Cambs 33 K5
Caynham Shrops 39 K7
Caythorpe Lincs 42 D1
Caythorpe Notts 51 P10
Cayton N York 67 M10
Ceannabeinne Highld 108 H3
Ceann a Bhaigh W Isls 111 a4
Ceannacroc Lodge Highld 98 C6
Cearsiadar W Isls 111 d2
Cefn Newpt 28 C10
Cefn-brith Conwy 55 N10
Cefn-bryn-brain Carmth 26 G6
Cefn-coed-y-cymmer Myr Td 27 L7
Cefn Cribwr Brdgnd 27 J11
Cefneithin Carmth 26 D6
Cefngorwydd Powys 37 P10
Cefn-mawr Wrexhm 48 F7
Cefn-y-pant Carmth 25 L4
Cellardyke Fife 87 L2
Cellarhead Staffs 50 C10
Cemaes IoA 54 E3
Cemmaes Powys 47 N9
Cemmaes Road Powys 47 N9
Cenarth Cerdgn 36 E11
Ceres Fife 93 M12
Cerne Abbas Dorset 7 P3
Cerney Wick Gloucs 18 F2
Cerrigydrudion Conwy 55 P11
Ceunant Gwynd 54 G8
Chaceley Gloucs 29 M3
Chacewater Cnwll 2 H6
Chackmore Bucks 31 P7
Chacombe Nhants 31 L5
Chadbury Worcs 30 D5
Chadderton Oldham 58 B12
Chaddesden C Derb 51 J12
Chaddesley Corbett Worcs 40 B11
Chaddlehanger Devon 5 L6
Chaddleworth W Berk 19 M5
Chadlington Oxon 31 J9
Chadshunt Warwks 31 J4
Chadwell Leics 42 B5
Chadwell Heath Gt Lon 21 P6
Chadwell St Mary Thurr 22 D7
Chadwick End Solhll 40 G11
Chaffcombe Somset 7 J2
Chafford Hundred Thurr 22 C7
Chagford Devon 5 N3
Chailey E Susx 11 N6
Chainhurst Kent 12 E1
Chaldon Surrey 21 L11
Chaldon Herring Dorset 8 B10
Chale IoW 9 N11
Chale Green IoW 9 N10
Chalfont Common Bucks 20 G5
Chalfont St Giles Bucks 20 F5
Chalfont St Peter Bucks 20 G5
Chalford Gloucs 29 M8
Chalford Wilts 18 C10
Chalgrove Oxon 19 Q2
Chalk Kent 22 D8
Chalkwell Kent 22 H10
Challaborough Devon 5 M4
Challacombe Devon 15 M4
Challoch D & G 69 K5
Challock Kent 23 J12

Chalton C Beds 32 E10
Chalton Hants 10 B6
Chalvey Slough 20 F7
Chalvington E Susx 11 P8
Chandler's Cross Herts 20 H4
Chandler's Ford Hants 9 M4
Channel Tunnel Terminal Kent 13 L3
Chantry Somset 17 Q6
Chantry Suffk 35 J7
Chapel Fife 86 F4
Chapel Allerton Leeds 58 H6
Chapel Allerton Somset 17 K6
Chapel Amble Cnwll 3 M1
Chapel Brampton Nhants 31 Q2
Chapel Chorlton Staffs 49 P7
Chapelend Way Essex 34 B8
Chapel-en-le-Frith Derbys 50 D5
Chapel Green Warwks 31 L3
Chapel Haddlesey N York 59 M8
Chapelhall N Lans 85 N9
Chapel Hill Abers 103 L8
Chapel Hill Lincs 52 H11
Chapel Hill N York 59 J5
Chapelhope Border 79 K5
Chapelknowe D & G 71 M2
Chapel Lawn Shrops 38 G6
Chapel-le-Dale N York 64 D11
Chapel Leigh Somset 16 F9
Chapel of Garioch Abers 102 F9
Chapel Rossan D & G 68 F9
Chapel Row W Berk 19 P6
Chapel St Leonards Lincs 53 N8
Chapel Stile Cumb 62 G2
Chapelton Angus 95 P4
Chapelton Angus 93 Q6
Chapelton Devon 15 K6
Chapelton S Lans 77 L2
Chapeltown Bl w D 57 N6
Chapeltown Moray 101 K10
Chapeltown Sheff 51 J2
Chapmanslade Wilts 18 C10
Chapmans Well Devon 4 H2
Chapmore End Herts 33 K12
Chappel Essex 34 E10
Chard Somset 7 J2
Chard Junction Somset 7 J2
Chardleigh Green Somset 7 J1
Chardstock Devon 7 J2
Charfield S Glos 29 J9
Charing Kent 23 J2
Charingworth Gloucs 30 G6
Charlbury Oxon 31 J9
Charlcombe BaNES 17 Q3
Charlcutt Wilts 18 E5
Charlecote Warwks 30 H3
Charlemont Sandw 40 D8
Charles Devon 15 M5
Charleston Angus 93 L6
Charlestown C Aber 95 Q2
Charlestown C Brad 58 F6
Charlestown Calder 58 C8
Charlestown Cnwll 3 M5
Charlestown Cnwll 3 M5
Charlestown Fife 86 C5
Charlestown Highld 105 M7
Charlestown Highld 107 K11
Charlestown Salfd 57 P8
Charlestown of Aberlour
  Moray 101 K6
Charles Tye Suffk 34 G6
Charlesworth Derbys 50 D3
Charlinch Somset 16 H8
Charlottetown Fife 93 K12
Charlton Gt Lon 21 N7
Charlton Nhants 31 M7
Charlton Nthumb 72 E4
Charlton Oxon 19 L3
Charlton Somset 16 H10
Charlton Somset 17 P6
Charlton W Susx 10 E7
Charlton Wilts 8 D3
Charlton Wilts 18 E3
Charlton Worcs 30 D5
Charlton Wrekin 49 L12
Charlton Abbots Gloucs 30 D8
Charlton Adam Somset 17 M9
Charlton All Saints Wilts 8 H3
Charlton Down Dorset 7 P4
Charlton Horethorne Somset 17 P10
Charlton Kings Gloucs 29 N5
Charlton Mackrell Somset 17 M9
Charlton Marshall Dorset 8 D6
Charlton Musgrove Somset 17 Q9
Charlton-on-Otmoor Oxon 31 M10
Charlton on the Hill Dorset 8 D6
Charlton St Peter Wilts 18 G9
Charlwood Hants 10 A4
Charlwood Surrey 11 K2
Charminster Dorset 7 P4
Charmouth Dorset 7 J4
Charndon Bucks 31 N9
Charney Bassett Oxon 19 L2
Charnock Richard Lancs 57 K6
Charnock Richard Services
  Lancs 57 K6
Charsfield Suffk 35 L5
Charter Alley Hants 19 P8
Charterhall Border 80 G5
Charterhouse Somset 17 M5
Chartershall Stirlg 85 N5
Chartham Kent 23 L11
Chartham Hatch Kent 23 L11
Chartridge Bucks 20 E3
Chart Sutton Kent 22 F12
Charvil Wokham 20 C8
Charwelton Nhants 31 M3
Chase Terrace Staffs 40 D5
Chasetown Staffs 40 D6
Chastleton Oxon 30 G8
Chasty Devon 14 F10
Chatburn Lancs 63 P12
Chatcull Staffs 49 P8
Chatham Medway 22 F9
Chatham Green Essex 22 E1
Chathill Nthumb 81 P8
Chatsworth House Derbys 50 H6
Chattenden Medway 22 F8
Chatteris Cambs 43 L11
Chatterton Lancs 57 P5
Chattisham Suffk 34 H8
Chatto Border 80 G10
Chatton Nthumb 81 M8
Chawleigh Devon 15 M9

Chawton Hants 10 B3
Cheadle Staffs 50 D11
Cheadle Stockp 57 Q10
Cheadle Hulme Stockp 57 Q10
Cheam Gt Lon 21 K10
Chearsley Bucks 31 Q11
Chebsey Staffs 49 Q9
Checkendon Oxon 19 Q4
Checkley Ches E 49 N6
Checkley Staffs 50 D12
Chedburgh Suffk 34 D5
Cheddar Somset 17 L5
Cheddington Bucks 32 D12
Cheddleton Staffs 50 C9
Cheddon Fitzpaine Somset 16 H9
Chedgrave Norfk 45 N9
Chedington Dorset 7 L2
Chediston Suffk 35 M2
Chedworth Gloucs 30 D10
Chedzoy Somset 17 J8
Cheetham Hill Manch 57 Q8
Cheldon Devon 15 M9
Chelford Ches E 49 P1
Chellaston C Derb 41 J2
Chellington Bed 32 D5
Chelmarsh Shrops 39 N5
Chelmer Village Essex 22 E2
Chelmondiston Suffk 35 K8
Chelmorton Derbys 50 E6
Chelmsford Essex 22 E3
Chelmsley Wood Solhll 40 F9
Chelsea Gt Lon 21 L7
Chelsfield Gt Lon 21 P9
Chelsworth Suffk 34 G7
Cheltenham Gloucs 29 N4
Chelveston Nhants 32 E3
Chelvey N Som 17 L3
Chelwood BaNES 17 P4
Chelwood Gate E Susx 11 N4
Cheney Longville Shrops 38 H5
Chenies Bucks 20 G4
Chepstow Mons 28 G9
Cherhill Wilts 18 F6
Cherington Gloucs 29 M8
Cherington Warwks 30 H6
Cheriton Hants 9 P2
Cheriton Kent 13 M3
Cheriton Pembks 24 H8
Cheriton Swans 26 B9
Cheriton Bishop Devon 5 P2
Cheriton Fitzpaine Devon 15 P10
Cherrington Wrekin 49 M10
Cherry Burton E R Yk 60 G6
Cherry Hinton Cambs 33 M5
Cherry Orchard Worcs 39 Q10
Cherry Willingham Lincs 52 E8
Chertsey Surrey 20 G9
Cherwell Valley Services
  Oxon 31 M8
Cheselbourne Dorset 8 B7
Chesham Bucks 20 F3
Chesham Bury 57 P6
Chesham Bois Bucks 20 F4
Cheshunt Herts 21 M3
Chesil Beach Dorset 7 N6
Chesley Hay Staffs 40 C6
Chessetts Wood Warwks 40 F11
Chessington Gt Lon 21 J10
Chessington World of
  Adventures Gt Lon 21 J10
Chester Ches W 48 H3
Chesterblade Somset 17 P7
Chesterfield Derbys 51 J6
Chesterfield Staffs 40 E6
Chesterhill Mdloth 86 H8
Chester-le-Street Dur 73 M9
Chester Moor Dur 73 M10
Chesters Border 80 E11
Chesters Border 80 E9
Chester Services Ches W 49 J1
Chesterton Cambs 33 M5
Chesterton Cambs 42 G10
Chesterton Gloucs 18 E1
Chesterton Oxon 31 M9
Chesterton Shrops 39 P3
Chesterton Staffs 49 P5
Chesterton Green Warwks 31 J3
Chesterwood Nthumb 72 E7
Chester Zoo Ches W 48 H2
Chestfield Kent 23 L9
Cheston Devon 5 N8
Cheswardine Shrops 49 N9
Cheswick Nthumb 81 L5
Chetnole Dorset 7 N2
Chettisham Cambs 43 N12
Chettle Dorset 8 D5
Chetton Shrops 39 M4
Chetwynd Wrekin 49 N10
Chetwynd Aston Wrekin 49 N11
Cheveley Cambs 34 B5
Chevening Kent 21 P11
Chevington Suffk 34 D5
Cheviot Hills 80 G12
Chevithorne Devon 16 D11
Chew Magna BaNES 17 N4
Chew Stoke BaNES 17 M4
Chewton Keynsham BaNES 17 P3
Chewton Mendip Somset 17 M5
Chicheley M Keyn 32 C7
Chichester W Susx 10 D8
Chickerell Dorset 7 P6
Chicklade Wilts 8 D2
Chidden Hants 9 Q4
Chiddingfold Surrey 10 F3
Chiddingly E Susx 12 B7
Chiddingstone Kent 11 P2
Chiddingstone Causeway
  Kent 11 Q1
Chideock Dorset 7 K4
Chidham W Susx 10 C8
Chidswell Kirk 58 H9
Chieveley W Berk 19 M6
Chieveley Services W Berk 19 N6
Chignall St James Essex 22 D2
Chignall Smealy Essex 22 D2
Chigwell Essex 21 N5
Chigwell Row Essex 21 P5
Chilbolton Hants 19 L11
Chilcomb Hants 9 N2
Chilcombe Dorset 7 M4
Chilcompton Somset 17 P6
Chilcote Leics 40 H5
Childer Thornton Ches W 56 G12

Child Okeford Dorset 8 C5
Childrey Oxon 19 L3
Child's Ercall Shrops 49 M9
Childswickham Worcs 30 E6
Childwall Lpool 56 H10
Chilfrome Dorset 7 N3
Chilgrove W Susx 10 D7
Chilham Kent 23 K11
Chillaton Devon 5 J4
Chillenden Kent 23 N11
Chillerton IoW 9 N10
Chillesford Suffk 35 N6
Chillington Devon 5 Q10
Chillington Somset 7 K1
Chilmark Wilts 8 E2
Chilmington Green Kent 13 J3
Chilson Oxon 30 H9
Chilsworthy Cnwll 5 J6
Chilsworthy Devon 14 F10
Chiltern Hills 20 C4
Chilthorne Domer Somset 17 M11
Chilton Bucks 31 P10
Chilton Dur 65 M2
Chilton Oxon 19 N4
Chilton Candover Hants 19 P11
Chilton Cantelo Somset 17 N10
Chilton Foliat Wilts 19 K6
Chilton Polden Somset 17 K7
Chilton Street Suffk 34 C7
Chilton Trinity Somset 16 H8
Chilwell Notts 41 L1
Chilworth Hants 9 L4
Chilworth Surrey 10 G1
Chimney Oxon 19 L1
Chineham Hants 19 Q9
Chingford Gt Lon 21 M5
Chinley Derbys 50 D4
Chinnor Oxon 20 C3
Chipnall Shrops 49 N8
Chippenham Cambs 33 Q3
Chippenham Wilts 18 D6
Chipperfield Herts 20 G3
Chipping Herts 33 K9
Chipping Lancs 63 L12
Chipping Campden Gloucs 30 F6
Chipping Norton Oxon 30 H8
Chipping Ongar Essex 22 B3
Chipping Sodbury S Glos 29 K11
Chipping Warden Nhants 31 L5
Chipstable Somset 16 E10
Chipstead Kent 21 P11
Chipstead Surrey 21 L11
Chirbury Shrops 38 F3
Chirk Wrexhm 48 F7
Chirnside Border 81 J3
Chirnsidebridge Border 80 H3
Chirton Wilts 18 F8
Chisbury Wilts 19 J7
Chiselborough Somset 17 L12
Chiseldon Swindn 18 H5
Chislehampton Oxon 19 P2
Chiserley Calder 58 D8
Chisholme Border 79 N6
Chislehurst Gt Lon 21 N9
Chislet Kent 23 N9
Chiswell Green Herts 21 J3
Chiswick Gt Lon 21 K7
Chisworth Derbys 50 C3
Chithurst W Susx 10 D5
Chittering Cambs 33 M3
Chitterne Wilts 18 E11
Chittlehamholt Devon 15 L7
Chittlehampton Devon 15 L7
Chittoe Wilts 18 E7
Chivelstone Devon 5 Q11
Chivenor Devon 15 J5
Chlenry D & G 68 F6
Chobham Surrey 20 F10
Cholderton Wilts 19 J11
Cholesbury Bucks 20 E3
Chollerton Nthumb 72 G6
Cholsey Oxon 19 P4
Cholstrey Herefs 39 J9
Chop Gate N York 66 D7
Choppington Nthumb 73 M4
Chopwell Gatesd 73 K8
Chorley Ches E 49 K5
Chorley Lancs 57 L5
Chorley Shrops 39 M5
Chorleywood Herts 20 G4
Chorleywood West Herts 20 G4
Chorlton Ches E 49 N5
Chorlton-cum-Hardy Manch 57 P9
Chorlton Lane Ches W 49 J6
Choulton Shrops 38 H5
Chrishall Essex 33 M8
Chrisswell Inver 84 D7
Christchurch BCP 8 H8
Christchurch Cambs 43 M10
Christchurch Newpt 28 D10
Christian Malford Wilts 18 E5
Christon N Som 17 K5
Christon Bank Nthumb 81 P9
Christow Devon 5 Q4
Chudleigh Devon 6 B6
Chudleigh Knighton Devon 6 B7
Chulmleigh Devon 15 M8
Church Lancs 57 N3
Churcham Gloucs 29 K5
Church Aston Wrekin 49 N11
Church Brampton Nhants 31 Q2
Church Broughton Derbys 40 G2
Church Cove Cnwll 2 G12
Church Crookham Hants 20 D12
Churchdown Gloucs 29 M5
Church Eaton Staffs 49 Q11
Church End C Beds 32 H8
Churchend Essex 23 J5
Church End Essex 34 C10
Church End Gt Lon 21 K5
Church Enstone Oxon 31 J8
Church Fenton N York 59 L6
Churchfield Sandw 40 D8
Churchgate Street Essex 21 P2
Church Green Devon 6 G4
Church Hanborough Oxon 31 K10
Church Houses N York 66 F7
Churchill Devon 6 H3
Churchill N Som 17 L4
Churchill Oxon 30 H8
Churchill Worcs 30 B4
Churchill Worcs 39 Q6
Churchinford Somset 6 G1

Church Knowle Dorset ...8 D10
Church Langton Leics ...41 Q8
Church Lawford Warwks ...41 L11
Church Leigh Staffs ...40 D1
Church Lench Worcs ...30 D4
Church Mayfield Staffs ...50 F11
Church Minshull Ches E ...49 N10
Church Norton W Susx ...10 E10
Churchover Warwks ...41 L10
Church Preen Shrops ...39 K3
Church Pulverbatch Shrops ...38 H2
Churchstanton Somset ...16 G12
Churchstoke Powys ...38 F4
Churchstow Devon ...5 P10
Church Stowe Nhants ...31 N3
Church Street Kent ...22 E8
Church Stretton Shrops ...39 J4
Churchtown Cnwll ...4 D5
Churchtown Derbys ...50 H8
Churchtown IoM ...56 d3
Churchtown Lancs ...63 J12
Church Village Rhondd ...27 M10
Church Warsop Notts ...51 M7
Churston Ferrers Torbay ...6 B10
Churt Surrey ...10 D3
Churton Ches W ...48 H4
Churwell Leeds ...58 H8
Chwilog Gwynd ...46 G4
Chyandour Cnwll ...2 D9
Cilcain Flints ...48 D3
Cilcennin Cerdgn ...36 H8
Cilfrew Neath ...26 G8
Cilfynydd Rhondd ...27 M9
Cilgerran Pembks ...36 C11
Cilmaengwyn Neath ...26 G7
Cilmery Powys ...38 B11
Cilsan Carmth ...26 E4
Cilycwm Carmth ...37 M11
Cimla Neath ...26 G9
Cinderford Gloucs ...28 H6
Cinder Hill Wolves ...40 B8
Cippenham Slough ...20 F7
Cirencester Gloucs ...18 F1
City Gt Lon ...21 M7
City Airport Gt Lon ...21 N7
Clabhach Ag & B ...88 F5
Clachaig Ag & B ...84 B6
Clachaig Inn Highld ...90 F5
Clachan Ag & B ...83 L10
Clachan Ag & B ...84 B3
Clachan Ag & B ...89 Q11
Clachan Ag & B ...90 H3
Clachan Highld ...96 G3
Clachan-a-Luib W Isls ...111 b4
Clachan Mor Ag & B ...88 C6
Clachan na Luib W Isls ...111 b4
Clachan of Campsie E Duns ...85 K7
Clachan-Seil Ag & B ...89 Q11
Clachnaharry Highld ...107 K11
Clachtoll Highld ...108 B9
Clacket Lane Services Surrey ...21 N11
Clackmannan Clacks ...85 Q5
Clackmannanshire Bridge
  Fife ...85 Q5
Clackmarras Moray ...101 K4
Clacton-on-Sea Essex ...23 M1
Cladich Ag & B ...90 F11
Cladswell Worcs ...30 D3
Claggan Highld ...89 P6
Claigan Highld ...104 C10
Clanfield Hants ...10 B6
Clanfield Oxon ...19 K1
Clanville Hants ...19 K10
Clanville Somset ...17 P9
Claonaig Ag & B ...83 N10
Clapgate Herts ...33 M10
Clapham Bed ...32 E6
Clapham Gt Lon ...21 L8
Clapham N York ...63 N8
Clapham W Susx ...10 H8
Clapton Somset ...7 K2
Clapton Somset ...17 P5
Clapton-in-Gordano N Som ...17 L2
Clapton-on-the-Hill Gloucs ...18 F9
Claravale Gatesd ...73 K7
Clarbeston Pembks ...25 J5
Clarbeston Road Pembks ...24 H5
Clarborough Notts ...51 Q4
Clare Suffk ...34 C7
Clarebrand D & G ...70 C3
Clarencefield D & G ...70 H2
Clarilaw Border ...80 C9
Clarkston E Rens ...85 J10
Clashmore Highld ...107 M5
Clashmore Highld ...108 B9
Clashnessie Highld ...108 B9
Clashnoir Moray ...101 J10
Clathy P & K ...92 E10
Clathymore P & K ...92 F10
Clatt Abers ...102 C9
Clatter Powys ...38 B4
Clatworthy Somset ...16 E9
Claughton Lancs ...57 K1
Claughton Lancs ...63 K8
Claughton Wirral ...56 F10
Claverdon Warwks ...30 G2
Claverham N Som ...17 L3
Clavering Essex ...33 M9
Claverley Shrops ...39 P4
Claverton BaNES ...18 B7
Clawdd-coch V Glam ...27 M12
Clawdd-newydd Denbgs ...48 C5
Clawton Devon ...14 F11
Claxby Lincs ...52 G5
Claxton N York ...59 P3
Claxton Norfk ...45 M9
Claybrooke Magna Leics ...41 L9
Clay Coton Nhants ...41 N11
Clay Cross Derbys ...51 K8
Claydon Oxon ...31 L4
Claydon Suffk ...35 J6
Claygate D & G ...79 N11
Claygate Kent ...12 E2
Claygate Surrey ...21 J10
Clayhall Gt Lon ...21 N5
Clayhanger Devon ...16 D10
Clayhidon Devon ...16 F11
Clayhill E Susx ...12 G5
Clayock Highld ...110 D4
Claypits Gloucs ...29 K7
Claypole Lincs ...42 C1
Clayton C Brad ...58 E7

Clayton Donc ...59 L11
Clayton W Susx ...11 L7
Clayton-le-Moors Lancs ...57 N3
Clayton-le-Woods Lancs ...57 K4
Clayton West Kirk ...58 H11
Clayworth Notts ...51 Q4
Cleadale Highld ...96 F11
Cleadon S Tyne ...73 P8
Cleadon Park S Tyne ...73 P7
Clearbrook Devon ...5 L7
Clearwell Gloucs ...28 G7
Cleasby N York ...65 M5
Cleat Ork ...111 h3
Cleatlam Dur ...65 K4
Cleator Cumb ...70 G11
Cleator Moor Cumb ...70 G11
Cleckheaton Kirk ...58 F8
Cleehill Shrops ...39 L7
Cleekhimin N Lans ...85 M10
Clee St Margaret Shrops ...39 K5
Cleethorpes NE Lin ...53 K2
Cleeton St Mary Shrops ...39 L6
Cleeve N Som ...17 L3
Cleeve Oxon ...19 Q5
Cleeve Hill Gloucs ...29 N4
Cleeve Prior Worcs ...30 E4
Cleghornie E Loth ...87 L5
Clehonger Herefs ...28 E2
Cleish P & K ...86 C3
Cleland N Lans ...85 N10
Clenamacrie Ag & B ...90 C9
Clenchwarton Norfk ...43 P6
Clenerty Abers ...102 G3
Clent Worcs ...40 B10
Cleobury Mortimer Shrops ...39 M7
Cleobury North Shrops ...39 L5
Cleongart Ag & B ...75 K5
Clephanton Highld ...107 N11
Clerkhill D & G ...79 L8
Cleuch-head D & G ...78 D8
Clevancy Wilts ...18 F6
Clevedon N Som ...17 K2
Cleveleys Lancs ...62 G12
Cleverton Wilts ...18 E4
Clewer Somset ...17 L6
Cley next the Sea Norfk ...44 H2
Cliburn Cumb ...64 B3
Cliddesden Hants ...19 Q10
Cliffe Medway ...22 E7
Cliffe N York ...59 P7
Cliff End E Susx ...12 H7
Cliffe Woods Medway ...22 E8
Clifford Herefs ...38 E11
Clifford Leeds ...59 K5
Clifford Chambers Warwks ...30 G4
Clifford's Mesne Gloucs ...29 J4
Clifton Bristl ...17 N2
Clifton C Beds ...32 G8
Clifton C Nott ...41 M1
Clifton C York ...59 N4
Clifton Calder ...58 F9
Clifton Cumb ...71 Q9
Clifton Derbys ...50 F11
Clifton Devon ...15 K4
Clifton Donc ...51 M2
Clifton Lancs ...57 J3
Clifton N York ...58 F5
Clifton Oxon ...31 L7
Clifton Worcs ...39 Q11
Clifton Campville Staffs ...40 G8
Clifton Hampden Oxon ...19 P2
Clifton Reynes M Keyn ...32 C6
Clifton upon Dunsmore
  Warwks ...41 M11
Clifton upon Teme Worcs ...39 N9
Cliftonville Kent ...23 Q8
Climping W Susx ...10 F9
Clink Somset ...18 B10
Clint N York ...58 H3
Clinterty C Aber ...102 H11
Clint Green Norfk ...44 G7
Clintmains Border ...80 E7
Clippesby Norfk ...45 N7
Clipsham Rutlnd ...42 D6
Clipston Nhants ...41 Q10
Clipston Notts ...41 N1
Clipstone C Beds ...32 D10
Clipstone Notts ...51 N8
Clitheroe Lancs ...57 N1
Clive Shrops ...49 K9
Clixby Lincs ...52 F3
Cloatley Wilts ...29 N10
Clocaenog Denbgs ...48 C5
Clochan Moray ...101 M3
Clodock Herefs ...28 C4
Clola Abers ...103 K6
Clophill C Beds ...32 F8
Clopton Nhants ...32 F1
Clopton Suffk ...35 K6
Clopton Corner Suffk ...35 K6
Clos du Valle Guern ...6 c1
Closeburn D & G ...78 E9
Closeburnmill D & G ...78 E9
Closworth Somset ...7 N2
Clothall Herts ...33 J9
Clotton Ches W ...49 K3
Clough Foot Calder ...58 B9
Clough Head Calder ...58 E9
Cloughton N York ...67 L8
Clousta Shet ...111 k4
Clova Angus ...94 F7
Clovelly Devon ...14 F7
Clovenfords Border ...79 P2
Clovulin Highld ...90 D4
Clowne Derbys ...51 L6
Clows Top Worcs ...39 N7
Cluanie Inn Highld ...97 Q7
Cluanie Lodge Highld ...97 Q7
Clugston D & G ...69 J7
Clun Shrops ...38 F6
Clunas Highld ...100 D6
Clunbury Shrops ...38 G6
Clunderwen Carmth ...25 K5
Clune Highld ...99 L4
Clunes Highld ...98 B10
Clungunford Shrops ...38 H6
Clunie P & K ...92 G6
Clunton Shrops ...38 G6
Cluny P & K ...86 F3
Clutton BaNES ...17 N4
Clutton Ches W ...49 J5
Clutton Hill BaNES ...17 P4

Clydach Mons ...27 P6
Clydach Swans ...26 F8
Clydach Vale Rhondd ...27 K9
Clydebank W Duns ...84 H8
Clyffe Pypard Wilts ...18 F5
Clynder Ag & B ...84 D6
Clyne Neath ...26 H8
Clynnog Fawr Gwynd ...54 E10
Clyro Powys ...38 E12
Clyst Honiton Devon ...6 D4
Clyst Hydon Devon ...6 D3
Clyst St George Devon ...6 D5
Clyst St Lawrence Devon ...6 D3
Clyst St Mary Devon ...6 C5
Cnoc W Isls ...111 d2
Cnwch Coch Cerdgn ...37 L5
Coad's Green Cnwll ...4 G5
Coalburn S Lans ...78 D2
Coalburns Gatesd ...73 K8
Coaley Gloucs ...29 K8
Coalhill Essex ...22 F4
Coalpit Heath S Glos ...29 J11
Coal Pool Wsall ...40 D7
Coalport Wrekin ...39 M2
Coalsnaughton Clacks ...85 Q4
Coaltown of Balgonie Fife ...86 G3
Coaltown of Wemyss Fife ...86 G3
Coalville Leics ...41 K5
Coanwood Nthumb ...72 C8
Coat Somset ...17 L11
Coatbridge N Lans ...85 M9
Coatdyke N Lans ...85 M9
Coate Swindn ...18 H4
Coate Wilts ...18 F8
Coates Cambs ...43 K9
Coates Gloucs ...29 N8
Coates Lincs ...52 C6
Coates W Susx ...10 F6
Cobbaton Devon ...15 K6
Coberley Gloucs ...29 N5
Cobham Kent ...22 D9
Cobham Surrey ...20 H10
Cobham Services Surrey ...20 H11
Cobnash Herefs ...39 J9
Cobo Guern ...6 b1
Cobridge C Stke ...49 Q5
Coburby Abers ...103 J3
Cockayne Hatley C Beds ...33 J6
Cock Bridge Abers ...101 K12
Cockburnspath Border ...87 P7
Cock Clarks Essex ...22 F3
Cockenzie and Port Seton
  E Loth ...86 H7
Cockerham Lancs ...63 J11
Cockermouth Cumb ...71 J9
Cockernhoe Herts ...32 G11
Cockett Swans ...26 E9
Cockfield Dur ...65 K3
Cockfield Suffk ...34 E6
Cockfosters Gt Lon ...21 L4
Cock Green Essex ...34 B11
Cocking W Susx ...10 E6
Cocking Causeway W Susx ...10 E6
Cockington Torbay ...6 B9
Cocklake Somset ...17 L6
Cockley Cley Norfk ...44 D8
Cock Marling E Susx ...12 H6
Cockpole Green Wokham ...20 C7
Cockshutt Shrops ...48 H9
Cockthorpe Norfk ...44 G2
Cockwood Devon ...6 D6
Cockyard Derbys ...50 D5
Coddenham Suffk ...35 J6
Coddington Herefs ...29 J3
Coddington Notts ...52 B11
Codford St Mary Wilts ...18 E11
Codford St Peter Wilts ...18 E11
Codicote Herts ...32 H11
Codmore Hill W Susx ...10 G6
Codnor Derbys ...51 K10
Codrington S Glos ...29 K11
Codsall Staffs ...39 Q2
Codsall Wood Staffs ...39 Q2
Coedpoeth Wrexhm ...48 F5
Coed Talon Flints ...48 F4
Coed-y-paen Mons ...28 D8
Coed-yr-ynys Powys ...27 N5
Coffinswell Devon ...6 B8
Cofton Devon ...6 C6
Cofton Hackett Worcs ...40 D11
Cogan V Glam ...16 G2
Cogenhoe Nhants ...32 B5
Cogges Oxon ...31 J11
Coggeshall Essex ...34 E11
Coignafearn Highld ...99 K5
Coilacriech Abers ...94 E3
Coilantogle Stirlg ...85 K2
Coillore Highld ...96 D3
Coity Brdgnd ...27 K11
Col W Isls ...111 d2
Colaboll Highld ...107 J1
Colan Cnwll ...3 K4
Colaton Raleigh Devon ...6 E5
Colbost Highld ...104 B11
Colburn N York ...65 L6
Colby Cumb ...64 C4
Colby IoM ...56 b6
Colchester Essex ...34 G10
Colchester Zoo Essex ...34 F11
Cold Ash W Berk ...19 N6
Cold Ashby Nhants ...41 P11
Cold Ashton S Glos ...17 Q2
Cold Aston Gloucs ...30 F9
Coldbackie Highld ...109 L4
Cold Brayfield M Keyn ...32 D6
Coldean Br & H ...11 M8
Coldeast Devon ...5 Q5
Colden Calder ...58 C8
Colden Common Hants ...9 N3
Cold Hanworth Lincs ...52 E6
Coldharbour Surrey ...11 J2
Cold Higham Nhants ...31 P4
Coldingham Border ...81 J2
Cold Kirby N York ...66 D10
Coldmeece Staffs ...49 Q8
Cold Norton Essex ...22 G4
Cold Overton Leics ...42 B7
Coldred Kent ...13 P1
Coldridge Devon ...15 M10
Coldstream Border ...80 H6
Coldwaltham W Susx ...10 G6
Coldwells Abers ...103 K7
Cole Somset ...17 P9

Colebatch Shrops ...38 G5
Colebrook Devon ...6 D2
Colebrooke Devon ...15 N11
Coleby Lincs ...52 D10
Coleby N Linc ...60 F9
Coleford Devon ...15 N11
Coleford Gloucs ...28 G6
Coleford Somset ...17 P6
Colegate End Norfk ...45 K11
Colehill Dorset ...8 F7
Coleman's Hatch E Susx ...11 N4
Colemere Shrops ...48 H7
Colemore Hants ...10 B4
Colenden P & K ...92 G9
Colerne Wilts ...18 B6
Colesbourne Gloucs ...30 D10
Coleshill Bucks ...20 F4
Coleshill Oxon ...19 J3
Coleshill Warwks ...40 G9
Coley BaNES ...17 N5
Colgate W Susx ...11 K4
Colinsburgh Fife ...87 J2
Colinton C Edin ...86 E8
Colintraive Ag & B ...83 Q7
Colkirk Norfk ...44 F5
Coll Ag & B ...88 F5
Coll W Isls ...111 d2
Collace P & K ...93 J8
Collafirth Shet ...111 k3
Coll Airport Ag & B ...88 E5
Collaton Devon ...5 P11
Collaton St Mary Torbay ...6 B10
College of Roseisle Moray ...100 H3
College Town Br For ...20 D10
Collessie Fife ...93 K11
Collier Row Gt Lon ...21 P5
Collier's End Herts ...33 L11
Collier Street Kent ...12 E2
Colliery Abers ...103 L9
Collin D & G ...70 G1
Collingbourne Ducis Wilts ...19 J9
Collingbourne Kingston Wilts ...19 J9
Collingham Leeds ...59 K5
Collingham Notts ...52 B10
Collington Herefs ...39 M9
Collingtree Nhants ...31 Q3
Collins Green Warrtn ...57 K9
Colliston Angus ...93 Q6
Colliton Devon ...6 D2
Collyweston Nhants ...42 E9
Colmonell S Ayrs ...68 F2
Colmworth Bed ...32 F6
Colnabaichin Abers ...101 K12
Colnbrook Slough ...20 G7
Colne Cambs ...33 L2
Colne Lancs ...58 B6
Colne Engaine Essex ...34 E10
Colney Norfk ...45 K8
Colney Heath Herts ...21 K3
Coln Rogers Gloucs ...30 E11
Coln St Aldwyns Gloucs ...30 F12
Coln St Dennis Gloucs ...30 E11
Colonsay Ag & B ...82 E4
Colonsay Airport Ag & B ...82 E5
Colpy Abers ...102 E8
Colquhar Border ...79 M1
Colsterworth Lincs ...42 D5
Colston Bassett Notts ...41 P2
Coltfield Moray ...100 H3
Coltishall Norfk ...45 L6
Colton Cumb ...62 G5
Colton Leeds ...59 J7
Colton N York ...59 M5
Colton Norfk ...44 H7
Colton Staffs ...40 D4
Colt's Hill Kent ...12 D2
Colvend D & G ...70 E5
Colwall Herefs ...29 K1
Colwell Nthumb ...72 G6
Colwich Staffs ...40 D4
Colwinston V Glam ...16 C2
Colworth W Susx ...10 E9
Colwyn Bay Conwy ...55 M6
Colyford Devon ...6 H4
Colyton Devon ...6 H4
Combe Oxon ...31 K10
Combe W Berk ...19 L8
Combe Down BaNES ...18 B8
Combe Fishacre Devon ...6 A9
Combe Florey Somset ...16 F9
Combe Hay BaNES ...17 Q4
Combeinteignhead Devon ...6 B8
Combe Martin Devon ...15 K3
Combe Raleigh Devon ...6 F3
Comberbach Ches W ...57 M12
Comberford Staffs ...40 F6
Comberton Cambs ...33 L5
Comberton Herefs ...39 J8
Combe St Nicholas Somset ...7 J1
Combrook Warwks ...30 H4
Combs Derbys ...50 D5
Combs Suffk ...34 H5
Combs Ford Suffk ...34 H5
Combwich Somset ...16 H7
Comers Abers ...95 L1
Comeytrowe Somset ...16 G10
Comhampton Worcs ...39 Q8
Commins Coch Powys ...47 N10
Commondale N York ...66 F5
Common End Cumb ...70 G10
Common Moor Cnwll ...4 F6
Compstall Stockp ...50 C3
Compstonend D & G ...69 P8
Compton Devon ...6 B9
Compton Hants ...9 M3
Compton Staffs ...39 P5
Compton Surrey ...10 F1
Compton W Berk ...19 N5
Compton W Susx ...10 C7
Compton Wilts ...18 G9
Compton Abbas Dorset ...8 C4
Compton Abdale Gloucs ...30 D10
Compton Bassett Wilts ...18 F5
Compton Beauchamp Oxon ...19 J4
Compton Bishop Somset ...17 K5
Compton Chamberlayne
  Wilts ...8 F2
Compton Dando BaNES ...17 P4
Compton Dundon Somset ...17 L9
Compton Durville Somset ...17 L11
Compton Greenfield S Glos ...28 G11
Compton Martin BaNES ...17 M5
Compton Pauncefoot Somset ...17 P10

Compton Valence Dorset ...7 N4
Comrie Fife ...86 B4
Comrie P & K ...92 B10
Conaglen House Highld ...90 E3
Concha Highld ...97 M4
Concraigie P & K ...92 G6
Conderton Worcs ...29 N2
Condicote Gloucs ...30 F8
Condorrat N Lans ...85 M8
Condover Shrops ...39 J2
Coney Hill Gloucs ...29 L5
Coneyhurst W Susx ...10 H5
Coneysthorpe N York ...66 G12
Coney Weston Suffk ...34 F2
Congerstone Leics ...41 J6
Congham Norfk ...44 B5
Congleton Ches E ...49 Q3
Congresbury N Som ...17 L4
Conheath D & G ...70 G2
Conicavel Moray ...100 F5
Coningsby Lincs ...52 H11
Conington Cambs ...33 K4
Conington Cambs ...42 H11
Conisbrough Donc ...51 L2
Conisholme Lincs ...53 L4
Coniston Cumb ...62 F3
Coniston E R Yk ...61 K7
Coniston Cold N York ...58 B3
Conistone N York ...58 C1
Connah's Quay Flints ...48 F2
Connel Ag & B ...90 C9
Connel Park E Ayrs ...77 K8
Connor Downs Cnwll ...2 E7
Conon Bridge Highld ...107 J10
Cononley N York ...58 C5
Consall Staffs ...50 C10
Consett Dur ...73 K10
Constable Burton N York ...65 L8
Constable Lee Lancs ...57 P4
Constantine Cnwll ...2 H9
Constantine Bay Cnwll ...3 K2
Contin Highld ...106 G10
Conwy Conwy ...55 L6
Conwy Castle Conwy ...55 L6
Conyer's Green Suffk ...34 E3
Cooden E Susx ...12 E8
Cookbury Devon ...14 G10
Cookham W & M ...20 E6
Cookham Dean W & M ...20 D6
Cookham Rise W & M ...20 E6
Cookhill Worcs ...30 D3
Cookley Suffk ...35 M2
Cookley Worcs ...39 Q6
Cookley Green Oxon ...20 B5
Cookney Abers ...95 P4
Cook's Green Essex ...35 K11
Cooks Green Suffk ...34 G6
Cooksmill Green Essex ...22 D3
Coolham W Susx ...10 H5
Cooling Medway ...22 E8
Coombe Cnwll ...3 L5
Coombe Devon ...6 C7
Coombe Devon ...6 E4
Coombe Gloucs ...29 K9
Coombe Hants ...9 Q4
Coombe Bissett Wilts ...8 G3
Coombe Cellars Devon ...6 B8
Coombe Hill Gloucs ...29 M4
Coombe Keynes Dorset ...8 C9
Coombe Pafford Torbay ...6 C9
Coombes W Susx ...11 J8
Coombes-Moor Herefs ...38 G9
Coombeswood Dudley ...40 C9
Coopersale Common Essex ...21 P3
Copdock Suffk ...35 J8
Copford Green Essex ...34 F11
Copgrove N York ...59 J2
Copister Shet ...111 k3
Cople Bed ...32 F7
Copley Dur ...65 J3
Copmanthorpe C York ...59 M5
Copmere End Staffs ...49 P9
Copp Lancs ...56 H2
Coppenhall Staffs ...40 B4
Copperhouse Cnwll ...2 E8
Coppingford Cambs ...32 G2
Copplestone Devon ...15 N10
Coppull Lancs ...57 K6
Copsale W Susx ...11 J5
Copster Green Lancs ...57 M3
Copston Magna Warwks ...41 L9
Cop Street Kent ...23 P10
Copt Hewick N York ...65 N12
Copthorne W Susx ...11 L3
Copt Oak Leics ...41 L5
Copythorne Hants ...9 K5
Corbets Tey Gt Lon ...22 C6
Corbière Jersey ...7 a2
Corbridge Nthumb ...73 J8
Corby Nhants ...42 C11
Corby Glen Lincs ...42 E5
Cordon N Ayrs ...75 Q6
Coreley Shrops ...39 L7
Corfe Somset ...16 G11
Corfe Castle Dorset ...8 E10
Corfe Mullen Dorset ...8 E8
Corfton Shrops ...39 J5
Corgarff Abers ...94 E1
Corhampton Hants ...9 Q4
Corlae D & G ...77 L10
Corley Warwks ...40 H9
Corley Services Warwks ...40 H9
Cormuir Angus ...94 E8
Cornard Tye Suffk ...34 E8
Cornforth Dur ...65 N1
Cornhill Abers ...102 D4
Cornhill-on-Tweed Nthumb ...81 J5
Cornholme Calder ...58 B8
Cornoigmore Ag & B ...88 C7
Cornsay Dur ...73 K11
Cornsay Colliery Dur ...73 L11
Corntown Highld ...107 J10
Corntown V Glam ...27 J12
Cornwall Airport Newquay
  Cnwll ...3 K3
Cornwell Oxon ...30 H8
Cornwood Devon ...5 M8
Cornworthy Devon ...6 Q8
Corpach Highld ...90 F2
Corpusty Norfk ...45 J4
Corrachree Abers ...94 H2
Corran Highld ...90 D4
Corran Highld ...97 L4

Corrie D & G	79	K10
Corrie N Ayrs	75	Q4
Corriecravie N Ayrs	75	P7
Corriegills N Ayrs	75	Q5
Corriegour Lodge Hotel Highld	98	C9
Corriemoille Highld	106	F9
Corrimony Highld	98	E3
Corringham Lincs	52	C5
Corringham Thurr	22	E6
Corris Gwynd	47	M9
Corris Uchaf Gwynd	47	M9
Corrow Ag & B	84	D3
Corry Highld	96	H5
Corscombe Devon	15	L11
Corscombe Dorset	7	M2
Corse Gloucs	29	K3
Corse Lawn Gloucs	29	L3
Corsham Wilts	18	C6
Corsindae Abers	102	F12
Corsley Wilts	18	C10
Corsley Heath Wilts	18	B10
Corsock D & G	78	C12
Corston BaNES	17	Q3
Corston Wilts	18	D4
Corstorphine C Edin	86	E7
Cortachy Angus	94	F9
Corton Suffk	45	Q10
Corton Wilts	18	D11
Corton Denham Somset	17	P10
Coruanan Highld	90	E3
Corwen Denbgs	48	C6
Coryton Devon	5	K4
Coryton Thurr	22	E6
Cosby Leics	41	M8
Coseley Dudley	40	C8
Cosgrove Nhants	32	B8
Cosham C Port	9	Q6
Cosheston Pembks	24	H7
Coshieville P & K	92	B6
Cossall Notts	51	L11
Cossington Leics	41	N5
Cossington Somset	17	J7
Costessey Norfk	45	K7
Costock Notts	41	M3
Coston Leics	42	B6
Coston Norfk	44	H8
Cote Oxon	19	L1
Cotebrook Ches W	49	L3
Cotehill Cumb	71	P5
Cotes Leics	41	M4
Cotesbach Leics	41	M10
Cotford St Luke Somset	16	G9
Cotgrave Notts	41	N1
Cothal Abers	102	H11
Cotham Notts	42	B1
Cotherstone Dur	64	H4
Cothill Oxon	19	M2
Cotleigh Devon	6	G3
Cotmanhay Derbys	51	L11
Coton Cambs	33	L5
Coton Nhants	41	P12
Coton Staffs	49	P10
Coton Clanford Staffs	49	Q10
Coton Hill Shrops	49	J11
Coton in the Elms Derbys	40	G4
Cotswold Airport Wilts	29	N9
Cotswolds	30	C11
Cotswold Wildlife Park & Gardens Oxon	30	G11
Cott Devon	5	Q7
Cottam Lancs	57	J3
Cottam Notts	52	B7
Cottenham Cambs	33	M4
Cottered Herts	33	K10
Cotteridge Birm	40	D10
Cotterstock Nhants	42	F11
Cottesbrooke Nhants	41	P11
Cottesmore Rutlnd	42	C7
Cottingham E R Yk	60	H7
Cottingham Nhants	42	B11
Cottingley C Brad	58	E6
Cottisford Oxon	31	N7
Cotton Suffk	34	H4
Cottown Abers	101	P9
Cottown Abers	102	G11
Cottown of Gight Abers	102	H7
Cotts Devon	5	K4
Coughton Warwks	30	E3
Coulaghailtro Ag & B	83	N4
Coulags Highld	97	N1
Coulby Newham Middsb	66	D5
Coull Abers	94	H2
Coulport Ag & B	84	D5
Coulsdon Gt Lon	21	L10
Coulston Wilts	18	D9
Coulter S Lans	78	G3
Coulton N York	66	E11
Coultra Fife	93	L10
Cound Shrops	39	K2
Coundon Dur	65	M2
Countersett N York	64	G9
Countess Wear Devon	6	C5
Countesswells C Aber	95	P2
Countesthorpe Leics	41	N8
Countisbury Devon	15	M3
Coupar Angus P & K	93	J7
Coupland Nthumb	81	K7
Cour Ag & B	75	M3
Courteachan Highld	97	J9
Courteenhall Nhants	31	Q4
Court Henry Carmth	26	D4
Courtsend Essex	23	K5
Courtway Somset	16	G8
Cousland Mdloth	86	H8
Cousley Wood E Susx	12	D4
Cove Ag & B	84	D5
Cove Border	87	P7
Cove Devon	16	C11
Cove Hants	20	D11
Cove Highld	105	M4
Cove Bay C Aber	95	Q2
Covehithe Suffk	35	Q1
Coven Staffs	40	B6
Coveney Cambs	33	M1
Covenham St Bartholomew Lincs	53	K5
Covenham St Mary Lincs	53	K5
Coventry Covtry	41	J10
Coverack Cnwll	2	H11
Coverack Bridges Cnwll	2	G9
Coverham N York	65	K9
Covington Cambs	32	F3
Covington S Lans	78	F2
Cowan Bridge Lancs	63	L7
Cowbeech E Susx	12	C7
Cowbit Lincs	43	J6
Cowbridge V Glam	16	D2
Cowden Kent	11	P3
Cowdenbeath Fife	86	D4
Cowers Lane Derbys	50	H10
Cowes IoW	9	N8
Cowesby N York	66	C9
Cowfold W Susx	11	K5
Cowhill S Glos	28	H9
Cowie Stirlg	85	P5
Cowley Devon	6	B4
Cowley Gloucs	29	N6
Cowley Gt Lon	20	G7
Cowley Oxon	31	M12
Cowling Lancs	57	L5
Cowling N York	58	C5
Cowling N York	65	M9
Cowlinge Suffk	34	B6
Cowpen Nthumb	73	N5
Cowplain Hants	10	B7
Cowshill Dur	72	F11
Cowslip Green N Som	17	L4
Cowthorpe N York	59	K4
Coxbank Ches E	49	M7
Coxbench Derbys	51	J11
Coxford Cnwll	14	C11
Coxford Norfk	44	E4
Coxheath Kent	22	E12
Coxhoe Dur	65	N1
Coxley Somset	17	M7
Coxley Wick Somset	17	M7
Coxtie Green Essex	22	C4
Coxwold N York	66	D11
Coychurch Brdgnd	27	K11
Coylton S Ayrs	76	G7
Coylumbridge Highld	99	N6
Coytrahen Brdgnd	27	J10
Crabbs Cross Worcs	30	D2
Crabtree W Susx	11	K5
Crackenthorpe Cumb	64	C3
Crackington Haven Cnwll	14	C11
Crackley Staffs	49	Q5
Crackleybank Shrops	49	N12
Cracoe N York	58	C3
Craddock Devon	6	E1
Cradley Dudley	40	C9
Cradley Herefs	39	N11
Cradley Heath Sandw	40	C9
Cradoc Powys	27	L3
Crafthole Cnwll	4	H9
Craggan Highld	100	F9
Cragganmore Moray	101	J7
Craghead Dur	73	L10
Cragside House & Garden Nthumb	73	J1
Crai Powys	27	J4
Craibstone Moray	101	P4
Craichie Angus	93	N6
Craig Angus	95	L10
Craig Highld	105	Q11
Craigbank E Ayrs	77	K8
Craigburn Border	86	F10
Craigcleuch D & G	79	M10
Craigdam Abers	102	H8
Craigdhu Ag & B	83	M2
Craigearn Abers	102	F11
Craigellachie Moray	101	K6
Craigend P & K	92	G10
Craigend Rens	84	H8
Craigendoran Ag & B	84	E6
Craigends Rens	84	G9
Craighlaw D & G	69	J6
Craighouse Ag & B	82	G9
Craigie P & K	92	G7
Craigie S Ayrs	76	G5
Craigiefold Abers	103	J3
Craigley D & G	70	C4
Craig Llangiwg Neath	26	G7
Craiglockhart C Edin	86	E7
Craigmillar C Edin	86	G7
Craigneston D & G	78	C10
Craigneuk N Lans	85	N10
Craigneuk N Lans	85	N9
Craignure Ag & B	89	P8
Craigo Angus	95	L8
Craigrothie Fife	93	L12
Craigruie Stirlg	91	M11
Craigton Angus	93	N7
Craigton C Aber	95	N2
Craigton E Rens	84	H11
Craigton of Airlie Angus	93	K6
Craik Border	79	M7
Crail Fife	87	L1
Crailing Border	80	F8
Craiselound N Linc	51	Q2
Crakehall N York	65	M9
Crambe N York	60	C2
Cramlington Nthumb	73	M5
Cramond C Edin	86	E7
Cramond Bridge C Edin	86	E7
Cranage Ches E	49	N2
Cranberry Staffs	49	P8
Cranborne Dorset	8	F5
Cranbourne Br For	20	E8
Cranbrook Devon	6	C4
Cranbrook Kent	12	F3
Cranfield C Beds	32	D8
Cranford Gt Lon	20	H7
Cranford St Andrew Nhants	32	D2
Cranford St John Nhants	32	D2
Cranham Gloucs	29	M6
Crank St Hel	57	J8
Cranleigh Surrey	10	G3
Cranmore Somset	17	P7
Cranoe Leics	41	Q8
Cransford Suffk	35	M4
Cranshaws Border	87	N9
Crantock Cnwll	3	K4
Cranwell Lincs	52	E12
Cranwich Norfk	44	C10
Cranworth Norfk	44	G8
Craobh Haven Ag & B	83	M2
Crarae Ag & B	83	Q4
Crask Inn Highld	109	J10
Crask of Aigas Highld	98	H2
Craster Nthumb	81	Q9
Cratfield Suffk	35	M2
Crathes Abers	95	M3
Crathie Abers	94	E3
Crathie Highld	98	H9
Crathorne N York	66	B6
Craven Arms Shrops	38	H5
Crawcrook Gatesd	73	K8
Crawford S Lans	78	F5
Crawfordjohn S Lans	78	E4
Crawley Hants	9	M1
Crawley Oxon	31	J10
Crawley W Susx	11	L3
Crawley Down W Susx	11	M3
Crawton Abers	95	P6
Cray N York	64	G10
Cray P & K	94	C8
Crayke N York	66	D12
Crays Hill Essex	22	E5
Creacombe Devon	15	P8
Creagan Inn Ag & B	90	D7
Creag Ghoraidh W Isls	111	b5
Creagorry W Isls	111	b5
Creaguaineach Lodge Highld	91	J3
Creaton Nhants	41	P12
Creca D & G	71	K2
Credenhill Herefs	39	J12
Crediton Devon	15	P11
Creebank D & G	69	J4
Creebridge D & G	69	K6
Creech Heathfield Somset	16	H10
Creech St Michael Somset	16	H10
Creed Cnwll	3	L6
Creekmouth Gt Lon	21	P7
Creeting St Mary Suffk	34	H5
Creeton Lincs	42	E6
Creetown D & G	69	L7
Cregneash IoM	56	a7
Creich Fife	93	K10
Creigiau Cardif	27	M11
Cremyll Cnwll	5	K9
Cressage Shrops	39	L2
Cressbrook Derbys	50	F6
Cresselly Pembks	25	J7
Cressex Bucks	20	D5
Cressing Essex	34	D11
Cresswell Nthumb	73	N3
Cresswell Pembks	25	J7
Cresswell Staffs	50	C11
Creswell Derbys	51	M6
Cretingham Suffk	35	K5
Cretshengan Ag & B	83	K9
Crewe Ches E	49	N4
Crewe-by-Farndon Ches W	48	H5
Crewe Green Ches E	49	N5
Crew Green Powys	48	G11
Crewkerne Somset	7	L2
Crewton C Derb	41	J2
Crianlarich Stirlg	91	K10
Cribyn Cerdgn	36	H9
Criccieth Gwynd	46	H4
Crich Derbys	51	J9
Crichton Mdloth	86	H9
Crick Nhants	41	N11
Crickadarn Powys	27	M1
Cricket St Thomas Somset	7	K2
Crickhowell Powys	27	P5
Cricklade Wilts	18	G3
Cricklewood Gt Lon	21	K6
Criddlestone Wakefd	58	H10
Crigglestone Wakefd	58	H10
Crimond Abers	103	L4
Crimplesham Norfk	43	Q8
Crimscote Warwks	30	G5
Crinaglack Highld	98	F2
Crinan Ag & B	83	L4
Crindledyke N Lans	85	N10
Cringleford Norfk	45	K8
Crinow Pembks	25	K6
Croachy Highld	99	J4
Crockenhill Kent	21	P9
Crocker End Oxon	20	B6
Crockernwell Devon	5	P2
Crockerton Wilts	18	C11
Crocketford D & G	70	D2
Crockham Hill Kent	21	N12
Croeserw Neath	27	J9
Croes-goch Pembks	24	E3
Croes-lan Cerdgn	36	F10
Croesor Gwynd	47	K3
Croesyceiliog Carmth	25	P5
Croesyceiliog Torfn	28	C9
Croft Leics	41	L8
Croft Lincs	53	N10
Croft Warrtn	57	L9
Croftamie Stirlg	84	H6
Crofton Wakefd	59	J9
Croft-on-Tees N York	65	M5
Croftown Highld	106	C5
Crofts Moray	101	K5
Crofts Bank Traffd	57	N9
Crofts of Dipple Moray	101	L4
Crofts of Haddo Abers	102	H7
Crofts of Savoch Abers	103	L4
Crofty Swans	26	C9
Croggan Ag & B	89	P10
Croglin Cumb	71	R6
Croick Highld	106	H4
Cromarty Highld	107	N8
Crombie Fife	86	C5
Cromdale Highld	100	G9
Cromer Herts	33	J10
Cromer Norfk	45	K2
Cromford Derbys	50	H9
Cromhall S Glos	29	J8
Cromor W Isls	111	d2
Cromra W Isls	111	d2
Cromwell Notts	51	B10
Cronberry E Ayrs	77	K6
Crondall Hants	10	C1
Cronton Knows	57	J10
Crook Cumb	63	J3
Crook Dur	65	L1
Crookedholm E Ayrs	76	H4
Crookes Sheff	51	J4
Crookham Nthumb	81	J6
Crookham W Berk	19	P7
Crookham Village Hants	20	C11
Crook Inn Border	78	H4
Crooklands Cumb	63	K5
Crook of Devon P & K	86	C2
Cropredy Oxon	31	L5
Cropston Leics	41	M5
Cropthorne Worcs	30	D5
Cropton N York	66	G9
Cropwell Bishop Notts	41	P1
Cropwell Butler Notts	51	P12
Cros W Isls	111	e1
Crosbost W Isls	111	d2
Crosby Cumb	70	H7
Crosby IoM	56	c5
Crosby N Linc	60	F10
Crosby Sefton	56	G8
Crosby Garret Cumb	63	N1
Crosby Ravensworth Cumb	64	B5
Croscombe Somset	17	N7
Cross Somset	17	K5
Crossaig Ag & B	75	M3
Crossapol Ag & B	88	C7
Cross Ash Mons	28	E5
Cross-at-Hand Kent	12	F2
Crossbost W Isls	111	d2
Crosscanonby Cumb	70	H7
Crossdale Street Norfk	45	K3
Cross Flatts C Brad	58	E6
Crossford Fife	86	C5
Crossford S Lans	77	N3
Crossgatehall E Loth	86	H8
Crossgates E Ayrs	76	F3
Crossgates Fife	86	D5
Cross Gates Leeds	59	J7
Crossgates N York	67	M10
Crossgill Lancs	63	K9
Cross Green Leeds	59	J7
Cross Green Suffk	34	E5
Cross Green Suffk	34	G6
Cross Hands Carmth	26	D6
Crosshands E Ayrs	76	H5
Crosshill Fife	86	E3
Crosshill S Ayrs	76	F9
Crosshouse E Ayrs	76	G4
Cross Houses Shrops	39	K1
Cross in Hand E Susx	12	C6
Cross Inn Cerdgn	36	F8
Cross Inn Cerdgn	37	J7
Cross Keys Ag & B	84	F6
Crosskeys Caerph	27	P9
Crosskirk Highld	110	B2
Cross Lane IoW	9	N9
Cross Lane Head Shrops	39	N3
Crosslee Rens	84	G9
Crossmichael D & G	70	C3
Cross of Jackston Abers	102	G8
Cross o' th' hands Derbys	50	H10
Crossroads Abers	95	J1
Crossroads Abers	95	M3
Cross Street Suffk	35	K2
Crosston Angus	93	N5
Cross Town Ches E	57	N12
Crossway Green Worcs	39	Q8
Crossways Dorset	8	B9
Crosswell Pembks	25	K2
Crosthwaite Cumb	62	H4
Croston Lancs	57	J5
Crostwick Norfk	45	L7
Crouch End Gt Lon	21	L6
Crouchston Wilts	8	F3
Crouch Hill Dorset	7	Q1
Croughton Nhants	31	M7
Crovie Abers	102	G3
Crowan Cnwll	2	F8
Crowborough E Susx	11	P4
Crowborough Warren E Susx	11	P4
Crowcombe Somset	16	F8
Crowdecote Derbys	50	E7
Crowden Derbys	50	E2
Crow Edge Barns	58	F12
Crowell Oxon	20	C4
Crowfield Suffk	35	J5
Crowhill E Loth	87	N7
Crow Hill Herefs	28	H4
Crowhurst E Susx	12	F7
Crowhurst Surrey	11	M1
Crowland Lincs	43	J7
Crowland Suffk	34	G3
Crowlas Cnwll	2	D8
Crowle N Linc	60	D10
Crowle Worcs	30	B3
Crowle Green Worcs	30	B3
Crowmarsh Gifford Oxon	19	Q3
Crown Corner Suffk	35	L3
Crownhill C Plym	5	K8
Crownpits Surrey	10	F2
Crownthorpe Norfk	44	H9
Crowntown Cnwll	2	F9
Crows-an-Wra Cnwll	2	B9
Crowthorne Wokham	20	D9
Crowton Ches W	49	L1
Croxdale Dur	73	M12
Croxden Staffs	50	E11
Croxley Green Herts	20	H4
Croxteth Lpool	56	H9
Croxton Cambs	33	J5
Croxton N Linc	61	J10
Croxton Norfk	44	E11
Croxton Norfk	44	G4
Croxton Staffs	49	P8
Croxton Kerrial Leics	42	B4
Croy Highld	107	N11
Croy N Lans	85	M7
Croyde Devon	14	H4
Croydon Cambs	33	K6
Croydon Gt Lon	21	L9
Crubenmore Highld	99	K10
Cruckmeole Shrops	38	H1
Cruckton Shrops	48	H12
Cruden Bay Abers	103	M7
Crudgington Wrekin	49	L11
Crudie Abers	102	G4
Crudwell Wilts	29	N9
Crumlin Caerph	27	P8
Crumplehorn Cnwll	4	F9
Crumpsall Manch	57	Q8
Crundale Kent	13	K1
Crux Easton Hants	19	M9
Crwbin Carmth	26	C6
Cryers Hill Bucks	20	E4
Crymych Pembks	25	L2
Crynant Neath	26	H7
Crystal Palace Gt Lon	21	M8
Cuaig Highld	105	K10
Cuan Ag & B	89	P12
Cubert Cnwll	2	H4
Cublington Bucks	32	B11
Cublington Herefs	28	E2
Cuckfield W Susx	11	L5
Cucklington Somset	17	R10
Cuckney Notts	51	M6
Cuddesdon Oxon	31	N12
Cuddington Bucks	31	Q11
Cuddington Ches W	49	L2
Cuddington Heath Ches W	49	J6
Cudham Gt Lon	21	N10
Cudliptown Devon	5	L4
Cudnell BCP	8	F7
Cudworth Barns	59	K11
Cudworth Somset	7	K1
Cuffley Herts	21	L3
Cuil Highld	90	D5
Culbokie Highld	107	K9
Culburnie Highld	98	G1
Culcabock Highld	107	L12
Culcharry Highld	100	D5
Culcheth Warrtn	57	M9
Culdrain Abers	101	P8
Culduie Highld	97	K2
Culford Suffk	34	D3
Culgaith Cumb	64	B2
Culham Oxon	19	N2
Culkein Highld	108	B8
Culkein Drumbeg Highld	108	C8
Culkerton Gloucs	29	N9
Cullen Moray	101	P2
Cullercoats N Tyne	73	P6
Cullerlie Abers	95	M2
Cullicudden Highld	107	K9
Cuillin Hills Highld	96	F5
Cullipool Ag & B	83	L1
Cullivoe Shet	111	k2
Culloden Highld	107	M12
Cullompton Devon	6	D2
Cullompton Services Devon	6	D2
Culm Davy Devon	16	F12
Culmington Shrops	39	J6
Culmstock Devon	16	E12
Culnacraig Highld	106	A2
Culnaightrie D & G	70	C5
Culnaknock Highld	104	G9
Culrain Highld	107	J4
Culross Fife	86	B5
Culroy S Ayrs	76	F8
Culsalmond Abers	102	E8
Culscadden D & G	69	L8
Culshabbin D & G	69	J8
Culswick Shet	111	j4
Cultercullen Abers	103	J9
Cults C Aber	95	P2
Culverstone Green Kent	22	D10
Culverthorpe Lincs	42	E3
Culworth Nhants	31	M5
Culzean Castle & Country Park S Ayrs	76	D8
Cumbernauld N Lans	85	M7
Cumbernauld Village N Lans	85	M7
Cumberworth Lincs	53	N8
Cuminestown Abers	102	G5
Cumledge Border	80	G3
Cummersdale Cumb	71	N5
Cummertrees D & G	71	J3
Cummingston Moray	100	H2
Cumnock E Ayrs	77	J7
Cumnor Oxon	31	L12
Cumrew Cumb	71	Q5
Cumrue D & G	78	H10
Cumwhinton Cumb	71	P5
Cumwhitton Cumb	71	Q5
Cundall N York	65	Q11
Cunninghamhead N Ayrs	76	F3
Cunningsburgh Shet	111	k4
Cupar Fife	93	L11
Cupar Muir Fife	93	L11
Curbar Derbys	50	G6
Curbridge Hants	9	N5
Curbridge Oxon	31	J11
Curdridge Hants	9	N5
Curdworth Warwks	40	F8
Curland Somset	16	H11
Curridge W Berk	19	N6
Currie C Edin	86	E8
Curry Mallet Somset	17	J10
Curry Rivel Somset	17	K10
Curtisden Green Kent	12	E3
Curtisknowle Devon	5	P9
Cury Cnwll	2	G10
Cushnie Abers	102	C11
Cusworth Donc	59	M12
Cutcloy D & G	69	L11
Cutcombe Somset	16	C8
Cuthill Highld	107	M5
Cutnall Green Worcs	39	Q8
Cutsdean Gloucs	30	D7
Cutthorpe Derbys	51	J6
Cuxham Oxon	19	Q2
Cuxton Medway	22	E9
Cuxwold Lincs	52	G4
Cwm Denbgs	56	C12
Cwmafan Neath	26	G9
Cwmaman Rhondd	27	L8
Cwmbach Carmth	25	M4
Cwmbâch Powys	27	N2
Cwmbach Rhondd	27	L8
Cwmbran Torfn	28	C9
Cwmcarn Caerph	27	P9
Cwmcarvan Mons	28	F7
Cwm-cou Cerdgn	36	E11
Cwm Crawnon Powys	27	N5
Cwmdare Rhondd	27	L7
Cwmdu Powys	27	P4
Cwmdu Swans	26	E9
Cwmduad Carmth	25	P3
Cwmfelin Brdgnd	27	J10
Cwmfelin Myr Td	27	M8
Cwmfelin Boeth Carmth	25	L5
Cwmfelinfach Caerph	27	P9
Cwmffrwd Carmth	25	P5
Cwmgiedd Powys	26	H6
Cwmgorse Carmth	26	F6
Cwmgwili Carmth	26	D6
Cwmhiraeth Carmth	26	N2
Cwm Llinau Powys	47	N9
Cwmllynfell Neath	26	G6
Cwmmawr Carmth	26	D6
Cwmparc Rhondd	27	K9
Cwmpengraig Carmth	25	N2
Cwmtillery Blae G	27	P7
Cwm-twrch Isaf Powys	26	G6
Cwm-twrch Uchaf Powys	26	H6
Cwm-y-glo Gwynd	54	H8
Cwmystwyth Cerdgn	37	N6
Cwrtnewydd Cerdgn	36	H10

Dunan Highld 96 G4
Dunan P & K 91 L5
Dunaverty Ag & B 75 K10
Dunball Somset 17 J7
Dunbar E Loth 87 M6
Dunbeath Highld 110 D9
Dunbeg Ag & B 90 B9
Dunblane Stirlg 85 N3
Dunbridge Fife 93 K11
Duncanston Highld 107 J10
Duncanstone Abers 102 D9
Dunchideock Devon 6 B5
Dunchurch Warwks 41 L12
Duncow D & G 78 F11
Duncrievie P & K 86 D1
Duncton W Susx 10 F6
Dundee C Dund 93 M9
Dundee Airport C Dund 93 L9
Dundon Somset 17 L9
Dundonald S Ayrs 76 F5
Dundonnell Highld 106 B5
Dundraw Cumb 71 K5
Dundreggan Highld 98 D6
Dundrennan D & G 70 C6
Dundry N Som 17 N3
Dunecht Abers 102 G12
Dunfermline Fife 86 C5
Dunfield Gloucs 18 G2
Dungate Kent 13 L6
Dungeness Kent 13 L6
Dunham Massey Traffd 57 N10
Dunham-on-the-Hill Ches W 49 J2
Dunham-on-Trent Notts 52 B8
Dunhampton Worcs 39 Q8
Dunham Town Traffd 57 N10
Dunham Woodhouses Traffd 57 N10
Dunholme Lincs 52 E7
Dunino Fife 93 P12
Dunipace Falk 85 N6
Dunkeld P & K 92 F7
Dunkerton BaNES 17 Q4
Dunkeswell Devon 6 F2
Dunkeswick N York 58 H5
Dunkirk Kent 23 L10
Dunkirk S Glos 18 B4
Dunk's Green Kent 22 C11
Dunlappie Angus 95 K8
Dunley Hants 19 P8
Dunley Worcs 39 P8
Dunlop E Ayrs 76 G2
Dunmaglass Highld 98 H5
Dunmore Falk 85 P5
Dunnet Highld 110 E2
Dunnichen Angus 93 N6
Dunning P & K 92 F11
Dunnington C York 59 P4
Dunnington E R Yk 61 K4
Dunnington Warwks 30 E4
Dunoon Ag & B 84 C7
Dunphail Moray 100 F7
Dunragit D & G 68 F7
Duns Border 80 G4
Dunsby Lincs 42 F5
Dunscore D & G 78 E11
Dunscroft Donc 59 P11
Dunsdale R & Cl 66 E4
Dunsden Green Oxon 20 B7
Dunsdon Devon 14 F9
Dunsfold Surrey 10 G3
Dunsford Devon 5 Q3
Dunshalt Fife 86 F1
Dunshillock Abers 103 K5
Dunsill Notts 51 L8
Dunsley N York 67 J5
Dunsley Staffs 39 Q5
Dunsmore Bucks 20 D3
Dunsop Bridge Lancs 63 M11
Dunstable C Beds 32 E11
Dunstall Staffs 40 F4
Dunstan Nthumb 81 Q9
Dunster Somset 16 D7
Duns Tew Oxon 31 L8
Dunston Gatesd 73 M8
Dunston Lincs 52 F10
Dunston Norfk 45 K9
Dunston Staffs 40 B4
Dunstone Devon 5 N9
Dunstone Devon 5 P5
Dunsville Donc 59 N11
Dunswell E R Yk 61 J7
Dunsyre S Lans 86 C11
Dunterton Devon 4 H4
Duntisbourne Abbots Gloucs 29 N7
Duntisbourne Rouse Gloucs 29 P7
Duntish Dorset 7 Q2
Duntocher W Duns 84 H8
Dunton Bucks 32 B11
Dunton C Beds 33 J7
Dunton Norfk 44 E4
Dunton Bassett Leics 41 M8
Dunton Green Kent 21 P11
Duntulm Highld 104 F7
Dunure S Ayrs 76 E8
Dunvant Swans 26 D9
Dunvegan Highld 104 C11
Dunwich Suffk 35 P3
Durgan Cnwll 2 H9
Durham Dur 73 M11
Durham Cathedral Dur 73 M11
Durham Services Dur 73 N12
Durham Tees Valley Airport S on T 65 P5
Durisdeer D & G 78 E8
Durisdeermill D & G 78 E7
Durleigh Somset 16 H8
Durley Hants 9 N4
Durley Wilts 19 J7
Durley Street Hants 9 N4
Durlock Kent 23 P10
Durlock Kent 23 P9
Durness Highld 108 G3
Durno Abers 102 F9
Duror Highld 90 D5
Durran Ag & B 83 P2
Durrington W Susx 10 H8
Durrington Wilts 18 H10
Dursley Gloucs 29 K8
Dursley Cross Gloucs 29 J5
Durston Somset 16 H9
Durweston Dorset 8 C6
Duston Nhants 31 Q2
Duthil Highld 99 P4
Dutton Ches W 57 L11
Duxford Cambs 33 M7

Duxford Oxon 19 L2
Duxford IWM Cambs 33 M7
Dwygyfylchi Conwy 55 K6
Dwyran IoA 54 F8
Dyce C Aber 103 J11
Dyfatty Carmth 26 B8
Dyffryn Ardudwy Gwynd 47 J6
Dyffryn Cellwen Neath 27 J4
Dyke Lincs 42 F5
Dyke Moray 100 F4
Dykehead Angus 93 J5
Dykehead Angus 94 F9
Dykehead N Lans 85 P10
Dykehead Stirlg 85 K4
Dykelands Abers 95 L8
Dykends Angus 93 J4
Dykeside Abers 102 F6
Dymchurch Kent 13 L4
Dymock Gloucs 29 J3
Dyrham S Glos 17 Q2
Dysart Fife 86 G4
Dyserth Denbgs 56 C11

E

Eagland Hill Lancs 62 H12
Eagle Lincs 52 C9
Eaglesfield Cumb 70 H9
Eaglesfield D & G 71 K1
Eaglesham E Rens 85 J11
Eagley Bolton 57 N6
Eakring Notts 51 P8
Ealand N Linc 60 D10
Ealing Gt Lon 21 J7
Eals Nthumb 72 C9
Eamont Bridge Cumb 71 Q9
Earby Lancs 58 B5
Earcroft Bl w D 57 M4
Eardington Shrops 39 N4
Eardisland Herefs 38 H9
Eardisley Herefs 38 F11
Eardiston Shrops 48 G9
Eardiston Worcs 39 M8
Earith Cambs 33 L2
Earlestown St Hel 57 L9
Earley Wokham 20 C8
Earlham Norfk 45 K8
Earlish Highld 104 E9
Earls Barton Nhants 32 C4
Earls Colne Essex 34 E10
Earls Common Worcs 30 C3
Earl's Croome Worcs 29 M1
Earlsdon Covtry 40 H10
Earlsferry Fife 87 J3
Earlsfield Gt Lon 21 K8
Earlsford Abers 102 H8
Earlsheaton Kirk 58 H9
Earl Shilton Leics 41 L7
Earl Soham Suffk 35 K4
Earl Sterndale Derbys 50 E7
Earlston Border 80 D6
Earlston E Ayrs 76 G4
Earlswood Surrey 21 L12
Earlswood Warwks 40 E11
Earnley W Susx 10 D10
Earsdon N Tyne 73 N6
Earsham Norfk 45 M11
Eartham W Susx 10 F8
Easby N York 66 E6
Easdale Ag & B 89 P11
Easebourne W Susx 10 E5
Easenhall Warwks 41 L10
Eashing Surrey 10 F2
Easington Bucks 31 P11
Easington Dur 73 P11
Easington E R Yk 61 P9
Easington R & Cl 66 G4
Easington Colliery Dur 73 Q11
Easington Lane Sundld 73 P10
Easingwold N York 59 M1
Eassie and Nevay Angus 93 M6
East Aberthaw V Glam 16 D3
East Allington Devon 5 P9
East Anstey Devon 15 P6
East Ardsley Leeds 58 H8
East Ashey IoW 9 P9
East Ashling W Susx 10 D8
East Ayton N York 67 L9
East Barkwith Lincs 52 G7
East Barming Kent 22 E11
East Barnby N York 66 H5
East Barnet Gt Lon 21 L4
East Barns E Loth 87 N7
East Barsham Norfk 44 F4
East Beckham Norfk 45 J3
East Bedfont Gt Lon 20 H8
East Bergholt Suffk 34 H9
East Bilney Norfk 44 F6
East Blatchington E Susx 11 P9
East Boldon S Tyne 73 P8
East Boldre Hants 9 L7
Eastbourne Darltn 65 N5
Eastbourne E Susx 12 C9
East Bradenham Norfk 44 F8
East Brent Somset 17 J6
Eastbridge Suffk 35 P4
East Bridgford Notts 51 P11
East Buckland Devon 15 L6
East Budleigh Devon 6 E6
Eastburn C Brad 58 D5
Eastbury W Berk 19 K5
East Butterwick N Linc 52 B3
Eastby N York 58 D4
East Calder W Loth 86 C8
East Carleton Norfk 45 K9
East Carlton Leeds 58 G5
East Carlton Nhants 42 B3
East Chaldon Dorset 8 B10
East Challow Oxon 19 L3
East Charleton Devon 5 P10
East Chelborough Dorset 7 M2
East Chiltington E Susx 11 M7
East Chinnock Somset 17 L12
East Chisenbury Wilts 18 G9
Eastchurch Kent 23 J8
East Clandon Surrey 20 G11
East Claydon Bucks 31 Q8
East Coker Somset 7 M1
Eastcombe Gloucs 29 M7
East Compton Somset 17 N7
East Cornworthy Devon 6 B10

Eastcote Gt Lon 20 H6
Eastcote Nhants 31 P4
Eastcote Solhll 40 G10
Eastcott Wilts 18 F9
East Cottingwith E R Yk 60 C6
Eastcourt Wilts 19 J8
East Cowes IoW 9 N8
East Cowick E R Yk 59 P9
East Cowton N York 65 N6
East Cranmore Somset 17 P7
East Dean E Susx 12 C9
East Dean Gloucs 28 H5
East Dean Hants 9 J3
East Dean W Susx 10 E7
East Drayton Notts 51 Q6
East Dulwich Gt Lon 21 M8
East Dundry N Som 17 N3
East Ella C KuH 61 H8
Eastend Essex 22 H5
East End Hants 9 L7
East End Hants 19 N8
East End Kent 12 G3
East End Oxon 31 K10
East End Somset 17 P6
Easter Balmoral Abers 94 E3
Easter Compton S Glos 28 G11
Easter Dalziel Highld 107 M11
Eastergate W Susx 10 F8
Easterhouse C Glas 85 L9
Easter Howgate Mdloth 86 F9
Easter Kinkell Highld 107 J10
Easter Moniack Highld 98 H1
Eastern Green Covtry 40 H10
Easter Ord Abers 95 N1
Easter Pitkierie Fife 87 L2
Easter Skeld Shet 111 k4
Easter Softlaw Border 80 G7
Easterton Wilts 18 F9
East Everleigh Wilts 18 H9
East Farleigh Kent 22 E11
East Farndon Nhants 41 Q9
East Ferry Lincs 52 B4
Eastfield N Lans 85 P9
Eastfield N York 67 M10
East Fortune E Loth 87 K6
East Garston W Berk 19 L5
Eastgate Dur 72 G12
Eastgate Lincs 42 F6
Eastgate Norfk 45 J5
East Goscote Leics 41 N5
East Grafton Wilts 19 J8
East Grimstead Wilts 9 J2
East Grinstead W Susx 11 N3
East Guldeford E Susx 12 H6
East Haddon Nhants 31 P1
East Hagbourne Oxon 19 N3
East Halton N Linc 61 K9
East Ham Gt Lon 21 N6
Easthampton Herefs 38 H9
East Hanney Oxon 19 M3
East Hanningfield Essex 22 F3
East Hardwick Wakefd 59 L9
East Harling Norfk 44 G11
East Harlsey N York 65 Q7
East Harnham Wilts 8 G2
East Harptree BaNES 17 N5
East Harting W Susx 10 C6
East Hatch Wilts 8 D2
East Hatley Cambs 33 J6
East Hauxwell N York 65 L9
East Haven Angus 93 P8
East Heckington Lincs 42 H2
East Hedleyhope Dur 73 K11
East Helmsdale Highld 110 B11
East Hendred Oxon 19 M3
East Heslerton N York 67 K11
East Hoathly E Susx 11 Q6
East Holme Dorset 8 D9
Easthope Shrops 39 K3
Easthorpe Essex 34 F11
East Horrington Somset 17 N6
East Horsley Surrey 20 H11
East Howe BCP 8 F8
East Huntspill Somset 17 J7
East Ilsley W Berk 19 N5
Eastington Devon 15 M9
Eastington Gloucs 29 K7
Eastington Gloucs 30 F10
East Keal Lincs 53 L10
East Kennett Wilts 18 G7
East Keswick Leeds 59 J5
East Kilbride S Lans 85 K11
East Kirkby Lincs 53 K10
East Knighton Dorset 8 B9
East Knoyle Wilts 8 C2
East Lambrook Somset 17 L11
Eastlands D & G 70 D2
East Langdon Kent 13 P2
East Langton Leics 41 Q8
East Lavant W Susx 10 D8
East Lavington W Susx 10 F6
East Layton N York 65 L5
Eastleach Martin Gloucs 30 G12
Eastleach Turville Gloucs 30 G11
East Leake Notts 41 M3
Eastleigh Devon 14 H6
Eastleigh Hants 9 M4
East Lexham Norfk 44 E6
Eastling Kent 23 J11
East Linton E Loth 87 L6
East Lockinge Oxon 19 M4
East Lound N Linc 52 B4
East Lulworth Dorset 8 C10
East Lutton N York 60 G1
East Lydford Somset 17 N9
East Malling Kent 22 E11
East Marden W Susx 10 D7
East Markham Notts 51 Q6
East Martin Hants 8 F4
East Marton N York 58 B4
East Meon Hants 10 B5
East Mersea Essex 23 K1
East Midlands Airport Leics 41 K3
East Molesey Surrey 21 J9
East Morden Dorset 8 D8
East Morton C Brad 58 E6
East Morton D & G 78 E8
East Ness N York 66 F10
Eastney C Port 9 Q7
Eastnor Herefs 29 K2
East Norton Leics 42 B9
Eastoft N Linc 60 D10
East Ogwell Devon 5 Q6

Easton Cambs 32 G3
Easton Devon 5 P3
Easton Dorset 7 Q8
Easton Hants 9 N2
Easton Lincs 42 D5
Easton Norfk 45 J7
Easton Somset 17 M6
Easton Suffk 35 L5
Easton Wilts 18 D6
Easton Grey Wilts 18 C4
Easton-in-Gordano N Som 17 M2
Easton Maudit Nhants 32 C5
Easton-on-the-Hill Nhants 42 E8
Easton Royal Wilts 18 H8
East Orchard Dorset 8 C4
East Peckham Kent 12 D1
East Pennard Somset 17 N8
East Portlemouth Devon 5 P11
East Prawle Devon 5 Q11
East Preston W Susx 10 H9
East Putford Devon 14 G8
East Quantoxhead Somset 16 F7
East Rainton Sundld 73 N10
East Ravendale NE Lin 52 H4
East Raynham Norfk 44 E5
Eastrea Cambs 43 J10
Eastriggs D & G 71 L3
East Rigton Leeds 59 J5
Eastrington E R Yk 60 D8
Eastrop Swindn 18 H3
East Rounton N York 65 Q6
East Rudham Norfk 44 D5
East Runton Norfk 45 K2
East Ruston Norfk 45 M5
Eastry Kent 23 P11
East Saltoun E Loth 87 J8
East Sheen Gt Lon 21 K8
East Shefford W Berk 19 L6
East Stockwith Lincs 52 B5
East Stoke Dorset 8 C9
East Stoke Notts 51 Q10
East Stour Dorset 8 B3
East Stourmouth Kent 23 N10
East Stowford Devon 15 L6
East Stratton Hants 19 P11
East Studdal Kent 23 P12
East Taphouse Cnwll 4 E7
East-the-Water Devon 14 H6
East Thirston Nthumb 73 L2
East Tilbury Thurr 22 D7
East Tisted Hants 10 B4
East Torrington Lincs 52 G6
East Tuddenham Norfk 44 H7
East Tytherley Hants 9 K2
East Tytherton Wilts 18 E6
East Village Devon 15 P10
Eastville Bristl 17 N2
Eastville Lincs 53 L11
East Walton Norfk 44 C6
East Week Devon 5 N2
Eastwell Leics 41 Q2
East Wellow Hants 9 K4
East Wemyss Fife 86 G3
East Whitburn W Loth 85 Q9
Eastwick Herts 21 N2
East Wickham Gt Lon 21 P7
East Williamston Pembks 25 J7
East Winch Norfk 44 B6
East Winterslow Wilts 9 J1
East Wittering W Susx 10 C9
East Witton N York 65 K9
Eastwood Notts 51 L10
Eastwood Sthend 22 G6
East Woodburn Nthumb 72 G4
East Woodhay Hants 19 N8
East Worldham Hants 10 C3
East Worthing W Susx 10 J8
East Wretham Norfk 44 F11
Eathorpe Warwks 31 K1
Eaton Ches E 49 Q3
Eaton Ches W 49 L3
Eaton Leics 42 B4
Eaton Norfk 45 K8
Eaton Notts 51 P5
Eaton Oxon 31 K12
Eaton Shrops 39 J4
Eaton Bray C Beds 32 D11
Eaton Constantine Shrops 39 L2
Eaton Green C Beds 32 D11
Eaton Hastings Oxon 19 J2
Eaton Mascott Shrops 39 K2
Eaton Socon Cambs 32 G5
Eaton upon Tern Shrops 49 M10
Ebberston N York 67 K10
Ebbesborne Wake Wilts 8 E3
Ebbw Vale Blae G 27 N6
Ebchester Dur 73 K9
Ebford Devon 6 D5
Ebley Gloucs 29 L7
Ebnal Ches W 49 J6
Ebrington Gloucs 30 F6
Ecchinswell Hants 19 N8
Ecclaw Border 87 P8
Ecclefechan D & G 71 K1
Eccles Border 80 G6
Eccles Kent 22 E10
Eccles Salfd 57 P8
Ecclesall Sheff 50 H4
Ecclesfield Sheff 51 J3
Eccleshall Staffs 49 P9
Eccleshill C Brad 58 F6
Ecclesmachan W Loth 86 C7
Eccles Road Norfk 44 G11
Eccleston Ches W 48 H3
Eccleston Lancs 57 J5
Eccleston St Hel 57 J8
Echt Abers 95 M2
Eckford Border 80 F8
Eckington Derbys 51 K5
Eckington Worcs 29 N1
Ecton Nhants 32 B4
Edale Derbys 50 E4
Eday Ork 111 h1
Eday Airport Ork 111 h1
Edburton W Susx 11 K7
Edderton Highld 107 L5
Eddleston Border 86 F11
Eddlewood S Lans 85 M11
Edenbridge Kent 11 N2
Edenfield Lancs 57 P5
Edenhall Cumb 71 Q8
Edenham Lincs 42 F6
Eden Park Gt Lon 21 M9

Eden Project Cnwll 3 M5
Edensor Derbys 50 G6
Edentaggart Ag & B 84 F4
Edenthorpe Donc 59 N11
Edern Gwynd 46 E4
Edgbaston Birm 40 D9
Edgcott Bucks 31 P9
Edgcott Somset 15 P4
Edge Gloucs 29 L6
Edgefield Norfk 44 H4
Edgefield Green Norfk 44 H4
Edgerton Kirk 58 F10
Edgeworth Gloucs 29 N7
Edgmond Wrekin 49 N10
Edgton Shrops 38 H5
Edgware Gt Lon 21 J5
Edgworth Bl w D 57 N5
Edinbane Highld 104 D11
Edinburgh C Edin 86 F7
Edinburgh Airport C Edin 86 D7
Edinburgh Castle C Edin 86 F7
Edinburgh Old & New Town C Edin 86 F7
Edinburgh Royal Botanic Gardens C Edin 86 F7
Edinburgh Zoo RZSS C Edin 86 E7
Edingale Staffs 40 G5
Edingham D & G 70 D3
Edingley Notts 51 P9
Edingthorpe Norfk 45 M4
Edingthorpe Green Norfk 45 M4
Edington Border 81 J3
Edington Nthumb 73 K4
Edington Somset 17 K8
Edington Wilts 18 D9
Edingworth Somset 17 J5
Edithmead Somset 17 J6
Edith Weston Rutlnd 42 D8
Edlesborough Bucks 32 D11
Edlingham Nthumb 81 M11
Edlington Lincs 52 H8
Edmondsham Dorset 8 F5
Edmondsley Dur 73 M10
Edmondthorpe Leics 42 C6
Edmonton Gt Lon 21 M5
Edmundbyers Dur 72 H10
Ednam Border 80 G6
Edradynate P & K 92 D5
Edrom Border 80 H3
Edstaston Shrops 49 K8
Edstone Warwks 30 F2
Edwalton Notts 41 N1
Edwinstowe Notts 51 N7
Edworth C Beds 32 H8
Edwyn Ralph Herefs 39 M9
Edzell Angus 95 K8
Edzell Woods Abers 95 K7
Efail-fach Neath 26 G9
Efail Isaf Rhondd 27 M11
Efailnewydd Gwynd 46 F4
Efailwen Carmth 25 K4
Efenechtyd Denbgs 48 C4
Effgill D & G 79 L9
Effingham Surrey 20 H11
Egerton Bolton 57 N6
Egerton Kent 12 H1
Eggborough N York 59 M9
Eggbuckland C Plym 5 K8
Eggesford Devon 15 M9
Eggington C Beds 32 D10
Egginton Derbys 40 H2
Egglescliffe S on T 65 P5
Eggleston Dur 64 H3
Egham Surrey 20 G8
Egleton Rutlnd 42 C8
Eglingham Nthumb 81 M9
Egloshayle Cnwll 3 M2
Egloskerry Cnwll 4 G3
Eglwysbach Conwy 55 L7
Eglwys Cross Wrexhm 49 J7
Eglwyswrw Pembks 25 K2
Egmanton Notts 51 Q7
Egremont Cumb 70 G12
Egremont Wirral 56 G9
Egton N York 66 H6
Egton Bridge N York 66 H6
Egypt Bucks 20 F6
Eigg Highld 96 F11
Eight Ash Green Essex 34 F10
Eilanreach Highld 97 L6
Eilean Donan Castle Highld 97 M5
Eisgein W Isls 111 d3
Eishken W Isls 111 d3
Elan Valley Powys 37 P7
Elan Village Powys 37 Q7
Elberton S Glos 28 H10
Elburton C Plym 5 L9
Eldersfield Worcs 29 L3
Elderslie Rens 84 H9
Eldon Dur 65 M2
Elerch Cerdgn 37 L4
Elfhill Abers 95 N5
Elford Staffs 40 F5
Elgin Moray 101 J3
Elgol Highld 96 G6
Elham Kent 13 M2
Elie Fife 87 K3
Elim IoA 54 E5
Eling Hants 9 L5
Elkesley Notts 51 P6
Elkstone Gloucs 29 N6
Ella Abers 102 E4
Ellacombe Torbay 6 C9
Elland Calder 58 E9
Ellary Ag & B 83 L7
Ellastone Staffs 50 E11
Ellel Lancs 63 J10
Ellemford Border 87 N9
Ellenabeich Ag & B 89 P11
Ellenhall Staffs 49 Q9
Ellen's Green Surrey 10 H3
Ellerbeck N York 66 B8
Ellerby N York 66 H5
Ellerdine Heath Wrekin 49 L10
Elleric Ag & B 90 E4
Ellerker E R Yk 60 F8
Ellerton E R Yk 60 C6
Ellerton N York 65 M7
Ellesborough Bucks 20 D3
Ellesmere Shrops 48 H8
Ellesmere Port Ches W 56 H12
Ellingham Norfk 45 N10
Ellingham Nthumb 81 N8

Ellingstring N York 65 L10
Ellington Cambs 32 G3
Ellington Nthumb 73 M3
Elliots Green Somset 18 B10
Ellisfield Hants 19 Q10
Ellishader Highld 104 G8
Ellistown Leics 41 K5
Ellon Abers 103 K8
Ellonby Cumb 71 N8
Elloughton E R Yk 60 G8
Ellwood Gloucs 28 G7
Elm Cambs 43 M8
Elmbridge Worcs 30 B1
Elmdon Essex 33 M8
Elmdon Solhll 40 F10
Elmer W Susx 10 F9
Elmers End Gt Lon 21 M9
Elmer's Green Lancs 57 J7
Elmesthorpe Leics 41 L8
Elmhurst Staffs 40 E5
Elmley Castle Worcs 29 N1
Elmley Lovett Worcs 39 Q8
Elmore Gloucs 29 K6
Elmore Back Gloucs 29 K5
Elm Park Gt Lon 21 Q6
Elmsett Suffk 34 H7
Elmstead Market Essex 34 H10
Elmsted Kent 13 L2
Elmstone Kent 23 N10
Elmstone Hardwicke Gloucs 29 M4
Elmswell E R Yk 60 G3
Elmswell Suffk 34 G4
Elmton Derbys 51 L6
Elphin Highld 108 E12
Elphinstone E Loth 86 H8
Elrick Abers 95 N1
Elrig D & G 69 J9
Elrington Nthumb 72 F8
Elsdon Nthumb 72 G3
Elsenham Essex 33 N10
Elsfield Oxon 31 M11
Elsham N Linc 60 H10
Elsing Norfk 44 H6
Elslack N York 58 B4
Elson Hants 9 P7
Elsrickle S Lans 86 C12
Elstead Surrey 10 E2
Elsted W Susx 10 D6
Elsthorpe Lincs 42 F5
Elston Notts 51 Q10
Elstow Bed 32 F7
Elstree Herts 21 J4
Elstronwick E R Yk 61 L7
Elswick Lancs 56 H2
Elswick N u Ty 73 M7
Elsworth Cambs 33 K4
Elterwater Cumb 62 G2
Eltham Gt Lon 21 N8
Eltisley Cambs 33 J5
Elton Cambs 42 F10
Elton Ches W 49 J1
Elton Derbys 50 G8
Elton Herefs 39 J7
Elton S on T 65 P4
Elton-on-the-Hill Notts 51 Q11
Eltringham Nthumb 73 J8
Elvanfoot S Lans 78 F5
Elvaston Derbys 41 K2
Elveden Suffk 34 D2
Elvetham Heath Hants 20 C11
Elvingston E Loth 87 J7
Elvington C York 60 C5
Elvington Kent 23 P12
Elwick Hartpl 66 C2
Elworth Ches E 49 N3
Elworthy Somset 16 E8
Ely Cambs 33 N1
Ely Cardif 16 F2
Emberton M Keyn 32 C6
Embleton Cumb 71 J9
Embleton Nthumb 81 P9
Embo Highld 107 N4
Emborough Somset 17 N6
Embo Street Highld 107 N4
Embsay N York 58 D4
Emery Down Hants 9 K6
Emley Kirk 58 G10
Emmington Oxon 20 C3
Emneth Norfk 43 M8
Emneth Hungate Norfk 43 N8
Empingham Rutlnd 42 D8
Empshott Hants 10 C4
Emsworth Hants 10 C8
Enborne W Berk 19 M7
Enborne Row W Berk 19 M7
Enderby Leics 41 M7
Endmoor Cumb 63 K5
Endon Staffs 50 B9
Endon Bank Staffs 50 B9
Enfield Gt Lon 21 M4
Enfield Lock Gt Lon 21 M4
Enfield Wash Gt Lon 21 M4
Enford Wilts 18 G9
Engine Common S Glos 29 J11
Englefield W Berk 19 Q6
Englefield Green Surrey 20 F8
English Bicknor Gloucs 28 G5
Englishcombe BaNES 17 Q4
English Frankton Shrops 49 J9
Enham Alamein Hants 19 L10
Enmore Somset 16 H8
Enmore Green Dorset 8 C3
Ennerdale Bridge Cumb 70 H11
Ensay Ag & B 88 H4
Ensbury BCP 8 F8
Ensdon Shrops 49 H11
Enstone Oxon 31 J8
Enterkinfoot D & G 78 E7
Enville Staffs 39 P5
Eochar W Isls 111 a5
Eòlaigearraidh W Isls 111 a6
Eoligarry W Isls 111 a6
Epney Gloucs 29 K6
Epperstone Notts 51 P10
Epping Essex 21 P3
Epping Green Essex 21 N3
Epping Upland Essex 21 N3
Eppleby N York 65 L5
Epsom Surrey 21 K10
Epwell Oxon 31 J6
Epworth N Linc 52 A3
Erbistock Wrexhm 48 G7

Erdington Birm 40 E8
Eridge Green E Susx 12 B3
Erines Ag & B 83 N7
Eriska Ag & B 90 C7
Eriskay W Isls 111 b6
Eriswell Suffk 34 C2
Erith Gt Lon 21 P7
Erlestoke Wilts 18 E9
Ermington Devon 5 M9
Erpingham Norfk 45 K4
Errogie Highld 98 H5
Errol P & K 93 J10
Erskine Rens 84 H8
Erskine Bridge Rens 84 H8
Ervie D & G 68 D5
Erwarton Suffk 35 K9
Erwood Powys 38 C12
Eryholme N York 65 N6
Eryrys Denbgs 48 E4
Escomb Dur 65 L3
Escrick N York 59 N5
Esgairgeiliog Powys 47 M9
Esh Dur 73 L11
Esher Surrey 21 J9
Eshott Nthumb 73 L2
Esh Winning Dur 73 L11
Eskadale Highld 98 F2
Eskbank Mdloth 86 G8
Eskdale Green Cumb 62 D3
Eskdalemuir D & G 79 L8
Esprick Lancs 56 H2
Essendine Rutlnd 42 F7
Essendon Herts 21 L2
Essich Highld 99 J2
Esslemont Abers 103 J8
Eston R & Cl 66 D4
Etal Nthumb 81 K6
Etchilhampton Wilts 18 F8
Etchingham E Susx 12 E5
Etchinghill Kent 13 M3
Etchinghill Staffs 40 D4
Eton W & M 20 F7
Eton Wick W & M 20 F7
Etruria C Stke 49 Q6
Etteridge Highld 99 K9
Ettersgill Dur 64 F3
Ettiley Heath Ches E 49 N4
Ettingshall Wolves 40 B8
Ettington Warwks 30 H4
Etton C Pete 42 G8
Etton E R Yk 60 G5
Ettrick Border 79 L6
Ettrickbridge Border 79 N4
Ettrickhill Border 79 L6
Etwall Derbys 40 H2
Euston Suffk 34 E2
Euxton Lancs 57 K5
Evanton Highld 107 K8
Evedon Lincs 42 F1
Evelix Highld 107 M4
Evenjobb Powys 38 F9
Evenley Nhants 31 N7
Evenlode Gloucs 30 G8
Evenwood Dur 65 K3
Evercreech Somset 17 P8
Everingham E R Yk 60 D6
Everleigh Wilts 18 H9
Eversholt C Beds 32 E9
Evershot Dorset 7 N2
Eversley Hants 20 C10
Eversley Cross Hants 20 C10
Everthorpe E R Yk 60 F7
Everton C Beds 32 H6
Everton Hants 9 K8
Everton Lpool 56 G9
Everton Notts 51 P3
Evertown D & G 71 M1
Evesbatch Herefs 39 M11
Evesham Worcs 30 D5
Evington C Leic 41 N6
Ewden Village Sheff 50 H2
Ewell Surrey 21 K10
Ewell Minnis Kent 13 N2
Ewelme Oxon 19 Q3
Ewen Gloucs 18 E2
Ewenny V Glam 27 J12
Ewerby Lincs 42 G1
Ewhurst Surrey 10 H3
Ewhurst Green E Susx 12 F5
Ewhurst Green Surrey 10 H3
Ewloe Flints 48 F3
Ewood Bl w D 57 M4
Eworthy Devon 5 J2
Ewshot Hants 20 D12
Ewyas Harold Herefs 28 D3
Exbourne Devon 15 K10
Exbury Hants 9 M7
Exebridge Somset 16 C10
Exelby N York 65 N9
Exeter Devon 6 C4
Exeter Airport Devon 6 D4
Exeter Services Devon 6 C4
Exford Somset 15 P5
Exfordsgreen Shrops 39 J2
Exhall Warwks 30 E3
Exhall Warwks 41 J9
Exlade Street Oxon 19 Q4
Exminster Devon 6 C5
Exmoor National Park 15 P4
Exmouth Devon 6 D6
Exning Suffk 33 Q4
Exton Devon 6 D5
Exton Hants 9 Q4
Exton Rutlnd 42 D7
Exton Somset 16 C9
Exwick Devon 6 B4
Eyam Derbys 50 G5
Eydon Nhants 31 M4
Eye C Pete 42 H9
Eye Herefs 39 J8
Eye Suffk 35 J3
Eyemouth Border 81 K2
Eyeworth C Beds 33 J7
Eyhorne Street Kent 22 G11
Eyke Suffk 35 M6
Eynesbury Cambs 32 H5
Eynsford Kent 21 N3
Eynsham Oxon 31 K11
Eype Dorset 7 L5
Eyre Highld 104 F10
Eythorne Kent 23 P12
Eyton Herefs 39 J9

Eyton Shrops 48 H10
Eyton on Severn Shrops 39 L2
Eyton upon the Weald
    Moors Wrekin 49 M11

F

Faccombe Hants 19 L8
Faceby N York 66 C7
Fachwen Powys 48 H10
Faddiley Ches E 49 L5
Fadmoor N York 66 F9
Faerdre Swans 26 F8
Faifley W Duns 84 H8
Failand N Som 17 M2
Failford S Ayrs 76 H6
Failsworth Oldham 50 B1
Fairbourne Gwynd 47 K8
Fairburn N York 59 L8
Fairfield Derbys 50 E6
Fairfield Worcs 40 C11
Fairford Gloucs 18 H1
Fair Green Norfk 43 Q6
Fairhaven Lancs 56 G4
Fair Isle Shet 111 m5
Fair Isle Airport Shet 111 m5
Fairlands Surrey 20 F11
Fairlie N Ayrs 84 D11
Fairlight E Susx 12 G7
Fairmile Devon 6 E4
Fairmile Surrey 20 H10
Fairmilehead C Edin 86 F8
Fairnilee Border 79 P3
Fair Oak Hants 9 N4
Fairoak Staffs 49 N8
Fair Oak Green Hants 19 Q8
Fairseat Kent 22 D10
Fairstead Essex 34 C12
Fairstead Norfk 43 Q6
Fairwarp E Susx 11 P5
Fairwater Cardif 27 N12
Fairy Cross Devon 14 G7
Fakenham Norfk 44 F4
Fakenham Magna Suffk 34 E2
Fala Mdloth 87 J9
Fala Dam Mdloth 87 J9
Faldingworth Lincs 52 F6
Faldouët Jersey 7 c2
Falfield S Glos 29 J9
Falkenham Suffk 35 L8
Falkirk Falk 85 P7
Falkirk Wheel Falk 85 P7
Falkland Fife 86 F2
Fallburn S Lans 78 F2
Fallin Stirlg 85 N5
Fallodon Nthumb 81 P9
Fallowfield Manch 57 Q9
Fallowfield Nthumb 72 G7
Falmer E Susx 11 M8
Falmouth Cnwll 3 J8
Falnash Border 79 N7
Falsgrave N York 67 M9
Falstone Nthumb 72 D4
Fanagmore Highld 108 D6
Fancott C Beds 32 E10
Fanellan Highld 98 G1
Fangdale Beck N York 66 D8
Fangfoss E R Yk 60 D4
Fanmore Ag & B 89 J7
Fannich Lodge Highld 106 D2
Fans Border 80 E6
Far Bletchley M Keyn 32 C9
Farcet Cambs 42 H10
Far Cotton Nhants 31 Q3
Fareham Hants 9 P6
Farewell Staffs 40 E5
Faringdon Oxon 19 K2
Farington Lancs 57 K4
Farlam Cumb 71 Q4
Farleigh N Som 17 M3
Farleigh Surrey 21 M10
Farleigh Hungerford Somset 18 B8
Farleigh Wallop Hants 19 Q10
Farlesthorpe Lincs 53 M8
Farleton Cumb 63 K6
Farleton Lancs 63 L8
Farley Staffs 50 E11
Farley Wilts 9 J2
Farley Green Surrey 10 G2
Farley Hill Wokham 20 C9
Farleys End Gloucs 29 K6
Farlington C Port 10 B8
Farlington N York 59 N1
Farlow Shrops 39 L6
Farmborough BaNES 17 P4
Farmcote Gloucs 30 D8
Farmington Gloucs 30 F10
Farmoor Oxon 31 L11
Far Moor Wigan 57 K7
Farmtown Moray 101 P5
Farnborough Gt Lon 21 N9
Farnborough Hants 20 E11
Farnborough W Berk 19 M4
Farnborough Warwks 31 K5
Farnborough Park Hants 20 E11
Farncombe Surrey 10 F2
Farndish Bed 32 D4
Farndon Ches W 48 H5
Farndon Notts 51 Q9
Farne Islands Nthumb 81 P6
Farnell Angus 93 Q5
Farnham Dorset 8 D5
Farnham Essex 33 M10
Farnham N York 59 J3
Farnham Suffk 35 M5
Farnham Surrey 10 D1
Farnham Common Bucks 20 F6
Farnham Royal Bucks 20 F6
Farningham Kent 22 B9
Farnley Leeds 58 G7
Farnley N York 58 G5
Farnley Tyas Kirk 58 F10
Farnsfield Notts 51 P9
Farnworth Bolton 57 N7
Farnworth Halton 57 K10
Far Oakridge Gloucs 29 N7
Farr Highld 99 J2
Farr Highld 99 M8
Farr Highld 109 M3
Farraline Highld 98 H5

Farrington Devon 6 D5
Farrington Gurney BaNES 17 P5
Far Sawrey Cumb 62 H3
Farsley Leeds 58 G7
Farthinghoe Nhants 31 M6
Farthingstone Nhants 31 N3
Fartown Kirk 58 F9
Fasnacloich Ag & B 90 D6
Fasnakyle Highld 98 D4
Fassfern Highld 90 D1
Fatfield Sundld 73 N9
Fauldhouse W Loth 85 Q10
Faulkbourne Essex 34 D12
Faulkland Somset 17 Q5
Fauls Shrops 49 L8
Faversham Kent 23 K10
Fawdington N York 66 B11
Fawdon N u Ty 73 M7
Fawkham Green Kent 22 C9
Fawler Oxon 31 J10
Fawley Bucks 20 C6
Fawley Hants 9 M6
Fawley W Berk 19 L5
Faxfleet E R Yk 60 E8
Faygate W Susx 11 K3
Fazakerley Lpool 56 G9
Fazeley Staffs 40 G7
Fearby N York 65 L10
Fearn Highld 107 N7
Fearnan P & K 91 Q7
Fearnbeg Highld 105 L9
Fearnmore Highld 105 K9
Fearnoch Ag & B 83 P7
Featherstone Staffs 40 C6
Featherstone Wakefd 59 K9
Feckenham Worcs 30 D2
Feering Essex 34 E11
Feetham N York 64 H7
Felbridge Surrey 11 M3
Felbrigg Norfk 45 K3
Felcourt Surrey 11 M2
Felden Herts 20 H3
Felindre Carmth 25 N2
Felindre Carmth 26 D5
Felindre Powys 38 D6
Felindre Swans 26 E8
Felindre Farchog Pembks 36 C11
Felinfoel Carmth 26 C8
Felingwmisaf Carmth 26 C4
Felingwmuchaf Carmth 26 C4
Felixkirk N York 66 C9
Felixstowe Suffk 35 L9
Felling Gatesd 73 M8
Felmersham Bed 32 E5
Felmingham Norfk 45 L4
Felpham W Susx 10 F9
Felsham Suffk 34 F5
Felsted Essex 34 B11
Feltham Gt Lon 20 H8
Felthamhill Surrey 20 H8
Felthorpe Norfk 45 J6
Felton Herefs 39 L11
Felton N Som 17 M3
Felton Nthumb 73 L2
Felton Butler Shrops 48 H11
Feltwell Norfk 44 B11
Fence Lancs 57 P2
Fence Rothm 51 K4
Fencott Oxon 31 M10
Fendike Corner Lincs 53 M10
Fen Ditton Cambs 33 M5
Fen Drayton Cambs 33 K3
Feniscliffe Bl w D 57 M4
Feniscowles Bl w D 57 M4
Feniton Devon 6 E3
Feniton Court Devon 6 F3
Fenn Green Shrops 39 P5
Fenn Street Medway 22 F8
Fenny Bentley Derbys 50 F10
Fenny Bridges Devon 6 F3
Fenny Compton Warwks 31 K4
Fenny Drayton Leics 41 J7
Fenstanton Cambs 33 K3
Fen Street Norfk 44 G10
Fenton Cambs 33 K2
Fenton Cumb 71 Q4
Fenton Lincs 52 B8
Fenton Lincs 52 C12
Fenton Notts 52 B6
Fenton Nthumb 81 K7
Fenton Barns E Loth 87 K6
Fenwick Donc 59 N10
Fenwick E Ayrs 76 H3
Fenwick Nthumb 73 J6
Fenwick Nthumb 81 M6
Feock Cnwll 3 J7
Feolin Ferry Ag & B 82 F8
Feorlin Ag & B 76 F3
Ferguslie N Ayrs 76 F3
Feriniquarrie Highld 104 B11
Fern Angus 94 H9
Ferndale Rhondd 27 L9
Ferndown Dorset 8 F7
Ferness Highld 100 E6
Fernham Oxon 19 K3
Fernhill Heath Worcs 39 Q9
Fernhurst W Susx 10 E4
Fernie Fife 93 K11
Ferniegair S Lans 85 M11
Fernilea Highld 96 D3
Fernilee Derbys 50 D5
Fernwood Notts 52 B12
Ferrensby N York 59 J3
Ferrindonald Highld 97 J7
Ferring W Susx 10 H9
Ferrybridge Services Wakefd 59 L9
Ferryden Angus 95 M9
Ferryhill Dur 65 M2
Ferryhill Station Dur 65 N2
Ferry Point Highld 107 M5
Ferryside Carmth 25 N6
Fersfield Norfk 44 H12
Fersit Highld 91 K2
Feshiebridge Highld 99 M8
Fetcham Surrey 21 J11
Fetlar Shet 111 m2
Fetterangus Abers 103 K5
Fettercairn Abers 95 K7
Fewston N York 58 G4
Ffairfach Carmth 26 E5
Ffair Rhos Cerdgn 37 M7
Ffarmers Carmth 37 K10
Ffawyddog Powys 27 P3
Ffestiniog Gwynd 47 K4
Ffestiniog Railway Gwynd 47 K4
Fforest Carmth 26 D7
Ffostrasol Cerdgn 36 F10

Ffrith Flints 48 F4
Ffynnongroyw Flints 56 D11
Fickleshole Surrey 21 M10
Fiddington Somset 16 G7
Fiddleford Dorset 8 B5
Fiddlers Green Cnwll 3 J5
Field Staffs 40 D2
Field Dalling Norfk 44 G3
Field Head Leics 41 L5
Fifehead Magdalen Dorset 8 B5
Fifehead Neville Dorset 8 B5
Fifehead St Quintin Dorset 8 B5
Fife Keith Moray 101 M5
Fifield Oxon 30 G9
Fifield W & M 20 E7
Figheldean Wilts 18 H10
Filby Norfk 45 P7
Filey N York 67 N10
Filgrave M Keyn 32 C7
Filkins Oxon 30 G12
Filleigh Devon 15 L6
Fillingham Lincs 52 D6
Fillongley Warwks 40 H9
Filton S Glos 28 H11
Fimber E R Yk 60 F3
Finavon Angus 93 N4
Fincham Norfk 44 B8
Finchampstead Wokham 20 C10
Fincharn Ag & B 83 N3
Finchdean Hants 10 B7
Finchingfield Essex 34 B9
Finchley Gt Lon 21 L5
Findern Derbys 40 H2
Findhorn Moray 100 G3
Findhorn Bridge Highld 99 M4
Findochty Moray 101 N2
Findo Gask P & K 92 E10
Findon Abers 95 Q3
Findon W Susx 10 H8
Findon Mains Highld 107 K8
Findon Valley W Susx 11 J8
Findrack House Abers 95 K2
Finedon Nhants 32 D3
Fingask P & K 92 H10
Fingest Bucks 20 C5
Finghall N York 65 L9
Fingland D & G 77 M7
Finglesham Kent 23 P11
Fingringhoe Essex 34 G11
Finlarig Stirlg 91 N9
Finmere Oxon 31 N7
Finnart P & K 91 M5
Finningham Suffk 34 H3
Finningley Donc 51 P2
Finsbay W Isls 111 c4
Finstall Worcs 40 C12
Finsthwaite Cumb 62 G5
Finstock Oxon 31 J10
Finstown Ork 111 h2
Fintry Abers 102 G4
Fintry Stirlg 85 K5
Finzean Abers 95 K4
Fionnphort Ag & B 88 G10
Fionnsbhagh W Isls 111 c4
Firbank Cumb 63 L4
Firbeck Rothm 51 M3
Firby N York 60 C2
Firby N York 65 M9
Firle E Susx 11 P8
Firsby Lincs 53 M10
Fir Tree Dur 65 K1
Fishbourne IoW 9 P8
Fishbourne W Susx 10 D8
Fishbourne Roman Palace W Susx 10 D8
Fishburn Dur 65 P2
Fishcross Clacks 85 P4
Fisherford Abers 102 E8
Fisherrow E Loth 86 G7
Fisher's Pond Hants 9 N4
Fisherton Highld 107 M11
Fisherton S Ayrs 76 E7
Fisherton de la Mere Wilts 18 E11
Fishery W & M 20 E7
Fishguard Pembks 24 G2
Fishlake Donc 59 P10
Fishnish Pier Ag & B 89 N7
Fishponds Bristl 17 P2
Fishtoft Lincs 43 K2
Fishtoft Drove Lincs 43 K1
Fishwick Lancs 57 K3
Fiskavaig Highld 96 C3
Fiskerton Lincs 52 F8
Fiskerton Notts 51 Q9
Fittleton Wilts 18 G10
Fittleworth W Susx 10 G6
Fitz Shrops 49 J11
Fitzhead Somset 16 F9
Fitzwilliam Wakefd 59 K10
Five Ash Down E Susx 11 P5
Five Ashes E Susx 12 B5
Fivehead Somset 17 J10
Fivelanes Cnwll 4 F4
Five Oak Green Kent 12 D2
Five Oaks Jersey 7 c2
Five Oaks W Susx 10 H4
Five Roads Carmth 26 C7
Flackwell Heath Bucks 20 E5
Fladbury Worcs 30 C5
Fladdabister Shet 111 k4
Flagg Derbys 50 F7
Flamborough E R Yk 67 Q12
Flamborough Head E R Yk 67 Q12
Flamingo Land Theme Park N York 66 H10
Flamstead Herts 20 H1
Flamstead End Herts 21 M3
Flansham W Susx 10 F9
Flanshaw Wakefd 58 H9
Flasby N York 58 C3
Flash Staffs 50 D7
Flashader Highld 104 D10
Flaunden Herts 20 G4
Flawborough Notts 42 B2
Flawith N York 59 L2
Flax Bourton N Som 17 M3
Flaxby N York 59 K3
Flaxley Gloucs 29 J6
Flaxpool Somset 16 F8
Flaxton N York 59 P2
Fleckney Leics 41 P8
Flecknoe Warwks 31 M2

Place	County	Page	Grid
Fledborough	Notts	52	B8
Fleet	Dorset	7	P6
Fleet	Hants	20	D11
Fleet	Lincs	43	L5
Fleet Hargate	Lincs	43	L5
Fleet Services	Hants	20	C11
Fleetwood	Lancs	62	G11
Fleggburgh	Norfk	45	P7
Flemingston	V Glam	16	D3
Flemington	S Lans	85	L10
Flempton	Suffk	34	D3
Fletchertown	Cumb	71	K7
Fletching	E Susx	11	N5
Flexbury	Cnwll	14	D10
Flexford	Surrey	20	E12
Flimby	Cumb	70	G8
Flimwell	E Susx	12	E4
Flint	Flints	48	E2
Flintham	Notts	51	Q10
Flinton	E R Yk	61	L7
Flitcham	Norfk	44	C5
Flitch Green	Essex	33	Q11
Flitton	C Beds	32	F9
Flitwick	C Beds	32	E9
Flixborough	N Linc	60	E10
Flixborough Stather	N Linc	60	E10
Flixton	N York	67	M10
Flixton	Suffk	45	M11
Flixton	Traffd	57	N9
Flockton	Kirk	58	G10
Flockton Green	Kirk	58	G10
Flodigarry	Highld	104	F7
Flookburgh	Cumb	62	G7
Flordon	Norfk	45	K10
Flore	Nhants	31	N3
Flowton	Suffk	34	H7
Flushing	Cnwll	3	J8
Fluxton	Devon	6	E4
Flyford Flavell	Worcs	30	C3
Fobbing	Thurr	22	E6
Fochabers	Moray	101	L4
Fochriw	Caerph	27	M7
Fockerby	N Linc	60	E9
Foddington	Somset	17	N9
Foel	Powys	48	B12
Foggathorpe	E R Yk	60	D6
Fogo	Border	80	G4
Fogwatt	Moray	101	K4
Foindle	Highld	108	D6
Folda	Angus	94	C8
Fole	Staffs	50	D12
Foleshill	Covtry	41	J10
Folke	Dorset	17	P12
Folkestone	Kent	13	N3
Folkingham	Lincs	42	F4
Folkington	E Susx	12	C8
Folksworth	Cambs	42	G11
Folkton	N York	67	M10
Folla Rule	Abers	102	F8
Follifoot	N York	59	J4
Folly Gate	Devon	15	K11
Fonthill Bishop	Wilts	8	D2
Fonthill Gifford	Wilts	8	D2
Fontmell Magna	Dorset	8	C4
Fontmell Parva	Dorset	8	C5
Fontwell	W Susx	10	F8
Foolow	Derbys	50	F5
Forbestown	Abers	101	M11
Forcett	N York	65	L5
Ford	Ag & B	83	N3
Ford	Bucks	31	Q11
Ford	Derbys	51	K5
Ford	Devon	14	G7
Ford	Gloucs	30	E8
Ford	Nthumb	81	K6
Ford	Somset	16	E9
Ford	Staffs	50	E9
Ford	W Susx	10	F8
Ford	Wilts	18	C6
Fordcombe	Kent	11	Q3
Fordell	Fife	86	D5
Forden	Powys	38	E2
Ford End	Essex	34	B12
Forder Green	Devon	5	Q6
Fordham	Cambs	33	Q3
Fordham	Essex	34	F10
Fordham	Norfk	43	P9
Fordingbridge	Hants	8	G5
Fordon	E R Yk	67	M11
Fordoun	Abers	95	M6
Fordstreet	Essex	34	F10
Ford Street	Somset	16	F11
Fordwich	Kent	23	M10
Fordyce	Abers	102	D3
Forebridge	Staffs	40	B3
Forest	Guern	6	b2
Forest Chapel	Ches E	50	C6
Forest Gate	Gt Lon	21	N6
Forest Green	Surrey	10	H2
Forest Hall	N Tyne	73	M6
Forest Hill	Gt Lon	21	M8
Forest Hill	Oxon	31	N11
Forest Lane Head	N York	59	J3
Forest Mill	Clacks	85	Q4
Forest of Bowland	Lancs	63	L10
Forest of Dean	Gloucs	28	H6
Forest Row	E Susx	11	N3
Forestside	W Susx	10	C7
Forest Town	Notts	51	M8
Forfar	Angus	93	M5
Forgandenny	P & K	92	G11
Forge Hammer	Torfn	28	C9
Forgie	Moray	101	M4
Forgieside	Moray	101	M5
Forgue	Abers	102	D6
Formby	Sefton	56	F7
Forncett End	Norfk	45	J10
Forncett St Mary	Norfk	45	J10
Forncett St Peter	Norfk	45	J10
Fornham All Saints	Suffk	34	E4
Fornham St Martin	Suffk	34	E4
Fornighty	Highld	100	E5
Forres	Moray	100	F4
Forsbrook	Staffs	50	C11
Forse	Highld	110	E8
Forsinard	Highld	109	Q7
Forss	Highld	110	B3
Fort Augustus	Highld	98	E7
Forteviot	P & K	92	F11
Forth	S Lans	85	Q11
Forthampton	Gloucs	29	M3
Forth Rail Bridge	C Edin	86	D6
Forth Road Bridge	Fife	86	D6
Fortingall	P & K	91	Q6
Forton	Hants	19	M11
Forton	Lancs	63	J11
Forton	Shrops	48	H11
Forton	Somset	7	J2
Forton	Staffs	49	N10
Fortrie	Abers	102	E6
Fortrose	Highld	107	M10
Fortuneswell	Dorset	7	P7
Fort William	Highld	90	F2
Forty Hill	Gt Lon	21	M4
Fosbury	Wilts	19	K8
Foscot	Oxon	30	G9
Fosdyke	Lincs	43	K4
Foss	P & K	92	B4
Fossebridge	Gloucs	30	E11
Foster Street	Essex	21	P2
Foston	Derbys	40	E2
Foston	Leics	41	N8
Foston	Lincs	42	C2
Foston	N York	59	P2
Foston on the Wolds	E R Yk	61	J3
Fotherby	Lincs	53	K5
Fotheringhay	Nhants	42	F10
Foula	Shet	111	j5
Foula Airport	Shet	111	j5
Foulden	Border	81	K3
Foulden	Norfk	44	C9
Foul End	Warwks	40	G8
Foulness Island	Essex	23	J5
Foulridge	Lancs	58	B6
Foulsham	Norfk	44	G5
Fountainhall	Border	87	J11
Four Ashes	Suffk	34	G3
Four Crosses	Powys	48	F10
Four Elms	Kent	11	P1
Four Forks	Somset	16	G8
Four Gotes	Cambs	43	M6
Four Lanes	Cnwll	2	G7
Four Marks	Hants	9	R1
Four Mile Bridge	IoA	54	C6
Four Oaks	Birm	40	E7
Four Oaks	Solhll	40	G10
Fourpenny	Highld	107	N4
Four Roads	Carmth	25	Q7
Fourstones	Nthumb	72	F7
Four Throws	Kent	12	F4
Fovant	Wilts	8	E2
Foveran	Abers	103	K9
Fowey	Cnwll	4	D9
Fowlhall	Kent	12	E2
Fowlis	Angus	93	K8
Fowlis Wester	P & K	92	D10
Fowlmere	Cambs	33	L7
Fownhope	Herefs	28	G3
Foxbar	Rens	84	H10
Foxcote	Somset	17	Q5
Foxdale	IoM	56	b5
Foxearth	Essex	34	D7
Foxfield	Cumb	62	E5
Foxhole	Cnwll	3	L5
Foxholes	N York	67	L11
Foxley	Norfk	44	H6
Foxt	Staffs	50	D10
Foxton	Cambs	33	L7
Foxton	Leics	41	P9
Foxton	N York	65	Q8
Foxwood	Shrops	39	L6
Foy	Herefs	28	H3
Foyers	Highld	98	G5
Foynesfield	Highld	100	D5
Fraddon	Cnwll	3	K4
Fradley	Staffs	40	F5
Fradswell	Staffs	40	C2
Fraisthorpe	E R Yk	61	K2
Framfield	E Susx	11	P6
Framingham Earl	Norfk	45	L9
Framingham Pigot	Norfk	45	L9
Framlingham	Suffk	35	L4
Frampton	Dorset	7	P4
Frampton	Lincs	43	K3
Frampton Cotterell	S Glos	29	J11
Frampton Mansell	Gloucs	29	N8
Frampton-on-Severn	Gloucs	29	K7
Framsden	Suffk	35	K5
Framwellgate Moor	Dur	73	M11
Franche	Worcs	39	P6
Frankby	Wirral	56	E10
Frankley	Worcs	40	C10
Frankley Services	Worcs	40	C10
Frankton	Warwks	41	K12
Frant	E Susx	12	C3
Fraserburgh	Abers	103	K2
Frating	Essex	34	H11
Frating Green	Essex	34	H11
Fratton	C Port	9	Q7
Freathy	Cnwll	5	J9
Freckenham	Suffk	33	Q3
Freckleton	Lancs	56	H3
Freeby	Leics	42	B6
Freefolk	Hants	19	N10
Freeland	Oxon	31	K10
Freethorpe	Norfk	45	N8
Freethorpe Common	Norfk	45	N8
Freiston	Lincs	43	L12
Fremington	Devon	15	J6
Fremington	N York	65	J7
Frenchay	S Glos	28	H12
Frenich	P & K	92	C4
Frensham	Surrey	10	D2
Freshfield	Sefton	56	F7
Freshford	Wilts	18	B8
Freshwater	IoW	9	K9
Fressingfield	Suffk	35	L2
Freston	Suffk	35	J8
Freswick	Highld	110	G2
Fretherne	Gloucs	29	K6
Frettenham	Norfk	45	L6
Freuchie	Fife	86	F2
Freystrop	Pembks	24	G6
Friar Park	Sandw	40	D8
Friday Bridge	Cambs	43	M8
Friday Street	Suffk	35	N5
Fridaythorpe	E R Yk	60	E3
Friendly	Calder	58	D8
Friern Barnet	Gt Lon	21	L5
Friesthorpe	Lincs	52	F6
Frieston	Lincs	42	D1
Frieth	Bucks	20	C5
Frilford	Oxon	19	M2
Frilsham	W Berk	19	P6
Frimley	Surrey	20	E10
Frindsbury	Medway	22	E9
Fring	Norfk	44	C3
Fringford	Oxon	31	N8
Frinsted	Kent	22	H11
Frinton-on-Sea	Essex	35	K11
Friockheim	Angus	93	Q6
Frisby on the Wreake	Leics	41	P4
Friskney	Lincs	53	M11
Friston	E Susx	11	B9
Friston	Suffk	35	N5
Fritchley	Derbys	51	J9
Fritham	Hants	9	J5
Frithelstock	Devon	14	H8
Frithelstock Stone	Devon	14	H8
Frithville	Lincs	53	K12
Frittenden	Kent	12	F2
Frittiscombe	Devon	5	Q10
Fritton	Norfk	45	K10
Fritton	Norfk	45	P9
Fritwell	Oxon	31	M8
Frizinghall	C Brad	58	F7
Frizington	Cumb	70	G11
Frocester	Gloucs	29	K8
Frodesley	Shrops	39	K2
Frodsham	Ches W	57	K12
Frogden	Border	80	G8
Frog End	Cambs	33	L7
Froggatt	Derbys	50	G5
Froghall	Staffs	50	D10
Frogmore	Devon	5	P10
Frognall	Lincs	42	G7
Frog Pool	Worcs	39	P8
Frogwell	Cnwll	4	H6
Frolesworth	Leics	41	L8
Frome	Somset	18	B10
Frome St Quintin	Dorset	7	N3
Fromes Hill	Herefs	39	M11
Froncysyllte	Wrexhm	48	F7
Fron-goch	Gwynd	47	P4
Fron Isaf	Wrexhm	48	F7
Frosterley	Dur	72	R12
Froxfield	Wilts	19	K7
Froxfield Green	Hants	10	B3
Fryern Hill	Hants	9	M4
Fryerning	Essex	22	D4
Fryton	N York	66	F11
Fuinary	Highld	89	M7
Fulbeck	Lincs	52	D12
Fulbourn	Cambs	33	N5
Fulbrook	Oxon	30	H10
Fulflood	Hants	9	M2
Fulford	C York	59	N4
Fulford	Somset	16	G9
Fulford	Staffs	50	C12
Fulham	Gt Lon	21	K8
Fulking	W Susx	11	L7
Fullarton	N Ayrs	76	F4
Fuller Street	Essex	34	C12
Fullerton	Hants	19	L11
Fulletby	Lincs	53	J8
Fullready	Warwks	30	H5
Full Sutton	E R Yk	60	D3
Fullwood	E Ayrs	76	G2
Fulmer	Bucks	20	F6
Fulmodeston	Norfk	44	G4
Fulnetby	Lincs	52	F7
Fulney	Lincs	43	J5
Fulstow	Lincs	53	K4
Fulwell	Sundld	73	P8
Fulwood	Lancs	57	K3
Fulwood	Sheff	50	H4
Fundenhall	Norfk	45	J10
Funtington	W Susx	10	C8
Funtullich	P & K	92	B9
Furley	Devon	6	H2
Furnace	Ag & B	83	Q3
Furnace	Carmth	26	C8
Furness Vale	Derbys	50	D4
Furneux Pelham	Herts	33	L10
Furzley	Hants	9	K4
Fyfield	Essex	22	C3
Fyfield	Hants	19	K10
Fyfield	Oxon	19	M2
Fyfield	Wilts	18	G7
Fyfield	Wilts	18	H8
Fylingthorpe	N York	67	K6
Fyning	W Susx	10	D5
Fyvie	Abers	102	G7

G

Place	County	Page	Grid
Gabroc Hill	E Ayrs	76	H2
Gaddesby	Leics	41	P5
Gaddesden Row	Herts	20	G2
Gadgirth	S Ayrs	76	G6
Gaerllwyd	Mons	28	E9
Gaerwen	IoA	54	F7
Gailes	N Ayrs	76	F4
Gailey	Staffs	40	B5
Gainford	Dur	65	L4
Gainsborough	Lincs	52	B5
Gainsborough	Suffk	35	K8
Gainsford End	Essex	34	C9
Gairloch	Highld	105	M7
Gairlochy	Highld	98	B11
Gairneybridge	P & K	86	D3
Gaitsgill	Cumb	71	N6
Galashiels	Border	80	C7
Galgate	Lancs	63	J10
Galhampton	Somset	17	P9
Gallanachbeg	Ag & B	90	B10
Gallanachmore	Ag & B	90	R10
Gallatown	Fife	86	G4
Galley Wood	Essex	22	E3
Gallovie	Highld	98	H10
Galloway Forest Park		69	L3
Gallowfauld	Angus	93	M7
Gallowhill	P & K	92	H8
Galltair	Highld	97	L5
Galmisdale	Highld	96	F11
Galmpton	Devon	5	M11
Galmpton	Torbay	6	B10
Galphay	N York	65	M11
Galston	E Ayrs	76	H4
Gamblesby	Cumb	72	B11
Gamlingay	Cambs	33	J6
Gamlingay Great Heath	Cambs	32	H6
Gamrie	Abers	102	G3
Gamston	Notts	51	N5
Gamston	Notts	51	P5
Ganavan Bay	Ag & B	90	B9
Ganllwyd	Gwynd	47	L4
Gannachy	Angus	95	K7
Ganstead	E R Yk	61	K7
Ganthorpe	N York	66	F12
Ganton	N York	67	L11
Garbity	Moray	101	L5
Garboldisham	Norfk	34	G1
Garbole	Highld	99	L4
Garchory	Abers	101	L12
Gardeners Green	Wokhm	20	D9
Gardenstown	Abers	102	G3
Garden Village	Sheff	50	H2
Garderhouse	Shet	111	k4
Gare Hill	Somset	18	B11
Garelochhead	Ag & B	84	D5
Garford	Oxon	19	M2
Garforth	Leeds	59	K7
Gargrave	N York	58	B4
Gargunnock	Stirlg	85	M4
Garlic Street	Norfk	45	K12
Garlieston	D & G	69	L9
Garlinge	Kent	23	P9
Garlinge Green	Kent	23	L11
Garlogie	Abers	95	M2
Garmond	Abers	102	G5
Garmouth	Moray	101	L3
Garmston	Shrops	39	L2
Garndolbenmaen	Gwynd	46	H3
Garrabost	W Isls	111	e2
Garrallan	E Ayrs	77	J7
Garras	Cnwll	2	G10
Garreg	Gwynd	47	K3
Garrigill	Cumb	72	D11
Garroch	D & G	69	N3
Garrochtrie	D & G	68	F10
Garrochty	Ag & B	84	B11
Garros	Highld	104	G9
Garsdale Head	Cumb	64	E8
Garsdon	Wilts	18	E4
Garshall Green	Staffs	40	C1
Garsington	Oxon	31	M12
Garstang	Lancs	63	J12
Garston	Herts	20	H4
Garston	Lpool	56	H11
Gartachossan	Ag & B	82	E10
Gartcosh	N Lans	85	L9
Garth	Powys	37	Q10
Garth	Wrexhm	48	F7
Garthamlock	C Glas	85	L9
Garthmyl	Powys	38	E3
Garthorpe	Leics	42	B6
Garthorpe	N Linc	60	E9
Garth Row	Cumb	63	K3
Gartly	Abers	102	C8
Gartmore	Stirlg	85	J4
Gartness	N Lans	85	N9
Gartness	Stirlg	84	H5
Gartocharn	W Duns	84	G6
Garton-on-the-Wolds	E R Yk	60	G3
Gartymore	Highld	110	B11
Garva Bridge	Highld	98	G9
Garvald	Border	86	C11
Garvald	E Loth	87	L7
Garvan	Highld	90	D2
Garvard	Ag & B	82	E5
Garve	Highld	106	G9
Garvellachs	Ag & B	83	K2
Garvestone	Norfk	44	G8
Garvock	Inver	84	E8
Garway	Herefs	28	E4
Garynahine	W Isls	111	c2
Garyvard	W Isls	111	d2
Gasper	Wilts	8	B2
Gastard	Wilts	18	C7
Gasthorpe	Norfk	34	F1
Gaston Green	Essex	33	N12
Gatcombe	IoW	9	N9
Gate Burton	Lincs	52	B7
Gateforth	N York	59	M8
Gatehead	E Ayrs	76	G4
Gate Helmsley	N York	59	P3
Gatehouse	Nthumb	72	E3
Gatehouse of Fleet	D & G	69	N7
Gateley	Norfk	44	F5
Gatenby	N York	65	N9
Gateshaw	Border	80	G9
Gateshead	Gatesd	73	M8
Gateside	Angus	93	M6
Gateside	E Rens	84	H10
Gateside	Fife	86	E1
Gateside	N Ayrs	84	F11
Gateslack	D & G	78	E8
Gatley	Stockp	57	Q10
Gattonside	Border	80	D7
Gatwick Airport	W Susx	11	L2
Gaulby	Leics	41	P7
Gauldry	Fife	93	L10
Gauldswell	P & K	93	J5
Gautby	Lincs	52	H8
Gavinton	Border	80	G4
Gawcott	Bucks	31	P7
Gawsworth	Ches E	50	B6
Gawthrop	Cumb	63	M5
Gawthwaite	Cumb	62	F5
Gaydon	Warwks	31	J4
Gayhurst	M Keyn	32	C7
Gayle	N York	64	F9
Gayles	N York	65	K6
Gayton	Nhants	31	P4
Gayton	Norfk	44	C6
Gayton	Staffs	40	C2
Gayton le Marsh	Lincs	53	L6
Gayton Thorpe	Norfk	44	C6
Gaywood	Norfk	43	Q6
Gazeley	Suffk	34	C4
Gearraidh Bhaird	W Isls	111	d2
Gearraidh na h-Aibhne	W Isls	111	c2
Geary	Highld	104	C9
Gedding	Suffk	34	F5
Geddington	Nhants	42	C12
Gedling	Notts	51	N11
Gedney	Lincs	43	L5
Gedney Broadgate	Lincs	43	L5
Gedney Drove End	Lincs	43	M4
Gedney Dyke	Lincs	43	L5
Gedney Hill	Lincs	43	K7
Geeston	Rutlnd	42	E8
Geirinis	W Isls	111	b5
Geldeston	Norfk	45	N10
Gellideg	Myr Td	27	L7
Gellifor	Denbgs	48	D3
Gelligaer	Caerph	27	N9
Gellilydan	Gwynd	47	L4
Gellinudd	Neath	26	G7
Gellyburn	P & K	92	G7
Gellywen	Carmth	25	M4
Gelston	D & G	70	C4
Gelston	Lincs	42	C2
Gembling	E R Yk	61	J3
Gentleshaw	Staffs	40	D5
Georgefield	D & G	79	L9
George Green	Bucks	20	F7
Georgeham	Devon	14	H4
Georgemas Junction Station	Highld	110	D4
George Nympton	Devon	15	M7
Georth	Ork	111	h2
Gerinish	W Isls	111	b5
Germansweek	Devon	5	J2
Gerrans	Cnwll	3	K8
Gerrards Cross	Bucks	20	G6
Gerrick	R & Cl	66	G5
Gestingthorpe	Essex	34	D8
Geuffordd	Powys	48	E11
Gidea Park	Gt Lon	21	Q5
Gidleigh	Devon	5	M3
Giffnock	E Rens	85	J10
Gifford	E Loth	87	K8
Giffordtown	Fife	93	K12
Giggleswick	N York	63	P9
Gigha	Ag & B	75	J3
Gilberdyke	E R Yk	60	E8
Gilchriston	E Loth	87	J8
Gilcrux	Cumb	70	H7
Gildersome	Leeds	58	G8
Gildingwells	Rothm	51	M4
Gilesgate Moor	Dur	73	N11
Gileston	V Glam	16	D3
Gilfach	Caerph	27	N8
Gilfach Goch	Brdgnd	27	K10
Gilfachrheda	Cerdgn	36	G8
Gilgarran	Cumb	70	G10
Gillamoor	N York	66	F9
Gillen	Highld	104	C9
Gillesbie	D & G	79	J9
Gilling East	N York	66	E11
Gillingham	Dorset	8	B3
Gillingham	Medway	22	F9
Gillingham	Norfk	45	N10
Gilling West	N York	65	L6
Gillock	Highld	110	E4
Gills	Highld	110	G2
Gilmanscleuch	Border	79	M5
Gilmerton	C Edin	86	F8
Gilmerton	P & K	92	D10
Gilmonby	Dur	64	H5
Gilmorton	Leics	41	M9
Gilsland	Nthumb	72	B7
Gilston	Border	87	J10
Gilston	Herts	21	N2
Gilwern	Mons	27	Q6
Gimingham	Norfk	45	L3
Gipping	Suffk	34	H4
Gipsey Bridge	Lincs	53	J12
Girdle Toll	N Ayrs	76	F3
Girlsta	Shet	111	k4
Girsby	N York	65	N6
Girthon	D & G	69	N8
Girton	Cambs	33	L4
Girton	Notts	52	B9
Girvan	S Ayrs	76	D10
Gisburn	Lancs	63	P11
Gisleham	Suffk	45	Q11
Gislingham	Suffk	34	H3
Gissing	Norfk	45	J11
Gittisham	Devon	6	F3
Gladestry	Powys	38	E10
Gladsmuir	E Loth	87	J7
Glais	Swans	26	F8
Glaisdale	N York	66	H6
Glamis	Angus	93	L6
Glanaman	Carmth	26	F6
Glandford	Norfk	44	H2
Glandwr	Pembks	25	L3
Glandyfi	Cerdgn	47	L11
Glanllynfi	Brdgnd	27	J10
Glan-rhyd	Powys	26	G7
Glanton	Nthumb	81	M10
Glanvilles Wootton	Dorset	7	P2
Glan-y-don	Flints	56	D11
Glapthorn	Nhants	42	E11
Glapwell	Derbys	51	L7
Glasbury	Powys	27	P2
Glascote	Staffs	40	G6
Glascwm	Powys	38	D10
Glasfryn	Conwy	55	N10
Glasgow	C Glas	85	K9
Glasgow Airport	Rens	84	H9
Glasgow Prestwick Airport	S Ayrs	76	F6
Glasgow Science Centre	C Glas	85	J9
Glasinfryn	Gwynd	54	H7
Glasnacardoch Bay	Highld	97	J9
Glasnakille	Highld	96	G7
Glasphein	Highld	104	B11
Glassford	S Lans	77	M2
Glasshouse	Gloucs	29	J5
Glasshouses	N York	58	F2
Glasslaw	Abers	102	H4
Glasson	Cumb	71	L4
Glasson	Lancs	63	J10
Glassonby	Cumb	72	B12
Glasterlaw	Angus	93	Q5
Glaston	Rutlnd	42	C9
Glastonbury	Somset	17	M8
Glatton	Cambs	42	G11
Glazebrook	Warrtn	57	M9
Glazebury	Warrtn	57	M9
Glazeley	Shrops	39	N5
Gleaston	Cumb	62	F7
Glebe	Highld	98	G5
Gledhow	Leeds	58	H6
Gledpark	D & G	69	P8
Gledrid	Shrops	48	F8
Glemsford	Suffk	34	D7
Glen Achulish	Highld	90	E5
Glenallachie	Moray	101	K7
Glenancross	Highld	97	J10
Glenaros House	Ag & B	89	L7
Glen Auldyn	IoM	56	d3
Glenbarr	Ag & B	75	J5
Glenbarry	Abers	102	D4
Glenbervie	Abers	95	M6
Glenboig	N Lans	85	M8
Glenborrodale	Highld	89	M4

172 Glenbranter – Gunby

Glenbranter Ag & B 84 B4
Glenbreck Border 78 H5
Glenbrittle Highld 96 E5
Glenbuck E Ayrs 77 M5
Glencally Angus 94 F8
Glencaple D & G 70 G2
Glencarse P & K 92 H10
Glencoe Highld 90 F5
Glencothe Border 78 H3
Glencraig Fife 86 E4
Glencrosh D & G 78 C10
Glendale Highld 104 B11
Glendaruel Ag & B 83 Q6
Glendevon P & K 86 B2
Glendoe Lodge Highld 98 E7
Glendoick P & K 93 J10
Glenduckie Fife 93 K11
Glenegedale Ag & B 74 D3
Glenelg Highld 97 L6
Glenerney Moray 100 F6
Glenfarg P & K 92 G12
Glenfield Leics 41 M6
Glenfinnan Highld 90 C1
Glenfintaig Lodge Highld 98 C10
Glenfoot P & K 92 H11
Glenfyne Lodge Ag & B 90 G12
Glengarnock N Ayrs 84 F11
Glengolly Highld 110 C3
Glengorm Castle Ag & B 89 K5
Glengrasco Highld 96 E1
Glenholm Border 78 H3
Glenhoul D & G 69 N2
Glenkin Ag & B 84 C7
Glenkindie Abers 101 N11
Glenlivet Moray 101 J9
Glenlochar D & G 70 C3
Glenlomond P & K 86 E2
Glenluce D & G 68 G7
Glenmassen Ag & B 84 B5
Glenmavis N Lans 85 M9
Glen Maye IoM 56 b5
Glenmore Highld 96 E2
Glenmore Lodge Highld 99 P7
Glen Nevis House Highld 90 F2
Glenochil Clacks 85 P4
Glen Parva Leics 41 M7
Glenquiech Angus 94 G9
Glenralloch Ag & B 83 M8
Glenridding Cumb 71 N11
Glenrothes Fife 86 F3
Glenshero Lodge Highld 98 H9
Glenstriven Ag & B 84 B7
Glentham Lincs 52 E5
Glentrool D & G 69 J4
Glen Trool Lodge D & G 69 K3
Glentruim Highld 99 K9
Glentworth Lincs 52 D6
Glenuig Highld 89 N2
Glenvarragill Highld 96 F2
Glen Vine IoM 56 c5
Glenwhilly D & G 68 G5
Glespin S Lans 78 D4
Glewstone Herefs 28 G4
Glinton C Pete 42 G8
Glooston Leics 41 Q8
Glossop Derbys 50 D3
Gloster Hill Nthumb 81 Q12
Gloucester Gloucs 29 L5
Gloucester Services Gloucs 29 L6
Gloucestershire Airport Gloucs 29 M5
Glusburn N York 58 D5
Glutt Lodge Highld 110 B8
Glympton Oxon 31 K9
Glynarthen Cerdgn 36 E10
Glyn Ceiriog Wrexhm 48 E7
Glyncoch Rhondd 27 M9
Glyncorrwg Neath 27 J8
Glynde E Susx 11 P8
Glyndyfrdwy Denbgs 48 D7
Glynneath Neath 27 J7
Glyntawe Powys 26 H5
Glynteg Carmth 25 N2
Gnosall Staffs 49 P10
Gnosall Heath Staffs 49 P10
Goadby Leics 41 Q7
Goadby Marwood Leics 41 R3
Goatacre Wilts 18 F5
Goathill Dorset 17 P11
Goathland N York 67 J7
Goathurst Somset 16 H8
Goat Lees Kent 13 K2
Gobowen Shrops 48 F8
Godalming Surrey 10 F2
Goddard's Green Kent 12 G3
Godmanchester Cambs 33 J3
Godmanstone Dorset 7 P4
Godmersham Kent 23 K12
Godney Somset 17 L7
Godolphin Cross Cnwll 2 F9
Godre'r-graig Neath 26 G7
Godshill IoW 9 N10
Godstone Surrey 21 M11
Goetre Mons 28 C7
Goff's Oak Herts 21 M3
Gogar C Edin 86 E7
Goginan Cerdgn 37 L4
Golan Gwynd 46 H3
Golant Cnwll 4 D8
Golberdon Cnwll 4 H6
Golborne Wigan 57 L8
Golcar Kirk 58 E10
Goldcliff Newpt 28 D11
Golden Green Kent 12 D1
Goldenhill C Stke 49 Q5
Golden Pot Hants 10 B2
Golders Green Gt Lon 21 K6
Goldhanger Essex 22 H2
Goldington Bed 32 F6
Goldsborough N York 59 J3
Goldsborough N York 67 J5
Golds Green Sandw 40 C8
Goldsithney Cnwll 2 E9
Goldthorpe Barns 59 L12
Goldworthy Devon 14 G7
Gollanfield Highld 107 N10
Golspie Highld 107 N3
Gomeldon Wilts 8 H1
Gomshall Surrey 10 H1
Gonalston Notts 51 P10
Gonerby Hill Foot Lincs 42 C3
Gonfirth Shet 111 k3
Good Easter Essex 22 D2
Gooderstone Norfk 44 C9
Goodleigh Devon 15 K5
Goodmanham E R Yk 60 F5
Goodmayes Gt Lon 21 P6
Goodnestone Kent 23 K10
Goodnestone Kent 23 N11
Goodrich Herefs 28 G5
Goodrington Torbay 6 B10
Goodshaw Lancs 57 P4
Goodwick Pembks 24 G2
Goodworth Clatford Hants 19 L11
Goole E R Yk 60 C9
Goom's Hill Worcs 30 D3
Goonbell Cnwll 2 G6
Goonhavern Cnwll 2 H5
Goonvrea Cnwll 2 G6
Goosecruives Abers 95 M5
Gooseford Devon 5 N2
Goose Green Essex 35 J10
Goose Green S Glos 17 P2
Gooseham Cnwll 14 E8
Goosey Oxon 19 L3
Goosnargh Lancs 57 K2
Goostrey Ches E 49 P2
Gordano Services N Som 17 M2
Gordon Border 80 E5
Gordon Arms Hotel Border 79 L4
Gordonstown Abers 102 D4
Gordonstown Abers 102 F7
Gorebridge Mdloth 86 G9
Gorefield Cambs 43 L7
Gores Wilts 18 G8
Gorey Jersey 7 c2
Goring Oxon 19 P5
Goring-by-Sea W Susx 10 H9
Gorleston-on-Sea Norfk 45 Q8
Gorrachie Abers 102 F4
Gorran Churchtown Cnwll 3 M7
Gorran Haven Cnwll 3 M7
Gorsedd Flints 56 D12
Gorse Hill Swindn 18 H4
Gorseinon Swans 26 D8
Gorsgoch Cerdgn 36 H9
Gorslas Carmth 26 D6
Gorsley Gloucs 29 J4
Gorsley Common Herefs 29 J4
Gorstan Highld 106 F9
Gorsten Ag & B 89 P9
Gorsty Hill Staffs 40 E2
Gorthleck Highld 98 G5
Gorton Manch 50 B2
Gosbeck Suffk 35 J5
Gosberton Lincs 43 J4
Gosfield Essex 34 D10
Gosforth Cumb 62 C2
Gosforth N u Ty 73 M7
Gosport Hants 9 Q7
Gossington Gloucs 29 K8
Gotham Notts 41 M2
Gotherington Gloucs 29 N3
Gotton Somset 16 H9
Goudhurst Kent 12 E3
Goulceby Lincs 53 J7
Gourdas Abers 102 G7
Gourdie C Dund 93 L8
Gourdon Abers 95 N7
Gourock Inver 84 D7
Govan C Glas 85 J9
Goveton Devon 5 P10
Govilon Mons 28 B6
Gowdall E R Yk 59 N9
Gower Highld 106 H10
Gower Swans 26 C10
Gowerton Swans 26 D9
Gowkhall Fife 86 C5
Goxhill E R Yk 61 K5
Goxhill N Linc 61 J9
Grabhair W Isls 111 d3
Graffham W Susx 10 E6
Grafham Cambs 32 G3
Grafham Surrey 10 G2
Grafton N York 59 K2
Grafton Oxon 19 J1
Grafton Shrops 48 H10
Grafton Worcs 29 N2
Grafton Flyford Worcs 30 C3
Grafton Regis Nhants 31 Q5
Grafton Underwood Nhants 32 D2
Grafty Green Kent 12 G1
Graig Conwy 55 L7
Graigfechan Denbgs 48 D5
Grain Medway 22 H7
Grainsby Lincs 53 J4
Grainthorpe Lincs 53 L4
Grampound Cnwll 3 L6
Grampound Road Cnwll 3 K5
Gramsdal W Isls 111 b5
Gramsdale W Isls 111 b5
Granborough Bucks 31 Q8
Granby Notts 41 Q1
Grandborough Warwks 31 L2
Grand Chemins Jersey 7 c2
Grandes Rocques Guern 6 b1
Grandtully P & K 92 D5
Grange Cumb 71 L11
Grange Medway 22 F9
Grange P & K 93 K10
Grange Crossroads Moray 101 N4
Grange Hall Moray 100 G3
Grangehall S Lans 78 F1
Grange Hill Essex 21 N5
Grangemill Derbys 50 G8
Grange Moor Kirk 58 G10
Grangemouth Falk 85 Q6
Grange of Lindores Fife 93 J11
Grange-over-Sands Cumb 62 H6
Grangepans Falk 86 B6
Grange Park Nhants 31 Q3
Grangetown R & Cl 66 D4
Grangetown Sundld 73 P9
Grange Villa Dur 73 M9
Gransmoor E R Yk 61 J3
Granston Pembks 24 F2
Grantchester Cambs 33 M6
Grantham Lincs 42 D3
Granton C Edin 86 F6
Grantown-on-Spey Highld 100 F9
Grantshouse Border 87 P8
Grappenhall Warrtn 57 M10
Grasby Lincs 52 F3
Grasmere Cumb 62 G1
Grasscroft Oldham 58 C12
Grassendale Lpool 56 H10
Grassington N York 58 D2
Grassmoor Derbys 51 K7
Grassthorpe Notts 52 B9
Grateley Hants 19 J11
Graveley Cambs 33 J4
Graveley Herts 32 H10
Gravelly Hill Birm 40 E9
Graveney Kent 23 K10
Gravesend Kent 22 D8
Gravir W Isls 111 d3
Grayingham Lincs 52 D4
Grayrigg Cumb 63 L3
Grays Thurr 22 C7
Grayshott Hants 10 E3
Grayswood Surrey 10 E3
Greasbrough Rothm 51 K2
Greasby Wirral 56 F10
Great Abington Cambs 33 N7
Great Addington Nhants 32 D2
Great Alne Warwks 30 E3
Great Altcar Lancs 56 G7
Great Amwell Herts 21 M2
Great Asby Cumb 64 C5
Great Ashfield Suffk 34 G4
Great Ayton N York 66 D5
Great Baddow Essex 22 E3
Great Badminton S Glos 18 B4
Great Bardfield Essex 34 B10
Great Barford Bed 32 G6
Great Barr Sandw 40 D8
Great Barrington Gloucs 30 G10
Great Barrow Ches W 49 J2
Great Barton Suffk 34 E4
Great Barugh N York 66 G10
Great Bavington Nthumb 72 H5
Great Bealings Suffk 35 K7
Great Bedwyn Wilts 19 J7
Great Bentley Essex 35 J11
Great Billing Nhants 32 B4
Great Bircham Norfk 44 C4
Great Blakenham Suffk 35 J6
Great Blencow Cumb 71 P8
Great Bolas Wrekin 49 M10
Great Bookham Surrey 21 J11
Great Bourton Oxon 31 L5
Great Bowden Leics 41 Q9
Great Bradley Suffk 34 B6
Great Braxted Essex 22 G1
Great Bricett Suffk 34 G6
Great Brickhill Bucks 32 C10
Great Bridgeford Staffs 40 B3
Great Brington Nhants 31 P2
Great Bromley Essex 34 H10
Great Broughton Cumb 70 H8
Great Broughton N York 66 D6
Great Budworth Ches W 57 M12
Great Burdon Darltn 65 N4
Great Burstead Essex 22 D5
Great Busby N York 66 D6
Great Carlton Lincs 53 L6
Great Casterton Rutlnd 42 E8
Great Chalfield Wilts 18 C7
Great Chart Kent 13 J2
Great Chatwell Staffs 49 P11
Great Chell C Stke 49 Q5
Great Chesterford Essex 33 N8
Great Cheverell Wilts 18 E9
Great Chishill Cambs 33 L8
Great Clacton Essex 35 K12
Great Clifton Cumb 70 G9
Great Coates NE Lin 61 L11
Great Comberton Worcs 29 N1
Great Corby Cumb 71 P5
Great Cornard Suffk 34 E8
Great Cowden E R Yk 61 L6
Great Coxwell Oxon 19 J3
Great Cransley Nhants 32 B2
Great Cressingham Norfk 44 E9
Great Crosthwaite Cumb 71 L10
Great Cubley Derbys 50 F12
Great Cumbrae Island N Ayrs 84 C10
Great Dalby Leics 41 Q5
Great Denham Bed 32 E7
Great Doddington Nhants 32 C4
Great Dunham Norfk 44 E7
Great Dunmow Essex 33 Q11
Great Durnford Wilts 18 G12
Great Easton Essex 33 P10
Great Easton Leics 42 C10
Great Eccleston Lancs 56 H2
Great Ellingham Norfk 44 G10
Great Elm Somset 17 Q6
Great Everdon Nhants 31 N3
Great Eversden Cambs 33 K6
Great Fencote N York 65 M8
Great Finborough Suffk 34 G5
Greatford Lincs 42 F7
Great Fransham Norfk 44 E7
Great Gaddesden Herts 20 G2
Greatgate Staffs 50 D11
Great Gidding Cambs 42 G12
Great Givendale E R Yk 60 E4
Great Glemham Suffk 35 M4
Great Glen Leics 41 P7
Great Gonerby Lincs 42 C3
Great Gransden Cambs 33 J5
Great Green Cambs 33 J7
Great Green Suffk 34 F5
Great Habton N York 66 G11
Great Hale Lincs 42 G2
Great Hallingbury Essex 33 N11
Greatham Hants 10 C4
Greatham Hartpl 66 C3
Greatham W Susx 10 G6
Great Hampden Bucks 20 D3
Great Harrowden Nhants 32 C3
Great Harwood Lancs 57 N3
Great Haseley Oxon 19 Q1
Great Hatfield E R Yk 61 K5
Great Haywood Staffs 40 D3
Great Heck N York 59 N9
Great Henny Essex 34 E8
Great Hinton Wilts 18 D8
Great Hockham Norfk 44 F10
Great Holland Essex 35 K11
Great Hollands Br For 20 D9
Great Horkesley Essex 34 F9
Great Hormead Herts 33 L10
Great Horton C Brad 58 F7
Great Horwood Bucks 31 Q7
Great Houghton Barns 59 K11
Great Houghton Nhants 32 B5
Great Hucklow Derbys 50 F5
Great Kelk E R Yk 61 J3
Great Kimble Bucks 20 D3
Great Kingshill Bucks 20 E4
Great Langdale Cumb 62 F2
Great Langton N York 65 N8
Great Leighs Essex 34 C12
Great Limber Lincs 52 G2
Great Linford M Keyn 32 C8
Great Livermere Suffk 34 E3
Great Longstone Derbys 50 G6
Great Lumley Dur 73 N10
Great Malvern Worcs 39 P11
Great Maplestead Essex 34 D9
Great Marton Bpool 56 G2
Great Massingham Norfk 44 D5
Great Milton Oxon 19 Q1
Great Missenden Bucks 20 E3
Great Mitton Lancs 57 N2
Great Mongeham Kent 23 Q12
Great Moulton Norfk 45 J11
Great Musgrave Cumb 64 D5
Great Ness Shrops 48 H10
Great Notley Essex 34 C11
Great Oak Mons 28 D6
Great Oakley Essex 35 K10
Great Oakley Nhants 42 C11
Great Offley Herts 32 G10
Great Ormside Cumb 64 C4
Great Orton Cumb 71 M5
Great Ouseburn N York 59 K2
Great Oxendon Nhants 41 Q10
Great Park N u Ty 73 L6
Great Parndon Essex 21 N2
Great Paxton Cambs 32 H4
Great Plumpton Lancs 56 H3
Great Plumstead Norfk 45 L7
Great Ponton Lincs 42 D4
Great Preston Leeds 59 K8
Great Raveley Cambs 33 J1
Great Rissington Gloucs 30 G10
Great Rollright Oxon 31 J7
Great Ryburgh Norfk 44 F5
Great Ryton Shrops 39 J2
Great Saling Essex 34 B10
Great Salkeld Cumb 71 Q8
Great Sampford Essex 33 Q9
Great Saughall Ches W 48 G2
Great Shefford W Berk 19 L6
Great Shelford Cambs 33 M6
Great Smeaton N York 65 N6
Great Snoring Norfk 44 F4
Great Somerford Wilts 18 E4
Great Soudley Shrops 49 N9
Great Stainton Darltn 65 N3
Great Stambridge Essex 22 H5
Great Staughton Cambs 32 G4
Great Steeping Lincs 53 M9
Great Stoke S Glos 28 H11
Greatstone-on-Sea Kent 13 L5
Great Strickland Cumb 71 Q10
Great Stukeley Cambs 32 H2
Great Sturton Lincs 52 H7
Great Swinburne Nthumb 72 G6
Great Tew Oxon 31 K8
Great Tey Essex 34 E10
Great Thurlow Suffk 34 B6
Great Torrington Devon 15 J8
Great Tosson Nthumb 72 H2
Great Totham Essex 22 G2
Great Totham Essex 22 G2
Great Urswick Cumb 62 F7
Great Wakering Essex 22 H6
Great Waldingfield Suffk 34 E7
Great Walsingham Norfk 44 F3
Great Waltham Essex 22 E2
Great Warley Essex 22 C5
Great Washbourne Gloucs 29 N2
Great Weeke Devon 5 P3
Great Wenham Suffk 34 H8
Great Whittington Nthumb 72 H6
Great Wigborough Essex 23 J1
Great Wilbraham Cambs 33 N5
Great Wishford Wilts 8 F1
Great Witcombe Gloucs 29 M6
Great Witley Worcs 39 N8
Great Wolford Warwks 30 G7
Greatworth Nhants 31 M6
Great Wratting Suffk 34 B7
Great Wymondley Herts 32 H10
Great Wyrley Staffs 40 C6
Great Yarmouth Norfk 45 Q8
Great Yeldham Essex 34 C8
Greenburn W Loth 85 Q10
Green End Herts 33 K11
Green End Herts 33 K9
Greenfield Ag & B 84 D5
Greenfield C Beds 32 F9
Greenfield Flints 56 E12
Greenfield Highld 98 B8
Greenfield Oldham 58 C12
Greenford Gt Lon 21 J7
Greengairs N Lans 85 N8
Greengates C Brad 58 G6
Greenham Somset 16 E11
Green Hammerton N York 59 L3
Greenhaugh Nthumb 72 E4
Greenhead Nthumb 72 C7
Green Heath Staffs 40 C5
Greenhill D & G 78 H11
Greenhill Falk 85 N7
Greenhill Kent 23 M9
Greenhill Leics 41 K5
Greenhill S Lans 78 F3
Greenhills S Lans 85 K11
Greenhithe Kent 22 C8
Greenholm E Ayrs 77 J4
Greenhouse Border 80 D9
Greenhow Hill N York 58 E2
Greenland Highld 110 E3
Greenland Sheff 51 K3
Greenlaw Border 80 F5
Greenlea D & G 70 G1
Greenloaning P & K 85 N2
Greenmount Bury 57 P6
Greenock Inver 84 E7
Greenodd Cumb 62 F6
Green Ore Somset 17 N6
Green Park Readg 20 B9
Green Quarter Cumb 63 J2
Greenshields S Lans 86 B12
Greenside Gatesd 73 K8
Greenside Kirk 58 F10
Greens Norton Nhants 31 P4
Greenstead Green Essex 34 D10
Green Street Herts 21 J4
Green Street Herts 33 M11
Green Tye Herts 33 M11
Greenway Somset 17 J10
Greenwich Gt Lon 21 M7
Greenwich Maritime Gt Lon 21 M7
Greet Gloucs 30 D7
Greete Shrops 39 L7
Greetham Lincs 53 K8
Greetham Rutlnd 42 D7
Greetland Calder 58 E9
Greinton Somset 17 K8
Grenaby IoM 56 b6
Grendon Nhants 32 C5
Grendon Warwks 40 H7
Grendon Underwood Bucks 31 P9
Grenoside Sheff 51 J3
Greosabhagh W Isls 111 c3
Gresford Wrexhm 48 G5
Gresham Norfk 45 J3
Greshornish Highld 104 D10
Gressenhall Norfk 44 F7
Gressenhall Green Norfk 44 F6
Gressingham Lancs 63 K8
Greta Bridge Dur 65 J5
Gretna D & G 71 M3
Gretna Green D & G 71 M2
Gretna Services D & G 71 L2
Gretton Gloucs 30 D7
Gretton Nhants 42 C10
Gretton Shrops 39 K3
Grewelthorpe N York 65 M11
Greyrigg D & G 78 H10
Greys Green Oxon 20 B6
Greysouthen Cumb 70 H9
Greystoke Cumb 71 P8
Greystone Angus 93 P7
Greywell Hants 20 B12
Griff Warwks 41 J9
Griffithstown Torfn 28 C8
Grimeford Village Lancs 57 L6
Grimesthorpe Sheff 51 J3
Grimethorpe Barns 59 K11
Grimister Shet 111 k2
Grimley Worcs 39 Q9
Grimmet S Ayrs 76 F8
Grimoldby Lincs 53 L6
Grimpo Shrops 48 G9
Grimsargh Lancs 57 L3
Grimsby NE Lin 61 M11
Grimscote Nhants 31 P4
Grimscott Cnwll 14 E10
Grimshader W Isls 111 d2
Grimsthorpe Lincs 42 F5
Grimston Leics 41 P3
Grimston Norfk 44 C5
Grimstone Dorset 7 P4
Grimstone End Suffk 34 F3
Grindale E R Yk 67 N12
Grindleford Derbys 50 G5
Grindleton Lancs 63 N11
Grindley Brook Shrops 49 K7
Grindlow Derbys 50 F5
Grindon Staffs 50 E9
Gringley on the Hill Notts 51 Q3
Grinsdale Cumb 71 M4
Grinshill Shrops 49 K10
Grinton N York 65 J7
Griomsiadar W Isls 111 d2
Grishipoll Ag & B 88 F5
Gristhorpe N York 67 M10
Griston Norfk 44 F9
Gritley Ork 111 h2
Grittenham Wilts 18 F4
Grittleton Wilts 18 C5
Grizebeck Cumb 62 E5
Grizedale Cumb 62 G4
Groby Leics 41 M6
Groes Conwy 55 Q8
Groes-faen Rhondd 27 M11
Groeslon Gwynd 54 F9
Groes-Wen Caerph 27 N10
Grogarry W Isls 111 a5
Grogport Ag & B 75 M4
Groigearraidh W Isls 111 a5
Gronant Flints 56 C11
Groombridge E Susx 11 Q3
Grosebay W Isls 111 c3
Grosmont Mons 28 E4
Grosmont N York 67 J6
Groton Suffk 34 F8
Grouville Jersey 7 c2
Grove Notts 51 Q5
Grove Oxon 19 L3
Grove Green Kent 22 F11
Grove Park Gt Lon 21 N8
Grovesend Swans 26 D8
Gruinard Highld 105 P4
Gruinart Ag & B 82 D9
Grula Highld 96 D4
Gruline Ag & B 89 L8
Grundisburgh Suffk 35 K6
Gruting Shet 111 j4
Grutness Shet 111 k5
Gualachulain Highld 90 F7
Guardbridge Fife 93 M11
Guarlford Worcs 39 P11
Guay P & K 92 E6
Guernsey Guern 6 b2
Guernsey Airport Guern 6 b2
Guestling Green E Susx 12 G7
Guestling Thorn E Susx 12 G6
Guestwick Norfk 44 H5
Guide Bridge Tamesd 50 B2
Guilden Morden Cambs 33 J7
Guilden Sutton Ches W 49 J2
Guildford Surrey 20 F12
Guildtown P & K 92 G8
Guilsborough Nhants 41 P11
Guilsfield Powys 48 E12
Guiltreehill S Ayrs 76 F8
Guineaford Devon 15 J5
Guisborough R & Cl 66 E4
Guiseley Leeds 58 G6
Guist Norfk 44 G5
Guiting Power Gloucs 30 E8
Gullane E Loth 87 J5
Gulval Cnwll 2 D9
Gulworthy Devon 5 K5
Gumfreston Pembks 25 J8
Gumley Leics 41 P9
Gunby Lincs 42 D6

Gundleton - Heaton 173

Gundleton Hants 9 Q2
Gun Hill E Susx 12 C7
Gunn Devon 15 L5
Gunnerside N York 64 G7
Gunnerton Nthumb 72 G6
Gunness N Linc 60 E11
Gunnislake Cnwll 5 J6
Gunnista Shet 111 k4
Gunthorpe C Pete 42 H9
Gunthorpe N Linc 52 B4
Gunthorpe Norfk 44 G3
Gunthorpe Notts 51 P11
Gunwalloe Cnwll 2 F10
Gurnard IoW 9 N8
Gurney Slade Somset 17 N6
Gurnos Powys 26 G7
Gussage All Saints Dorset 8 E5
Gussage St Andrew Dorset 8 E5
Gussage St Michael Dorset 8 E5
Guston Kent 13 P2
Gutcher Shet 111 k2
Guthrie Angus 93 P5
Guyhirn Cambs 43 L8
Guyzance Nthumb 81 P12
Gwaenysgor Flints 56 C11
Gwalchmai IoA 54 E6
Gwaun-Cae-Gurwen Carmth 26 F6
Gweek Cnwll 2 G9
Gwenddwr Powys 38 C12
Gwennap Cnwll 2 H7
Gwennap Mining District Cnwll 2 H7
Gwernaffield Flints 48 E3
Gwernesney Mons 28 E8
Gwernogle Carmth 26 D3
Gwernymynydd Flints 48 E3
Gwersyllt Wrexhm 48 G5
Gwespyr Flints 56 C11
Gwinear Cnwll 2 E8
Gwithian Cnwll 2 E7
Gwyddelwern Denbgs 48 C6
Gwyddgrug Carmth 26 C2
Gwytherin Conwy 55 N8

H

Habberley Shrops 38 H2
Habberley Worcs 39 P6
Habergham Lancs 57 P3
Habertoft Lincs 53 N9
Habrough NE Lin 61 K10
Hacconby Lincs 42 F5
Haceby Lincs 42 E3
Hacheston Suffk 35 M5
Hackbridge Gt Lon 21 L9
Hackenthorpe Sheff 51 K4
Hackford Norfk 44 H9
Hackforth N York 65 M8
Hackland Ork 111 h2
Hackleton Nhants 32 B6
Hacklinge Kent 23 Q11
Hackness N York 67 L9
Hackney Gt Lon 21 M6
Hackthorn Lincs 52 E7
Hackthorpe Cumb 71 Q10
Hadden Border 80 G7
Haddenham Bucks 20 B2
Haddenham Cambs 33 M2
Haddington E Loth 87 K7
Haddington Lincs 52 D10
Haddiscoe Norfk 45 P10
Haddon Cambs 42 G10
Hadfield Derbys 50 D2
Hadham Ford Herts 33 M11
Hadleigh Essex 22 F6
Hadleigh Suffk 34 G8
Hadley Worcs 39 Q8
Hadley Wrekin 49 M12
Hadley End Staffs 40 F4
Hadley Wood Gt Lon 21 L4
Hadlow Kent 22 D12
Hadlow Down E Susx 11 Q5
Hadnall Shrops 49 K10
Hadrian's Wall 72 G6
Hadstock Essex 33 N7
Hadzor Worcs 30 B2
Haggersta Shet 111 k4
Haggerston Nthumb 81 L5
Haggs Falk 85 N7
Hagley Herefs 28 G1
Hagley Worcs 40 B10
Hagworthingham Lincs 53 K9
Haile Cumb 62 B1
Hailey Oxon 31 J10
Hailsham E Susx 12 C8
Hail Weston Cambs 32 G4
Hainault Gt Lon 21 P5
Hainford Norfk 45 K6
Hainton Lincs 52 H6
Haisthorpe E R Yk 61 J2
Hakin Pembks 24 F7
Halam Notts 51 P9
Halbeath Fife 86 D5
Halberton Devon 6 D1
Halcro Highld 110 E4
Hale Cumb 63 J6
Hale Halton 57 J11
Hale Hants 8 H4
Hale Surrey 10 D1
Hale Traffd 57 P10
Hale Barns Traffd 57 P10
Hales Norfk 45 N10
Hales Staffs 49 N8
Halesowen Dudley 40 C10
Hales Place Kent 23 M10
Hale Street Kent 22 D12
Halesworth Suffk 35 N2
Halewood Knows 57 J10
Halford Devon 5 Q5
Halford Warwks 30 H5
Halfpenny Green Staffs 39 P4
Halfway House Shrops 48 G12
Halfway Houses Kent 22 H8
Halifax Calder 58 E8
Halket E Ayrs 84 G11
Halkirk Highld 110 D4
Halkyn Flints 48 E2
Hall E Rens 84 G11
Halland E Susx 11 P6
Hallaton Leics 42 B10
Hallatrow BaNES 17 P5
Hallbankgate Cumb 72 B8
Hall Dunnerdale Cumb 62 E3
Hallen S Glos 28 G11
Hallgarth Dur 73 N11
Hallglen Falk 85 P7
Hall Green Birm 40 E10
Hallin Highld 104 C9
Halling Medway 22 E10
Hallington Lincs 53 K6
Hallington Nthumb 72 H6
Halliwell Bolton 57 M6
Halloughton Notts 51 P9
Hallow Worcs 39 P9
Hall's Green Herts 33 J10
Hallyne Border 79 K2
Halmore Gloucs 29 J8
Halnaker W Susx 10 E8
Halsall Lancs 56 G6
Halse Nhants 31 M6
Halse Somset 16 F9
Halsetown Cnwll 2 D7
Halsham E R Yk 61 M8
Halstead Essex 34 D10
Halstead Kent 21 P10
Halstead Leics 41 Q6
Halstock Dorset 7 M2
Haltham Lincs 53 J10
Halton Bucks 20 E2
Halton Halton 57 K11
Halton Lancs 63 J8
Halton Leeds 59 J7
Halton Nthumb 72 H7
Halton Wrexhm 48 F7
Halton East N York 58 D4
Halton Gill N York 64 F11
Halton Holegate Lincs 53 L9
Halton Lea Gate Nthumb 72 C8
Halton Shields Nthumb 72 H7
Halton West N York 63 Q10
Haltwhistle Nthumb 72 D7
Halvergate Norfk 45 N8
Halwell Devon 5 Q9
Halwill Devon 14 H11
Halwill Junction Devon 14 H11
Ham Devon 6 H3
Ham Gloucs 29 J8
Ham Gt Lon 21 J8
Ham Kent 23 P11
Ham Somset 16 H10
Ham Wilts 19 K8
Hambleden Bucks 20 C6
Hambledon Hants 9 Q4
Hambledon Surrey 10 F3
Hamble-le-Rice Hants 9 N6
Hambleton Lancs 56 G1
Hambleton N York 59 M7
Hambridge Somset 17 K10
Hambrook W Susx 10 C8
Hameringham Lincs 53 K9
Hamerton Cambs 32 G2
Ham Green Worcs 30 D2
Hamilton S Lans 85 M11
Hamilton Services (northbound) S Lans 85 M10
Hamlet Dorset 7 N2
Hammersmith Gt Lon 21 K7
Hammerwich Staffs 40 E6
Hammoon Dorset 8 B5
Hamnavoe Shet 111 k4
Hampden Park E Susx 12 C9
Hampnett Gloucs 30 E10
Hampole Donc 59 L11
Hampreston Dorset 8 F7
Hampstead Gt Lon 21 L6
Hampstead Norreys W Berk 19 N5
Hampsthwaite N York 58 H3
Hampton C Pete 42 G10
Hampton Gt Lon 21 J9
Hampton Kent 23 M9
Hampton Shrops 39 N5
Hampton Swindn 18 H3
Hampton Worcs 30 D5
Hampton Bishop Herefs 28 G2
Hampton Court Palace Gt Lon 21 J9
Hampton Heath Ches W 49 J5
Hampton-in-Arden Solhll 40 G10
Hampton Lovett Worcs 30 B2
Hampton Lucy Warwks 30 G3
Hampton Magna Warwks 30 H2
Hampton Park Wilts 8 H2
Hampton Poyle Oxon 31 L10
Hampton Wick Gt Lon 21 J9
Hamptworth Wilts 9 J4
Hamsey E Susx 11 N7
Hamstall Ridware Staffs 40 E4
Hamstead Birm 40 D8
Hamstead Marshall W Berk 19 M7
Hamsterley Dur 65 K2
Hamsterley Dur 73 K9
Hamstreet Kent 13 J4
Ham Street Somset 17 M8
Hamworthy BCP 8 E8
Hanbury Staffs 40 F2
Hanbury Worcs 30 C2
Hanchurch Staffs 49 Q7
Handa Island Highld 108 C6
Hand and Pen Devon 6 E4
Handbridge Ches W 48 H3
Handcross W Susx 11 L4
Handforth Ches E 57 Q11
Handley Ches W 49 J4
Handley Derbys 51 J8
Handsworth Birm 40 D9
Handsworth Sheff 51 K4
Hanford C Stke 49 Q7
Hanging Heaton Kirk 58 G9
Hanging Houghton Nhants 41 Q11
Hanging Langford Wilts 18 F12
Hangleton Br & H 11 L8
Hanham S Glos 17 P2
Hankelow Ches E 49 M6
Hankerton Wilts 29 N9
Hanley C Stke 50 B10
Hanley Castle Worcs 39 Q12
Hanley Child Worcs 39 M8
Hanley Swan Worcs 39 P12
Hanley William Worcs 39 M8
Hanlith N York 58 B2
Hanmer Wrexhm 49 J7
Hannaford Devon 15 K6
Hannington Hants 19 N9
Hannington Nhants 32 B3
Hannington Swindn 18 H3
Hannington Wick Swindn 18 H2
Hanslope M Keyn 32 B7
Hanthorpe Lincs 42 F5
Hanwell Gt Lon 21 J7
Hanwell Oxon 31 K5
Hanwood Shrops 49 J12
Hanworth Gt Lon 20 H8
Hanworth Norfk 45 K3
Happendon S Lans 78 E3
Happendon Services S Lans 78 D3
Happisburgh Norfk 45 N4
Happisburgh Common Norfk 45 N4
Hapsford Ches W 49 J1
Hapton Lancs 57 P3
Hapton Norfk 45 K10
Harberton Devon 5 Q8
Harbertonford Devon 5 Q8
Harbledown Kent 23 L10
Harborne Birm 40 D10
Harborough Magna Warwks 41 L10
Harbottle Nthumb 81 K12
Harbourneford Devon 5 P7
Harburn W Loth 86 C9
Harbury Warwks 31 J3
Harby Leics 41 Q2
Harby Notts 52 C8
Harcombe Devon 6 B6
Harcombe Devon 6 F5
Harcombe Bottom Devon 7 J4
Harden C Brad 58 E6
Harden Wsall 40 D7
Hardenhuish Wilts 18 D6
Hardgate Abers 95 N2
Hardgate D & G 70 D3
Hardgate W Duns 84 H8
Hardham W Susx 10 G6
Hardingham Norfk 44 H8
Hardingstone Nhants 31 Q3
Hardington Somset 17 Q5
Hardington Mandeville Somset 7 M1
Hardington Marsh Somset 7 M2
Hardington Moor Somset 7 M1
Hardisworthy Devon 14 E7
Hardley Hants 9 M6
Hardley Street Norfk 45 N9
Hardraw N York 64 F8
Hardstoft Derbys 51 K8
Hardway Hants 9 Q7
Hardway Somset 17 Q8
Hardwick Bucks 32 B11
Hardwick Cambs 33 L5
Hardwick Nhants 32 C3
Hardwick Norfk 45 K11
Hardwick Oxon 31 J11
Hardwick Oxon 31 M7
Hardwick Wsall 40 E7
Hardwicke Gloucs 29 L6
Hardwicke Gloucs 29 M4
Hardwick Hall Derbys 51 L7
Hardy's Green Essex 34 F11
Hare Croft C Brad 58 E7
Harefield Gt Lon 20 G5
Hare Green Essex 34 H10
Hare Hatch Wokham 20 C7
Harehill Derbys 40 F1
Harehills Leeds 59 J7
Harelaw Border 80 C9
Harelaw D & G 79 N12
Harescombe Gloucs 29 L6
Haresfield Gloucs 29 L6
Harestock Hants 9 M2
Hare Street Essex 21 N2
Hare Street Herts 33 L10
Harewood Leeds 58 H5
Harewood End Herefs 28 F4
Harford Devon 5 M8
Hargrave Ches W 49 J3
Hargrave Nhants 32 E3
Hargrave Suffk 34 C5
Harkstead Suffk 35 K9
Harlaston Staffs 40 G5
Harlaxton Lincs 42 C4
Harlech Gwynd 47 J5
Harlech Castle Gwynd 47 J5
Harlescott Shrops 49 J11
Harlesden Gt Lon 21 K6
Harlesthorpe Derbys 51 L5
Harleston Devon 5 Q10
Harleston Norfk 45 L12
Harleston Suffk 34 G5
Harlestone Nhants 31 P2
Harle Syke Lancs 57 Q2
Harley Rothm 51 J2
Harley Shrops 39 L2
Harlington C Beds 32 E10
Harlington Donc 51 L1
Harlington Gt Lon 20 H7
Harlosh Highld 96 C2
Harlow Essex 21 N2
Harlow Carr RHS N York 58 H4
Harlow Hill Nthumb 73 J7
Harlthorpe E R Yk 60 C6
Harlton Cambs 33 L6
Harlyn Cnwll 3 K1
Harman's Cross Dorset 8 E10
Harmby N York 65 K9
Harmer Green Herts 33 J12
Harmer Hill Shrops 49 J10
Harmston Lincs 52 D10
Harnage Shrops 39 K2
Harnhill Gloucs 18 F1
Harold Hill Gt Lon 21 Q5
Haroldston West Pembks 24 F6
Haroldswick Shet 111 m2
Harold Wood Gt Lon 22 B5
Harome N York 66 F10
Harpenden Herts 21 J1
Harpford Devon 6 E5
Harpham E R Yk 61 J2
Harpley Norfk 44 D5
Harpley Worcs 39 M9
Harpole Nhants 31 P2
Harpsdale Highld 110 D5
Harpswell Lincs 52 D5
Harpurhey Manch 57 Q8
Harraby Cumb 71 N5
Harracott Devon 15 K6
Harrapool Highld 97 J5
Harras Cumb 70 F11
Harrietfield P & K 92 E9
Harrietsham Kent 22 G11
Harringay Gt Lon 21 L6
Harrington Cumb 70 G9
Harrington Lincs 53 L8
Harrington Nhants 41 Q10
Harringworth Nhants 42 D10
Harris W Isls 111 c3
Harrogate N York 58 H3
Harrold Bed 32 D5
Harrow Gt Lon 21 J6
Harrowbarrow Cnwll 5 J6
Harrowgate Village Darltn 65 N4
Harrow Green Suffk 34 E6
Harrow on the Hill Gt Lon 21 J6
Harrow Weald Gt Lon 21 J5
Harston Cambs 33 L6
Harston Leics 42 B4
Harswell E R Yk 60 E6
Hart Hartpl 66 C1
Hartburn Nthumb 73 J4
Hartburn S on T 65 Q4
Hartest Suffk 34 D6
Hartfield E Susx 11 P3
Hartford Cambs 33 J3
Hartford Ches W 49 L2
Hartfordbridge Hants 20 C10
Hartford End Essex 34 B12
Hartforth N York 65 L6
Hartgrove Dorset 8 C4
Harthill Ches W 49 J4
Harthill N Lans 85 Q9
Harthill Rothm 51 L5
Harthope D & G 78 G6
Hartington Derbys 50 F8
Hartland Devon 14 E7
Hartland Quay Devon 14 D7
Hartlebury Worcs 39 Q7
Hartlepool Hartpl 66 C2
Hartley Cumb 64 E6
Hartley Kent 12 F3
Hartley Kent 22 C9
Hartley Wespall Hants 20 B10
Hartley Wintney Hants 20 C11
Hartlip Kent 22 G9
Harton N York 60 C2
Harton S Tyne 73 P7
Hartpury Gloucs 29 L4
Hartshead Kirk 58 F9
Hartshead Moor Services Calder 58 F8
Hartshill C Stke 49 Q6
Hartshill Warwks 41 J8
Hartshorne Derbys 41 J4
Hartwell Nhants 32 B6
Hartwith N York 58 G2
Hartwood N Lans 85 P10
Hartwoodmyres Border 79 N4
Harvel Kent 22 D10
Harvington Worcs 30 D4
Harvington Worcs 39 Q7
Harwell Notts 51 P3
Harwell Oxon 19 N3
Harwich Essex 35 L9
Harwood Dale N York 67 L8
Harworth Notts 51 N3
Hasbury Dudley 40 C10
Hascombe Surrey 10 G3
Haselbech Nhants 41 P11
Haselbury Plucknett Somset 7 L1
Haseley Warwks 30 G1
Haselor Warwks 30 E3
Hasfield Gloucs 29 L4
Haskayne Lancs 56 G7
Hasketon Suffk 35 L6
Haslemere Surrey 10 E4
Haslingden Lancs 57 P4
Haslingfield Cambs 33 L6
Haslington Ches E 49 N4
Hassingham Norfk 45 N8
Hassocks W Susx 11 L7
Hassop Derbys 50 G6
Haster Highld 110 G5
Hastingleigh Kent 13 L2
Hastings E Susx 12 G7
Hastingwood Essex 21 P2
Hastoe Herts 20 E2
Haswell Dur 73 P11
Haswell Plough Dur 73 P11
Hatch Beauchamp Somset 17 J11
Hatch End Gt Lon 21 J5
Hatchmere Ches W 49 K2
Hatch Warren Hants 19 Q10
Hatcliffe NE Lin 52 H4
Hatfield Donc 59 P11
Hatfield Herefs 39 L9
Hatfield Herts 21 K2
Hatfield Broad Oak Essex 33 N12
Hatfield Heath Essex 21 Q1
Hatfield Peverel Essex 22 F2
Hatfield Woodhouse Donc 59 P11
Hatford Oxon 19 K2
Hatherden Hants 19 K10
Hatherleigh Devon 15 J10
Hathern Leics 41 L3
Hatherop Gloucs 30 F11
Hathersage Derbys 50 G5
Hathersage Booths Derbys 50 G5
Hatherton Ches E 49 M6
Hatherton Staffs 40 C5
Hatley St George Cambs 33 J6
Hatt Cnwll 5 J7
Hattersley Tamesd 50 C2
Hatton Abers 103 L7
Hatton Angus 93 N7
Hatton Derbys 40 G2
Hatton Gt Lon 20 H8
Hatton Lincs 52 H7
Hatton Shrops 39 J4
Hatton Warrtn 57 L11
Hatton Warwks 30 G1
Hatton of Fintray Abers 102 H11
Haugh E Ayrs 76 H6
Haugham Lincs 53 K7
Haughhead E Duns 85 K7
Haughley Suffk 34 G4
Haughley Green Suffk 34 G4
Haugh of Glass Moray 101 M7
Haugh of Urr D & G 70 D3
Haughs of Kinnaird Angus 93 Q4
Haughton Ches E 49 L4
Haughton Shrops 48 H9
Haughton Staffs 49 Q10
Haughton le Skerne Darltn 65 N4
Haultwick Herts 33 K11
Haunton Staffs 40 G5
Hauxton Cambs 33 M6
Havant Hants 10 B8
Havenstreet IoW 9 P8
Havercroft Wakefd 59 K10
Haverfordwest Pembks 24 G6
Haverhill Suffk 33 Q7
Haverigg Cumb 62 D6
Havering-atte-Bower Gt Lon 21 P5
Haversham M Keyn 32 B8
Haverthwaite Cumb 62 G5
Havyatt N Som 17 L4
Hawarden Flints 48 G3
Hawbush Green Essex 34 D11
Hawen Cerdgn 36 F10
Hawes N York 64 F9
Hawe's Green Norfk 45 L9
Hawford Worcs 39 Q9
Hawick Border 80 C10
Hawkchurch Devon 7 J3
Hawkedon Suffk 34 D6
Hawkeridge Wilts 18 C9
Hawkesbury S Glos 18 B4
Hawkesbury Upton S Glos 18 B4
Hawkhurst Kent 12 F4
Hawkinge Kent 13 N3
Hawkley Hants 10 C4
Hawkridge Somset 15 P6
Hawkshead Cumb 62 G3
Hawkshead Hill Cumb 62 G3
Hawksland S Lans 78 D2
Hawkstone Shrops 49 L9
Hawkswick N York 64 G12
Hawksworth Leeds 58 F6
Hawksworth Notts 51 Q11
Hawkwell Essex 22 G5
Hawley Hants 20 D10
Hawling Gloucs 30 E9
Hawnby N York 66 D9
Haworth C Brad 58 D6
Hawstead Suffk 34 E5
Hawthorn Dur 73 P10
Hawthorn Hill Lincs 52 H11
Hawton Notts 52 B12
Haxby C York 59 N3
Haxey N Linc 51 Q2
Haydock St Hel 57 K9
Haydon Bridge Nthumb 72 F7
Haydon Wick Swindn 18 G4
Hayes Gt Lon 20 H7
Hayes Gt Lon 21 N9
Hayes End Gt Lon 20 H7
Hayfield Ag & B 90 E10
Hayfield Derbys 50 D4
Hayhillock Angus 93 N7
Hayle Cnwll 2 E8
Hayle Port Cnwll 2 E8
Hayley Green Dudley 40 C10
Hayling Island Hants 10 B9
Hayne Devon 5 P3
Haynes C Beds 32 F8
Haynes Church End C Beds 32 F8
Haynes West End C Beds 32 F8
Hay-on-Wye Powys 27 P1
Hayscastle Pembks 24 F4
Hayscastle Cross Pembks 24 F4
Hay Street Herts 33 L10
Hayton Cumb 70 H7
Hayton Cumb 71 Q4
Hayton E R Yk 60 E5
Hayton Notts 51 Q4
Haytor Vale Devon 5 P5
Haytown Devon 14 G8
Haywards Heath W Susx 11 M5
Haywood Donc 59 N10
Hazelbank S Lans 77 P3
Hazelbury Bryan Dorset 7 Q2
Hazeleigh Essex 22 G3
Hazel Grove Stockp 50 B4
Hazelton Walls Fife 93 L10
Hazelwood Derbys 51 J10
Hazlemere Bucks 20 E4
Hazlerigg N u Ty 73 M6
Hazleton Gloucs 30 E9
Heacham Norfk 44 B3
Headbourne Worthy Hants 9 N2
Headcorn Kent 12 G2
Headingley Leeds 58 H7
Headington Oxon 31 M11
Headlam Dur 65 L4
Headlesscross N Lans 85 Q10
Headless Cross Worcs 30 D2
Headley Hants 10 D3
Headley Hants 19 N8
Headley Surrey 21 K11
Headley Down Hants 10 D3
Headon Notts 51 Q5
Heads Nook Cumb 71 P5
Heage Derbys 51 J10
Healaugh N York 59 L5
Healaugh N York 64 H7
Heald Green Stockp 57 Q10
Heale Somset 16 H11
Heale Somset 17 K10
Healey N York 65 L10
Healeyfield Dur 73 J10
Healing NE Lin 61 L11
Heamoor Cnwll 2 C9
Heanor Derbys 51 K10
Heanton Punchardon Devon 15 J5
Heapham Lincs 52 C6
Heart of Scotland Services N Lans 85 Q9
Heasley Mill Devon 15 M6
Heaste Highld 96 H6
Heath Derbys 51 K7
Heath Wakefd 59 J9
Heath and Reach C Beds 32 D10
Heathcote Derbys 50 F8
Heather Leics 41 K5
Heathfield E Susx 12 C6
Heathfield Somset 16 F10
Heath Green Worcs 40 E12
Heath Hall D & G 78 G11
Heath Hayes & Wimblebury Staffs 40 D5
Heath Hill Shrops 49 N11
Heathrow Airport Gt Lon 20 H8
Heathton Shrops 39 P4
Heath Town Wolves 40 B7
Heatley Warrtn 57 N10
Heaton C Brad 58 F7
Heaton N u Ty 73 M7
Heaton Staffs 50 C8

174 Heaton Chapel – Hook

Heaton Chapel Stockp 57 Q9
Heaton Mersey Stockp 57 Q10
Heaton Norris Stockp 50 B3
Heaton's Bridge Lancs 56 H6
Heaverham Kent 22 C10
Heavitree Devon 6 C4
Hebburn S Tyne 73 N7
Hebden N York 58 D2
Hebden Bridge Calder 58 C8
Hebing End Herts 33 K11
Hebron Carmth 25 L4
Hebron Nthumb 73 L3
Heckfield Hants 20 B10
Heckfield Green Suffk 35 K2
Heckfordbridge Essex 34 F11
Heckington Lincs 42 G2
Heckmondwike Kirk 58 G9
Heddington Wilts 18 E7
Heddon-on-the-Wall Nthumb 73 K7
Hedenham Norfk 45 M10
Hedge End Hants 9 N5
Hedgerley Bucks 20 F6
Hedging Somset 17 J9
Hedley on the Hill Nthumb 73 J8
Hednesford Staffs 40 C5
Hedon E R Yk 61 K8
Hedsor Bucks 20 E6
Heeley Sheff 51 J4
Heglibister Shet 111 k4
Heighington Darltn 65 M3
Heighington Lincs 52 E9
Heightington Worcs 39 N7
Heiton Border 80 F7
Hele Devon 6 D3
Hele Devon 15 J3
Helensburgh Ag & B 84 E6
Helenton S Ayrs 76 G5
Helford Cnwll 2 H9
Helford Passage Cnwll 2 H9
Helhoughton Norfk 44 E5
Helions Bumpstead Essex 33 Q8
Helland Cnwll 3 N2
Hellescott Cnwll 4 G3
Hellesdon Norfk 45 K7
Hellidon Nhants 31 M3
Hellifield N York 63 Q10
Hellingly E Susx 12 C7
Helmdon Nhants 31 N5
Helme Kirk 58 E10
Helmingham Suffk 35 K5
Helmsdale Highld 110 B11
Helmshore Lancs 57 P5
Helmsley N York 66 E10
Helperby N York 59 K1
Helperthorpe N York 67 K12
Helpringham Lincs 42 G3
Helpston C Pete 42 G8
Helsby Ches W 49 J1
Helston Cnwll 2 F9
Helstone Cnwll 4 D4
Helton Cumb 71 Q10
Hemel Hempstead Herts 20 G2
Hemerdon Devon 5 L8
Hemingbrough N York 59 P7
Hemingby Lincs 53 J8
Hemingford Abbots Cambs 33 J3
Hemingford Grey Cambs 33 J3
Hemingstone Suffk 35 J6
Hemington Leics 41 L2
Hemington Nhants 42 F12
Hemington Somset 17 Q5
Hemley Suffk 35 L8
Hemlington Middsb 66 C5
Hempnall Norfk 45 L10
Hempnall Green Norfk 45 L10
Hempriggs Moray 100 H3
Hempstead Essex 33 Q8
Hempstead Medway 22 F9
Hempstead Norfk 44 H3
Hempstead Norfk 45 N5
Hempton Norfk 44 E4
Hempton Oxon 31 K7
Hemsby Norfk 45 P6
Hemswell Lincs 52 D5
Hemswell Cliff Lincs 52 D5
Hemsworth Wakefd 59 K10
Hemyock Devon 16 F12
Henbury Bristl 28 G11
Hendon Gt Lon 21 K5
Hendon Sundld 73 P9
Hendy Carmth 26 D7
Henfield W Susx 11 K6
Hengoed Caerph 27 N9
Hengoed Powys 38 E10
Hengrave Suffk 34 D3
Henham Essex 33 N10
Heniarth Powys 38 D1
Henlade Somset 16 H10
Henley Dorset 7 Q2
Henley Somset 17 L9
Henley Suffk 35 J6
Henley W Susx 10 E5
Henley Green Covtry 41 J10
Henley-in-Arden Warwks 30 F2
Henley-on-Thames Oxon 20 C6
Henley's Down E Susx 12 E7
Henllan Cerdgn 36 F11
Henllan Denbgs 55 Q7
Henllys Torfn 28 B9
Henlow C Beds 32 H8
Henlow Camp C Beds 32 G9
Hennock Devon 5 Q4
Henny Street Essex 34 E8
Henryd Conwy 55 L6
Henry's Moat (Castell Hendre) Pembks 24 H4
Hensall N York 59 N9
Henshaw Nthumb 72 D7
Hensingham Cumb 70 G11
Henstead Suffk 45 P11
Hensting Hants 9 N3
Henstridge Somset 17 Q11
Henstridge Ash Somset 17 Q11
Henton Oxon 20 C3
Henton Somset 17 L7
Henwick Worcs 39 Q10
Henwood Cnwll 4 G5
Heol-y-Cyw Brdgnd 27 K11
Hepple Nthumb 72 H1
Hepscott Nthumb 73 L4
Heptonstall Calder 58 C8
Hepworth Kirk 58 F11
Hepworth Suffk 34 G2
Herbrandston Pembks 24 F7
Hereford Herefs 28 F2
Hereson Kent 23 Q9
Heribusta Highld 104 E8
Heriot Border 86 H10
Hermiston C Edin 86 E8
Hermitage Border 79 P9
Hermitage Dorset 7 P2
Hermitage W Berk 19 N6
Hermon Carmth 25 N3
Hermon Pembks 25 L3
Herne Kent 23 M9
Herne Bay Kent 23 M9
Herne Hill Gt Lon 21 L8
Herne Pound Kent 22 D11
Hernhill Kent 23 K10
Herodsfoot Cnwll 4 F7
Heronsford S Ayrs 68 F3
Herriard Hants 19 Q10
Herringfleet Suffk 45 P9
Herringswell Suffk 34 C3
Herringthorpe Rothm 51 K3
Herrington Sundld 73 P9
Hersden Kent 23 M10
Hersham Surrey 20 H9
Herstmonceux E Susx 12 D7
Herston Dorset 8 E10
Herston Ork 111 h3
Hertford Herts 21 M2
Hertford Heath Herts 21 M2
Hertingfordbury Herts 21 L2
Hesketh Bank Lancs 57 J4
Hesketh Lane Lancs 57 L1
Hesket Newmarket Cumb 71 M7
Hesleden Dur 73 Q12
Heslington C York 59 N4
Hessay C York 59 M4
Hessenford Cnwll 4 G8
Hessett Suffk 34 F4
Hessle E R Yk 60 H8
Hessle Wakefd 59 K9
Hest Bank Lancs 63 J8
Heston Gt Lon 20 H7
Heston Services Gt Lon 20 H7
Hestwall Ork 111 g2
Heswall Wirral 56 F11
Hethe Oxon 31 N8
Hethersett Norfk 45 J8
Hethersgill Cumb 71 P3
Hett Dur 73 M12
Hetton N York 58 C3
Hetton-le-Hole Sundld 73 N10
Heugh Nthumb 73 J6
Heughhead Abers 101 M11
Heugh Head Border 87 Q9
Heveningham Suffk 35 M3
Hever Kent 11 P2
Heversham Cumb 63 J5
Hevingham Norfk 45 K6
Hewas Water Cnwll 3 L6
Hewelsfield Gloucs 28 G8
Hewish Somset 7 K2
Hewood Dorset 7 J3
Hexham Nthumb 72 G7
Hextable Kent 21 P8
Hexthorpe Donc 51 M1
Hexton Herts 32 F10
Hexworthy Cnwll 4 H4
Hexworthy Devon 5 N6
Heybridge Essex 22 D4
Heybridge Essex 22 G2
Heybrook Bay Devon 5 K9
Heydon Cambs 33 M8
Heydon Norfk 45 J5
Heydour Lincs 42 E3
Heylipoll Ag & B 88 B7
Heylor Shet 111 j3
Heysham Lancs 62 H9
Heyshott W Susx 10 E6
Heytesbury Wilts 18 D11
Heythrop Oxon 31 J8
Heywood Rochdl 57 Q6
Heywood Wilts 18 C9
Hibaldstow N Linc 52 D3
Hickleton Donc 59 L12
Hickling Norfk 45 N5
Hickling Notts 41 P2
Hickling Green Norfk 45 N5
Hickstead W Susx 11 L6
Hidcote Bartrim Gloucs 30 F5
Hidcote Boyce Gloucs 30 F6
High Ackworth Wakefd 59 K9
Higham Barns 58 H11
Higham Derbys 51 K8
Higham Kent 12 C1
Higham Kent 22 E8
Higham Lancs 57 P2
Higham Suffk 34 C4
Higham Suffk 34 G9
Higham Ferrers Nhants 32 D3
Higham Gobion C Beds 32 F9
Higham Hill Gt Lon 21 M5
Higham on the Hill Leics 41 J8
Highampton Devon 14 H10
Highams Park Gt Lon 21 M5
High Ardwell D & G 68 E9
High Auldgirth D & G 78 E10
High Bankhill Cumb 71 Q7
High Beach Essex 21 N4
High Bentham N York 63 M8
High Bickington Devon 15 K7
High Biggins Cumb 63 L6
High Blantyre S Lans 85 L10
High Bonnybridge Falk 85 N7
High Bray Devon 15 M5
Highbridge Somset 17 J6
Highbrook W Susx 11 M4
High Brooms Kent 12 C2
Highburton Kirk 58 F10
Highbury Gt Lon 21 L6
Highbury Somset 17 Q6
High Catton E R Yk 60 C4
Highclere Hants 19 M8
Highcliffe BCP 8 H8
High Coniscliffe Darltn 65 M5
High Crosby Cumb 71 P4
High Cross E Ayrs 76 G3
High Cross Hants 10 B5
High Cross Herts 33 K11
High Cross Warwks 30 G1
High Drummore D & G 68 F11
High Easter Essex 22 C1
High Ellington N York 65 L10
Higher Ansty Dorset 8 B6
Higher Bartle Lancs 57 J3
Higher Bockhampton Dorset 7 Q4
Higher Brixham Torbay 6 C10
High Ercall Wrekin 49 L11
Higher Chillington Somset 7 K2
Higher Folds Wigan 57 M8
Higher Gabwell Devon 6 C8
Higher Heysham Lancs 62 H9
Higher Irlam Salfd 57 N9
Higher Kinnerton Flints 48 G4
Higher Muddiford Devon 15 K5
Higher Penwortham Lancs 57 K3
Higher Prestacott Devon 14 G11
Higher Town Cnwll 3 J6
Higher Town Cnwll 3 M4
Higher Town IoS 2 c1
Higher Walton Lancs 57 L4
Higher Walton Warrtn 57 L10
Higher Wambrook Somset 6 H2
Higher Waterston Dorset 7 Q4
Higher Wheelton Lancs 57 L4
Higher Whitley Ches W 57 L11
Higher Wincham Ches W 57 M12
Higher Wraxhall Dorset 7 N3
Higher Wych Ches W 49 J6
High Etherley Dur 65 L2
Highfield Gatesd 73 K8
Highfield N Ayrs 76 E2
Highfields Caldecote Cambs 33 K5
High Garrett Essex 34 C10
Highgate Gt Lon 21 L6
Highgate Kent 12 F4
High Grantley N York 65 M12
High Green Norfk 45 J11
High Green Norfk 45 J8
High Green Sheff 51 J2
High Halden Kent 12 H3
High Halstow Medway 22 F8
High Ham Somset 17 K9
High Harrington Cumb 70 G9
High Harrogate N York 58 H3
High Hatton Shrops 49 L9
High Hauxley Nthumb 73 M1
High Hawsker N York 67 K6
High Hesket Cumb 71 P6
High Hoyland Barns 58 H11
High Hurstwood E Susx 11 P5
High Hutton N York 60 D1
High Ireby Cumb 71 K7
High Kilburn N York 66 D10
High Lands Dur 65 K3
Highlane Derbys 51 K4
High Lane Stockp 50 C4
High Lanes Cnwll 2 E8
Highleadon Gloucs 29 K4
High Legh Ches E 57 M11
Highleigh W Susx 10 D9
High Leven S on T 66 C5
Highley Shrops 39 N5
High Littleton BaNES 17 P5
High Lorton Cumb 71 J9
High Marnham Notts 52 B9
High Melton Donc 51 L1
High Mickley Nthumb 73 J8
Highmoor Oxon 20 B6
Highmoor Cross Oxon 20 B6
Highnam Gloucs 29 L5
High Newport Sundld 73 P9
High Newton Cumb 62 H5
High Newton-by-the-Sea Nthumb 81 P8
High Nibthwaite Cumb 62 F4
High Offley Staffs 49 P9
High Ongar Essex 22 C3
High Onn Staffs 49 P11
High Park Corner Essex 34 G11
High Pennyvenie E Ayrs 76 H9
High Pittington Dur 73 N11
High Roding Essex 33 P12
High Salvington W Susx 10 H8
High Spen Gatesd 73 K8
Highsted Kent 22 H10
High Street Cnwll 3 L5
Highstreet Kent 23 L10
Highstreet Green Surrey 10 F3
Hightae D & G 78 H11
Highter's Heath Birm 40 E10
Hightown Sefton 56 F7
Hightown Green Suffk 34 F5
High Toynton Lincs 53 J9
High Valleyfield Fife 86 B5
Highweek Devon 6 B8
Highwood Essex 22 D3
Highwood Hill Gt Lon 21 K5
Highworth Swindn 18 H3
High Wray Cumb 62 G3
High Wych Herts 21 P1
High Wycombe Bucks 20 D5
Hilborough Norfk 44 D9
Hilcott Wilts 18 G8
Hildenborough Kent 21 R12
Hilden Park Kent 12 C1
Hildersham Cambs 33 N7
Hilderstone Staffs 40 C1
Hilderthorpe E R Yk 61 K2
Hilgay Norfk 43 P9
Hill S Glos 28 H9
Hill Warwks 31 L2
Hillam N York 59 L8
Hill Brow Hants 10 C5
Hillbutts Dorset 8 E7
Hill Chorlton Staffs 49 P7
Hillcliffane Derbys 50 H10
Hill Common Somset 16 F10
Hilldyke Lincs 43 K1
Hill End Fife 86 C3
Hillend Fife 86 D5
Hill End Gloucs 29 M2
Hillend Mdloth 86 F8
Hillend N Lans 85 N9
Hillesden Bucks 31 P8
Hillesley Gloucs 29 K10
Hillfarrance Somset 16 F10
Hill Green Kent 22 G10
Hillhead Abers 102 D8
Hill Head Hants 9 P6
Hillhead S Lans 78 F2
Hillhead of Cocklaw Abers 103 M6
Hilliclay Highld 110 D3
Hillingdon Gt Lon 20 H6
Hillington C Glas 85 J9
Hillington Norfk 44 C5
Hillmorton Warwks 41 M11
Hill of Beath Fife 86 D4
Hill of Fearn Highld 107 N6
Hillowton D & G 70 C3
Hill Ridware Staffs 40 E4
Hillside Abers 95 Q3
Hillside Angus 95 L9
Hill Side Kirk 58 F10
Hills Town Derbys 51 L6
Hillstreet Hants 9 K4
Hillswick Shet 111 j3
Hill Top Sandw 40 C8
Hill Top Wakefd 59 J10
Hillwell Shet 111 k5
Hilmarton Wilts 18 E6
Hilperton Wilts 18 C8
Hilsea C Port 9 Q6
Hilston E R Yk 61 M7
Hilton Border 81 J4
Hilton Cambs 33 J4
Hilton Cumb 64 D4
Hilton Derbys 40 G2
Hilton Dorset 8 B6
Hilton Dur 65 L3
Hilton S on T 66 C5
Hilton Shrops 39 P3
Hilton of Cadboll Highld 107 P7
Hilton Park Services Staffs 40 C6
Himbleton Worcs 30 C3
Himley Staffs 39 Q4
Hincaster Cumb 63 K5
Hinchley Wood Surrey 21 J9
Hinckley Leics 41 K8
Hinderclay Suffk 34 G2
Hinderwell N York 66 H4
Hindhead Surrey 10 E3
Hindhead Tunnel Surrey 10 E3
Hindley Wigan 57 L7
Hindlip Worcs 39 Q9
Hindolveston Norfk 44 G4
Hindon Wilts 8 D2
Hindringham Norfk 44 G3
Hingham Norfk 44 G9
Hinstock Shrops 49 M9
Hintlesham Suffk 34 H7
Hinton Herefs 28 D2
Hinton Nhants 31 M4
Hinton S Glos 17 Q2
Hinton Shrops 38 H1
Hinton Ampner Hants 9 P2
Hinton Blewett BaNES 17 N5
Hinton Charterhouse BaNES 18 B8
Hinton-in-the-Hedges Nhants 31 M6
Hinton Martell Dorset 8 E6
Hinton on the Green Worcs 30 D6
Hinton Parva Swindn 19 J4
Hinton St George Somset 7 K1
Hinton St Mary Dorset 8 B4
Hinton Waldrist Oxon 19 L2
Hints Staffs 40 F6
Hinwick Bed 32 D5
Hinxhill Kent 13 K2
Hinxton Cambs 33 M7
Hinxworth Herts 32 H8
Hipperholme Calder 58 E8
Hipswell N York 65 L7
Hirn Abers 95 M2
Hirnant Powys 48 B10
Hirst Nthumb 73 M4
Hirst Courtney N York 59 N8
Hirwaun Rhondd 27 K7
Hiscott Devon 15 J7
Histon Cambs 33 M4
Hitcham Suffk 34 G6
Hitcham Causeway Suffk 34 G6
Hitcham Street Suffk 34 G6
Hitchin Herts 32 H10
Hither Green Gt Lon 21 M8
Hittisleigh Devon 5 P2
Hive E R Yk 60 E7
Hixon Staffs 40 D3
Hoaden Kent 23 N10
Hoar Cross Staffs 40 F3
Hoarwithy Herefs 28 G3
Hoath Kent 23 M9
Hobarris Shrops 38 F6
Hobkirk Border 80 D11
Hobson Dur 73 L9
Hoby Leics 41 P4
Hockering Norfk 44 H7
Hockerton Notts 51 Q9
Hockley Essex 22 G5
Hockley Heath Solhll 40 F11
Hockliffe C Beds 32 D10
Hockwold cum Wilton Norfk 44 C11
Hockworthy Devon 16 D11
Hoddesdon Herts 21 M2
Hoddlesden Bl w D 57 N4
Hoddom Cross D & G 71 J2
Hoddom Mains D & G 71 J2
Hodgeston Pembks 24 H8
Hodnet Shrops 49 L9
Hodsock Notts 51 N4
Hodsoll Street Kent 22 D10
Hodson Swindn 18 H5
Hodthorpe Derbys 51 M5
Hoe Norfk 44 G6
Hogben's Hill Kent 23 K11
Hoggeston Bucks 32 B10
Hoggrill's End Warwks 40 G8
Hoghton Lancs 57 L4
Hognaston Derbys 50 G10
Hogsthorpe Lincs 53 N8
Holbeach Lincs 43 K5
Holbeach Bank Lincs 43 K5
Holbeach Clough Lincs 43 K5
Holbeach Drove Lincs 43 K7
Holbeach Hurn Lincs 43 L5
Holbeach St Johns Lincs 43 K6
Holbeach St Mark's Lincs 43 L4
Holbeach St Matthew Lincs 43 L4
Holbeck Notts 51 M6
Holberrow Green Worcs 30 D3
Holbeton Devon 5 M9
Holborn Gt Lon 21 L7
Holbrook Derbys 51 J11
Holbrook Suffk 35 J9
Holbrooks Covtry 41 J10
Holbury Hants 9 M6
Holcombe Devon 6 C7
Holcombe Somset 17 P6
Holcombe Rogus Devon 16 E11
Holcot Nhants 32 B3
Holden Lancs 63 P11
Holdenby Nhants 31 P1
Holder's Green Essex 33 Q10
Holdgate Shrops 39 K4
Holdingham Lincs 42 F1
Holditch Dorset 7 J3
Holemoor Devon 14 H10
Holford Somset 16 F7
Holgate C York 59 N4
Holker Cumb 62 G6
Holkham Norfk 44 E2
Hollacombe Devon 14 G10
Holland Fen Lincs 52 H12
Holland-on-Sea Essex 35 K12
Hollandstoun Ork 111 i1
Hollee D & G 71 L2
Hollesley Suffk 35 M7
Hollicombe Torbay 6 B9
Hollingbourne Kent 22 G11
Hollingbury Br & H 11 L8
Hollingdon Bucks 32 C10
Hollington Derbys 50 G11
Hollington Staffs 50 D11
Hollingworth Tamesd 50 D2
Hollinsclough Staffs 50 E7
Hollins End Sheff 51 J4
Hollins Green Warrtn 57 M10
Hollinswood Wrekin 39 N1
Hollocombe Devon 15 L9
Holloway Derbys 51 J9
Holloway Gt Lon 21 L6
Hollowell Nhants 41 P11
Hollowmoor Heath Ches W 49 J2
Hollows D & G 79 N12
Hollybush Caerph 27 N7
Hollybush E Ayrs 76 G8
Hollybush Herefs 29 K2
Hollym E R Yk 61 N8
Holmbridge Kirk 58 E11
Holmbury St Mary Surrey 10 H2
Holmbush Cnwll 3 M5
Holmcroft Staffs 40 B3
Holme Cambs 42 H11
Holme Cumb 63 K6
Holme Kirk 58 E11
Holme N York 65 P10
Holme Notts 52 B10
Holme Chapel Lancs 57 Q3
Holme Hale Norfk 44 E8
Holme Lacy Herefs 28 G2
Holme Marsh Herefs 38 G10
Holme next the Sea Norfk 44 B2
Holme on the Wolds E R Yk 60 G5
Holme Pierrepont Notts 51 N11
Holmer Herefs 28 F1
Holmer Green Bucks 20 E4
Holme St Cuthbert Cumb 70 H6
Holmes Chapel Ches E 49 N3
Holmesfield Derbys 50 H5
Holmeswood Lancs 56 H5
Holmethorpe Surrey 21 L12
Holme upon Spalding Moor E R Yk 60 D6
Holmewood Derbys 51 K7
Holmfirth Kirk 58 F11
Holmhead E Ayrs 77 J7
Holmpton E R Yk 61 N9
Holmrook Cumb 62 C3
Holmside Dur 73 L10
Holne Devon 5 N6
Holnicote Somset 16 C6
Holsworthy Devon 14 F10
Holsworthy Beacon Devon 14 G9
Holt Dorset 8 F6
Holt Norfk 44 H3
Holt Wilts 18 C8
Holt Worcs 39 P9
Holt Wrexhm 48 H5
Holtby C York 59 P4
Holt End Worcs 40 E12
Holt Heath Worcs 39 P9
Holton Oxon 31 N11
Holton Somset 17 P10
Holton Suffk 35 N2
Holton cum Beckering Lincs 52 G7
Holton le Clay Lincs 53 J3
Holton le Moor Lincs 52 F4
Holton St Mary Suffk 34 H8
Holwell Dorset 7 Q1
Holwell Herts 32 G9
Holwell Leics 41 Q3
Holwell Oxon 30 G11
Holwick Dur 64 G3
Holybourne Hants 10 B2
Holyhead IoA 54 C5
Holy Island IoA 54 C5
Holy Island Nthumb 81 N5
Holy Island Nthumb 81 N6
Holymoorside Derbys 51 J7
Holyport W & M 20 E7
Holystone Nthumb 72 G1
Holytown N Lans 85 M10
Holywell C Beds 32 E12
Holywell Cambs 33 K3
Holywell Cnwll 2 H4
Holywell Dorset 7 N2
Holywell Flints 48 E1
Holywell Green Calder 58 E9
Holywell Lake Somset 16 F11
Holywell Row Suffk 34 B2
Holywood D & G 78 F11
Holywood Village D & G 78 F11
Homer Shrops 39 L2
Homersfield Suffk 45 L11
Homington Wilts 8 G3
Honeybourne Worcs 30 E5
Honeychurch Devon 15 L10
Honeystreet Wilts 18 G8
Honey Tye Suffk 34 F9
Honiley Warwks 40 G11
Honing Norfk 45 M5
Honingham Norfk 45 H7
Honington Lincs 42 D2
Honington Suffk 34 E2
Honington Warwks 30 H5
Honiton Devon 6 F3
Honley Kirk 58 F10
Hooe C Plym 5 K9
Hooe E Susx 12 E7
Hoo Green Ches E 57 N11
Hoohill Bpool 56 G2
Hook E R Yk 60 D8

Hook Gt Lon	21	J9
Hook Hants	20	B11
Hook Pembks	24	G6
Hook Wilts	18	F4
Hooke Dorset	7	M3
Hook Green Kent	12	D3
Hook Norton Oxon	31	J7
Hookway Devon	15	P11
Hooley Surrey	21	L11
Hoo St Werburgh Medway	22	F8
Hooton Levitt Rothm	51	M3
Hooton Pagnell Donc	59	L11
Hooton Roberts Rothm	51	L2
Hope Derbys	50	F4
Hope Devon	5	N11
Hope Flints	48	F4
Hope Staffs	50	E9
Hope Bagot Shrops	39	L7
Hope Bowdler Shrops	39	J4
Hopehouse Border	79	L5
Hopeman Moray	100	H2
Hope Mansell Herefs	28	H5
Hopesay Shrops	38	H5
Hope under Dinmore Herefs	39	K10
Hopgrove C York	59	N3
Hopperton N York	59	K3
Hopstone Shrops	39	P4
Hopton Derbys	50	H9
Hopton Staffs	40	C3
Hopton Suffk	34	G2
Hopton Cangeford Shrops	39	K6
Hopton Castle Shrops	38	G6
Hoptonheath Shrops	38	H6
Hopton on Sea Norfk	45	Q9
Hopton Wafers Shrops	39	M6
Hopwas Staffs	40	F6
Hopwood Worcs	40	D11
Hopwood Park Services		
Worcs	40	D11
Horam E Susx	12	C6
Horbling Lincs	42	G3
Horbury Wakefd	58	H9
Horden Dur	73	Q11
Hordle Hants	9	J8
Hordley Shrops	48	H8
Horfield Bristl	17	N2
Horham Suffk	35	K3
Horkesley Heath Essex	34	G10
Horkstow N Linc	60	G9
Horley Oxon	31	K5
Horley Surrey	11	L2
Hornblotton Green Somset	17	N9
Hornby Lancs	63	L8
Hornby N York	65	L8
Hornby N York	65	P6
Horncastle Lincs	53	J9
Hornchurch Gt Lon	21	Q6
Horncliffe Nthumb	81	K4
Horndean Border	81	J4
Horndean Hants	10	B7
Horndon Devon	5	L4
Horndon on the Hill Thurr	22	D6
Horne Surrey	11	M2
Horner Somset	16	B7
Horning Norfk	45	M6
Horninghold Leics	42	B10
Horninglow Staffs	40	G3
Horningsea Cambs	33	M4
Horningsham Wilts	18	B11
Horningtoft Norfk	44	F5
Horns Cross Devon	14	G7
Hornsea E R Yk	61	K5
Hornsey Gt Lon	21	L5
Hornton Oxon	31	K5
Horrabridge Devon	5	K6
Horringer Suffk	34	D4
Horrocksford Lancs	63	N12
Horsebridge Devon	5	J5
Horsebridge E Susx	12	C7
Horsebridge Hants	9	L2
Horsehay Wrekin	39	M1
Horseheath Cambs	33	P7
Horsehouse N York	65	J10
Horsell Surrey	20	F10
Horseman's Green Wrexhm	49	J7
Horsey Norfk	45	P5
Horsey Somset	17	J8
Horsford Norfk	45	K6
Horsforth Leeds	58	H6
Horsham W Susx	11	J4
Horsham Worcs	39	N9
Horsham St Faith Norfk	45	K7
Horsington Lincs	52	H9
Horsington Somset	17	Q10
Horsley Derbys	51	J11
Horsley Gloucs	29	L8
Horsley Nthumb	72	F2
Horsley Nthumb	73	J7
Horsleycross Street Essex	35	J10
Horsleyhill Border	80	C9
Horsley Woodhouse Derbys	51	K11
Horsmonden Kent	12	E2
Horspath Oxon	31	M12
Horstead Norfk	45	L6
Horsted Keynes W Susx	11	M5
Horton Bucks	32	D11
Horton Dorset	8	F6
Horton Lancs	63	Q11
Horton Nhants	32	B6
Horton S Glos	18	A4
Horton Somset	17	J12
Horton Staffs	50	C8
Horton Swans	26	C10
Horton W & M	20	G8
Horton Wilts	18	F7
Horton Wrekin	49	M11
Horton-cum-Studley Oxon	31	N10
Horton Green Ches W	49	J5
Horton-in-Ribblesdale N York	64	E12
Horton Kirby Kent	22	C9
Horwich Bolton	57	M6
Horwood Devon	15	J6
Hoscote Border	79	N6
Hose Leics	41	Q2
Hosh P & K	85	N2
Hoswick Shet	111	k5
Hotham E R Yk	60	F7
Hothfield Kent	13	J2
Hoton Leics	41	N11
Hough Ches E	49	N5
Hougham Lincs	42	C2
Hough Green Halton	57	J10
Hough-on-the-Hill Lincs	42	D2

Houghton Cambs	33	J3
Houghton Hants	9	K2
Houghton Pembks	24	H7
Houghton W Susx	10	G7
Houghton Conquest C Beds	32	F8
Houghton Green E Susx	12	H5
Houghton-le-Spring Sundld	73	N10
Houghton on the Hill Leics	41	P6
Houghton Regis C Beds	32	E10
Houghton St Giles Norfk	44	F3
Hound Green Hants	20	B10
Houndslow Border	80	E5
Houndwood Border	87	Q9
Hounslow Gt Lon	21	J8
Househill Highld	100	D4
Houses Hill Kirk	58	G10
Housieside Abers	103	J9
Houston Rens	84	G9
Houstry Highld	110	D8
Houton Ork	111	g2
Hove Br & H	11	L8
Hoveringham Notts	51	P10
Hoveton Norfk	45	M6
Hovingham N York	66	F11
How Caple Herefs	28	H3
Howden E R Yk	60	D8
Howden-le-Wear Dur	65	L2
Howe Highld	110	F4
Howe N York	65	P10
Howe Norfk	45	L9
Howe Green Essex	22	E3
Howegreen Essex	22	G3
Howell Lincs	42	G2
Howe of Teuchar Abers	102	G6
Howes D & G	71	K3
Howe Street Essex	22	E1
Howe Street Essex	34	B9
Howey Powys	38	C9
Howgate Cumb	70	G10
Howgate Mdloth	86	F10
Howick Nthumb	81	Q10
Howlett End Essex	33	P9
Howley Somset	6	H2
How Mill Cumb	71	Q4
Howmore W Isls	111	a5
Hownam Border	80	G9
Howsham N Linc	52	E3
Howsham N York	60	C2
Howtel Nthumb	81	J7
How Wood Herts	21	J3
Howwood Rens	84	G10
Hoxa Ork	111	h3
Hoxne Suffk	35	K2
Hoy Ork	111	g3
Hoylake Wirral	56	E10
Hoyland Barns	51	J1
Hoylandswaine Barns	58	H12
Hubberston Pembks	24	F7
Huby N York	58	H5
Huby N York	59	M2
Hucclecote Gloucs	29	M5
Hucking Kent	22	G10
Hucknall Notts	51	M10
Huddersfield Kirk	58	F10
Huddington Worcs	30	C3
Hudswell N York	65	K7
Huggate E R Yk	60	F3
Hughenden Valley Bucks	20	D4
Hughley Shrops	39	K3
Hugh Town IoS	2	c2
Huish Devon	15	J9
Huish Wilts	18	G7
Huish Champflower Somset	16	E9
Huish Episcopi Somset	17	L10
Hùisinis W Isls	111	b3
Huisinish W Isls	111	b3
Hulcott Bucks	32	C12
Hulham Devon	6	D6
Hulland Derbys	50	G10
Hulland Ward Derbys	50	G10
Hullavington Wilts	18	D4
Hullbridge Essex	22	F4
Hull, Kingston upon C KuH	61	J8
Hulme Manch	57	Q9
Hulme Staffs	50	C10
Hulme Wartn	57	L9
Hulme End Staffs	50	E8
Hulme Walfield Ches E	49	Q3
Hulton Lane Ends Bolton	57	M7
Hulverstone IoW	9	L9
Hulver Street Suffk	45	P11
Humber Bridge N Linc	60	H8
Humberside Airport N Linc	61	J11
Humberston NE Lin	53	K3
Humberstone C Leic	41	N6
Humbie E Loth	87	J7
Humbleton E R Yk	61	L7
Humby Lincs	42	E4
Hume Border	80	F6
Humshaugh Nthumb	72	G6
Huna Highld	110	G2
Huncote Leics	41	M7
Hundalee Border	80	E9
Hunderthwaite Dur	64	H4
Hundleby Lincs	53	L9
Hundleton Pembks	24	G8
Hundon Suffk	34	C7
Hundred House Powys	38	C10
Hungarton Leics	41	P6
Hungerford Somset	16	E7
Hungerford W Berk	19	L6
Hungerford Newtown W Berk	19	L6
Hungerstone Herefs	28	E2
Hunmanby N York	67	N11
Hunningham Warwks	31	J1
Hunsbury Hill Nhants	31	Q3
Hunsdon Herts	21	N1
Hunsingore N York	59	K4
Hunslet Leeds	58	H7
Hunsonby Cumb	64	B1
Hunstanton Norfk	43	Q3
Hunstanworth Dur	72	G10
Hunsterson Ches E	49	M6
Hunston Suffk	34	F3
Hunston W Susx	10	D9
Hunstrete BaNES	17	P4
Hunsworth Kirk	58	F8
Hunter's Quay Ag & B	84	C7
Huntham Somset	17	J10
Hunthill Lodge Angus	94	H7
Huntingdon Cambs	33	J3
Huntingfield Suffk	35	M2
Huntington C York	59	N3

Huntington Ches W	48	H3
Huntington E Loth	87	J7
Huntington Herefs	38	F10
Huntington Staffs	40	C5
Huntingtowerfield P & K	92	G9
Huntley Gloucs	29	J5
Huntly Abers	102	C7
Hunton Kent	22	E12
Hunton N York	65	L8
Huntscott Somset	16	C7
Huntsham Devon	16	D11
Huntshaw Devon	15	J7
Huntspill Somset	17	J7
Huntstile Somset	16	H9
Huntworth Somset	17	J9
Hunwick Dur	65	L2
Hunworth Norfk	44	H3
Hurdcott Wilts	8	H1
Hurdsfield Ches E	50	B6
Hurley W & M	20	D6
Hurley Warwks	40	G8
Hurley Common Warwks	40	G7
Hurlford E Ayrs	76	H4
Hurn BCP	8	G7
Hursley Hants	9	M3
Hurst Wokham	20	C8
Hurstbourne Priors Hants	19	M10
Hurstbourne Tarrant Hants	19	L9
Hurst Green E Susx	12	E5
Hurst Green Essex	34	H12
Hurst Green Lancs	57	M2
Hurst Green Surrey	11	N12
Hurst Hill Dudley	40	B4
Hurstpierpoint W Susx	11	L6
Hurstwood Lancs	57	Q3
Hurtiso Ork	111	h2
Hurworth-on-Tees Darltn	65	N5
Hurworth Place Darltn	65	N5
Husbands Bosworth Leics	41	N10
Husborne Crawley C Beds	32	D9
Husthwaite N York	66	D11
Huthwaite Notts	51	L8
Huttoft Lincs	53	N8
Hutton Border	81	J4
Hutton E R Yk	60	H4
Hutton Essex	22	D4
Hutton Lancs	57	J4
Hutton N Som	17	J4
Hutton Buscel N York	67	L10
Hutton Conyers N York	65	N11
Hutton Cranswick E R Yk	60	H4
Hutton End Cumb	71	P7
Hutton Henry Dur	65	Q1
Hutton-le-Hole N York	66	G9
Hutton Lowcross R & Cl	66	E5
Hutton Magna Dur	65	K5
Hutton Roof Cumb	63	K6
Hutton Roof Cumb	71	M8
Hutton Rudby N York	66	C6
Hutton Sessay N York	66	C11
Hutton Wandesley N York	59	L4
Huxham Devon	6	C4
Huxley Ches W	49	K3
Huyton Knows	57	J10
Hycemoor Cumb	62	C4
Hyde Tamesd	50	C2
Hyde Heath Bucks	20	E4
Hyde Lea Staffs	40	B4
Hylands House & Park Essex	22	D3
Hyndford Bridge S Lans	78	E1
Hynish Ag & B	88	B8
Hyssington Powys	38	F4
Hythe Essex	34	G10
Hythe Hants	9	M6
Hythe Kent	13	M3
Hythe End W & M	20	G8

I

Ibberton Dorset	8	B6
Ible Derbys	50	G9
Ibsley Hants	8	H5
Ibstock Leics	41	K5
Ibstone Bucks	20	C5
Ibthorpe Hants	19	L9
Iburndale N York	67	J6
Ibworth Hants	19	P9
Ichrachan Ag & B	90	D9
Ickburgh Norfk	44	D10
Ickenham Gt Lon	20	H6
Ickford Bucks	31	N11
Ickham Kent	23	N10
Ickleford Herts	32	H9
Icklesham E Susx	12	G6
Ickleton Cambs	33	M7
Icklingham Suffk	34	C3
Ickornshaw N York	58	C5
Ickwell Green C Beds	32	G7
Icomb Gloucs	30	G9
Idbury Oxon	30	G9
Iddesleigh Devon	15	K9
Ide Devon	6	B5
Ideford Devon	6	B7
Ide Hill Kent	21	P11
Iden E Susx	12	H5
Iden Green Kent	12	E3
Iden Green Kent	12	F4
Idle C Brad	58	F6
Idless Cnwll	3	J6
Idlicote Warwks	30	H5
Idmiston Wilts	18	H12
Idole Carmth	25	P6
Idridgehay Derbys	50	H10
Idrigill Highld	104	E9
Idstone Oxon	19	J4
Iffley Oxon	31	M12
Ifield W Susx	11	K3
Ifold W Susx	10	G4
Iford BCP	8	G8
Iford E Susx	11	N8
Ifton Mons	28	F10
Ightfield Shrops	49	L7
Ightham Kent	22	C11
Ilam Staffs	50	F10
Ilchester Somset	17	M10
Ilderton Nthumb	81	L9
Ilford Gt Lon	21	N6
Ilford Somset	17	K11
Ilfracombe Devon	15	J3
Ilkeston Derbys	51	L11
Ilketshall St Andrew Suffk	45	N11

Ilketshall St Margaret Suffk	45	M11
Ilkley C Brad	58	E5
Illand Cnwll	4	G5
Illey Dudley	40	C10
Illogan Cnwll	2	G7
Illston on the Hill Leics	41	P7
Ilmer Bucks	20	C3
Ilmington Warwks	30	G5
Ilminster Somset	17	J12
Ilsington Devon	5	Q5
Ilston Swans	26	D10
Ilton N York	65	L11
Ilton Somset	17	J11
Imachar N Ayrs	75	N4
Immingham NE Lin	61	K10
Immingham Dock NE Lin	61	K10
Impington Cambs	33	M4
Ince Ches W	57	J12
Ince Blundell Sefton	56	G8
Ince-in-Makerfield Wigan	57	J7
Inchbae Lodge Hotel Highld	106	G8
Inchbare Angus	95	K8
Inchberry Moray	101	L4
Incheril Highld	105	Q9
Inchinnan Rens	84	H8
Inchlaggan Highld	98	B8
Inchmichael P & K	93	J9
Inchmore Highld	107	J12
Inchnadamph Highld	108	E10
Inchture P & K	93	K9
Inchyra P & K	92	H10
Indian Queens Cnwll	3	K4
Ingatestone Essex	22	D4
Ingbirchworth Barns	58	G11
Ingestre Staffs	40	C3
Ingham Lincs	52	D6
Ingham Norfk	45	N5
Ingham Suffk	34	E3
Ingham Corner Norfk	45	N5
Ingleby Derbys	41	J3
Ingleby Arncliffe N York	66	C7
Ingleby Barwick S on T	66	C5
Ingleby Greenhow N York	66	E6
Ingleigh Green Devon	15	K10
Inglesbatch BaNES	17	Q4
Inglesham Swindn	18	H2
Ingleston D & G	70	F3
Ingleton Dur	65	L4
Ingleton N York	63	M7
Inglewhite Lancs	57	K2
Ingoe Nthumb	73	J6
Ingol Lancs	57	K3
Ingoldisthorpe Norfk	44	B4
Ingoldmells Lincs	53	N9
Ingoldsby Lincs	42	E4
Ingram Nthumb	81	L10
Ingrave Essex	22	D5
Ingrow C Brad	58	D6
Ings Cumb	63	J3
Ingst S Glos	28	G10
Ingthorpe Rutlnd	42	E8
Ingworth Norfk	45	K4
Inkberrow Worcs	30	D3
Inkersall Green Derbys	51	K6
Inkhorn Abers	103	J7
Inkpen W Berk	19	L7
Inkstack Highld	110	F2
Innellan Ag & B	84	C8
Innerleithen Border	79	M2
Innerleven Fife	86	H3
Innermessan D & G	68	E6
Innerwick E Loth	87	N7
Innesmill Moray	101	K3
Insch Abers	102	E9
Insh Highld	99	M8
Inshes Highld	99	K1
Inskip Lancs	57	J2
Instow Devon	14	H6
Intake Sheff	51	K4
Inver Abers	94	D4
Inver Highld	107	P6
Inver P & K	92	F7
Inverailort Highld	97	K12
Inverallochy Abers	103	L3
Inveran Highld	107	J3
Inveraray Ag & B	84	B2
Inverarish Highld	96	G3
Inverarity Angus	93	M6
Inverarnan Stirlg	91	J11
Inverasdale Highld	105	M5
Inverbeg Ag & B	84	F4
Inverbervie Abers	95	N7
Inverboyndie Abers	102	E3
Invercreran Lodge Ag & B	90	D7
Inverdruie Highld	99	N6
Inveresk E Loth	86	G7
Inveresragan Ag & B	90	D8
Inverey Abers	94	B4
Inverfarigaig Highld	98	G4
Inverfolla Ag & B	90	C7
Invergarry Highld	98	D8
Invergeldie P & K	91	Q10
Invergloy Highld	98	C10
Invergordon Highld	107	L8
Invergowrie P & K	93	L9
Inverguseran Highld	97	K8
Inverie Highld	97	K9
Inverinan Ag & B	90	D11
Inverinate Highld	97	N5
Inverkeilor Angus	93	R6
Inverkeithing Fife	86	D5
Inverkeithny Abers	102	E6
Inverkip Inver	84	D8
Inverkirkaig Highld	108	B10
Inverlael Highld	106	C5
Inverlair Highld	98	D11
Inverliever Lodge Ag & B	83	N2
Inverlochy Ag & B	90	G10
Invermark Angus	94	G6
Invermoriston Highld	98	F5
Invernaver Highld	109	M4
Inverneill Ag & B	83	M4
Inverness Highld	107	L12
Inverness Airport Highld	107	M11
Invernettie Abers	103	M6
Invernoaden Ag & B	84	C4
Inveroran Hotel Ag & B	90	H7
Inverquharity Angus	93	M4
Inverquhomery Abers	103	L6
Inverroy Highld	98	C11
Inversanda Highld	90	C4

Invershiel Highld	97	N6
Invershin Highld	107	J3
Invershore Highld	110	F8
Inversnaid Hotel Stirlg	84	F2
Inverugie Abers	103	M6
Inveruglas Ag & B	84	F2
Inveruglass Highld	99	M8
Inverurie Abers	102	G10
Inwardleigh Devon	15	K11
Inworth Essex	34	E12
Iochdar W Isls	111	a5
Iona Ag & B	88	G10
Iping W Susx	10	D5
iPort Logistics Park Donc	51	N2
Ipplepen Devon	5	Q7
Ipsden Oxon	19	Q4
Ipstones Staffs	50	D10
Ipswich Suffk	35	J7
Irby Wirral	56	F11
Irby in the Marsh Lincs	53	M10
Irby upon Humber NE Lin	52	H3
Irchester Nhants	32	D4
Ireby Cumb	71	K7
Ireby Lancs	63	M7
Ireleth Cumb	62	E6
Ireshopeburn Dur	72	F12
Irlam Salfd	57	N9
Irnham Lincs	42	E5
Iron Acton S Glos	29	J11
Ironbridge Wrekin	39	M2
Ironbridge Gorge Wrekin	39	M2
Ironmacannie D & G	69	P4
Ironville Derbys	51	K9
Irstead Norfk	45	M6
Irthington Cumb	71	P4
Irthlingborough Nhants	32	D3
Irton N York	67	L10
Irvine N Ayrs	76	F4
Isauld Highld	110	A3
Isbister Shet	111	k2
Isbister Shet	111	m3
Isfield E Susx	11	N6
Isham Nhants	32	C3
Isington Hants	10	C2
Islay Ag & B	82	E10
Islay Airport Ag & B	74	D3
Isle Abbotts Somset	17	J11
Isle Brewers Somset	17	K11
Isleham Cambs	33	Q2
Isle of Dogs Gt Lon	21	M7
Isle of Grain Medway	22	G7
Isle of Lewis W Isls	111	d2
Isle of Man IoM	56	c4
Isle of Man Ronaldsway		
Airport IoM	56	b7
Isle of Mull Ag & B	89	M8
Isle of Purbeck Dorset	8	E10
Isle of Sheppey Kent	23	J9
Isle of Skye Highld	96	E3
Isle of Thanet Kent	23	P9
Isle of Walney Cumb	62	E8
Isle of Whithorn D & G	69	L10
Isle of Wight IoW	9	N9
Isleornsay Highld	97	J7
Isles of Scilly IoS	2	c2
Isles of Scilly St Mary's		
Airport IoS	2	c2
Islesteps D & G	70	F2
Isleworth Gt Lon	21	J8
Isley Walton Leics	41	K3
Islibhig W Isls	111	b2
Islington Gt Lon	21	L6
Islip Nhants	32	E2
Islip Oxon	31	M10
Islivig W Isls	111	b2
Isombridge Wrekin	49	L11
Istead Rise Kent	22	D9
Itchen Abbas Hants	9	N2
Itchen Stoke Hants	9	P2
Itchingfield W Susx	11	J4
Itteringham Norfk	45	J4
Itton Mons	28	F9
Itton Common Mons	28	F9
Ivegill Cumb	71	N6
Iver Bucks	20	G7
Iver Heath Bucks	20	G6
Iveston Dur	73	K10
Ivinghoe Bucks	32	D12
Ivinghoe Aston Bucks	32	D12
Ivington Herefs	39	J10
Ivybridge Devon	5	M8
Ivychurch Kent	13	K5
Ivy Hatch Kent	22	C11
Iwade Kent	22	H9
Iwerne Courtney Dorset	8	C5
Iwerne Minster Dorset	8	C5
Ixworth Suffk	34	F3
Ixworth Thorpe Suffk	34	F3

J

Jack-in-the-Green Devon	6	D4
Jackton S Lans	85	K11
Jacobstow Cnwll	4	D2
Jacobstowe Devon	15	K10
Jameston Pembks	25	J8
Jamestown Highld	106	H10
Jamestown W Duns	84	G6
Janetstown Highld	110	E8
Janetstown Highld	110	G5
Jardine Hall D & G	78	H10
Jarrow S Tyne	73	N7
Jasper's Green Essex	34	C10
Jawcraig Falk	85	P7
Jaywick Essex	23	M1
Jedburgh Border	80	E9
Jeffreyston Pembks	25	J7
Jemimaville Highld	107	M8
Jerbourg Guern	6	c2
Jersey Jersey	7	b1
Jersey Airport Jersey	7	a2
Jesmond N u Ty	73	M7
Jevington E Susx	12	C9
Jockey End Herts	20	G2
Jodrell Bank Ches E	49	P2
John Lennon Airport Lpool	56	H11
John o' Groats Highld	110	H2
Johnshaven Abers	95	N8
Johnston Pembks	24	G6
Johnstone D & G	79	L8

Johnstone Rens....84 G9
Johnstonebridge D & G....78 H9
Johnstown Carmth....25 P5
Johnstown Wrexhm....48 F6
Joppa C Edin....86 G7
Joppa Cerdgn....37 J7
Joppa S Ayrs....76 G7
Jordanston Pembks....24 G3
Joyden's Wood Kent....21 P8
Juniper Nthumb....72 G8
Juniper Green C Edin....86 E8
Jura Ag & B....82 G6
Jurassic Coast Devon....7 J5
Jurby IoM....56 c2

K

Kaber Cumb....64 E5
Kaimend S Lans....86 B11
Kames Ag & B....83 P8
Kames E Ayrs....77 L6
Kea Cnwll....3 J7
Keadby N Linc....60 E10
Keal Cotes Lincs....53 K10
Kearsley Bolton....57 N7
Kearsney Kent....13 P2
Kearstwick Cumb....63 L6
Kedington Suffk....34 B7
Kedleston Derbys....50 H11
Keelby Lincs....61 K11
Keele Staffs....49 P6
Keele Services Staffs....49 P6
Keelham C Brad....58 E7
Keeston Pembks....24 F5
Keevil Wilts....18 D8
Kegworth Leics....41 L3
Kehelland Cnwll....2 F7
Keig Abers....102 D10
Keighley C Brad....58 D6
Keilarsbrae Clacks....85 P4
Keillour P & K....92 E9
Keiloch Abers....94 C4
Keils Ag & B....82 G8
Keinton Mandeville Somset....17 M9
Keir Mill D & G....78 E9
Keisley Cumb....64 D3
Keiss Highld....110 G4
Keith Moray....101 N5
Keithick P & K....93 J7
Keithock Angus....95 K8
Keithtown Highld....106 H10
Kelbrook Lancs....58 B5
Kelby Lincs....42 E2
Keld N York....64 F7
Kelfield N York....59 N6
Kelham Notts....51 Q9
Kelhead D & G....71 J2
Kellamergh Lancs....56 H3
Kellas Angus....93 M8
Kellas Moray....101 J5
Kellaton Devon....5 Q11
Kelling Norfk....44 H2
Kellington N York....59 M8
Kelloe Dur....73 N12
Kelloholm D & G....77 M8
Kells Cumb....70 F11
Kelly Devon....5 J4
Kelmarsh Nhants....41 Q10
Kelmscott Oxon....19 J2
Kelsale Suffk....35 N4
Kelsall Ches W....49 K2
Kelshall Herts....33 K9
Kelsick Cumb....71 K5
Kelso Border....80 G7
Kelstedge Derbys....51 J7
Kelstern Lincs....53 J5
Kelston BaNES....17 Q3
Keltneyburn P & K....92 B6
Kelton D & G....70 D4
Kelty Fife....86 D4
Kelvedon Essex....34 E11
Kelvedon Hatch Essex....22 C4
Kelynack Cnwll....2 B9
Kemback Fife....93 M11
Kemberton Shrops....39 N2
Kemble Gloucs....29 P8
Kemerton Worcs....29 N2
Kemeys Commander Mons....28 D7
Kemnay Abers....102 F11
Kempley Gloucs....29 J3
Kempley Green Gloucs....29 J3
Kempsey Worcs....39 Q11
Kempsford Gloucs....18 H2
Kempshott Hants....19 P10
Kempston Bed....32 E7
Kempton Shrops....38 G5
Kemp Town Br & H....11 M8
Kemsing Kent....22 B10
Kenardington Kent....13 J4
Kenchester Herefs....38 H12
Kencot Oxon....30 G12
Kendal Cumb....63 K4
Kenfig Brdgnd....26 H11
Kenfig Hill Brdgnd....26 H11
Kenilworth Warwks....40 H12
Kenley Gt Lon....21 L10
Kenley Shrops....39 K3
Kenmore Highld....105 L10
Kenmore P & K....92 B6
Kenn Devon....6 C6
Kenn N Som....17 K3
Kennacraig Ag & B....83 M9
Kennall Vale Cnwll....2 H8
Kennerleigh Devon....15 P10
Kennet Clacks....85 Q5
Kennethmont Abers....102 D9
Kennett Cambs....34 B3
Kennford Devon....6 C5
Kenninghall Norfk....44 G11
Kennington Kent....13 K2
Kennington Oxon....19 N1
Kennoway Fife....86 G2
Kenny Somset....17 J11
Kenny Hill Suffk....33 Q2
Kennythorpe N York....60 D2
Kenovay Ag & B....88 C7
Kensaleyre Highld....104 F11
Kensington Gt Lon....21 L7
Kensington Palace Gt Lon....21 K7
Kensworth Common C Beds....32 E12
Kentallen Highld....90 D5

Kentchurch Herefs....28 E4
Kentford Suffk....34 B4
Kentisbeare Devon....6 E2
Kentisbury Devon....15 L4
Kentish Town Gt Lon....21 L6
Kentmere Cumb....63 J2
Kenton Devon....6 C6
Kenton Gt Lon....21 J6
Kenton N u Ty....73 L7
Kenton Suffk....35 K4
Kenton Bankfoot N u Ty....73 L7
Kentra Highld....89 N3
Kentsboro Hants....19 K11
Kent's Green Gloucs....29 K4
Kent's Oak Hants....9 K3
Kenwyn Cnwll....3 J6
Keoldale Highld....108 G3
Keppoch Highld....97 M5
Kepwick N York....66 C8
Keresley Covtry....40 H10
Kerrera Ag & B....89 Q10
Kerry Powys....38 D4
Kerrycroy Ag & B....84 B10
Kersbrook Devon....6 E4
Kersey Suffk....34 G7
Kershader W Isls....111 d4
Kerswell Devon....6 E2
Kerswell Green Worcs....39 Q11
Kesgrave Suffk....35 K7
Kessingland Suffk....45 Q11
Kestle Cnwll....3 L6
Kestle Mill Cnwll....3 J4
Keston Gt Lon....21 N9
Keswick Cumb....71 L10
Keswick Norfk....45 K8
Kettering Nhants....32 C2
Ketteringham Norfk....45 J9
Kettins P & K....93 J7
Kettlebaston Suffk....34 F6
Kettlebridge Fife....86 G2
Kettlebrook Staffs....40 G6
Kettleburgh Suffk....35 L5
Kettleholm D & G....79 J12
Kettleshulme Ches E....50 C5
Kettlesing N York....58 G3
Kettlesing Bottom N York....58 G3
Kettlestone Norfk....44 F4
Kettlethorpe Lincs....52 C8
Kettletoft Ork....111 i1
Kettlewell N York....64 H11
Ketton Rutlnd....42 E8
Kew Gt Lon....21 J7
Kew Royal Botanic Gardens Gt Lon....21 J7
Kewstoke N Som....17 J4
Kexby C York....60 C4
Kexby Lincs....52 C6
Key Green Ches E....50 B7
Keyham Leics....41 P6
Keyhaven Hants....9 K8
Keyingham E R Yk....61 L8
Keymer W Susx....11 L7
Keynsham BaNES....17 P3
Keysoe Bed....32 F4
Keysoe Row Bed....32 F5
Keyston Cambs....32 F2
Keyworth Notts....41 N2
Kibblesworth Gatesd....73 M9
Kibworth Beauchamp Leics....41 P8
Kibworth Harcourt Leics....41 P8
Kidbrooke Gt Lon....21 N7
Kidderminster Worcs....39 Q6
Kidlington Oxon....31 L10
Kidmore End Oxon....20 B7
Kidsdale D & G....69 L10
Kidsgrove Staffs....49 Q5
Kidwelly Carmth....25 P7
Kiel Crofts Ag & B....90 C8
Kielder Nthumb....72 B3
Kielder Forest....72 B4
Kiells Ag & B....82 F8
Kilbarchan Rens....84 G9
Kilbeg Highld....97 J8
Kilberry Ag & B....83 K9
Kilbirnie N Ayrs....84 E11
Kilbride Ag & B....83 L7
Kilbride Ag & B....83 Q9
Kilbuiack Moray....100 G4
Kilburn Derbys....51 J10
Kilburn Gt Lon....21 K6
Kilburn N York....66 D10
Kilby Leics....41 N8
Kilchamaig Ag & B....83 M10
Kilchattan Ag & B....82 E4
Kilchattan Ag & B....84 B11
Kilcheran Ag & B....89 Q8
Kilchoan Highld....89 K4
Kilchoman Ag & B....82 C9
Kilchrenan Ag & B....90 E10
Kilconquhar Fife....87 J2
Kilcot Gloucs....29 J4
Kilcoy Highld....107 J11
Kilcreggan Ag & B....84 D6
Kildale N York....66 E5
Kildalloig Ag & B....75 L8
Kildary Highld....107 M7
Kildavaig Ag & B....83 Q9
Kildavanan Ag & B....83 Q9
Kildonan Highld....109 Q10
Kildonan N Ayrs....75 Q8
Kildonan Lodge Highld....109 Q10
Kildonnan Highld....96 F11
Kildrochet House D & G....68 E7
Kildrummy Abers....101 N10
Kildwick N York....58 D5
Kilfinan Ag & B....83 P7
Kilfinnan Highld....98 C9
Kilgetty Pembks....25 K7
Kilgrammie S Ayrs....76 E10
Kilgwrrwg Common Mons....28 F8
Kilham E R Yk....60 H2
Kilkenneth Ag & B....88 B7
Kilkenzie Ag & B....75 K7
Kilkerran Ag & B....75 L8
Kilkhampton Cnwll....14 D9
Killamarsh Derbys....51 L5
Killay Swans....26 H3
Killean Ag & B....75 K5
Killearn Stirlg....85 H3
Killen Highld....107 L10
Killerby Darltn....65 L4
Killerton Devon....6 C3
Killichonan P & K....91 N4

Killiechonate Highld....98 C11
Killiechronan Ag & B....89 L7
Killiecrankie P & K....92 D3
Killilan Highld....97 N4
Killimster Highld....110 G4
Killin Stirlg....91 N9
Killinghall N York....58 H3
Killington Cumb....63 L5
Killington Lake Services Cumb....63 L4
Killingworth N Tyne....73 M6
Killochyett Border....87 J12
Kilmacolm Inver....84 F8
Kilmahog Stirlg....85 K2
Kilmahumaig Ag & B....83 L4
Kilmaluag Highld....104 F7
Kilmany Fife....93 L10
Kilmarnock E Ayrs....76 G4
Kilmartin Ag & B....83 M3
Kilmaurs E Ayrs....76 G3
Kilmelford Ag & B....83 M1
Kilmersdon Somset....17 Q6
Kilmeston Hants....9 P3
Kilmichael Ag & B....75 K7
Kilmichael Glassary Ag & B....83 N4
Kilmichael of Inverlussa Ag & B....83 L6
Kilmington Devon....6 H4
Kilmington Wilts....18 B12
Kilmington Common Wilts....8 B1
Kilmington Street Wilts....8 B1
Kilmorack Highld....106 H12
Kilmore Ag & B....90 B10
Kilmore Highld....97 J8
Kilmory Ag & B....83 K7
Kilmory Highld....89 L3
Kilmory N Ayrs....75 P8
Kilmuir Highld....104 C11
Kilmuir Highld....104 E8
Kilmuir Highld....107 L11
Kilmuir Highld....107 M7
Kilmun Ag & B....84 C6
Kilnave Ag & B....82 D8
Kilncadzow S Lans....77 P2
Kildown Kent....12 E3
Kilninver Ag & B....89 Q11
Kilnsea E R Yk....61 P10
Kilnsey N York....58 C1
Kilnwick E R Yk....60 G4
Kiloran Ag & B....82 E4
Kilpatrick N Ayrs....75 P8
Kilpeck Herefs....28 E3
Kilpin E R Yk....60 D8
Kilrenny Fife....87 L2
Kilsby Nhants....41 M12
Kilspindie P & K....93 J9
Kilstay D & G....68 F10
Kilsyth N Lans....85 M7
Kiltarlity Highld....98 G2
Kilton R & Cl....66 F4
Kilton Thorpe R & Cl....66 F4
Kilvaxter Highld....104 E8
Kilve Somset....16 F7
Kilvington Notts....42 B2
Kilwinning N Ayrs....76 E3
Kimberley Norfk....44 H8
Kimberley Notts....51 L11
Kimberworth Rothm....51 K3
Kimblesworth Dur....73 M10
Kimbolton Cambs....32 F4
Kimbolton Herefs....39 K9
Kimcote Leics....41 N9
Kimmeridge Dorset....8 D10
Kimpton Hants....19 J10
Kimpton Herts....32 H11
Kinbrace Highld....109 Q6
Kinbuck Stirlg....85 N3
Kincaple Fife....93 N11
Kincardine Fife....85 Q5
Kincardine Highld....107 K5
Kincardine Bridge Fife....85 Q5
Kincardine O'Neil Abers....95 K3
Kincorth C Aber....95 Q2
Kincorth House Moray....100 F3
Kincraig Highld....99 M7
Kincraigie P & K....92 E6
Kindallachan P & K....92 E6
Kinerarach Ag & B....75 J2
Kineton Gloucs....30 D4
Kineton Warwks....31 J4
Kinfauns P & K....92 H10
Kingarth Ag & B....84 B10
Kingcausie Abers....95 P3
Kingcoed Mons....28 E7
Kingerby Lincs....52 F5
Kingham Oxon....30 H8
Kingholm Quay D & G....70 F2
Kinghorn Fife....86 F5
Kinglassie Fife....86 E3
Kingoodie P & K....93 L9
Kingsand Cnwll....5 J9
Kingsbarns Fife....93 Q12
Kingsbridge Devon....5 P10
Kingsbridge Somset....16 D8
King's Bromley Staffs....40 E4
Kingsburgh Highld....104 E10
Kingsbury Gt Lon....21 J5
Kingsbury Warwks....40 G8
Kingsbury Episcopi Somset....17 L11
King's Caple Herefs....28 G3
Kingsclere Hants....19 N8
King's Cliffe Nhants....42 E10
Kings Clipstone Notts....51 N7
Kingscote Gloucs....29 L9
Kingscott Devon....15 J8
King's Coughton Warwks....30 E3
Kingscross N Ayrs....75 Q6
Kingsdon Somset....17 M10
Kingsdown Kent....13 Q1
Kingsdown Swindn....18 H3
Kingsdown Wilts....18 B7
Kingseat Abers....103 J9
Kingseat Fife....86 D4
Kingsey Bucks....20 C3
Kingsfold W Susx....11 J4
Kingsford E Ayrs....76 G3
Kingsford Worcs....39 P5
Kingsgate Kent....23 Q8
Kingshall Street Suffk....34 F4
King's Heath Birm....40 E10
Kings Hill Kent....22 E10
King's Hill Wsall....40 C8

Kings House Hotel Highld....90 H5
Kingshurst Solhll....40 F9
Kingskerswell Devon....6 B8
Kingskettle Fife....86 G1
Kingsland Herefs....39 J9
Kingsland IoA....54 C5
Kings Langley Herts....20 H3
Kingsley Ches W....49 K1
Kingsley Hants....10 C3
Kingsley Staffs....50 D10
Kingsley Green W Susx....10 E4
Kingsley Park Nhants....31 Q2
King's Lynn Norfk....43 P6
Kings Meaburn Cumb....64 B4
King's Mills Guern....6 b2
Kingsmuir Angus....93 N6
Kings Muir Border....79 L2
Kingsmuir Fife....87 K1
Kingsnorth Kent....13 J3
King's Norton Birm....40 D10
King's Norton Leics....41 P7
Kings Nympton Devon....15 M8
King's Pyon Herefs....38 H11
Kings Ripton Cambs....33 J2
King's Somborne Hants....9 L2
King's Stag Dorset....7 Q1
King's Stanley Gloucs....29 L7
King's Sutton Nhants....31 L6
Kingstanding Birm....40 E8
Kingsteignton Devon....6 B8
Kingsthorne Herefs....28 F3
Kingsthorpe Nhants....31 Q2
Kingston Cambs....33 K6
Kingston Cnwll....4 H5
Kingston Devon....5 M10
Kingston Devon....7 Q2
Kingston Dorset....8 E10
Kingston E Loth....87 K6
Kingston IoW....9 N10
Kingston Kent....23 M12
Kingston Bagpuize Oxon....19 L2
Kingston Blount Oxon....20 B4
Kingston by Sea W Susx....11 K8
Kingston Deverill Wilts....18 C12
Kingstone Herefs....28 E2
Kingstone Somset....17 K12
Kingstone Staffs....40 D2
Kingston Lacy House & Gardens Dorset....8 E7
Kingston Lisle Oxon....19 K4
Kingston near Lewes E Susx....11 N8
Kingston on Soar Notts....41 L2
Kingston on Spey Moray....101 L3
Kingston Russell Dorset....7 N5
Kingston St Mary Somset....16 G9
Kingston Seymour N Som....17 K3
Kingston upon Hull C KuH....61 J8
Kingston upon Thames Gt Lon....21 J9
King's Walden Herts....32 G11
Kingswear Devon....6 B11
Kingswells C Aber....95 P1
Kings Weston Bristl....28 G12
Kingswinford Dudley....40 B9
Kingswood Bucks....31 P9
Kingswood Gloucs....29 K9
Kingswood S Glos....17 P2
Kingswood Somset....16 F8
Kingswood Surrey....21 K11
Kingswood Warwks....40 F12
Kingswood Common Staffs....39 Q2
Kings Worthy Hants....9 N2
Kingthorpe Lincs....52 G8
Kington Herefs....38 F10
Kington S Glos....28 H10
Kington Worcs....30 C3
Kington Langley Wilts....18 D5
Kington Magna Dorset....8 B3
Kington St Michael Wilts....18 D5
Kingussie Highld....99 L8
Kingweston Somset....17 M9
Kinharrachie Abers....103 J8
Kinharvie D & G....70 F3
Kinkell Bridge P & K....92 D11
Kinknockie Abers....103 L7
Kinleith C Edin....86 E8
Kinlet Shrops....39 N6
Kinloch Highld....96 E9
Kinloch Highld....108 G3
Kinloch Highld....109 K5
Kinloch P & K....92 H6
Kinlochard Stirlg....84 H3
Kinlochbervie Highld....108 E4
Kinlocheil Highld....90 D1
Kinlochewe Highld....105 Q9
Kinloch Hourn Highld....97 N8
Kinlochlaggan Highld....98 G10
Kinlochleven Highld....90 G4
Kinlochmoidart Highld....89 P2
Kinlochnanuagh Highld....97 K11
Kinloch Rannoch P & K....91 P5
Kinloss Moray....100 G3
Kinmel Bay Conwy....55 P5
Kinmuck Abers....102 H10
Kinmundy Abers....103 J10
Kinnabus Ag & B....74 D4
Kinnadie Abers....103 K6
Kinnaird P & K....92 H9
Kinneff Abers....95 N6
Kinnelhead D & G....78 G8
Kinnell Angus....93 Q5
Kinnerley Shrops....48 G10
Kinnersley Herefs....38 G11
Kinnersley Worcs....39 Q12
Kinnerton Powys....38 E9
Kinnesswood P & K....86 E2
Kinnordy Angus....93 L5
Kinoulton Notts....41 N2
Kinross P & K....86 D2
Kinrossie P & K....92 H8
Kinross Services P & K....86 D2
Kinsham Herefs....38 G8
Kinsham Worcs....29 N2
Kinsley Wakefd....59 K10
Kinson BCP....8 F8
Kintail Highld....97 P5
Kintbury W Berk....19 L7
Kintessack Moray....100 F4
Kintillo P & K....92 H11
Kinton Herefs....38 H7
Kinton Shrops....48 G10
Kintore Abers....102 G11
Kintour Ag & B....74 F3

Kintra Ag & B....74 D3
Kintra Ag & B....88 H10
Kintraw Ag & B....83 M3
Kintyre Ag & B....75 L5
Kinveachy Highld....99 N5
Kinver Staffs....39 Q5
Kippax Leeds....59 K7
Kippen Stirlg....85 L4
Kippford D & G....70 D5
Kipping's Cross Kent....12 D3
Kirbister Shet....111 h2
Kirby Bedon Norfk....45 L8
Kirby Bellars Leics....41 Q4
Kirby Cane Norfk....45 N10
Kirby Cross Essex....35 K11
Kirby Grindalythe N York....60 F1
Kirby Hill N York....59 K1
Kirby Hill N York....65 K6
Kirby Knowle N York....66 C9
Kirby-le-Soken Essex....35 K11
Kirby Misperton N York....66 H10
Kirby Muxloe Leics....41 M6
Kirby Underdale E R Yk....60 D3
Kirby Wiske N York....65 P9
Kirdford W Susx....10 G5
Kirk Highld....110 F4
Kirkabister Shet....111 k4
Kirkandrews D & G....69 N9
Kirkandrews upon Eden Cumb....71 M4
Kirkbampton Cumb....71 L4
Kirkbean D & G....70 F4
Kirk Bramwith Donc....59 N10
Kirkbride Cumb....71 K4
Kirkbuddo Angus....93 N7
Kirkburn Border....79 L2
Kirkburn E R Yk....60 G3
Kirkburton Kirk....58 G10
Kirkby Knows....56 H8
Kirkby Lincs....52 F5
Kirkby N York....66 D6
Kirkby Fleetham N York....65 M8
Kirkby Green Lincs....52 F11
Kirkby-in-Ashfield Notts....51 L8
Kirkby-in-Furness Cumb....62 E6
Kirkby la Thorpe Lincs....42 F2
Kirkby Lonsdale Cumb....63 L6
Kirkby Malham N York....58 B3
Kirkby Mallory Leics....41 L7
Kirkby Malzeard N York....65 M11
Kirkbymoorside N York....66 F9
Kirkby on Bain Lincs....53 J10
Kirkby Overblow N York....59 J4
Kirkby Stephen Cumb....64 E6
Kirkby Thore Cumb....64 B3
Kirkby Underwood Lincs....42 F5
Kirkby Wharf N York....59 L6
Kirkcaldy Fife....86 F4
Kirkcambeck Cumb....71 Q2
Kirkchrist D & G....69 P8
Kirkcolm D & G....68 D5
Kirkconnel D & G....77 M8
Kirkconnell D & G....70 F2
Kirkcowan D & G....69 J7
Kirkcudbright D & G....69 P8
Kirkdale Lpool....56 G9
Kirk Deighton N York....59 K4
Kirk Ella E R Yk....60 H8
Kirkfieldbank S Lans....77 P3
Kirkgunzeon D & G....70 E3
Kirk Hallam Derbys....51 L11
Kirkham Lancs....56 H3
Kirkham N York....60 D2
Kirkhamgate Wakefd....58 H9
Kirk Hammerton N York....59 L3
Kirkhaugh Nthumb....72 D10
Kirkheaton Kirk....58 F9
Kirkheaton Nthumb....73 H5
Kirkhill Highld....107 J12
Kirkhope S Lans....78 F7
Kirkibost Highld....96 G6
Kirkinch P & K....93 K6
Kirkinner D & G....69 K8
Kirkintilloch E Duns....85 L8
Kirk Ireton Derbys....50 H10
Kirkland Cumb....70 H11
Kirkland Cumb....77 M8
Kirkland D & G....78 D10
Kirkland D & G....78 G10
Kirk Langley Derbys....50 H11
Kirkleatham R & Cl....66 E3
Kirklevington S on T....66 B5
Kirkley Suffk....45 Q10
Kirklington N York....65 N10
Kirklington Notts....51 P8
Kirklinton Cumb....71 N3
Kirkliston C Edin....86 D7
Kirkmabreck D & G....69 L7
Kirkmaiden D & G....68 F10
Kirk Merrington Dur....65 M2
Kirk Michael IoM....56 c4
Kirkmichael P & K....94 B9
Kirkmichael S Ayrs....76 F9
Kirkmuirhill S Lans....77 N3
Kirknewton Nthumb....81 J8
Kirknewton W Loth....86 D8
Kirkney Abers....101 P8
Kirk of Shotts N Lans....85 P9
Kirkoswald Cumb....71 Q7
Kirkoswald S Ayrs....76 D9
Kirkpatrick D & G....78 E10
Kirkpatrick Durham D & G....70 C2
Kirkpatrick-Fleming D & G....71 L2
Kirk Sandall Donc....59 N11
Kirksanton Cumb....62 D6
Kirk Smeaton N York....59 M10
Kirkstall Leeds....58 H7
Kirkstead Lincs....52 H10
Kirkstile Abers....102 C8
Kirkstile D & G....79 M10
Kirkstyle Highld....110 G2
Kirkthorpe Wakefd....59 J9
Kirkton Abers....102 E9
Kirkton Abers....102 F11
Kirkton D & G....78 F11
Kirkton Fife....93 L10
Kirkton Highld....97 L4
Kirkton Highld....97 N2
Kirkton P & K....92 E11
Kirkton Manor Border....79 K2
Kirkton of Airlie Angus....93 K5
Kirkton of Auchterhouse Angus....93 L7
Kirkton of Barevan Highld....107 N11

Kirkton of Collace P & K....92 H8
Kirkton of Durris Abers....95 M3
Kirkton of Glenbuchat Abers....101 M11
Kirkton of Glenisla Angus....94 D9
Kirkton of Kingoldrum Angus....93 L5
Kirkton of Lethendy P & K....92 G7
Kirkton of Logie Buchan Abers....103 K8
Kirkton of Maryculter Abers....95 P3
Kirkton of Menmuir Angus....95 J8
Kirkton of Monikie Angus....93 N7
Kirkton of Rayne Abers....102 F8
Kirkton of Skene Abers....95 N1
Kirkton of Tealing Angus....93 M7
Kirkton of Tough Abers....102 D11
Kirktown Abers....103 K3
Kirktown Abers....103 M5
Kirktown of Alvah Abers....102 E4
Kirktown of Bourtie Abers....102 G9
Kirktown of Deskford Moray....101 P3
Kirktown of Fetteresso Abers....95 P5
Kirktown of Mortlach Moray....101 L7
Kirktown of Slains Abers....103 L9
Kirkurd Border....86 D12
Kirkwall Ork....111 h2
Kirkwall Airport Ork....111 h2
Kirkwhelpington Nthumb....72 H4
Kirk Yetholm Border....80 H8
Kirmington N Linc....61 J11
Kirmond le Mire Lincs....52 H5
Kirn Ag & B....84 C7
Kirriemuir Angus....93 L5
Kirstead Green Norfk....45 L10
Kirtlebridge D & G....71 K2
Kirtling Cambs....34 B5
Kirtling Green Cambs....34 B5
Kirtlington Oxon....31 L9
Kirtomy Highld....109 N3
Kirton Lincs....43 K3
Kirton Notts....51 P7
Kirton Suffk....35 L8
Kirtonhill W Duns....84 G7
Kirton in Lindsey N Linc....52 D4
Kirwaugh D & G....69 K8
Kishorn Highld....97 L2
Kislingbury Nhants....31 P3
Kittisford Somset....16 E10
Kitt's Green Birm....40 F9
Kittybrewster C Aber....95 Q1
Kivernoll Herefs....28 F3
Kiveton Park Rothm....51 L4
Knaith Lincs....52 B6
Knap Corner Dorset....8 B3
Knaphill Surrey....20 F10
Knapp Somset....17 J10
Knapton C York....59 M4
Knapton N York....67 J11
Knapton Norfk....45 M4
Knapwell Cambs....33 K4
Knaresborough N York....59 J3
Knarsdale Nthumb....72 C9
Knaven Abers....103 J6
Knayton N York....66 B9
Knebworth Herts....33 J11
Knedlington E R Yk....60 C8
Kneesall Notts....51 P7
Kneeton Notts....51 P10
Knelston Swans....26 C10
Knenhall Staffs....50 B12
Knightcote Warwks....31 K4
Knightley Staffs....49 P9
Knighton C Leic....41 N7
Knighton Dorset....7 N1
Knighton Powys....38 F7
Knighton Somset....16 G7
Knighton Staffs....49 N7
Knighton Staffs....49 N9
Knighton on Teme Worcs....39 L7
Knightwick Worcs....39 N10
Knill Herefs....38 F9
Knipoch Ag & B....90 B10
Knipton Leics....42 B4
Kniveton Derbys....50 G10
Knock Cumb....64 C3
Knock Highld....97 J7
Knock Moray....102 C5
Knock W Isls....111 d2
Knock Castle N Ayrs....84 D9
Knockdee Highld....110 D4
Knockdow Ag & B....84 B8
Knockdown Wilts....18 C3
Knockeen S Ayrs....76 E11
Knockenkelly N Ayrs....75 Q7
Knockentiber E Ayrs....76 G4
Knockholt Kent....21 P10
Knockholt Pound Kent....21 P10
Knockin Shrops....48 G10
Knockinlaw E Ayrs....76 G4
Knocknain D & G....68 C6
Knockrome Ag & B....82 H6
Knocksharry IoM....56 b4
Knocksheen D & G....69 N3
Knockvennie Smithy D & G....70 C2
Knodishall Suffk....35 N4
Knodishall Common Suffk....35 P5
Knole Somset....17 L10
Knolls Green Ches E....57 P11
Knolton Wrexhm....48 H7
Knook Wilts....18 D11
Knossington Leics....42 B8
Knott End-on-Sea Lancs....62 G11
Knotting Bed....32 E4
Knotting Green Bed....32 E4
Knottingley Wakefd....59 L9
Knotty Ash Lpool....56 H9
Knowbury Shrops....39 L7
Knowe D & G....69 J5
Knowehead D & G....69 N2
Knoweside S Ayrs....76 E8
Knowes of Elrick Abers....102 F5
Knowle Bristl....17 N3
Knowle Devon....6 D2
Knowle Devon....6 E6
Knowle Devon....15 J3
Knowle Devon....15 N10
Knowle Shrops....39 L7
Knowle Solhll....40 F11
Knowle Somset....16 C7

Knowlefield Cumb....71 N4
Knowle Green Lancs....57 L2
Knowle St Giles Somset....7 J1
Knowl Hill W & M....20 D7
Knowsley Knows....56 H9
Knowsley Safari Park Knows....57 J9
Knowstone Devon....15 P7
Knox Bridge Kent....12 F2
Knoydart Highld....97 L8
Knucklas Powys....38 F7
Knuston Nhants....32 D4
Knutsford Ches E....57 N12
Knutsford Services Ches E....57 N12
Krumlin Calder....58 D9
Kuggar Cnwll....2 G11
Kyleakin Highld....97 K4
Kyle of Lochalsh Highld....97 K4
Kylerhea Highld....97 L5
Kylesku Highld....108 E8
Kylesmorar Highld....97 L10
Kyles Scalpay W Isls....111 c3
Kylestrome Highld....108 E8
Kynnersley Wrekin....49 M11
Kyrewood Worcs....39 L8

L

Lacasaigh W Isls....111 d2
Lacasdal W Isls....111 d2
Laceby NE Lin....52 H3
Lacey Green Bucks....20 D4
Lach Dennis Ches W....49 N2
Lackford Suffk....34 D3
Lackford Green Suffk....34 D3
Lacock Wilts....18 D7
Ladbroke Warwks....31 K4
Laddingford Kent....12 E1
Ladock Cnwll....3 K5
Lady Ork....111 i1
Ladybank Fife....93 K12
Ladygill S Lans....78 F4
Lady Hall Cumb....62 E5
Ladykirk Border....81 J5
Ladywood Birm....40 D9
Ladywood Worcs....39 Q9
La Fontenelle Guern....6 c1
Lag D & G....78 D10
Laga Highld....89 N4
Lagavulin Ag & B....74 F4
Lagg N Ayrs....75 P7
Laggan Highld....98 D3
Laggan Highld....99 J9
Lagganlia Highld....99 M8
La Grève de Lecq Jersey....7 a1
Laid Highld....108 H4
Laide Highld....105 N4
Laig Highld....96 F11
Laigh Clunch E Ayrs....76 H2
Laigh Fenwick E Ayrs....76 H3
Laigh Glenmuir E Ayrs....77 K7
Laighstonehall S Lans....85 M11
Laindon Essex....22 D5
Lairg Highld....107 J2
Laisterdyke C Brad....58 F7
Lake IoW....9 P10
Lake Wilts....18 G11
Lake District Cumb....71 K12
Lake District National Park Cumb....71 K12
Lakenheath Suffk....44 B12
Lakes End Norfk....43 N10
Laleston Brdgnd....27 J11
Lamarsh Essex....34 E9
Lamas Norfk....45 L5
Lambden Border....80 G5
Lamberhurst Kent....12 D3
Lamberhurst Down Kent....12 D3
Lamberton Border....81 K3
Lambeth Gt Lon....21 L7
Lambfair Green Suffk....34 B6
Lambley Notts....51 N10
Lambley Nthumb....72 C8
Lambourn W Berk....19 K5
Lambourne End Essex....21 P5
Lambs Green W Susx....11 K3
Lamerton Devon....5 K5
Lamesley Gatesd....73 M8
Lamington S Lans....78 F3
Lamlash N Ayrs....75 Q6
Lamonby Cumb....71 N8
Lamorna Cnwll....2 C10
Lamorran Cnwll....3 K7
Lampeter Cerdgn....37 J10
Lampeter Velfrey Pembks....25 K6
Lamphey Pembks....24 H8
Lamplugh Cumb....70 H10
Lamport Nhants....41 Q11
Lamyatt Somset....17 P8
Lanark S Lans....77 P3
Lancaster Lancs....63 J9
Lancaster Services Lancs....63 J9
Lanchester Dur....73 L10
Lancing W Susx....11 J8
L'Ancresse Guern....6 c1
Landbeach Cambs....33 M4
Landcross Devon....14 H7
Landerberry Abers....95 M2
Landford Wilts....9 J4
Land-hallow Highld....110 E8
Landimore Swans....26 C9
Landkey Devon....15 K6
Landore Swans....26 F9
Landrake Cnwll....4 H7
Land's End Airport Cnwll....2 B9
Landulph Cnwll....5 J7
Lane Cnwll....3 J4
Laneast Cnwll....4 F4
Lane End Bucks....20 D5
Lane End Kent....22 C8
Lane End Wilts....18 B10
Lane Ends Derbys....40 G1
Laneham Notts....52 B8
Lanehead Dur....72 F11
Lane Head Dur....65 K9
Lane Head Wsall....40 C7
Lane Side Lancs....57 P4
Langal Highld....89 P3
Langaller Somset....16 H10
Langar Notts....51 Q5
Langbank Rens....84 G8
Langbar N York....58 E5

Langcliffe N York....63 P8
Langdale End N York....67 K8
Langdon Hills Essex....22 D6
Langdown Hants....9 M6
Langdyke Fife....86 G2
Langenhoe Essex....34 G11
Langford C Beds....32 H8
Langford Devon....6 D3
Langford Essex....22 G2
Langford Notts....52 B10
Langford Oxon....30 G12
Langford Budville Somset....16 F10
Langham Essex....34 G9
Langham Norfk....44 G2
Langham Rutlnd....42 B7
Langham Suffk....34 F3
Langho Lancs....57 N3
Langholm D & G....79 M11
Langland Swans....26 E10
Langlee Border....80 C7
Langley Hants....9 M7
Langley Herts....32 H11
Langley Kent....22 F11
Langley Nthumb....72 E8
Langley Slough....20 G7
Langley Somset....16 E9
Langley W Susx....10 D4
Langley Warwks....30 F2
Langley Burrell Wilts....18 D6
Langley Green Essex....34 E11
Langley Marsh Somset....16 E9
Langley Mill Derbys....51 K10
Langley Park Dur....73 L11
Langley Street Norfk....45 N9
Langley Upper Green Essex....33 M9
Langney E Susx....12 D9
Langold Notts....51 N4
Langore Cnwll....4 G3
Langport Somset....17 K10
Langrick Lincs....43 J1
Langridge BaNES....17 Q3
Langrigg Cumb....71 J6
Langrish Hants....10 B5
Langsett Barns....50 G2
Langside P & K....92 B11
Langstone Hants....10 B8
Langthorne N York....65 M8
Langthorpe N York....59 K1
Langthwaite N York....64 H7
Langtoft E R Yk....60 H2
Langtoft Lincs....42 G7
Langton Dur....65 L4
Langton Lincs....52 H9
Langton Lincs....53 L9
Langton N York....60 D2
Langton by Wragby Lincs....52 G7
Langton Green Kent....12 B3
Langton Herring Dorset....7 N6
Langton Matravers Dorset....8 E10
Langtree Devon....14 H8
Langwathby Cumb....71 R8
Langwell Highld....106 C2
Langwell House Highld....110 D10
Langwith Derbys....51 M6
Langwith Junction Derbys....51 L7
Langworth Lincs....52 F8
Lanhydrock House & Gardens Cnwll....3 N3
Lanivet Cnwll....3 M3
Lanlivery Cnwll....3 N4
Lanner Cnwll....2 G7
Lanreath Cnwll....4 E8
Lansallos Cnwll....4 E9
Lanteglos Cnwll....4 D4
Lanteglos Highway Cnwll....4 E9
Lanton Border....80 E9
Lanton Nthumb....81 K7
Lapford Devon....15 M9
Laphroaig Ag & B....74 E4
Lapley Staffs....49 Q11
Lapworth Warwks....40 F12
Larachbeg Highld....89 N6
Larbert Falk....85 P6
Largie Abers....102 D8
Largiemore Ag & B....83 P6
Largoward Fife....87 J1
Largs N Ayrs....84 D10
Largybeg N Ayrs....75 Q7
Largymore N Ayrs....75 Q7
Larkfield Inver....84 D7
Larkfield Kent....22 E10
Larkhall S Lans....77 M2
Larkhill Wilts....18 G11
Larling Norfk....44 G11
La Rocque Jersey....7 c2
Lartington Dur....64 H4
Lasham Hants....19 Q11
Lasswade Mdloth....86 G8
Lastingham N York....66 G9
Latchford Warrtn....57 L10
Latchingdon Essex....22 G4
Latchley Cnwll....5 J5
Lathbury M Keyn....32 C7
Latheron Highld....110 E8
Latheronwheel Highld....110 E8
Lathones Fife....87 J1
Latimer Bucks....20 G4
Latteridge S Glos....29 J10
Lattiford Somset....17 Q10
Latton Wilts....18 G2
Lauder Border....80 C5
Laugharne Carmth....25 M6
Laughterton Lincs....52 B8
Laughton E Susx....11 P7
Laughton Leics....41 P9
Laughton Lincs....42 D4
Laughton Lincs....52 B6
Laughton Common Rothm....51 L4
Laughton-en-le-Morthen Rothm....51 M4
Launcells Cnwll....4 H4
Launton Oxon....31 N9
Laurencekirk Abers....95 L7
Laurieston D & G....69 P6
Laurieston Falk....85 Q7
Lavendon M Keyn....32 D6
Lavenham Suffk....34 F7
Lavernock V Glam....16 G3
Laversdale Cumb....71 P3
Laverstock Wilts....8 H2
Laverstoke Hants....19 N10
Laverton Gloucs....30 E7
Laverton N York....65 M11

Laverton Somset....18 B9
La Villette Guern....6 b2
Lavister Wrexhm....48 G4
Law S Lans....85 N11
Lawers P & K....91 Q8
Lawford Essex....34 H9
Lawford Somset....16 F8
Law Hill S Lans....85 N11
Lawhitton Cnwll....4 H4
Lawkland N York....63 P8
Lawley Wrekin....39 M1
Lawrence Weston Bristl....28 G11
Lawrenny Pembks....24 H7
Lawshall Suffk....34 E6
Laxay W Isls....111 d2
Laxdale W Isls....111 d2
Laxey IoM....56 d4
Laxfield Suffk....35 L3
Laxford Bridge Highld....108 E6
Laxo Shet....111 k3
Laxton E R Yk....60 D8
Laxton Nhants....42 D10
Laxton Notts....51 Q7
Laycock C Brad....58 D6
Layer Breton Essex....34 F12
Layer-de-la-Haye Essex....34 F11
Layer Marney Essex....34 F12
Layham Suffk....34 G8
Laymore Dorset....7 K2
Laytham E R Yk....60 D6
Lazenby Cumb....71 Q7
Lazonby Cumb....71 Q7
Lea Derbys....51 J8
Lea Herefs....28 H4
Lea Lincs....52 B6
Lea Shrops....38 G4
Lea Wilts....18 E4
Leachkin Highld....107 K12
Leadburn Border....86 F10
Leadenham Lincs....52 D11
Leaden Roding Essex....22 C1
Leadgate Dur....73 K9
Leadhills S Lans....78 E6
Leafield Oxon....30 H10
Leagrave Luton....32 F11
Leake Common Side Lincs....53 L11
Lealholm N York....66 G6
Lealt Highld....104 G9
Lea Marston Warwks....40 G8
Leamington Hastings Warwks....31 K1
Leamington Spa Warwks....30 H2
Leap Cross E Susx....12 C7
Learney Abers....95 K2
Leasgill Cumb....63 J5
Leasingham Lincs....42 F1
Leasingthorne Dur....65 M2
Leatherhead Surrey....21 J11
Leathley N York....58 G5
Leaton Shrops....49 J10
Leaveland Kent....23 J11
Leavenheath Suffk....34 F8
Leavening N York....60 D2
Leaves Green Gt Lon....21 N10
Lebberston N York....67 M10
Le Bourg Guern....6 b2
Lechlade on Thames Gloucs....18 H2
Lecht Gruinart Ag & B....82 D8
Leck Lancs....63 M6
Leckbuie P & K....91 Q8
Leckford Hants....19 L12
Leckhampstead Bucks....31 Q6
Leckhampstead W Berk....19 M5
Leckhampstead Thicket W Berk....19 M5
Leckhampton Gloucs....29 N5
Leckmelm Highld....106 C4
Leconfield E R Yk....60 H5
Ledaig Ag & B....90 C8
Ledburn Bucks....32 C11
Ledbury Herefs....29 J2
Ledgemoor Herefs....38 H11
Ledmore Highld....108 E12
Ledsham Ches W....59 L8
Ledsham Leeds....59 K8
Ledston Leeds....59 K8
Ledwell Oxon....31 K8
Lee Devon....14 H3
Lee Gt Lon....21 M8
Leebotwood Shrops....39 J3
Lee Brockhurst Shrops....49 K9
Leece Cumb....62 E8
Lee Chapel Essex....22 E6
Lee Clump Bucks....20 E3
Leeds Kent....22 G11
Leeds Leeds....58 H7
Leeds Bradford Airport Leeds....58 G6
Leeds Castle Kent....22 G11
Leeds Skelton Lake Services Leeds....59 J7
Leedstown Cnwll....2 E8
Leek Staffs....50 C9
Leek Wootton Warwks....30 H1
Lee Mill Devon....5 M8
Leeming N York....65 N9
Leeming Bar N York....65 N9
Leeming Bar Rest Area N York....65 M9
Lee-on-the-Solent Hants....9 P7
Lees Derbys....50 H12
Lees Oldham....58 C12
Lees Green Derbys....50 H12
Leesthorpe Leics....42 B7
Leeswood Flints....48 F4
Leftwich Ches W....49 M2
Legbourne Lincs....53 L6
Legerwood Border....80 D5
Legoland W & M....20 F8
Legsby Lincs....52 G6
Leicester C Leic....41 N6
Leicester Forest East Services Leics....41 M7
Leigh Dorset....7 N2
Leigh Gloucs....29 M4
Leigh Kent....21 P12
Leigh Surrey....11 K1
Leigh Wigan....57 M8
Leigh Wilts....18 F3
Leigh Worcs....39 P10
Leigh Beck Essex....22 H5
Leigh Delamere Wilts....18 C5
Leigh Delamere Services Wilts....18 D5
Leigh Green Kent....12 H4
Leigh Knoweglass S Lans....77 K2

Leigh-on-Sea Sthend....22 G6
Leigh Park Dorset....8 F7
Leigh Park Hants....10 B8
Leigh Sinton Worcs....39 P11
Leighswood Wsall....40 D7
Leighterton Gloucs....29 L9
Leighton Powys....38 F2
Leighton Shrops....39 L2
Leighton Bromswold Cambs....32 G2
Leighton Buzzard C Beds....32 D10
Leigh upon Mendip Somset....17 Q6
Leigh Woods N Som....17 N2
Leinthall Earls Herefs....39 J8
Leinthall Starkes Herefs....38 H8
Leintwardine Herefs....38 H7
Leire Leics....41 M9
Leiston Suffk....35 N4
Leith C Edin....86 F7
Leitholm Border....80 G5
Lelant Cnwll....2 E8
Lelley E R Yk....61 L7
Lempitlaw Border....80 G7
Lemreway W Isls....111 d3
Lemsford Herts....21 K2
Lenchwick Worcs....30 D5
Lendalfoot S Ayrs....68 E2
Lendrick Terrace Abers....103 M7
Lenham Kent....22 H11
Lenham Heath Kent....22 H12
Lenie Highld....98 G4
Lennel Border....80 H6
Lennox Plunton D & G....69 N8
Lennoxtown E Duns....85 K7
Lent Bucks....20 E7
Lenton C Nott....51 M11
Lenton Lincs....42 E4
Lenwade Norfk....44 H6
Lenzie E Duns....85 L8
Leochel-Cushnie Abers....102 C12
Leominster Herefs....39 J9
Leonard Stanley Gloucs....29 L7
Lephin Highld....104 B11
Leppington N York....60 D2
Lepton Kirk....58 G10
Lerags Ag & B....90 B10
L'Erée Guern....6 a2
Lerryn Cnwll....4 E8
Lerwick Shet....111 k4
Lesbury Nthumb....81 P10
Leslie Abers....102 D9
Leslie Fife....86 F2
Lesmahagow S Lans....78 D2
Lesnewth Cnwll....4 E3
Les Quartiers Guern....6 c1
Les Quennevais Jersey....7 a2
Lessingham Norfk....45 N5
Lessonhall Cumb....71 K5
Leswalt D & G....68 D6
L'Etacq Jersey....7 a1
Letchmore Heath Herts....21 J4
Letchworth Garden City Herts....32 H9
Letcombe Bassett Oxon....19 L4
Letcombe Regis Oxon....19 L4
Letham Angus....93 P6
Letham Border....80 F11
Letham Falk....85 P6
Letham Fife....93 K11
Letham Grange Angus....93 Q6
Lethenty Abers....102 D10
Lethenty Abers....102 H7
Letheringham Suffk....35 L5
Letheringsett Norfk....44 H3
Letterewe Highld....105 P7
Letterfearn Highld....97 M5
Letterfinlay Lodge Hotel Highld....98 C10
Letters Highld....106 C4
Lettershaw S Lans....78 E5
Letterston Pembks....24 G3
Lettoch Highld....99 Q5
Lettoch Highld....100 H8
Letton Herefs....38 G11
Letty Green Herts....21 L2
Letwell Rothm....51 M4
Leuchars Fife....93 M10
Leumrabhagh W Isls....111 d3
Leurbost W Isls....111 d2
Levan Inver....84 D7
Levedale Staffs....40 B4
Leven E R Yk....61 J5
Leven Fife....86 H3
Levens Cumb....63 J5
Levens Green Herts....33 K11
Levenshulme Manch....57 Q9
Levenwick Shet....111 k5
Leverburgh W Isls....111 c4
Leverington Cambs....43 M7
Leverstock Green Herts....20 H3
Leverton Lincs....43 L1
Le Villocq Guern....6 b1
Levington Suffk....35 K8
Levisham N York....67 J8
Lew Oxon....31 J11
Lewannick Cnwll....4 F4
Lewdown Devon....5 K3
Lewes E Susx....11 N7
Leweston Pembks....24 G4
Lewisham Gt Lon....21 M8
Lewiston Highld....98 G4
Lewistown Brdgnd....27 K10
Lewknor Oxon....20 B4
Leworthy Devon....5 K3
Lewson Street Kent....23 J10
Lewtrenchard Devon....5 K3
Lexden Essex....34 F10
Lexworthy Somset....16 H8
Leybourne Kent....22 D10
Leyburn N York....65 K9
Leygreen Herts....32 G10
Ley Hill Bucks....20 F3
Leyland Lancs....57 K4
Leylodge Abers....102 G11
Leys Abers....103 K5
Leys P & K....93 J7
Leysdown-on-Sea Kent....23 K8
Leysmill Angus....93 Q6
Leys of Cossans Angus....93 L6
Leysters Herefs....39 K8
Leyton Gt Lon....21 M6
Leytonstone Gt Lon....21 N6
Lezant Cnwll....4 H5
Lhanbryde Moray....101 K3

178 Libanus – Llanymynech

Libanus Powys 27 L4
Libberton S Lans 78 G1
Liberton C Edin 86 F8
Lichfield Staffs 40 E5
Lickey Worcs 40 C11
Lickey End Worcs 40 C11
Lickfold W Susx 10 E5
Liddesdale Highld 89 Q4
Liddington Swindn 18 H5
Lidgate Suffk 34 C5
Lidlington C Beds 32 E8
Liff Angus 93 L8
Lifford Birm 40 D10
Lifton Devon 5 J3
Liftondown Devon 4 H3
Lighthorne Warwks 31 J3
Lighthorne Heath Warwks 31 J3
Lightwater Surrey 20 E10
Lightwater Valley Theme Park N York 65 M11
Lightwood C Stke 50 B11
Lilbourne Nhants 41 M11
Lilleshall Wrekin 49 N11
Lilley Herts 32 G10
Lilliesleaf Border 80 C8
Lillingstone Dayrell Bucks 31 P6
Lillingstone Lovell Bucks 31 P6
Lillington Dorset 7 P1
Lilliput BCP 8 F9
Lilstock Somset 16 F7
Limbury Luton 32 F11
Limekilnburn S Lans 77 M2
Limekilns Fife 86 C5
Limerigg Falk 85 P8
Limerstone IoW 9 M10
Lime Street Worcs 29 L3
Limington Somset 17 M10
Limmerhaugh E Ayrs 77 K6
Limpenhoe Norfk 45 N8
Limpley Stoke Wilts 18 B8
Limpsfield Surrey 21 N11
Limpsfield Chart Surrey 21 N11
Linby Notts 51 M9
Linchmere W Susx 10 D4
Lincluden D & G 78 F12
Lincoln Lincs 52 D8
Lincomb Worcs 39 P8
Lindale Cumb 62 H6
Lindal in Furness Cumb 62 F7
Lindfield W Susx 11 M5
Lindford Hants 10 D3
Lindley Kirk 58 E9
Lindores Fife 93 K11
Lindridge Worcs 39 M8
Lindsell Essex 33 Q10
Lindsey Suffk 34 G7
Lindsey Tye Suffk 34 G7
Lingdale R & Cl 66 F4
Lingen Herefs 38 G8
Lingfield Surrey 11 M2
Lingfield Common Surrey 11 M2
Lingwood Norfk 45 M8
Liniclate W Isls 111 b5
Linicro Highld 104 E8
Linkend Worcs 29 L3
Linkenholt Hants 19 L8
Linkinhorne Cnwll 4 G5
Linktown Fife 86 F4
Linkwood Moray 101 K3
Linley Shrops 38 G4
Linley Green Herefs 39 M10
Linlithgow W Loth 86 B6
Linsidemore Highld 107 J3
Linslade C Beds 32 C10
Linstead Parva Suffk 35 M2
Linstock Cumb 71 N4
Linthurst Worcs 40 D11
Linthwaite Kirk 58 E10
Lintlaw Border 87 Q9
Lintmill Moray 101 P3
Linton Border 80 G8
Linton Cambs 33 P7
Linton Derbys 40 H4
Linton Herefs 28 H4
Linton Kent 22 F12
Linton Leeds 59 K5
Linton N York 58 C2
Linton Hill Herefs 29 J4
Linton-on-Ouse N York 59 L3
Linwood Lincs 52 G6
Linwood Rens 84 G9
Lionacleit W Isls 111 b5
Lional W Isls 111 e1
Liphook Hants 10 D4
Liscard Wirral 56 F9
Liscombe Somset 15 P5
Liskeard Cnwll 4 F7
Lismore Ag & B 90 B7
Liss Hants 10 C5
Lissett E R Yk 61 K3
Lissington Lincs 52 G6
Lisvane Cardif 27 P11
Liswerry Newpt 28 D10
Litcham Norfk 44 E6
Litchborough Nhants 31 N4
Litchfield Hants 19 M9
Litherland Sefton 56 G8
Litlington Cambs 33 K8
Litlington E Susx 11 Q9
Little Abington Cambs 33 N7
Little Addington Nhants 32 D3
Little Airies D & G 69 K9
Little Alne Warwks 30 F2
Little Altcar Sefton 56 F7
Little Amwell Herts 21 M2
Little Aston Staffs 40 E7
Little Ayton N York 66 D5
Little Baddow Essex 22 F2
Little Badminton S Glos 18 B4
Little Bampton Cumb 71 L5
Little Bardfield Essex 33 Q9
Little Barford Bed 32 H5
Little Barningham Norfk 45 J4
Little Barrington Gloucs 30 G10
Little Barrow Ches W 49 J2
Little Bavington Nthumb 72 H5
Little Bedwyn Wilts 19 K7
Little Bentley Essex 35 J10
Little Berkhamsted Herts 21 L2
Little Billing Nhants 32 B4
Little Billington C Beds 32 D11
Little Birch Herefs 28 F3
Little Blakenham Suffk 34 H7
Little Blencow Cumb 71 P8
Little Bloxwich Wsall 40 D6
Little Bognor W Susx 10 G6
Little Bollington Ches E 57 N10
Little Bookham Surrey 20 H11
Littleborough Notts 52 B7
Littleborough Rochdl 58 C10
Littlebourne Kent 23 N11
Little Bourton Oxon 31 L5
Little Braxted Essex 22 G1
Little Brechin Angus 95 J9
Littlebredy Dorset 7 N5
Little Brickhill M Keyn 32 C9
Little Brington Nhants 31 P2
Little Bromley Essex 34 H10
Little Budworth Ches W 49 L3
Littleburn Highld 107 K10
Little Burstead Essex 22 D5
Littlebury Essex 33 N8
Littlebury Green Essex 33 M8
Little Bytham Lincs 42 E6
Little Carlton Lincs 53 L6
Little Casterton Rutlnd 42 E8
Little Cawthorpe Lincs 53 K6
Little Chalfont Bucks 20 F4
Little Chart Kent 12 H2
Little Chesterford Essex 33 N8
Little Cheverell Wilts 18 E9
Little Chishill Cambs 33 L8
Little Clacton Essex 35 J11
Little Clifton Cumb 70 H9
Little Coates NE Lin 53 J2
Little Comberton Worcs 30 C5
Little Common E Susx 12 E8
Little Compton Warwks 30 H7
Little Cornard Suffk 34 E8
Little Cowarne Herefs 39 L11
Little Coxwell Oxon 19 K3
Little Crakehall N York 65 M9
Little Cressingham Norfk 44 E9
Little Crosby Sefton 56 G8
Little Cubley Derbys 50 F12
Little Dalby Leics 41 Q5
Littledean Gloucs 29 J6
Little Dewchurch Herefs 28 F3
Little Ditton Cambs 33 Q5
Little Downham Cambs 43 N12
Little Driffield E R Yk 60 H3
Little Dunham Norfk 44 E7
Little Dunkeld P & K 92 F7
Little Dunmow Essex 33 Q11
Little Durnford Wilts 8 G1
Little Easton Essex 33 P11
Little Eaton Derbys 51 J11
Little Ellingham Norfk 44 G9
Little Everdon Nhants 31 N3
Little Eversden Cambs 33 L6
Little Faringdon Oxon 19 J1
Little Fencote N York 65 M8
Little Fenton N York 59 M7
Littleferry Highld 107 N4
Little Fransham Norfk 44 E7
Little Gaddesden Herts 20 F2
Little Glemham Suffk 35 M5
Little Gorsley Herefs 29 J4
Little Gransden Cambs 33 J6
Little Green Somset 17 Q6
Little Hadham Herts 33 M11
Little Hale Lincs 42 G2
Little Hallam Derbys 51 L11
Little Hallingbury Essex 33 N12
Littleham Devon 6 D6
Littleham Devon 14 H7
Littlehampton W Susx 10 G9
Little Harrowden Nhants 32 C3
Little Haseley Oxon 19 Q1
Little Haven Pembks 24 F6
Littlehaven W Susx 11 J4
Little Hay Staffs 40 E7
Little Haywood Staffs 40 D3
Littlehempston Devon 5 Q7
Little Hereford Herefs 39 K8
Little Horkesley Essex 34 F9
Little Hormead Herts 33 L10
Little Horsted E Susx 11 P6
Little Horton C Brad 58 F7
Little Horwood Bucks 32 B10
Little Houghton Barns 59 K11
Little Houghton Nhants 32 B5
Little Hucklow Derbys 50 F5
Little Hutton N York 66 C11
Little Irchester Nhants 32 C4
Little Keyford Somset 18 B10
Little Kimble Bucks 20 D3
Little Kineton Warwks 31 J4
Little Kingshill Bucks 20 E4
Little Knox D & G 70 D4
Little Langdale Cumb 62 G2
Little Langford Wilts 18 F12
Little Leigh Ches W 49 L1
Little Leighs Essex 34 C12
Little Lever Bolton 57 N7
Little Linford M Keyn 32 B7
Little Load Somset 17 L10
Little London Cambs 43 L10
Little London E Susx 12 C6
Little London Hants 19 L10
Little London Hants 19 Q8
Little Longstone Derbys 50 F6
Little Maplestead Essex 34 D9
Little Marcle Herefs 29 J2
Little Marlow Bucks 20 E6
Little Massingham Norfk 44 D5
Little Melton Norfk 45 J8
Littlemill Abers 94 E3
Littlemill Highld 100 E5
Little Mill Mons 28 C8
Little Milton Oxon 19 Q1
Little Missenden Bucks 20 E4
Littlemore Oxon 31 M12
Little Musgrave Cumb 64 D5
Little Ness Shrops 48 H10
Little Newcastle Pembks 24 G3
Little Newsham Dur 65 K4
Little Norton Somset 17 L11
Little Oakley Essex 35 K10
Little Oakley Nhants 42 C11
Little Orton Cumb 71 M5
Littleover C Derb 41 J1
Little Packington Warwks 40 G9
Little Paxton Cambs 32 H4
Little Petherick Cnwll 3 K2
Little Plumstead Norfk 45 M7
Little Ponton Lincs 42 D4
Littleport Cambs 43 P11
Little Preston Nhants 31 N4
Littler Ches W 49 L3
Little Raveley Cambs 33 J2
Little Reedness E R Yk 60 D9
Little Ribston N York 59 J4
Little Rissington Gloucs 30 F9
Little Rollright Oxon 30 H7
Little Ryburgh Norfk 44 F5
Little Salkeld Cumb 71 Q8
Little Sampford Essex 33 Q9
Little Saughall Ches W 48 G2
Little Saxham Suffk 34 D4
Little Scatwell Highld 106 F10
Little Shelford Cambs 33 M6
Little Singleton Lancs 56 G2
Little Skipwith N York 59 P6
Little Smeaton N York 59 M10
Little Snoring Norfk 44 F4
Little Sodbury S Glos 18 A4
Little Somborne Hants 9 L2
Little Somerford Wilts 18 E4
Little Soudley Shrops 49 N9
Little Stainton Darltn 65 N4
Little Stanney Ches W 48 H1
Little Staughton Bed 32 F4
Little Steeping Lincs 53 M10
Little Stoke Staffs 40 B2
Littlestone-on-Sea Kent 13 L5
Little Stonham Suffk 35 J5
Little Stretton Leics 41 P7
Little Stretton Shrops 39 J4
Little Strickland Cumb 71 Q10
Little Stukeley Cambs 32 H2
Little Sugnall Staffs 49 P8
Little Swinburne Nthumb 72 G5
Little Sypland D & G 70 B5
Little Tew Oxon 31 J8
Little Tey Essex 34 E11
Little Thetford Cambs 33 N2
Little Thorpe Dur 73 Q11
Littlethorpe Leics 41 M7
Littlethorpe N York 59 J1
Little Thurlow Suffk 34 B6
Little Thurrock Thurr 22 D7
Littleton Ches W 48 H3
Littleton D & G 69 P7
Littleton Hants 9 M2
Littleton Somset 17 L9
Littleton Surrey 20 H9
Littleton Drew Wilts 18 C5
Littleton of Airlie Angus 93 L5
Littleton-on-Severn S Glos 28 H10
Littleton Panell Wilts 18 E9
Little Torrington Devon 15 J8
Littletown Dur 73 N11
Little Town Lancs 57 M2
Little Urswick Cumb 62 F7
Little Wakering Essex 22 H6
Little Walden Essex 33 N8
Little Waldingfield Suffk 34 F7
Little Walsingham Norfk 44 F3
Little Waltham Essex 22 E2
Little Weighton E R Yk 60 G7
Little Wenlock Wrekin 39 M2
Little Weston Somset 17 N10
Little Whitefield IoW 9 P9
Littlewick Green W & M 20 D7
Little Wilbraham Cambs 33 N5
Little Witcombe Gloucs 29 M6
Little Witley Worcs 39 P8
Little Wittenham Oxon 19 P3
Little Wolford Warwks 30 H7
Little Woodcote Gt Lon 21 L10
Littleworth Oxon 19 K2
Littleworth Staffs 40 C3
Littleworth Worcs 30 B4
Little Wymington Bed 32 D4
Little Wymondley Herts 32 H10
Little Wyrley Staffs 40 D6
Little Yeldham Essex 34 C8
Littley Green Essex 34 B12
Litton Derbys 50 F6
Litton N York 64 G11
Litton Somset 17 N5
Litton Cheney Dorset 7 M5
Liurbost W Isls 111 d2
Liverpool Lpool 56 G10
Liverpool Maritime Mercantile City Lpool 56 G10
Liversedge Kirk 58 G9
Liverton Devon 5 Q5
Liverton R & Cl 66 G4
Livingston W Loth 86 C8
Livingston Village W Loth 86 C8
Lixwm Flints 48 D2
Lizard Cnwll 2 G12
Llanaelhaearn Gwynd 46 F3
Llanafan Cerdgn 37 L6
Llanafan-Fawr Powys 37 Q9
Llanallgo IoA 54 G5
Llanarmon Dyffryn Ceiriog Wrexhm 48 D8
Llanarmon-yn-Ial Denbgs 48 E4
Llanarth Cerdgn 36 G8
Llanarth Mons 28 D6
Llanarthne Carmth 26 D5
Llanasa Flints 56 C11
Llanbadarn Fawr Cerdgn 37 K4
Llanbadarn Fynydd Powys 38 C6
Llanbadoc Mons 28 D8
Llanbeder Newpt 28 D10
Llanbedr Gwynd 47 J6
Llanbedr Powys 27 P5
Llanbedr-Dyffryn-Clwyd Denbgs 48 D4
Llanbedrgoch IoA 54 G5
Llanbedrog Gwynd 46 E5
Llanbedr-y-Cennin Conwy 55 L7
Llanberis Gwynd 54 H9
Llanbethêry V Glam 16 D3
Llanbister Powys 38 C7
Llanblethian V Glam 16 D2
Llanboidy Carmth 25 L4
Llanbradach Caerph 27 N10
Llanbrynmair Powys 47 P10
Llancadle V Glam 16 D3
Llancarfan V Glam 16 E3
Llancloudy Herefs 28 F5
Llandaff Cardif 27 N12
Llandanwg Gwynd 47 J5
Llanddaniel Fab IoA 54 G7
Llanddarog Carmth 26 C5
Llanddeiniol Cerdgn 37 J6
Llanddeiniolen Gwynd 54 G8
Llandderfel Gwynd 47 R4
Llanddeusant IoA 54 D5
Llanddew Powys 27 M3
Llanddewi Swans 26 B10
Llanddewi Brefi Cerdgn 37 L9
Llanddewi Rhydderch Mons 28 D6
Llanddewi Velfrey Pembks 25 K5
Llanddewi Ystradenni Powys 38 C8
Llanddoged Conwy 55 L8
Llanddona IoA 54 H5
Llanddowror Carmth 25 M6
Llanddulas Conwy 55 N6
Llanddwywe Gwynd 47 J6
Llanddyfnan IoA 54 G6
Llandefaelog-Tre'r-Graig Powys 27 N3
Llandefalle Powys 27 M2
Llandegfan IoA 54 H6
Llandegla Denbgs 48 E5
Llandegley Powys 38 D9
Llandegveth Mons 28 D9
Llandeilo Carmth 26 E4
Llandeilo Graban Powys 38 C12
Llandeloy Pembks 24 F4
Llandenny Mons 28 E7
Llandevaud Newpt 28 E10
Llandevenny Mons 28 E10
Llandinam Powys 38 B5
Llandissilio Pembks 25 K5
Llandogo Mons 28 F7
Llandough V Glam 16 D2
Llandough V Glam 16 F2
Llandovery Carmth 26 G2
Llandow V Glam 16 C2
Llandre Carmth 37 L11
Llandre Cerdgn 37 K4
Llandre Isaf Pembks 25 K3
Llandrillo Denbgs 48 B7
Llandrillo-yn-Rhos Conwy 55 M5
Llandrindod Wells Powys 38 C9
Llandrinio Powys 48 F11
Llandudno Conwy 55 L5
Llandudno Junction Conwy 55 L6
Llandulas Powys 37 P11
Llandwrog Gwynd 54 F9
Llandybie Carmth 26 E6
Llandyfaelog Carmth 25 P6
Llandyfriog Cerdgn 36 F11
Llandygai Gwynd 54 H7
Llandygwydd Cerdgn 36 D11
Llandyrnog Denbgs 48 C3
Llandyssil Powys 38 E3
Llandysul Cerdgn 36 G11
Llanedeyrn Cardif 27 P11
Llaneglwys Powys 27 M2
Llanegryn Gwynd 47 K9
Llanegwad Carmth 26 D4
Llaneilian IoA 54 F3
Llanelian-yn-Rhôs Conwy 55 M6
Llanelidan Denbgs 48 C5
Llanelieu Powys 27 P3
Llanellen Mons 28 C6
Llanelli Carmth 26 C8
Llanelltyd Gwynd 47 L7
Llanelwedd Powys 38 B10
Llanenddwyn Gwynd 47 J6
Llanengan Gwynd 46 E6
Llanerchymedd IoA 54 F5
Llanerfyl Powys 38 B1
Llanfachraeth IoA 54 D5
Llanfachreth Gwynd 47 M6
Llanfaelog IoA 54 D7
Llanfaelrhys Gwynd 46 D6
Llanfaethlu IoA 54 D4
Llanfair Gwynd 47 J5
Llanfair Caereinion Powys 38 C2
Llanfair Clydogau Cerdgn 37 K9
Llanfair Dyffryn Clwyd Denbgs 48 D4
Llanfairfechan Conwy 55 K6
Llanfairpwllgwyngyll IoA 54 G7
Llanfair Talhaiarn Conwy 55 N7
Llanfair Waterdine Shrops 38 E6
Llanfairynghornwy IoA 54 D4
Llanfair-yn-Neubwll IoA 54 D6
Llanfallteg Carmth 25 K5
Llanfallteg West Carmth 25 K5
Llanfarian Cerdgn 37 J5
Llanfechain Powys 48 E10
Llanfechell IoA 54 E4
Llanferres Denbgs 48 E4
Llan Ffestiniog Gwynd 47 L3
Llanfihangel-ar-arth Carmth 36 G11
Llanfihangel Glyn Myfyr Conwy 55 P10
Llanfihangel Nant Bran Powys 27 K2
Llanfihangel Rhydithon Powys 38 D8
Llanfihangel Rogiet Mons 28 E10
Llanfihangel-y-Creuddyn Cerdgn 37 L5
Llanfihangel-yng-Ngwynfa Powys 48 C11
Llanfihangel yn Nhowyn IoA 54 D6
Llanfilo Powys 27 N3
Llanfoist Mons 28 C6
Llanfor Gwynd 47 Q4
Llanfrechfa Torfn 28 C9
Llanfrynach Powys 27 M4
Llanfwrog Denbgs 48 D4
Llanfwrog IoA 54 D5
Llanfyllin Powys 48 D10
Llanfynydd Carmth 26 D4
Llanfynydd Flints 48 F4
Llanfyrnach Pembks 25 L3
Llangadfan Powys 48 B12
Llangadog Carmth 26 F3
Llangadwaladr IoA 54 E7
Llangaffo IoA 54 F7
Llangammarch Wells Powys 37 Q10
Llangan V Glam 27 K12
Llangarron Herefs 28 F5
Llangathen Carmth 26 D4
Llangattock Powys 27 P5
Llangattock Lingoed Mons 28 D5
Llangedwyn Powys 48 E10
Llangefni IoA 54 F6
Llangeinor Brdgnd 27 J10
Llangeitho Cerdgn 37 K8
Llangeler Carmth 36 F11
Llangelynin Gwynd 47 J9
Llangennech Carmth 26 D8
Llangennith Swans 25 P9
Llangernyw Conwy 55 N7
Llangian Gwynd 46 E5
Llangloffan Pembks 24 F3
Llanglydwen Carmth 25 L4
Llangoed IoA 54 H6
Llangollen Denbgs 48 E7
Llangolman Pembks 25 K4
Llangors Powys 27 N4
Llangower Gwynd 47 P5
Llangrannog Cerdgn 36 E9
Llangristiolus IoA 54 F6
Llangrove Herefs 28 F5
Llangunllo Powys 38 E7
Llangunnor Carmth 25 P5
Llangurig Powys 37 P5
Llangwm Conwy 47 Q3
Llangwm Mons 28 E8
Llangwm Pembks 24 H6
Llangwnnadl Gwynd 46 D5
Llangwyryfon Cerdgn 37 K6
Llangybi Cerdgn 37 K9
Llangybi Gwynd 46 G3
Llangybi Mons 28 D9
Llangyndeyrn Carmth 26 B6
Llangynhafal Denbgs 48 D3
Llangynidr Powys 27 N5
Llangynin Carmth 25 M5
Llangynog Carmth 25 N6
Llangynog Powys 48 B9
Llangynwyd Brdgnd 27 J10
Llanhamlach Powys 27 M4
Llanharan Rhondd 27 L11
Llanharry Rhondd 27 L11
Llanhennock Mons 28 D9
Llanhilleth Blae G 27 P8
Llanidloes Powys 37 Q4
Llaniestyn Gwynd 46 E5
Llanigon Powys 27 P2
Llanilar Cerdgn 37 K5
Llanilid Rhondd 27 K11
Llanina Cerdgn 36 G8
Llanishen Cardif 27 N11
Llanishen Mons 28 F7
Llanllechid Gwynd 55 J7
Llanllowell Mons 28 D8
Llanllugan Powys 38 C2
Llanllwch Carmth 25 P5
Llanllwchaiarn Powys 38 D4
Llanllwni Carmth 36 H11
Llanllyfni Gwynd 54 F10
Llanmadoc Swans 25 Q9
Llanmaes V Glam 16 D3
Llanmartin Newpt 28 D10
Llanmiloe Carmth 25 M7
Llannefydd Conwy 55 P7
Llannon Carmth 26 D7
Llannor Gwynd 46 F4
Llanon Cerdgn 36 H7
Llanover Mons 28 C7
Llanpumsaint Carmth 25 P3
Llanrhaeadr-ym-Mochnant Powys 48 D9
Llanrhian Pembks 24 E3
Llanrhidian Swans 26 C9
Llanrhychwyn Conwy 55 L8
Llanrhyddlad IoA 54 D4
Llanrhystud Cerdgn 37 J6
Llanrug Gwynd 54 G8
Llanrumney Cardif 27 P11
Llanrwst Conwy 55 L8
Llansadurnen Carmth 25 M6
Llansadwrn Carmth 26 F3
Llansadwrn IoA 54 H6
Llansaint Carmth 25 P7
Llansamlet Swans 26 F8
Llansanffraid Glan Conwy Conwy 55 L6
Llansannan Conwy 55 N8
Llansantffraed Powys 27 N4
Llansantffraed-Cwmdeuddwr Powys 37 Q7
Llansantffraed-in-Elvel Powys 38 C10
Llansantffraid Cerdgn 36 H7
Llansantffraid-ym-Mechain Powys 48 E10
Llansawel Carmth 26 E2
Llansilin Powys 48 E9
Llansoy Mons 28 E8
Llanspyddid Powys 27 L3
Llanstadwell Pembks 24 G7
Llansteffan Carmth 25 N6
Llantarnam Torfn 28 C9
Llanteg Pembks 25 L6
Llanthewy Skirrid Mons 28 D5
Llanthony Mons 28 C4
Llantilio-Crossenny Mons 28 D6
Llantilio Pertholey Mons 28 C5
Llantrisant Mons 28 D9
Llantrisant Rhondd 27 L11
Llantrithyd V Glam 16 E2
Llantwit Fardre Rhondd 27 M10
Llantwit Major V Glam 16 C3
Llanuwchllyn Gwynd 47 P5
Llanvaches Newpt 28 E9
Llanvair Discoed Mons 28 E9
Llanvapley Mons 28 D6
Llanvetherine Mons 28 D5
Llanvihangel Crucorney Mons 28 C5
Llanwddyn Powys 48 B10
Llanwenog Cerdgn 36 H10
Llanwern Newpt 28 D10
Llanwinio Carmth 25 M4
Llanwnda Gwynd 54 F9
Llanwnda Pembks 24 G2
Llanwnnen Cerdgn 37 J10
Llanwnog Powys 38 B4
Llanwrda Carmth 26 F3
Llanwrin Powys 47 M9
Llanwrthwl Powys 37 Q7
Llanwrtyd Wells Powys 37 P10
Llanwyddelan Powys 38 C2
Llanyblodwel Shrops 48 E10
Llanybri Carmth 25 N6
Llanybydder Carmth 36 H10
Llanycefn Pembks 25 J4
Llanychaer Pembks 24 H2
Llanymawddwy Gwynd 47 P7
Llanymynech Powys 48 F10

Llanynghenedl IoA....54 D5
Llanynys Denbgs....48 C3
Llanyre Powys....38 B9
Llanystumdwy Gwynd....46 H4
Llanywern Powys....27 M3
Llawhaden Pembks....25 J5
Llawryglyn Powys....37 Q3
Llay Wrexhm....48 G4
Llechrhyd Caerph....27 M7
Llechryd Cerdgn....36 D11
Lledrod Cerdgn....37 K6
Lleyn Peninsula Gwynd....46 E4
Llithfaen Gwynd....46 F3
Lloc Flints....56 D12
Llowes Powys....27 P1
Llwydcoed Rhondd....27 L7
Llwydiarth Powys....48 B11
Llwyncelyn Cerdgn....36 G8
Llwyndafydd Cerdgn....36 F9
Llwyngwril Gwynd....47 J9
Llwynmawr Wrexhm....48 E7
Llwynypia Rhondd....27 L9
Llynclys Shrops....48 F10
Llynfaes IoA....54 E6
Llysfaen Conwy....55 N6
Llyswen Powys....27 N2
Llysworney V Glam....16 C2
Llys-y-frân Pembks....24 H4
Llywel Powys....27 J3
Loan Falk....85 Q7
Loanhead Mdloth....86 F8
Loaningfoot D & G....70 F4
Loans S Ayrs....76 F5
Lobhillcross Devon....5 K3
Lochailort Highld....97 K12
Lochaline Highld....89 N7
Lochans D & G....68 E7
Locharbriggs D & G....78 G11
Lochavich Ag & B....90 C12
Lochawe Ag & B....90 F10
Loch Baghasdail W Isls....111 b6
Lochboisdale W Isls....111 b6
Lochbuie Ag & B....89 M10
Lochcarron Highld....97 M2
Lochdon Ag & B....89 P9
Lochdonhead Ag & B....89 P9
Lochead Ag & B....83 L7
Lochearnhead Stirlg....91 N10
Lochee C Dund....93 L8
Loch Eil Highld....90 E1
Locheilside Station Highld....90 D1
Lochend Highld....98 H2
Lochfoot D & G....70 E2
Lochgair Ag & B....83 P8
Lochgelly Fife....86 E4
Lochgilphead Ag & B....83 N5
Lochgoilhead Ag & B....84 D3
Lochieheads Fife....93 J11
Lochill Moray....101 K3
Lochindorb Lodge Highld....100 E8
Lochinver Highld....108 C10
Loch Lomond and The
    Trossachs National Park....84 H1
Loch Loyal Lodge Highld....109 L6
Lochluichart Highld....106 F9
Lochmaben D & G....78 H11
Lochmaddy W Isls....111 b4
Loch nam Madadh W Isls....111 b4
Loch Ness Highld....98 G4
Lochore Fife....86 E3
Loch Portain W Isls....111 b4
Lochportain W Isls....111 b4
Lochranza N Ayrs....75 P3
Loch Sgioport W Isls....111 b5
Lochside Abers....95 M8
Lochside D & G....78 F12
Lochside Highld....107 N11
Lochslin Highld....107 N6
Lochton S Ayrs....68 H3
Lochty Angus....95 J9
Lochty Fife....87 K1
Lochuisge Highld....89 Q5
Lochwinnoch Rens....84 F10
Lochwood D & G....78 H9
Lockengate Cnwll....3 M4
Lockerbie D & G....79 J11
Lockeridge Wilts....18 G7
Lockerley Hants....9 K3
Locking N Som....17 J4
Locking Stumps Warrtn....57 M9
Lockington E R Yk....60 G5
Lockleywood Shrops....49 M9
Locksbottom Gt Lon....21 N9
Locks Heath Hants....9 N6
Lockton N York....67 J9
Loddington Leics....41 B9
Loddington Nhants....32 B2
Loddiswell Devon....5 P9
Loddon Norfk....45 M9
Lode Cambs....33 N4
Lode Heath Solhll....40 F10
Loders Dorset....7 L4
Lodsworth W Susx....10 E5
Lofthouse Leeds....59 J8
Lofthouse N York....65 K11
Lofthouse Gate Wakefd....59 J8
Loftus R & Cl....66 G4
Logan E Ayrs....77 K7
Loganlea W Loth....86 B9
Loggerheads Staffs....49 N8
Logie Angus....95 L8
Logie Fife....93 M10
Logie Moray....100 F5
Logie Coldstone Abers....94 G2
Logie Newton Abers....102 E7
Logie Pert Angus....95 L8
Logierait P & K....92 E5
Logierieve Abers....103 J9
Login Carmth....25 K4
Lolworth Cambs....33 L4
Lonbain Highld....105 K10
Londesborough E R Yk....60 E5
London Gt Lon....21 M7
London Apprentice Cnwll....3 M6
London City Airport
    Gt Lon....21 N7
London Colney Herts....21 J3
Londonderry N York....65 N9
London Gateway Services
    Gt Lon....21 K5

London Gatwick Airport
    W Susx....11 L2
London Heathrow Airport
    Gt Lon....20 H8
London Luton Airport Luton....32 G11
London Oxford Airport Oxon....31 L10
London Southend Airport
    Essex....22 G5
London Stansted Airport
    Essex....33 N11
Londonthorpe Lincs....42 D3
London Zoo ZSL Gt Lon....21 L6
Londubh Highld....105 M6
Lonemore Highld....105 L6
Long Ashton N Som....17 M3
Long Bank Worcs....39 N7
Long Bennington Lincs....42 B2
Longbenton N Tyne....73 M7
Longborough Gloucs....30 F8
Long Bredy Dorset....7 N5
Longbridge Birm....40 D11
Longbridge Deverill Wilts....18 C11
Long Buckby Nhants....31 N1
Longburton Dorset....7 P1
Long Clawson Leics....41 Q3
Longcliffe Derbys....50 G9
Longcombe Devon....5 Q8
Long Compton Staffs....49 Q10
Long Compton Warwks....30 H7
Longcot Oxon....19 J3
Long Crendon Bucks....31 B2
Long Crichel Dorset....8 E4
Longden Shrops....38 H2
Long Ditton Surrey....21 J9
Longdon Staffs....40 E5
Longdon Worcs....29 L2
Longdon Green Staffs....40 E5
Longdon upon Tern Wrekin....49 L11
Longdown Devon....6 B5
Longdowns Cnwll....2 H8
Long Duckmanton Derbys....51 K6
Long Eaton Derbys....41 L2
Longfield Kent....22 C9
Longford Covtry....41 J10
Longford Derbys....50 G12
Longford Gloucs....29 L5
Longford Shrops....49 M8
Longford Wrekin....49 N10
Longforgan P & K....93 K9
Longformacus Border....87 K10
Longframlington Nthumb....73 K1
Long Green Ches W....49 J2
Longham Dorset....8 F7
Longham Norfk....44 F7
Long Hanborough Oxon....31 K10
Longhaven Abers....103 M2
Longhirst Nthumb....73 L3
Longhope Gloucs....29 J5
Longhope Ork....111 g3
Longhorsley Nthumb....73 K2
Longhoughton Nthumb....81 Q10
Long Itchington Warwks....31 K2
Longlane Derbys....50 G12
Long Lawford Warwks....41 L11
Longlevens Gloucs....29 L5
Longleys P & K....93 K7
Long Load Somset....17 L10
Longmanhill Abers....102 F3
Long Marston Herts....20 E1
Long Marston N York....59 L4
Long Marston Warwks....30 F4
Long Marton Cumb....64 C3
Long Melford Suffk....34 E7
Longmoor Camp Hants....10 C4
Longmorn Moray....101 K4
Longmoss Ches E....50 B6
Long Newnton Gloucs....29 M9
Longnewton Border....80 D8
Long Newton E Loth....87 K8
Longnewton S on T....65 P4
Longney Gloucs....29 K6
Longniddry E Loth....87 J7
Longnor Shrops....39 J3
Longnor Staffs....50 E7
Longparish Hants....19 M10
Long Preston N York....63 Q9
Longridge Lancs....57 L2
Longridge W Loth....85 Q9
Longriggend N Lans....85 N8
Long Riston E R Yk....61 J5
Longrock Cnwll....2 D9
Longsdon Staffs....50 C9
Longside Abers....103 L6
Longstanton Cambs....33 L4
Longstock Hants....19 L12
Longstowe Cambs....33 K6
Long Stratton Norfk....45 K10
Long Street M Keyn....32 B7
Longstreet Wilts....18 G9
Long Sutton Hants....10 B1
Long Sutton Lincs....43 L5
Long Sutton Somset....17 L10
Longthorpe C Pete....42 G9
Long Thurlow Suffk....34 G3
Longthwaite Cumb....71 N10
Longton Lancs....57 J4
Longton C Stke....50 C9
Longtown Cumb....71 N2
Longtown Herefs....28 C3
Longueville Jersey....7 c2
Longville in the Dale Shrops....39 K4
Long Waste Wrekin....49 L11
Long Whatton Leics....41 L3
Longwick Bucks....20 C3
Long Wittenham Oxon....19 P3
Longwitton Nthumb....73 J3
Longwood D & G....70 B4
Longworth Oxon....19 L2
Longyester E Loth....87 K8
Lonmay Abers....103 L4
Lonmore Highld....104 C12
Looe Cnwll....4 F9
Loose Kent....22 F11
Loosley Row Bucks....20 D4
Lootcherbrae Abers....102 D5
Lopen Somset....17 K12
Loppington Shrops....49 J9
Lordshill C Soton....9 L4
Lords Wood Medway....22 F10
Lornty P & K....92 H6
Loscoe Derbys....51 K10
Losgaintir W Isls....111 c3

Lossiemouth Moray....101 K2
Lostock Gralam Ches W....49 M1
Lostock Green Ches W....49 M1
Lostwithiel Cnwll....4 D8
Lothbeg Highld....107 L11
Lothersdale N York....58 C5
Lothmore Highld....110 A12
Loudwater Bucks....20 E5
Loughborough Leics....41 M4
Loughor Swans....26 D8
Loughton Essex....21 N4
Loughton M Keyn....32 B8
Lound Lincs....42 F6
Lound Notts....51 P4
Lound Suffk....45 Q9
Lount Leics....41 K4
Louth Lincs....53 K6
Lover Wilts....8 H4
Loversall Donc....51 M2
Loveston Pembks....25 J7
Lovington Somset....17 N9
Low Ackworth Wakefd....59 K10
Low Barbeth D & G....68 D4
Low Bentham N York....63 M8
Low Biggins Cumb....63 L6
Low Borrowbridge Cumb....63 L3
Low Bradfield Sheff....50 H3
Low Bradley N York....58 D5
Low Burnham N Linc....52 A3
Lowca Cumb....70 F10
Low Catton E R Yk....60 C4
Low Crosby Cumb....71 P4
Lowdham Notts....51 P10
Low Dinsdale Darltn....65 N5
Lower Aisholt Somset....16 G8
Lower Ansty Dorset....8 B4
Lower Apperley Gloucs....29 M4
Lower Arboll Highld....107 P6
Lower Ashton Devon....6 A6
Lower Assendon Oxon....20 C6
Lower Badcall Highld....108 D7
Lower Bartle Lancs....57 J3
Lower Basildon W Berk....19 Q5
Lower Beeding W Susx....11 K5
Lower Benefield Nhants....42 E11
Lower Bentley Worcs....30 C2
Lower Boddington Nhants....31 L4
Lower Bourne Surrey....10 D2
Lower Brailes Warwks....30 H6
Lower Breakish Highld....97 J5
Lower Broadheath Worcs....39 P10
Lower Broxwood Herefs....38 G10
Lower Bullingham Herefs....28 F2
Lower Burgate Hants....8 H4
Lower Caldecote C Beds....32 H7
Lower Chapel Powys....27 L2
Lower Chicksgrove Wilts....8 E2
Lower Chute Wilts....19 K9
Lower Clapton Gt Lon....21 M6
Lower Clent Worcs....40 B10
Lower Cumberworth Kirk....58 G11
Lower Darwen Bl w D....57 M4
Lower Dean Bed....32 F3
Lower Diabaig Highld....105 L9
Lower Dicker E Susx....12 B7
Lower Down Shrops....38 G5
Lower Dunsforth N York....59 K2
Lower Egleton Herefs....39 L11
Lower End M Keyn....32 D8
Lower Eythorne Kent....23 P12
Lower Failand N Som....17 M2
Lower Farringdon Hants....10 B3
Lower Feltham Gt Lon....20 H8
Lower Froyle Hants....10 C2
Lower Gabwell Devon....6 C8
Lower Gledfield Highld....107 K4
Lower Godney Somset....17 L7
Lower Gornal Dudley....40 B8
Lower Gravenhurst C Beds....32 G9
Lower Green Herefs....12 C3
Lower Green Kent....12 D2
Lower Halstow Kent....22 G9
Lower Hamworthy BCP....8 E8
Lower Hardres Kent....23 M11
Lower Hartwell Bucks....20 C2
Lower Hergest Herefs....38 F10
Lower Heyford Oxon....31 L8
Lower Heysham Lancs....62 H9
Lower Houses Kirk....58 F10
Lower Irlam Salfd....57 N9
Lower Killeyan Ag & B....74 D4
Lower Langford N Som....17 L4
Lower Largo Fife....86 H2
Lower Leigh Staffs....50 D1
Lower Loxhore Devon....15 K5
Lower Lydbrook Gloucs....28 G5
Lower Lye Herefs....38 H8
Lower Machen Newpt....27 P10
Lower Merridge Somset....16 G8
Lower Middleton Cheney
    Nhants....31 L6
Lower Moor Worcs....30 C5
Lower Morton S Glos....28 H9
Lower Nazeing Essex....21 N3
Lower Oddington Gloucs....30 G8
Lower Penarth V Glam....16 G3
Lower Penn Staffs....39 Q3
Lower Peover Ches E....49 N1
Lower Place Rochdl....58 B10
Lower Quinton Warwks....30 F5
Lower Raydon Suffk....34 G8
Lower Roadwater Somset....16 D8
Lower Seagry Wilts....18 E5
Lower Shelton C Beds....32 E8
Lower Shiplake Oxon....20 C8
Lower Shuckburgh Warwks....31 L2
Lower Slaughter Gloucs....30 F9
Lower Standen Kent....13 N3
Lower Stanton St Quintin
    Wilts....18 D5
Lower Stoke Medway....22 G8
Lower Stondon C Beds....32 G9
Lower Stone Gloucs....29 J9
Lower Stow Bedon Norfk....44 F10
Lower Street Norfk....45 L3
Lower Street Suffk....34 J6
Lower Swanwick Hants....9 N5
Lower Swell Gloucs....30 G8
Lower Tasburgh Norfk....45 K10
Lower Tean Staffs....50 D12
Lower Town Devon....5 P5
Lower Town Pembks....24 G2
Lower Upham Hants....9 N4

Lower Weare Somset....17 K5
Lower Welson Herefs....38 F11
Lower Westmancote Worcs....29 N2
Lower Whatley Somset....17 Q6
Lower Whitley Ches W....57 L11
Lower Wield Hants....19 Q11
Lower Willingdon E Susx....12 C9
Lower Withington Ches E....49 P2
Lower Woodford Wilts....8 G1
Lower Wraxhall Dorset....7 N3
Lowesby Leics....41 Q6
Lowestoft Suffk....45 Q10
Loweswater Cumb....71 J10
Low Fell Gatesd....73 M8
Lowfield Heath W Susx....11 L3
Low Gartachorrans Stirlg....84 H6
Low Grantley N York....65 M12
Low Ham Somset....17 L9
Low Harrogate N York....58 H3
Low Hesket Cumb....71 P6
Low Hutton N York....60 D1
Lowick Nhants....32 E1
Lowick Nthumb....81 L6
Lowick Green Cumb....62 F5
Low Lorton Cumb....71 J9
Low Marnham Notts....52 B9
Low Mill N York....66 F8
Low Moorsley Sundld....73 N10
Low Moresby Cumb....70 G10
Low Newton Cumb....62 H6
Low Row Cumb....72 B8
Low Row N York....64 H7
Low Salchrie D & G....68 D6
Low Santon N Linc....60 G10
Lowsonford Warwks....30 F1
Low Tharston Norfk....45 K10
Lowther Cumb....71 Q10
Lowthorpe E R Yk....61 J3
Lowton Somset....16 G11
Lowton Common Wigan....57 L8
Low Torry Fife....86 B5
Low Worsall N York....65 P5
Low Wray Cumb....62 G2
Loxbeare Devon....16 C11
Loxhill Surrey....10 G3
Loxhore Devon....15 K4
Loxley Warwks....30 H4
Loxton N Som....17 K5
Loxwood W Susx....10 H4
Lubenham Leics....41 P9
Luccombe Somset....16 C7
Luccombe Village IoW....9 P10
Lucker Nthumb....81 N8
Luckett Cnwll....5 J5
Lucking Street Essex....34 D9
Luckington Wilts....18 C4
Lucklawhill Fife....93 M10
Luckwell Bridge Somset....16 B8
Lucton Herefs....38 H8
Ludag W Isls....111 b6
Ludborough Lincs....53 J4
Ludbrook Devon....5 N9
Ludchurch Pembks....25 K6
Luddenden Calder....58 D8
Luddenden Foot Calder....58 D8
Luddesdown Kent....22 D9
Luddington N Linc....60 E10
Luddington Warwks....30 F4
Luddington in the Brook
    Nhants....42 F12
Ludford Lincs....52 H5
Ludford Shrops....39 K7
Ludgershall Bucks....31 P10
Ludgershall Wilts....19 J9
Ludgvan Cnwll....2 D8
Ludham Norfk....45 N6
Ludlow Shrops....39 K7
Ludney Somset....7 K1
Ludwell Wilts....8 D3
Ludworth Dur....73 P11
Luffness E Loth....87 J6
Lugar E Ayrs....77 K7
Luggate Burn E Loth....87 L7
Luggiebank N Lans....85 M8
Lugton E Ayrs....84 G11
Lugwardine Herefs....28 G1
Luib Highld....96 G4
Lulham Herefs....28 E1
Lullington Derbys....40 G5
Lullington Somset....18 B9
Lulsgate Bottom N Som....17 M3
Lulsley Worcs....39 N10
Lumb Calder....58 D9
Lumby N York....59 K7
Lumphanan Abers....95 J2
Lumphinnans Fife....86 E4
Lumsden Abers....101 N10
Lunan Angus....95 L10
Lunanhead Angus....93 N5
Luncarty P & K....92 G9
Lund E R Yk....60 G5
Lund N York....59 P7
Lundie Angus....93 K8
Lundin Links Fife....86 H2
Lundin Mill Fife....86 H2
Lundy Devon....14 C3
Lunga Ag & B....83 K2
Lunna Shet....111 k3
Lunsford Kent....22 E10
Lunsford's Cross E Susx....12 E7
Lunt Sefton....56 G8
Luppitt Devon....6 F2
Lupset Wakefd....58 H9
Lupton Cumb....63 K5
Lurgashall W Susx....10 F5
Lurley Devon....16 C12
Luscombe Devon....5 Q8
Luskentyre W Isls....111 c3
Luss Ag & B....84 F1
Lussagiven Ag & B....83 J6
Lusta Highld....104 C10
Lustleigh Devon....5 Q4
Luston Herefs....38 H9
Luthermuir Abers....95 L8
Luthrie Fife....93 K10
Luton Devon....6 B7
Luton Devon....6 C3
Luton Luton....32 F11
Luton Medway....22 F9
Luton Airport Luton....32 G11
Lutterworth Leics....41 M9
Lutton Devon....5 M8

Lutton Devon....5 N7
Lutton Lincs....43 M5
Lutton Nhants....42 G11
Luxborough Somset....16 D8
Luxulyan Cnwll....3 M4
Luxulyan Valley Cnwll....3 N4
Lybster Highld....110 F8
Lydbury North Shrops....38 G5
Lydd Kent....13 K6
Lydd Airport Kent....13 K6
Lydden Kent....13 N2
Lydden Kent....23 Q9
Lyddington Rutlnd....42 C10
Lydeard St Lawrence Somset....16 F9
Lydford Devon....5 K3
Lydford on Fosse Somset....17 N9
Lydgate Calder....58 B8
Lydham Shrops....38 G4
Lydiard Millicent Wilts....18 G4
Lydiard Tregoze Swindn....18 G4
Lydiate Sefton....56 G7
Lydiate Ash Worcs....40 C11
Lydlinch Dorset....17 Q12
Lydney Gloucs....28 H7
Lydstep Pembks....25 J8
Lye Dudley....40 B10
Lye Green E Susx....11 P4
Lye Green Warwks....30 G2
Lye's Green Wilts....18 B10
Lyford Oxon....19 L2
Lymbridge Green Kent....13 L2
Lyme Regis Dorset....7 J4
Lyminge Kent....13 M2
Lymington Hants....9 K8
Lyminster W Susx....10 G8
Lymm Warrtn....57 M10
Lymm Services Warrtn....57 M11
Lympne Kent....13 L3
Lympsham Somset....17 J5
Lympstone Devon....6 D6
Lynchat Highld....99 L8
Lynch Green Norfk....45 J8
Lyndhurst Hants....9 K6
Lyndon Rutlnd....42 C8
Lyndon Green Birm....40 F9
Lyne Border....79 K1
Lyne Surrey....20 G9
Lyneal Shrops....49 J8
Lyneham Oxon....30 H9
Lyneham Wilts....18 F5
Lynemouth Nthumb....73 N3
Lyne of Skene Abers....102 G12
Lyness Ork....111 g3
Lyng Norfk....44 H6
Lyng Somset....17 J9
Lynmouth Devon....15 M3
Lynsted Kent....22 H10
Lynton Devon....15 M3
Lyon's Gate Dorset....7 P2
Lyonshall Herefs....38 G10
Lytchett Matravers Dorset....8 D8
Lytchett Minster Dorset....8 D8
Lyth Highld....110 F3
Lytham Lancs....56 G4
Lytham St Annes Lancs....56 G4
Lythe N York....67 J5
Lythmore Highld....110 C3

M

Maaruig W Isls....111 c3
Mabe Burnthouse Cnwll....2 H8
Mablethorpe Lincs....53 N6
Macclesfield Ches E....50 B6
Macduff Abers....102 F3
Macharioch Ag & B....75 L9
Machen Caerph....27 P10
Machrie N Ayrs....75 N5
Machrihanish Ag & B....75 J8
Machrins Ag & B....82 E4
Machroes Gwynd....46 E6
Machynlleth Powys....47 M10
Machynys Carmth....26 C8
Mackworth Derbys....50 H12
Macmerry E Loth....87 J7
Madderty P & K....92 E10
Maddiston Falk....85 Q7
Madeley Staffs....49 P6
Madeley Wrekin....39 M2
Madingley Cambs....33 L5
Madley Herefs....28 E2
Madresfield Worcs....39 P11
Madron Cnwll....2 C9
Maenclochog Pembks....25 J4
Maendy V Glam....16 D2
Maentwrog Gwynd....47 L3
Maen-y-groes Cerdgn....36 F8
Maer Staffs....49 P7
Maerdy Conwy....48 B8
Maerdy Rhondd....27 K8
Maesbrook Shrops....48 F10
Maesbury Shrops....48 F9
Maesbury Marsh Shrops....48 G9
Maesllyn Cerdgn....36 F10
Maesteg Brdgnd....27 J10
Maesybont Carmth....26 D5
Maesycwmmer Caerph....27 N9
Maggieknockater Moray....101 L6
Magham Down E Susx....12 D7
Maghull Sefton....56 G8
Magna Park Leics....41 M9
Magor Mons....28 E10
Magor Services Mons....28 E10
Maidenbower W Susx....11 L3
Maiden Bradley Wilts....18 B11
Maidencombe Torbay....6 C8
Maidenhayne Devon....6 H4
Maiden Head N Som....17 N3
Maidenhead W & M....20 E7
Maiden Newton Dorset....7 N4
Maidens S Ayrs....76 D9
Maiden's Green Br For....20 E8
Maiden Wells Pembks....24 G8
Maidford Nhants....31 N4
Maids Moreton Bucks....31 P7
Maidstone Kent....22 F11
Maidstone Services Kent....22 G11
Maidwell Nhants....41 Q11
Mail Shet....111 k4
Maindee Newpt....28 C10
Mainland Ork....111 h2

Mainland Shet 111 k4
Mainsforth Dur 65 N2
Mains of Balhall Angus 94 H8
Mains of Balnakettle Abers ...95 K7
Mains of Dalvey Highld 100 H8
Mains of Haulkerton Abers ...95 L7
Mains of Lesmoir Abers 101 N9
Mains of Melgunds Angus 93 P5
Mainsriddle D & G 70 F4
Mainstone Shrops 38 F5
Maisemore Gloucs 29 L5
Major's Green Worcs 40 E11
Malborough Devon 5 P11
Maldon Essex 22 G3
Malham N York 58 B2
Maligar Highld 104 J9
Mallaig Highld 97 J9
Mallaigvaig Highld 97 J9
Malleny Mills C Edin 86 E8
Malltraeth IoA 54 E7
Mallwyd Gwynd 47 P8
Malmesbury Wilts 18 D4
Malmsmead Devon 15 N3
Malpas Ches W 49 J6
Malpas Cnwll 3 J7
Malpas Newpt 28 C10
Maltby Rothm 51 M3
Maltby S on T 66 C5
Maltby le Marsh Lincs 53 M7
Maltman's Hill Kent 12 H2
Malton N York 66 H12
Malvern Worcs 39 P11
Malvern Hills 39 P12
Malvern Link Worcs 39 P11
Malvern Wells Worcs 29 K1
Mamble Worcs 39 M7
Mamhilad Mons 28 C7
Manaccan Cnwll 2 H10
Manafon Powys 38 C2
Mànais W Isls 111 c3
Manaton Devon 5 P4
Manby Lincs 53 L6
Mancetter Warwks 40 H7
Manchester Manch 57 Q8
Manchester Airport Manch ...57 P11
Mancot Flints 48 G3
Mandally Highld 98 D8
Manea Cambs 43 M11
Maney Birm 40 E8
Manfield N York 65 L5
Mangersta W Isls 111 b2
Mangotsfield S Glos 17 Q2
Mangurstadh W Isls 111 b2
Manish W Isls 111 c3
Manley Ches W 49 J2
Manmoel Caerph 27 P7
Mannal Ag & B 88 C4
Manningford Bohune Wilts ...18 G8
Manningford Bruce Wilts 18 G8
Manningham C Brad 58 F7
Mannings Heath W Susx 11 K4
Mannington Dorset 8 F6
Manningtree Essex 34 H9
Mannofield C Aber 95 Q2
Manorbier Pembks 25 J8
Manorbier Newton Pembks ...24 H8
Manorhill Border 80 F7
Manorowen Pembks 24 G2
Manor Park Gt Lon 21 N6
Mansell Gamage Herefs 38 H12
Mansell Lacy Herefs 38 H11
Mansfield E Ayrs 77 K4
Mansfield Notts 51 M8
Mansfield Woodhouse Notts ...51 M7
Manston Dorset 8 C4
Manston Kent 23 Q9
Manston Leeds 59 J7
Manswood Dorset 8 E6
Manthorpe Lincs 42 F7
Manton N Linc 52 D3
Manton Rutlnd 42 C8
Manton Wilts 18 H7
Manuden Essex 33 M10
Maperton Somset 17 P10
Maplebeck Notts 51 P8
Mapledurham Oxon 19 R5
Mapledurwell Hants 20 B12
Maplehurst W Susx 11 J5
Maplescombe Kent 22 C9
Mapleton Derbys 50 F10
Mapperley Derbys 51 K11
Mapperley Park C Nott 51 M11
Mapperton Dorset 7 M3
Mappleborough Green
  Warwks 30 E2
Mappleton E R Yk 61 L5
Mapplewell Barns 59 J11
Mappowder Dorset 7 Q2
Màraig W Isls 111 c3
Marazion Cnwll 2 D9
Marbhig W Isls 111 d2
Marbury Ches E 49 K6
March Cambs 43 L10
March S Lans 78 G6
Marcham Oxon 19 M2
Marchamley Shrops 49 L9
Marchington Staffs 40 F2
Marchwiel Wrexhm 48 G6
Marchwood Hants 9 L5
Marcross V Glam 16 C3
Marden Herefs 39 K11
Marden Kent 12 E2
Marden Wilts 18 G8
Marden Thorn Kent 12 F2
Mardy Mons 28 C5
Mareham le Fen Lincs 53 J10
Mareham on the Hill Lincs ...53 J9
Marehill W Susx 10 G6
Maresfield E Susx 11 P5
Marfleet C KuH 61 K8
Marford Wrexhm 48 G4
Margam Neath 26 H11
Margaret Marsh Dorset 8 B4
Margaretting Essex 22 D3
Margaretting Tye Essex 22 D4
Margate Kent 23 Q8
Margnaheglish N Ayrs 75 Q6
Margrie D & G 69 N8
Margrove Park R & Cl 66 F4
Marham Norfk 44 B7
Marhamchurch Cnwll 14 D10
Marholm C Pete 42 G9
Mariansleigh Devon 15 M7

Marine Town Kent 22 H8
Marionburgh Abers 95 L1
Marishader Highld 104 G9
Maristow Devon 5 K7
Marjoriebanks D & G 78 H11
Mark Somset 17 K6
Markbeech Kent 11 P2
Markby Lincs 53 M7
Mark Cross E Susx 12 C4
Market Bosworth Leics 41 K6
Market Deeping Lincs 42 G7
Market Drayton Shrops 49 M8
Market Harborough Leics 41 Q9
Market Lavington Wilts 18 E9
Market Overton Rutlnd 42 C6
Market Rasen Lincs 52 G5
Market Stainton Lincs 52 H7
Market Warsop Notts 51 M7
Market Weighton E R Yk 60 F6
Market Weston Suffk 34 G2
Markfield Leics 41 L5
Markham Caerph 27 N8
Markham Moor Notts 51 Q6
Markinch Fife 86 G2
Markington N York 58 H2
Markle E Loth 87 L6
Marksbury BaNES 17 P4
Marks Tey Essex 34 E11
Markyate Herts 32 F12
Marlborough Wilts 18 H7
Marlcliff Warwks 30 E4
Marldon Devon 6 B9
Marlesford Suffk 35 M5
Marlingford Norfk 45 J8
Marloes Pembks 24 E7
Marlow Bucks 20 D6
Marlow Bottom Bucks 20 D6
Marlpit Hill Kent 11 N1
Marnhull Dorset 8 B4
Marple Stockp 50 C3
Marr Donc 59 L12
Marrick N York 65 J7
Marsden Kirk 58 D10
Marsden S Tyne 73 P7
Marshalswick Herts 21 J2
Marsham Norfk 45 K5
Marsh Baldon Oxon 19 P2
Marshborough Kent 23 P11
Marshbrook Shrops 38 H4
Marshchapel Lincs 53 K4
Marshfield Newpt 28 B11
Marshfield S Glos 18 B6
Marshgate Cnwll 6 E2
Marsh Gibbon Bucks 31 N9
Marsh Green Devon 6 E4
Marsh Green Kent 11 N2
Marshland St James Norfk 43 N8
Marsh Lane Derbys 51 K5
Marsh Street Somset 16 D7
Marshwood Dorset 7 K3
Marske N York 65 K7
Marske-by-the-Sea R & Cl ...66 E4
Marston Herefs 38 G10
Marston Lincs 42 C2
Marston Oxon 31 M11
Marston Staffs 40 B3
Marston Staffs 40 E9
Marston Wilts 18 E9
Marston Green Solhll 40 F9
Marston Magna Somset 17 N10
Marston Meysey Wilts 18 G2
Marston Montgomery Derbys ...50 F12
Marston Moretaine C Beds ...32 E8
Marston on Dove Derbys 40 G2
Marston St Lawrence Nhants ...31 M6
Marston Trussell Nhants 41 P9
Marstow Herefs 28 G5
Marsworth Bucks 20 E1
Marten Wilts 19 K8
Martham Norfk 45 P6
Martin Hants 8 F4
Martin Kent 23 Q1
Martin Lincs 52 G10
Martinhoe Devon 15 L3
Martin Hussingtree Worcs 39 Q9
Martinstown Dorset 7 P5
Martlesham Suffk 35 L7
Martlesham Heath Suffk 35 L7
Martletwy Pembks 24 H6
Martley Worcs 39 N9
Martock Somset 17 L11
Marton Ches E 49 Q2
Marton E R Yk 61 K6
Marton Lincs 52 B7
Marton Middsb 66 D4
Marton N York 59 K2
Marton N York 66 G10
Marton Shrops 38 F2
Marton Warwks 31 K1
Marton-le-Moor N York 65 P12
Martyr Worthy Hants 9 N2
Marvig W Isls 111 d2
Marwick Ork 111 g2
Marwood Devon 15 J5
Marybank Highld 106 H10
Maryburgh Highld 107 J10
Marygold Border 87 P9
Maryhill C Glas 85 J8
Marykirk Abers 95 L8
Marylebone Gt Lon 21 L7
Marylebone Wigan 57 J7
Marypark Moray 101 J7
Maryport Cumb 70 G8
Maryport D & G 68 F11
Marystow Devon 5 J4
Mary Tavy Devon 5 K4
Maryton Angus 95 L10
Marywell Abers 95 J3
Marywell Abers 95 Q3
Marywell Angus 93 Q6
Masham N York 65 L10
Masongill N York 63 M7
Mastin Moor Derbys 51 L5
Matching Green Essex 21 Q2
Matching Tye Essex 21 P2
Matfen Nthumb 73 J6
Matfield Kent 12 D2
Mathern Mons 28 F9
Mathon Herefs 39 N11
Mathry Pembks 24 F3
Matlask Norfk 45 J3
Matlock Derbys 50 H8

Matlock Bath Derbys 50 H8
Matson Gloucs 29 L5
Mattersey Notts 51 P3
Mattingley Hants 20 B10
Mattishall Norfk 44 H7
Mattishall Burgh Norfk 44 H7
Mauchline E Ayrs 76 H6
Maud Abers 103 J6
Maufant Jersey 7 c1
Maugersbury Gloucs 30 G8
Maughold IoM 56 e3
Mauld Highld 98 E2
Maulden C Beds 32 F8
Maulds Meaburn Cumb 64 B4
Maunby N York 65 N9
Maundown Somset 16 E9
Mautby Norfk 45 P7
Mavesyn Ridware Staffs 40 E4
Mavis Enderby Lincs 53 K9
Mawbray Cumb 70 G6
Mawdesley Lancs 57 J6
Mawdlam Brdgnd 26 H11
Mawgan Cnwll 2 G10
Mawgan Porth Cnwll 3 J3
Mawla Cnwll 2 G6
Mawnan Cnwll 2 H9
Mawnan Smith Cnwll 2 H9
Mawsley Nhants 32 B2
Maxey C Pete 42 G8
Maxstoke Warwks 40 G9
Maxton Border 80 E7
Maxton Kent 13 P2
Maxworthy Cnwll 4 G2
May Bank Staffs 49 Q6
Maybole S Ayrs 76 E8
Maybury Surrey 20 G10
Mayfield E Susx 12 C5
Mayfield Mdloth 86 G8
Mayfield Staffs 50 F10
Mayford Surrey 20 F11
May Hill Gloucs 29 J5
Mayland Essex 22 H3
Maylandsea Essex 22 H3
Maynard's Green E Susx 12 C6
Maypole Birm 40 E10
Maypole Green Norfk 45 N10
Maypole Green Suffk 34 F5
Meadgate BaNES 17 P5
Meadle Bucks 20 C3
Meadowfield Dur 73 M11
Meadwell Devon 5 J4
Mealabost W Isls 111 d2
Meanwood Leeds 58 H6
Meare Somset 17 L7
Meare Green Somset 16 H10
Meare Green Somset 17 J10
Mearns E Rens 85 J11
Mears Ashby Nhants 32 B4
Measham Leics 41 J5
Meath Green Surrey 11 L2
Meathop Cumb 62 H6
Meavaig W Isls 111 c2
Meavy Devon 5 L6
Medbourne Leics 42 B10
Meddon Devon 14 E8
Meden Vale Notts 51 M6
Medmenham Bucks 20 D6
Medomsley Dur 73 K9
Medstead Hants 9 Q12
Medway Services Medway 22 G10
Meerbrook Staffs 50 C8
Meesden Herts 33 L9
Meeth Devon 15 J9
Meeting House Hill Norfk 45 M5
Meidrim Carmth 25 M5
Meifod Powys 48 D11
Meigle P & K 93 K6
Meikle Carco D & G 77 N8
Meikle Earnock S Lans 85 M11
Meikle Ferry Highld 107 M5
Meikle Kilmory Ag & B 83 R10
Meikle Obney P & K 92 F8
Meikleour P & K 92 H7
Meikle Wartle Abers 102 F8
Meinciau Carmth 26 B6
Meir C Stke 50 C11
Melbost W Isls 111 d2
Melbourn Cambs 33 L7
Melbourne Derbys 41 J3
Melbourne E R Yk 60 D5
Melbury Abbas Dorset 8 C4
Melbury Bubb Dorset 7 N2
Melbury Osmond Dorset 7 N2
Melchbourne Bed 32 E4
Melcombe Bingham Dorset 8 B6
Meldon Devon 5 L2
Meldon Nthumb 73 K4
Meldreth Cambs 33 L7
Meldrum Stirlg 85 M3
Melfort Ag & B 90 B12
Meliden Denbgs 56 C11
Melin-y-wig Denbgs 48 B6
Melkinthorpe Cumb 71 Q9
Melkridge Nthumb 72 D7
Melksham Wilts 18 D7
Melling Lancs 63 L7
Melling Sefton 56 H8
Mellis Suffk 34 H2
Mellon Charles Highld 105 M4
Mellon Udrigle Highld 105 N3
Mellor Lancs 57 M3
Mellor Stockp 50 C3
Mellor Brook Lancs 57 M3
Mells Somset 17 Q6
Melmerby Cumb 72 B12
Melmerby N York 65 J9
Melmerby N York 65 N11
Melness Highld 109 K4
Melplash Dorset 7 L3
Melrose Border 80 D7
Melsetter Ork 111 g3
Melsonby N York 65 L7
Meltham Kirk 58 E11
Melton E R Yk 60 H8
Melton Suffk 35 L6
Melton Constable Norfk 44 H4
Melton Mowbray Leics 41 Q4
Melton Ross N Linc 60 H11
Melvaig Highld 105 L5
Melverley Shrops 48 G11
Melvich Highld 109 N4
Membury Devon 6 H3

Memsie Abers 103 K3
Memus Angus 93 M4
Menai Bridge IoA 54 H7
Mendham Suffk 45 L12
Mendip Hills 17 M5
Mendlesham Suffk 34 H4
Mendlesham Green Suffk 34 H4
Menheniot Cnwll 4 G7
Mennock D & G 77 N9
Menston C Brad 58 F5
Menstrie Clacks 85 P4
Mentmore Bucks 32 C11
Meoble Highld 97 L11
Meole Brace Shrops 49 J12
Meonstoke Hants 9 Q4
Meopham Kent 22 D9
Mepal Cambs 33 M1
Meppershall C Beds 32 G9
Mere Ches E 57 N11
Mere Wilts 8 C2
Mere Brow Lancs 56 H5
Mereclough Lancs 57 Q3
Mere Green Birm 40 E7
Mereworth Kent 22 D11
Meriden Solhll 40 G10
Merkadale Highld 96 D4
Merley BCP 8 F7
Merrion Pembks 24 G8
Merriott Somset 7 L1
Merrow Surrey 20 G12
Merry Hill Herts 21 J5
Merryhill Wolves 40 B7
Merrymeet Cnwll 4 G7
Mersea Island Essex 23 K1
Mersey Crossing Halton 57 K11
Mersham Kent 13 K3
Merstham Surrey 21 L11
Merston W Susx 10 E9
Merstone IoW 9 N9
Merther Cnwll 3 L5
Merthyr Cynog Powys 27 L2
Merthyr Mawr Brdgnd 27 J12
Merthyr Tydfil Myr Td 27 M7
Merthyr Vale Myr Td 27 M8
Merton Devon 15 J9
Merton Gt Lon 21 K9
Merton Norfk 44 E9
Merton Oxon 31 M9
Meshaw Devon 15 N8
Messing Essex 34 E11
Messingham N Linc 52 C3
Metfield Suffk 35 L1
Metherell Cnwll 5 J6
Metheringham Lincs 52 F10
Methil Fife 86 H3
Methilhill Fife 86 G3
Methlick Abers 102 H7
Methven P & K 92 F9
Methwold Norfk 44 C10
Methwold Hythe Norfk 44 B10
Mettingham Suffk 45 M11
Metton Norfk 45 K3
Mevagissey Cnwll 3 M6
Mexborough Donc 51 L2
Mey Highld 110 F2
Meysey Hampton Gloucs 18 G1
Miabhaig W Isls 111 c2
Michaelchurch Herefs 28 F4
Michaelchurch Escley Herefs ...28 D3
Michaelstone-y-Fedw Newpt ...27 P11
Michaelston-le-Pit V Glam ...16 F2
Michaelstow Cnwll 4 D4
Micheldever Hants 19 N11
Micheldever Station Hants ...19 N11
Michelmersh Hants 9 L3
Mickfield Suffk 35 J4
Micklebring Donc 51 L2
Mickleby N York 66 H5
Micklefield Leeds 59 K7
Mickleham Surrey 21 J11
Mickleover C Derb 40 H1
Mickleton Dur 64 H3
Mickleton Gloucs 30 F5
Mickletown Leeds 59 K8
Mickle Trafford Ches W 49 J2
Mickley N York 65 M11
Mickley Square Nthumb 73 J8
Mid Ardlaw Abers 103 K3
Mid Beltie Abers 95 K2
Mid Calder W Loth 86 C8
Mid Clyth Highld 110 F8
Mid Culbeuchly Abers 102 E3
Middle Aston Oxon 31 L8
Middle Barton Oxon 31 K8
Middlebie D & G 71 K1
Middlebridge P & K 92 D3
Middle Chinnock Somset 7 L1
Middle Claydon Bucks 31 P8
Middlecroft Derbys 51 K6
Middleham N York 65 K9
Middle Handley Derbys 51 K5
Middlehill Wilts 18 B7
Middlehope Shrops 39 J4
Middle Kames Ag & B 83 N5
Middle Littleton Worcs 30 E5
Middlemarsh Dorset 7 P2
Middle Mayfield Staffs 50 F10
Middle Rasen Lincs 52 F5
Middle Rocombe Devon 6 B8
Middlesbrough Middsb 66 C4
Middleshaw Cumb 63 K4
Middlesmoor N York 65 J11
Middle Stoke Medway 22 G8
Middlestone Dur 65 M2
Middlestown Wakefd 58 H10
Middlethird Border 80 F5
Middleton Ag & B 88 B7
Middleton Derbys 50 G8
Middleton Derbys 50 H9
Middleton Essex 34 E8
Middleton Hants 19 M11
Middleton Herefs 39 K8
Middleton Leeds 58 H8
Middleton N York 58 F4
Middleton N York 66 H10
Middleton Nhants 42 B11
Middleton Norfk 43 Q6
Middleton Nthumb 73 J4
Middleton P & K 86 B2
Middleton Rochdl 57 Q7
Middleton Shrops 39 K6

Middleton Suffk 35 N3
Middleton Swans 25 P10
Middleton Warwks 40 F7
Middleton Cheney Nhants 31 L6
Middleton-in-Teesdale Dur ...64 G3
Middleton Moor Suffk 35 N4
Middleton One Row Darltn ...65 P5
Middleton-on-Sea W Susx 10 F9
Middleton on the Hill Herefs ...39 K8
Middleton on the Wolds
  E R Yk 60 G4
Middleton Park C Aber 103 J11
Middleton Quernhow N York ...65 N10
Middleton St George Darltn ...65 N5
Middleton Scriven Shrops 39 M5
Middleton Stoney Oxon 31 M9
Middleton Tyas N York 65 M6
Middle Town IoS 2 b3
Middletown Powys 48 F11
Middle Tysoe Warwks 31 J5
Middle Wallop Hants 19 K12
Middlewich Ches E 49 N3
Middle Winterslow Wilts 9 J2
Middlewood Cnwll 4 G5
Middle Woodford Wilts 18 G12
Middlewood Green Suffk 34 H5
Middlezoy Somset 17 K9
Midford BaNES 18 B8
Midgham W Berk 19 P7
Midgley Calder 58 D8
Midgley Wakefd 58 H10
Midhopestones Sheff 50 G2
Midhurst W Susx 10 E6
Mid Lavant W Susx 10 D8
Midlem Border 80 C8
Mid Mains Highld 98 F2
Midpark Ag & B 83 Q10
Midsomer Norton BaNES 17 P5
Midtown Highld 109 K4
Mid Yell Shet 111 k2
Migdale Highld 107 K4
Migvie Abers 94 G1
Milborne Port Somset 17 P11
Milborne St Andrew Dorset ...8 C8
Milborne Wick Somset 17 P11
Milbourne Nthumb 73 K5
Milbourne Wilts 18 D4
Milburn Cumb 64 C2
Milbury Heath S Glos 29 J10
Milby N York 59 K1
Milcombe Oxon 31 K5
Mildenhall Suffk 34 B2
Mildenhall Wilts 18 H6
Mileham Norfk 44 F6
Mile Oak Br & H 11 K8
Milesmark Fife 86 C5
Miles Platting Manch 57 Q8
Mile Town Kent 22 H8
Milfield Nthumb 81 K7
Milford Derbys 51 J10
Milford Devon 14 E7
Milford Staffs 40 C4
Milford Surrey 10 F2
Milford Haven Pembks 24 F7
Milford on Sea Hants 9 K8
Milkwall Gloucs 28 G7
Milland W Susx 10 D4
Mill Bank Calder 58 D9
Millbreck Abers 103 K6
Millbridge Surrey 10 D2
Millbrook C Beds 32 E8
Millbrook C Soth 9 L5
Millbrook Cnwll 5 J9
Millbrook Jersey 7 b2
Mill Brow Stockp 50 C3
Millbuie Abers 102 G6
Millbuie Highld 107 J11
Millcorner E Susx 12 G5
Millcraig Highld 107 K4
Milldale Staffs 50 F9
Mill End Bucks 20 C6
Mill End Herts 33 K9
Millerhill Mdloth 86 G8
Miller's Dale Derbys 50 F6
Millerston C Glas 85 L9
Mill Green Cambs 33 P7
Mill Green Essex 22 D3
Mill Green Lincs 42 H5
Mill Green Suffk 34 F8
Mill Green Suffk 34 G5
Mill Green Suffk 35 J5
Millhalf Herefs 38 F11
Millheugh S Lans 77 M2
Mill Hill Gt Lon 21 K5
Millhouse Ag & B 83 P8
Millhousebridge D & G 78 H10
Millhouse Green Barns 58 G12
Millhouses Sheff 51 J4
Milliken Park Rens 84 G9
Millington E R Yk 60 E4
Millmeece Staffs 49 Q8
Mill of Drummond P & K 92 C11
Mill of Haldane W Duns 84 G6
Millom Cumb 62 D6
Millport N Ayrs 83 C11
Mill Street Suffk 34 H4
Millthrop Cumb 63 M4
Milltimber C Aber 95 P2
Milltown Abers 101 K12
Milltown Abers 101 N11
Milltown D & G 71 M1
Milltown Devon 15 K4
Milltown Highld 97 J2
Milltown of Auchindoun
  Moray 101 L7
Milltown of Campfield Abers ...95 L1
Milltown of Edinvillie Moray ...101 K7
Milltown of Rothiemay Moray ...102 C5
Milnathort P & K 86 D2
Milngavie E Duns 85 J7
Milnrow Rochdl 58 B10
Milnthorpe Cumb 63 J6
Milovaig Highld 104 B11
Milson Shrops 39 M7
Milstead Kent 22 H10
Milston Wilts 18 H10
Milthorpe Nhants 31 N5
Milton C Stke 50 B10
Milton Cambs 33 M4
Milton Cumb 71 Q3
Milton D & G 68 G8
Milton D & G 70 D4

Milton Derbys....................40 H3
Milton Highld....................98 G3
Milton Highld...................107 J11
Milton Highld...................107 M7
Milton Highld...................110 G5
Milton Inver.....................84 F8
Milton Kent......................22 D8
Milton Moray....................101 J10
Milton Moray....................101 P3
Milton N Som.....................17 J4
Milton Notts.....................51 P6
Milton Oxon......................19 N3
Milton Oxon......................31 L7
Milton P & K.....................94 B9
Milton Pembks....................24 H8
Milton Somset....................17 L10
Milton Stirlg....................84 H3
Milton W Duns....................84 G7
Milton Abbas Dorset...............8 B7
Milton Abbot Devon................5 J4
Milton Bridge Mdloth.............86 F9
Milton Bryan C Beds..............32 D10
Milton Clevedon Somset...........17 P8
Milton Combe Devon................5 K7
Milton Damerel Devon.............14 G9
Milton Ernest Bed................32 E5
Milton Green Ches W..............49 J4
Milton Hill Oxon.................19 M3
Milton Keynes M Keyn.............32 C8
Milton Lilbourne Wilts...........18 H8
Milton Malsor Nhants.............31 Q3
Milton Morenish P & K............91 P8
Milton of Auchinhove Abers.......95 J2
Milton of Balgonie Fife..........86 G3
Milton of Buchanan Stirlg........84 G5
Milton of Campsie E Duns.........85 L7
Milton of Finavon Angus..........93 N4
Milton of Leys Highld............99 K1
Milton of Murtle C Aber..........95 P2
Milton on Stour Dorset............8 B2
Milton Regis Kent................22 H9
Milton-under-Wychwood
  Oxon...........................30 H9
Milverton Somset.................16 F10
Milverton Warwks.................30 H2
Milwich Staffs...................40 C2
Minard Ag & B....................83 P4
Minchinhampton Gloucs............29 M8
Minehead Somset..................16 C6
Minera Wrexhm....................48 F5
Minety Wilts.....................18 F3
Minffordd Gwynd..................47 J4
Mingarrypark Highld..............89 N3
Miningsby Lincs..................53 K10
Minions Cnwll.....................4 G6
Minishant S Ayrs.................76 F8
Minllyn Gwynd....................47 P8
Minnigaff D & G..................69 K6
Minnonie Abers..................102 G4
Minskip N York...................59 K2
Minstead Hants....................9 K5
Minsted W Susx...................10 D6
Minster Kent.....................23 P9
Minsterley Shrops................38 G2
Minster Lovell Oxon..............30 H10
Minster-on-Sea Kent..............23 J8
Minsterworth Gloucs..............29 K5
Minterne Magna Dorset.............7 P2
Minting Lincs....................52 H8
Mintlaw Abers...................103 K6
Minto Border.....................80 D9
Minton Shrops....................38 H4
Mirehouse Cumb...................70 F11
Mireland Highld.................110 G4
Mirfield Kirk....................58 G9
Miserden Gloucs..................29 N7
Miskin Rhondd....................27 L11
Misson Notts.....................51 P2
Misterton Notts..................51 Q2
Misterton Somset..................7 L2
Mistley Essex....................35 J9
Mitcham Gt Lon...................21 L9
Mitcheldean Gloucs...............29 J5
Mitchell Cnwll....................3 J5
Mitchellslacks D & G.............78 F9
Mitchel Troy Mons................28 F6
Mitford Nthumb...................73 L4
Mithian Cnwll.....................2 H5
Mixbury Oxon.....................31 N7
Mobberley Ches E.................57 P11
Mobberley Staffs.................50 D11
Mochdre Powys....................38 C4
Mochrum D & G....................69 J9
Mockbeggar Kent..................12 E1
Mockerkin Cumb...................70 H10
Modbury Devon.....................5 N9
Moddershall Staffs...............50 B12
Moelfre IoA......................54 G4
Moelfre Powys....................48 E9
Moffat D & G.....................78 H7
Moggerhanger C Beds..............32 G6
Moira Leics......................40 H4
Molash Kent......................23 K11
Mol-chlach Highld................96 E7
Mold Flints......................48 E3
Moldgreen Kirk...................58 F10
Molehill Green Essex.............33 P10
Molescroft E R Yk................60 H6
Molesworth Cambs.................32 F2
Moll Highld......................96 G4
Molland Devon....................15 N6
Mollington Ches W................48 H2
Mollington Oxon..................31 K5
Mollinsburn N Lans...............85 M6
Mondynes Abers...................95 M6
Monewden Suffk...................35 L5
Moneydie P & K...................92 F9
Moniaive D & G...................78 C10
Monifieth Angus..................93 N8
Monikie Angus....................93 N7
Monimail Fife....................93 K11
Monken Hadley Gt Lon.............21 K4
Monk Fryston N York..............59 L8
Monkhide Herefs..................39 L12
Monkhill Cumb....................71 M4
Monkhopton Shrops................39 L4
Monkland Herefs..................39 J10
Monkleigh Devon..................14 H7
Monknash V Glam..................16 C3
Monkokehampton Devon.............15 K10
Monkseaton N Tyne................73 N6
Monks Eleigh Suffk...............34 F7
Monk's Gate W Susx...............11 K5

Monks Heath Ches E...............49 Q1
Monk Sherborne Hants.............19 Q9
Monksilver Somset................16 E8
Monks Kirby Warwks...............41 L10
Monk Soham Suffk.................35 K4
Monks Risborough Bucks...........20 D3
Monksthorpe Lincs................53 M9
Monk Street Essex................33 P10
Monkswood Mons...................28 D8
Monkton Devon.....................6 G3
Monkton Kent.....................23 P9
Monkton S Ayrs...................76 F6
Monkton S Tyne...................73 N7
Monkton Combe BaNES..............18 B8
Monkton Deverill Wilts...........18 C12
Monkton Farleigh Wilts...........18 B7
Monkton Heathfield Somset........16 H10
Monkton Wyld Dorset...............7 J4
Monkwearmouth Sundld.............73 P8
Monkwood Hants....................9 Q2
Monmore Green Wolves.............40 B7
Monmouth Mons....................28 F6
Monnington on Wye Herefs.........38 G12
Monreith D & G...................69 J10
Montacute Somset.................17 M11
Montford Shrops..................48 H11
Montford Bridge Shrops...........48 H11
Montgarrie Abers................102 D10
Montgomery Powys.................38 E3
Montrose Angus...................95 L9
Mont Saint Guern..................6 b2
Monxton Hants....................19 K11
Monyash Derbys...................50 F7
Monymusk Abers..................102 F11
Monzie P & K.....................92 C9
Moodiesburn N Lans...............85 L8
Moonzie Fife.....................93 L11
Moor Allerton Leeds..............58 H6
Moorby Lincs.....................53 J10
Moor Crichel Dorset...............8 E6
Moordown BCP......................8 G8
Moore Halton.....................57 L11
Moor End Calder..................58 D8
Moorends Donc....................59 P10
Moorhead C Brad..................58 F6
Moorhouse Cumb...................71 M4
Moorhouse Notts..................51 Q7
Moorhouse Bank Surrey............21 N11
Moorlinch Somset.................17 K8
Moor Monkton N York..............59 L3
Moorsholm R & Cl.................66 F5
Moorside Border..................84 B4
Moorswater Cnwll..................4 F7
Moorthorpe Wakefd................59 L11
Moortown Leeds...................58 H6
Moortown Lincs...................52 F4
Morangie Highld.................107 M6
Morar Highld.....................97 J10
Morborne Cambs...................42 G10
Morchard Bishop Devon............15 N10
Morcombelake Dorset...............7 K4
Morcott Rutlnd...................42 D9
Morda Shrops.....................48 F9
Morden Dorset.....................8 D8
Morden Gt Lon....................21 K9
Mordiford Herefs.................28 F3
Mordon Dur.......................65 N3
More Shrops......................38 G4
Morebath Devon...................16 C10
Morebattle Border................80 G8
Morecambe Lancs..................62 H8
Moredon Swindn...................18 G4
Morefield Highld................106 B4
Morehall Kent....................13 N3
Moreleigh Devon...................5 P9
Morenish P & K...................91 N8
Morestead Hants...................9 N3
Moreton Dorset....................8 B9
Moreton Essex....................21 Q3
Moreton Herefs...................39 J8
Moreton Oxon.....................20 B3
Moreton Wirral...................56 F10
Moreton Corbet Shrops............49 K10
Moretonhampstead Devon............5 P3
Moreton-in-Marsh Gloucs..........30 G2
Moreton Jeffries Herefs..........39 L11
Moreton Morrell Warwks...........30 H3
Moreton on Lugg Herefs...........39 J11
Moreton Pinkney Nhants...........31 M4
Moreton Say Shrops...............49 L8
Moreton Valence Gloucs...........29 K6
Morfa Nefyn Gwynd................46 E4
Morham E Loth....................87 K7
Morland Cumb.....................64 B3
Morley Ches E....................57 P11
Morley Derbys....................51 K11
Morley Leeds.....................58 H8
Morley Green Ches E..............57 P11
Morley St Botolph Norfk..........44 H9
Morningside C Edin...............86 F7
Morningside N Lans...............85 N11
Morningthorpe Norfk..............45 K10
Morpeth Nthumb...................73 L4
Morphie Abers....................95 L8
Morrey Staffs....................40 E4
Morriston Swans..................26 F8
Morston Norfk....................44 G2
Mortehoe Devon...................14 H3
Morthen Rothm....................51 L3
Mortimer W Berk..................19 Q7
Mortimer West End Hants..........19 Q7
Mortlake Gt Lon..................21 K8
Morton Cumb......................71 N5
Morton Derbys....................51 K8
Morton Lincs.....................42 F5
Morton Lincs.....................52 B5
Morton Notts.....................51 Q9
Morton Shrops....................48 F9
Morton-on-Swale N York...........65 N6
Morton on the Hill Norfk.........45 J6
Morvah Cnwll......................2 B8
Morval Cnwll......................4 F7
Morvich Highld...................97 N5
Morville Shrops..................39 M4
Morwenstow Cnwll.................14 D8
Mosborough Sheff.................51 K5
Moscow E Ayrs....................76 H4
Moseley Birm.....................40 E10
Moseley Wolves...................40 C7
Moseley Worcs....................39 P9
Moss Ag & B......................88 B7
Moss Donc........................59 N10
Mossat Abers....................101 N10
Mossbank Shet...................111 k3

Moss Bank St Hel.................57 K8
Mossbay Cumb.....................70 G9
Mossblown S Ayrs.................76 G6
Mossburnford Border..............80 F10
Mossdale D & G...................69 P5
Mossdale E Ayrs..................76 H9
Moss Edge Lancs..................62 H12
Mossend N Lans...................85 M10
Mossley Tamesd...................50 C1
Mosspaul Hotel Border............79 N8
Moss-side Highld................100 D4
Mosstodloch Moray...............101 L4
Mossyard D & G...................69 M8
Mossy Lea Lancs..................57 K6
Mosterton Dorset..................7 L2
Moston Manch.....................57 Q8
Mostyn Flints....................56 D11
Motcombe Dorset...................8 C3
Mothecombe Devon..................5 M10
Motherby Cumb....................71 N9
Motherwell N Lans................85 M10
Motspur Park Gt Lon..............21 K9
Mottingham Gt Lon................21 N8
Mottisfont Hants..................9 K3
Mottistone Hants..................9 K3
Mottistone IoW....................9 L10
Mottram in Longdendale
  Tamesd.........................50 C2
Mottram St Andrew Ches E.........57 Q12
Mouldsworth Ches W...............49 J2
Moulin P & K.....................92 E4
Moulsecoomb Br & H...............11 M8
Moulsford Oxon...................19 P4
Moulsoe M Keyn...................32 C8
Moultavie Highld................107 K2
Moulton Ches W...................49 M2
Moulton Lincs....................43 K5
Moulton N York...................65 M6
Moulton Nhants...................32 B4
Moulton Suffk....................34 B4
Moulton V Glam...................16 E3
Moulton Chapel Lincs.............43 J4
Moulton St Mary Norfk............45 N8
Moulton Seas End Lincs...........43 K5
Mount Cnwll.......................4 E6
Mount C Brad.....................58 E7
Mountain Ash Rhondd..............27 L8
Mountain Cross Border............86 D11
Mount Ambrose Cnwll...............2 G7
Mount Bures Essex................34 E9
Mountfield E Susx................12 E6
Mountgerald Highld..............107 J10
Mount Hawke Cnwll.................2 G6
Mountjoy Cnwll....................3 K4
Mount Lothian Mdloth.............86 F10
Mountnessing Essex...............22 D4
Mounton Mons.....................28 F9
Mount Pleasant Derbys............51 J10
Mount Pleasant Suffk.............34 C7
Mountsorrel Leics................41 M5
Mount Tabor Calder...............58 D8
Mousehole Cnwll...................2 C9
Mouswald D & G...................70 H2
Mow Cop Ches E...................49 Q4
Mowhaugh Border..................80 H9
Mowmacre Hill C Leic.............41 N6
Mowsley Leics....................41 N9
Moy Highld.......................98 F11
Moy Highld.......................99 L3
Moyle Highld.....................97 M6
Moylegrove Pembks................36 B10
Muasdale Ag & B..................75 K4
Muchalls Abers...................95 P4
Much Birch Herefs................28 F3
Much Cowarne Herefs..............39 L11
Much Dewchurch Herefs............28 F3
Muchelney Somset.................17 L10
Muchelney Ham Somset.............17 L10
Much Hadham Herts................33 L11
Much Hoole Lancs.................57 J4
Muchlarnick Cnwll.................4 F8
Much Marcle Herefs...............28 H3
Much Wenlock Shrops..............39 L3
Muck Highld......................89 J1
Muckleburgh Collection
  Norfk..........................44 H2
Mucklestone Staffs...............49 N7
Muckton Lincs....................53 L7
Muddiford Devon..................15 K5
Muddles Green E Susx.............12 B7
Mudeford BCP......................8 H8
Mudford Somset...................17 N11
Mudford Sock Somset..............17 M11
Mugdock Stirlg...................85 J2
Mugeary Highld...................96 E2
Mugginton Derbys.................50 H11
Muirden Abers...................102 F5
Muirdrum Angus...................93 P8
Muiresk Abers...................102 F5
Muirhead Angus...................93 L8
Muirhead Fife....................86 F2
Muirhead N Lans..................85 L8
Muirhouses Falk..................86 B6
Muirkirk E Ayrs..................77 L6
Muirmill Stirlg..................85 M6
Muir of Fowlis Abers............102 D11
Muir of Miltonduff Moray........101 J4
Muir of Ord Highld..............107 J11
Muirshearlich Highld.............98 A11
Muirtack Abers..................103 K7
Muirton P & K....................85 Q1
Muirton Mains Highld............106 H10
Muirton of Ardblair P & K........92 H7
Muker N York.....................64 G7
Mulbarton Norfk..................45 K9
Mulben Moray....................101 L5
Mull Ag & B......................89 M8
Mullardoch Highld................98 C3
Mullion Cnwll.....................2 G11
Mullion Cove Cnwll................2 F11
Mumby Lincs......................53 N8
Munderfield Row Herefs...........39 M10
Munderfield Stocks Herefs........39 M11
Mundesley Norfk..................45 M3
Mundford Norfk...................44 D10
Mundham Norfk....................45 M9
Mundon Hill Essex................22 G3
Mungrisdale Cumb.................71 M9
Munlochy Highld.................107 K10
Munnoch N Ayrs...................76 E2
Munsley Herefs...................29 J1
Munslow Shrops...................39 K5
Murchington Devon.................5 N3

Murcott Oxon.....................31 N10
Murkle Highld...................110 D3
Murlaggan Highld.................97 P10
Murroes Angus....................93 N8
Murrow Cambs.....................43 L8
Murston Kent.....................22 H9
Murthill Angus...................93 N4
Murthly P & K....................92 G7
Murton C York....................59 P4
Murton Cumb......................64 D3
Murton Dur.......................73 P10
Murton Nthumb....................81 K5
Musbury Devon.....................6 H4
Musselburgh E Loth...............86 G7
Muston Leics.....................42 B3
Muston N York....................67 N10
Muswell Hill Gt Lon..............21 L5
Mutehill D & G...................69 P8
Mutford Suffk....................45 P11
Muthill P & K....................92 C11
Mybster Highld..................110 D5
Myddfai Carmth...................26 G3
Myddle Shrops....................49 J10
Mydroilyn Cerdgn.................36 G9
Mylor Cnwll.......................3 J8
Mylor Bridge Cnwll................3 J8
Mynachlog-ddu Pembks.............25 K3
Mynydd-bach Mons.................28 F9
Mynydd-Bach Swans................26 E8
Mynyddgarreg Carmth..............25 P7
Mynydd Isa Flints................48 F3
Myrebird Abers...................95 M3
Myredykes Border.................72 B2
Mytchett Surrey..................20 E11
Mytholm Calder...................58 C8
Mytholmroyd Calder...............58 D8
Myton-on-Swale N York............59 K2

N

Naast Highld....................105 M6
Na Buirgh W Isls................111 c3
Naburn C York....................59 N5
Nackington Kent..................23 M11
Nacton Suffk.....................35 K8
Nafferton E R Yk.................60 H3
Nailbourne Somset................16 G9
Nailsea N Som....................17 L3
Nailstone Leics..................41 K6
Nailsworth Gloucs................29 L8
Nairn Highld....................100 D4
Nannerch Flints..................48 D2
Nanpantan Leics..................41 L4
Nanpean Cnwll.....................3 L5
Nanstallon Cnwll..................3 M3
Nanternis Cerdgn.................36 F8
Nantgaredig Carmth...............26 C5
Nantglyn Denbgs..................55 Q8
Nantmel Powys....................38 B8
Nantmor Gwynd....................47 K3
Nant Peris Gwynd.................54 H9
Nantwich Ches E..................49 M5
Nantyglo Blae G..................27 P6
Nant-y-moel Brdgnd...............27 K9
Naphill Bucks....................20 D4
Napton on the Hill Warwks........31 L2
Narberth Pembks..................25 J6
Narborough Leics.................41 M7
Narborough Norfk.................44 C7
Nasareth Gwynd...................54 F10
Naseby Nhants....................41 P10
Nash Bucks.......................32 B9
Nash Newpt.......................28 D11
Nash Shrops......................39 L7
Nassington Nhants................42 F10
Nateby Cumb......................64 D6
Nateby Lancs.....................63 J12
National Memorial
  Arboretum Staffs...............40 F5
National Motor Museum
  (Beaulieu) Hants...............9 L6
National Space Centre C Leic....41 N6
Natland Cumb.....................63 K4
Naughton Suffk...................34 G7
Naunton Gloucs...................30 E9
Naunton Worcs....................29 M2
Naunton Beauchamp Worcs..........30 C4
Navenby Lincs....................52 E10
Navestock Essex..................21 Q4
Navestock Side Essex.............22 C4
Navidale Highld.................110 B11
Navity Highld...................107 M8
Nawton N York....................66 F9
Nayland Suffk....................34 F9
Nazeing Essex....................21 N3
Neap Shet.......................111 k4
Near Cotton Staffs...............50 E10
Near Sawrey Cumb.................62 G3
Neasden Gt Lon...................21 K6
Neasham Darltn...................65 N5
Neath Neath......................26 G8
Neatham Hants....................10 C3
Neatishead Norfk.................45 M6
Nebo Cerdgn......................37 J7
Nebo Conwy.......................55 M9
Nebo Gwynd.......................54 F10
Nebo IoA.........................54 F4
Necton Norfk.....................44 E8
Nedd Highld.....................108 C8
Nedging Suffk....................34 G7
Nedging Tye Suffk................34 G6
Needham Norfk....................45 K11
Needham Market Suffk.............34 H6
Needingworth Cambs...............33 K3
Neen Savage Shrops...............39 M6
Neen Sollars Shrops..............39 M7
Neenton Shrops...................39 M5
Nefyn Gwynd......................46 E4
Neilston E Rens..................84 H10
Nelson Caerph....................27 M9
Nelson Lancs.....................57 Q2
Nemphlar S Lans..................77 P3
Nempnett Thrubwell BaNES.........17 M4
Nenthall Cumb....................72 E11
Nenthead Cumb....................72 E11
Nenthorn Border..................80 F6
Nerabus Ag & B...................82 C11
Nercwys Flints...................48 E4
Nerston S Lans...................85 L10
Nesbit Nthumb....................81 K7
Nesfield N York..................58 E4

Nesscliffe Shrops................48 H10
Neston Ches W....................56 F12
Neston Wilts.....................18 C7
Netchwood Shrops.................39 L4
Nether Abington S Lans...........78 F4
Nether Alderley Ches E...........49 Q1
Netheravon Wilts.................18 G10
Nether Blainslie Border..........80 D5
Netherbrae Abers................102 G4
Nether Broughton Leics...........41 P3
Netherburn S Lans................77 N2
Netherbury Dorset.................7 L3
Netherby N York..................59 J5
Nether Cerne Dorset...............7 P4
Nethercleuch D & G...............79 J10
Nether Compton Dorset............17 N11
Nether Crimond Abers............102 H10
Nether Dallachy Moray...........101 M3
Netherend Gloucs.................28 G8
Netherfield E Susx...............12 E6
Netherfield Notts................51 N11
Nether Fingland S Lans...........78 F6
Netherhampton Wilts...............8 G2
Nether Handwick Angus............93 L7
Nether Haugh Rothm...............51 K2
Netherhay Dorset..................7 K2
Nether Headon Notts..............51 Q5
Nether Heage Derbys..............51 J10
Nether Heyford Nhants............31 P3
Nether Kellet Lancs..............63 J8
Nether Kinmundy Abers...........103 L6
Nether Langwith Notts............51 M6
Netherley Abers..................95 P4
Nethermill D & G.................78 G10
Nethermuir Abers................103 J6
Netherne-on-the-Hill Surrey.....21 L11
Netheroyd Hill Kirk..............58 F9
Nether Padley Derbys.............50 G5
Nether Poppleton C York..........59 M4
Netherseal Derbys................40 H5
Nether Silton N York.............66 C8
Nether Stowey Somset.............16 G8
Netherthong Kirk.................58 F11
Netherthorpe Angus...............93 P4
Netherton Devon...................6 B8
Netherton Dudley.................40 C9
Netherton Kirk...................58 F10
Netherton N Lans.................85 N11
Netherton Nthumb.................81 K11
Netherton P & K..................92 H5
Netherton Sefton.................56 G8
Netherton Stirlg.................85 J7
Netherton Wakefd.................58 H10
Nethertown Cumb..................62 B1
Nethertown Highld...............110 G1
Nethertown Staffs................40 E4
Netherurd Border.................86 D12
Nether Wallop Hants..............19 K12
Nether Wasdale Cumb..............62 D2
Nether Westcote Gloucs...........30 G9
Nether Whitacre Warwks...........40 G8
Nether Whitecleuch S Lans........78 D5
Nether Winchendon Bucks..........31 Q10
Netherwitton Nthumb..............73 K3
Nethy Bridge Highld..............99 Q5
Netley Hants......................9 M6
Netley Marsh Hants................9 K5
Nettlebed Oxon...................20 B6
Nettlebridge Somset..............17 P6
Nettlecombe Dorset................7 M4
Nettleden Herts..................20 G2
Nettleham Lincs..................52 E8
Nettlestead Kent.................22 D11
Nettlestead Green Kent...........22 D12
Nettlestone IoW...................9 Q8
Nettlesworth Dur.................73 M10
Nettleton Lincs..................52 G4
Nettleton Wilts..................18 B5
Netton Wilts.....................18 G12
Nevern Pembks....................36 B11
Nevill Holt Leics................42 B10
New Abbey D & G..................70 F3
New Aberdour Abers..............103 J3
New Addington Gt Lon.............21 M10
Newall Leeds.....................58 G5
New Alresford Hants...............9 P2
New Alyth P & K..................93 J6
Newark C Pete....................42 H9
Newark Ork......................111 i1
Newark-on-Trent Notts............52 B11
New Arley Warwks.................40 H9
Newarthill N Lans................85 N10
New Ash Green Kent...............22 C9
New Balderton Notts..............52 B11
New Barn Kent....................22 C9
New Barnet Gt Lon................21 L4
Newbattle Mdloth.................86 G8
New Bewick Nthumb................81 M9
Newbie D & G.....................71 K3
Newbiggin Cumb...................64 B2
Newbiggin Cumb...................71 P9
Newbiggin Cumb...................71 Q6
Newbiggin Dur....................64 G3
Newbiggin N York.................64 H9
Newbiggin-by-the-Sea
  Nthumb.........................73 N4
Newbigging Angus.................93 K7
Newbigging Angus.................93 M8
Newbigging Angus.................93 N8
Newbigging S Lans................86 B11
Newbiggin-on-Lune Cumb...........63 N2
New Bilton Warwks................41 L11
Newbold Derbys...................51 J6
Newbold on Avon Warwks...........41 L11
Newbold on Stour Warwks..........30 G5
Newbold Pacey Warwks.............30 H3
Newbold Verdon Leics.............41 K6
New Bolingbroke Lincs............53 K11
Newborough C Pete................42 H8
Newborough IoA...................54 F8
Newborough Staffs................40 F3
New Boultham Lincs...............52 D8
Newbourne Suffk..................35 L8
New Bradwell M Keyn..............32 B8
New Brampton Derbys..............51 J6
New Brancepeth Dur...............73 M11
Newbridge C Edin.................86 D7
Newbridge Caerph.................27 P8
Newbridge Cnwll...................2 C9
Newbridge D & G..................78 F11
Newbridge Hants...................9 K4
Newbridge IoW.....................9 M9
Newbridge Green Worcs............29 L2

Newbridge-on-Wye Powys....38 B9
New Brighton Wirral....56 F9
Newbrough Nthumb....72 F7
New Buckenham Norfk....44 H11
Newbuildings Devon....15 N10
Newburgh Abers....103 K4
Newburgh Abers....103 K9
Newburgh Fife....93 J11
Newburgh Lancs....57 J6
Newburn N u Ty....73 L7
Newbury Somset....17 Q6
Newbury W Berk....19 M7
Newbury Park Gt Lon....21 N6
Newby Cumb....64 B4
Newby Lancs....63 P11
Newby N York....63 N8
Newby N York....66 C5
Newby N York....67 L9
Newby Bridge Cumb....62 G3
Newby East Cumb....71 P4
New Byth Abers....102 H5
Newby West Cumb....71 M5
Newcastle Mons....28 E5
Newcastle Shrops....38 F5
Newcastle Airport Nthumb....73 L6
Newcastle Emlyn Carmth....36 E11
Newcastleton Border....79 P10
Newcastle-under-Lyme
  Staffs....49 Q6
Newcastle upon Tyne N u Ty....73 M7
Newchapel Pembks....36 D11
Newchapel Surrey....11 M2
Newchurch IoW....9 P9
Newchurch Kent....13 K4
Newchurch Mons....28 E8
Newchurch Powys....38 E11
Newchurch Staffs....40 F3
New Costessey Norfk....45 K7
Newcraighall C Edin....86 G7
New Crofton Wakefd....59 K10
New Cross Gt Lon....21 M7
New Cross Somset....17 K11
New Cumnock E Ayrs....77 K8
New Deer Abers....103 J6
New Denham Bucks....20 G6
Newdigate Surrey....11 K2
New Duston Nhants....31 Q2
New Earswick C York....59 N3
New Edlington Donc....51 M2
New Elgin Moray....101 J3
New Ellerby E R Yk....61 K6
Newell Green Br For....20 E8
New Eltham Gt Lon....21 N8
New End Worcs....30 D3
Newenden Kent....12 G5
New England C Pete....42 H9
Newent Gloucs....29 J4
New Ferry Wirral....56 G10
Newfield Dur....65 L2
Newfield Highld....107 N7
New Fletton C Pete....42 H9
New Forest National Park....9 K6
Newgale Pembks....24 E4
New Galloway D & G....69 P4
Newgate Street Herts....21 L3
New Gilston Fife....87 J1
New Grimsby IoS....2 b1
Newhall Ches E....49 L6
New Hartley Nthumb....73 N5
Newhaven C Edin....86 F7
Newhaven E Susx....11 N9
New Haw Surrey....20 G10
New Hedges Pembks....25 K8
New Holland N Linc....61 J9
Newholm N York....67 J5
New Houghton Derbys....51 L7
New Houghton Norfk....44 D5
Newhouse N Lans....85 N10
New Hutton Cumb....63 K4
Newick E Susx....11 N6
Newington Kent....13 M3
Newington Kent....22 G9
Newington Oxon....19 Q2
New Inn Carmth....26 C2
New Inn Torfn....28 C8
New Invention Shrops....38 F6
New Lakenham Norfk....45 K8
New Lanark S Lans....78 E1
New Lanark Village S Lans....78 E1
Newland C KuH....61 J7
Newland Gloucs....28 G6
Newland N York....59 P8
Newland Somset....15 P5
Newland Worcs....39 P11
Newlandrig Mdloth....86 H9
Newlands Border....79 Q9
Newlands Nthumb....73 J9
Newlands of Dundurcas
  Moray....101 L5
New Langholm D & G....79 M11
New Leake Lincs....53 L11
New Leeds Abers....103 J11
New Lodge Barns....59 J11
New Longton Lancs....57 K4
New Luce D & G....68 G6
Newlyn Cnwll....2 C9
Newmachar Abers....103 J10
Newmains N Lans....85 N10
New Malden Gt Lon....21 K9
Newman's Green Suffk....34 E7
Newmarket Suffk....33 Q4
Newmarket W Isls....111 d2
New Marske R & Cl....66 E4
New Marston Oxon....31 M11
New Mill Abers....95 N5
Newmill Border....79 P6
New Mill Cnwll....2 C8
New Mill Kirk....58 F11
Newmill Moray....101 N5
Newmillerdam Wakefd....59 J10
Newmills C Edin....86 E8
New Mills Derbys....50 D4
Newmills Fife....86 B5
Newmills Mons....28 F7
New Mills Powys....38 C2
Newmiln P & K....92 G9
Newmilns E Ayrs....77 J4
New Milton Hants....9 J8
New Mistley Essex....35 J9
New Moat Pembks....25 J4
Newney Green Essex....22 D3
Newnham Hants....20 B11

Newnham Herts....33 J8
Newnham Kent....23 J11
Newnham Nhants....31 M3
Newnham Bridge Worcs....39 M8
Newnham on Severn Gloucs....29 J6
New Ollerton Notts....51 P7
New Oscott Birm....40 E8
New Pitsligo Abers....103 J4
Newport Cnwll....4 H3
Newport E R Yk....60 F7
Newport Essex....33 N9
Newport Gloucs....29 J8
Newport Highld....110 D10
Newport IoW....9 N9
Newport Newpt....28 C10
Newport Pembks....25 J2
Newport Wrekin....49 N10
Newport-on-Tay Fife....93 M9
Newport Pagnell M Keyn....32 C7
Newport Pagnell Services
  M Keyn....32 C7
New Prestwick S Ayrs....76 F6
New Quay Cerdgn....36 F8
Newquay Cnwll....3 J4
Newquay Zoo Cnwll....3 J4
New Rackheath Norfk....45 L7
New Radnor Powys....38 E9
New Ridley Nthumb....73 J8
New Romney Kent....13 K5
New Rossington Donc....51 N2
New Sauchie Clacks....85 P4
Newseat Abers....102 F8
Newsham Lancs....57 K2
Newsham N York....65 K5
Newsham N York....65 P9
Newsham Nthumb....73 N5
New Sharlston Wakefd....59 J9
Newsholme E R Yk....60 C8
New Silksworth Sundld....73 P9
Newsome Kirk....58 F10
New Somerby Lincs....42 D3
Newstead Border....80 D7
Newstead Notts....51 L9
Newstead Nthumb....81 N8
New Stevenston N Lans....85 M10
New Swanage Dorset....8 F10
Newthorpe Notts....51 L10
New Thundersley Essex....22 F5
Newton Ag & B....83 Q4
Newton Border....80 E9
Newton Brdgnd....26 H12
Newton C Beds....32 H7
Newton Cambs....33 M4
Newton Cambs....43 M7
Newton Ches W....48 H2
Newton Ches W....49 J4
Newton Cumb....62 E7
Newton Derbys....51 K8
Newton Herefs....28 D3
Newton Herefs....39 K10
Newton Highld....107 J11
Newton Highld....107 M11
Newton Highld....107 M8
Newton Highld....110 D3
Newton Lancs....42 F3
Newton Mdloth....86 G8
Newton Moray....100 H3
Newton Moray....101 J3
Newton Nhants....42 C12
Newton Norfk....44 D7
Newton Notts....51 P11
Newton Nthumb....73 J7
Newton S Lans....78 F3
Newton S Lans....85 L10
Newton Sandw....40 D8
Newton Staffs....40 D3
Newton Suffk....34 F8
Newton W Loth....86 C6
Newton Warwks....41 M10
Newton Abbot Devon....6 B8
Newton Arlosh Cumb....71 K5
Newton Aycliffe Dur....65 M3
Newton Bewley Hartpl....66 C3
Newton Blossomville M Keyn....32 D6
Newton Bromswold Nhants....32 E4
Newton Burgoland Leics....41 J4
Newton by Toft Lincs....52 F6
Newton Ferrers Devon....5 L7
Newton Ferry W Isls....111 b4
Newton Flotman Norfk....45 K9
Newtongrange Mdloth....86 G8
Newton Green Mons....28 F9
Newton Harcourt Leics....41 N2
Newton Heath Manch....57 Q8
Newtonhill Abers....95 P4
Newton-in-Bowland Lancs....63 M11
Newton Kyme N York....59 L5
Newton-le-Willows N York....65 L9
Newton-le-Willows St Hel....57 L9
Newtonloan Mdloth....86 G9
Newton Longville Bucks....32 C9
Newton Mearns E Rens....85 J11
Newtonmill Angus....95 K8
Newtonmore Highld....99 K8
Newton Morrell N York....65 M5
Newton of Balcanquhal P & K....92 H12
Newton of Balcormo Fife....87 K2
Newton of Belltrees Rens....84 F10
Newton-on-Ouse N York....59 L3
Newton-on-Rawcliffe N York....66 H9
Newton-on-the-Moor
  Nthumb....81 N12
Newton on Trent Lincs....52 B8
Newton Poppleford Devon....6 E5
Newton Purcell Oxon....31 N7
Newton Regis Warwks....40 H6
Newton Reigny Cumb....71 P8
Newton St Cyres Devon....15 Q11
Newton St Faith Norfk....45 K6
Newton St Loe BaNES....17 Q3
Newton St Petrock Devon....14 G9
Newton Solney Derbys....40 H3
Newton Stacey Hants....19 M11
Newton Stewart D & G....69 K6
Newton Tony Wilts....19 J11
Newton Tracey Devon....15 J6
Newton under Roseberry
  R & Cl....66 D5
Newton upon Derwent E R Yk....60 C5
Newton Valence Hants....10 B4
Newton Wamphray D & G....78 H9
Newton with Scales Lancs....57 J3
Newtown BCP....8 F8

Newtown Cumb....70 H6
Newtown Cumb....71 P3
Newtown D & G....77 M10
Newtown Devon....6 E3
Newtown Devon....15 N10
Newtown Gloucs....29 J8
Newtown Hants....9 Q5
Newtown Herefs....39 L12
Newtown Highld....98 E7
Newtown IoW....9 M8
Newtown Nthumb....81 L8
Newtown Powys....38 C4
Newtown Shrops....49 J8
Newtown Somset....6 H1
Newtown Staffs....50 B8
Newtown Wigan....57 K7
Newtown Worcs....39 Q10
Newtown Linford Leics....41 M5
Newtown St Boswells Border....80 D7
New Tredegar Caerph....27 N8
New Trows S Lans....77 N4
Newtyle Angus....93 K7
New Walsoken Cambs....43 M8
New Waltham NE Lin....53 J3
New Winton E Loth....87 J7
Newyork Ag & B....83 P2
New York Lincs....53 J10
New York N Tyne....73 N6
Neyland Pembks....24 H7
Nicholashayne Devon....16 E11
Nicholaston Swans....26 C10
Nidd N York....58 H3
Nigg C Aber....95 Q2
Nigg Highld....107 N7
Nigg Ferry Highld....107 N8
Ninebanks Nthumb....72 E9
Nine Elms Swindn....18 G4
Ninfield E Susx....12 E7
Ningwood IoW....9 L9
Nisbet Border....80 F8
Nisbet Hill Border....80 H4
Niton IoW....9 N11
Nitshill C Glas....85 J10
Nocton Lincs....52 F10
Noke Oxon....31 M10
Nolton Pembks....24 F5
Nolton Haven Pembks....24 F5
No Man's Heath Ches W....49 K6
No Man's Heath Warwks....40 H5
Nomansland Devon....15 P9
Nomansland Wilts....9 J4
Noneley Shrops....49 J9
Nonington Kent....23 N11
Nook Cumb....63 K6
Norbiton Gt Lon....21 K9
Norbury Ches E....49 K6
Norbury Derbys....50 F11
Norbury Gt Lon....21 L9
Norbury Shrops....38 G4
Norbury Staffs....49 P10
Norchard Worcs....39 Q8
Nordelph Norfk....43 N9
Nordley Shrops....39 M3
Norfolk Broads Norfk....45 P8
Norham Nthumb....81 J9
Norley Ches W....49 K2
Norleywood Hants....9 L7
Normanby Lincs....52 E6
Normanby N Linc....60 F10
Normanby R & Cl....66 D4
Normanby le Wold Lincs....52 G5
Normandy Surrey....20 E11
Norman's Green Devon....6 E5
Normanton C Derb....41 J2
Normanton Leics....42 B2
Normanton Notts....51 P9
Normanton Wakefd....59 J9
Normanton le Heath Leics....41 J5
Normanton on Cliffe Lincs....42 D2
Normanton on Soar Notts....41 L3
Normanton on the Wolds
  Notts....41 N2
Normanton on Trent Notts....52 B9
Norris Green Lpool....56 H9
Norris Hill Leics....41 J4
Norristhorpe Kirk....58 G9
Northall Bucks....32 D11
Northallerton N York....65 P8
Northam C Sotn....9 M5
Northam Devon....14 H6
Northampton Nhants....31 Q2
Northampton Worcs....39 Q8
Northampton Services Nhants....31 Q3
North Anston Rothm....51 M4
North Ascot Br For....20 E9
North Aston Oxon....31 L8
Northaw Herts....21 L3
Northay Somset....6 H1
North Baddesley Hants....9 L4
North Ballachulish Highld....90 H4
North Barrow Somset....17 N9
North Barsham Norfk....44 F3
Northbay W Isls....111 a7
North Benfleet Essex....22 F5
North Berwick E Loth....87 K5
North Boarhunt Hants....9 P5
Northborough C Pete....42 G8
Northbourne Kent....23 P11
North Bovey Devon....5 P4
North Bradley Wilts....18 C9
North Brentor Devon....5 K4
North Brewham Somset....17 Q8
Northbrook Hants....19 N11
North Buckland Devon....14 H4
North Burlingham Norfk....45 N7
North Cadbury Somset....17 P10
North Carlton Lincs....52 D7
North Carlton Notts....51 N4
North Cave E R Yk....60 F7
North Cerney Gloucs....30 D11
North Chailey E Susx....11 N6
Northchapel W Susx....10 F4
North Charford Hants....8 H4
North Charlton Nthumb....81 N9
North Cheam Gt Lon....21 K9
North Cheriton Somset....17 Q10
North Chideock Dorset....7 K4
North Cliffe E R Yk....60 F7
North Clifton Notts....52 B8
North Cockerington Lincs....53 L5

North Connel Ag & B....90 C9
North Cornelly Brdgnd....26 H11
North Cotes Lincs....53 K4
Northcott Devon....4 H2
Northcourt Oxon....19 N2
North Cove Suffk....45 P11
North Cowton N York....65 M6
North Crawley M Keyn....32 D7
North Creake Norfk....44 E3
North Curry Somset....17 J10
North Dalton E R Yk....60 F4
North Deighton N York....59 K4
Northdown Kent....23 Q8
North Downs....22 H11
North Duffield N York....59 P6
North Elmham Norfk....44 G6
North Elmsall Wakefd....59 L10
North End C Port....9 Q7
North End Essex....33 Q11
North End Hants....8 G4
North End Hants....19 N5
North End W Susx....10 F8
Northend Warwks....31 J4
Northenden Manch....57 P10
North Erradale Highld....105 J3
North Evington C Leic....41 N6
North Fambridge Essex....22 G4
North Ferriby E R Yk....60 G7
Northfield Birm....40 D10
Northfield C Aber....95 P1
Northfield E R Yk....60 H8
Northfields Lincs....42 E8
Northfleet Kent....22 D8
North Frodingham E R Yk....61 J4
North Gorley Hants....8 H5
North Green Suffk....35 M4
North Greetwell Lincs....52 E8
North Grimston N York....60 E1
North Hayling Hants....10 B8
North Hill Cnwll....4 G5
North Hillingdon Gt Lon....20 H6
North Hinksey Village Oxon....31 L11
North Holmwood Surrey....11 J2
North Huish Devon....5 P8
North Hykeham Lincs....52 D9
Northiam E Susx....12 G5
Northill C Beds....32 G7
Northington Hants....19 P12
North Kelsey Lincs....52 F3
North Kessock Highld....107 L11
North Killingholme N Linc....61 K10
North Kilvington N York....65 Q10
North Kilworth Leics....41 N10
North Kyme Lincs....52 G11
North Landing E R Yk....67 Q12
Northlands Lincs....53 K11
Northleach Gloucs....30 E10
North Lee Bucks....20 D2
Northleigh Devon....6 G4
North Leigh Oxon....31 K10
North Leverton with
  Habblesthorpe Notts....52 B7
Northlew Devon....15 J11
North Littleton Worcs....30 E5
North Lopham Norfk....44 G12
North Luffenham Rutlnd....42 D9
North Marden W Susx....10 D6
North Marston Bucks....31 Q9
North Middleton Mdloth....86 G9
North Millbrex Abers....102 H6
North Milmain D & G....68 E8
North Molton Devon....15 M6
Northmoor Oxon....19 M1
North Moreton Oxon....19 P3
Northmuir Angus....93 L5
North Mundham W Susx....10 E9
North Muskham Notts....52 B10
North Newbald E R Yk....60 F6
North Newington Oxon....31 K6
North Newnton Wilts....18 G8
North Newton Somset....17 J9
Northney Hants....10 B8
North Nibley Gloucs....29 K9
Northolt Gt Lon....21 J6
Northolt Airport Gt Lon....20 H6
Northop Flints....48 E2
Northop Hall Flints....48 F2
North Ormesby Middsb....66 D4
North Ormsby Lincs....53 J5
Northorpe Kirk....58 G9
Northorpe Lincs....42 H3
Northorpe Lincs....52 C4
North Otterington N York....65 P9
North Owersby Lincs....52 F5
Northowram Calder....58 E8
North Perrott Somset....7 L2
North Petherton Somset....16 H9
North Petherwin Cnwll....4 G3
North Pickenham Norfk....44 E8
North Piddle Worcs....30 C3
North Poorton Dorset....7 M3
Northport Dorset....8 D9
North Queensferry Fife....86 D6
North Rauceby Lincs....42 E2
Northrepps Norfk....45 L3
North Reston Lincs....53 L6
North Rigton N York....58 H4
North Rode Ches E....50 B7
North Roe Shet....111 k3
North Ronaldsay Ork....111 i1
North Ronaldsay Airport Ork....111 i1
North Runcton Norfk....43 Q6
North Scarle Lincs....52 C9
North Shian Ag & B....90 C7
North Shields N Tyne....73 N7
North Shoebury Sthend....22 H6
North Shore Bpool....56 F2
North Side C Pete....43 J9
North Somercotes Lincs....53 L4
North Stainley N York....65 M11
North Stifford Thurr....22 D7
North Stoke BaNES....17 Q3
North Stoke Oxon....19 Q4
North Stoke W Susx....10 G7
North Street Kent....23 K10
North Street W Berk....19 Q6
North Sunderland Nthumb....81 P7
North Tamerton Cnwll....14 F11
North Tawton Devon....15 L10
North Third Stirlg....85 M9
North Thoresby Lincs....53 J4
North Tolsta W Isls....111 e1
Northton W Isls....111 b3

North Town Devon....15 J9
North Town Somset....17 N7
North Town W & M....20 E7
North Tuddenham Norfk....44 G7
North Uist W Isls....111 a4
Northumberland National
  Park Nthumb....72 E5
North Walsham Norfk....45 L4
North Waltham Hants....19 P10
North Warnborough Hants....20 B12
North Weald Bassett Essex....21 P3
North Wheatley Notts....51 Q4
Northwich Ches W....49 M2
North Widcombe BaNES....17 N5
North Willingham Lincs....52 G6
North Wingfield Derbys....51 K7
North Witham Lincs....42 D6
Northwold Norfk....44 C10
Northwood C Stke....50 B10
Northwood Gt Lon....20 H5
Northwood IoW....9 N8
Northwood Shrops....49 J8
Northwood Green Gloucs....29 J5
North Wootton Dorset....17 P2
North Wootton Norfk....43 Q5
North Wootton Somset....17 N7
North Wraxall Wilts....18 B6
North York Moors National
  Park....66 G7
Norton Donc....59 M10
Norton E Susx....11 P9
Norton Gloucs....29 M4
Norton Halton....57 K11
Norton Nhants....31 N2
Norton Notts....51 M6
Norton Powys....38 F8
Norton S on T....66 C3
Norton Sheff....51 J5
Norton Shrops....39 N3
Norton Suffk....34 F4
Norton Swans....26 E10
Norton W Susx....10 E8
Norton Wilts....18 C4
Norton Worcs....30 D5
Norton Worcs....39 Q10
Norton Bavant Wilts....18 D11
Norton Canes Staffs....40 D6
Norton Canes Services Staffs....40 D6
Norton Canon Herefs....38 H11
Norton Disney Lincs....52 C10
Norton Fitzwarren Somset....16 G10
Norton Green IoW....9 K9
Norton Hawkfield BaNES....17 N4
Norton Heath Essex....22 C3
Norton in Hales Shrops....49 N7
Norton-Juxta-Twycross Leics....41 J6
Norton-le-Clay N York....65 P12
Norton-le-Moors C Stke....50 B9
Norton Lindsey Warwks....30 G2
Norton Little Green Suffk....34 F4
Norton Malreward BaNES....17 N3
Norton-on-Derwent N York....66 H12
Norton St Philip Somset....18 B9
Norton Subcourse Norfk....45 N9
Norton sub Hamdon Somset....17 L11
Norwell Notts....51 Q8
Norwell Woodhouse Notts....51 Q8
Norwich Norfk....45 K8
Norwich Airport Norfk....45 K7
Norwick Shet....111 m2
Norwood Clacks....85 P4
Norwood Green Gt Lon....21 J7
Norwood Hill Surrey....11 K2
Norwoodside Cambs....43 L9
Noss Mayo Devon....5 L10
Nosterfield N York....65 M10
Nostie Highld....97 M4
Notgrove Gloucs....30 E9
Nottage Brdgnd....26 H12
Nottingham C Nott....51 M11
Notton Wakefd....59 J10
Notton Wilts....18 D6
Noutard's Green Worcs....39 P8
Nuffield Oxon....19 Q4
Nunburnholme E R Yk....60 E5
Nuneaton Warwks....41 J8
Nunhead Gt Lon....21 M8
Nun Monkton N York....59 L3
Nunney Somset....17 Q7
Nunnington N York....66 F10
Nunsthorpe NE Lin....53 J2
Nunthorpe C York....59 N4
Nunthorpe Middsb....66 D5
Nunthorpe Village Middsb....66 D5
Nunton Wilts....8 H3
Nunwick N York....65 N11
Nursling Hants....9 L4
Nutbourne W Susx....10 C8
Nutbourne W Susx....10 H6
Nutfield Surrey....21 L12
Nuthall Notts....51 M11
Nuthampstead Herts....33 L9
Nuthurst W Susx....11 J5
Nutley E Susx....11 N5
Nuttall Bury....57 P5
Nybster Highld....110 G3
Nyetimber W Susx....10 E9
Nyewood W Susx....10 C6
Nymans W Susx....11 L4
Nymet Rowland Devon....15 M9
Nymet Tracey Devon....15 M11
Nympsfield Gloucs....29 L8
Nynehead Somset....16 F10
Nyton W Susx....10 E8

O

Oadby Leics....41 N7
Oad Street Kent....22 G10
Oakamoor Staffs....50 D11
Oakbank W Loth....86 C8
Oak Cross Devon....15 J11
Oakdale Caerph....27 P8
Oake Somset....16 F10
Oaken Staffs....39 Q2
Oakenclough Lancs....63 K11
Oakengates Wrekin....49 M12
Oakenshaw Dur....73 L12
Oakenshaw Kirk....58 F8
Oakford Cerdgn....36 G9

Oakford – Penrice 183

Oakford Devon 16 C11
Oakham Rutlnd 42 C8
Oakhanger Hants 10 C3
Oakhill Somset 17 P6
Oakington Cambs 33 L4
Oaklands Herts 33 J12
Oakle Street Gloucs 29 K5
Oakley Bed 32 E6
Oakley Bucks 31 N10
Oakley Fife 86 B4
Oakley Hants 19 P9
Oakley Suffk 35 J2
Oakridge Lynch Gloucs 29 M7
Oaksey Wilts 29 P9
Oakthorpe Leics 40 H5
Oakwood C Derb 51 J12
Oakworth C Brad 58 D6
Oare Kent 23 J10
Oare Somset 15 N3
Oare Wilts 18 H7
Oasby Lincs 42 E3
Oath Somset 17 K10
Oathlaw Angus 93 N4
Oatlands Park Surrey 20 H9
Oban Ag & B 90 B9
Oban Airport Ag & B 90 C8
Obley Shrops 38 G6
Obney P & K 92 F8
Oborne Dorset 17 P11
Occold Suffk 35 J3
Occumster Highld 110 F8
Ochiltree E Ayrs 76 H7
Ockbrook Derbys 41 K1
Ocker Hill Sandw 40 C8
Ockham Surrey 20 H11
Ockle Highld 89 L3
Ockley Surrey 11 J3
Ocle Pychard Herefs 39 L11
Odcombe Somset 17 M11
Odd Down BaNES 17 Q4
Oddingley Worcs 30 B3
Oddington Oxon 31 M10
Odell Bed 32 D5
Odiham Hants 20 C12
Odsal C Brad 58 F8
Odsey Cambs 33 J8
Odstock Wilts 8 G3
Odstone Leics 41 K6
Offchurch Warwks 31 J2
Offenham Worcs 30 D5
Offerton Stockp 50 B3
Offham E Susx 11 N7
Offham Kent 22 D11
Offham W Susx 10 G8
Offord Cluny Cambs 32 H4
Offord D'Arcy Cambs 32 H4
Offton Suffk 34 H6
Offwell Devon 6 G3
Ogbourne Maizey Wilts 18 H6
Ogbourne St Andrew Wilts 18 H6
Ogbourne St George Wilts 18 H6
Ogle Nthumb 73 K5
Oglet Lpool 56 H11
Ogmore V Glam 16 B2
Ogmore-by-Sea V Glam 16 B2
Ogmore Vale Brdgnd 27 K10
Okeford Fitzpaine Dorset 8 B5
Okehampton Devon 5 M2
Oker Side Derbys 50 H8
Okewood Hill Surrey 11 J3
Old Nhants 32 B3
Old Aberdeen C Aber 95 Q1
Old Alresford Hants 9 P1
Oldany Highld 108 C8
Old Arley Warwks 40 H8
Old Auchenbrack D & G 77 M11
Old Basford C Nott 51 M11
Old Basing Hants 19 Q9
Old Beetley Norfk 44 F6
Oldberrow Warwks 30 E2
Old Bewick Nthumb 81 M9
Old Bolingbroke Lincs 53 K9
Old Bramhope Leeds 58 G5
Old Brampton Derbys 51 J6
Old Bridge of Urr D & G 70 C3
Old Buckenham Norfk 44 H10
Old Burghclere Hants 19 M8
Oldbury Sandw 40 C9
Oldbury Shrops 39 N4
Oldbury Warwks 40 H8
Oldbury-on-Severn S Glos 28 H9
Oldbury on the Hill Gloucs 18 B3
Old Byland N York 66 D9
Old Cantley Donc 51 N1
Oldcastle Mons 28 C4
Old Catton Norfk 45 K7
Old Clee NE Lin 53 J2
Old Cleeve Somset 16 E7
Old Colwyn Conwy 55 M6
Oldcotes Notts 51 N3
Old Coulsdon Gt Lon 21 L11
Old Dailly S Ayrs 76 D10
Old Dalby Leics 41 P3
Old Deer Abers 103 K6
Old Edlington Donc 51 M2
Old Ellerby E R Yk 61 K6
Old Felixstowe Suffk 35 M9
Oldfield Worcs 39 Q8
Old Fletton C Pete 42 H10
Oldford Somset 18 B10
Old Forge Herefs 28 G5
Old Grimsby IoS 2 b1
Old Hall Green Herts 33 L11
Oldham Oldham 58 B12
Oldhamstocks E Loth 87 N7
Old Harlow Essex 21 P2
Old Hunstanton Norfk 44 B2
Old Hurst Cambs 33 J2
Old Hutton Cumb 63 K5
Old Inns Services N Lans 85 N7
Old Kilpatrick W Duns 84 H8
Old Knebworth Herts 32 H11
Old Lakenham Norfk 45 K8
Oldland S Glos 17 P2
Old Langho Lancs 57 N2
Old Leake Lincs 53 L12
Old Malton N York 66 H11
Oldmeldrum Abers 102 H9
Oldmill Cnwll 4 H5
Old Milverton Warwks 30 H1
Oldmixon N Som 17 J5
Old Newton Suffk 34 H4
Old Portlethen Abers 95 Q3
Old Radford C Nott 51 M11
Old Radnor Powys 38 F9
Old Rayne Abers 102 E9
Old Romney Kent 13 K5
Old Shoreham W Susx 11 K8
Oldshoremore Highld 108 D4
Old Sodbury S Glos 29 K11
Old Somerby Lincs 42 D4
Oldstead N York 66 D10
Old Stratford Nhants 31 Q6
Old Struan P & K 92 C3
Old Swinford Dudley 40 B10
Old Thirsk N York 66 B10
Old Town Cumb 63 L5
Old Town E Susx 12 C9
Old Town IoS 2 c2
Old Trafford Traffd 57 P9
Oldwall Cumb 71 P4
Oldwalls Swans 26 C9
Old Warden C Beds 32 G7
Old Weston Cambs 32 F2
Old Wick Highld 110 G6
Old Windsor W & M 20 F8
Old Wives Lees Kent 23 K11
Old Woking Surrey 20 G11
Olgrinmore Highld 110 C5
Olive Green Staffs 40 E4
Oliver's Battery Hants 9 M2
Ollaberry Shet 111 k3
Ollach Highld 96 F3
Ollerton Ches E 57 P12
Ollerton Notts 51 P7
Ollerton Shrops 49 M9
Olney M Keyn 32 C6
Olrig House Highld 110 E3
Olton Solhll 40 F10
Olveston S Glos 28 H10
Ombersley Worcs 39 Q8
Ompton Notts 51 P7
Onchan IoM 56 d5
Onecote Staffs 50 D9
Onibury Shrops 39 J6
Onich Highld 90 E4
Onllwyn Neath 26 H6
Onneley Staffs 49 N6
Onslow Green Essex 33 Q12
Onslow Village Surrey 20 F12
Onston Ches W 49 L1
Opinan Highld 105 L7
Orbliston Moray 101 L4
Orbost Highld 96 B2
Orby Lincs 53 M9
Orchard Portman Somset 16 H10
Orcheston Wilts 18 F10
Orcop Herefs 28 F4
Orcop Hill Herefs 28 F4
Ord Abers 102 E4
Ordhead Abers 102 E12
Ordie Abers 94 G2
Ordiequish Moray 101 L4
Ordsall Notts 51 P5
Ore E Susx 12 G7
Orford Suffk 35 N6
Orford Warrtn 57 L10
Organford Dorset 8 D8
Orkney Islands Ork 111 h2
Orkney Neolithic Ork 111 g2
Orlestone Kent 13 J3
Orleton Herefs 39 J8
Orleton Worcs 39 M8
Orlingbury Nhants 32 C3
Ormesby R & Cl 66 D4
Ormesby St Margaret Norfk 45 P7
Ormesby St Michael Norfk 45 P7
Ormiscaig Highld 105 M4
Ormiston E Loth 86 H8
Ormsaigmore Highld 89 K4
Ormsary Ag & B 83 L8
Ormskirk Lancs 56 H7
Oronsay Ag & B 82 E5
Orphir Ork 111 h2
Orpington Gt Lon 21 P9
Orrell Sefton 56 G9
Orrell Wigan 57 K7
Orroland D & G 70 C6
Orsett Thurr 22 D7
Orslow Staffs 49 P11
Orston Notts 51 Q11
Orton Cumb 63 L1
Orton Nhants 32 B2
Orton Staffs 39 Q3
Orton Longueville C Pete 42 G10
Orton-on-the-Hill Leics 40 H6
Orton Waterville C Pete 42 G10
Orwell Cambs 33 K6
Osbaldeston Lancs 57 M3
Osbaldwick C York 59 N4
Osbaston Leics 41 K6
Osbaston Shrops 48 G10
Osborne House IoW 9 N8
Osbournby Lincs 42 F3
Oscroft Ches W 49 J3
Ose Highld 96 C2
Osgathorpe Leics 41 K4
Osgodby Lincs 52 F5
Osgodby N York 59 N7
Osgodby N York 67 M9
Oskaig Highld 96 G3
Oskamull Ag & B 89 K8
Osmaston Derbys 50 G11
Osmington Dorset 7 Q6
Osmington Mills Dorset 7 Q6
Osmondthorpe Leeds 59 J7
Osmotherley N York 66 C7
Osney Oxon 31 L11
Ospringe Kent 23 J10
Ossett Wakefd 58 H9
Ossington Notts 51 Q7
Osterley Gt Lon 21 J7
Oswaldkirk N York 66 E10
Oswaldtwistle Lancs 57 N4
Oswestry Shrops 48 F9
Otairnis W Isls 111 b4
Otford Kent 21 Q10
Otham Kent 22 F11
Othery Somset 17 K9
Otley Leeds 58 G5
Otley Suffk 35 K5
Otterbourne Hants 9 M3
Otterburn N York 63 Q9
Otterburn Nthumb 72 F3
Otter Ferry Ag & B 83 P6
Otterham Cnwll 4 E3
Otterhampton Somset 16 H7
Otternish W Isls 111 b4
Ottershaw Surrey 20 G9
Otterswick Shet 111 k3
Otterton Devon 6 E6
Ottery St Mary Devon 6 E4
Ottinge Kent 13 M2
Ottringham E R Yk 61 M8
Oughterside Cumb 71 J7
Oughtibridge Sheff 50 H3
Oughtrington Warrtn 57 M10
Oulston N York 66 D11
Oulton Cumb 71 K5
Oulton Norfk 45 J4
Oulton Staffs 40 B1
Oulton Suffk 45 Q10
Oulton Broad Suffk 45 Q10
Oulton Street Norfk 45 J5
Oundle Nhants 42 E11
Ounsdale Staffs 39 Q4
Our Dynamic Earth C Edin 86 F7
Ousby Cumb 64 B1
Ousden Suffk 34 C5
Ousefleet E R Yk 60 E9
Ouston Dur 73 M9
Outgate Cumb 62 G3
Outhgill Cumb 64 E7
Outhill Warwks 30 E2
Outlane Kirk 58 E9
Out Rawcliffe Lancs 56 H1
Out Skerries Shet 111 m3
Outwell Norfk 43 N8
Outwood Surrey 11 L2
Outwoods Staffs 49 P10
Ouzlewell Green Leeds 59 J8
Ovenden Calder 58 E8
Over Cambs 33 L3
Over Ches W 49 M3
Overbury Worcs 29 N2
Overcombe Dorset 7 Q6
Over Compton Dorset 17 N11
Over Haddon Derbys 50 G7
Over Hulton Bolton 57 M7
Over Kellet Lancs 63 K8
Over Kiddington Oxon 31 K9
Overleigh Somset 17 L8
Over Norton Oxon 30 H8
Over Peover Ches E 49 P1
Overpool Ches W 56 H12
Overscaig Highld 108 H10
Overseal Derbys 40 H4
Over Silton N York 66 C8
Oversland Kent 23 K11
Overstone Nhants 32 B4
Over Stowey Somset 16 G8
Overstrand Norfk 45 L3
Over Stratton Somset 17 L11
Overthorpe Nhants 31 L6
Overton C Aber 102 H11
Overton Hants 19 N10
Overton Lancs 62 H9
Overton N York 59 M3
Overton Shrops 39 J7
Overton Swans 26 B10
Overton Wakefd 58 H10
Overton Wrexhm 48 G7
Overtown N Lans 85 N11
Over Wallop Hants 19 K11
Over Whitacre Warwks 40 G8
Over Worton Oxon 31 K8
Oving Bucks 32 A11
Oving W Susx 10 E8
Ovingdean Br & H 11 M8
Ovingham Nthumb 73 J7
Ovington Dur 65 K5
Ovington Essex 34 C8
Ovington Hants 9 P2
Ovington Norfk 44 F9
Ovington Nthumb 73 J7
Ower Hants 9 K4
Owermoigne Dorset 8 B9
Owlerton Sheff 51 J3
Owlsmoor Br For 20 D10
Owlswick Bucks 20 C3
Owmby Lincs 52 E6
Owmby Lincs 52 F3
Owslebury Hants 9 N3
Owston Donc 59 M11
Owston Leics 41 Q6
Owston Ferry N Linc 52 B4
Owstwick E R Yk 61 M7
Owthorne E R Yk 61 N8
Owthorpe Notts 41 P2
Owton Manor Hartpl 66 C2
Oxborough Norfk 44 C9
Oxcombe Lincs 53 K7
Oxenholme Cumb 63 K4
Oxenhope C Brad 58 D7
Oxen Park Cumb 62 G5
Oxenpill Somset 17 L7
Oxenton Gloucs 29 N3
Oxenwood Wilts 19 K8
Oxford Oxon 31 L11
Oxford Airport Oxon 31 L10
Oxford Services Oxon 31 N12
Oxgangs C Edin 86 F8
Oxhey Herts 20 H4
Oxhill Dur 73 L9
Oxhill Warwks 30 H5
Oxley Wolves 40 B7
Oxley Green Essex 22 H1
Oxlode Cambs 43 M11
Oxnam Border 80 F9
Oxnead Norfk 45 K5
Oxshott Surrey 21 J10
Oxspring Barns 50 H1
Oxted Surrey 21 N11
Oxton Border 80 C4
Oxton N York 59 L5
Oxton Notts 51 N9
Oxton Wirral 56 F10
Oxwich Swans 26 C10
Oxwich Green Swans 26 C10
Oykel Bridge Highld 106 F3
Oyne Abers 102 E9
Oystermouth Swans 26 E10

P

Pabail W Isls 111 e2
Packington Leics 41 J5
Packmoor C Stke 49 Q5
Padanaram Angus 93 M5
Padbury Bucks 31 Q7
Paddington Gt Lon 21 L7
Paddlesworth Kent 13 M3
Paddlesworth Kent 22 D10
Paddock Wood Kent 12 D2
Padiham Lancs 57 P3
Padside N York 58 F3
Padstow Cnwll 3 K1
Padworth W Berk 19 Q7
Pagham W Susx 10 E9
Paglesham Essex 22 H5
Paignton Torbay 6 B10
Pailton Warwks 41 L10
Painscastle Powys 38 D11
Painshawfield Nthumb 73 J8
Painsthorpe E R Yk 60 E3
Painswick Gloucs 29 M6
Painter's Forstal Kent 23 J10
Paisley Rens 84 H9
Pakefield Suffk 45 Q11
Pakenham Suffk 34 F4
Paley Street W & M 20 E7
Palfrey Wsall 40 D7
Palgrave Suffk 35 J2
Pallington Dorset 8 B8
Palmarsh Kent 13 L4
Palmerston E Ayrs 76 H7
Palnackie D & G 70 D4
Palnure D & G 69 L6
Palterton Derbys 51 L7
Pamber End Hants 19 Q8
Pamber Green Hants 19 Q8
Pamber Heath Hants 19 Q8
Pamington Gloucs 29 N3
Pamphill Dorset 8 E7
Pampisford Cambs 33 N7
Panbride Angus 93 P8
Pancrasweek Devon 14 F10
Pandy Mons 28 D4
Pandy Tudur Conwy 55 M8
Panfield Essex 34 C10
Pangbourne W Berk 19 Q5
Pangdean W Susx 11 L7
Pannal N York 58 H4
Pannal Ash N York 58 H4
Pant Shrops 48 F10
Pantasaph Flints 48 D1
Pant-ffrwyth Brdgnd 27 K11
Pant Glas Gwynd 46 H2
Pantglas Powys 47 M10
Panton Lincs 52 H7
Pantside Caerph 27 P8
Pant-y-dwr Powys 37 R6
Pantymwyn Flints 48 E3
Panxworth Norfk 45 M7
Papa Stour Shet 111 j3
Papa Stour Airport Shet 111 j4
Papa Westray Ork 111 h1
Papa Westray Airport Ork 111 h1
Papcastle Cumb 70 H8
Papigoe Highld 110 H5
Papple E Loth 87 L7
Papplewick Notts 51 M9
Papworth Everard Cambs 33 J4
Papworth St Agnes Cambs 33 J4
Par Cnwll 3 N5
Parbold Lancs 57 J6
Parbrook Somset 17 N8
Parc Gwynd 47 P5
Parc Seymour Newpt 28 E9
Pardshaw Cumb 70 H9
Parham Suffk 35 M5
Park D & G 78 E10
Park Nthumb 72 C8
Park Corner Oxon 20 B6
Parkend Gloucs 28 H7
Parker's Green Kent 12 C1
Park Farm Kent 13 J3
Parkgate Ches W 56 F12
Parkgate D & G 78 G10
Park Gate Hants 9 N6
Park Gate Leeds 58 F6
Parkgate Surrey 11 K2
Parkhall W Duns 84 H8
Parkham Devon 14 G7
Parkmill Swans 26 D10
Park Royal Gt Lon 21 K7
Parkside Dur 73 Q10
Parkside N Lans 85 N10
Parkstone BCP 8 F8
Park Street Herts 21 J3
Parracombe Devon 15 L3
Parson Drove Cambs 43 L8
Parson's Heath Essex 34 G10
Partick C Glas 85 J9
Partington Traffd 57 N9
Partney Lincs 53 L9
Parton Cumb 70 F10
Partridge Green W Susx 11 J6
Parwich Derbys 50 F9
Passenham Nhants 32 A8
Paston C Pete 42 H9
Paston Norfk 45 M4
Patcham Br & H 11 L8
Patching W Susx 10 H8
Patchway S Glos 28 H11
Pateley Bridge N York 58 F2
Pathhead Fife 86 F4
Pathhead Mdloth 86 H9
Path of Condie P & K 92 G12
Patna E Ayrs 76 G8
Patney Wilts 18 F8
Patrick IoM 56 b5
Patrick Brompton N York 65 L8
Patricroft Salfd 57 N8
Patrington E R Yk 61 M9
Patrington Haven E R Yk 61 M9
Patrixbourne Kent 23 M11
Patterdale Cumb 71 N11
Pattingham Staffs 39 P3
Pattishall Nhants 31 P4
Pattiswick Green Essex 34 D11
Paul Cnwll 2 C9
Paulerspury Nhants 31 Q5
Paull E R Yk 61 K8
Paulton BaNES 17 P5
Paultons Park Hants 9 K4
Pauperhaugh Nthumb 73 K2
Pavenham Bed 32 E5
Pawlett Somset 16 H7
Paxford Gloucs 30 F6
Paxton Border 81 K4
Payhembury Devon 6 E3
Paythorne Lancs 63 P10
Peacehaven E Susx 11 N9
Peak District National Park 50 F3
Peak Forest Derbys 50 E5
Peakirk C Pete 42 G8
Peasedown St John BaNES 17 Q5
Peasemore W Berk 19 M5
Peasenhall Suffk 35 M3
Pease Pottage W Susx 11 L4
Pease Pottage Services W Susx 11 L4
Peaslake Surrey 10 H2
Peasley Cross St Hel 57 K9
Peasmarsh E Susx 12 H5
Peathill Abers 103 J3
Peat Inn Fife 87 J1
Peatling Magna Leics 41 N8
Peatling Parva Leics 41 N9
Pebmarsh Essex 34 E9
Pebsham E Susx 12 F8
Pebworth Worcs 30 F5
Pecket Well Calder 58 C8
Peckforton Ches E 49 K4
Peckham Gt Lon 21 M8
Peckleton Leics 41 L7
Pedlinge Kent 13 L3
Pedmore Dudley 40 B10
Pedwell Somset 17 K8
Peebles Border 79 L2
Peel IoM 56 b4
Peene Kent 13 M3
Pegsdon C Beds 32 G9
Pegswood Nthumb 73 M4
Pegwell Kent 23 Q9
Peinchorran Highld 96 G3
Peinlich Highld 104 F10
Peldon Essex 34 G12
Pelsall Wsall 40 D6
Pelton Dur 73 M9
Pelynt Cnwll 4 F8
Pemberton Carmth 26 D8
Pemberton Wigan 57 K7
Pembrey Carmth 25 P8
Pembridge Herefs 38 H9
Pembroke Pembks 24 H8
Pembroke Dock Pembks 24 G7
Pembrokeshire Coast National Park Pembks 24 E5
Pembury Kent 12 D2
Pen-allt Herefs 28 G3
Penallt Mons 28 F6
Penally Pembks 25 K8
Penarth V Glam 16 G2
Pen-bont Rhydybeddau Cerdgn 37 L4
Penbryn Cerdgn 36 E9
Pencader Carmth 25 Q2
Pencaitland E Loth 87 J8
Pencarnisiog IoA 54 D6
Pencarreg Carmth 37 J10
Pencelli Powys 27 M4
Penclawdd Swans 26 D9
Pencoed Brdgnd 27 K11
Pencombe Herefs 39 L10
Pencraig Herefs 28 G5
Pencraig Powys 48 B9
Pendeen Cnwll 2 B8
Penderyn Rhondd 27 K7
Pendine Carmth 25 L7
Pendlebury Salfd 57 P8
Pendleton Lancs 57 N2
Pendock Worcs 29 K3
Pendoggett Cnwll 4 C4
Pendomer Somset 7 M1
Pendoylan V Glam 16 E2
Penegoes Powys 47 M10
Pen-ffordd Pembks 25 J4
Pengam Caerph 27 N8
Pengam Cardif 27 P12
Penge Gt Lon 21 M8
Pengelly Cnwll 4 D4
Penhallow Cnwll 2 H5
Penhalvean Cnwll 2 G8
Penhill Swindn 18 H3
Penhow Newpt 28 E10
Penicuik Mdloth 86 F9
Penifiler Highld 96 F2
Peninver Ag & B 75 L7
Penistone Barns 50 G1
Penkill S Ayrs 76 D10
Penkridge Staffs 40 B5
Penley Wrexhm 48 H7
Penllyn V Glam 16 C2
Penmachno Conwy 55 L10
Penmaen Caerph 27 P8
Penmaen Swans 26 D10
Penmaenmawr Conwy 55 K6
Penmaenpool Gwynd 47 L7
Penmark V Glam 16 E3
Penmynydd IoA 54 G6
Pennal Gwynd 47 L10
Pennan Abers 102 H3
Pennant Powys 47 P10
Pennar Pembks 24 G8
Pennerley Shrops 38 G3
Pennines 58 C7
Pennington Cumb 62 F6
Penorth Powys 27 M4
Penn Street Bucks 20 E4
Penny Bridge Cumb 62 F5
Pennycross Ag & B 89 L10
Pennyghael Ag & B 89 L10
Pennyglen S Ayrs 76 E8
Pennymoor Devon 15 P9
Pennywell Sundld 73 P9
Penparc Cerdgn 36 D10
Penperlleni Mons 28 C7
Penpoll Cnwll 4 E8
Penponds Cnwll 2 F7
Penpont D & G 78 D9
Pen-rhiw Pembks 36 D11
Penrhiwceiber Rhondd 27 M8
Pen Rhiwfawr Neath 26 G6
Penrhiwllan Cerdgn 36 F11
Penrhiwpal Cerdgn 36 F10
Penrhos Gwynd 46 F5
Penrhos Mons 28 E6
Penrhyn Bay Conwy 55 M5
Penrhyn-coch Cerdgn 37 K4
Penrhyndeudraeth Gwynd 47 K4
Penrice Swans 26 C10

Penrioch N Ayrs 75 N4
Penrith Cumb 71 Q9
Penrose Cnwll 3 K2
Penruddock Cumb 71 N9
Penryn Cnwll 2 H8
Pensarn Conwy 55 P6
Pensax Worcs 39 N8
Penselwood Somset 17 R9
Pensford BaNES 17 N4
Pensham Worcs 30 C5
Penshaw Sundld 73 N9
Penshurst Kent 11 Q2
Pensilva Cnwll 4 G6
Pensnett Dudley 40 B9
Pentewan Cnwll 3 M6
Pentir Gwynd 54 H8
Pentire Cnwll 2 H4
Pentlow Essex 34 D7
Pentney Norfk 44 C7
Pentonbridge Cumb 79 P12
Penton Mewsey Hants 19 K10
Pentraeth IoA 54 G6
Pentre Mons 28 E8
Pentre Rhondd 27 K9
Pentre Shrops 48 G11
Pentrebach Myr Td 27 M7
Pentre-bach Powys 27 J3
Pentre Berw IoA 54 F7
Pentrecelyn Denbgs 48 D5
Pentre-celyn Powys 47 P9
Pentre-chwyth Swans 26 F9
Pentre-cwrt Carmth 25 P2
Pentredwr Denbgs 48 E6
Pentrefelin Gwynd 47 J4
Pentrefoelas Conwy 55 M10
Pentregat Cerdgn 36 F9
Pentre-Gwenlais Carmth 26 E5
Pentre Hodrey Shrops 38 G6
Pentre Llanrhaeadr Denbgs 48 C3
Pentre Meyrick V Glam 16 C2
Pentre-tafarn-y-fedw Conwy 55 M8
Pentrich Derbys 51 J9
Pentridge Dorset 8 F4
Pentwyn Cardif 27 P11
Pen-twyn Mons 28 F7
Pentwynmaur Caerph 27 P9
Pentyrch Cardif 27 M11
Penwithick Cnwll 3 M5
Penybanc Carmth 26 E4
Penybont Powys 38 C8
Pen-y-bont Powys 48 E10
Penybontfawr Powys 48 C9
Pen-y-bryn Pembks 36 C11
Penycae Wrexhm 48 F6
Pen-y-clawdd Mons 28 E7
Pen-y-coedcae Rhondd 27 M10
Penycwm Pembks 24 E4
Pen-y-felin Flints 48 D2
Penyffordd Flints 48 F4
Pen-y-Garnedd Powys 48 C10
Pen-y-graig Gwynd 46 C5
Penygraig Rhondd 27 L10
Penygroes Carmth 26 D6
Penygroes Gwynd 54 F10
Pen-y-Mynydd Carmth 26 C7
Penymynydd Flints 48 F3
Penysarn IoA 54 G4
Pen-y-stryt Denbgs 48 E5
Penywaun Rhondd 27 K7
Penzance Cnwll 2 D9
Peopleton Worcs 30 C4
Peplow Shrops 49 L9
Perceton N Ayrs 76 F4
Percyhorner Abers 103 K3
Perham Down Wilts 19 J10
Periton Somset 16 C7
Perivale Gt Lon 21 J6
Perkins Village Devon 6 D5
Perlethorpe Notts 51 N6
Perranarworthal Cnwll 2 H7
Perranporth Cnwll 2 H5
Perranuthnoe Cnwll 2 D9
Perranwell Cnwll 2 H7
Perranzabuloe Cnwll 2 H5
Perry Birm 40 E8
Perry Cambs 32 G4
Perry Barr Birm 40 E8
Perry Green Wilts 18 E3
Pershall Staffs 49 P9
Pershore Worcs 30 C5
Pertenhall Bed 32 F4
Perth P & K 92 G10
Perthy Shrops 48 G8
Perton Herefs 28 H2
Perton Staffs 39 Q3
Peterborough C Pete 42 H9
Peterborough Services Cambs 42 G10
Peterchurch Herefs 28 D2
Peterculter C Aber 95 N2
Peterhead Abers 103 M6
Peterlee Dur 73 Q11
Petersfield Hants 10 B5
Peter's Green Herts 32 G11
Petersham Gt Lon 21 J8
Peters Marland Devon 14 H9
Peterstone Wentlooge Newpt 28 B11
Peterston-super-Ely V Glam 16 E2
Peterstow Herefs 28 G4
Peter Tavy Devon 5 K5
Petham Kent 23 L12
Petherwin Gate Cnwll 4 G3
Petrockstow Devon 15 J9
Pett E Susx 12 G7
Pettaugh Suffk 35 J5
Petterden Angus 93 M7
Pettinain S Lans 77 Q3
Pettistree Suffk 35 L6
Petton Devon 16 D10

Phoenix Green Hants 20 C11
Pibsbury Somset 17 L10
Pickburn Donc 59 L11
Pickering N York 66 H10
Pickford Covtry 40 H10
Pickhill N York 65 N10
Picklescott Shrops 38 H3
Pickmere Ches E 57 M12
Pickney Somset 16 G9
Pickwell Leics 42 B7
Pickworth Lincs 42 F4
Pickworth Rutlnd 42 E7
Picton Ches W 48 H2
Picton N York 65 P6
Piddinghoe E Susx 11 N9
Piddington Nhants 32 B6
Piddington Oxon 31 N10
Piddlehinton Dorset 7 Q4
Piddletrenthide Dorset 7 Q3
Pidley Cambs 33 K2
Piercebridge Darltn 65 L4
Pierowall Ork 111 h1
Pilgrims Hatch Essex 22 C4
Pilham Lincs 52 C5
Pillaton Cnwll 4 H7
Pillerton Hersey Warwks 30 H4
Pillerton Priors Warwks 30 H5
Pilley Barns 51 J11
Pilley Hants 9 K7
Pillgwenlly Newpt 28 C10
Pilling Lancs 62 H11
Pilning S Glos 28 G10
Pilsbury Derbys 50 E7
Pilsdon Dorset 7 K3
Pilsley Derbys 50 G6
Pilsley Derbys 51 K8
Pilson Green Norfk 45 N7
Piltdown E Susx 11 N5
Pilton Devon 15 K5
Pilton Nhants 42 E12
Pilton Rutlnd 42 D9
Pilton Somset 17 N7
Pimlico Herts 20 H3
Pimperne Dorset 8 D5
Pinchbeck Lincs 43 J5
Pin Green Herts 33 J10
Pinhoe Devon 6 C4
Pinley Green Warwks 30 G2
Pinminnoch S Ayrs 76 D11
Pinmore S Ayrs 76 D11
Pinn Devon 6 E5
Pinner Gt Lon 20 H5
Pinner Green Gt Lon 20 H5
Pinvin Worcs 30 C4
Pinwherry S Ayrs 68 G2
Pinxton Derbys 51 L9
Pipe and Lyde Herefs 39 J2
Pipe Aston Herefs 39 J7
Pipe Gate Shrops 49 N7
Piperdam Angus 93 K8
Piperhill Highld 100 D5
Pipewell Nhants 42 B11
Pirbright Surrey 20 F11
Pirnie Border 80 E8
Pirnmill N Ayrs 75 N4
Pirton Herts 32 G9
Pishill Oxon 20 B5
Pistyll Gwynd 46 E3
Pitblae Abers 103 K3
Pitcairngreen P & K 92 F9
Pitcalnie Highld 107 N7
Pitcaple Abers 102 F9
Pitcairity Angus 94 F8
Pitchcombe Gloucs 29 L7
Pitchcott Bucks 31 Q9
Pitchford Shrops 39 K2
Pitch Green Bucks 20 C3
Pitchroy Moray 101 J7
Pitcombe Somset 17 P9
Pitcox E Loth 87 M7
Pitfichie Abers 102 E11
Pitglassie Abers 102 F6
Pitgrudy Highld 107 N4
Pitlessie Fife 86 G1
Pitlochry P & K 92 D4
Pitmachie Abers 102 E9
Pitmain Highld 99 L8
Pitmedden Abers 103 J9
Pitmedden Garden Abers 103 J9
Pitminster Somset 16 G11
Pitmuies Angus 93 P6
Pitmunie Abers 102 E11
Pitney Somset 17 L9
Pitroddie P & K 93 J10
Pitscottie Fife 93 M11
Pitsea Essex 22 E6
Pitsford Nhants 31 Q1
Pitstone Bucks 20 F1
Pittarrow Abers 95 M7
Pittenweem Fife 87 K2
Pitteuchar Fife 86 F3
Pittodrie House Hotel Abers 102 F9
Pitton Wilts 8 H2
Pittulie Abers 103 K3
Pity Me Dur 73 M10
Pixham Surrey 21 J12
Plains N Lans 85 N9
Plaish Shrops 39 K3
Plaistow Gt Lon 21 N6
Plaistow W Susx 10 G4
Plaitford Hants 9 J4
Plawsworth Dur 73 M10
Plaxtol Kent 22 C11
Playden E Susx 12 H6
Playford Suffk 35 K7
Play Hatch Oxon 20 B7
Playing Place Cnwll 3 J7
Playley Green Gloucs 29 K3
Plealey Shrops 38 H2
Plean Stirlg 85 P5
Pleasance Fife 93 J12
Pleasington Bl w D 57 M4
Pleasley Derbys 51 L7
Pleasurewood Hills Suffk 45 Q10
Plemstall Ches W 49 J2
Pleshey Essex 22 D1
Plockton Highld 97 L3
Plowden Shrops 38 H5
Pluckley Kent 12 H2
Pluckley Thorne Kent 12 H2
Plumbland Cumb 71 J7
Plumley Ches E 49 N1
Plumpton Cumb 71 P7

Plumpton E Susx 11 M7
Plumpton Nhants 31 N5
Plumpton Green E Susx 11 M6
Plumstead Gt Lon 21 N7
Plumstead Norfk 45 J3
Plumtree Notts 41 N2
Plungar Leics 41 Q1
Plurenden Kent 12 H3
Plush Dorset 7 Q3
Plwmp Cerdgn 36 F9
Plymouth C Plym 5 K8
Plympton C Plym 5 L8
Plymstock C Plym 5 L9
Plymtree Devon 6 E3
Pockley N York 66 F9
Pocklington E R Yk 60 D4
Podimore Somset 17 M10
Podington Bed 32 D4
Podmore Staffs 49 P8
Pointon Lincs 42 G4
Pokesdown BCP 8 G8
Polbain Highld 105 L10
Polbathic Cnwll 4 H8
Polbeth W Loth 86 B9
Poldark Mine Cnwll 2 G9
Polebrook Nhants 42 F11
Polegate E Susx 12 C8
Polesden Lacey Surrey 21 J11
Polesworth Warwks 40 H7
Polglass Highld 105 Q2
Polgooth Cnwll 3 M5
Polgown D & G 77 M9
Poling W Susx 10 G8
Poling Corner W Susx 10 G8
Polkerris Cnwll 4 D9
Pollington E R Yk 59 N9
Polloch Highld 89 Q3
Pollokshaws C Glas 85 J10
Pollokshields C Glas 85 J9
Polmassick Cnwll 3 L6
Polmont Falk 85 Q7
Polnish Highld 97 K12
Polperro Cnwll 4 F9
Polruan Cnwll 4 F9
Polstead Suffk 34 G8
Poltalloch Ag & B 83 M4
Poltimore Devon 6 C4
Polton Mdloth 86 F8
Polwarth Border 80 G4
Polyphant Cnwll 4 G4
Polzeath Cnwll 4 H4
Pomathorn Mdloth 86 F9
Pondersbridge Cambs 43 J10
Ponders End Gt Lon 21 M4
Ponsanooth Cnwll 2 H8
Ponsworthy Devon 5 N5
Pont Abraham Services Carmth 26 D7
Pontamman Carmth 25 Q6
Pontantwn Carmth 25 Q6
Pontardawe Neath 26 F7
Pontarddulais Swans 26 D7
Pont-ar-gothi Carmth 26 C5
Pontarsais Carmth 25 Q3
Pontblyddyn Flints 48 F4
Pontcysyllte Aqueduct Wrexhm 48 F7
Pontefract Wakefd 59 L9
Ponteland Nthumb 73 L6
Ponterwyd Cerdgn 37 M4
Pontesbury Shrops 38 H2
Pontesford Shrops 38 H2
Pontfadog Wrexhm 48 E7
Pontfaen Pembks 24 H3
Pont-faen Powys 27 L3
Pontgarreg Cerdgn 36 F9
Ponthenri Carmth 26 C7
Ponthir Torfn 28 C9
Ponthirwaun Cerdgn 36 D10
Pontllanfraith Caerph 27 P9
Pontlliw Swans 26 E8
Pontllyfni Gwynd 54 F10
Pontlottyn Caerph 27 N7
Pontnêddfêchan Neath 27 J7
Pontnewydd Torfn 28 C9
Pontrhydfendigaid Cerdgn 37 M7
Pontrhydyfen Neath 26 H9
Pont-rhyd-y-groes Cerdgn 37 M6
Pontrilas Herefs 28 D4
Pont Robert Powys 48 C11
Pontshaen Cerdgn 36 G10
Pontsticill Myr Td 27 M6
Pontwelly Carmth 36 G11
Pontyates Carmth 26 C7
Pontyberem Carmth 26 C6
Pontybodkin Flints 48 F4
Pontyclun Rhondd 27 L11
Pontycymer Brdgnd 27 J9
Pontymister Caerph 27 P10
Pont-y-pant Conwy 55 L10
Pontypool Torfn 28 C8
Pontypridd Rhondd 27 M10
Pontywaun Caerph 27 P9
Pool Cnwll 2 G7
Poole BCP 8 G8
Poole Keynes Gloucs 18 E2
Poolewe Highld 105 M6
Pooley Bridge Cumb 71 P10
Poolfold Staffs 50 B8
Poolhill Gloucs 29 K3
Pool in Wharfedale Leeds 58 G5
Pool of Muckhart Clacks 86 B3
Pool Street Essex 34 C8
Poplar Gt Lon 21 M7
Porchfield IoW 9 M8
Poringland Norfk 45 L9
Porkellis Cnwll 2 G8
Porlock Somset 15 Q3
Porlock Weir Somset 15 P3
Portachoillan Ag & B 83 L10
Port-an-Eorna Highld 97 K4
Port Appin Ag & B 90 C7
Port Askaig Ag & B 82 F8
Portavadie Ag & B 83 P8
Port Bannatyne Ag & B 84 B9
Portbury N Som 17 M2
Port Carlisle Cumb 71 K3
Port Charlotte Ag & B 82 C10
Portchester Hants 9 Q6
Port Driseach Ag & B 83 Q8
Port Ellen Ag & B 74 E4
Port Elphinstone Abers 102 H10
Portencalzie D & G 68 D5
Portencross N Ayrs 76 C2

Port Erin IoM 56 a6
Portesham Dorset 7 N5
Portessie Moray 101 N3
Port Eynon Swans 26 C10
Portfield Gate Pembks 24 G6
Portgate Devon 5 J4
Port Gaverne Cnwll 4 C4
Port Glasgow Inver 84 F7
Portgordon Moray 101 M3
Portgower Highld 110 B11
Porth Cnwll 3 J4
Porth Rhondd 27 L9
Porthallow Cnwll 2 H10
Porthallow Cnwll 4 F9
Porthcawl Brdgnd 26 H12
Porthcothan Cnwll 3 K2
Porthcurno Cnwll 2 B10
Port Henderson Highld 105 L7
Porthgain Pembks 24 E3
Porthgwarra Cnwll 2 B10
Porthill Staffs 49 Q6
Porthkerry V Glam 16 E3
Porthleven Cnwll 2 F9
Porthmadog Gwynd 47 J4
Porth Navas Cnwll 2 H9
Porthoustock Cnwll 3 J10
Porthpean Cnwll 3 M5
Porthtowan Cnwll 2 G6
Porthyrhyd Carmth 26 C5
Portincaple Ag & B 84 D4
Portington E R Yk 60 D7
Portinnisherrich Ag & B 83 P2
Portinscale Cumb 71 L10
Port Isaac Cnwll 4 C4
Portishead N Som 17 L2
Portknockie Moray 101 N2
Portland Dorset 7 P8
Portlethen Abers 95 Q3
Portling D & G 70 E5
Portloe Cnwll 3 L7
Port Logan D & G 68 E10
Portmahomack Highld 107 Q5
Port Mary D & G 70 C6
Portmeirion Gwynd 47 J4
Portmellon Cnwll 3 M7
Port Mòr Highld 89 J1
Portnacroish Ag & B 90 C6
Portnaguran W Isls 111 e2
Portnahaven Ag & B 74 B2
Portnalong Highld 96 D3
Portnancon Highld 108 H4
Port nan Giùran W Isls 111 e2
Port nan Long W Isls 111 b4
Port Nis W Isls 111 e1
Portobello C Edin 86 G7
Portobello Wolves 40 C7
Port of Menteith Stirlg 85 K3
Port of Ness W Isls 111 e1
Porton Wilts 18 H12
Portpatrick D & G 68 D8
Port Quin Cnwll 4 B4
Port Ramsay Ag & B 90 B7
Portreath Cnwll 2 F6
Portreath Harbour Cnwll 2 F6
Portree Highld 96 F2
Port Righ Ag & B 75 M5
Port St Mary IoM 56 b7
Portscatho Cnwll 3 K8
Portsea C Port 9 Q7
Portskerra Highld 109 Q3
Portskewett Mons 28 F10
Portslade Br & H 11 K8
Portslade-by-Sea Br & H 11 L8
Portslogan D & G 68 D7
Portsmouth C Port 9 Q7
Portsmouth Calder 58 B8
Portsmouth Dockyard C Port 9 Q7
Port Soderick IoM 56 c6
Portsonachan Hotel Ag & B 90 E11
Portsoy Abers 102 D3
Port Sunlight Wirral 56 G11
Portswood C Sotn 9 M5
Port Talbot Neath 26 G10
Port Tennant Swans 26 G9
Portuairk Highld 89 K3
Portway Sandw 40 C9
Portway Worcs 40 E11
Port Wemyss Ag & B 74 B3
Port William D & G 69 J9
Portwrinkle Cnwll 4 H9
Portyerrock D & G 69 L10
Poslingford Suffk 34 C7
Posso Border 79 K3
Postbridge Devon 5 N4
Postcombe Oxon 20 B4
Postling Kent 13 M3
Postwick Norfk 45 L8
Potarch Abers 95 J3
Potten End Herts 20 G2
Potter Brompton N York 67 L11
Potterhanworth Lincs 52 F9
Potterhanworth Booths Lincs 52 F9
Potter Heigham Norfk 45 N6
Potterne Wilts 18 E8
Potterne Wick Wilts 18 E8
Potters Bar Herts 21 K3
Potters Corner Kent 13 J2
Potters Crouch Herts 21 H3
Potters Marston Leics 41 L8
Potterspury Nhants 31 Q5
Potter Street Essex 21 P2
Potterton Abers 103 K11
Potto N York 66 C6
Potton C Beds 32 H6
Pott Shrigley Ches E 50 C5
Poughill Cnwll 14 D10
Poughill Devon 15 P3
Poulner Hants 8 H6
Poulshot Wilts 18 E8
Poulton Gloucs 18 G1
Poulton Wirral 56 F10
Poulton-le-Fylde Lancs 56 G2
Poundbury Dorset 7 P5
Poundffald Swans 26 D9
Pound Green E Susx 11 P5
Pound Green Suffk 34 C6
Pound Hill W Susx 11 L3
Poundon Bucks 31 N8
Poundsgate Devon 5 N6
Poundstock Cnwll 14 D11
Pouton D & G 69 L9
Povey Cross Surrey 11 L2

Powburn Nthumb 81 M10
Powderham Devon 6 C6
Powerstock Dorset 7 M4
Powfoot D & G 71 J3
Powick Worcs 39 Q10
Powmill P & K 86 B3
Poxwell Dorset 7 Q6
Poyle Slough 20 G7
Poynings W Susx 11 L7
Poyntington Dorset 17 P11
Poynton Ches E 50 B4
Poynton Green Wrekin 49 K10
Praa Sands Cnwll 2 E9
Praze-an-Beeble Cnwll 2 F8
Prees Shrops 49 K8
Preesall Lancs 62 G11
Prees Green Shrops 49 K8
Prees Heath Shrops 49 K7
Prees Higher Heath Shrops 49 K8
Pren-gwyn Cerdgn 36 G10
Prenteg Gwynd 47 J3
Prescot Knows 57 J9
Prescott Devon 16 E12
Presnerb Angus 94 C8
Prestatyn Denbgs 56 C11
Prestbury Ches E 50 B5
Prestbury Gloucs 29 N4
Presteigne Powys 38 G8
Prestleigh Somset 17 P7
Preston Border 87 P10
Preston Br & H 11 L8
Preston Devon 6 B7
Preston Dorset 7 Q6
Preston E R Yk 61 K7
Preston Gloucs 18 G1
Preston Herts 32 H10
Preston Kent 23 K10
Preston Kent 23 N10
Preston Lancs 57 K3
Preston Nthumb 81 P8
Preston Rutlnd 42 C9
Preston Somset 16 E8
Preston Torbay 6 B9
Preston Wilts 18 F5
Preston Bagot Warwks 30 F2
Preston Bissett Bucks 31 P8
Preston Bowyer Somset 16 F10
Preston Brockhurst Shrops 49 K9
Preston Brook Halton 57 K11
Preston Candover Hants 19 Q11
Preston Capes Nhants 31 M3
Preston Green Warwks 30 F2
Preston Gubbals Shrops 49 J10
Preston on Stour Warwks 30 G4
Preston on the Hill Halton 57 K11
Preston on Wye Herefs 38 D1
Prestonpans E Loth 86 H7
Preston Patrick Cumb 63 K5
Preston Plucknett Somset 17 M11
Preston St Mary Suffk 34 F6
Preston-under-Scar N York 65 J8
Preston upon the Weald Moors Wrekin 49 M11
Preston Wynne Herefs 39 K11
Prestwich Bury 57 P7
Prestwick S Ayrs 76 F6
Prestwick Airport S Ayrs 76 F6
Prestwood Bucks 20 E4
Prickwillow Cambs 33 P1
Priddy Somset 17 M6
Priest Hutton Lancs 63 K7
Priestland E Ayrs 77 J4
Priest Weston Shrops 38 F3
Primrosehill Border 87 P10
Primrose Hill Dudley 40 C9
Primsidemill Border 80 H8
Prince of Wales Bridge Mons 28 F10
Princes Risborough Bucks 20 D3
Princethorpe Warwks 41 K12
Princetown Devon 5 M5
Priors Hardwick Warwks 31 L3
Priorslee Wrekin 49 N12
Priors Marston Warwks 31 L3
Priors Norton Gloucs 29 M4
Priors Park Gloucs 29 M3
Priston BaNES 17 Q4
Prittlewell Sthend 22 G6
Privett Hants 10 B5
Prixford Devon 15 J5
Probus Cnwll 3 K6
Prora E Loth 87 K6
Prospect Cumb 71 J7
Prospidnick Cnwll 2 F8
Protstonhill Abers 102 H3
Prudhoe Nthumb 73 K8
Pubil P & K 91 L7
Publow BaNES 17 P4
Puckeridge Herts 33 L11
Puckington Somset 17 K11
Pucklechurch S Glos 17 Q2
Puddington Ches W 48 G2
Puddington Devon 15 P9
Puddletown Dorset 7 Q4
Pudsey Leeds 58 G7
Pulborough W Susx 10 G6
Pulford Ches W 48 G4
Pulham Dorset 7 Q3
Pulham Market Norfk 45 K11
Pulham St Mary Norfk 45 K11
Pulloxhill C Beds 32 F9
Pulverbatch Shrops 38 H2
Pumpherston W Loth 86 C8
Pumsaint Carmth 37 K11
Puncheston Pembks 24 H3
Puncknowle Dorset 7 M5
Punnett's Town E Susx 12 C6
Purbrook Hants 10 B8
Purfleet-on-Thames Thurr 22 B7
Puriton Somset 17 J7
Purleigh Essex 22 G3
Purley Gt Lon 21 L10
Purley on Thames W Berk 19 Q5
Purse Caundle Dorset 17 Q11
Purton Somset 7 K2
Purton Gloucs 29 J7
Purton Gloucs 29 J7
Purton Wilts 18 G3
Purton Stoke Wilts 18 G3
Pury End Nhants 31 P5
Pusey Oxon 19 L2
Putley Herefs 28 H2
Putley Green Herefs 28 H2
Putney Gt Lon 21 K8

Puttenham *Surrey* 10 E1
Puxley *Nhants* 31 Q6
Puxton *N Som* 17 K4
Pwll *Carmth* 26 C8
Pwll-glâs *Denbgs* 48 C5
Pwllgloyw *Powys* 27 L3
Pwllheli *Gwynd* 46 F4
Pwllmeyric *Mons* 28 F9
Pwll-trap *Carmth* 25 M5
Pwll-y-glaw *Neath* 26 H9
Pye Bridge *Derbys* 51 K9
Pyecombe *W Susx* 11 L7
Pyle *Brdgnd* 26 H11
Pyleigh *Somset* 16 F9
Pylle *Somset* 17 N8
Pymoor *Cambs* 43 M11
Pymore *Dorset* 7 L4
Pyrford *Surrey* 20 G10
Pyrton *Oxon* 20 B4
Pytchley *Nhants* 32 C2
Pyworthy *Devon* 14 F10

Q

Quadring *Lincs* 42 H4
Quadring Eaudike *Lincs* 43 J4
Quainton *Bucks* 31 Q9
Quantock Hills *Somset* 16 G8
Quarff *Shet* 111 k4
Quarley *Hants* 19 J11
Quarndon *Derbys* 51 J11
Quarrier's Village *Inver* 84 F9
Quarrington *Lincs* 42 F2
Quarrington Hill *Dur* 73 N12
Quarry Bank *Dudley* 40 B9
Quarrywood *Moray* 101 J3
Quarter *N Ayrs* 84 D10
Quarter *S Lans* 85 M11
Quatford *Shrops* 39 N4
Quatt *Shrops* 39 N5
Quebec *Dur* 73 L11
Quedgeley *Gloucs* 29 L6
Queen Adelaide *Cambs* 33 P1
Queenborough *Kent* 22 H8
Queen Camel *Somset* 17 N10
Queen Charlton *BaNES* 17 P3
Queen Elizabeth Forest Park *Stirlg* 84 H3
Queen Elizabeth II Bridge *Thurr* 22 C8
Queenhill *Worcs* 29 M2
Queen Oak *Dorset* 8 B2
Queen's Bower *IoW* 9 P9
Queensbury *C Brad* 58 E7
Queensferry *Flints* 48 G2
Queensferry Crossing *Fife* 86 D6
Queenslie *C Glas* 85 L9
Queen's Park *Bed* 32 E6
Queen's Park *Essex* 22 D4
Queen's Park *Nhants* 31 Q2
Queenzieburn *N Lans* 85 L7
Quendon *Essex* 33 N10
Queniborough *Leics* 41 N5
Quenington *Gloucs* 30 F12
Queslett *Birm* 40 E8
Quethiock *Cnwll* 4 G7
Quidenham *Norfk* 44 G11
Quidhampton *Wilts* 8 G2
Quinton *Nhants* 31 R4
Quintrell Downs *Cnwll* 3 J4
Quixwood *Border* 87 P9
Quoig *P & K* 92 C10
Quorn *Leics* 41 M4
Quothquan *S Lans* 78 G2
Quoyburray *Ork* 111 h2
Quoyloo *Ork* 111 g2

R

Raasay *Highld* 96 G2
Rachan Mill *Border* 79 J3
Rachub *Gwynd* 55 J7
Rackenford *Devon* 15 P8
Rackham *W Susx* 10 G7
Rackheath *Norfk* 45 L7
Racks *D & G* 70 G1
Rackwick *Ork* 111 g3
Radbourne *Derbys* 40 H1
Radcliffe *Bury* 57 P7
Radcliffe on Trent *Notts* 51 N11
Radclive *Bucks* 31 P7
Raddery *Highld* 107 L9
Radernie *Fife* 87 J1
Radford *Covtry* 41 J10
Radford Semele *Warwks* 31 J2
Radlett *Herts* 21 J4
Radley *Oxon* 19 N2
Radley Green *Essex* 22 D3
Radnage *Bucks* 20 C4
Radstock *BaNES* 17 P5
Radstone *Nhants* 31 N6
Radway *Warwks* 31 J5
Radwell *Bed* 32 E5
Radwell *Herts* 32 H9
Radwinter *Essex* 33 P8
Radyr *Cardif* 27 N11
Rafford *Moray* 100 G4
RAF Museum Cosford *Shrops* 39 P2
RAF Museum Hendon *Gt Lon* 21 K5
Ragdale *Leics* 41 P4
Raglan *Mons* 28 E7
Ragnall *Notts* 52 B8
Raigbeg *Highld* 99 M4
Rainbow Hill *Worcs* 39 Q10
Rainford *St Hel* 57 J8
Rainham *Gt Lon* 21 Q7
Rainham *Medway* 22 F9
Rainhill *St Hel* 57 J9
Rainhill Stoops *St Hel* 57 J10
Rainow *Ches E* 50 C6
Rainton *N York* 65 P11
Rainworth *Notts* 51 N8
Rait *P & K* 93 J9
Raithby *Lincs* 53 K6
Raithby *Lincs* 53 L9
Rake *Hants* 10 C5
Ralia *Highld* 99 K9
Ramasaig *Highld* 96 A2
Rame *Cnwll* 3 G8

Rame *Cnwll* 5 J9
Rampisham *Dorset* 7 N3
Rampside *Cumb* 62 E8
Rampton *Cambs* 33 L3
Rampton *Notts* 52 B7
Ramsbottom *Bury* 57 P5
Ramsbury *Wilts* 19 J6
Ramscraigs *Highld* 110 D9
Ramsdean *Hants* 10 B5
Ramsdell *Hants* 19 P8
Ramsden *Oxon* 31 J10
Ramsden Bellhouse *Essex* 22 E5
Ramsey *Cambs* 43 J11
Ramsey *Essex* 35 K10
Ramsey *IoM* 56 e3
Ramsey Forty Foot *Cambs* 43 K11
Ramsey Heights *Cambs* 43 J12
Ramsey Island *Essex* 23 J3
Ramsey Island *Pembks* 24 C4
Ramsey Mereside *Cambs* 43 J11
Ramsey St Mary's *Cambs* 43 J11
Ramsgate *Kent* 23 Q9
Ramsgill *N York* 65 K12
Ramshope *Nthumb* 80 G12
Ramshorn *Staffs* 50 E10
Ramsnest Common *Surrey* 10 F4
Ranby *Lincs* 52 H7
Ranby *Notts* 51 P5
Rand *Lincs* 52 F7
Randwick *Gloucs* 29 L7
Ranfurly *Rens* 84 G9
Rangemore *Staffs* 40 F3
Rangeworthy *S Glos* 29 J10
Rankinston *E Ayrs* 76 H8
Rannoch Station *P & K* 91 L5
Ranscombe *Somset* 16 C7
Ranskill *Notts* 51 P4
Ranton *Staffs* 49 Q10
Ranton Green *Staffs* 49 Q10
Ranworth *Norfk* 45 M7
Raploch *Stirlg* 85 N4
Rapness *Ork* 111 h1
Rascarrel *D & G* 70 D6
Rashfield *Ag & B* 84 C6
Rashwood *Worcs* 30 B2
Raskelf *N York* 66 C12
Rastrick *Calder* 58 F9
Ratagan *Highld* 97 N6
Ratby *Leics* 41 L6
Ratcliffe Culey *Leics* 41 J7
Ratcliffe on Soar *Notts* 41 L2
Ratcliffe on the Wreake *Leics* 41 N5
Rathen *Abers* 103 K3
Rathillet *Fife* 93 L10
Rathmell *N York* 63 P9
Ratho *C Edin* 86 D7
Ratho Station *C Edin* 86 D7
Rathven *Moray* 101 N3
Ratley *Warwks* 31 J3
Ratling *Kent* 23 N11
Ratlinghope *Shrops* 38 H3
Rattar *Highld* 110 F2
Rattery *Devon* 5 P7
Rattlesden *Suffk* 34 F5
Ratton Village *E Susx* 12 C9
Rattray *P & K* 92 H6
Raunds *Nhants* 32 E3
Ravenfield *Rothm* 51 L2
Ravenglass *Cumb* 62 C3
Raveningham *Norfk* 45 N10
Ravenscar *N York* 67 L7
Ravenscraig *N Lans* 85 N10
Ravensden *Bed* 32 F6
Ravenshead *Notts* 51 M9
Ravensthorpe *Kirk* 58 G9
Ravensthorpe *Nhants* 41 P12
Ravenstone *Leics* 41 K5
Ravenstone *M Keyn* 32 C6
Ravenstonedale *Cumb* 63 N2
Ravenstruther *S Lans* 77 Q3
Ravensworth *N York* 65 K6
Rawcliffe *C York* 59 N4
Rawcliffe *E R Yk* 59 P9
Rawdon *Leeds* 58 G6
Rawling Street *Kent* 22 H10
Rawmarsh *Rothm* 51 K2
Rawreth *Essex* 22 F5
Rawridge *Devon* 6 G2
Rawtenstall *Lancs* 57 P4
Raydon *Suffk* 34 H8
Rayleigh *Essex* 22 F5
Rayne *Essex* 34 C11
Raynes Park *Gt Lon* 21 K9
Reach *Cambs* 33 P4
Read *Lancs* 57 P2
Reading *Readg* 20 B8
Reading Services *W Berk* 20 A9
Reading Street *Kent* 12 H4
Reading Street *Kent* 23 Q9
Reagill *Cumb* 64 B4
Rearquhar *Highld* 107 M4
Rearsby *Leics* 41 P5
Reawla *Cnwll* 2 F8
Reay *Highld* 110 A3
Reculver *Kent* 23 N9
Red Ball *Devon* 16 E11
Redberth *Pembks* 25 J7
Redbourn *Herts* 20 H2
Redbourne *N Linc* 52 D4
Redbrook *Gloucs* 28 G6
Redbrook *Wrexhm* 49 K6
Redbrook Street *Kent* 12 H3
Redburn *Highld* 100 G6
Redcar *R & C* 66 E3
Redcastle *D & G* 70 D3
Redcastle *Highld* 107 J11
Redding *Falk* 85 Q7
Reddingmuirhead *Falk* 85 Q7
Reddish *Stockp* 50 B3
Redditch *Worcs* 30 D1
Rede *Suffk* 34 D5
Redenhall *Norfk* 45 L12
Redesmouth *Nthumb* 72 F5
Redford *Abers* 95 M7
Redford *Angus* 93 P6
Redford *W Susx* 10 D5
Redfordgreen *Border* 79 M6
Redgate *Rhondd* 27 L10
Redgorton *P & K* 92 G9
Redgrave *Suffk* 34 H2
Redhill *Abers* 95 M1
Red Hill *BCP* 8 G8
Redhill *Herts* 33 J9

Redhill *N Som* 17 M4
Redhill *Surrey* 21 L12
Redisham *Suffk* 45 N12
Redland *Bristl* 17 N2
Redland *Ork* 111 h2
Redlingfield *Suffk* 35 K3
Redlingfield Green *Suffk* 35 K3
Red Lodge *Suffk* 34 B3
Redlynch *Somset* 17 Q9
Redlynch *Wilts* 8 H3
Redmarley *Worcs* 39 N8
Redmarley D'Abitot *Gloucs* 29 K3
Redmarshall *S on T* 65 P4
Redmile *Leics* 42 B3
Redmire *N York* 65 J8
Redmyre *Abers* 95 M6
Rednal *Shrops* 48 G9
Redpath *Border* 80 D7
Red Point *Highld* 105 K8
Red Roses *Carmth* 25 L6
Red Row *Nthumb* 73 M2
Redruth *Cnwll* 2 G7
Redstone *P & K* 92 H8
Red Street *Staffs* 49 P5
Red Wharf Bay *IoA* 54 G5
Redwick *Newpt* 28 E11
Redwick *S Glos* 28 G10
Redworth *Darltn* 65 M3
Reed *Herts* 33 K9
Reedham *Norfk* 45 N9
Reedness *E R Yk* 60 D9
Reeds Holme *Lancs* 57 P4
Reepham *Lincs* 52 E8
Reepham *Norfk* 44 H5
Reeth *N York* 65 J7
Reeves Green *Solhll* 40 H11
Regil *N Som* 17 M4
Reiff *Highld* 108 A11
Reigate *Surrey* 21 K12
Reighton *N York* 67 N11
Reinigeadal *W Isls* 111 c3
Reisque *Abers* 103 J10
Reiss *Highld* 110 G5
Relubbus *Cnwll* 2 E8
Relugas *Moray* 100 F5
Remenham *Wokham* 20 C6
Remenham Hill *Wokam* 20 C6
Rempstone *Notts* 41 M3
Rendcomb *Gloucs* 30 D11
Rendham *Suffk* 35 M4
Rendlesham *Suffk* 35 M6
Renfrew *Rens* 84 H9
Renhold *Bed* 32 F6
Renishaw *Derbys* 51 K5
Rennington *Nthumb* 81 P9
Renton *W Duns* 84 G7
Renwick *Cumb* 72 B11
Repps *Norfk* 45 N6
Repton *Derbys* 40 H3
Reraig *Highld* 97 L4
Resaurie *Highld* 107 L12
Resipole Burn *Highld* 89 P4
Reskadinnick *Cnwll* 2 F7
Resolis *Highld* 107 L8
Resolven *Neath* 26 H8
Rest and be thankful *Ag & B* 84 D2
Reston *Border* 87 R9
Reswallie *Angus* 93 N3
Retford *Notts* 51 P5
Rettendon *Essex* 22 F4
Revesby *Lincs* 53 J10
Rewe *Devon* 6 C3
Rew Street *IoW* 9 M8
Reymerston *Norfk* 44 G8
Reynalton *Pembks* 25 J7
Reynoldston *Swans* 26 C10
Rezare *Cnwll* 4 H5
Rhandirmwyn *Carmth* 37 M11
Rhayader *Powys* 37 Q7
Rheindown *Highld* 106 H11
Rhenigidale *W Isls* 111 c3
Rhes-y-cae *Flints* 48 E2
Rhewl *Denbgs* 48 C4
Rhewl *Denbgs* 48 D6
Rhicarn *Highld* 108 C10
Rhiconich *Highld* 108 E5
Rhicullen *Highld* 107 L7
Rhigos *Rhondd* 27 K7
Rhives *Highld* 107 N3
Rhiwbina *Cardif* 27 N11
Rhiwderyn *Newpt* 28 B10
Rhiwlas *Gwynd* 54 H8
Rhoden Green *Kent* 12 D2
Rhodes Minnis *Kent* 13 M2
Rhodiad-y-brenin *Pembks* 24 D4
Rhonehouse *D & G* 70 C4
Rhoose *V Glam* 16 E3
Rhos *Carmth* 25 P2
Rhos *Neath* 26 G8
Rhoscolyn *IoA* 54 C6
Rhoscrowther *Pembks* 24 F8
Rhosesmor *Flints* 48 E2
Rhosgoch *Powys* 38 E11
Rhoshill *Pembks* 36 C11
Rhoshirwaun *Gwynd* 46 C5
Rhoslefain *Gwynd* 47 J9
Rhosllanerchrugog *Wrexhm* 48 F6
Rhosmeirch *IoA* 54 F6
Rhosneigr *IoA* 54 D7
Rhosnesni *Wrexhm* 48 G5
Rhôs-on-Sea *Conwy* 55 M5
Rhossili *Swans* 25 P10
Rhostryfan *Gwynd* 54 G9
Rhostyllen *Wrexhm* 48 F6
Rhosybol *IoA* 54 F4
Rhos-y-gwaliau *Gwynd* 47 Q4
Rhosymedre *Wrexhm* 48 F7
Rhu *Ag & B* 84 E6
Rhuallt *Denbgs* 48 C1
Rhubodach *Ag & B* 83 Q8
Rhuddlan *Denbgs* 55 Q6
Rhue *Highld* 106 B3
Rhunahaorine *Ag & B* 75 K3
Rhyd *Gwynd* 47 K3
Rhydargaeau *Carmth* 25 Q4
Rhydcymerau *Carmth* 26 D2
Rhyd-Ddu *Gwynd* 54 H10
Rhydlewis *Cerdgn* 36 F10
Rhydowen *Cerdgn* 36 G10
Rhyd-uchaf *Gwynd* 47 P4
Rhyd-y-clafdy *Gwynd* 46 F4
Rhyd-y-foel *Conwy* 55 N6
Rhydfro *Neath* 26 F7

Rhyd-y-groes *Gwynd* 54 H8
Rhyd-y-pennau *Cerdgn* 37 K4
Rhyl *Denbgs* 55 Q5
Rhymney *Caerph* 27 N7
Rhynd *P & K* 92 H10
Rhynie *Abers* 101 P9
Rhynie *Highld* 107 P6
Ribbesford *Worcs* 39 P7
Ribbleton *Lancs* 57 K3
Ribchester *Lancs* 57 M2
Riby *Lincs* 52 H3
Riccall *N York* 59 N6
Riccarton *Border* 79 Q9
Riccarton *E Ayrs* 76 G4
Richards Castle *Herefs* 39 J8
Richmond *Gt Lon* 21 J8
Richmond *N York* 65 L7
Richmond *Sheff* 51 K4
Rickerscote *Staffs* 40 B4
Rickford *N Som* 17 L4
Rickham *Devon* 5 P11
Rickinghall *Suffk* 34 H2
Rickling Green *Essex* 33 N10
Rickmansworth *Herts* 20 G5
Riddell *Border* 80 C8
Riddlecombe *Devon* 15 K8
Riddlesden *C Brad* 58 E5
Ridge *Dorset* 8 D9
Ridge *Herts* 21 K4
Ridge *Wilts* 8 D2
Ridge Lane *Warwks* 40 H8
Ridgeway *Derbys* 51 K5
Ridgewell *Essex* 34 C8
Ridgewood *E Susx* 11 P6
Ridgmont *C Beds* 32 D9
Riding Mill *Nthumb* 72 H8
Ridlington *Norfk* 45 M4
Ridlington *Rutlnd* 42 C9
Ridsdale *Nthumb* 72 G4
Rievaulx *N York* 66 E9
Rigg *D & G* 71 L3
Riggend *N Lans* 85 M8
Righoul *Highld* 100 D5
Rigsby *Lincs* 53 L8
Rigside *S Lans* 78 E2
Riley Green *Lancs* 57 L4
Rilla Mill *Cnwll* 4 G5
Rillington *N York* 67 J11
Rimington *Lancs* 63 P11
Rimpton *Somset* 17 N10
Rimswell *E R Yk* 61 M8
Rinaston *Pembks* 24 H4
Ringford *D & G* 69 Q7
Ringland *Norfk* 45 J7
Ringmer *E Susx* 11 N7
Ringmore *Devon* 5 N10
Ringmore *Devon* 6 C8
Ringorm *Moray* 101 K6
Ringsfield *Suffk* 45 N11
Ringsfield Corner *Suffk* 45 N11
Ringshall *Herts* 20 F1
Ringshall *Suffk* 34 G6
Ringshall Stocks *Suffk* 34 H6
Ringstead *Nhants* 32 E2
Ringstead *Norfk* 44 B3
Ringwood *Hants* 8 H6
Ringwould *Kent* 13 Q1
Rinmore *Abers* 101 M11
Ripe *E Susx* 11 P7
Ripley *Derbys* 51 K10
Ripley *Hants* 8 H7
Ripley *N York* 58 H3
Ripley *Surrey* 20 G11
Riplington *Hants* 9 Q3
Ripon *N York* 65 N12
Rippingale *Lincs* 42 F5
Ripple *Kent* 23 Q12
Ripple *Worcs* 29 M2
Ripponden *Calder* 58 D9
Risabus *Ag & B* 74 D4
Risbury *Herefs* 39 K10
Risby *Suffk* 34 C4
Risca *Caerph* 27 P9
Rise *E R Yk* 61 K6
Risegate *Lincs* 42 H4
Riseley *Bed* 32 F4
Riseley *Wokham* 20 B10
Rishangles *Suffk* 35 J3
Rishton *Lancs* 57 N3
Rishworth *Calder* 58 D9
Risley *Derbys* 41 L1
Risley *Warrtn* 57 M9
Risplith *N York* 58 G1
River *Kent* 13 P2
River *W Susx* 10 F5
Riverford *Highld* 107 J10
Riverhead *Kent* 21 P11
Rivington *Lancs* 57 L6
Rivington Services *Lancs* 57 L6
Roade *Nhants* 31 Q4
Roadmeetings *S Lans* 77 P2
Roadside *E Ayrs* 77 K7
Roadside *Highld* 110 D4
Roadwater *Somset* 16 D8
Roag *Highld* 96 C2
Roan of Craigoch *S Ayrs* 76 E9
Roath *Cardif* 27 P12
Roberton *Border* 79 N6
Roberton *S Lans* 78 F3
Robertsbridge *E Susx* 12 E5
Roberttown *Kirk* 58 G9
Robeston Wathen *Pembks* 25 J5
Robgill Tower *D & G* 71 L2
Robin Hood's Bay *N York* 67 K6
Roborough *Devon* 5 K7
Roborough *Devon* 15 K8
Robroyston *C Glas* 85 K8
Roby *Knows* 56 H10
Rocester *Staffs* 50 E11
Roch *Pembks* 24 F5
Rochdale *Rochdl* 58 B10
Roche *Cnwll* 3 L4
Rochester *Medway* 22 E9
Rochester *Nthumb* 72 E2
Rochford *Essex* 22 G5
Rochford *Worcs* 39 L8
Rock *Cnwll* 3 L1
Rock *Nthumb* 81 P9
Rock *Worcs* 39 N7
Rockbeare *Devon* 6 D4
Rockbourne *Hants* 8 G5
Rockcliffe *Cumb* 71 M4

Rockcliffe *D & G* 70 D5
Rockend *Torbay* 6 C9
Rock Ferry *Wirral* 56 G10
Rockfield *Highld* 107 Q6
Rockfield *Mons* 28 F6
Rockford *Devon* 15 N3
Rockhampton *S Glos* 28 H9
Rockhill *Shrops* 38 F6
Rockingham *Nhants* 42 C10
Rockland All Saints *Norfk* 44 G10
Rockland St Mary *Norfk* 45 M8
Rockland St Peter *Norfk* 44 G9
Rockley *Notts* 51 Q6
Rockliffe *Lancs* 57 Q4
Rockville *Ag & B* 84 D5
Rockwell End *Bucks* 20 C6
Rodborough *Gloucs* 29 L7
Rodbourne *Swindn* 18 G4
Rodbourne *Wilts* 18 D4
Rodden *Dorset* 7 N6
Rode *Somset* 18 B9
Rode Heath *Ches E* 49 P4
Rodel *W Isls* 111 c4
Roden *Wrekin* 49 L11
Rodhuish *Somset* 16 D8
Rodington *Wrekin* 49 L11
Rodington Heath *Wrekin* 49 L11
Rodley *Gloucs* 29 K6
Rodley *Leeds* 58 G6
Rodmarton *Gloucs* 29 N8
Rodmell *E Susx* 11 N8
Rodmersham *Kent* 22 H10
Rodmersham Green *Kent* 22 H10
Rodney Stoke *Somset* 17 L6
Rodsley *Derbys* 50 G11
Roecliffe *N York* 59 J2
Roe Green *Herts* 21 K2
Roe Green *Herts* 33 K9
Roehampton *Gt Lon* 21 K8
Roffey *W Susx* 11 K4
Rogart *Highld* 107 M2
Rogate *W Susx* 10 D5
Rogerstone *Newpt* 28 C10
Roghadal *W Isls* 111 c4
Rogiet *Mons* 28 E10
Roke *Oxon* 19 Q3
Roker *Sundld* 73 P8
Rollesby *Norfk* 45 P7
Rolleston *Leics* 41 Q7
Rolleston *Notts* 51 Q9
Rolleston on Dove *Staffs* 40 G3
Rolston *E R Yk* 61 L5
Rolvenden *Kent* 12 G4
Rolvenden Layne *Kent* 12 G4
Romaldkirk *Dur* 64 H3
Romanby *N York* 65 P8
Romanno Bridge *Border* 86 D11
Romansleigh *Devon* 15 M7
Romesdal *Highld* 104 E10
Romford *Dorset* 8 F5
Romford *Gt Lon* 21 P5
Romiley *Stockp* 50 C3
Romsey *Cambs* 33 M5
Romsey *Hants* 9 L3
Romsley *Shrops* 39 P5
Romsley *Worcs* 40 C10
Rona *Highld* 105 J10
Ronachan *Ag & B* 83 L11
Rookhope *Dur* 72 G11
Rookley *IoW* 9 N9
Rooks Bridge *Somset* 17 K5
Rooks Nest *Somset* 16 E9
Rookwith *N York* 65 L9
Roos *E R Yk* 61 M7
Roothams Green *Bed* 32 F5
Ropley *Hants* 9 Q2
Ropley Dean *Hants* 9 Q2
Ropsley *Lincs* 42 E4
Rora *Abers* 103 L5
Rorrington *Shrops* 38 F3
Rosarie *Moray* 101 M5
Rose *Cnwll* 2 H5
Rose Ash *Devon* 15 N7
Rosebank *S Lans* 77 N2
Rosebush *Pembks* 25 J3
Rosedale Abbey *N York* 66 G8
Rose Green *Essex* 34 E10
Rose Green *Suffk* 34 F7
Rose Green *Suffk* 34 F8
Rose Green *W Susx* 10 E9
Rosehall *Highld* 106 H2
Rosehearty *Abers* 103 J2
Rose Hill *Lancs* 57 P3
Roseisle *Moray* 100 H3
Roselands *E Susx* 12 C9
Rosemarket *Pembks* 24 G7
Rosemarkie *Highld* 107 M10
Rosemary Lane *Devon* 16 F12
Rosemount *P & K* 92 H7
Rosenannon *Cnwll* 3 L3
Rosewell *Mdloth* 86 F9
Roseworth *S on T* 65 Q3
Rosgill *Cumb* 71 Q11
Roskhill *Highld* 96 C1
Rosley *Cumb* 71 M6
Roslin *Mdloth* 86 F9
Rosliston *Derbys* 40 H4
Rosneath *Ag & B* 84 E6
Ross *D & G* 69 P9
Rossett *Wrexhm* 48 G4
Rossett Green *N York* 58 H4
Rossington *Donc* 51 N2
Ross-on-Wye *Herefs* 28 H4
Roster *Highld* 110 F7
Rosthorne *Ches E* 57 N11
Rosthwaite *Cumb* 71 L11
Roston *Derbys* 50 F11
Rosyth *Fife* 86 D5
Rothbury *Nthumb* 73 J1
Rotherby *Leics* 41 P4
Rotherfield *E Susx* 12 B4
Rotherfield Greys *Oxon* 20 B7
Rotherfield Peppard *Oxon* 20 B7
Rotherham *Rothm* 51 K3
Rothersthorpe *Nhants* 31 Q3
Rotherwick *Hants* 20 B11
Rothes *Moray* 101 K5
Rothesay *Ag & B* 84 C9
Rothiebrisbane *Abers* 102 G7
Rothiemurchus Lodge *Highld* 99 P7
Rothienorman *Abers* 102 F7
Rothley *Leics* 41 N5
Rothmaise *Abers* 102 F8

Rothwell Leeds	59	J8
Rothwell Lincs	52	G4
Rothwell Nhants	32	B1
Rottal Lodge Angus	94	F7
Rottingdean Br & H.	11	M9
Rottington Cumb	70	F11
Roucan D & G	78	G12
Rougham Norfk	44	D6
Rougham Suffk	34	E4
Rough Common Kent	23	L10
Roughpark Abers	101	L11
Roughton Lincs	53	J9
Roughton Norfk	45	K3
Roughton Shrops	39	N4
Roundbush Green Essex	22	C1
Round Green Luton	32	F11
Roundham Somset	7	K2
Roundhay Leeds	59	J6
Rounds Green Sandw	40	C9
Roundswell Devon	15	J6
Roundway Wilts	18	E7
Roundyhill Angus	93	L5
Rousay Ork	111	h1
Rousdon Devon	6	H5
Rousham Oxon	31	L8
Rous Lench Worcs	30	D4
Routenburn N Ayrs	84	D10
Routh E R Yk	61	J6
Row Cumb	63	J4
Rowanburn D & G	79	N12
Rowardennan Stirlg	84	F4
Rowarth Derbys	50	D3
Rowberrow Somset	17	L5
Rowde Wilts	18	E8
Rowen Conwy	55	L7
Rowfoot Nthumb	72	C8
Rowhedge Essex	34	G11
Rowington Warwks	30	G1
Rowland Derbys	50	G6
Rowland's Castle Hants	10	B7
Rowlands Gill Gatesd	73	L8
Rowledge Surrey	10	D2
Rowley Dur	73	J10
Rowley Regis Sandw	40	C9
Rowlstone Herefs	28	D4
Rowly Surrey	10	G2
Rowner Hants	9	P7
Rowney Green Worcs	40	D12
Rownhams Hants	9	L4
Rownhams Services Hants	9	L4
Rowrah Cumb	70	H10
Rowsham Bucks	32	C12
Rowsley Derbys	50	G7
Rowston Lincs	52	F11
Rowton Ches W	49	J3
Rowton Wrekin	49	L10
Roxburgh Border	80	F7
Roxby N Linc	60	F10
Roxton Bed	32	G6
Roxwell Essex	22	D2
Royal Leamington Spa Warwks	30	H2
Royal Sutton Coldfield Birm	40	E8
Royal Tunbridge Wells Kent	12	C2
Royal Wootton Bassett Wilts	18	F4
Royal Yacht Britannia C Edin	86	F6
Roy Bridge Highld	98	C11
Roydon Essex	21	N2
Roydon Norfk	34	H1
Roydon Norfk	44	B5
Roydon Hamlet Essex	21	N2
Royston Barns	59	J11
Royston Herts	33	K8
Royton Oldham	58	B11
Rozel Jersey	7	c1
Ruabon Wrexhm	48	F6
Ruaig Ag & B	88	D6
Ruan Lanihorne Cnwll	3	K7
Ruan Major Cnwll	2	G11
Ruan Minor Cnwll	2	G11
Ruardean Gloucs	28	H5
Ruardean Hill Gloucs	28	H5
Ruardean Woodside Gloucs	28	H5
Rubery Birm	40	C11
Rubha Ban W Isls	111	b6
Ruckhall Herefs	28	E2
Ruckinge Kent	13	K4
Ruckley Shrops	39	K3
Rudby Ches W	66	C6
Rudchester Nthumb	73	K7
Ruddington Notts	41	M2
Rudge Somset	18	C9
Rudgeway S Glos	28	H10
Rudgwick W Susx	10	H4
Rudheath Ches W	49	M2
Rudley Green Essex	22	G3
Rudloe Wilts	18	C6
Rudry Caerph	27	P10
Rudston E R Yk	61	J1
Rudyard Staffs	50	C8
Ruecastle Border	80	E9
Rufford Lancs	57	J6
Rufford Abbey Notts	51	N7
Rufforth C York	59	M4
Rugby Warwks	41	L11
Rugby Services Warwks	41	L10
Rugeley Staffs	40	D4
Ruigh'riabhach Highld	105	Q4
Ruisgarry W Isls	111	h4
Ruishton Somset	16	H10
Ruisigearraidh W Isls	111	h4
Ruislip Gt Lon	20	H6
Rùm Highld	96	D9
Rumbach Moray	101	M5
Rumbling Bridge P & K	86	B3
Rumburgh Suffk	35	M1
Rumford Cnwll	3	K2
Rumford Falk	85	Q7
Rumney Cardif	27	P11
Runcorn Halton	57	K11
Runcton W Susx	10	E9
Runcton Holme Norfk	43	P8
Runfold Surrey	10	D1
Runhall Norfk	44	H8
Runham Norfk	45	P7
Runnington Somset	16	F10
Runswick N York	66	H4
Runtaleave Angus	94	E8
Runwell Essex	22	F5
Ruscombe Wokham	20	C8
Rushall Herefs	28	H3
Rushall Norfk	45	K12
Rushall Wilts	18	G9

Rushall Wsall	40	D7
Rushbrooke Suffk	34	E5
Rushbury Shrops	39	K4
Rushden Herts	33	K9
Rushden Nhants	32	D4
Rushenden Kent	22	H8
Rushford Norfk	34	F1
Rush Green Essex	23	M1
Rush Green Gt Lon	21	P6
Rush Green Warrtn	57	M10
Rushlake Green E Susx	12	D6
Rushmere Suffk	45	P11
Rushmoor Surrey	10	E3
Rushock Worcs	40	B12
Rusholme Manch	57	Q9
Rushton Nhants	42	B12
Rushton Spencer Staffs	50	C8
Rushwick Worcs	39	P10
Rushyford Dur	65	M2
Ruskie Stirlg	85	K3
Ruskington Lincs	52	F12
Rusland Cumb	62	G5
Rusper W Susx	11	K3
Ruspidge Gloucs	29	J6
Russell's Water Oxon	20	B5
Russ Hill Surrey	11	K3
Rusthall Kent	12	C3
Rustington W Susx	10	G9
Ruston N York	67	K10
Ruston Parva E R Yk	60	H2
Ruswarp N York	67	J5
Rutherford Border	80	E7
Rutherglen S Lans	85	K10
Ruthernbridge Cnwll	3	M3
Ruthin Denbgs	48	D4
Ruthrieston C Aber	95	Q2
Ruthven Abers	101	P6
Ruthven Angus	93	K6
Ruthven Highld	99	L8
Ruthven Highld	99	M3
Ruthvoes Cnwll	3	K4
Ruthwell D & G	70	H3
Ruyton-XI-Towns Shrops	48	H10
Ryal Nthumb	72	H6
Ryall Dorset	7	K4
Ryall Worcs	29	M1
Ryarsh Kent	22	D10
Rydal Cumb	62	G2
Ryde IoW	9	P8
Rye E Susx	12	H6
Rye Foreign E Susx	12	H5
Rye Street Worcs	29	K2
Ryhall Rutlnd	42	E7
Ryhill Wakefd	59	J10
Ryhope Sundld	73	P9
Ryland Lincs	52	E7
Rylands Notts	41	M1
Rylstone N York	58	C3
Ryme Intrinseca Dorset	7	N1
Ryther N York	59	M6
Ryton Gatesd	73	K7
Ryton Shrops	39	N2
Ryton-on-Dunsmore Warwks	41	J11
RZSS Edinburgh Zoo C Edin	86	E7

S

Sabden Lancs	57	P2
Sacombe Herts	33	K11
Sacriston Dur	73	M10
Sadberge Daﬂtn	65	N4
Saddell Ag & B	75	L6
Saddington Leics	41	P8
Saddle Bow Norfk	43	P7
Saddlescombe W Susx	11	L7
Saffron Walden Essex	33	N8
Sageston Pembks	25	J7
Saham Hills Norfk	44	E9
Saham Toney Norfk	44	E9
Saighton Ches W	49	J3
St Abbs Border	81	J1
St Agnes Border	87	M9
St Agnes Cnwll	2	G5
St Agnes IoS	2	b3
St Agnes Mining District Cnwll	2	G6
St Albans Herts	21	J2
St Allen Cnwll	3	J5
St Andrew Guern	6	b2
St Andrews Fife	93	N11
St Andrews Botanic Garden Fife	93	N11
St Andrews Major V Glam	16	F2
St Andrews Well Dorset	7	L4
St Anne's Lancs	56	G3
St Ann's D & G	78	H9
St Ann's Chapel Cnwll	5	J6
St Ann's Chapel Cnwll	5	N10
St Anthony-in-Meneage Cnwll	2	H10
St Anthony's Hill E Susx	12	D9
St Arvans Mons	28	F9
St Asaph Denbgs	48	B1
St Athan V Glam	16	D3
St Aubin Jersey	7	b2
St Austell Cnwll	3	M5
St Bees Cumb	70	F12
St Blazey Cnwll	3	N5
St Boswells Border	80	D7
St Brelade Jersey	7	a2
St Brelade's Bay Jersey	7	a2
St Breock Cnwll	3	L2
St Breward Cnwll	4	D5
St Briavels Gloucs	28	G7
St Brides Major V Glam	16	B2
St Brides-super-Ely V Glam	27	M12
St Brides Wentlooge Newpt	28	C11
St Budeaux C Plym	5	K8
Saintbury Gloucs	30	E6
St Buryan Cnwll	2	C9
St Catherines Ag & B	84	C2
St Chloe Gloucs	29	L8
St Clears Carmth	25	M5
St Cleer Cnwll	4	F6
St Clement Cnwll	3	J7
St Clement Jersey	7	c2
St Clether Cnwll	4	F4
St Colmac Ag & B	83	Q9
St Columb Major Cnwll	3	K3
St Columb Minor Cnwll	3	J4
St Columb Road Cnwll	3	K4

St Combs Abers	103	L3
St Cross South Elmham Suffk	45	L12
St Cyrus Abers	95	M8
St David's P & K	92	E10
St Davids Pembks	24	D4
St Davids Cathedral Pembks	24	D4
St Day Cnwll	2	G7
St Dennis Cnwll	3	L4
St Dogmaels Pembks	36	C10
St Dominick Cnwll	5	J6
St Donats V Glam	16	C3
St Endellion Cnwll	4	C5
St Enoder Cnwll	3	K4
St Erme Cnwll	3	J6
St Erney Cnwll	4	H8
St Erth Cnwll	2	E8
St Erth Praze Cnwll	2	E8
St Ervan Cnwll	3	K2
St Eval Cnwll	3	K3
St Ewe Cnwll	3	L6
St Fagans Cardif	27	N12
St Fagans: National History Museum Cardif	27	N12
St Fergus Abers	103	M5
St Fillans P & K	91	Q10
St Florence Pembks	25	J8
St Gennys Cnwll	14	C11
St George Conwy	55	P6
St Georges N Som	17	K4
St George's V Glam	16	E2
St Germans Cnwll	4	H8
St Giles in the Wood Devon	15	J8
St Giles-on-the-Heath Devon	4	H3
St Harmon Powys	38	B7
St Helen Auckland Dur	65	L3
St Helen's E Susx	12	G7
St Helens IoW	9	Q9
St Helens St Hel	57	K9
St Helier Gt Lon	21	L9
St Helier Jersey	7	b2
St Hilary Cnwll	2	E9
St Hilary V Glam	16	D2
St Ippolyts Herts	32	H10
St Ishmael's Pembks	24	E7
St Issey Cnwll	3	L2
St Ive Cnwll	4	G6
St Ives Cambs	33	K3
St Ives Cnwll	2	D7
St James's End Nhants	31	Q3
St James South Elmham Suffk	35	M1
St Jidgey Cnwll	3	L2
St John Cnwll	5	J9
St John Jersey	7	b1
St John's E Susx	11	P4
St John's IoM	56	b5
St John's Kent	21	Q11
St Johns Surrey	20	F10
St Johns Worcs	39	Q10
St John's Chapel Devon	15	J6
St John's Chapel Dur	72	F12
St John's Fen End Norfk	43	N7
St John's Kirk S Lans	78	F2
St John's Town of Dalry D & G	69	N3
St John's Wood Gt Lon	21	L6
St Judes IoM	56	d3
St Just Cnwll	2	B9
St Just-in-Roseland Cnwll	3	J8
St Just Mining District Cnwll	2	B8
St Katherines Abers	102	G8
St Keverne Cnwll	2	H10
St Kew Cnwll	3	M1
St Kew Highway Cnwll	3	M1
St Keyne Cnwll	4	F7
St Lawrence Essex	23	J3
St Lawrence IoW	9	N11
St Lawrence Jersey	7	b1
St Lawrence Kent	23	Q9
St Leonards Bucks	20	E3
St Leonards Dorset	8	G6
St Leonards E Susx	12	F8
St Levan Cnwll	2	B9
St Lythans V Glam	16	F2
St Mabyn Cnwll	3	M2
St Madoes P & K	92	H10
St Margarets Herefs	28	D3
St Margarets Herts	21	M2
St Margaret's at Cliffe Kent	13	Q2
St Margaret's Hope Ork	111	h3
St Margaret South Elmham Suffk	45	M12
St Marks IoM	56	c6
St Martin Cnwll	4	G8
St Martin Cnwll	2	H10
St Martin Guern	6	b2
St Martin Jersey	7	c1
St Martin's IoS	2	c1
St Martin's P & K	92	H9
St Martin's Shrops	48	G8
St Mary Jersey	7	a1
St Mary Bourne Hants	19	M10
St Marychurch Torbay	6	C9
St Mary Church V Glam	16	D2
St Mary Cray Gt Lon	21	P9
St Mary in the Marsh Kent	13	K5
St Mary's IoS	2	c2
St Mary's Ork	111	h2
St Mary's Bay Kent	13	L5
St Mary's Hoo Medway	22	F7
St Mary's Platt Kent	22	D11
St Maughans Green Mons	28	F5
St Mawes Cnwll	3	J8
St Mawgan Cnwll	3	K3
St Mellion Cnwll	5	J7
St Mellons Cardif	27	P11
St Merryn Cnwll	3	K2
St Michael Caerhays Cnwll	3	L7
St Michael Church Somset	17	J9
St Michael Penkevil Cnwll	3	J7
St Michaels Kent	12	H3
St Michaels Worcs	39	L8
St Michael's Mount Cnwll	2	D9
St Michael's on Wyre Lancs	57	J1
St Minver Cnwll	3	L1
St Monans Fife	87	J2
St Neot Cnwll	4	E6
St Neots Cambs	32	H5
St Newlyn East Cnwll	3	J5
St Nicholas Pembks	24	F3
St Nicholas V Glam	16	E2
St Nicholas-at-Wade Kent	23	N9
St Ninians Stirlg	85	N5
St Olaves Norfk	45	P9

St Osyth Essex	23	L1
St Ouen Jersey	7	a1
St Owen's Cross Herefs	28	G4
St Paul's Cray Gt Lon	21	P9
St Paul's Walden Herts	32	H11
St Peter Jersey	7	a1
St Peter Port Guern	6	c2
St Peter's Guern	6	b2
St Peter's Kent	23	Q9
St Peter's Hill Cambs	33	J3
St Pinnock Cnwll	4	F7
St Quivox S Ayrs	76	F6
St Sampson Guern	6	c1
St Saviour Guern	6	b2
St Saviour Jersey	7	b2
St Stephen Cnwll	3	L5
St Stephens Cnwll	4	H3
St Stephens Cnwll	5	J8
St Teath Cnwll	4	D5
St Thomas Devon	6	B5
St Tudy Cnwll	3	N1
St Twynnells Pembks	24	G8
St Veep Cnwll	4	E8
St Vigeans Angus	93	Q7
St Wenn Cnwll	3	L3
St Weonards Herefs	28	F4
Salcombe Devon	5	P11
Salcombe Regis Devon	6	F5
Salcott-cum-Virley Essex	23	J1
Sale Traffd	57	P9
Saleby Lincs	53	M7
Sale Green Worcs	30	B3
Salehurst E Susx	12	E5
Salem Cerdgn	37	L4
Salen Ag & B	89	M7
Salen Highld	89	N4
Salford C Beds	32	D8
Salford Oxon	30	H8
Salford Salfd	57	P8
Salford Priors Warwks	30	E4
Salfords Surrey	11	L2
Salhouse Norfk	45	M7
Saline Fife	86	B4
Salisbury Wilts	8	G2
Salisbury Plain Wilts	18	F10
Salkeld Dykes Cumb	71	Q7
Sallachy Highld	107	J1
Salle Norfk	45	J5
Salmonby Lincs	53	K8
Salperton Gloucs	30	E9
Salsburgh N Lans	85	N9
Salt Staffs	40	C2
Saltaire C Brad	58	F6
Saltaire C Brad	58	F6
Saltash Cnwll	5	J8
Saltburn Highld	107	M8
Saltburn-by-the-Sea R & Cl	66	F4
Saltby Leics	42	C5
Saltcoats N Ayrs	76	D3
Saltcotes Lancs	56	G4
Saltdean Br & H	11	M9
Salterbeck Cumb	70	G9
Salterforth Lancs	58	B5
Salterswall Ches W	49	L3
Salterton Wilts	18	G12
Saltfleet Lincs	53	M5
Saltfleetby All Saints Lincs	53	M5
Saltfleetby St Clement Lincs	53	M5
Saltfleetby St Peter Lincs	53	M5
Saltford BaNES	17	P3
Salthouse Norfk	44	H2
Saltley Birm	40	E9
Saltmarshe E R Yk	60	D8
Saltney Flints	48	H3
Salton N York	66	G10
Saltrens Devon	14	H7
Saltwood Kent	13	M3
Salvington W Susx	10	H8
Salwarpe Worcs	39	Q9
Salway Ash Dorset	7	L4
Sambourne Warwks	30	D2
Sambrook Wrekin	49	N9
Sampford Arundel Somset	16	F11
Sampford Brett Somset	16	E7
Sampford Courtenay Devon	15	L11
Sampford Moor Somset	16	F11
Sampford Peverell Devon	16	D12
Sampford Spiney Devon	5	L6
Samsonlane Ork	111	i2
Samuelston E Loth	87	J7
Sanaigmore Ag & B	82	C8
Sancreed Cnwll	2	C9
Sancton E R Yk	60	F6
Sandaig Highld	97	K8
Sandal Magna Wakefd	59	J9
Sanday Ork	111	i1
Sanday Airport Ork	111	i1
Sandbach Ches E	49	N4
Sandbach Services Ches E	49	P4
Sandbank Ag & B	84	C6
Sandbanks BCP	8	F9
Sandend Abers	102	D3
Sanderstead Gt Lon	21	M10
Sandford Cumb	64	D4
Sandford Devon	15	P10
Sandford Dorset	8	D9
Sandford Hants	8	H5
Sandford IoW	9	N10
Sandford N Som	17	K4
Sandford S Lans	77	M3
Sandford-on-Thames Oxon	19	N1
Sandford Orcas Dorset	17	P11
Sandford St Martin Oxon	31	K8
Sandgate Kent	13	M3
Sandhaven Abers	103	K2
Sandhead D & G	68	E8
Sand Hills Leeds	59	J6
Sandhills Oxon	31	M11
Sandhills Surrey	10	F3
Sandhoe Nthumb	72	H7
Sand Hole E R Yk	60	D6
Sandholme E R Yk	60	E7
Sandhurst Br For	20	D10
Sandhurst Gloucs	29	M4
Sandhurst Kent	12	F4
Sand Hutton N York	59	P3
Sandhutton N York	65	P10
Sandiacre Derbys	51	L12
Sandilands Lincs	53	N7
Sandleheath Hants	8	G4
Sandleigh Oxon	19	M1
Sandley Dorset	8	B3

Sandness Shet	111	j4
Sandon Essex	22	E3
Sandon Herts	33	K9
Sandon Staffs	40	C2
Sandon Bank Staffs	40	C2
Sandown IoW	9	P9
Sandplace Cnwll	4	F8
Sandridge Herts	21	J2
Sandringham Norfk	44	B4
Sandsend N York	67	J5
Sandtoft N Linc	60	D11
Sandway Kent	22	H12
Sandwich Kent	23	P10
Sandwick Shet	111	k5
Sandwick W Isls	111	d2
Sandwith Cumb	70	F11
Sandy C Beds	32	G6
Sandyford D & G	79	K9
Sandygate Devon	6	B7
Sandygate IoM	56	d3
Sandyhills D & G	70	E5
Sandylands Lancs	62	H9
Sandy Lane Wilts	18	E7
Sandy Park Devon	5	P3
Sangobeg Highld	108	H3
Sangomore Highld	108	H3
Sankyn's Green Worcs	39	P8
Sanna Highld	89	K3
Sanndabhaig W Isls	111	d2
Sannox N Ayrs	75	Q4
Sanquhar D & G	77	N8
Santon Bridge Cumb	62	C2
Santon Downham Suffk	44	D11
Sapcote Leics	41	L8
Sapey Common Herefs	39	M8
Sapiston Suffk	34	F2
Sapley Cambs	33	J2
Sapperton Gloucs	29	N7
Sapperton Lincs	42	E4
Saracen's Head Lincs	43	K5
Sarclet Highld	110	G7
Sarisbury Hants	9	N5
Sarn Powys	38	E4
Sarnau Cerdgn	36	E9
Sarnau Powys	48	E11
Sarn Mellteyrn Gwynd	46	D5
Sarn Park Services Brdgnd	27	J11
Saron Carmth	26	E6
Saron Gwynd	54	G8
Sarratt Herts	20	G4
Sarre Kent	23	N9
Sarsden Oxon	30	H9
Satley Dur	73	K11
Satterleigh Devon	15	L9
Satterthwaite Cumb	62	G4
Sauchen Abers	102	F11
Saucher P & K	92	H8
Sauchieburn Abers	95	L7
Saul Gloucs	29	K7
Saundby Notts	52	B6
Saundersfoot Pembks	25	K7
Saunderton Bucks	20	C3
Saunton Devon	14	H5
Sausthorpe Lincs	53	L9
Savile Town Kirk	58	G9
Sawbridge Warwks	31	L2
Sawbridgeworth Herts	21	P1
Sawdon N York	67	K9
Sawley Lancs	63	P11
Sawley N York	58	G1
Sawston Cambs	33	M7
Sawtry Cambs	42	G12
Saxby Leics	42	B6
Saxby Lincs	52	E6
Saxby All Saints N Linc	60	G10
Saxelbye Leics	41	P4
Saxham Street Suffk	34	H5
Saxilby Lincs	52	C8
Saxlingham Norfk	44	G3
Saxlingham Green Norfk	45	L10
Saxlingham Nethergate Norfk	45	K10
Saxlingham Thorpe Norfk	45	K9
Saxmundham Suffk	35	N4
Saxondale Notts	51	N5
Saxon Street Cambs	34	B5
Saxtead Suffk	35	L4
Saxtead Green Suffk	35	L4
Saxtead Little Green Suffk	35	L4
Saxthorpe Norfk	45	J4
Saxton N York	59	L6
Sayers Common W Susx	11	L6
Scackleton N York	66	F11
Scadabay W Isls	111	c3
Scadabhagh W Isls	111	c3
Scafell Pike Cumb	62	E2
Scaftworth Notts	51	P3
Scagglethorpe N York	67	J11
Scalasaig Ag & B	82	E4
Scalby E R Yk	60	E8
Scalby N York	67	L9
Scaldwell Nhants	41	Q11
Scaleby Cumb	71	P3
Scalebyhill Cumb	71	P3
Scales Cumb	62	F2
Scales Cumb	71	M9
Scalford Leics	41	Q3
Scaling N York	66	H5
Scalloway Shet	111	k4
Scalpay Highld	96	H4
Scalpay W Isls	111	c3
Scamblesby Lincs	53	J7
Scamodale Highld	90	B2
Scampston N York	67	J11
Scampton Lincs	52	D7
Scaniport Highld	99	J2
Scapegoat Hill Kirk	58	E10
Scarba Ag & B	83	K3
Scarborough N York	67	M9
Scarcewater Cnwll	3	K5
Scarcliffe Derbys	51	L7
Scarcroft Leeds	59	J6
Scarfskerry Highld	110	F2
Scarinish Ag & B	88	C7
Scarisbrick Lancs	56	H6
Scarning Norfk	44	F7
Scarrington Notts	51	Q11
Scartho NE Lin	53	J3
Scatsta Airport Shet	111	k3
Scaur D & G	70	E5
Scawby N Linc	52	D3
Scawsby Donc	59	M12
Scawthorpe Donc	59	M11
Scawton N York	66	D10

Place	County	Page	Grid
Scayne's Hill	W Susx	11	M5
Scethrog	Powys	27	M4
Scholar Green	Ches E	49	Q4
Scholes	Kirk	58	F11
Scholes	Leeds	59	J6
Scholes	Rothm	51	K2
Scholes	Wigan	57	L7
Scissett	Kirk	58	G11
Scleddau	Pembks	24	G2
Scofton	Notts	51	N5
Scole	Norfk	35	J4
Scone	P & K	92	H9
Sconser	Highld	96	F4
Scoonie	Fife	86	H2
Scopwick	Lincs	52	F11
Scoraig	Highld	105	Q3
Scorborough	E R Yk	60	H5
Scorrier	Cnwll	2	G7
Scorton	Lancs	63	J11
Scorton	N York	65	M7
Scotby	Cumb	71	P5
Scotch Corner	N York	65	L6
Scotch Corner Rest Area	N York	65	L6
Scotforth	Lancs	63	J9
Scothern	Lincs	52	E7
Scotlandwell	P & K	86	E2
Scotscalder Station	Highld	110	C5
Scot's Gap	Nthumb	73	J4
Scotsmill	Abers	102	D10
Scotstoun	C Glas	85	J9
Scotswood	N u Ty	73	L7
Scotter	Lincs	52	C4
Scotterthorpe	Lincs	52	C3
Scottish Seabird Centre	E Loth	87	K5
Scottish Wool Centre	Stirlg	85	J3
Scotton	Lincs	52	C4
Scotton	N York	59	J3
Scotton	N York	65	L8
Scoulton	Norfk	44	G9
Scourie	Highld	108	D6
Scourie More	Highld	108	D7
Scousburgh	Shet	111	k5
Scrabster	Highld	110	C2
Scraesburgh	Border	80	F9
Scrane End	Lincs	43	L2
Scraptoft	Leics	41	P6
Scratby	Norfk	45	Q4
Scrayingham	N York	60	C3
Scredington	Lincs	42	F3
Scremby	Lincs	53	M9
Scremerston	Nthumb	81	L4
Screveton	Notts	51	Q11
Scriven	N York	59	J3
Scrooby	Notts	51	P3
Scropton	Derbys	40	G2
Scrub Hill	Lincs	52	H11
Scruton	N York	65	N8
Scullomie	Highld	109	L4
Sculthorpe	Norfk	44	E4
Scunthorpe	N Linc	60	F11
Seaborough	Dorset	7	K2
Seabridge	Staffs	49	Q6
Seabrook	Kent	13	M3
Seaburn	Sundld	73	P8
Seacombe	Wirral	56	G10
Seacroft	Leeds	59	J7
Seafield	W Loth	86	B8
Seaford	E Susx	11	P9
Seaforth	Sefton	56	G9
Seagrave	Leics	41	N4
Seaham	Dur	73	P10
Seahouses	Nthumb	81	P7
Seal	Kent	22	B11
Sealand	Flints	48	G2
Seale	Surrey	10	E1
Seamer	N York	66	C5
Seamer	N York	67	L10
Seamill	N Ayrs	76	D2
Sea Palling	Norfk	45	N5
Searby	Lincs	52	F3
Seasalter	Kent	23	L9
Seascale	Cumb	62	B3
Seathwaite	Cumb	62	E3
Seatoller	Cumb	71	L11
Seaton	Cnwll	4	G8
Seaton	Cumb	70	G8
Seaton	Devon	6	H5
Seaton	E R Yk	61	K5
Seaton	Kent	23	N10
Seaton	Nthumb	73	N5
Seaton	Rutlnd	42	C9
Seaton Carew	Hartpl	66	D2
Seaton Delaval	Nthumb	73	N6
Seaton Ross	E R Yk	60	D6
Seaton Sluice	Nthumb	73	N5
Seatown	Dorset	7	K4
Seatown	Moray	101	K2
Seave Green	N York	66	D7
Seaview	IoW	9	Q8
Seaville	Cumb	71	J5
Seavington St Mary	Somset	17	K12
Seavington St Michael	Somset	17	K12
Sebastopol	Torfn	28	C8
Sebergham	Cumb	71	M7
Seckington	Warwks	40	H6
Second Severn Crossing	Mons	28	F10
Sedbergh	Cumb	63	M4
Sedbury	Gloucs	28	G9
Sedbusk	N York	64	F8
Sedgeberrow	Worcs	30	D6
Sedgebrook	Lincs	42	C3
Sedgefield	Dur	65	P2
Sedgeford	Norfk	44	B3
Sedgehill	Wilts	8	C2
Sedgemoor Services	Somset	17	J5
Sedgley	Dudley	40	B8
Sedgley Park	Bury	57	P8
Sedgwick	Cumb	63	K5
Sedlescombe	E Susx	12	F6
Sedrup	Bucks	20	C2
Seend	Wilts	18	D8
Seend Cleeve	Wilts	18	D8
Seer Green	Bucks	20	F5
Seething	Norfk	45	M9
Sefton	Sefton	56	G9
Seighford	Staffs	49	Q9
Seion	Gwynd	54	H8
Seisdon	Staffs	39	Q3
Selattyn	Shrops	48	F8
Selborne	Hants	10	C4
Selby	N York	59	N7
Selham	W Susx	10	E6
Selhurst	Gt Lon	21	M9
Selkirk	Border	79	P3
Sellack	Herefs	28	G4
Sellafield Station	Cumb	62	B2
Sellafirth	Shet	111	k2
Sellindge	Kent	13	L3
Selling	Kent	23	K11
Sells Green	Wilts	18	D8
Selly Oak	Birm	40	D10
Selmeston	E Susx	11	P8
Selsdon	Gt Lon	21	M10
Selsey	W Susx	10	D10
Selside	N York	64	E11
Selsley	Gloucs	29	L7
Selsted	Kent	13	N2
Selston	Notts	51	K11
Selworthy	Somset	16	C6
Semer	Suffk	34	G7
Semington	Wilts	18	D8
Semley	Wilts	8	D3
Send	Surrey	20	G11
Senghenydd	Caerph	27	N10
Sennen	Cnwll	2	B10
Sennen Cove	Cnwll	2	B9
Sennybridge	Powys	27	K3
Sessay	N York	66	C11
Setchey	Norfk	43	Q7
Seton Mains	E Loth	87	J7
Settle	N York	63	P9
Settrington	N York	67	J12
Sevenhampton	Gloucs	30	D9
Sevenhampton	Swindn	18	H3
Seven Kings	Gt Lon	21	P6
Sevenoaks	Kent	21	Q11
Sevenoaks Weald	Kent	21	Q12
Seven Sisters	Neath	26	H7
Seven Star Green	Essex	34	F10
Severn Beach	S Glos	28	G10
Severn Bridge	S Glos	28	G10
Severn Stoke	Worcs	39	Q12
Severn View Services	S Glos	28	G10
Sevington	Kent	13	K2
Sewards End	Essex	33	P8
Sewell	C Beds	32	E11
Sewerby	E R Yk	61	L1
Seworgan	Cnwll	2	G9
Sewstern	Leics	42	C6
Sgalpaigh	W Isls	111	c3
Sgiogarstaigh	W Isls	111	e1
Shabbington	Bucks	31	P11
Shackerstone	Leics	41	J6
Shackleford	Surrey	10	E2
Shader	W Isls	111	d1
Shadforth	Dur	73	N11
Shadingfield	Suffk	45	P12
Shadoxhurst	Kent	13	J3
Shadwell	Leeds	59	J6
Shadwell	Norfk	44	F12
Shaftenhoe End	Herts	33	L8
Shaftesbury	Dorset	8	C3
Shafton	Barns	59	K11
Shakerley	Wigan	57	M8
Shalbourne	Wilts	19	K7
Shalden	Hants	10	B2
Shaldon	Devon	6	C8
Shalfleet	IoW	9	M9
Shalford	Essex	34	C10
Shalford	Surrey	10	G1
Shalford Green	Essex	34	B10
Shalmsford Street	Kent	23	L11
Shalstone	Bucks	31	N6
Shamley Green	Surrey	10	G2
Shandford	Angus	94	H9
Shandon	Ag & B	84	E6
Shandwick	Highld	107	P7
Shangton	Leics	41	Q8
Shanklin	IoW	9	P10
Shantron	Ag & B	84	F5
Shap	Cumb	71	Q11
Shapinsay	Ork	111	h2
Shapwick	Dorset	8	D7
Shapwick	Somset	17	K8
Shard End	Birm	40	F9
Shardlow	Derbys	41	K2
Shareshill	Staffs	40	C6
Sharlston	Wakefd	59	K9
Sharmans Cross	Solhll	40	F10
Sharnbrook	Bed	32	E5
Sharnford	Leics	41	L8
Sharoe Green	Lancs	57	K3
Sharow	N York	65	N12
Sharpenhoe	C Beds	32	F10
Sharperton	Nthumb	81	K12
Sharpness	Gloucs	29	J8
Sharrington	Norfk	44	G3
Shatterford	Worcs	39	P6
Shaugh Prior	Devon	5	L7
Shavington	Ches E	49	M5
Shaw	Oldham	58	C11
Shaw	Swindn	18	G4
Shaw	W Berk	19	N7
Shaw	Wilts	18	D7
Shawbirch	Wrekin	49	M11
Shawbost	W Isls	111	d1
Shawbury	Shrops	49	K10
Shawell	Leics	41	M10
Shawford	Hants	9	M3
Shawhead	D & G	70	E1
Shaw Mills	N York	58	G2
Shawsburn	S Lans	77	N2
Shearington	D & G	70	G3
Shearsby	Leics	41	N8
Shearston	Somset	16	H9
Shebbear	Devon	14	H9
Shebdon	Staffs	49	N9
Shebster	Highld	110	B3
Shedfield	Hants	9	P5
Sheen	Staffs	50	E8
Sheepridge	Kirk	58	F9
Sheepscar	Leeds	58	H7
Sheepscombe	Gloucs	29	M6
Sheepstor	Devon	5	L6
Sheepwash	Devon	14	H10
Sheepy Magna	Leics	41	J7
Sheepy Parva	Leics	41	J7
Sheering	Essex	21	P1
Sheerness	Kent	22	H8
Sheerwater	Surrey	20	G10
Sheet	Hants	10	C5
Sheffield	Sheff	51	J4
Sheffield Park	E Susx	11	N5
Shefford	C Beds	32	G8
Sheigra	Highld	108	D4
Sheinton	Shrops	39	L2
Shelderton	Shrops	38	H6
Sheldon	Birm	40	F9
Sheldon	Derbys	50	F7
Sheldon	Devon	6	F2
Sheldwich	Kent	23	K11
Shelfanger	Norfk	45	J12
Shelford	Notts	51	P11
Shelley	Kirk	58	G11
Shelley	Suffk	34	G8
Shellingford	Oxon	19	K3
Shellow Bowells	Essex	22	C2
Shelsley Beauchamp	Worcs	39	N9
Shelsley Walsh	Worcs	39	N9
Shelton	Bed	32	E3
Shelton	Norfk	45	K11
Shelton	Notts	42	B2
Shelton Lock	C Derb	41	J2
Shelton Under Harley	Staffs	49	P7
Shelve	Shrops	38	G3
Shelwick	Herefs	28	F1
Shenfield	Essex	22	C4
Shenington	Oxon	31	J5
Shenley	Herts	21	J4
Shenley Brook End	M Keyn	32	B9
Shenley Church End	M Keyn	32	B9
Shenmore	Herefs	28	D2
Shennanton	D & G	69	J6
Shenstone	Staffs	40	E6
Shenstone	Worcs	39	Q7
Shenton	Leics	41	J7
Shenval	Moray	101	J8
Shephall	Herts	33	J11
Shepherd's Bush	Gt Lon	21	K7
Shepherdswell	Kent	13	N1
Shepley	Kirk	58	G11
Shepperton	Surrey	20	H9
Shepreth	Cambs	33	L7
Shepshed	Leics	41	L4
Shepton Beauchamp	Somset	17	K11
Shepton Mallet	Somset	17	N7
Shepton Montague	Somset	17	P9
Shepway	Kent	22	F11
Sheraton	Dur	66	C1
Sherborne	Dorset	17	P11
Sherborne	Gloucs	30	F10
Sherborne	Somset	17	N5
Sherborne St John	Hants	19	Q9
Sherbourne	Warwks	30	H2
Sherburn	Dur	73	N11
Sherburn	N York	67	K11
Sherburn Hill	Dur	73	N11
Sherburn in Elmet	N York	59	L7
Shere	Surrey	10	H1
Shereford	Norfk	44	E4
Sherfield English	Hants	9	K3
Sherfield on Loddon	Hants	20	B10
Sherford	Devon	5	Q10
Sheriffhales	Shrops	49	N11
Sheriff Hutton	N York	59	P2
Sheringham	Norfk	45	J2
Shernborne	Norfk	44	B4
Sherrington	Wilts	18	E11
Sherston	Wilts	18	C4
Sherwood	C Nott	51	M11
Sherwood Forest	Notts	51	N8
Shetland Islands	Shet	111	k4
Shettleston	C Glas	85	L9
Shevington	Wigan	57	K7
Shevington Vale	Wigan	57	K7
Sheviock	Cnwll	4	H8
Shibden Head	C Brad	58	E8
Shide	IoW	9	N9
Shidlaw	Nthumb	80	H6
Shiel Bridge	Highld	97	N6
Shieldaig	Highld	105	M10
Shieldhill	D & G	78	G11
Shieldhill	Falk	85	P7
Shieldhill House Hotel	S Lans	78	G2
Shields	N Lans	85	N11
Shielfoot	Highld	89	N3
Shielhill	Angus	93	M4
Shielhill	Inver	84	D8
Shifnal	Shrops	39	N1
Shilbottle	Nthumb	81	P11
Shildon	Dur	65	M3
Shillford	E Rens	84	H10
Shillingford	Devon	16	D10
Shillingford	Oxon	19	P3
Shillingford Abbot	Devon	6	B5
Shillingford St George	Devon	6	B5
Shillingstone	Dorset	8	C5
Shillington	C Beds	32	G9
Shilton	Oxon	30	H11
Shilton	Warwks	41	K9
Shimpling	Norfk	45	J12
Shimpling	Suffk	34	E6
Shimpling Street	Suffk	34	E6
Shincliffe	Dur	73	N11
Shiney Row	Sundld	73	N9
Shinfield	Wokham	20	B9
Shinness	Highld	109	J11
Shipbourne	Kent	22	C11
Shipdham	Norfk	44	F8
Shipham	Somset	17	L5
Shiphay	Torbay	6	B9
Shiplake	Oxon	20	C7
Shipley	C Brad	58	F6
Shipley	W Susx	11	J5
Shipley Bridge	Surrey	11	L3
Shipmeadow	Suffk	45	N11
Shippon	Oxon	19	N2
Shipston-on-Stour	Warwks	30	G6
Shipton	Gloucs	30	D9
Shipton	N York	59	M3
Shipton	Shrops	39	K4
Shipton Bellinger	Hants	19	J10
Shipton Gorge	Dorset	7	M5
Shipton Green	W Susx	10	C9
Shipton Moyne	Gloucs	29	M10
Shipton-on-Cherwell	Oxon	31	L10
Shiptonthorpe	E R Yk	60	E5
Shipton-under-Wychwood	Oxon	30	H9
Shirburn	Oxon	20	B4
Shirdley Hill	Lancs	56	G6
Shirebrook	Derbys	51	L7
Shiregreen	Sheff	51	J3
Shirehampton	Bristl	28	G12
Shiremoor	N Tyne	73	N6
Shirenewton	Mons	28	F9
Shireoaks	Notts	51	M5
Shirland	Derbys	51	K8
Shirley	C Soton	9	L5
Shirley	Derbys	50	G11
Shirley	Gt Lon	21	M9
Shirley	Solhll	40	E10
Shirrell Heath	Hants	9	P5
Shirwell	Devon	15	K5
Shiskine	N Ayrs	75	N6
Shobdon	Herefs	38	H9
Shobrooke	Devon	15	N11
Shoby	Leics	41	P4
Shocklach	Ches W	48	H5
Shoeburyness	Sthend	22	H6
Sholden	Kent	23	Q11
Sholing	C Sotn	9	M5
Shop	Cnwll	14	D8
Shoreditch	Gt Lon	21	M6
Shoreditch	Somset	16	H10
Shoreham	Kent	21	P10
Shoreham-by-Sea	W Susx	11	K8
Shorley	Hants	9	P3
Shorne	Kent	22	E8
Shortgate	E Susx	11	P7
Short Heath	Birm	40	D9
Short Heath	Wsall	40	C7
Shortlanesend	Cnwll	3	J6
Shortlees	E Ayrs	76	G4
Shortwood	S Glos	29	J12
Shorwell	IoW	9	M10
Shoscombe	BaNES	17	Q5
Shotesham	Norfk	45	L10
Shotgate	Essex	22	F5
Shotley	Suffk	35	K9
Shotley Bridge	Dur	73	J9
Shotley Gate	Suffk	35	L9
Shottenden	Kent	23	K11
Shottery	Warwks	30	F3
Shotteswell	Warwks	31	K5
Shottisham	Suffk	35	M7
Shottle	Derbys	50	H10
Shotton	Dur	73	P11
Shotton	Flints	48	F2
Shotton Colliery	Dur	73	P11
Shotts	N Lans	85	P10
Shotwick	Ches W	48	G2
Shougle	Moray	101	J4
Shouldham	Norfk	44	B8
Shouldham Thorpe	Norfk	43	Q8
Shoulton	Worcs	39	P9
Shrawardine	Shrops	48	H11
Shrawley	Worcs	39	P8
Shrewley	Warwks	30	G1
Shrewsbury	Shrops	49	J11
Shrewton	Wilts	18	F11
Shripney	W Susx	10	F9
Shrivenham	Oxon	19	J3
Shropham	Norfk	44	G10
Shroton	Dorset	8	C5
Shucknall	Herefs	28	G1
Shudy Camps	Cambs	33	P7
Shuna	Ag & B	83	L2
Shurdington	Gloucs	29	N5
Shurlock Row	W & M	20	D8
Shurrery	Highld	110	B4
Shurrery Lodge	Highld	110	B4
Shurton	Somset	16	G7
Shustoke	Warwks	40	G8
Shute	Devon	6	H4
Shute	Devon	15	Q11
Shutford	Oxon	31	J6
Shut Heath	Staffs	49	Q10
Shuthonger	Gloucs	29	M2
Shutlanger	Nhants	31	Q4
Shuttington	Warwks	40	G6
Shuttlewood	Derbys	51	L6
Shuttleworth	Bury	57	P5
Siabost	W Isls	111	d1
Siadar	W Isls	111	e1
Sibbertoft	Nhants	41	P10
Sibford Ferris	Oxon	31	J6
Sibford Gower	Oxon	31	J6
Sible Hedingham	Essex	34	C9
Sibley's Green	Essex	33	P10
Sibsey	Lincs	53	K12
Sibson	Cambs	42	F10
Sibson	Leics	41	J7
Sibster	Highld	110	G5
Sibthorpe	Notts	51	Q10
Sibthorpe	Notts	51	Q6
Sibton	Suffk	35	M3
Sicklesmere	Suffk	34	E5
Sicklinghall	N York	59	J5
Sidbury	Devon	6	F4
Sidbury	Shrops	39	M5
Sidcot	N Som	17	K5
Sidcup	Gt Lon	21	P8
Siddington	Ches E	49	Q2
Siddington	Gloucs	18	F2
Sidestrand	Norfk	45	L3
Sidford	Devon	6	F5
Sidlesham	W Susx	10	D9
Sidley	E Susx	12	E8
Sidmouth	Devon	6	F5
Sigglesthorne	E R Yk	61	K5
Sigingstone	V Glam	16	C2
Silchester	Hants	19	Q8
Sileby	Leics	41	N5
Silecroft	Cumb	62	D6
Silfield	Norfk	45	J9
Silkstone	Barns	58	H11
Silkstone Common	Barns	58	H12
Silk Willoughby	Lincs	42	F2
Silloth	Cumb	70	H5
Silpho	N York	67	L8
Silsden	C Brad	58	D5
Silsoe	C Beds	32	F9
Silton	Dorset	8	B2
Silverburn	Mdloth	86	E9
Silverdale	Lancs	63	J7
Silverdale	Staffs	49	P6
Silver End	Essex	34	D11
Silverford	Abers	102	G3
Silverstone	Nhants	31	P5
Silverton	Devon	6	C3
Silvington	Shrops	39	L6
Simonburn	Nthumb	72	F6
Simonsbath	Somset	15	N4
Simonstone	Lancs	57	P2
Simprim	Border	80	H5
Simpson	M Keyn	32	C9
Simpson Cross	Pembks	24	F5
Sinclair's Hill	Border	80	H4
Sinclairston	E Ayrs	76	H7
Sinderby	N York	65	N10
Sinderland Green	Traffd	57	N10
Sindlesham	Wokham	20	C9
Sinfin	C Derb	41	J2
Singleton	Kent	13	J2
Singleton	Lancs	56	H2
Singleton	W Susx	10	E7
Singlewell	Kent	22	D8
Sinnahard	Abers	101	N11
Sinnington	N York	66	G9
Sinton	Worcs	39	P9
Sinton	Worcs	39	Q9
Sinton Green	Worcs	39	P9
Sissinghurst	Kent	12	F3
Siston	S Glos	17	P2
Sithney	Cnwll	2	F9
Sittingbourne	Kent	22	H10
Six Ashes	Shrops	39	P4
Sixhills	Lincs	52	G6
Six Mile Bottom	Cambs	33	P5
Sixpenny Handley	Dorset	8	E4
Skaill	Ork	111	h2
Skara Brae	Ork	111	g2
Skares	Abers	77	J7
Skateraw	Abers	95	P4
Skateraw	E Loth	87	N7
Skeabost	Highld	104	F11
Skeeby	N York	65	L7
Skeffington	Leics	41	Q7
Skeffling	E R Yk	61	N9
Skegby	Notts	51	L8
Skegby	Notts	52	B9
Skegness	Lincs	53	P10
Skelbo	Highld	107	N4
Skelbo Street	Highld	107	N4
Skelbrooke	Donc	59	L10
Skeldyke	Lincs	43	K3
Skellingthorpe	Lincs	52	D8
Skellow	Donc	59	M11
Skelmanthorpe	Kirk	58	G11
Skelmersdale	Lancs	57	J7
Skelmorlie	N Ayrs	84	D9
Skelpick	Highld	109	M5
Skelston	D & G	78	D10
Skelton	C York	59	M3
Skelton	Cumb	71	N8
Skelton	E R Yk	60	D8
Skelton	R & Cl	66	F4
Skelton on Ure	N York	59	J1
Skelwith Bridge	Cumb	62	G2
Skendleby	Lincs	53	M9
Skene House	Abers	102	G12
Skenfrith	Mons	28	E5
Skerne	E R Yk	60	H3
Skerray	Highld	109	L3
Skerricha	Highld	108	E5
Skerton	Lancs	63	J9
Sketchley	Leics	41	K8
Sketty	Swans	26	E9
Skewsby	N York	66	E12
Skiall	Highld	110	B3
Skidby	E R Yk	60	H7
Skigersta	W Isls	111	e1
Skilgate	Somset	16	D10
Skillington	Lincs	42	C5
Skinburness	Cumb	71	J4
Skinflats	Falk	85	Q6
Skinidin	Highld	104	C11
Skipness	Ag & B	83	N10
Skipper's Bridge	D & G	79	M11
Skipsea	E R Yk	61	K3
Skipton	N York	58	C4
Skipton-on-Swale	N York	65	P10
Skipwith	N York	59	P6
Skirlaugh	E R Yk	61	K6
Skirling	Border	78	H2
Skirmett	Bucks	20	C5
Skirpenbeck	E R Yk	60	D3
Skirwith	Cumb	64	B2
Skirza	Highld	110	H3
Skokholm Island	Pembks	24	D7
Skomer Island	Pembks	24	D7
Skulamus	Highld	97	J5
Skye Green	Essex	34	E11
Skye of Curr	Highld	99	P4
Slack	Calder	58	C8
Slackbuie	Highld	99	K1
Slacks of Cairnbanno	Abers	102	H6
Slad	Gloucs	29	M7
Slade	Devon	15	J3
Slade Green	Gt Lon	21	Q7
Slade Hooton	Rothm	51	M3
Slaggyford	Nthumb	72	C9
Slaidburn	Lancs	63	N10
Slaithwaite	Kirk	58	E10
Slaley	Nthumb	72	H8
Slamannan	Falk	85	P8
Slapton	Bucks	32	D11
Slapton	Devon	5	Q10
Slapton	Nhants	31	N5
Slaugham	W Susx	11	K5
Slaughterford	Wilts	18	C6
Slawston	Leics	41	R8
Sleaford	Hants	10	C3
Sleaford	Lincs	42	F2
Sleagill	Cumb	64	B4
Sleapford	Wrekin	49	L11
Sleasdairidh	Highld	107	K3
Sledmere	E R Yk	60	F2
Sleetbeck	Cumb	79	P12
Sleights	N York	67	J6
Slickly	Highld	110	F3
Sliddery	N Ayrs	75	P7
Sligachan	Highld	96	F4
Sligrachan	Ag & B	84	C3
Slimbridge	Gloucs	29	K7
Slindon	Staffs	49	P8
Slindon	W Susx	10	F8
Slinfold	W Susx	10	H4
Slingsby	N York	66	F11
Slip End	C Beds	32	F11
Slip End	Herts	33	J8
Slipton	Nhants	32	D2
Slitting Mill	Staffs	40	D4
Slockavullin	Ag & B	83	M4
Sloncombe	Devon	5	P3
Sloothby	Lincs	53	M8
Slough	Slough	20	F7
Slough Green	Somset	16	H11
Slumbay	Highld	97	M2
Slyfield	Surrey	20	F11

Slyne Lancs ...63 J8
Smailholm Border ...80 E7
Smallburgh Norfk ...45 M5
Smallburn E Ayrs ...77 L6
Small Dole W Susx ...11 K7
Smalley Derbys ...51 K11
Smallfield Surrey ...11 L2
Small Heath Birm ...40 E9
Small Hythe Kent ...12 H4
Smallridge Devon ...7 J3
Smallthorne C Stke ...50 B10
Smallworth Norfk ...34 G1
Smannell Hants ...19 L10
Smarden Kent ...12 G2
Smarden Bell Kent ...12 G2
Smart's Hill Kent ...11 Q2
Smeatharpe Devon ...6 G1
Smeeth Kent ...13 K3
Smeeton Westerby Leics ...41 P8
Smerral Highld ...110 D8
Smestow Staffs ...39 Q4
Smethwick Sandw ...40 D9
Smirisary Highld ...89 N2
Smisby Derbys ...41 J4
Smithfield Cumb ...71 P3
Smith's Green Essex ...33 Q8
Smithstown Highld ...105 L6
Smithton Highld ...107 L12
Smoo Highld ...108 H3
Smythe's Green Essex ...34 F11
Snade D & G ...78 D10
Snailbeach Shrops ...38 G2
Snailwell Cambs ...33 Q4
Snainton N York ...67 K10
Snaith E R Yk ...59 N9
Snape N York ...65 M10
Snape Suffk ...35 N5
Snape Street Suffk ...35 N5
Snaresbrook Gt Lon ...21 N5
Snarestone Leics ...41 J5
Snarford Lincs ...52 F7
Snargate Kent ...13 J4
Snave Kent ...13 K4
Sneaton N York ...67 J6
Snelland Lincs ...52 F7
Snelston Derbys ...50 F11
Snetterton Norfk ...44 G11
Snettisham Norfk ...44 B4
Snitter Nthumb ...81 L12
Snitterby Lincs ...52 E5
Snitterfield Warwks ...30 G3
Snitton Shrops ...39 K7
Snodland Kent ...22 E10
Snowdon Gwynd ...54 H10
Snowdonia National Park ...47 N5
Snow End Herts ...33 L9
Snowshill Gloucs ...30 E7
Soake Hants ...9 Q5
Soay Highld ...96 E7
Soberton Hants ...9 Q4
Soberton Heath Hants ...9 P5
Sockburn Darltn ...65 N6
Soham Cambs ...33 P3
Solas W Isls ...111 b4
Soldridge Hants ...9 Q1
Sole Street Kent ...22 D9
Sole Street Kent ...23 L12
Solihull Solhll ...40 F10
Sollas W Isls ...111 b4
Sollers Dilwyn Herefs ...38 H10
Sollers Hope Herefs ...28 H3
Solva Pembks ...24 E4
Solwaybank D & G ...79 L12
Somerby Leics ...41 R5
Somerby Lincs ...52 F3
Somercotes Derbys ...51 K9
Somerford BCP ...8 H8
Somerford Keynes Gloucs ...18 E2
Somerley W Susx ...10 D9
Somerleyton Suffk ...45 P10
Somersal Herbert Derbys ...40 F1
Somersby Lincs ...53 K8
Somersham Cambs ...33 K2
Somersham Suffk ...34 H7
Somerton Oxon ...31 L8
Somerton Somset ...17 L9
Somerton Suffk ...34 D6
Sompting W Susx ...11 J8
Sonning Wokham ...20 C8
Sonning Common Oxon ...20 B7
Sopley Hants ...8 H7
Sopwell Herts ...21 J3
Sopworth Wilts ...18 C4
Sorbie D & G ...69 J8
Sordale Highld ...110 D4
Sorisdale Ag & B ...88 G4
Sorn E Ayrs ...77 J6
Sornhill E Ayrs ...77 J4
Sortat Highld ...110 F3
Sotby Lincs ...52 H7
Sotterley Suffk ...45 P12
Soughton Flints ...48 E3
Soulbury Bucks ...32 C10
Soulby Cumb ...64 D8
Souldern Oxon ...31 M7
Souldrop Bed ...32 E4
Sound Ches E ...49 L6
Sound Muir Moray ...101 M5
Soundwell S Glos ...17 P2
Sourton Devon ...5 L3
Soutergate Cumb ...62 E6
South Acre Norfk ...44 D7
South Alkham Kent ...13 N2
Southall Gt Lon ...20 H7
South Allington Devon ...5 Q11
South Alloa Falk ...85 P5
Southam Gloucs ...29 N4
Southam Warwks ...31 K2
Southampton C Sotn ...9 M5
Southampton Airport Hants ...9 M4
South Anston Rothm ...51 L4
South Ashford Kent ...13 J2
South Baddesley Hants ...9 L7
South Bank C York ...59 N4
South Barrow Somset ...17 N9
South Beddington Gt Lon ...21 L10
South Benfleet Essex ...22 F6
Southborough Gt Lon ...21 N9
Southborough Kent ...12 C2
Southbourne BCP ...8 H8
Southbourne W Susx ...10 C8
South Bramwith Donc ...59 N11

South Brent Devon ...5 N8
South Brewham Somset ...17 Q8
South Broomhill Nthumb ...73 M3
Southburgh Norfk ...44 G8
South Burlingham Norfk ...45 N8
Southburn E R Yk ...60 H4
South Cadbury Somset ...17 P10
South Carlton Lincs ...52 D8
South Carlton Notts ...51 N4
South Cave E R Yk ...60 F7
South Cerney Gloucs ...18 F2
South Chailey E Susx ...11 N6
South Charlton Nthumb ...81 N9
South Cheriton Somset ...17 Q10
South Church Dur ...65 L2
Southchurch Sthend ...22 H6
South Cliffe E R Yk ...60 F7
South Clifton Notts ...52 B9
South Cockerington Lincs ...53 L6
South Cornelly Brdgnd ...26 H11
Southcott Cnwll ...4 F2
Southcott Devon ...5 P4
Southcourt Bucks ...20 D2
South Cove Suffk ...35 P1
South Creake Norfk ...44 E3
South Croxton Leics ...41 P5
South Dalton E R Yk ...60 G5
South Darenth Kent ...22 C9
South Dell W Isls ...111 d1
South Downs National Park ...11 M8
South Duffield N York ...59 P7
South Earlswood Surrey ...11 L1
Southease E Susx ...11 N8
South Elkington Lincs ...53 J6
South Elmsall Wakefd ...59 L11
Southend Ag & B ...75 K10
Southend Airport Essex ...22 G5
Southend-on-Sea Sthend ...22 H6
Southernden Leics ...41 P7
Southerness D & G ...70 F5
South Erradale Highld ...105 L7
Southerton Devon ...6 E5
Southery Norfk ...43 P10
South Fambridge Essex ...22 G5
South Ferriby N Linc ...60 G9
South Field E R Yk ...60 H8
Southfield Falk ...85 P8
Southfleet Kent ...22 C8
Southgate Gt Lon ...21 L5
Southgate Swans ...26 D10
South Gorley Hants ...8 H5
South Gosforth N u Ty ...73 M7
South Green Essex ...22 D5
South Green Kent ...22 G10
South Green Norfk ...44 H7
South Gyle C Edin ...86 E7
South Hanningfield Essex ...22 E4
South Harting W Susx ...10 C6
South Hayling Hants ...10 B9
South Heath Bucks ...20 E3
South Heighton E Susx ...11 N9
South Hetton Dur ...73 P10
South Hiendley Wakefd ...59 K10
South Hill Cnwll ...4 H5
South Hinksey Oxon ...31 L12
South Holmwood Surrey ...11 J2
South Hornchurch Gt Lon ...21 P6
South Huish Devon ...5 N11
South Hykeham Lincs ...52 D9
South Hylton Sundld ...73 N9
Southill C Beds ...32 G8
Southington Hants ...19 N10
South Kelsey Lincs ...52 E4
South Kessock Highld ...107 L11
South Killingholme N Linc ...61 K10
South Kilvington N York ...65 Q10
South Kilworth Leics ...41 N10
Southkirkby Wakefd ...59 K11
South Kyme Lincs ...52 G12
Southleigh Devon ...6 G4
South Leigh Oxon ...31 K11
South Leverton Notts ...52 A7
South Littleton Worcs ...30 E5
South Lopham Norfk ...34 G1
South Luffenham Rutlnd ...42 D9
South Lynn Norfk ...43 P6
South Malling E Susx ...11 N7
South Marston Swindn ...18 H3
South Merstham Surrey ...21 L11
South Milford N York ...59 L7
South Milton Devon ...5 N10
South Mimms Herts ...21 K3
South Mimms Services Herts ...21 K4
Southminster Essex ...23 J4
South Molton Devon ...15 M7
South Moor Dur ...73 L9
Southmoor Oxon ...19 L2
South Moreton Oxon ...19 P3
Southmuir Angus ...93 L5
South Mundham W Susx ...10 E9
South Newbald E R Yk ...60 F7
South Newington Oxon ...31 K7
South Newton Wilts ...8 G1
South Nitshill C Glas ...85 J10
South Normanton Derbys ...51 K9
South Norwood Gt Lon ...21 M9
South Ockendon Thurr ...22 C6
Southoe Cambs ...32 H4
Southolt Suffk ...35 K3
South Ormsby Lincs ...53 L8
Southorpe C Pete ...42 F9
South Otterington N York ...65 P9
Southover Dorset ...7 N4
South Owersby Lincs ...52 F5
Southowram Calder ...58 G9
South Park Surrey ...11 K1
South Perrott Dorset ...7 L2
South Petherton Somset ...17 L11
South Petherwin Cnwll ...4 G4
South Pickenham Norfk ...44 E8
South Pill Cnwll ...5 J8
South Pool Devon ...5 N10
South Poorton Dorset ...7 M4
Southport Sefton ...56 G5
South Queensferry C Edin ...86 D6
South Rauceby Lincs ...42 E2
South Raynham Norfk ...44 E5
South Reddish Stockp ...50 B3
Southrepps Norfk ...45 L3
South Reston Lincs ...53 L6
Southrey Lincs ...52 G9
South Ronaldsay Ork ...111 h3
Southrop Gloucs ...30 G12

Southrope Hants ...19 Q10
South Runcton Norfk ...43 Q8
South Scarle Notts ...52 B10
Southsea C Port ...10 Q7
South Shian Ag & B ...90 C7
South Shields S Tyne ...73 P7
South Shore Bpool ...56 F3
Southside Dur ...65 K3
South Stainley N York ...58 H2
South Stifford Thurr ...22 C7
South Stoke BaNES ...17 Q4
South Stoke Oxon ...19 P4
South Stoke W Susx ...10 G7
South Street Kent ...23 K10
South Street Kent ...23 L9
South Tarbrax S Lans ...86 B10
South Tawton Devon ...5 N2
South Tehidy Cnwll ...2 F7
South Thoresby Lincs ...53 L7
Southtown Norfk ...45 Q8
South Uist W Isls ...111 b6
Southwaite Cumb ...71 P6
Southwaite Services Cumb ...71 P6
South Walsham Norfk ...45 N7
Southwark Gt Lon ...21 L7
South Warnborough Hants ...10 B1
Southwater W Susx ...11 J5
Southway C Plym ...5 K7
South Weald Essex ...22 C5
Southwell Notts ...51 P9
South Weston Oxon ...20 B4
South Wheatley Notts ...51 Q4
Southwick Hants ...9 Q6
Southwick Nhants ...42 E10
Southwick Sundld ...73 P8
Southwick W Susx ...11 K8
Southwick Wilts ...18 C9
South Widcombe BaNES ...17 N5
South Wigston Leics ...41 N7
South Willingham Lincs ...52 H6
South Wingfield Derbys ...51 J9
South Witham Lincs ...42 D6
Southwold Suffk ...35 Q2
South Woodham Ferrers Essex ...22 F4
South Wootton Norfk ...43 Q5
South Wraxall Wilts ...18 C7
South Zeal Devon ...5 N2
Sovereign Harbour E Susx ...12 D9
Sowerby Calder ...58 D9
Sowerby N York ...66 B10
Sowerby Bridge Calder ...58 D9
Sowood Calder ...58 E9
Sowton Devon ...5 K7
Sowton Devon ...6 D4
Soyland Town Calder ...58 D9
Spain's End Essex ...33 Q8
Spalding Lincs ...43 J5
Spaldington E R Yk ...60 D7
Spaldwick Cambs ...32 G3
Spalford Notts ...52 B9
Spanby Lincs ...42 F3
Sparham Norfk ...44 H6
Spark Bridge Cumb ...62 F5
Sparkford Somset ...17 N10
Sparkhill Birm ...40 E10
Sparkwell Devon ...5 M8
Sparrowpit Derbys ...50 E5
Sparrows Green E Susx ...12 D4
Sparsholt Hants ...9 M2
Sparsholt Oxon ...19 L4
Spaunton N York ...66 G9
Spaxton Somset ...16 G8
Spean Bridge Highld ...98 C11
Spearywell Hants ...9 K2
Speen Bucks ...20 D4
Speen W Berk ...19 M7
Speeton N York ...67 N11
Speke Lpool ...56 H11
Speldhurst Kent ...12 B2
Spellbrook Herts ...33 M12
Spencers Wood Wokham ...20 B9
Spen Green Ches E ...49 P4
Spennithorne N York ...65 K9
Spennymoor Dur ...65 M2
Spetchley Worcs ...30 B4
Spetisbury Dorset ...8 D7
Spexhall Suffk ...35 N2
Spey Bay Moray ...101 L3
Speybridge Highld ...100 G9
Speyview Moray ...101 K6
Spilsby Lincs ...53 L9
Spinkhill Derbys ...51 L5
Spinningdale Highld ...107 L4
Spital Wirral ...56 G11
Spital Hill Donc ...51 N3
Spittal E Loth ...87 J6
Spittal Highld ...110 D5
Spittal Nthumb ...81 N4
Spittal Pembks ...24 H4
Spittalfield P & K ...92 G7
Spittal of Glenmuick Abers ...94 E5
Spittal of Glenshee P & K ...92 B7
Spittal-on-Rule Border ...80 D7
Spixworth Norfk ...45 L7
Splatt Devon ...15 K10
Splayne's Green E Susx ...11 N5
Splott Cardif ...16 G2
Spofforth N York ...59 J4
Spondon C Derb ...41 K1
Spooner Row Norfk ...44 H10
Sporle Norfk ...44 E7
Spott E Loth ...87 M7
Spottiswoode Border ...87 E4
Spratton Nhants ...41 Q12
Spreakley Surrey ...10 D2
Spreyton Devon ...15 M11
Spriddlestone Devon ...5 L9
Spridlington Lincs ...52 E6
Springburn C Glas ...85 K8
Springfield D & G ...71 M2
Springfield Essex ...22 F2
Springfield Fife ...93 L12
Springholm D & G ...70 D2
Springside N Ayrs ...76 F4
Springthorpe Lincs ...52 C5
Springwell Sundld ...73 M8

Sproxton Leics ...42 C5
Sproxton N York ...66 E10
Spurstow Ches E ...49 K4
Spyway Dorset ...7 M4
Stableford Shrops ...39 N3
Stacey Bank Sheff ...50 H3
Stackhouse N York ...63 P8
Stackpole Pembks ...24 H9
Stackpole Elidor Pembks ...24 H8
Staddiscombe C Plym ...5 L9
Stadhampton Oxon ...19 Q2
Stadhlaigearraidh W Isls ...111 a5
Staffield Cumb ...71 Q7
Staffin Highld ...104 G8
Stafford Staffs ...40 B3
Stafford Services (northbound) Staffs ...40 B2
Stafford Services (southbound) Staffs ...40 B2
Stagsden Bed ...32 E7
Stainburn Cumb ...70 G9
Stainby Lincs ...42 C5
Staincross Barns ...59 J11
Staindrop Dur ...65 K4
Staines-upon-Thames Surrey ...20 G8
Stainforth Donc ...59 N10
Stainforth N York ...63 P8
Staining Lancs ...56 G2
Stainland Calder ...58 E9
Stainsacre N York ...67 K6
Stainton Cumb ...63 K5
Stainton Cumb ...71 P9
Stainton Donc ...51 M3
Stainton Dur ...65 J4
Stainton Middsb ...66 C5
Stainton by Langworth Lincs ...52 F7
Staintondale N York ...67 L7
Stainton le Vale Lincs ...52 H5
Stainton with Adgarley Cumb ...62 F7
Stair E Ayrs ...76 G6
Stairhaven D & G ...68 G8
Staithes N York ...66 H4
Stakes Hants ...10 B8
Stalbridge Dorset ...17 Q11
Stalbridge Weston Dorset ...17 Q11
Stalham Norfk ...45 N5
Stalisfield Green Kent ...23 J11
Stallen Dorset ...17 N11
Stallingborough NE Lin ...61 K11
Stalmine Lancs ...62 G12
Stalybridge Tamesd ...50 C2
Stambourne Essex ...34 C8
Stambourne Green Essex ...34 B8
Stamford Lincs ...42 E8
Stamford Nthumb ...81 P9
Stamford Bridge Ches W ...49 J3
Stamford Bridge E R Yk ...60 C3
Stamfordham Nthumb ...73 J6
Stamford Hill Gt Lon ...21 M6
Stanbridge C Beds ...32 D11
Stanbury C Brad ...58 D6
Stand N Lans ...85 M8
Standburn Falk ...85 Q7
Standeford Staffs ...40 B6
Standen Kent ...12 G3
Standerwick Somset ...18 B10
Standford Hants ...10 D3
Standingstone Cumb ...70 H8
Standish Wigan ...57 K6
Standlake Oxon ...31 K12
Standon Hants ...9 M3
Standon Herts ...33 L11
Standon Staffs ...49 P8
Stane N Lans ...85 P10
Stanfield Norfk ...44 F6
Stanford C Beds ...32 G8
Stanford Kent ...13 L3
Stanford Bishop Herefs ...39 M10
Stanford Bridge Worcs ...39 N8
Stanford Dingley W Berk ...19 P6
Stanford in the Vale Oxon ...19 K3
Stanford le Hope Thurr ...22 D7
Stanford on Avon Nhants ...41 N10
Stanford on Soar Notts ...41 M3
Stanford on Teme Worcs ...39 N8
Stanfree Derbys ...51 L6
Stanghow R & Cl ...66 F4
Stanground C Pete ...42 H10
Stanhoe Norfk ...44 D3
Stanhope Border ...79 J3
Stanhope Dur ...72 H11
Stanhope Kent ...13 J2
Stanion Nhants ...42 D11
Stanley Derbys ...51 K11
Stanley Dur ...73 L9
Stanley P & K ...92 G8
Stanley Staffs ...50 B9
Stanley Crook Dur ...73 L12
Stanley Pontlarge Gloucs ...30 D7
Stanmer Br & H ...11 M7
Stanmore Gt Lon ...21 J5
Stanmore Hants ...9 M3
Stannersburn Nthumb ...72 D4
Stanningfield Suffk ...34 E5
Stannington Nthumb ...73 L5
Stannington Sheff ...50 H4
Stannington Station Nthumb ...73 L5
Stansbatch Herefs ...38 G9
Stansfield Suffk ...34 C6
Stanstead Suffk ...34 D7
Stanstead Abbotts Herts ...21 M2
Stansted Kent ...22 C10
Stansted Airport Essex ...33 N11
Stansted Mountfitchet Essex ...33 N10
Stanton Gloucs ...30 D7
Stanton Nthumb ...73 K3
Stanton Staffs ...50 F10
Stanton Suffk ...34 F3
Stanton by Bridge Derbys ...41 J3
Stanton by Dale Derbys ...51 L12
Stanton Drew BaNES ...17 N4
Stanton Fitzwarren Swindn ...18 H3
Stanton Harcourt Oxon ...31 K11
Stanton in Peak Derbys ...50 G7
Stanton Lacy Shrops ...39 J6
Stanton Lees Derbys ...50 G8
Stanton Long Shrops ...39 L4
Stanton-on-the-Wolds Notts ...41 N2
Stanton Prior BaNES ...17 P4
Stanton St Bernard Wilts ...18 G8
Stanton St John Oxon ...31 M11
Stanton St Quintin Wilts ...18 D5
Stanton Street Suffk ...34 F4

Stanton under Bardon Leics ...41 L5
Stanton upon Hine Heath Shrops ...49 K10
Stanton Wick BaNES ...17 N4
Stanway Essex ...34 F11
Stanway Gloucs ...30 D7
Stanwell Surrey ...20 G8
Stanwick Nhants ...32 E3
Stanwix Cumb ...71 N4
Staoinebrig W Isls ...111 a5
Stape N York ...66 H8
Stapeley Ches E ...49 M5
Stapenhill Staffs ...40 G3
Staple Kent ...23 P11
Staple Cross Devon ...16 D11
Staplecross E Susx ...12 F5
Staplefield W Susx ...11 L5
Staple Fitzpaine Somset ...16 H11
Stapleford Cambs ...33 M6
Stapleford Herts ...33 K12
Stapleford Leics ...42 B6
Stapleford Lincs ...52 C11
Stapleford Notts ...51 L12
Stapleford Wilts ...18 F12
Stapleford Abbotts Essex ...21 P5
Staplegrove Somset ...16 G10
Staplehay Somset ...16 G10
Staplehurst Kent ...12 F2
Staplers IoW ...9 N9
Staplestreet Kent ...23 K10
Stapleton Herefs ...38 G8
Stapleton Leics ...41 K7
Stapleton N York ...65 M5
Stapleton Shrops ...39 J2
Stapleton Somset ...17 L11
Stapley Somset ...16 G12
Staploe Bed ...32 G5
Staplow Herefs ...29 J1
Star Fife ...86 G2
Star Pembks ...25 M2
Star Somset ...17 L5
Starbeck N York ...59 J3
Starbotton N York ...64 G11
Starcross Devon ...6 C6
Stareton Warwks ...41 J12
Starlings Green Essex ...33 M9
Starston Norfk ...45 K12
Startforth Dur ...65 J4
Startley Wilts ...18 D4
Statenborough Kent ...23 P11
Statham Warrtn ...57 M10
Stathe Somset ...17 K9
Stathern Leics ...41 Q2
Staunton Gloucs ...28 G6
Staunton Gloucs ...29 K3
Staunton on Arrow Herefs ...38 G9
Staunton on Wye Herefs ...38 G12
Staveley Cumb ...63 J3
Staveley Derbys ...51 K6
Staveley N York ...59 J2
Staveley-in-Cartmel Cumb ...62 H5
Staverton Devon ...5 Q7
Staverton Gloucs ...29 M4
Staverton Nhants ...31 M2
Staverton Wilts ...18 C8
Stawell Somset ...17 K8
Stawley Somset ...16 E10
Staxigoe Highld ...110 H5
Staxton N York ...67 L10
Staynall Lancs ...62 G12
Stean N York ...65 J11
Stearsby N York ...66 E12
Steart Somset ...16 H7
Stebbing Essex ...33 Q11
Stechford Birm ...40 F9
Stedham W Susx ...10 D5
Steelend Fife ...86 B4
Steele Road Border ...79 Q9
Steen's Bridge Herefs ...39 K10
Steep Hants ...10 C5
Steep Lane Calder ...58 D9
Steeple Dorset ...8 E9
Steeple Essex ...23 J3
Steeple Ashton Wilts ...18 D9
Steeple Aston Oxon ...31 L8
Steeple Bumpstead Essex ...34 B8
Steeple Claydon Bucks ...31 P8
Steeple Gidding Cambs ...42 G1
Steeple Langford Wilts ...18 F12
Steeple Morden Cambs ...33 J8
Steeton C Brad ...58 D5
Stein Highld ...104 C10
Stelling Minnis Kent ...13 M1
Stembridge Somset ...17 L11
Stenalees Cnwll ...3 M4
Stenhouse D & G ...77 N11
Stenhousemuir Falk ...85 P6
Stenscholt Highld ...104 F8
Stenson Fields Derbys ...41 J2
Stenton E Loth ...87 M7
Steornabhagh W Isls ...111 d2
Stepaside Pembks ...25 K7
Stepford D & G ...78 E11
Stepney Gt Lon ...21 M7
Steppingley C Beds ...32 E9
Stepps N Lans ...85 L8
Sternfield Suffk ...35 N5
Stert Wilts ...18 F8
Stetchworth Cambs ...33 Q5
Stevenage Herts ...32 H10
Stevenston N Ayrs ...76 E3
Steventon Hants ...19 P10
Steventon Oxon ...19 M3
Steventon End Essex ...33 Q7
Stevington Bed ...32 E6
Stewartby Bed ...32 F7
Stewartfield S Lans ...85 K11
Stewarton Ag & B ...75 K8
Stewarton E Ayrs ...76 G3
Stewkley Bucks ...32 C10
Stewley Somset ...17 J11
Steyning W Susx ...11 J7
Steynton Pembks ...24 G7
Stibb Cnwll ...14 D9
Stibbard Norfk ...44 G5
Stibb Cross Devon ...14 H8
Stibb Green Wilts ...19 J8
Stibbington Cambs ...42 F9
Stichill Border ...80 F6
Sticker Cnwll ...3 L5
Stickford Lincs ...53 K10
Sticklepath Devon ...5 M2
Stickney Lincs ...53 K11
Stiffkey Norfk ...44 F2

Place	County	Page	Grid
Stifford Clays	Thurr	22	C7
Stilligarry	W Isls	111	a5
Stillingfleet	N York	59	N6
Stillington	N York	59	N1
Stillington	S on T	65	P3
Stilton	Cambs	42	G11
Stinchcombe	Gloucs	29	K8
Stinsford	Dorset	7	Q5
Stiperstones	Shrops	38	G3
Stirchley	Wrekin	39	M1
Stirling	Abers	103	M6
Stirling	Stirlg	85	N4
Stirling Castle	Stirlg	85	N4
Stirling Services	Stirlg	85	N5
Stirtloe	Cambs	32	H4
Stirton	N York	58	C4
Stisted	Essex	34	D10
Stithians	Cnwll	2	G8
Stivichall	Covtry	41	J11
Stixwould	Lincs	52	H9
St Michaels	Fife	93	M10
Stoak	Ches W	48	H2
Stobo	Border	79	K2
Stoborough	Dorset	8	D9
Stobs Castle	Border	80	C11
Stobswood	Nthumb	73	L2
Stock	Essex	22	E4
Stock	N Som	17	L4
Stockbridge	Hants	9	L1
Stockbridge	W Susx	10	D8
Stockbriggs	S Lans	77	N4
Stockbury	Kent	22	G10
Stockcross	W Berk	19	M7
Stockerston	Leics	42	B9
Stock Green	Worcs	30	C3
Stocking	Herefs	28	H3
Stockingford	Warwks	41	J8
Stocking Pelham	Herts	33	M10
Stockland	Devon	6	H2
Stockland Bristol	Somset	16	H7
Stockleigh English	Devon	15	P10
Stockleigh Pomeroy	Devon	15	P10
Stockley	Wilts	18	E7
Stocklinch	Somset	17	K11
Stockport	Stockp	50	B3
Stocksbridge	Sheff	50	H2
Stocksfield	Nthumb	73	J8
Stockton	Herefs	39	K9
Stockton	Norfk	45	N10
Stockton	Shrops	39	N3
Stockton	Warwks	31	K2
Stockton	Wilts	18	E12
Stockton	Wrekin	49	P11
Stockton Brook	Staffs	50	B9
Stockton Heath	Warrtn	57	L10
Stockton-on-Tees	S on T	66	C4
Stockton on Teme	Worcs	39	N8
Stockton on the Forest	C York	59	P3
Stockwell End	Wolves	40	B7
Stockwood	Bristl	17	P3
Stockwood	Dorset	7	N2
Stock Wood	Worcs	30	D3
Stodmarsh	Kent	23	N10
Stody	Norfk	44	H3
Stoer	Highld	108	B9
Stoford	Somset	17	N12
Stoford	Wilts	8	F1
Stogumber	Somset	16	E8
Stogursey	Somset	16	G7
Stoke	Covtry	41	J10
Stoke	Devon	14	C7
Stoke	Hants	19	B9
Stoke	Hants	9	L9
Stoke	Medway	22	G8
Stoke Abbott	Dorset	7	L3
Stoke Albany	Nhants	42	B11
Stoke Ash	Suffk	35	J3
Stoke Bardolph	Notts	51	N11
Stoke Bliss	Worcs	39	M9
Stoke Bruerne	Nhants	31	Q4
Stoke-by-Clare	Suffk	34	C7
Stoke-by-Nayland	Suffk	34	G9
Stoke Canon	Devon	6	C3
Stoke Charity	Hants	19	N11
Stoke Climsland	Cnwll	4	H5
Stoke Cross	Herefs	39	L11
Stoke D'Abernon	Surrey	20	H10
Stoke Doyle	Nhants	42	E11
Stoke Dry	Rutlnd	42	C10
Stoke Edith	Herefs	28	H1
Stoke Farthing	Wilts	8	F2
Stoke Ferry	Norfk	44	B9
Stoke Fleming	Devon	6	B11
Stokeford	Dorset	8	C9
Stoke Gabriel	Devon	6	B10
Stoke Gifford	S Glos	28	H11
Stoke Golding	Leics	41	K7
Stoke Goldington	M Keyn	32	B7
Stokeham	Notts	52	A7
Stoke Hammond	Bucks	32	C10
Stoke Holy Cross	Norfk	45	K9
Stokeinteignhead	Devon	6	C8
Stoke Lacy	Herefs	39	L11
Stoke Lyne	Oxon	31	M8
Stoke Mandeville	Bucks	20	D2
Stokenchurch	Bucks	20	C4
Stoke Newington	Gt Lon	21	M6
Stokenham	Devon	5	Q10
Stoke-on-Trent	C Stke	50	B10
Stoke Orchard	Gloucs	29	M3
Stoke Poges	Bucks	20	F6
Stoke Prior	Herefs	39	K10
Stoke Prior	Worcs	30	C11
Stoke Rivers	Devon	15	L5
Stoke Rochford	Lincs	42	D5
Stoke Row	Oxon	20	B6
Stoke St Gregory	Somset	17	J10
Stoke St Mary	Somset	16	H10
Stoke St Michael	Somset	17	P6
Stoke St Milborough	Shrops	39	K5
Stokesby	Norfk	45	N7
Stokesley	N York	66	C6
Stoke sub Hamdon	Somset	17	L11
Stoke Talmage	Oxon	20	B4
Stoke Trister	Somset	17	Q9
Stoke upon Tern	Shrops	49	M9
Stolford	Somset	16	G7
Stondon Massey	Essex	22	C4
Stone	Bucks	20	C2
Stone	Gloucs	29	J9
Stone	Rothm	51	M3
Stone	Staffs	40	B1
Stone	Worcs	39	Q7
Stone Allerton	Somset	17	K6
Ston Easton	Somset	17	N5
Stonebridge	N Som	17	K4
Stonebridge	Warwks	40	G10
Stonebroom	Derbys	51	K8
Stone Cross	Kent	23	P11
Stoneferry	C KuH	61	J7
Stonefield Castle Hotel	Ag & B	83	N8
Stonegate	E Susx	12	D4
Stonegrave	N York	66	F11
Stonehaven	Abers	95	P5
Stonehenge	Wilts	18	G11
Stonehouse	C Plym	5	K9
Stonehouse	Gloucs	29	L7
Stonehouse	S Lans	77	M3
Stone in Oxney	Kent	12	H5
Stoneleigh	Warwks	41	J11
Stonesby	Leics	42	B5
Stonesfield	Oxon	31	K10
Stones Green	Essex	35	J10
Stone Street	Kent	22	C11
Stone Street	Suffk	35	N1
Stonewells	Moray	101	K3
Stoneybridge	W Isls	111	a5
Stoneyburn	W Loth	86	B9
Stoneygate	Leics	41	N7
Stoneykirk	D & G	68	E8
Stoney Middleton	Derbys	50	G6
Stoney Stanton	Leics	41	L8
Stoney Stoke	Somset	17	Q9
Stoney Stratton	Somset	17	P8
Stoneywood	C Aber	103	J11
Stoneywood	Falk	85	N6
Stonham Aspal	Suffk	35	J5
Stonnall	Staffs	40	E6
Stonor	Oxon	20	B6
Stonton Wyville	Leics	41	Q8
Stonybreck	Shet	111	m5
Stony Houghton	Derbys	51	L7
Stony Stratford	M Keyn	32	B8
Stoodleigh	Devon	15	L6
Stoodleigh	Devon	16	C11
Stop 24 Services	Kent	13	L3
Stopham	W Susx	10	G6
Stopsley	Luton	32	F11
Stornoway	W Isls	111	d2
Stornoway Airport	W Isls	111	d2
Storridge	Herefs	39	N11
Storrington	W Susx	10	H7
Storth	Cumb	63	J6
Storwood	E R Yk	60	C5
Stotfield	Moray	101	J2
Stotfold	C Beds	32	H9
Stottesdon	Shrops	39	M5
Stoughton	Leics	41	N7
Stoughton	Surrey	20	F12
Stoughton	W Susx	10	C7
Stoulton	Worcs	30	B4
Stourbridge	Dudley	40	B10
Stourhead	Wilts	8	B1
Stourpaine	Dorset	8	C5
Stourport-on-Severn	Worcs	39	P7
Stour Provost	Dorset	8	B3
Stour Row	Dorset	8	B3
Stourton	Staffs	39	Q5
Stourton	Warwks	30	H6
Stourton	Wilts	8	B1
Stourton Caundle	Dorset	17	Q12
Stove	Shet	111	k5
Stoven	Suffk	35	P1
Stow	Border	87	J12
Stow	Lincs	52	C7
Stow Bardolph	Norfk	43	P8
Stow Bedon	Norfk	44	F10
Stowbridge	Norfk	43	P8
Stow-cum-Quy	Cambs	33	N5
Stowe	Shrops	38	F7
Stowe-by-Chartley	Staffs	40	D3
Stowell	Somset	17	P10
Stowey	BaNES	17	N4
Stowford	Devon	5	J3
Stowford	Devon	5	F5
Stowlangtoft	Suffk	34	F3
Stow Longa	Cambs	32	G3
Stow Maries	Essex	22	H4
Stowmarket	Suffk	34	H5
Stow-on-the-Wold	Gloucs	30	F8
Stowting	Kent	13	L2
Stowupland	Suffk	34	H5
Straad	Ag & B	83	Q9
Straanruie	Highld	99	P6
Strachan	Abers	95	L4
Strachur	Ag & B	84	B3
Stradbroke	Suffk	35	K3
Stradishall	Suffk	34	C6
Stradsett	Norfk	43	Q8
Stragglethorpe	Lincs	52	C11
Straiton	Mdloth	86	F8
Straiton	S Ayrs	76	G9
Straloch	Abers	102	H10
Straloch	P & K	92	F3
Stramshall	Staffs	40	E1
Strang	IoM	56	c5
Strangeways	Salfd	57	P8
Strangford	Herefs	28	G4
Stranraer	D & G	68	E7
Stratfield Mortimer	W Berk	19	Q7
Stratfield Saye	Hants	20	B10
Stratfield Turgis	Hants	20	B10
Stratford	Gt Lon	21	M6
Stratford St Andrew	Suffk	35	M5
Stratford St Mary	Suffk	34	H9
Stratford sub Castle	Wilts	8	G2
Stratford Tony	Wilts	8	F3
Stratford-upon-Avon	Warwks	30	G3
Strath	Highld	105	L6
Strathan	Highld	108	C10
Strathan	Highld	109	K3
Strathaven	S Lans	77	L3
Strathblane	Stirlg	85	J7
Strathcanaird	Highld	106	C3
Strathcarron	Highld	97	N2
Strathcoil	Ag & B	89	N9
Strathdon	Abers	101	L11
Strathkinness	Fife	93	M11
Strathloanhead	W Loth	85	Q8
Strathmashie House	Highld	98	H10
Strathmiglo	Fife	86	E1
Strathpeffer	Highld	106	H10
Strathtay	P & K	92	D5
Strathwhillan	N Ayrs	75	Q5
Strathy	Highld	109	P3
Strathy Inn	Highld	109	P3
Strathyre	Stirlg	91	N11
Stratton	Cnwll	14	E10
Stratton	Dorset	7	P4
Stratton	Gloucs	30	D12
Stratton Audley	Oxon	31	N8
Stratton-on-the-Fosse	Somset	17	P6
Stratton St Margaret	Swindn	18	H4
Stratton St Michael	Norfk	45	K10
Stratton Strawless	Norfk	45	K6
Streat	E Susx	11	M7
Streatham	Gt Lon	21	L8
Streatley	C Beds	32	F10
Streatley	W Berk	19	P5
Street	Devon	6	G5
Street	Somset	17	L8
Street Ashton	Warwks	41	L10
Street Dinas	Shrops	48	G7
Street End	Kent	23	M11
Street End	W Susx	10	D9
Streethay	Staffs	40	F5
Streetlam	N York	65	N7
Streetly End	Cambs	33	P7
Street on the Fosse	Somset	17	N8
Strelitz	P & K	92	H8
Strelley	Notts	51	L11
Strensall	C York	59	N3
Strensham Services (northbound)	Worcs	29	M1
Strensham Services (southbound)	Worcs	29	M2
Stretcholt	Somset	16	H7
Strete	Devon	5	R10
Stretford	Traffd	57	P9
Strethall	Essex	33	M8
Stretham	Cambs	33	N2
Strettington	W Susx	10	E8
Stretton	Derbys	51	K8
Stretton	Rutlnd	42	D7
Stretton	Staffs	40	B5
Stretton	Staffs	40	G3
Stretton	Warrtn	57	L11
Stretton Grandison	Herefs	39	L12
Stretton-on-Dunsmore	Warwks	41	K11
Stretton on Fosse	Warwks	30	G6
Stretton Sugwas	Herefs	28	E1
Stretton under Fosse	Warwks	41	L10
Stretton Westwood	Shrops	39	L3
Strichen	Abers	103	K4
Stringston	Somset	16	G7
Strixton	Nhants	32	C4
Stroat	Gloucs	28	G8
Strollamus	Highld	96	H4
Stroma	Highld	110	G1
Stromeferry	Highld	97	M3
Stromness	Ork	111	g2
Stronaba	Highld	98	B11
Stronachlachar	Stirlg	84	G2
Stronafian	Ag & B	83	Q6
Stronchrubie	Highld	108	E11
Strone	Ag & B	84	D6
Strone	Highld	98	A11
Strone	Highld	98	G4
Stronmilchan	Ag & B	90	F10
Stronsay	Ork	111	i2
Stronsay Airport	Ork	111	i2
Strontian	Highld	89	Q4
Strood	Medway	22	E9
Stroud	Gloucs	29	L7
Stroud	Hants	10	B5
Stroud Green	Gloucs	29	L7
Stroxton	Lincs	42	C4
Struan	Highld	96	D3
Struan	P & K	92	B3
Strumpshaw	Norfk	45	M8
Strutherhill	S Lans	77	M2
Struthers	Fife	86	H1
Struy	Highld	98	E2
Stuartfield	Abers	103	K6
Stubbington	Hants	9	P6
Stubbins	Lancs	57	P5
Stubton	Lincs	42	C1
Stuckton	Hants	8	H5
Studham	C Beds	32	E12
Studland	Dorset	8	F10
Studley	Warwks	30	E2
Studley	Wilts	18	E6
Studley Common	Warwks	30	E2
Studley Roger	N York	65	N12
Studley Royal	N York	65	M12
Studley Royal Park & Fountains Abbey	N York	58	H1
Stuntney	Cambs	33	N2
Sturmer	Essex	34	B7
Sturminster Common	Dorset	8	B5
Sturminster Marshall	Dorset	8	D7
Sturminster Newton	Dorset	8	B5
Sturry	Kent	23	M10
Sturton	N Linc	52	D3
Sturton by Stow	Lincs	52	C7
Sturton le Steeple	Notts	52	B6
Stuston	Suffk	35	J2
Stutton	N York	59	L6
Stutton	Suffk	35	J9
Styal	Ches E	57	Q11
Stynie	Moray	101	L3
Styrrup	Notts	51	N3
Succoth	Ag & B	84	E2
Suckley	Worcs	39	N10
Sudborough	Nhants	32	D1
Sudbourne	Suffk	35	N6
Sudbrook	Lincs	42	D2
Sudbrook	Mons	28	F10
Sudbrooke	Lincs	52	E8
Sudbury	Derbys	40	F2
Sudbury	Gt Lon	21	J6
Sudbury	Suffk	34	E8
Suffield	N York	67	L8
Suffield	Norfk	45	K4
Sugnall	Staffs	49	P8
Sugwas Pool	Herefs	28	E1
Suisnish	Highld	96	H6
Sulby	IoM	56	d3
Sulgrave	Nhants	31	M5
Sulham	W Berk	19	Q6
Sulhamstead	W Berk	19	Q7
Sullom	Shet	111	k3
Sullom Voe	Shet	111	k3
Sully	V Glam	16	F3
Sumburgh Airport	Shet	111	k5
Summerbridge	N York	58	G3
Summercourt	Cnwll	3	K5
Summerfield	Norfk	44	C3
Summerhill	Pembks	25	K7
Summerhouse	Darltn	65	L4
Summersdale	W Susx	10	D8
Summerseat	Bury	57	P6
Summertown	Oxon	31	L11
Sunbury-on-Thames	Surrey	20	H9
Sundaywell	D & G	78	D11
Sunderland	Ag & B	82	C9
Sunderland	Cumb	71	J8
Sunderland	Lancs	62	H10
Sunderland	Sundld	73	P9
Sunderland Bridge	Dur	73	M12
Sundhope	Border	79	M4
Sundon Park	Luton	32	F10
Sundridge	Kent	21	P11
Sunningdale	W & M	20	F9
Sunninghill	W & M	20	F9
Sunningwell	Oxon	19	N1
Sunniside	Dur	73	K12
Sunniside	Gatesd	73	L8
Sunnyhill	C Derb	41	J2
Sunnyhurst	Bl w D	57	M4
Sunnylaw	Stirlg	85	N4
Sunnymead	Oxon	31	L11
Surbiton	Gt Lon	21	J9
Surfleet	Lincs	43	J5
Surlingham	Norfk	45	M8
Surrex	Essex	34	E11
Sustead	Norfk	45	K3
Susworth	Lincs	52	B3
Sutcombe	Devon	14	F9
Sutcombemill	Devon	14	F9
Sutterby	Lincs	53	L8
Sutterton	Lincs	43	J3
Sutton	C Beds	32	H7
Sutton	C Pete	42	F9
Sutton	Cambs	33	M2
Sutton	Devon	5	N10
Sutton	E Susx	11	P9
Sutton	Gt Lon	21	K9
Sutton	Kent	23	P12
Sutton	N York	59	L8
Sutton	Norfk	45	N5
Sutton	Notts	51	Q12
Sutton	Oxon	31	K11
Sutton	Shrops	39	N5
Sutton	Shrops	49	J12
Sutton	Staffs	49	N10
Sutton	Suffk	35	M7
Sutton	W Susx	10	F7
Sutton-at-Hone	Kent	22	B9
Sutton Bassett	Nhants	41	Q9
Sutton Benger	Wilts	18	D5
Sutton Bonington	Notts	41	L3
Sutton Bridge	Lincs	43	M6
Sutton Cheney	Leics	41	K7
Sutton Coldfield	Birm	40	E8
Sutton Courtenay	Oxon	19	N2
Sutton cum Lound	Notts	51	P4
Sutton Green	Surrey	20	G11
Sutton Heath	Suffk	35	M7
Sutton Howgrave	N York	65	N10
Sutton-in-Ashfield	Notts	51	L8
Sutton-in-Craven	N York	58	D5
Sutton Maddock	Shrops	39	N2
Sutton Mallet	Somset	17	K8
Sutton Mandeville	Wilts	8	E2
Sutton Montis	Somset	17	P10
Sutton-on-Hull	C KuH	61	J7
Sutton on Sea	Lincs	53	N7
Sutton-on-the-Forest	N York	59	M2
Sutton on the Hill	Derbys	40	G2
Sutton on Trent	Notts	52	B9
Sutton St Edmund	Lincs	43	L7
Sutton St James	Lincs	43	L6
Sutton St Nicholas	Herefs	39	K11
Sutton Scotney	Hants	19	M11
Sutton-under-Brailes	Warwks	30	H6
Sutton-under-Whitestonecliffe	N York	66	C10
Sutton upon Derwent	E R Yk	60	C5
Sutton Valence	Kent	12	F2
Sutton Veny	Wilts	18	D11
Sutton Waldron	Dorset	8	C4
Sutton Weaver	Ches W	57	K11
Sutton Wick	BaNES	17	N4
Sutton Wick	Oxon	19	N2
Swaby	Lincs	53	L7
Swadlincote	Derbys	40	H4
Swaffham	Norfk	44	D8
Swaffham Bulbeck	Cambs	33	N4
Swaffham Prior	Cambs	33	P4
Swafield	Norfk	45	L4
Swainby	N York	66	C7
Swainshill	Herefs	28	E1
Swainsthorpe	Norfk	45	K9
Swainswick	BaNES	18	B7
Swalcliffe	Oxon	31	J6
Swalecliffe	Kent	23	L9
Swallow	Lincs	52	H3
Swallow Beck	Lincs	52	D9
Swallowcliffe	Wilts	8	E3
Swallowfield	Wokham	20	B9
Swallownest	Rothm	51	K4
Swampton	Hants	19	M9
Swanage	Dorset	8	F10
Swanbourne	Bucks	32	B10
Swan Green	Ches W	49	N12
Swanland	E R Yk	60	G8
Swanley	Kent	21	P9
Swanley Village	Kent	21	Q9
Swanmore	Hants	9	P4
Swannington	Leics	41	K4
Swannington	Norfk	45	J6
Swanpool	Lincs	52	D9
Swanscombe	Kent	22	C8
Swansea	Swans	26	E9
Swansea Airport	Swans	26	D9
Swansea West Services	Swans	26	E9
Swanton Abbot	Norfk	45	L5
Swanton Morley	Norfk	44	G6
Swanton Novers	Norfk	44	G4
Swan Village	Sandw	40	C8
Swanwick	Derbys	51	K9
Swanwick	Hants	9	N5
Swarby	Lincs	42	F2
Swardeston	Norfk	45	K9
Swarkestone	Derbys	41	J2
Swarland	Nthumb	81	N12
Swarraton	Hants	19	P12
Swarthmoor	Cumb	62	F6
Swaton	Lincs	42	G3
Swavesey	Cambs	33	K3
Sway	Hants	9	J7
Swayfield	Lincs	42	E5
Swaythling	C Sotn	9	M4
Sweetham	Devon	15	Q11
Sweethaws	E Susx	11	P4
Sweets	Cnwll	4	E2
Sweetshouse	Cnwll	3	N4
Swefling	Suffk	35	M4
Swepstone	Leics	41	J5
Swerford	Oxon	31	J7
Swettenham	Ches E	49	P3
Swilland	Suffk	35	K6
Swillington	Leeds	59	J7
Swimbridge	Devon	15	L6
Swimbridge Newland	Devon	15	K6
Swinbrook	Oxon	30	H10
Swincliffe	N York	58	G3
Swinderby	Lincs	52	C10
Swindon	Gloucs	29	N4
Swindon	Staffs	39	Q4
Swindon	Swindn	18	G4
Swine	E R Yk	61	K7
Swinefleet	E R Yk	60	D9
Swineshead	Bed	32	F4
Swineshead	Lincs	43	J3
Swiney	Highld	110	E8
Swinford	Leics	41	M10
Swingfield Minnis	Kent	13	N2
Swingfield Street	Kent	13	N2
Swingleton Green	Suffk	34	F7
Swinhoe	Nthumb	81	P8
Swinithwaite	N York	65	J9
Swinside	Cumb	71	K10
Swinstead	Lincs	42	E5
Swinton	Border	80	H5
Swinton	N York	65	L10
Swinton	N York	66	G11
Swinton	Rothm	51	K2
Swinton	Salfd	57	P8
Swiss Valley	Carmth	26	C8
Swithland	Leics	41	M5
Swordale	Highld	107	J8
Swordland	Highld	97	L10
Swordly	Highld	109	N3
Swynnerton	Staffs	49	Q8
Swyre	Dorset	7	M5
Sychtyn	Powys	38	B1
Syde	Gloucs	29	N6
Sydenham	Gt Lon	21	M8
Sydenham	Oxon	20	B3
Sydenham Damerel	Devon	5	J5
Syderstone	Norfk	44	D4
Sydling St Nicholas	Dorset	7	P3
Sydmonton	Hants	19	N8
Syerston	Notts	51	Q10
Sykehouse	Donc	59	N10
Symbister	Shet	111	k3
Symington	S Ayrs	76	G5
Symington	S Lans	78	G2
Symondsbury	Dorset	7	L4
Symonds Yat (West)	Herefs	28	G5
Syre	Highld	109	M7
Syreford	Gloucs	30	D9
Syresham	Nhants	31	N6
Syston	Leics	41	N5
Syston	Lincs	42	D2
Sytchampton	Worcs	39	Q8
Sywell	Nhants	32	B4

T

Place	County	Page	Grid
Tackley	Oxon	31	L9
Tacolneston	Norfk	45	J10
Tadcaster	N York	59	L5
Taddington	Derbys	50	F6
Tadley	Hants	19	P8
Tadlow	Cambs	33	J7
Tadmarton	Oxon	31	K6
Tadpole	Swindn	18	G3
Tadworth	Surrey	21	K11
Taff's Well	Rhondd	27	N11
Taibach	Neath	26	G10
Tain	Highld	107	M6
Tain	Highld	110	E3
Takeley	Essex	33	P11
Takeley Street	Essex	33	N11
Talaton	Devon	6	E3
Talbenny	Pembks	24	E6
Talbot Village	BCP	8	F8
Taleford	Devon	6	E4
Talerddig	Powys	47	Q10
Talgarreg	Cerdgn	36	G9
Talgarth	Powys	27	N3
Talisker	Highld	96	D4
Talke	Staffs	49	P5
Talke Pits	Staffs	49	P5
Talkin	Cumb	71	Q4
Talladale	Highld	105	N4
Talla Linnfoots	Border	79	J5
Tallaminnock	S Ayrs	76	G10
Tallarn Green	Wrexhm	49	J6
Tallentire	Cumb	70	H8
Talley	Carmth	26	E3
Tallington	Lincs	42	F8
Talmine	Highld	109	K3
Talog	Carmth	25	N4
Talsarn	Cerdgn	37	J9
Talsarnau	Gwynd	47	K4
Talskiddy	Cnwll	3	K3
Talwrn	IoA	54	G6
Tal-y-bont	Cerdgn	37	K3
Tal-y-Bont	Conwy	55	L7
Talybont	Gwynd	47	J9
Tal-y-bont	Gwynd	54	H7
Talybont-on-Usk	Powys	27	N4
Tal-y-Cafn	Conwy	55	L7
Tal-y-coed	Mons	28	E6
Talysarn	Gwynd	54	G10
Tamar Valley Mining District	Devon	5	J7
Tamerton Foliot	C Plym	5	K7
Tamworth	Staffs	40	G6
Tamworth Services	Warwks	40	G7
Tandridge	Surrey	21	M12
Tanfield	Dur	73	L9
Tanfield Lea	Dur	73	L9
Tangasdale	W Isls	111	a7
Tangley	Hants	19	K9
Tangmere	W Susx	10	E8
Tankerness	Ork	111	h2

Tankersley Barns 51 J2
Tankerton Kent 23 L9
Tannach Highld 110 G6
Tannachie Abers 95 N5
Tannadice Angus 93 N4
Tanner's Green Worcs 40 E11
Tannington Suffk 35 L4
Tannochside N Lans 85 L10
Tansley Derbys 51 J8
Tansor Nhants 42 F11
Tantobie Dur 73 L9
Tanworth in Arden Warwks 40 E12
Tan-y-groes Cerdgn 36 E10
Taobh Tuath W Isls 111 b3
Taplow Bucks 20 E7
Tarbert Ag & B 75 J3
Tarbert Ag & B 83 N8
Tarbert W Isls 111 c3
Tarbet Ag & B 84 F3
Tarbet Highld 97 L10
Tarbet Highld 108 D6
Tarbolton S Ayrs 76 G6
Tarbrax S Lans 86 B10
Tardebigge Worcs 30 D1
Tarfside Angus 94 H6
Tarland Abers 94 H2
Tarleton Lancs 57 J5
Tarlton Gloucs 29 N8
Tarnock Somset 17 K5
Tarporley Ches W 49 K3
Tarrant Crawford Dorset 8 D6
Tarrant Gunville Dorset 8 D5
Tarrant Hinton Dorset 8 D5
Tarrant Keyneston Dorset 8 D6
Tarrant Launceston Dorset 8 D5
Tarrant Monkton Dorset 8 D6
Tarrant Rawston Dorset 8 D6
Tarrant Rushton Dorset 8 D6
Tarring Neville E Susx 11 N8
Tarrington Herefs 28 H1
Tarskavaig Highld 96 H7
Tarves Abers 102 H8
Tarvin Ches W 49 J3
Tasburgh Norfk 45 K10
Tatenhill Staffs 40 G3
Tathwell Lincs 53 K6
Tatsfield Surrey 21 N11
Tattenhall Ches W 49 J4
Tatterford Norfk 44 E5
Tattersett Norfk 44 E4
Tattershall Lincs 52 H11
Tattershall Thorpe Lincs 52 H10
Tattingstone Suffk 35 J8
Tattingstone White Horse
  Suffk 35 J8
Tatton Park Ches E 57 N11
Tatworth Somset 7 J2
Tauchers Moray 101 M5
Taunton Somset 16 G10
Taunton Deane Services
  Somset 16 G11
Taverham Norfk 45 J7
Tavernspite Pembks 25 L6
Tavistock Devon 5 K5
Tavistock Devon 5 K5
Taw Green Devon 15 L11
Tawstock Devon 15 K6
Taxal Derbys 50 D5
Tay Bridge C Dund 93 M9
Taychreggan Hotel Ag & B 90 E11
Tay Forest Park P & K 92 B2
Tayinloan Ag & B 75 K4
Taynton Gloucs 29 J4
Taynton Oxon 30 G10
Taynuilt Ag & B 90 D9
Tayport Fife 93 M9
Tayvallich Ag & B 83 L5
Tealby Lincs 52 G5
Tealing Angus 93 M7
Team Valley Gatesd 73 M8
Teangue Highld 97 J7
Teanord Highld 107 K9
Tebay Cumb 63 L2
Tebay Services Cumb 63 L2
Tebworth C Beds 32 E10
Tedburn St Mary Devon 5 Q2
Teddington Gloucs 29 N3
Teddington Gt Lon 21 J8
Tedstone Delamere Herefs 39 M9
Tedstone Wafer Herefs 39 M9
Teeton Nhants 41 P12
Teffont Evias Wilts 8 E2
Teffont Magna Wilts 8 E2
Tegryn Pembks 25 L3
Teigh Rutlnd 42 C7
Teigngrace Devon 6 B7
Teignmouth Devon 6 C8
Teindside Border 79 P7
Telford Wrekin 39 M1
Telford Services Shrops 39 N1
Tellisford Somset 18 B9
Telscombe E Susx 11 N8
Tempar P & K 91 Q5
Templand D & G 78 H10
Temple Cnwll 4 E5
Temple Mdloth 86 G9
Temple Bar Cerdgn 37 J9
Temple Cloud BaNES 17 P5
Templecombe Somset 17 Q10
Temple Grafton Warwks 30 E3
Temple Guiting Gloucs 30 E8
Temple Hirst N York 59 N8
Temple Normanton Derbys 51 K7
Temple of Fiddes Abers 95 N5
Temple Sowerby Cumb 64 B3
Templeton Devon 15 Q9
Templeton Pembks 25 K6
Templetown Dur 73 K10
Tempsford C Beds 32 G6
Tenbury Wells Worcs 39 L8
Tenby Pembks 25 K8
Tendring Essex 35 J11
Tendring Green Essex 35 J10
Tendring Heath Essex 35 J10
Ten Mile Bank Norfk 43 P10
Tenterden Kent 12 H4
Terling Essex 22 F1
Ternhill Shrops 49 L8
Terregles D & G 78 F12
Terrington N York 66 F12
Terrington St Clement Norfk 43 N6
Terrington St John Norfk 43 N7
Teston Kent 22 E11

Testwood Hants 9 L5
Tetbury Gloucs 29 M9
Tetchill Shrops 48 H8
Tetcott Devon 14 F11
Tetford Lincs 53 K8
Tetney Lincs 53 K4
Tetsworth Oxon 20 B3
Tettenhall Wolves 40 B7
Tettenhall Wood Wolves 39 Q3
Teversal Notts 51 L8
Teversham Cambs 33 M5
Tewin Herts 21 L1
Tewkesbury Gloucs 29 M3
Teynham Kent 23 J10
Thackley C Brad 58 F6
Thainstone Abers 102 G10
Thakeham W Susx 10 H6
Thame Oxon 20 B3
Thames Ditton Surrey 21 J9
Thamesmead Gt Lon 21 P7
Thamesport Medway 22 G8
Thanington Kent 23 L11
Thankerton S Lans 78 F2
Tharston Norfk 45 K10
Thatcham W Berk 19 N7
Thaxted Essex 33 P9
Theakston N York 65 N9
Thealby N Linc 60 F9
Theale Somset 17 L7
Theale W Berk 19 Q6
Thearne E R Yk 61 J6
The Beeches Gloucs 18 F1
Theberton Suffk 35 P4
The Braes Highld 96 G3
The Bridge Kent 22 B8
The Broads 45 P8
The Brunt E Loth 87 M7
The Bungalow IoM 56 d4
The Burf Worcs 39 P8
The City Bucks 20 C4
The Common Wilts 9 J2
Theddingworth Leics 41 P9
Theddlethorpe All Saints
  Lincs 53 M6
Theddlethorpe St Helen Lincs 53 M6
The Deep C KuH 61 J8
The Den N Ayrs 76 F2
The Forstal Kent 13 K3
The Green Cumb 62 D5
The Green Essex 34 C11
The Green N York 66 H6
The Green Wilts 8 C2
The Headland Hartpl 66 D1
The Hill Cumb 62 D5
The Lee Bucks 20 E3
The Lhen IoM 56 d2
Thelnetham Suffk 34 G2
The Lochs Moray 101 L3
Thelveton Norfk 35 J1
Thelwall Warrtn 57 M10
Themelthorpe Norfk 45 H5
The Middles Dur 73 L9
The Moor Kent 12 F4
The Mumbles Swans 26 E10
The Murray S Lans 85 K11
The Neuk Abers 95 M3
Thenford Nhants 31 M6
The Reddings Gloucs 29 M5
Therfield Herts 33 K8
The Ross P & K 92 B10
The Spring Warwks 40 H11
The Stocks Kent 12 H5
The Strand Wilts 18 D8
Thetford Norfk 44 E12
Thetford Forest Park 44 D11
Theydon Bois Essex 21 N4
Thickwood Wilts 18 C6
Thimbleby Lincs 53 J9
Thimbleby N York 66 C8
Thingwall Wirral 56 F11
Thirkleby N York 66 C10
Thirlby N York 66 C10
Thirlestane Border 80 D5
Thirn N York 65 L9
Thirsk N York 65 Q10
Thistleton Lancs 56 H2
Thistleton Rutlnd 42 D6
Thistley Green Suffk 33 Q2
Thixendale N York 60 E3
Thockrington Nthumb 72 G5
Tholomas Drove Cambs 43 L8
Tholthorpe N York 59 L2
Thomastown Abers 102 D7
Thompson Norfk 44 F10
Thomshill Moray 101 J4
Thongsbridge Kirk 58 F11
Thoralby N York 64 H9
Thoresway Lincs 52 G4
Thorganby Lincs 52 H4
Thorganby N York 59 P6
Thorgill N York 66 G7
Thorington Suffk 35 N2
Thorington Street Suffk 34 G9
Thorlby N York 58 C4
Thorley Herts 33 M11
Thorley Street IoW 9 L9
Thormanby N York 66 C11
Thornaby-on-Tees S on T 66 C4
Thornage Norfk 44 H3
Thornborough Bucks 31 Q7
Thornborough N York 65 N10
Thornbury C Brad 58 G7
Thornbury Devon 14 G9
Thornbury Herefs 39 L9
Thornbury S Glos 28 H10
Thornby Nhants 41 P11
Thorncliff Staffs 50 D8
Thorncombe Dorset 7 K3
Thorndon Suffk 35 J4
Thorndon Cross Devon 5 L2
Thorne Donc 59 P10
Thorner Leeds 59 J6
Thorne St Margaret Somset 16 E11
Thorney C Pete 43 J8
Thorney Notts 52 C8
Thorney Somset 17 L10
Thorney Hill Hants 8 H7
Thorney Island W Susx 10 C9
Thornfalcon Somset 16 H10
Thornford Dorset 17 N12
Thorngrafton Nthumb 72 E7
Thorngumbald E R Yk 61 L7

Thornham Norfk 44 C2
Thornham Magna Suffk 34 H3
Thornham Parva Suffk 35 J3
Thornhaugh C Pete 42 F9
Thornhill C Soton 9 M5
Thornhill Cumb 62 B1
Thornhill D & G 78 E9
Thornhill Derbys 50 G4
Thornhill Kirk 58 G9
Thornhill Stirlg 85 L3
Thornholme E R Yk 61 J2
Thornicombe Dorset 8 C6
Thornington Nthumb 81 J7
Thornley Dur 73 K12
Thornley Dur 73 P11
Thornliebank E Rens 85 J10
Thorns Suffk 34 C6
Thornsett Derbys 50 D4
Thornthwaite Cumb 71 K9
Thornthwaite N York 58 F3
Thornton Angus 93 M6
Thornton Bucks 31 Q7
Thornton C Brad 58 E7
Thornton E R Yk 60 D5
Thornton Fife 86 F3
Thornton Lancs 56 G1
Thornton Leics 41 L6
Thornton Middsb 66 C5
Thornton Nthumb 81 K5
Thornton Curtis N Linc 61 J7
Thorntonhall S Lans 85 K11
Thornton Heath Gt Lon 21 L9
Thornton Hough Wirral 56 F11
Thornton-in-Craven N York 58 B5
Thornton in Lonsdale N York 63 M7
Thornton-le-Beans N York 65 P9
Thornton-le-Clay N York 59 P2
Thornton-le-Dale N York 67 J10
Thornton le Moor Lincs 52 F4
Thornton-le-Moor N York 65 P9
Thornton-le-Moors Ches W 48 H1
Thornton-le-Street N York 65 N7
Thorntonloch E Loth 87 N7
Thornton Rust N York 64 G9
Thornton Steward N York 65 L9
Thornton Watlass N York 65 M9
Thorndykes Border 80 E5
Thornythwaite Cumb 71 N10
Thoroton Notts 51 Q11
Thorp Arch Leeds 59 K5
Thorpe Derbys 50 F10
Thorpe E R Yk 60 G5
Thorpe N York 58 D2
Thorpe Notts 51 Q10
Thorpe Surrey 20 G9
Thorpe Abbotts Norfk 35 K2
Thorpe Arnold Leics 41 Q4
Thorpe Audlin Wakefd 59 L10
Thorpe Bassett N York 67 J11
Thorpe Bay Sthend 22 H6
Thorpe by Water Rutlnd 42 C10
Thorpe Constantine Staffs 40 H6
Thorpe End Norfk 45 L7
Thorpe Green Essex 35 J11
Thorpe Green Suffk 34 F6
Thorpe Hesley Rothm 51 J2
Thorpe in Balne Donc 59 N11
Thorpe Langton Leics 41 Q8
Thorpe Lea Surrey 20 G8
Thorpe-le-Soken Essex 35 K11
Thorpe le Street E R Yk 60 E5
Thorpe Malsor Nhants 32 C2
Thorpe Mandeville Nhants 31 M5
Thorpe Market Norfk 45 L3
Thorpe Marriot Norfk 45 K7
Thorpe Morieux Suffk 34 F6
Thorpeness Suffk 35 P5
Thorpe on the Hill Lincs 52 C9
Thorpe Park Surrey 20 G9
Thorpe St Andrew Norfk 45 L8
Thorpe St Peter Lincs 53 M10
Thorpe Salvin Rothm 51 M5
Thorpe Satchville Leics 41 Q5
Thorpe Thewles S on T 65 P3
Thorpe Tilney Lincs 52 G11
Thorpe Underwood N York 59 L3
Thorpe Waterville Nhants 32 E1
Thorpe Willoughby N York 59 M7
Thorrington Essex 34 H11
Thorverton Devon 6 C3
Thrandeston Suffk 35 J2
Thrapston Nhants 32 E2
Threapwood Ches W 48 H6
Threapwood Staffs 50 D11
Threave S Ayrs 76 F9
Three Bridges W Susx 11 L3
Three Chimneys Kent 12 G3
Three Cocks Powys 27 N2
Three Crosses Swans 26 D9
Three Cups Corner E Susx 12 D6
Threekingham Lincs 42 F3
Three Leg Cross E Susx 12 D4
Three Legged Cross Dorset 8 F6
Three Mile Cross Wokham 20 B9
Threemilestone Cnwll 2 H6
Threemiletown W Loth 86 C7
Three Oaks E Susx 12 G7
Threlkeld Cumb 71 M9
Threshers Bush Essex 21 P2
Threshfield N York 58 C2
Thrigby Norfk 45 P7
Thrintoft N York 65 N8
Thriplow Cambs 33 M7
Throcking Herts 33 K10
Throckley N u Ty 73 K7
Throckmorton Worcs 30 C4
Throop BCP 8 G8
Thropton Nthumb 81 H1
Throsk Stirlg 85 P5
Throughgate D & G 78 E11
Throwleigh Devon 5 N3
Throwley Forstal Kent 23 J11
Thrumpton Notts 41 L2
Thrumster Highld 110 G6
Thrunscoe NE Lin 53 K2
Thrupp Gloucs 29 M7
Thrussington Leics 41 P4
Thruxton Hants 19 K10
Thruxton Herefs 28 E2
Thrybergh Rothm 51 K2
Thulston Derbys 41 K2
Thundersley Essex 22 F6
Thurcaston Leics 41 M5

Thurcroft Rothm 51 L3
Thurgarton Norfk 45 K3
Thurgarton Notts 51 P10
Thurgoland Barns 50 H1
Thurlaston Leics 41 L7
Thurlaston Warwks 41 L12
Thurlbear Somset 16 H11
Thurlby Lincs 42 F6
Thurlby Lincs 52 C10
Thurlby Lincs 53 M8
Thurleigh Bed 32 F5
Thurlestone Devon 5 N10
Thurloxton Somset 16 H9
Thurlstone Barns 58 G12
Thurlton Norfk 45 N9
Thurmaston Leics 41 N5
Thurnby Leics 41 N6
Thurne Norfk 45 N7
Thurnham Kent 22 F11
Thurning Nhants 42 F12
Thurning Norfk 44 H4
Thurnscoe Barns 59 L11
Thurrock Services Thurr 22 C7
Thursby Cumb 71 M5
Thursford Norfk 44 G4
Thursley Surrey 10 E3
Thurso Highld 110 D3
Thurstaston Wirral 56 F11
Thurston Suffk 34 F4
Thurstonfield Cumb 71 M4
Thurstonland Kirk 58 F11
Thurton Norfk 45 M9
Thurvaston Derbys 50 G12
Thuxton Norfk 44 G8
Thwaite N York 64 F7
Thwaite Suffk 35 J4
Thwaite Head Cumb 62 G4
Thwaite St Mary Norfk 45 M10
Thwing E R Yk 67 M12
Tibbermore P & K 92 F10
Tibbers D & G 78 E9
Tibberton Gloucs 29 K4
Tibberton Worcs 30 B3
Tibberton Wrekin 49 M10
Tibenham Norfk 45 J11
Tibshelf Derbys 51 K8
Tibshelf Services Derbys 51 K8
Tibthorpe E R Yk 60 G3
Ticehurst E Susx 12 E4
Tichborne Hants 9 P2
Tickencote Rutlnd 42 E8
Tickenham N Som 17 L2
Tickhill Donc 51 N3
Ticklerton Shrops 39 J4
Ticknall Derbys 41 J3
Tickton E R Yk 60 H6
Tiddington Oxon 31 P12
Tiddington Warwks 30 G3
Tidebrook E Susx 12 C4
Tideford Cnwll 4 H8
Tideswell Derbys 50 F6
Tidmarsh W Berk 19 Q6
Tidmington Warwks 30 H6
Tidworth Wilts 19 J10
Tiers Cross Pembks 24 F6
Tiffield Nhants 31 P4
Tigerton Angus 95 J8
Tigh a' Ghearraidh W Isls 111 a4
Tigharry W Isls 111 a4
Tighnabruaich Ag & B 83 P8
Tigley Devon 5 P7
Tilbrook Cambs 32 F3
Tilbury Thurr 22 D8
Tile Cross Birm 40 F9
Tile Hill Covtry 40 H11
Tilehurst Readg 19 Q6
Tilford Surrey 10 E2
Tilgate W Susx 11 L3
Tilham Street Somset 17 M8
Tillicoultry Clacks 85 Q4
Tillietudlem S Lans 77 N3
Tillingham Essex 23 J3
Tillington Herefs 39 J12
Tillington W Susx 10 F6
Tillington Common Herefs 39 J11
Tillybirloch Abers 95 L1
Tillyfourie Abers 102 E11
Tillygreig Abers 103 J10
Tillyrie P & K 86 D2
Tilmanstone Kent 23 P12
Tilney All Saints Norfk 43 P6
Tilney High End Norfk 43 N6
Tilney St Lawrence Norfk 43 N7
Tilshead Wilts 18 F10
Tilstock Shrops 49 K7
Tilston Ches W 49 J5
Tilstone Fearnall Ches W 49 K4
Tilsworth C Beds 32 E11
Tilton on the Hill Leics 41 Q6
Tiltups End Gloucs 29 L8
Timberland Lincs 52 G10
Timbersbrook Ches E 50 B8
Timberscombe Somset 16 C7
Timble N York 58 F4
Timpanheck D & G 71 M1
Timperley Traffd 57 P10
Timsbury BaNES 17 P4
Timsbury Hants 9 L3
Timsgarry W Isls 111 c2
Timsgearraidh W Isls 111 c2
Timworth Suffk 34 E3
Timworth Green Suffk 34 E3
Tincleton Dorset 8 B8
Tindale Cumb 72 B8
Tingewick Bucks 31 P7
Tingrith C Beds 32 E9
Tingwall Airport Shet 111 k4
Tingwell Ork 111 h2
Tinhay Devon 5 J3
Tinsley Sheff 51 K3
Tinsley Green W Susx 11 L3
Tintagel Cnwll 4 C3
Tintern Mons 28 F8
Tintinhull Somset 17 M11
Tintwistle Derbys 50 D2
Tinwald D & G 78 G11
Tinwell Rutlnd 42 E8
Tipton Sandw 40 C8
Tipton Green Sandw 40 C8
Tipton St John Devon 6 E5
Tiptree Essex 34 E2

Tiptree Heath Essex 22 G1
Tirabad Powys 37 P11
Tiree Ag & B 88 C7
Tiree Airport Ag & B 88 C7
Tiretigan Ag & B 83 K9
Tirley Gloucs 29 L3
Tiroran Ag & B 89 K10
Tirphil Caerph 27 N7
Tirril Cumb 71 P9
Tisbury Wilts 8 D2
Tissington Derbys 50 F9
Titchberry Devon 14 E6
Titchfield Hants 9 P6
Titchmarsh Nhants 32 E2
Titchwell Norfk 44 C2
Tithby Notts 51 P12
Titley Herefs 38 G9
Titsey Surrey 21 N11
Titson Cnwll 14 E10
Tittensor Staffs 49 Q7
Tittleshall Norfk 44 E6
Titton Worcs 39 P7
Tiverton Ches W 49 K4
Tiverton Devon 6 C1
Tivetshall St Margaret Norfk 45 K11
Tivetshall St Mary Norfk 45 J11
Tixall Staffs 40 C3
Tixover Rutlnd 42 D9
Toab Shet 111 k5
Tobermory Ag & B 89 L5
Toberonochy Ag & B 83 L2
Tobha Mòr W Isls 111 a5
Tocher Abers 102 F8
Tochieneal Moray 101 P3
Tockenham Wilts 18 F5
Tockholes Bl w D 57 M4
Tockington S Glos 28 H10
Tockwith N York 59 L4
Todber Dorset 8 B4
Toddington C Beds 32 E10
Toddington Gloucs 30 D7
Toddington Services C Beds 32 E10
Todenham Gloucs 30 G7
Todhills Angus 93 M7
Todhills Rest Area Cumb 71 N3
Todmorden Calder 58 C8
Todwick Rothm 51 L4
Toft Cambs 33 K5
Toft Lincs 42 F6
Toft Shet 111 k3
Toft Hill Dur 65 K2
Toft Monks Norfk 45 N10
Toft next Newton Lincs 52 E5
Toftrees Norfk 44 E5
Togston Nthumb 73 M1
Tokavaig Highld 96 H7
Tokers Green Oxon 20 B7
Tolastadh bho Thuath W Isls 111 e1
Tolland Somset 16 E9
Tollard Royal Wilts 8 D4
Toll Bar Donc 59 M11
Toller Fratrum Dorset 7 N4
Toller Porcorum Dorset 7 N3
Tollerton N York 59 L2
Tollerton Notts 41 N1
Tollesbury Essex 23 J2
Tolleshunt D'Arcy Essex 22 H2
Tolleshunt Knights Essex 22 H1
Tolleshunt Major Essex 22 H2
Toll of Birness Abers 103 K8
Tolpuddle Dorset 8 B8
Tolworth Gt Lon 21 J9
Tomatin Highld 99 M4
Tomchrasky Highld 98 C5
Tomdoun Highld 98 B8
Tomich Highld 98 D4
Tomich Highld 107 J11
Tomich Highld 107 K6
Tomich Highld 107 L8
Tomintoul Moray 101 J9
Tomnacross Highld 98 G2
Tomnavoulin Moray 101 J9
Tonbridge Kent 12 C2
Tondu Brdgnd 27 J11
Tonedale Somset 16 F11
Tong C Brad 58 G7
Tong Kent 23 J11
Tong Shrops 39 P1
Tong W Isls 111 d2
Tonge Leics 41 K3
Tongham Surrey 10 E1
Tongland D & G 69 Q8
Tong Norton Shrops 39 P1
Tongue Highld 109 K4
Tongwynlais Cardif 27 N11
Tonmawr Neath 26 H9
Tonna Neath 26 G8
Tonwell Herts 33 K12
Tonypandy Rhondd 27 L9
Tonyrefail Rhondd 27 L10
Toot Baldon Oxon 19 P1
Toot Hill Essex 21 P3
Toothill Swindn 18 G4
Tooting Gt Lon 21 L8
Tooting Bec Gt Lon 21 L8
Topcliffe N York 65 P11
Topcroft Norfk 45 L10
Topcroft Street Norfk 45 L10
Toppesfield Essex 34 C8
Toprow Norfk 45 J9
Topsham Devon 6 C5
Torbeg N Ayrs 75 N6
Torboll Highld 107 M3
Torbreck Highld 99 J2
Torbryan Devon 6 B6
Torcastle Highld 90 F2
Torcross Devon 5 Q10
Tore Highld 107 K10
Torinturk Ag & B 83 M9
Torksey Lincs 52 B7
Torlundy Highld 90 F2
Tormarton S Glos 18 B5
Tormore N Ayrs 75 N6
Tornagrain Highld 107 M11
Torness Highld 98 H4
Toronto Dur 65 L2
Torpenhow Cumb 71 K7
Torphichen W Loth 86 A7
Torphins Abers 95 K2
Torpoint Cnwll 5 J9
Torquay Torbay 6 C9
Torquhan Border 87 J11

Place	Location	Page	Grid
Torran	Highld	104	H11
Torrance	E Duns	85	K8
Torranyard	N Ayrs	76	F3
Torridon	Highld	105	N10
Torridon House	Highld	105	M10
Torrin	Highld	96	G5
Torrisdale	Ag & B	75	M5
Torrisdale	Highld	109	M4
Torrish	Highld	110	A11
Torrisholme	Lancs	63	J9
Torrobull	Highld	107	K2
Torry	C Aber	95	Q2
Torryburn	Fife	86	B5
Torteval	Guern	6	a2
Torthorwald	D & G	78	G12
Tortington	W Susx	10	G8
Torton	Worcs	39	Q7
Tortworth	S Glos	29	J9
Torvaig	Highld	96	F2
Torver	Cumb	62	F4
Torwood	Falk	85	P6
Torwoodlee	Border	79	P2
Torworth	Notts	51	P4
Toscaig	Highld	97	J3
Toseland	Cambs	33	J4
Tosside	Lancs	63	P10
Tostock	Suffk	34	F4
Totaig	Highld	104	B11
Tote	Highld	104	F11
Tote	Highld	104	G9
Totland	IoW	9	K9
Totley	Sheff	50	H5
Totley Brook	Sheff	50	H5
Totnes	Devon	5	Q7
Toton	Notts	41	L1
Totronald	Ag & B	88	E5
Totscore	Highld	104	E8
Tottenham	Gt Lon	21	M5
Tottenhill	Norfk	43	Q7
Totteridge	Gt Lon	21	K5
Totternhoe	C Beds	32	E11
Tottington	Bury	57	P6
Totton	Hants	9	L5
Toulton	Somset	16	G9
Toulvaddie	Highld	107	P6
Tovil	Kent	22	F11
Toward	Ag & B	84	C8
Toward Quay	Ag & B	84	B9
Towcester	Nhants	31	P4
Towednack	Cnwll	2	D7
Tower of London	Gt Lon	21	M7
Towersey	Oxon	20	B3
Towie	Abers	101	N11
Tow Law	Dur	73	K11
Town End	Cambs	43	L10
Townend	W Duns	84	G7
Townhead	Barns	50	F1
Townhead	D & G	78	G10
Townhead of Greenlaw	D & G	70	C3
Townhill	Fife	86	D4
Town Littleworth	E Susx	11	N6
Townshend	Cnwll	2	E8
Town Street	Suffk	44	C11
Town Yetholm	Border	80	H8
Towthorpe	C York	59	N3
Towton	N York	59	L6
Towyn	Conwy	55	P6
Toxteth	Lpool	56	G10
Toynton All Saints	Lincs	53	L10
Toy's Hill	Kent	21	P12
Trabboch	E Ayrs	76	G7
Trabbochburn	E Ayrs	76	H7
Tradespark	Highld	100	D4
Trafford Park	Traffd	57	P9
Trallong	Powys	27	K3
Tranent	E Loth	86	H7
Tranmere	Wirral	56	G10
Trantelbeg	Highld	109	Q5
Trantlemore	Highld	109	Q5
Trap	Carmth	26	E5
Traprain	E Loth	87	L7
Traquair	Border	79	M3
Trawden	Lancs	58	B6
Trawsfynydd	Gwynd	47	L4
Trealaw	Rhondd	27	L9
Treales	Lancs	56	H3
Trearddur Bay	IoA	54	C6
Trebetherick	Cnwll	4	B5
Treborough	Somset	16	D8
Trebullett	Cnwll	4	H5
Treburley	Cnwll	4	H5
Trecastle	Powys	27	J3
Trecwn	Pembks	24	G3
Trecynon	Rhondd	27	L7
Tredegar	Blae G	27	N7
Tredington	Gloucs	29	M3
Tredington	Warwks	30	H5
Tredunnock	Mons	28	D9
Treen	Cnwll	2	B10
Treeton	Rothm	51	K4
Trefasser	Pembks	24	F2
Trefecca	Powys	27	N3
Trefechan	Myr Td	27	L7
Trefeglwys	Powys	37	Q3
Treffgarne	Pembks	24	G4
Treffgarne Owen	Pembks	24	F4
Trefilan	Cerdgn	37	J8
Trefin	Pembks	24	E3
Trefnant	Denbgs	48	B2
Trefonen	Shrops	48	F9
Trefor	Gwynd	46	F3
Treforest	Rhondd	27	M10
Trefriw	Conwy	55	L8
Tregadillett	Cnwll	4	G4
Tregare	Mons	28	E6
Tregaron	Cerdgn	37	L8
Tregarth	Gwynd	54	H7
Tregeare	Cnwll	4	F3
Tregeiriog	Wrexhm	48	D8
Tregele	IoA	54	E3
Treglemais	Pembks	24	E3
Tregonetha	Cnwll	3	L3
Tregonning & Gwinear Mining District	Cnwll	2	E9
Tregony	Cnwll	3	K6
Tregorrick	Cnwll	3	M5
Tregoyd	Powys	27	P2
Tre-groes	Cerdgn	36	G10
Tregynon	Powys	38	C3
Tre-gynwr	Carmth	25	P5
Trehafod	Rhondd	27	L10
Trehan	Cnwll	5	J8
Treharris	Myr Td	27	M9

Place	Location	Page	Grid
Treherbert	Rhondd	27	K8
Trekenner	Cnwll	4	H5
Treknow	Cnwll	4	D3
Trelawnyd	Flints	56	C11
Trelech	Carmth	25	M3
Treleddyd-fawr	Pembks	24	D3
Trelewis	Myr Td	27	M9
Trelights	Cnwll	4	B4
Trelill	Cnwll	4	C5
Trellech	Mons	28	F7
Trelogan	Flints	56	D11
Tremadog	Gwynd	47	J4
Tremail	Cnwll	4	E3
Tremain	Cerdgn	36	D10
Tremaine	Cnwll	4	F3
Tremar	Cnwll	4	G6
Trematon	Cnwll	5	J8
Tremeirchion	Denbgs	48	C2
Trenance	Cnwll	3	J3
Trenance	Cnwll	3	L2
Trench	Wrekin	49	M11
Trenear	Cnwll	2	G9
Treneglos	Cnwll	4	F3
Trent	Dorset	17	N11
Trentham	C Stke	49	Q7
Trentishoe	Devon	15	L3
Trent Vale	C Stke	49	Q6
Treoes	V Glam	27	K12
Treorchy	Rhondd	27	K8
Trequite	Cnwll	3	M1
Trerhyngyll	V Glam	27	L12
Trerulefoot	Cnwll	4	H8
Tresaith	Cerdgn	36	E9
Tresco	IoS	2	b2
Trescowe	Cnwll	2	E9
Tresean	Cnwll	2	H4
Tresham	Gloucs	29	L9
Treshnish Isles	Ag & B	88	G7
Tresillian	Cnwll	3	K6
Treskinnick Cross	Cnwll	14	D11
Tresmeer	Cnwll	4	F3
Tresparrett	Cnwll	4	E2
Tressait	P & K	92	C4
Tresta	Shet	111	k4
Tresta	Shet	111	m2
Treswell	Notts	52	A7
Tre Taliesin	Cerdgn	37	L3
Trethevey	Cnwll	4	D3
Trethewey	Cnwll	2	B10
Trethurgy	Cnwll	3	M5
Tretire	Herefs	28	F4
Tretower	Powys	27	P5
Treuddyn	Flints	48	F4
Trevalga	Cnwll	4	D3
Trevalyn	Wrexhm	48	H4
Trevarrian	Cnwll	3	J3
Treveal	Cnwll	2	H4
Treveighan	Cnwll	4	D4
Trevellas Downs	Cnwll	2	H5
Trevelmond	Cnwll	4	F7
Treverva	Cnwll	2	H9
Trevescan	Cnwll	2	B10
Treviscoe	Cnwll	3	L5
Trevone	Cnwll	3	K1
Trevor	Wrexhm	48	F7
Trewalder	Cnwll	4	D4
Trewarmett	Cnwll	4	D3
Trewavas Mining District	Cnwll	2	E9
Trewen	Cnwll	4	F4
Trewint	Cnwll	4	F4
Trewithian	Cnwll	3	K8
Trewoon	Cnwll	3	L5
Treyford	W Susx	10	D6
Trimdon	Dur	65	P1
Trimdon Colliery	Dur	65	P1
Trimdon Grange	Dur	65	P1
Trimingham	Norfk	45	L3
Trimley St Martin	Suffk	35	L8
Trimley St Mary	Suffk	35	L8
Trimsaran	Carmth	26	B7
Trimstone	Devon	15	J4
Trinafour	P & K	91	Q4
Tring	Herts	20	E2
Trinity	Angus	95	K9
Trinity	Jersey	7	b1
Trinity Gask	P & K	92	E11
Triscombe	Somset	16	F8
Trislaig	Highld	90	E2
Trispen	Cnwll	3	J6
Tritlington	Nthumb	73	L3
Trochry	P & K	92	E7
Troedyraur	Cerdgn	36	E10
Troedyrhiw	Myr Td	27	M8
Troon	Cnwll	2	F8
Troon	S Ayrs	76	F5
Tropical World Roundhay Park	Leeds	59	J6
Trossachs	Stirlg	84	H2
Trossachs Pier	Stirlg	84	H2
Troston	Suffk	34	E3
Trotshill	Worcs	30	B3
Trottiscliffe	Kent	22	D10
Trotton	W Susx	10	D5
Troutbeck	Cumb	62	H2
Troutbeck Bridge	Cumb	62	H3
Troway	Derbys	51	K5
Trowbridge	Wilts	18	C8
Trowell	Notts	51	L11
Trowell Services	Notts	51	L11
Trowle Common	Wilts	18	C8
Trowse Newton	Norfk	45	L8
Trudoxhill	Somset	17	Q7
Trull	Somset	16	G10
Trumpan	Highld	104	C9
Trumpet	Herefs	28	H2
Trumpington	Cambs	33	M6
Trunch	Norfk	45	L3
Truro	Cnwll	3	J6
Trusham	Devon	6	B6
Trusley	Derbys	40	G1
Trusthorpe	Lincs	53	N6
Trysull	Staffs	39	Q4
Tubney	Oxon	19	M2
Tuckenhay	Devon	5	Q8
Tuckhill	Shrops	39	P5
Tuckingmill	Cnwll	2	F7
Tuckingmill	Wilts	8	D2
Tuckton	BCP	8	G8
Tuddenham	Suffk	34	C3
Tuddenham	Suffk	35	K7
Tudeley	Kent	12	C2
Tudhoe	Dur	65	M1

Place	Location	Page	Grid
Tudweiliog	Gwynd	46	D4
Tuffley	Gloucs	29	L6
Tufton	Hants	19	M10
Tufton	Pembks	24	H3
Tugby	Leics	41	Q7
Tugford	Shrops	39	K5
Tughall	Nthumb	81	P8
Tullibody	Clacks	85	P4
Tullich	Abers	94	F3
Tullich	Highld	99	J4
Tullich	Highld	107	P7
Tulliemet	P & K	92	E5
Tulloch	Abers	102	G8
Tullochgorm	Ag & B	83	P4
Tulloch Station	Highld	98	E11
Tullymurdoch	P & K	92	H5
Tullynessle	Abers	102	D10
Tulse Hill	Gt Lon	21	L8
Tumble	Carmth	26	D6
Tumby	Lincs	53	J10
Tumby Woodside	Lincs	53	J11
Tummel Bridge	P & K	92	B4
Tunbridge Wells	Kent	12	C3
Tundergarth	D & G	79	J11
Tunga	W Isls	111	d2
Tunley	BaNES	17	Q4
Tunstall	E R Yk	61	M7
Tunstall	Kent	22	H10
Tunstall	Lancs	63	L7
Tunstall	N York	65	L8
Tunstall	Norfk	45	N8
Tunstall	Staffs	49	P9
Tunstall	Suffk	35	M6
Tunstall	Sundld	73	P9
Tunstead	Derbys	50	E6
Tunstead	Norfk	45	L6
Tunstead Milton	Derbys	50	D5
Tupsley	Herefs	28	G2
Turgis Green	Hants	20	B10
Turkdean	Gloucs	30	E9
Tur Langton	Leics	41	Q8
Turleigh	Wilts	18	B8
Turnastone	Herefs	28	D2
Turnberry	S Ayrs	76	D9
Turnditch	Derbys	50	H10
Turners Hill	W Susx	11	M3
Turnhouse	C Edin	86	D7
Turnworth	Dorset	8	B6
Turriff	Abers	102	F5
Turton Bottoms	Bl w D	57	N6
Turves	Cambs	43	K10
Turvey	Bed	32	D6
Turville	Bucks	20	C5
Turweston	Bucks	31	N6
Tushielaw Inn	Border	79	L5
Tutbury	Staffs	40	G2
Tutshill	Gloucs	28	G9
Tuttington	Norfk	45	K5
Tuxford	Notts	51	Q6
Twatt	Ork	111	g2
Twatt	Shet	111	k4
Twechar	E Duns	85	L7
Tweedbank	Border	80	C7
Tweedmouth	Nthumb	81	L4
Tweedsmuir	Border	78	H4
Twelveheads	Cnwll	2	H7
Twemlow Green	Ches E	49	P2
Twenty	Lincs	42	G6
Twerton	BaNES	17	Q4
Twickenham	Gt Lon	21	J8
Twigworth	Gloucs	29	L4
Twineham	W Susx	11	K6
Twinstead	Essex	34	E9
Twitchen	Devon	15	N6
Two Dales	Derbys	50	H8
Two Gates	Staffs	40	G7
Two Waters	Herts	20	G3
Twycross	Leics	41	J6
Twycross Zoo	Leics	40	H6
Twyford	Bucks	31	P8
Twyford	Hants	9	N3
Twyford	Leics	41	Q5
Twyford	Norfk	44	G5
Twyford	Wokham	20	C8
Twynholm	D & G	69	P8
Twyning Green	Gloucs	29	M2
Twynllanan	Carmth	26	G4
Twywell	Nhants	32	D2
Tyberton	Herefs	28	D2
Tyburn	Birm	40	F8
Tycroes	Carmth	26	E6
Tycrwyn	Powys	48	C10
Tydd Gote	Lincs	43	M6
Tydd St Giles	Cambs	43	L6
Tydd St Mary	Lincs	43	M6
Tye Green	Essex	33	P9
Tyldesley	Wigan	57	M8
Tyler Hill	Kent	23	L10
Tylorstown	Rhondd	27	L9
Ty-nant	Conwy	48	B6
Tyndrum	Stirlg	91	J9
Ty-n-dwr	Denbgs	48	E7
Tynemouth	N Tyne	73	P7
Tyne Tunnel	S Tyne	73	N7
Tynron	D & G	77	N11
Tyntesfield	N Som	17	M2
Tynygraig	Cerdgn	37	L6
Ty'n-y-Groes	Conwy	55	L7
Tyrie	Abers	103	J3
Tyringham	M Keyn	32	C7
Tyseley	Birm	40	E9
Tythegston	Brdgnd	27	J11
Tytherington	Ches E	50	B6
Tytherington	S Glos	29	J10
Tytherington	Wilts	18	D11
Tytherleigh	Devon	7	J3
Tytherton Lucas	Wilts	18	D6
Tywardreath	Cnwll	3	N5
Tywyn	Gwynd	47	J10

U

Place	Location	Page	Grid
Ubbeston Green	Suffk	35	M3
Ubley	BaNES	17	M5
Uckfield	E Susx	11	P6
Uckinghall	Worcs	29	M2
Uckington	Gloucs	29	M4
Uddingston	S Lans	85	L10
Uddington	S Lans	78	E3
Udimore	E Susx	12	G6
Udny Green	Abers	103	J9

Place	Location	Page	Grid
Udny Station	Abers	103	J9
Uffculme	Devon	16	E12
Uffington	Lincs	42	F8
Uffington	Oxon	19	K3
Uffington	Shrops	49	K11
Ufford	C Pete	42	F8
Ufford	Suffk	35	L6
Ufton	Warwks	31	Q7
Ufton Nervet	W Berk	19	Q7
Ugadale	Ag & B	75	L6
Ugborough	Devon	5	N8
Uggeshall	Suffk	35	P2
Ugglebarnby	N York	67	J6
Ughill	Sheff	50	G3
Ugley	Essex	33	N10
Ugley Green	Essex	33	N10
Ugthorpe	N York	66	H5
Uibhist A Deas	W Isls	111	b6
Uibhist A Tuath	W Isls	111	a4
Uig	Ag & B	88	E5
Uig	Highld	104	B10
Uig	Highld	104	E9
Uig	W Isls	111	c2
Uigshader	Highld	104	F12
Uisken	Ag & B	89	J11
Ulbster	Highld	110	G7
Ulceby	Lincs	53	L8
Ulceby	N Linc	61	J10
Ulceby Skitter	N Linc	61	J10
Ulcombe	Kent	12	G1
Uldale	Cumb	71	L7
Uley	Gloucs	29	K8
Ulgham	Nthumb	73	M3
Ullapool	Highld	106	B4
Ullenhall	Warwks	30	E1
Ulleskelf	N York	59	M6
Ullesthorpe	Leics	41	L9
Ulley	Rothm	51	L4
Ullingswick	Herefs	39	L11
Ullinish Lodge Hotel	Highld	96	C3
Ullock	Cumb	70	H10
Ullswater	Cumb	71	N10
Ullswater Steamers	Cumb	71	N11
Ulpha	Cumb	62	E4
Ulrome	E R Yk	61	K3
Ulsta	Shet	111	k3
Ulva	Ag & B	89	J8
Ulverley Green	Solhll	40	F10
Ulverston	Cumb	62	F6
Ulwell	Dorset	8	F10
Ulzieside	D & G	77	N9
Umberleigh	Devon	15	K7
Unapool	Highld	108	E8
Underbarrow	Cumb	63	J4
Undercliffe	C Brad	58	F7
Underdale	Shrops	49	J11
Underriver	Kent	22	B11
Underwood	Notts	51	L10
Undy	Mons	28	E10
Union Mills	IoM	56	c5
Unst	Shet	111	m2
Unstone	Derbys	51	J5
Upavon	Wilts	18	G9
Upchurch	Kent	22	G9
Upcott	Devon	15	N6
Up Exe	Devon	6	C3
Upgate	Norfk	45	J6
Uphall	Dorset	7	M3
Uphall	W Loth	86	C7
Upham	Devon	15	Q9
Upham	Hants	9	N4
Uphampton	Herefs	38	H9
Uphampton	Worcs	39	Q8
Uphill	N Som	17	J5
Up Holland	Lancs	57	K7
Uplawmoor	E Rens	84	G11
Upleadon	Gloucs	29	K4
Upleatham	R & Cl	66	E4
Uploders	Dorset	7	M4
Uplowman	Devon	16	D11
Uplyme	Devon	7	J4
Up Marden	W Susx	10	C7
Upminster	Gt Lon	22	C6
Up Mudford	Somset	17	N11
Up Nately	Hants	20	B11
Upottery	Devon	6	G2
Upper Affcot	Shrops	39	J5
Upper Arley	Worcs	39	N6
Upper Badcall	Highld	108	D7
Upper Basildon	W Berk	19	P5
Upper Beeding	W Susx	11	K7
Upper Benefield	Nhants	42	E11
Upper Bentley	Worcs	30	C2
Upper Bighouse	Highld	109	Q4
Upper Boddington	Nhants	31	L4
Upper Brailes	Warwks	30	H6
Upper Broadheath	Worcs	39	P10
Upper Broughton	Notts	41	P3
Upper Bucklebury	W Berk	19	P7
Upper Burgate	Hants	8	H4
Upperby	Cumb	71	N5
Upper Caldecote	C Beds	32	G7
Upper Chapel	Powys	27	L1
Upper Chicksgrove	Wilts	8	E2
Upper Chute	Wilts	19	K9
Upper Clapton	Gt Lon	21	M6
Upper Clatford	Hants	19	L11
Upper Cound	Shrops	39	K2
Upper Cumberworth	Kirk	58	G11
Upper Dallachy	Moray	101	M3
Upper Deal	Kent	23	Q11
Upper Dean	Bed	32	F4
Upper Denby	Kirk	58	G11
Upper Dicker	E Susx	11	P7
Upper Dounreay	Highld	110	B3
Upper Dovercourt	Essex	35	K9
Upper Drumbane	Stirlg	85	J2
Upper Dunsforth	N York	59	K2
Upper Eashing	Surrey	10	F2
Upper Eathie	Highld	107	M9
Upper Egleton	Herefs	39	M12
Upper Elkstone	Staffs	50	D8
Upper Ellastone	Staffs	50	E11
Upper Farringdon	Hants	10	B3
Upper Framilode	Gloucs	29	K6
Upper Froyle	Hants	10	C2
Upperglen	Highld	104	D11
Upper Godney	Somset	17	L7
Upper Gravenhurst	C Beds	32	G8
Upper Green	W Berk	19	L7
Upper Grove Common	Herefs	28	G4
Upper Hale	Surrey	10	D1

Place	Location	Page	Grid
Upper Halliford	Surrey	20	H9
Upper Hambleton	Rutlnd	42	C8
Upper Harbledown	Kent	23	L10
Upper Hartfield	E Susx	11	P3
Upper Hatherley	Gloucs	29	M5
Upper Heaton	Kirk	58	F9
Upper Helmsley	N York	59	P3
Upper Hergest	Herefs	38	F10
Upper Heyford	Nhants	31	P3
Upper Heyford	Oxon	31	L8
Upper Hill	Herefs	39	J10
Upper Hopton	Kirk	58	G9
Upper Hulme	Staffs	50	D8
Upper Inglesham	Swindn	18	H2
Upper Killay	Swans	26	D9
Upper Kinchrackine	Ag & B	90	G10
Upper Knockando	Moray	101	J6
Upper Lambourn	W Berk	19	K5
Upper Landywood	Staffs	40	C6
Upper Langford	N Som	17	L4
Upper Langwith	Derbys	51	L6
Upper Largo	Fife	87	J2
Upper Leigh	Staffs	50	D12
Upper Lochton	Abers	95	L3
Upper Longdon	Staffs	40	D5
Upper Lybster	Highld	110	F8
Upper Lydbrook	Gloucs	28	H6
Upper Lye	Herefs	38	H8
Uppermill	Oldham	58	C11
Upper Milton	Worcs	39	P7
Upper Minety	Wilts	18	E3
Upper Mulben	Moray	101	L5
Upper Netchwood	Shrops	39	L4
Upper Nobut	Staffs	40	D1
Upper Norwood	W Susx	10	F6
Upper Oddington	Gloucs	30	G8
Upper Poppleton	C York	59	M4
Upper Ratley	Hants	9	K3
Upper Rissington	Gloucs	30	G9
Upper Rochford	Worcs	39	L8
Upper Ruscoe	D & G	69	N6
Upper Sapey	Herefs	39	M8
Upper Seagry	Wilts	18	D5
Upper Shelton	C Beds	32	E7
Upper Sheringham	Norfk	45	J2
Upper Skelmorlie	N Ayrs	84	D9
Upper Slaughter	Gloucs	30	F9
Upper Soudley	Gloucs	28	H6
Upper Standen	Kent	13	N3
Upper Stoke	Norfk	45	L9
Upper Stondon	C Beds	32	G9
Upper Stowe	Nhants	31	N3
Upper Street	Hants	8	H4
Upper Street	Norfk	45	M6
Upper Street	Norfk	45	M6
Upper Street	Suffk	34	C6
Upper Street	Suffk	34	H6
Upper Sundon	C Beds	32	F10
Upper Swell	Gloucs	30	F8
Upper Tean	Staffs	50	D11
Upperthong	Kirk	58	F11
Upperton	W Susx	10	F5
Upper Town	Herefs	39	L11
Uppertown	Highld	110	G1
Upper Town	N Som	17	M3
Upper Town	Suffk	34	F4
Upper Tumble	Carmth	26	D6
Upper Tysoe	Warwks	31	J5
Upper Victoria	Angus	93	P8
Upper Wardington	Oxon	31	L5
Upper Welland	Worcs	29	K1
Upper Wellingham	E Susx	11	N7
Upper Weybread	Suffk	35	K2
Upper Wield	Hants	19	Q11
Upper Winchendon	Bucks	31	Q10
Upper Woodford	Wilts	18	G12
Upper Wraxall	Wilts	18	B6
Uppingham	Rutlnd	42	C9
Uppington	Shrops	39	L1
Upsall	N York	66	C9
Upsettlington	Border	81	J5
Upshire	Essex	21	N4
Up Somborne	Hants	9	L2
Upstreet	Kent	23	N10
Upton	Bucks	31	Q10
Upton	C Pete	42	G9
Upton	Cambs	32	H2
Upton	Ches W	48	H2
Upton	Cnwll	4	G6
Upton	Devon	5	N10
Upton	Devon	6	E13
Upton	Dorset	7	Q6
Upton	Dorset	8	E8
Upton	Halton	57	J10
Upton	Hants	9	L4
Upton	Hants	19	L9
Upton	Leics	41	J7
Upton	Lincs	52	C6
Upton	Norfk	45	N7
Upton	Notts	51	Q5
Upton	Notts	51	Q8
Upton	Oxon	19	N4
Upton	Slough	20	F7
Upton	Somset	16	D9
Upton	Somset	17	L10
Upton	Wakefd	59	L10
Upton	Wirral	56	F10
Upton Bishop	Herefs	28	H4
Upton Cheyney	S Glos	17	Q3
Upton Cressett	Shrops	39	M4
Upton Grey	Hants	10	B1
Upton Hellions	Devon	15	P10
Upton Lovell	Wilts	18	D11
Upton Magna	Shrops	49	K11
Upton Noble	Somset	17	Q8
Upton Pyne	Devon	6	C3
Upton St Leonards	Gloucs	29	M6
Upton Scudamore	Wilts	18	C10
Upton Snodsbury	Worcs	30	C4
Upton-upon-Severn	Worcs	29	M1
Upton Warren	Worcs	30	B1
Upwaltham	W Susx	10	F7
Upwell	Norfk	43	N9
Upwood	Cambs	43	J12
Urchfont	Wilts	18	F8
Urmston	Traffd	57	P9
Urquhart	Moray	101	K3
Urquhart Castle	Highld	98	G4
Urra	N York	66	E6
Urray	Highld	106	H10
Uryside	Abers	102	G10
Usan	Angus	95	M10
Ushaw Moor	Dur	73	M11

Usk Mons 28 D8
Usselby Lincs 52 F5
Usworth Sundld 73 N8
Utkinton Ches W 49 K3
Utley C Brad 58 D5
Uton Devon 15 P11
Utterby Lincs 53 K5
Uttoxeter Staffs 40 E2
Uxbridge Gt Lon 20 G6
Uyeasound Shet 111 m2
Uzmaston Pembks 24 G6

V

Vale Guern 6 c1
Valley IoA 54 D6
Valtos Highld 104 G9
Valtos W Isls 111 c2
Vange Essex 22 E6
Vatsetter Shet 111 k2
Vatten Highld 96 C2
Vaynor Myr Td 27 L6
Veensgarth Shet 111 k4
Velindre Powys 27 P2
Venngreen Devon 14 G9
Venn Ottery Devon 6 E5
Ventnor IoW 9 P11
Venton Devon 5 M8
Vernham Dean Hants 19 K9
Vernham Street Hants 19 L8
Verwood Dorset 8 G5
Veryan Cnwll 3 K7
Vickerstown Cumb 62 E8
Victoria Cnwll 3 L4
Vidlin Shet 111 k3
Viewfield Moray 101 K3
Viewpark N Lans 85 M10
Vigo Kent 22 D10
Village de Putron Guern 6 c2
Vines Cross E Susx 12 C6
Virginia Water Surrey 20 G9
Virginstow Devon 4 H2
Vobster Somset 17 Q6
Voe Shet 111 k3
Vowchurch Herefs 28 D2

W

Waberthwaite Cumb 62 C4
Wackerfield Dur 65 K3
Wacton Norfk 45 K10
Wadborough Worcs 30 B5
Waddesdon Bucks 31 Q10
Waddesdon Manor Bucks 31 Q10
Waddeton Devon 6 B10
Waddingham Lincs 52 E4
Waddington Lancs 63 N12
Waddington Lincs 52 D9
Waddon Gt Lon 21 L9
Wadebridge Cnwll 3 L2
Wadeford Somset 7 J1
Wadenhoe Nhants 42 E12
Wadesmill Herts 33 K12
Wadhurst E Susx 12 D4
Wadshelf Derbys 50 H6
Wadworth Donc 51 M2
Wainfleet All Saints Lincs 53 N10
Wainfleet St Mary Lincs 53 N10
Wainhouse Corner Cnwll 4 E2
Wainscott Medway 22 E9
Wainstalls Calder 58 D8
Waitby Cumb 64 D6
Waithe Lincs 53 J4
Wakefield Wakefd 59 J9
Wake Green Birm 40 E10
Wakehurst Place W Susx 11 M4
Wakerley Nhants 42 D9
Wakes Colne Essex 34 E10
Walberswick Suffk 35 P2
Walberton W Susx 10 F8
Walbutt D & G 70 C2
Walcombe Somset 17 M6
Walcot Lincs 42 F3
Walcot Shrops 49 L11
Walcot Swindn 18 H4
Walcote Leics 41 M10
Walcot Green Norfk 35 J1
Walcott Lincs 52 G11
Walcott Norfk 45 M4
Walden Stubbs N York 59 M10
Walderslade Medway 22 F10
Walderton W Susx 10 C7
Walditch Dorset 7 L4
Waldridge Dur 73 M10
Waldringfield Suffk 35 L7
Waldron E Susx 12 B6
Wales Rothm 51 L4
Wales Somset 17 N10
Walesby Lincs 52 G5
Walesby Notts 51 P6
Walford Herefs 28 G5
Walford Herefs 38 H7
Walford Heath Shrops 49 J10
Walgherton Ches E 49 M6
Walgrave Nhants 32 B3
Walkden Salfd 57 N8
Walker N u Ty 73 M7
Walkerburn Border 79 M2
Walkeringham Notts 51 Q3
Walkerith Lincs 52 B5
Walkern Herts 33 J10
Walker's Heath Birm 40 D10
Walkerton Fife 86 F3
Walkford BCP 8 H8
Walkhampton Devon 5 L6
Walkington E R Yk 60 G6
Walkley Sheff 51 J3
Walk Mill Lancs 57 Q3
Walkwood Worcs 30 D2
Wall Nthumb 72 G7
Wall Staffs 40 E6
Wallacetown S Ayrs 76 E10
Wallacetown S Ayrs 76 F6
Wallands Park E Susx 11 N7
Wallasey Wirral 56 F9
Wallasey (Kingsway) Tunnel Wirral 56 G9
Wall Heath Dudley 40 B9
Wallingford Oxon 19 P3

Wallington Gt Lon 21 L9
Wallington Hants 9 P6
Wallington Herts 33 J9
Wallington Heath Wsall 40 C6
Wallisdown BCP 8 F8
Walliswood Surrey 10 H3
Walls Shet 111 j4
Wallsend N Tyne 73 N7
Wallyford E Loth 86 H7
Walmer Kent 23 Q12
Walmer Bridge Lancs 57 J4
Walmley Birm 40 F8
Walmley Ash Birm 40 F8
Walpole Suffk 35 M2
Walpole Cross Keys Norfk 43 N6
Walpole Highway Norfk 43 N7
Walpole St Andrew Norfk 43 N6
Walpole St Peter Norfk 43 N6
Walsall Wsall 40 D7
Walsden Calder 58 C9
Walsgrave on Sowe Covtry 41 J10
Walsham le Willows Suffk 34 G3
Walshford N York 59 K4
Walsoken Norfk 43 M7
Walston S Lans 86 C12
Walsworth Herts 32 H10
Walter's Ash Bucks 20 D4
Waltham Kent 13 L1
Waltham NE Lin 53 J3
Waltham Abbey Essex 21 M4
Waltham Chase Hants 9 P4
Waltham Cross Herts 21 M4
Waltham on the Wolds Leics 42 B5
Waltham St Lawrence W & M 20 D7
Walthamstow Gt Lon 21 M5
Walton C Pete 42 H9
Walton Cumb 71 Q3
Walton Derbys 51 J7
Walton Leeds 59 K5
Walton Leics 41 N9
Walton M Keyn 32 C9
Walton Powys 38 F9
Walton Somset 17 L8
Walton Suffk 35 L9
Walton W Susx 10 D8
Walton Wakefd 59 J10
Walton Wrekin 49 L10
Walton Cardiff Gloucs 29 M3
Walton East Pembks 24 H4
Walton Highway Norfk 43 M7
Walton-in-Gordano N Som 17 K2
Walton-le-Dale Lancs 57 K4
Walton-on-Thames Surrey 20 H9
Walton-on-the-Hill Staffs 40 C4
Walton-on-the-Hill Surrey 21 K11
Walton-on-the-Naze Essex 35 L11
Walton on the Wolds Leics 41 N4
Walton-on-Trent Derbys 40 G4
Walton Park N Som 17 K2
Walton West Pembks 24 F6
Walworth Darltn 65 M4
Walworth Gt Lon 21 M7
Walwyn's Castle Pembks 24 F6
Wambrook Somset 6 H2
Wanborough Surrey 10 F2
Wanborough Swindn 18 H4
Wandsworth Gt Lon 21 K8
Wangford Suffk 35 P2
Wanlip Leics 41 N5
Wanlockhead D & G 78 E6
Wannock E Susx 12 C8
Wansford C Pete 42 F9
Wansford E R Yk 60 H3
Wanshurst Green Kent 12 F2
Wanstead Gt Lon 21 N6
Wanstrow Somset 17 Q7
Wanswell Gloucs 29 J8
Wantage Oxon 19 L3
Wappenbury Warwks 41 J12
Wappenham Nhants 31 N5
Warbleton E Susx 12 C6
Warborough Oxon 19 P3
Warboys Cambs 33 K2
Warbreck Bpool 56 G2
Warbstow Cnwll 4 F3
Warburton Traffd 57 M10
Warcop Cumb 64 D5
Warden Nthumb 72 G7
Ward End Birm 40 E9
Wardington Oxon 31 L5
Wardle Ches E 49 L4
Wardle Rochdl 58 B10
Wardley Gatesd 73 N8
Wardley Rutlnd 42 B9
Wardlow Derbys 50 F6
Wardy Hill Cambs 33 M1
Ware Herts 21 M1
Wareham Dorset 8 D9
Warehorne Kent 13 J4
Warenford Nthumb 81 N8
Wareside Herts 21 N1
Waresley Cambs 33 J6
Warfield Br For 20 E8
Warfleet Devon 6 B11
Wargrave Wokham 20 C7
Warham Norfk 44 F2
Wark Nthumb 72 F5
Wark Nthumb 80 H6
Warkleigh Devon 15 L7
Warkton Nhants 32 C2
Warkworth Nhants 31 L6
Warkworth Nthumb 81 P11
Warlaby N York 65 N8
Warleggan Cnwll 4 E6
Warley Town Calder 58 D8
Warlingham Surrey 21 M10
Warmfield Wakefd 59 J9
Warmingham Ches E 49 N4
Warmington Nhants 42 F11
Warmington Warwks 31 K5
Warminster Wilts 18 C10
Warmley S Glos 17 P2
Warmsworth Donc 51 M1
Warmwell Dorset 7 Q5
Warner Bros. Studio Tour Herts 20 H4
Warnford Hants 9 Q3
Warnham W Susx 11 J4
Warningcamp W Susx 10 G8
Warninglid W Susx 11 K5
Warren Ches E 50 B6
Warren Pembks 24 G8
Warrenhill S Lans 78 F2

Warren Row W & M 20 D7
Warren Street Kent 22 H11
Warrington M Keyn 32 C6
Warrington Warrtn 57 L10
Warriston C Edin 86 F7
Warsash Hants 9 N6
Warslow Staffs 50 E8
Warter E R Yk 60 E4
Warthermaske N York 65 L10
Warthill N York 59 P3
Wartling E Susx 12 D8
Wartnaby Leics 41 P3
Warton Lancs 56 H3
Warton Lancs 63 J7
Warton Warwks 40 H6
Warwick Warwks 30 H2
Warwick Bridge Cumb 71 P4
Warwick Castle Warwks 30 H2
Warwick Services Warwks 31 J3
Wasbister Ork 111 h1
Wasdale Head Cumb 62 E1
Washaway Cnwll 3 M2
Washbourne Devon 5 Q8
Washbrook Suffk 35 J8
Washfield Devon 16 C11
Washford Somset 16 E7
Washford Pyne Devon 15 N9
Washingborough Lincs 52 E8
Washington Sundld 73 N9
Washington W Susx 10 H7
Washington Services Gatesd 73 M9
Washwood Heath Birm 40 E9
Wasperton Warwks 30 H3
Wass N York 66 D10
Wast Water Cumb 62 D2
Watchet Somset 16 E7
Watchfield Oxon 19 J3
Watchgate Cumb 63 K3
Water Devon 5 P4
Waterbeach Cambs 33 M4
Waterbeach W Susx 10 E8
Waterbeck D & G 79 L12
Water End E R Yk 60 D6
Waterfall Staffs 50 E9
Waterfoot Ag & B 75 M5
Waterfoot E Rens 85 J11
Waterfoot Lancs 57 Q5
Waterford Herts 21 L1
Waterheads Border 86 F11
Waterhouses Staffs 50 E10
Wateringbury Kent 22 E11
Waterloo Highld 97 J5
Waterloo N Lans 85 N11
Waterloo P & K 92 F8
Waterloo Pembks 24 G7
Waterloo Sefton 56 G8
Waterlooville Hants 10 B7
Watermead Bucks 20 D1
Watermillock Cumb 71 P10
Water Newton Cambs 42 G10
Water Orton Warwks 40 F8
Waterperry Oxon 31 N11
Waterrow Somset 16 E10
Watersfield W Susx 10 G6
Waterside Bl w D 57 N4
Waterside E Ayrs 76 G9
Waterside E Ayrs 76 H3
Waterside E Duns 85 L8
Waterstein Highld 104 A11
Waterstock Oxon 31 N11
Waterston Pembks 24 G7
Water Stratford Bucks 31 P7
Waters Upton Wrekin 49 L10
Watford Herts 20 H4
Watford Nhants 31 N1
Watford Gap Services Nhants 31 N1
Wath N York 58 F1
Wath N York 65 N11
Wath upon Dearne Rothm 51 K1
Watlington Norfk 43 P7
Watlington Oxon 20 B5
Watten Highld 110 F5
Wattisfield Suffk 34 G2
Wattisham Suffk 34 G6
Watton Dorset 7 L4
Watton E R Yk 60 H4
Watton Norfk 44 F9
Watton-at-Stone Herts 33 K11
Wattston N Lans 85 N8
Wattsville Caerph 27 P9
Waulkmill Abers 95 K4
Waunarlwydd Swans 26 E9
Waunfawr Cerdgn 37 K4
Waunfawr Gwynd 54 G9
Wavendon M Keyn 32 C8
Waverbridge Cumb 71 K6
Waverton Ches W 49 J3
Waverton Cumb 71 K6
Wawne E R Yk 61 J6
Waxham Norfk 45 P5
Wayford Somset 7 K2
Waytown Dorset 7 L4
Way Village Devon 15 Q9
Weacombe Somset 16 F7
Weald Oxon 19 K1
Wealdstone Gt Lon 21 J5
Weardley Leeds 58 H5
Weare Somset 17 K5
Weare Giffard Devon 14 H7
Wearhead Dur 72 F11
Wearne Somset 17 K9
Weasenham All Saints Norfk 44 E6
Weasenham St Peter Norfk 44 E5
Weaste Salfd 57 P8
Weaverham Ches W 49 L1
Weaverthorpe N York 67 L12
Webheath Worcs 30 D2
Wedderlairs Abers 102 H8
Weddington Warwks 41 J8
Wedhampton Wilts 18 F8
Wedmore Somset 17 L6
Wednesbury Sandw 40 C8
Wednesfield Wolves 40 C7
Weedon Bucks 32 B12
Weedon Bec Nhants 31 N3
Weedon Lois Nhants 31 N5
Weeford Staffs 40 F6
Weeke Hants 9 M2
Weekley Nhants 32 C1
Week St Mary Cnwll 4 E11
Weel E R Yk 60 H6
Weeley Essex 35 J11
Weeley Heath Essex 35 J11

Weem P & K 92 C6
Weethley Warwks 30 D3
Weeting Norfk 44 C11
Weeton E R Yk 61 N9
Weeton Lancs 56 H2
Weeton N York 58 H5
Weetwood Leeds 58 H6
Weir Lancs 57 Q4
Weir Quay Devon 5 J7
Weisdale Shet 111 k4
Welborne Norfk 44 H7
Welbourn Lincs 52 D11
Welburn N York 60 C1
Welbury N York 65 P7
Welby Lincs 42 D3
Welcombe Devon 14 E8
Weldon Nhants 42 D11
Welford Nhants 41 N10
Welford W Berk 19 L6
Welford-on-Avon Warwks 30 F4
Welham Leics 41 Q8
Welham Notts 51 Q5
Welham Green Herts 21 K3
Well Hants 10 C2
Well Lincs 53 M8
Well N York 65 M10
Welland Worcs 29 L2
Wellbank Angus 93 N8
Wellesbourne Warwks 30 H3
Well Head Herts 32 H10
Welling Gt Lon 21 P8
Wellingborough Nhants 32 C3
Wellingham Norfk 44 E6
Wellingore Lincs 52 E11
Wellington Cumb 62 C2
Wellington Herefs 39 J11
Wellington Somset 16 F11
Wellington Wrekin 49 M12
Wellington Heath Herefs 29 J1
Wellow BaNES 17 Q5
Wellow IoW 9 L9
Wellow Notts 51 P7
Wells Somset 17 M7
Wells-next-the-Sea Norfk 44 F2
Wellstye Green Essex 33 Q11
Welltree P & K 92 E10
Wellwood Fife 86 C5
Welney Norfk 43 N10
Welshampton Shrops 48 H8
Welsh Frankton Shrops 48 G8
Welsh Newton Herefs 28 F5
Welshpool Powys 38 E1
Welsh St Donats V Glam 16 D2
Welton Cumb 71 M6
Welton E R Yk 60 G8
Welton Lincs 52 E7
Welton Nhants 31 N2
Welton le Marsh Lincs 53 M9
Welton le Wold Lincs 53 J6
Welwick E R Yk 61 N9
Welwyn Herts 33 H12
Welwyn Garden City Herts 21 K2
Wem Shrops 49 K9
Wembdon Somset 16 H8
Wembley Gt Lon 21 J6
Wembury Devon 5 L9
Wembworthy Devon 15 L9
Wemyss Bay Inver 84 D8
Wendens Ambo Essex 33 N9
Wendlebury Oxon 31 M9
Wendling Norfk 44 F7
Wendover Bucks 20 D2
Wendron Cnwll 2 G9
Wendron Mining District Cnwll 2 G8
Wendy Cambs 33 K7
Wenhaston Suffk 35 N2
Wennington Cambs 33 J2
Wennington Gt Lon 22 B7
Wennington Lancs 63 L8
Wensley Derbys 50 H8
Wensley N York 65 J9
Wentbridge Wakefd 59 L10
Wentnor Shrops 38 H4
Wentworth Cambs 33 M2
Wentworth Rothm 51 J2
Wenvoe V Glam 16 F2
Weobley Herefs 38 H10
Wepham W Susx 10 G8
Wereham Norfk 43 P9
Werrington C Pete 42 G9
Werrington Cnwll 4 H3
Wervin Ches W 48 H2
Wesham Lancs 56 H3
Wessington Derbys 51 J8
West Acre Norfk 44 C7
West Alvington Devon 5 P10
West Anstey Devon 15 P6
West Ashby Lincs 53 J8
West Ashling W Susx 10 D8
West Ashton Wilts 18 C9
West Auckland Dur 65 L3
West Ayton N York 67 L9
West Bagborough Somset 16 G9
West Bank Halton 57 K11
West Barkwith Lincs 52 G7
West Barnby N York 66 H5
West Barns E Loth 87 M6
West Barsham Norfk 44 E4
West Bay Dorset 7 L5
West Beckham Norfk 45 J3
West Bedfont Surrey 20 H8
Westbere Kent 23 M10
West Bergholt Essex 34 F10
West Bexington Dorset 7 M5
West Bilney Norfk 44 B7
West Blatchington Br & H 11 L8
West Boldon S Tyne 73 P8
Westborough Lincs 42 C2
Westbourne BCP 8 F8
Westbourne W Susx 10 C8
West Bowling C Brad 58 F7
West Bradenham Norfk 44 F8
West Bradford Lancs 63 N12
West Bradley Somset 17 M8
West Bretton Wakefd 58 H10
West Bridgford Notts 51 N12
West Bromwich Sandw 40 D8
Westbrook Kent 23 Q8
Westbrook W Berk 19 M6
West Buckland Devon 15 L6
West Buckland Somset 16 G11
West Burrafirth Shet 111 j4

West Burton N York 64 H9
Westbury Bucks 31 N7
Westbury Shrops 38 G1
Westbury Wilts 18 C9
Westbury Leigh Wilts 18 C10
Westbury-on-Severn Gloucs 29 J6
Westbury-on-Trym Bristl 28 G12
Westbury-sub-Mendip Somset 17 M6
West Butterwick N Linc 52 B3
Westby Lancs 56 H3
West Byfleet Surrey 20 G10
West Cairngaan D & G 68 F10
West Caister Norfk 45 Q7
West Calder W Loth 86 B9
West Camel Somset 17 N10
West Chaldon Dorset 8 B10
West Challow Oxon 19 L3
West Charleton Devon 5 P10
West Chiltington W Susx 10 H6
West Chinnock Somset 17 L12
West Clandon Surrey 20 G11
West Cliffe Kent 13 Q2
West Coker Somset 17 M12
Westcombe Somset 17 N7
West Compton Somset 17 N7
West Compton Abbas Dorset 7 N4
Westcote Gloucs 30 G9
Westcote Barton Oxon 31 K8
Westcott Bucks 31 Q10
Westcott Devon 6 D2
Westcott Surrey 11 J2
West Cottingwith N York 59 P6
Westcourt Wilts 19 J8
West Cowick E R Yk 59 P9
West Cross Swans 26 E10
West Curthwaite Cumb 71 M6
West Dean W Susx 10 D7
West Dean Wilts 9 J3
West Deeping Lincs 42 G8
West Derby Lpool 56 H9
West Dereham Norfk 43 P8
West Down Devon 15 J4
Westdowns Cnwll 4 C4
West Drayton Gt Lon 20 G7
West Drayton Notts 51 P6
West Dunnet Highld 110 E2
West Ella E R Yk 60 H8
West End Bed 32 E4
West End Hants 9 M5
West End N Som 17 L3
West End Norfk 45 Q7
West End Surrey 20 F10
West End Surrey 20 H10
West End Wilts 8 E3
West End Green Hants 19 Q8
Wester Aberchalder Highld 98 H5
Westerdale Highld 110 D5
Westerdale N York 66 F6
Westerfield Suffk 35 K7
Westergate W Susx 10 F8
Westerham Kent 21 N11
Westerhope N u Ty 73 L7
Westerland Devon 6 B9
Westerleigh S Glos 29 J11
Western Isles W Isls 111 c3
Wester Ochiltree W Loth 86 B7
Wester Pitkierie Fife 87 K2
Wester Ross Highld 105 L3
Westerton of Rossie Angus 93 R5
Westerwick Shet 111 j4
West Farleigh Kent 22 E11
West Farndon Nhants 31 M4
West Felton Shrops 48 G9
Westfield BaNES 17 P5
Westfield Cumb 70 G9
Westfield E Susx 12 F7
Westfield Highld 110 C3
Westfield N Lans 85 M8
Westfield Norfk 44 G8
Westfield Surrey 20 G11
Westfield W Loth 85 Q8
Westfields Herefs 28 F1
Westfields of Rattray P & K 92 H6
Westgate Dur 72 G12
Westgate N Linc 60 D11
Westgate-on-Sea Kent 23 N8
West Grafton Wilts 19 J8
West Green Hants 20 C11
West Grimstead Wilts 8 H3
West Grinstead W Susx 11 J5
West Haddlesey N York 59 M8
West Haddon Nhants 41 N12
West Hagbourne Oxon 19 N3
West Hagley Worcs 40 B10
Westhall Suffk 35 N1
West Hallam Derbys 51 K11
West Halton N Linc 60 F9
Westham Dorset 7 P7
West Ham Gt Lon 21 N6
Westham Somset 17 K6
Westhampnett W Susx 10 E8
West Handley Derbys 51 K5
West Hanney Oxon 19 L3
West Hanningfield Essex 22 E4
West Harnham Wilts 8 G2
West Harptree BaNES 17 M5
West Harting W Susx 10 C6
West Hatch Somset 16 H11
West Hatch Wilts 8 D2
West Haven Angus 93 P8
Westhay Somset 17 L7
West Heath Birm 40 D11
West Helmsdale Highld 110 B11
West Hendred Oxon 19 M3
West Heslerton N York 67 K11
West Hewish N Som 17 K4
Westhide Herefs 39 L12
Westhill Abers 95 N1
West Hill Devon 6 E4
Westhill Highld 107 L3
West Hoathly W Susx 11 M4
West Holme Dorset 8 D9
Westhope Herefs 39 J11
Westhope Shrops 39 J5
West Horndon Essex 22 D5
Westhorpe Lincs 42 H4
Westhorpe Suffk 34 G4
West Horrington Somset 17 N6
West Horsley Surrey 20 H11

West Hougham Kent 13 N3
Westhoughton Bolton 57 M7
Westhouse N York 63 M7
Westhouses Derbys 51 K8
West Howe BCP 8 F8
Westhumble Surrey 21 J11
West Huntingtower P & K 92 G10
West Huntspill Somset 17 J7
West Hythe Kent 13 L3
West Ilsley W Berk 19 M4
West Itchenor W Susx 10 C9
West Kennett Wilts 18 G7
West Kilbride N Ayrs 76 D2
West Kingsdown Kent 22 C10
West Kington Wilts 18 B5
West Kirby Wirral 56 E10
West Knapton N York 67 J11
West Knighton Dorset 7 Q5
West Knoyle Wilts 8 C2
Westlake Devon 5 M9
West Lambrook Somset 17 K11
West Langdon Kent 13 P1
West Lavington W Susx 10 E6
West Lavington Wilts 18 E9
West Layton N York 65 K5
West Leake Notts 41 M3
Westleigh Devon 14 H6
Westleigh Devon 16 E11
West Leigh Somset 16 F9
Westleton Suffk 35 P3
West Lexham Norfk 44 D6
Westley Suffk 34 D4
Westley Waterless Cambs 33 P5
West Lilling N York 59 P2
Westlington Bucks 31 Q11
West Linton Border 86 D10
Westlinton Cumb 71 N3
West Littleton S Glos 18 B5
West Lockinge Oxon 19 M4
West Lulworth Dorset 8 B10
West Lutton N York 60 F1
West Lydford Somset 17 N9
West Lyng Somset 17 J9
West Lynn Norfk 43 P6
West Malling Kent 22 D10
West Malvern Worcs 39 N11
West Marden W Susx 10 C7
West Markham Notts 51 Q6
Westmarsh Kent 23 P10
West Marsh NE Lin 61 L11
West Marton N York 58 B4
West Melbury Dorset 8 C4
West Meon Hants 9 Q3
West Mersea Essex 23 J2
Westmeston E Susx 11 M7
West Midland Safari Park Worcs 39 P7
Westmill Herts 33 K10
West Milton Dorset 7 M4
Westminster Gt Lon 21 L7
Westminster Abbey & Palace Gt Lon 21 L7
West Molesey Surrey 21 J9
West Monkton Somset 16 H9
West Moors Dorset 8 F6
West Morden Dorset 8 D8
West Morriston Border 80 E6
West Mudford Somset 17 N11
Westmuir Angus 93 L5
West Ness N York 66 F10
Westnewton Cumb 71 J6
West Newton E R Yk 61 L6
West Newton Norfk 44 B5
West Newton Somset 16 H9
West Norwood Gt Lon 21 L8
Westoe S Tyne 73 P7
West Ogwell Devon 5 Q6
Weston BaNES 17 Q3
Weston Ches E 49 M4
Weston Devon 6 F3
Weston Devon 6 F5
Weston Hants 10 B6
Weston Herts 33 J10
Weston Lincs 43 J5
Weston N York 58 F5
Weston Nhants 31 N5
Weston Notts 51 Q7
Weston Shrops 39 L4
Weston Shrops 48 F9
Weston Staffs 40 C3
Weston W Berk 19 L6
Weston Beggard Herefs 28 G1
Westonbirt Gloucs 18 C3
Weston by Welland Nhants 41 Q8
Weston Colville Cambs 33 P6
Weston Corbett Hants 10 B1
Weston Coyney C Stke 50 C11
Weston Favell Nhants 32 B4
Weston Green Cambs 33 P6
Weston Heath Shrops 49 P11
Westoning C Beds 32 E9
Weston-in-Gordano N Som 17 L2
Weston Jones Staffs 49 N10
Weston Longville Norfk 45 J7
Weston Lullingfields Shrops 48 H9
Weston-on-the-Green Oxon 31 M9
Weston Park Staffs 49 P12
Weston Patrick Hants 10 B1
Weston Rhyn Shrops 48 F8
Weston-sub-Edge Gloucs 30 E6
Weston-super-Mare N Som 17 J4
Weston Turville Bucks 20 D2
Weston-under-Lizard Staffs 49 P12
Weston under Penyard Herefs 28 H4
Weston-under-Redcastle Shrops 49 K9
Weston under Wetherley Warwks 41 J12
Weston Underwood Derbys 50 H11
Weston Underwood M Keyn 32 C6
Weston-upon-Trent Derbys 41 K2
Westonzoyland Somset 17 J8
West Orchard Dorset 8 B4
West Overton Wilts 18 G7
Westow N York 60 D2
West Park Abers 95 N3
West Parley Dorset 8 G7
West Peckham Kent 22 D11
West Pelton Dur 73 M9
West Pennard Somset 17 M8
West Pentire Cnwll 2 H4
West Porlock Somset 15 P3

Westport Somset 17 K11
West Putford Devon 14 G8
West Quantoxhead Somset 16 F7
Westquarter Falk 85 Q7
West Rainton Dur 73 N10
West Rasen Lincs 52 F5
Westray Ork 111 h1
Westray Airport Ork 111 h1
West Raynham Norfk 44 E5
Westrigg W Loth 85 Q9
Westrop Swindn 18 H3
West Rounton N York 65 P6
West Row Suffk 34 B3
West Rudham Norfk 44 D5
West Runton Norfk 45 K2
Westruther Border 80 E4
West Saltoun E Loth 87 J8
West Sandford Devon 15 N10
West Sandwick Shet 111 k3
West Scrafton N York 65 J10
West Stafford Dorset 7 Q5
West Stockwith Notts 52 B5
West Stoke W Susx 10 D8
West Stour Dorset 8 B3
West Stourmouth Kent 23 N10
West Stow Suffk 34 D3
West Stowell Wilts 18 G8
West Street Suffk 34 G3
West Tanfield N York 65 M10
West Taphouse Cnwll 4 E7
West Tarbert Ag & B 83 M9
West Tarring W Susx 10 H8
West Thirston Nthumb 73 L2
West Thorney W Susx 10 C9
West Thorpe Notts 41 N3
West Thurrock Thurr 22 C7
West Tilbury Thurr 22 D7
West Tisted Hants 9 Q2
West Torrington Lincs 52 G7
West Town Hants 10 B9
West Town N Som 17 L3
West Tytherley Hants 9 J2
West Walton Norfk 43 M7
Westward Cumb 71 L6
Westward Ho! Devon 14 H6
Westwell Kent 13 J1
Westwell Oxon 30 G11
Westwell Leacon Kent 13 J1
West Wellow Hants 9 K4
West Wembury Devon 5 L9
West Wemyss Fife 86 G4
Westwick Cambs 33 L4
West Wickham Cambs 33 P6
West Wickham Gt Lon 21 M9
West Williamston Pembks 24 H7
West Winch Norfk 43 Q6
West Winterslow Wilts 9 J2
West Wittering W Susx 10 C9
West Witton N York 65 J9
Westwood Devon 6 D3
Westwood Kent 23 Q9
Westwood Wilts 18 B8
West Woodburn Nthumb 72 F4
West Woodhay W Berk 19 L8
Westwoodside N Linc 51 Q2
West Worldham Hants 10 C3
West Worthing W Susx 11 J9
West Wratting Cambs 33 P6
West Wylam Nthumb 73 K8
Wetheral Cumb 71 P5
Wetherby Leeds 59 K5
Wetherby Services N York 59 K4
Wetherden Suffk 34 G4
Wetheringsett Suffk 35 J4
Wethersfield Essex 34 B9
Wetherup Street Suffk 35 J4
Wetley Rocks Staffs 50 C10
Wettenhall Ches E 49 L4
Wetton Staffs 50 E9
Wetwang E R Yk 60 F3
Wetwood Staffs 49 P8
Wexcombe Wilts 19 J8
Weybourne Norfk 45 J2
Weybourne Surrey 10 D1
Weybread Suffk 35 L1
Weybread Street Suffk 35 L2
Weybridge Surrey 20 H9
Weycroft Devon 7 J3
Weydale Highld 110 E3
Weyhill Hants 19 K10
Weymouth Dorset 7 Q7
Whaddon Bucks 32 B9
Whaddon Cambs 33 K7
Whaddon Gloucs 29 L6
Whaddon Wilts 8 H3
Whaddon Wilts 18 C8
Whaley Derbys 51 L6
Whaley Bridge Derbys 50 D5
Whaley Thorns Derbys 51 M6
Whaligoe Highld 110 G6
Whalley Lancs 57 N2
Whalsay Shet 111 m3
Whalton Nthumb 73 K5
Whaplode Lincs 43 K6
Whaplode Drove Lincs 43 K7
Wharf Warwks 31 K4
Wharfe N York 63 P8
Wharles Lancs 57 J2
Wharley End C Beds 32 D7
Wharncliffe Side Sheff 50 H2
Wharram-le-Street N York 60 E2
Wharton Ches W 49 M3
Wharton Herefs 39 J10
Whashton N York 65 K6
Whasset Cumb 63 K6
Whatcote Warwks 30 H5
Whateley Warwks 40 G7
Whatfield Suffk 34 G7
Whatley Somset 7 J2
Whatley Somset 17 Q6
Whatley's End S Glos 28 H11
Whatlington E Susx 12 F6
Whatton-in-the-Vale Notts 51 Q11
Whauphill D & G 69 K8
Wheal Peevor Cnwll 2 G6
Wheatacre Norfk 45 P10
Wheathampstead Herts 21 J1
Wheatley Hants 10 C3
Wheatley Oxon 31 N11
Wheatley Hill Dur 73 P11
Wheatley Hills Donc 59 N12
Wheaton Aston Staffs 49 Q11

Wheddon Cross Somset 16 C8
Wheeler's Green Wokham 20 C8
Wheelock Ches E 49 N4
Wheelton Lancs 57 L5
Wheldrake C York 59 P5
Whelford Gloucs 18 H2
Whelpley Hill Bucks 20 F3
Whempstead Herts 33 K11
Whenby N York 66 E12
Whepstead Suffk 34 D5
Wherstead Suffk 35 J8
Wherwell Hants 19 L11
Wheston Derbys 50 F5
Whetsted Kent 12 D2
Whetstone Gt Lon 21 L5
Whetstone Leics 41 M7
Whicham Cumb 62 D6
Whichford Warwks 30 H7
Whickham Gatesd 73 L8
Whiddon Down Devon 5 N2
Whigstreet Angus 93 N6
Whilton Nhants 31 N2
Whimple Devon 6 E4
Whimpwell Green Norfk 45 N4
Whinburgh Norfk 44 G8
Whinnieliggate D & G 70 B5
Whinnyfold Abers 103 M8
Whippingham IoW 9 N8
Whipsnade C Beds 32 E12
Whipsnade Zoo ZSL C Beds 32 E12
Whipton Devon 6 C4
Whisby Lincs 52 C9
Whissendine Rutlnd 42 B7
Whissonsett Norfk 44 F5
Whistlefield Ag & B 84 D4
Whistlefield Inn Ag & B 84 C5
Whistley Green Wokham 20 C8
Whiston Knows 57 J9
Whiston Nhants 32 C5
Whiston Rothm 51 K3
Whiston Staffs 40 B5
Whiston Staffs 50 D10
Whitbeck Cumb 62 D5
Whitbourne Herefs 39 N10
Whitburn S Tyne 73 P8
Whitburn W Loth 85 Q9
Whitby Ches W 48 H1
Whitby N York 67 J5
Whitchester Border 87 N9
Whitchurch BaNES 17 N3
Whitchurch Bucks 32 B11
Whitchurch Cardif 27 N11
Whitchurch Devon 5 K5
Whitchurch Hants 19 M10
Whitchurch Herefs 28 G5
Whitchurch Oxon 19 Q5
Whitchurch Pembks 24 D4
Whitchurch Shrops 49 K7
Whitchurch Canonicorum Dorset 7 K4
Whitchurch Hill Oxon 19 Q5
Whitcombe Dorset 7 Q5
Whitcot Shrops 38 H4
Whitcott Keysett Shrops 38 F5
Whiteacre Heath Warwks 40 G8
White Ball Somset 16 E11
Whitebridge Highld 98 G6
Whitebrook Mons 28 G7
Whitebushes Surrey 11 L1
Whitecairns Abers 103 J10
Whitechapel Gt Lon 21 M7
White Chapel Lancs 57 K1
White Colne Essex 34 E10
Whitecraig E Loth 86 G8
Whitecrook D & G 68 F7
White Cross Cnwll 2 G10
Whitecross Falk 85 R7
Whiteface Highld 107 L5
Whitefarland N Ayrs 75 N4
Whitefaulds S Ayrs 76 E8
Whitefield Bury 57 P7
Whitefield Somset 16 E9
Whiteford Abers 102 F9
Whitegate Ches W 49 L2
Whitehall Ork 111 i2
Whitehaven Cumb 70 F11
Whitehill Hants 10 C4
Whitehills Abers 102 E3
Whitehouse Abers 102 E11
Whitehouse Ag & B 83 M10
Whitehouse Common Birm 40 D7
Whitekirk E Loth 87 L6
White Lackington Dorset 7 Q3
Whitelackington Somset 17 K11
White Ladies Aston Worcs 30 B4
Whiteleaf Bucks 20 D3
Whiteley Hants 9 N5
Whiteley Bank IoW 9 P10
Whitemire Moray 100 F5
Whitemoor C Nott 51 M11
Whitemoor Cnwll 3 L4
Whiteness Shet 111 k4
White Notley Essex 34 D11
Whiteparish Wilts 9 J3
White Pit Lincs 53 L7
Whiterashes Abers 102 H9
White Roding Essex 22 C1
Whiterow Highld 110 G6
Whiterow Moray 100 F4
Whiteshill Gloucs 29 L7
Whitesmith E Susx 11 Q7
Whitestaunton Somset 6 H1
Whitestone Warwks 41 J9
Whitestone Cross Devon 5 B4
White Waltham W & M 20 D7
Whitewell Lancs 63 M11
Whitfield C Dund 93 M8
Whitfield Kent 13 P2
Whitfield Nhants 31 N6
Whitfield Nthumb 72 E8
Whitfield S Glos 28 J9
Whitford Devon 6 H4
Whitford Flints 56 D12
Whitgift E R Yk 60 E9
Whitgreave Staffs 49 B2
Whithorn D & G 69 L10
Whiting Bay N Ayrs 75 Q7
Whitkirk Leeds 59 J7
Whitland Carmth 25 L5
Whitlaw Border 80 C10
Whitletts S Ayrs 76 F6
Whitley N York 59 M9
Whitley Readg 20 B8
Whitley Sheff 51 J2

Whitley Wilts 18 C7
Whitley Bay N Tyne 73 N6
Whitley Chapel Nthumb 72 G8
Whitley Lower Kirk 58 G10
Whitminster Gloucs 29 K7
Whitmore Staffs 49 P7
Whitnage Devon 16 D11
Whitnash Warwks 31 J2
Whitney-on-Wye Herefs 38 F11
Whitsbury Hants 8 G4
Whitsome Border 81 J4
Whitson Newpt 28 D11
Whitstable Kent 23 L9
Whitstone Cnwll 14 E11
Whittingham Nthumb 81 M10
Whittingslow Shrops 38 H4
Whittington Derbys 51 J6
Whittington Gloucs 30 D9
Whittington Lancs 63 L7
Whittington Norfk 44 B9
Whittington Shrops 48 G9
Whittington Staffs 39 Q5
Whittington Staffs 40 F6
Whittington Warwks 40 H7
Whittington Worcs 39 Q10
Whittlebury Nhants 31 P5
Whittle-le-Woods Lancs 57 L5
Whittlesey Cambs 43 J10
Whittlesford Cambs 33 M7
Whitton N Linc 60 F8
Whitton Nthumb 73 J1
Whitton Powys 38 F8
Whitton S on T 65 P3
Whitton Shrops 39 L7
Whittonstall Nthumb 73 J9
Whitway Hants 19 M8
Whitwell Derbys 51 M5
Whitwell Herts 32 H11
Whitwell IoW 9 N10
Whitwell N York 65 M7
Whitwell Rutlnd 42 D8
Whitwell-on-the-Hill N York 60 C2
Whitwell Street Norfk 44 H6
Whitwick Leics 41 K4
Whitworth Lancs 58 B9
Whixall Shrops 49 K8
Whixley N York 59 K3
Whorlton Dur 65 K5
Whorlton N York 65 K9
Whyle Herefs 39 K9
Whyteleafe Surrey 21 M10
Wibsey C Brad 58 F7
Wibtoft Warwks 41 L9
Wichelstowe Swindn 18 G4
Wichenford Worcs 39 P9
Wichling Kent 22 H11
Wick BCP 8 H8
Wick Highld 110 G5
Wick S Glos 17 Q2
Wick V Glam 16 C2
Wick W Susx 10 G8
Wick Worcs 30 C5
Wicken Cambs 33 P3
Wicken Nhants 31 N6
Wicken Bonhunt Essex 33 N9
Wickenby Lincs 52 F7
Wicken Green Village Norfk 44 D4
Wickersley Rothm 51 L3
Wicker Street Green Suffk 34 F7
Wickford Essex 22 E5
Wickham Hants 9 N5
Wickham W Berk 19 L6
Wickham Bishops Essex 22 G2
Wickhambreaux Kent 23 N10
Wickhambrook Suffk 34 C6
Wickhamford Worcs 30 E6
Wickham Green Suffk 34 H3
Wickham Market Suffk 35 M5
Wickhampton Norfk 45 N8
Wickham St Paul Essex 34 D9
Wickham Skeith Suffk 34 H3
Wickham Street Suffk 34 H3
Wick John o' Groats Airport Highld 110 G5
Wicklewood Norfk 44 H9
Wickmere Norfk 45 J4
Wick St Lawrence N Som 17 K3
Wicksteed Park Nhants 32 C2
Wickwar S Glos 29 J10
Widdington Essex 33 N9
Widdrington Nthumb 73 M3
Widdrington Station Nthumb 73 M3
Widecombe in the Moor Devon 5 P5
Widegates Cnwll 4 G8
Widemouth Bay Cnwll 14 D10
Wide Open N Tyne 73 M6
Widford Essex 22 E3
Widford Herts 33 L12
Widmer End Bucks 20 E4
Widmerpool Notts 41 N2
Widmore Gt Lon 21 N9
Widnes Halton 57 K10
Widworthy Devon 6 G3
Wigan Wigan 57 L7
Wigborough Somset 17 L12
Wiggaton Devon 6 E4
Wiggenhall St Germans Norfk 43 P7
Wiggenhall St Mary Magdalen Norfk 43 P7
Wiggenhall St Mary the Virgin Norfk 43 P7
Wigginton C York 59 N3
Wigginton Herts 20 F2
Wigginton Oxon 31 K7
Wigginton Staffs 40 G6
Wigglesworth N York 63 P10
Wiggonby Cumb 71 L5
Wiggonholt W Susx 10 G6
Wighill N York 59 L5
Wighton Norfk 44 F3
Wightwick Wolves 39 Q3
Wigley Hants 9 K4
Wigmore Herefs 38 H8
Wigmore Medway 22 F9
Wigsley Notts 52 C9
Wigsthorpe Nhants 42 F12
Wigston Leics 41 N7
Wigston Fields Leics 41 N6
Wigston Parva Leics 41 L9
Wigthorpe Notts 51 M4
Wigtoft Lincs 43 J3
Wigton Cumb 71 L6
Wigtown D & G 69 L7
Wike Leeds 59 J5

Wilbarston Nhants 42 B11
Wilberfoss E R Yk 60 C4
Wilburton Cambs 33 M2
Wilby Nhants 32 C4
Wilby Norfk 44 G11
Wilby Suffk 35 L3
Wilcot Wilts 18 G8
Wilcott Shrops 48 H10
Wildboarclough Ches E 50 C7
Wilden Bed 32 F6
Wilden Worcs 39 P7
Wildmanbridge S Lans 85 N11
Wildmill Brdgnd 27 J11
Wildmoor Worcs 40 D11
Wildsworth Lincs 52 B4
Wilford C Nott 51 M12
Wilkesley Ches E 49 L7
Wilkhaven Highld 107 Q5
Wilkieston W Loth 86 D8
Willand Devon 6 D1
Willaston Ches E 49 M5
Willaston Ches W 56 G12
Willen M Keyn 32 C8
Willenhall Covtry 41 J11
Willenhall Wsall 40 D7
Willerby E R Yk 60 H7
Willerby N York 67 L10
Willersey Gloucs 30 E6
Willersley Herefs 38 G11
Willesborough Kent 13 K2
Willesborough Lees Kent 13 K2
Willesden Gt Lon 21 K6
Willesley Wilts 18 C3
Willett Somset 16 F9
Willey Shrops 39 M3
Willey Warwks 41 L9
Willey Green Surrey 20 F12
Williamscot Oxon 31 L5
Willian Herts 32 H9
Willingale Essex 22 C2
Willingdon E Susx 12 C9
Willingham Cambs 33 L3
Willingham by Stow Lincs 52 C6
Willingham St Mary Suffk 45 P12
Willington Bed 32 G6
Willington Derbys 40 H2
Willington Dur 65 L1
Willington Kent 22 F11
Willington N Tyne 73 N7
Willington Warwks 30 H6
Willitoft E R Yk 60 C7
Williton Somset 16 E7
Willoughby Lincs 53 M8
Willoughby Warwks 31 M1
Willoughby-on-the-Wolds Notts 41 N3
Willoughby Waterleys Leics 41 M8
Willoughton Lincs 52 D5
Willows Green Essex 34 C11
Willtown Somset 17 K10
Wilmcote Warwks 30 F3
Wilmington Devon 6 G3
Wilmington E Susx 12 B8
Wilmington Kent 22 Q8
Wilmslow Ches E 57 Q11
Wilpshire Lancs 57 M3
Wilsden C Brad 58 E6
Wilsford Lincs 42 E2
Wilsford Wilts 18 G11
Wilsford Wilts 8 G8
Wilshaw Kirk 58 E11
Wilsill N York 58 F2
Wilson Leics 41 K3
Wilsontown S Lans 85 Q11
Wilstead Bed 32 F7
Wilsthorpe Lincs 42 F7
Wilstone Herts 20 E1
Wilton Herefs 28 G4
Wilton N York 67 J10
Wilton R & Cl 66 E4
Wilton Wilts 8 G2
Wilton Wilts 19 J8
Wilton Dean Border 80 C10
Wimbish Green Essex 33 P9
Wimbledon Gt Lon 21 K8
Wimblington Cambs 43 L10
Wimboldsley Ches W 49 M3
Wimborne Minster Dorset 8 E7
Wimborne St Giles Dorset 8 F5
Wimbotsham Norfk 43 P8
Wimpole Cambs 33 K6
Wimpstone Warwks 30 G4
Wincanton Somset 17 Q9
Winchburgh W Loth 86 C7
Winchcombe Gloucs 30 D8
Winchelsea E Susx 12 H6
Winchester Hants 9 N2
Winchester Services Hants 9 N1
Winchet Hill Kent 12 E2
Winchfield Hants 20 C11
Winchmore Hill Bucks 20 E4
Winchmore Hill Gt Lon 21 L5
Wincle Ches E 50 C7
Wincobank Sheff 51 J3
Windermere Cumb 62 H3
Windermere Jetty Cumb 62 H3
Winderton Warwks 31 J6
Windhill Highld 107 J11
Windlesham Surrey 20 E9
Windmill Cnwll 3 K2
Windmill Hill E Susx 12 D7
Windmill Hill Somset 16 H11
Windrush Gloucs 30 F10
Windsole Abers 102 D4
Windsor W & M 20 F7
Windsor Castle W & M 20 F7
Windsoredge Gloucs 29 L8
Windsor Green Suffk 34 E6
Windygates Fife 86 G3
Wineham W Susx 11 K6
Winestead E R Yk 61 M8
Winfarthing Norfk 45 J11
Winford IoW 9 P9
Winford N Som 17 M3
Winforton Herefs 38 F11
Winfrith Newburgh Dorset 8 B9
Wing Bucks 32 C11
Wing Rutlnd 42 C9
Wingate Dur 73 P12
Wingerworth Derbys 51 J7
Wingfield C Beds 32 E10
Wingfield Suffk 35 K2
Wingfield Wilts 18 B9

Wingham Kent 23 N11
Wingrave Bucks 32 C11
Winkburn Notts 51 P8
Winkfield Br For 20 E8
Winkfield Row Br For 20 E8
Winkhill Staffs 50 D9
Winkleigh Devon 15 L9
Winksley N York 65 M12
Winlaton Gatesd 73 L8
Winless Highld 110 G5
Winmarleigh Lancs 63 J11
Winnall Hants 9 N2
Winnersh Wokham 20 C8
Winnington Ches W 49 M1
Winscombe N Som 17 K5
Winsford Ches W 49 M3
Winsford Somset 16 B8
Winsham Somset 7 K2
Winshill Staffs 40 H3
Winshwen Swans 26 F9
Winskill Cumb 64 B1
Winsley Wilts 18 B8
Winslow Bucks 31 Q8
Winson Gloucs 30 E11
Winsor Hants 9 K5
Winster Cumb 62 H4
Winster Derbys 50 G8
Winston Dur 65 K4
Winston Suffk 35 K5
Winstone Gloucs 29 N6
Winswell Devon 15 J9
Winterborne Came Dorset 7 Q5
Winterborne Clenston Dorset 8 C6
Winterborne Houghton Dorset 8 B6
Winterborne Kingston Dorset 8 C7
Winterborne Monkton Dorset 7 P5
Winterborne Stickland Dorset 8 C6
Winterborne Whitechurch Dorset 8 C7
Winterborne Zelston Dorset 8 D7
Winterbourne S Glos 28 H11
Winterbourne W Berk 19 M6
Winterbourne Abbas Dorset 7 N5
Winterbourne Bassett Wilts 18 G6
Winterbourne Dauntsey Wilts 8 H1
Winterbourne Earls Wilts 8 H1
Winterbourne Gunner Wilts 8 H1
Winterbourne Monkton Wilts 18 G6
Winterbourne Steepleton Dorset 7 P5
Winterbourne Stoke Wilts 18 F11
Winterburn N York 58 C3
Winteringham N Linc 60 F9
Winterley Ches E 49 N4
Winterslow Wilts 9 J2
Winterton N Linc 60 F9
Winterton-on-Sea Norfk 45 P6
Winthorpe Notts 52 B11
Winton BCP 8 G8
Winton Cumb 64 E5
Wintringham Cambs 32 H5
Wintringham N York 67 J11
Winwick Cambs 32 F1
Winwick Nhants 41 N11
Winwick Warrtn 57 L9
Wirksworth Derbys 50 H9
Wirral 56 F10
Wirswall Ches E 49 K6
Wisbech Cambs 43 M8
Wisbech St Mary Cambs 43 L8
Wisborough Green W Susx 10 G5
Wiseman's Bridge Pembks 25 K7
Wiseton Notts 51 Q3
Wishaw N Lans 85 N11
Wishaw Warwks 40 F8
Wisley Garden RHS Surrey 20 G10
Wispington Lincs 52 H8
Wissett Suffk 35 M2
Wissington Suffk 34 F9
Wistanstow Shrops 38 H5
Wistanswick Shrops 49 M9
Wistaston Ches E 49 M5
Wistaston Green Ches E 49 M5
Wiston Pembks 24 H5
Wiston S Lans 78 F3
Wiston W Susx 11 J7
Wistow Cambs 33 J1
Wistow N York 59 N7
Wiswell Lancs 57 N2
Witcham Cambs 33 M2
Witchampton Dorset 8 E6
Witchford Cambs 33 N2
Witcombe Somset 17 L10
Witham Essex 22 G1
Witham Friary Somset 17 Q7
Witham on the Hill Lincs 42 F6
Witham St Hughs Lincs 52 C10
Withcall Lincs 53 J6
Withdean Br & H 11 L8
Witherenden Hill E Susx 12 D5
Witheridge Devon 15 N8
Witherley Leics 41 J7
Withern Lincs 53 L7
Withernsea E R Yk 61 N8
Withernwick E R Yk 61 K6
Withersdale Street Suffk 35 L1
Withersfield Suffk 33 Q7
Witherslack Cumb 62 H5
Withiel Cnwll 3 M3
Withiel Florey Somset 16 D9
Withington Gloucs 30 D10
Withington Herefs 39 K12
Withington Manch 57 Q9
Withington Shrops 49 L11
Withington Staffs 40 D1
Withleigh Devon 6 B1
Withnell Lancs 57 L4
Withybed Green Worcs 40 D11
Withybrook Warwks 41 K10
Withycombe Somset 16 D7
Withyham E Susx 11 P3
Withypool Somset 15 P5
Withywood Bristl 6 N3
Witley Surrey 10 F3
Witnesham Suffk 35 K6
Witney Oxon 31 K11
Wittering C Pete 42 F9
Wittersham Kent 12 H5
Witton Birm 40 E8
Witton Norfk 45 M4
Witton Norfk 45 M8
Witton Gilbert Dur 73 M10

Witton le Wear Dur 65 K2
Witton Park Dur 65 L2
Wiveliscombe Somset 16 E9
Wivelrod Hants 19 R12
Wivelsfield E Susx 11 M6
Wivelsfield Green E Susx 11 M6
Wivenhoe Essex 34 G11
Wiveton Norfk 44 G2
Wix Essex 35 J10
Wixams Bed 32 F7
Wixford Warwks 30 E3
Wixoe Suffk 34 C8
Woburn C Beds 32 D9
Woburn Safari Park C Beds 32 D9
Woburn Sands M Keyn 32 D9
Woking Surrey 20 G10
Wokingham Wokham 20 D9
Woldingham Surrey 21 M11
Wold Newton E R Yk 67 M11
Wold Newton NE Lin 53 J4
Wolfclyde S Lans 78 G2
Wolferton Norfk 43 Q4
Wolfhill P & K 92 H8
Wolf's Castle Pembks 24 G4
Wolfsdale Pembks 24 G5
Wollaston Dudley 40 B9
Wollaston Nhants 32 C4
Wollaston Shrops 48 G11
Wollaton C Nott 51 M11
Wollaton Hall & Park C Nott 51 M11
Wollerton Shrops 49 L9
Wollescote Dudley 40 B10
Wolseley Bridge Staffs 40 D4
Wolsingham Dur 73 J12
Wolstanton Staffs 49 Q6
Wolston Warwks 41 K11
Wolvercote Oxon 31 L11
Wolverhampton Wolves 40 B7
Wolverhampton Halfpenny Green Airport Staffs 39 P4
Wolverley Worcs 39 P6
Wolverton Hants 19 P8
Wolverton M Keyn 32 B8
Wolverton Warwks 30 G2
Wolverton Wilts 8 B2
Wolvesnewton Mons 28 E8
Wolvey Warwks 41 K9
Wolvey Heath Warwks 41 K9
Wolviston S on T 66 C3
Wombleton N York 66 F10
Wombourne Staffs 39 Q4
Wombwell Barns 51 K1
Womenswold Kent 23 N12
Womersley N York 59 M9
Wonersh Surrey 10 G2
Wonford Devon 6 C5
Wonston Dorset 7 Q2
Wonston Hants 19 M11
Wooburn Bucks 20 E6
Wooburn Green Bucks 20 E6
Woodacott Devon 14 G9
Woodall Rothm 51 L5
Woodall Services Rothm 51 L5
Woodbastwick Norfk 45 M7
Wood Bevington Warwks 30 D4
Woodborough Notts 51 N10
Woodborough Wilts 18 G8
Woodbridge Suffk 35 L7
Woodbury Devon 6 D5
Woodbury Salterton Devon 6 D5
Woodchester Gloucs 29 L8
Woodchurch Kent 12 H3
Woodcombe Somset 16 C6
Woodcote Gt Lon 21 L10
Woodcote Oxon 19 Q4
Woodcote Wrekin 49 P11
Woodcroft Gloucs 28 G9
Wood Dalling Norfk 44 H5
Woodditton Cambs 33 Q5
Woodeaton Oxon 31 M10
Wood End Gt Lon 20 H7
Wood End Herts 33 K10
Woodend Highld 89 Q4
Woodend Nhants 31 N4
Woodend W Loth 85 Q8
Wood End W Susx 10 D8
Wood End Warwks 40 E11
Wood End Wolves 40 C7
Wood Enderby Lincs 53 J10
Woodfalls Wilts 8 H4
Woodford Cnwll 14 D9
Woodford Gloucs 29 J9
Woodford Gt Lon 21 N5
Woodford Nhants 32 D2
Woodford Stockp 50 B4
Woodford Bridge Gt Lon 21 N5
Woodford Green Gt Lon 21 N5
Woodford Halse Nhants 31 M4
Woodford Wells Gt Lon 21 N5
Woodgate Birm 40 D10
Woodgate Devon 16 E12
Woodgate W Susx 10 F8
Woodgate Worcs 30 C2
Wood Green Gt Lon 21 L5
Woodgreen Hants 8 H4
Woodhall N York 64 H9
Woodhall Spa Lincs 52 H10
Woodham Bucks 31 P9
Woodham Surrey 20 G10
Woodham Ferrers Essex 22 F4
Woodham Mortimer Essex 22 F3
Woodham Walter Essex 22 F3
Wood Hayes Wolves 40 C7
Woodhead Abers 102 H7
Woodhill Shrops 39 N5
Woodhill Somset 17 J10
Woodhorn Nthumb 73 N4
Woodhouse Leeds 58 H7
Woodhouse Leics 41 M5
Woodhouse Sheff 51 K4
Woodhouse Wakefd 59 J9
Woodhouse Eaves Leics 41 M5
Woodhouselee Mdloth 86 F8
Woodhouselees D & G 71 N1
Woodhouses Oldham 50 B1
Woodhouses Staffs 40 F4
Woodhurst Cambs 33 K2
Woodingdean Br & H 11 M8
Woodkirk Leeds 58 H8
Woodland Abers 103 J9
Woodland Devon 5 J8
Woodland Devon 5 Q6
Woodland Dur 65 J3

Woodland S Ayrs 76 C11
Woodlands Donc 59 M11
Woodlands Dorset 8 F5
Woodlands Hants 9 K5
Woodlands N York 59 J3
Woodlands of Durris Abers 95 N3
Woodlands Park W & M 20 D7
Woodland View Sheff 50 H3
Woodleigh Devon 5 P9
Woodley Wokham 20 C8
Woodmancote Gloucs 29 K8
Woodmancote Gloucs 29 N4
Woodmancote Gloucs 30 D11
Woodmancote W Susx 10 C8
Woodmancote W Susx 11 K7
Woodmancott Hants 19 P11
Woodmansey E R Yk 60 H6
Woodmansgreen W Susx 10 D5
Woodmansterne Surrey 21 L10
Woodmanton Devon 6 D5
Woodnesborough Kent 23 P11
Woodnewton Nhants 42 E10
Wood Norton Norfk 44 G5
Woodplumpton Lancs 57 J2
Woodrising Norfk 44 G9
Wood's Corner E Susx 12 D6
Woodseaves Staffs 49 P9
Woodsetts Rothm 51 M4
Woodsford Dorset 8 A8
Wood's Green E Susx 12 D4
Woodside Br For 20 E8
Woodside Fife 86 H1
Woodside Gt Lon 21 M9
Woodside P & K 93 J7
Woodstock Oxon 31 K10
Woodston C Pete 42 H10
Wood Street Norfk 45 N6
Wood Street Village Surrey 20 F12
Woodton Norfk 45 L10
Woodtown Devon 14 G7
Woodville Derbys 40 H4
Wood Walton Cambs 32 H1
Woofferton Shrops 39 K8
Wookey Somset 17 M7
Wookey Hole Somset 17 M8
Wool Dorset 8 C9
Woolacombe Devon 14 H4
Woolage Green Kent 23 N12
Woolaston Gloucs 28 G8
Woolaston Common Gloucs 28 G8
Woolavington Somset 17 J7
Woolbeding W Susx 10 D5
Woolbrook Devon 6 F5
Wooler Nthumb 81 L8
Woolfardisworthy Devon 14 F7
Woolfardisworthy Devon 15 P9
Woolfords S Lans 86 B10
Woolhampton W Berk 19 P7
Woolhope Herefs 28 H2
Woolland Dorset 8 B6
Woolley BaNES 17 Q3
Woolley Cambs 32 G2
Woolley Wakefd 58 H10
Woolley Edge Services Wakefd 58 H10
Woolmere Green Worcs 30 C2
Woolmer Green Herts 33 J11
Woolminstone Somset 7 K2
Woolpit Suffk 34 F4
Woolstaston Shrops 39 J3
Woolsthorpe by Belvoir Lincs 42 B4
Woolsthorpe-by-Colsterworth Lincs 42 D5
Woolston C Sotn 9 M5
Woolston Shrops 48 G9
Woolston Somset 16 E8
Woolston Somset 17 P9
Woolston Warrtn 57 M10
Woolstone Gloucs 29 N3
Woolstone M Keyn 32 C8
Woolston Green Devon 5 Q7
Woolton Lpool 56 H10
Woolton Hill Hants 19 M8
Woolverstone Suffk 35 K8
Woolverton Somset 18 B9
Woolwich Gt Lon 21 N7
Woonton Herefs 38 G10
Woore Shrops 49 N7
Wootten Green Suffk 35 K3
Wootton Bed 32 E7
Wootton Kent 13 N2
Wootton N Linc 61 J10
Wootton Nhants 31 Q3
Wootton Oxon 19 N1
Wootton Oxon 31 K9
Wootton Staffs 50 E10
Wootton Bassett Wilts 18 F4
Wootton Bridge IoW 9 P8
Wootton Courtenay Somset 16 C7
Wootton Fitzpaine Dorset 7 K4
Wootton Rivers Wilts 18 H8
Wootton St Lawrence Hants 19 P9
Wootton Wawen Warwks 30 F2
Worcester Worcs 39 Q10
Worcester Park Gt Lon 21 K9
Wordsley Dudley 40 B9
Worfield Shrops 39 N3
Workington Cumb 70 G9
Worksop Notts 51 N5
Worlaby N Linc 60 H10
Worlds End Hants 9 Q5
Worlds End W Susx 11 L6
Worle N Som 17 J4
Worleston Ches E 49 M4
Worlingham Suffk 45 P11
Worlington Devon 15 N9
Worlington Suffk 34 B3
Worlingworth Suffk 35 K3
Wormbridge Herefs 28 E3
Wormegay Norfk 43 Q7
Wormelow Tump Herefs 28 F3
Wormhill Derbys 50 E6
Wormingford Essex 34 F9
Worminghall Bucks 31 N11
Wormington Gloucs 30 D6
Wormit Fife 93 M9
Wormleighton Warwks 31 K4
Wormley Herts 21 M3
Wormley Surrey 10 F3
Wormshill Kent 22 G11
Wormsley Herefs 38 H11
Worplesdon Surrey 20 F11

Worrall Sheff 50 H3
Worsbrough Barns 51 J1
Worsbrough Bridge Barns 59 J12
Worsbrough Dale Barns 59 J12
Worsley Salfd 57 N8
Worstead Norfk 45 M5
Worsthorne Lancs 57 Q3
Worston Devon 5 M9
Worston Lancs 57 P1
Worth Kent 23 P11
Wortham Suffk 34 H2
Worthen Shrops 38 G2
Worthenbury Wrexhm 48 H6
Worthing Norfk 44 G6
Worthing W Susx 11 J9
Worthington Leics 41 K4
Worth Matravers Dorset 8 E11
Wortley Barns 50 H2
Wortley Leeds 58 H7
Worton N York 64 G9
Worton Wilts 18 E8
Wortwell Norfk 45 L12
Wotton-under-Edge Gloucs 29 K9
Wotton Underwood Bucks 31 P10
Woughton on the Green M Keyn 32 C8
Wouldham Kent 22 E9
Wrabness Essex 35 K9
Wrafton Devon 15 J5
Wragby Lincs 52 G7
Wragby Wakefd 59 K10
Wrangaton Devon 5 N9
Wrangle Lincs 53 L12
Wrangway Somset 16 F11
Wrantage Somset 17 J10
Wrawby N Linc 52 E2
Wraxall N Som 17 L2
Wraxall Somset 17 N8
Wray Lancs 63 L8
Wraysbury W & M 20 G8
Wrayton Lancs 63 L7
Wrea Green Lancs 56 H3
Wreay Cumb 71 N6
Wrecclesham Surrey 10 D2
Wrekenton Gatesd 73 M8
Wrelton N York 66 G9
Wrenbury Ches E 49 L6
Wreningham Norfk 45 J9
Wrentham Suffk 45 Q12
Wrenthall Shrops 38 H2
Wressle E R Yk 60 C7
Wressle N Linc 52 D2
Wrestlingworth C Beds 33 J7
Wretton Norfk 44 B9
Wrexham Wrexhm 48 G5
Wrexham Industrial Estate Wrexhm 48 H5
Wribbenhall Worcs 39 P7
Wrinehill Staffs 49 N6
Wrington N Som 17 L4
Writhlington BaNES 17 Q5
Writtle Essex 22 D3
Wrockwardine Wrekin 49 L11
Wroot N Linc 60 C12
Wrose C Brad 58 F6
Wrotham Kent 22 C10
Wroughton Swindn 18 G5
Wroxall IoW 9 P10
Wroxall Warwks 40 G12
Wroxeter Shrops 39 K1
Wroxham Norfk 45 L6
Wroxton Oxon 31 K6
Wyaston Derbys 50 F11
Wyberton Lincs 43 K2
Wyboston Bed 32 G5
Wybunbury Ches E 49 M5
Wychbold Worcs 30 B2
Wychnor Staffs 40 F4
Wyck Rissington Gloucs 30 F9
Wycliffe Dur 65 K5
Wycoller Lancs 58 C6
Wycomb Leics 41 Q3
Wycombe Marsh Bucks 20 E5
Wyddial Herts 33 L9
Wye Kent 13 K1
Wyke C Brad 58 F8
Wyke Dorset 8 B3
Wyke Champflower Somset 17 P8
Wykeham N York 67 L10
Wyken Covtry 41 J10
Wyken Shrops 39 N3
Wyke Regis Dorset 7 P7
Wykey Shrops 48 H9
Wylam Nthumb 73 K7
Wylde Green Birm 40 E8
Wylye Wilts 18 E12
Wymeswold Leics 41 N3
Wymington Bed 32 D4
Wymondham Leics 42 C6
Wymondham Norfk 45 J9
Wynford Eagle Dorset 7 N4
Wyre Piddle Worcs 30 C5
Wysall Notts 41 N3
Wythall Worcs 40 E11
Wytham Oxon 31 L11
Wythenshawe Manch 57 P10
Wyton Cambs 33 J3
Wyton E R Yk 61 K7
Wyverstone Suffk 34 G3
Wyverstone Street Suffk 34 G4

Y

Yaddlethorpe N Linc 52 C3
Yafforth N York 65 N8
Yalberton Torbay 6 B10
Yalding Kent 22 E12
Yanwath Cumb 71 Q9
Yanworth Gloucs 30 E10
Yapham E R Yk 60 D4
Yapton W Susx 10 F9
Yarborough N Som 17 K5
Yarburgh Lincs 53 K5
Yarcombe Devon 6 H2
Yard Devon 15 N7
Yardley Birm 40 E9
Yardley Gobion Nhants 31 Q5
Yardley Hastings Nhants 32 C5
Yardley Wood Birm 40 E10
Yarkhill Herefs 39 L12
Yarley Somset 17 M7

Yarlington Somset 17 P9
Yarm S on T 65 P5
Yarmouth IoW 9 L9
Yarnbrook Wilts 18 C9
Yarnfield Staffs 49 Q8
Yarnscombe Devon 15 K7
Yarnton Oxon 31 L10
Yarpole Herefs 39 J8
Yarrow Border 79 M4
Yarrow Feus Border 79 M4
Yarrowford Border 79 N3
Yarwell Nhants 42 F9
Yate S Glos 29 J11
Yateley Hants 20 D10
Yatesbury Wilts 18 F6
Yattendon W Berk 19 P6
Yatton Herefs 38 H8
Yatton N Som 17 L3
Yatton Keynell Wilts 18 C5
Yaverland IoW 9 Q9
Yaxham Norfk 44 G7
Yaxley Cambs 42 H10
Yaxley Suffk 35 J2
Yazor Herefs 38 H11
Yeading Gt Lon 20 H7
Yeadon Leeds 58 G6
Yealand Conyers Lancs 63 J7
Yealand Redmayne Lancs 63 J7
Yealmpton Devon 5 M9
Yearsley N York 66 E11
Yeaton Shrops 48 H10
Yeaveley Derbys 50 F11
Yeavering Nthumb 81 K7
Yedingham N York 67 J10
Yelford Oxon 31 J12
Yell Shet 111 k3
Yelling Cambs 33 J4
Yelvertoft Nhants 41 N11
Yelverton Devon 5 L6
Yelverton Norfk 45 L9
Yenston Somset 17 Q11
Yeoford Devon 15 N11
Yeolmbridge Cnwll 4 G3
Yeovil Somset 17 M11
Yeovil Marsh Somset 17 M11
Yeovilton Somset 17 M10
Yesnaby Ork 111 g2
Yetminster Dorset 7 N1
Yettington Devon 6 E5
Yetts o'Muckhart Clacks 86 B2
Yew Tree Sandw 40 D8
Y Felinheli Gwynd 54 G7
Y Ferwig Cerdgn 36 C10
Y Ffôr Gwynd 46 G4
Yielden Bed 32 E4
Yieldshields S Lans 77 P2
Yiewsley Gt Lon 20 G7
Ynys Gwynd 47 K4
Ynysboeth Rhondd 27 M9
Ynysddu Caerph 27 P9
Ynyshir Rhondd 27 L9
Ynystawe Swans 26 F8
Ynysybwl Rhondd 27 M9
Yockleton Shrops 48 H12
Yokefleet E R Yk 60 E8
Yoker C Glas 84 H8
York C York 59 N4
Yorkletts Kent 23 L10
Yorkley Gloucs 28 H7
Yorkshire Dales National Park 64 F11
York Town Surrey 20 D10
Youlgreave Derbys 50 G7
Youlthorpe E R Yk 60 D3
Youlton N York 59 L2
Yoxall Staffs 40 F4
Yoxford Suffk 35 N3
Y Rhiw Gwynd 46 D6
Ysbyty Ifan Conwy 55 M10
Ysbyty Ystwyth Cerdgn 37 M6
Ysceifiog Flints 48 C2
Ystalyfera Neath 26 G7
Ystrad Rhondd 27 L9
Ystrad Aeron Cerdgn 36 H9
Ystradfellte Powys 27 K6
Ystradgynlais Powys 26 H6
Ystrad Meurig Cerdgn 37 L7
Ystrad Mynach Caerph 27 N9
Ystradowen V Glam 27 L12
Ythanbank Abers 103 J10
Ythanwells Abers 102 E7
Ythsie Abers 103 J8

Z

Zeal Monachorum Devon 15 M10
Zeals Wilts 8 B2
Zelah Cnwll 3 J5
Zennor Cnwll 2 C7
Zouch Notts 41 L3
ZSL London Zoo Gt Lon 21 L6
ZSL Whipsnade Zoo C Beds 32 E12